The Life and Art

of ANDREW DUCROW

&

The Romantic Age of the English Circus

FRONTISPIECE. "Mr. Ducrow and Miss Woolford as Flora & Zephyr on the Double Ropes." The second part of the ballet after the rustic characters Gatz and Ida had been "metamorphosed" into the deities of the title and Ducrow flew above Flora's scallop-shell temple.

Mr DUCROW AND MISS WOOLFORD

FLORA & ZEPHYR on the DOUBLE ROPES

London Published by R.LLOYD, Dramatic Repository, 40 Gibson St.
Lambeth.

THE LIFE AND ART OF
ANDREW DUCROW

& the romantic age

of the English Circus

BY A. H. SAXON

Archon Books   *1978*

Library of Congress Cataloging in Publication Data

Saxon, A   H
    The life and art of Andrew Ducrow and the romantic age
of the English circus.

    Bibliography: p.
    Includes index.
    1. Ducrow, Andrew, 1793–1842. 2. Circus—England
—History. 3. Horsemanship. 4. Performing arts—Eng-
land—History. 5. Entertainers—England—Biography. I.
Title.
GV1811.D78S39   791.3′092′4 [B]   77-13010
ISBN 0-208-01651-1

© Arthur H. Saxon 1978

First published 1978 as an Archon Book,

an imprint of The Shoe String Press, Inc.,

Hamden, Connecticut 06514

Printed in the United States of America

To the Memory of My Grandmother
MARY WITHERS HARTLEY
"the same that oft in childhood solac'd me"

Contents

List of Illustrations

PLATE 4. "Mr. Ducrow and Miss Woolford as the Tyrolean Sheppard [sic] and Swiss Milkmaid." Theatrical portrait published by R. Lloyd. Theatre Museum, Victoria and Albert Museum.   *facing page 320*

BLACK AND WHITE FIGURES IN THE TEXT

Prologue

IN THE SECOND HALF of the eighteenth century pleasure-loving Londoners witnessed the birth of a new amusement. Although the majority of its acts, including tumbling, juggling, ropedancing, trick riding, and trained animal performances, dated from antiquity, in the past there had been no attempt to bring them together as a distinct entertainment that could stand on its own. The Englishman Philip Astley, a former sergeant major who had begun practicing trick riding while serving as horse breaker to his regiment, was responsible for this innovation. At the time of his discharge Astley was presented with a white charger, and with this and two other horses that he bought and trained, he and his wife began exhibiting trick horsemanship, together with the astonishing feats of the "Little Military Learned Horse," in an open field in Lambeth during the spring of 1768. By consensus this date marks the founding of the circus.[1]

The following year Astley secured a piece of land at the junction of Westminster Bridge Road and Stangate Street. It was here, a short distance to the south of the Thames, that the famous Astley's

Amphitheatre stood (although thrice burned down and renamed after successive owners) until 1893. The history of this building, as well as that of its rival the Royal Circus, has been told elsewhere,[2] but as circuses in the eighteenth and early nineteenth centuries were in several respects different from those of today, a few remarks are in order. To begin with, nearly all these establishments, including those erected in the larger provincial towns, were permanent structures; and although Astley had started out by giving performances in the open air, by the 1780s they were completely enclosed. To be sure, the solidity and safety of their construction often left much to be desired. It is not unusual to read in contemporary accounts of a season being ruined when a roof was suddenly discovered to be less than waterproof and the pit and ring beneath were unexpectedly deluged and turned to mud; of inadequately supported galleries collapsing under the weight of spectators with frightful consequences; or of a roof being blown down upon the audience in the midst of a storm. Philip Astley himself was not guiltless of these jerry-building practices. The third London amphitheatre he built was said to pose a problem for all the city's architects and builders. Despite the reassuring appearance of a brick facade and gorgeous interior embellishments, no one could understand how the roof and ceiling, composed of nothing more substantial than fir poles and spars from old ships held together with ropes and tenpenny nails and covered with painted canvas, remained up. In 1841 this huge structure, like its two predecessors, caught fire and was entirely consumed in three quarters of an hour.

The interior arrangement of these amphitheatres or circuses was not dissimilar to that found in theatres of the same period. Spectators had their choice among pit, boxes, and galleries; the only difference was that a large portion of the pit was reserved for the ride or circle, enclosed by a barrier some four feet high. It was Astley, again, who was probably the first to perform in an enclosed ring of fixed diameter, both he and his predecessors in trick horsemanship having previously exhibited in fields and riding schools. No doubt the dimensions of his first roofed amphitheatre contributed to this development. Another factor, although hardly original with Astley, was the discovery that by training his horse to canter in a circle at constant speed, the standing rider, while both he and his horse were leaning slightly inward, could effectively utilize centrifugal force to help maintain his balance. Since the radius of the circle was one of the determining factors in the amount of force exerted and riders and their mounts, then as now, traveled widely, the diameter of the ring soon became standardized at thirteen and a half meters or around forty-four feet, a dimension that still obtains in most circuses. Remarkable, too, is the fact that as early as 1782, when the Royal Circus first opened its doors, scenic stages were a part of these establishments (there were exceptions among provincial circuses, however). By the first decade of the nineteenth century these stages had grown to formidable dimensions. The third Astley's Amphitheatre (fig. 1), the circus that stood from 1804 to 1841 and with which this book is largely concerned, possessed an auditorium whose wall-to-wall width was a modest sixty-five feet. Its stage, however, said to be the largest in England, was described in 1808 as measuring one hundred thirty feet in width.[3] In 1818 an adjustable proscenium was installed by which the stage opening could be increased in full view of the audience from forty to sixty feet. Immense platforms, running the entire width of the stage and capable of supporting galloping horsemen and even carriages, could be raised and lowered mechanically and were masked by scenery representing battlements, bridges, and mountains.[4]

As is obvious from this description, early circus programs were substantially different from those of today. They did not include legitimate drama (that is, plays whose dialogue could be in prose, unaccompanied by music or recitative), since in London the patent theatres of Drury Lane and Covent Garden, together with the summer theatre in the Haymarket, claimed a monopoly on this type of drama until the Theatre Regulation Act of 1843. However, the annual licenses granted to Astley's and the Royal Circus, "for public dancing and music" and "for other public entertainments of the like kind," were broadly interpreted to include not only displays of equestrianism, but a variety of subdramatic entertainments as well.[5] Originally these consisted of burlettas, pantomimes, and ballets d'action for whose performance a separate "dramatic" company (as opposed to the "equestrian" company) of professional actors, singers, and dancers was engaged. At the same time the circus artists, in keeping with the versatility that has always been expected of them, frequently helped out also. Thus a graceful equestrienne might interpret the role of a young prince in the opening stage spectacle, adding a piquant note by dressing in close-fitting breeches, while a featured ropedancer or strongman might appear as Harlequin or a bereaved father in the

FIG. 1. Pugin and Rowlandson's depiction of the third Astley's Amphitheatre as it appeared in the early nineteenth century. Rowlandson's figures give a particularly graphic idea of the different classes who attended the Amphitheatre.

afterpiece. Such doubling of roles was even more general after the turn of the century, by which time the distinction between the two types of company had begun breaking down and circus stages had increased in size to accommodate more ambitious forms of entertainment. Prominent among these later productions, beginning in 1807 with *The Brave Cossack, or Perfidy Punished,* were the spectacles known as hippodramas, equestrianized melodramas in which riders and their mounts engaged in combat and galloped across the stage, and the horses themselves often appeared as "stars"—rescuing infants and heroines, identifying and apprehending villains, scampering up precipices, dancing, falling down and playing dead—and, as more than one critic took perverse delight in pointing out, frequently surpassed their two-footed colleagues in histrionic abilities.

By the early years of the nineteenth century the format of programs at Astley's had become standardized and ran something like the following. At 6:30 the curtain rose on the featured piece, a hippodrama with some resounding title like *The Brave Cossack, The Blood Red Knight,* or *Uranda the Enchanter of the Steel Castle.* At 8:30 half-price was taken, and the spectators so admitted, if the house was full, were let into the empty ring where they witnessed the concluding scenes of the spectacle. Next came the "Scenes in the Circle," lasting some forty-five minutes and including the acts we associate with the circus today—gymnasts, contortionists, clowns, strongmen—and always featuring a fine display of horsemanship. The action then reverted to the stage where a burletta, pantomime, or pedestrian melodrama rounded out the evening's bill. The musical accompaniment was provided by an orchestra stationed between the ring and the stage, and it was not unusual for the entertainments to conclude after midnight or even, during the initial representations of a hippodrama or pantomime, after 1:00 A.M. For the Amphitheatre, or "*Ample*-theatre," as visitors sometimes referred to it, believed in giving its patrons their money's worth. The heavy reliance on stage entertainments also explains the frequent appearances of circus companies in so many theatres of the nineteenth century. Both Covent Garden and Drury Lane eventually went over to producing hippodramas of their own, engaging equestrians from Astley's and elsewhere, and it was standard procedure for touring circuses to perform at regular theatres—not excepting theatres royal—in towns that did not possess circus buildings. On these occasions a part of the pit might be converted into a ring, but just as often the circle was dispensed with and performances were confined to the stage. The same arrangements prevailed in America, where even the prestigious Park Theatre in New York was occupied for a period in 1817 by the company of the English circus manager James West.[6]

All of this, however, is getting slightly ahead of the time when Philip Astley, dressed in his military uniform and brandishing a sword, rode outside his first amphitheatre, bawling its attractions to amused passersby. In the early years of the circus trick horsemanship formed the nucleus of every program, and contemporary bills, newspaper advertisements, and occasional prints have preserved some idea of the variety of feats exhibited by Astley and his wife and their numerous competitors. There we encounter them, exciting our admiration and often our risibility, ever straining to surpass their troublesome rivals, boasting in no uncertain terms of their ability to ride with one foot on the saddle and the other on the head (or in the mouth), bestride two horses in full gallop, or balance head downward on a pint bottle atop a rushing steed, at the same time firing a pistol at some distant target. My personal favorites among these early curiosities are those pertaining to the apiarist Daniel Wildman, who in 1772 was advertised to ride at Astley's with a swarm of bees covering his head and face. Wildman must have communicated the secret of his strange act to Mrs. Astley, for she is billed to ride on the same program with a swarm on her arm in imitation of a lady's muff—an accomplishment she obviously improved upon, for three years later, after Wildman had departed, I find her frequently advertised to ride with no less than three hives of bees as partners![7] Voltige acts, in which the rider leaps on and off his moving horse, were also popular from the earliest period, while a burlesque and dramatic element was quickly injected through brief equestrian scenes depicting the disastrous attempts of a tailor to mount a horse and gallop off to a waiting customer ("The Taylor Riding to Brentford"), the equally inept horsemanship of a French messenger, and a drunken sailor on the road to Portsmouth.[8] Besides equestrianism, Astley presented a wide variety of other acts, such as gymnasts forming a human pyramid (known as the "Egyptian Pyramid" or "Force of Hercules," after which Astley named his house Hercules Hall), the sagacious tricks of the Little Military Learned Horse, ropedancing, antics of the clown, tumbling and leaping (the latter usually accomplished with a "trampoline" or springboard by which the leaper was able to clear such formidable obstacles as mounted horsemen and ranks of soldiers with fixed bayonets), even fireworks and balloon ascensions.

Like most of London's minor theatres until the mid-nineteenth century, Astley's and the Royal Circus were licensed as summer houses and traditionally remained open from Easter Monday until the end of September or early October. The fall and winter months were generally spent on tour, with Astley either taking his company to the Continent (his Amphithéâtre Astley in Paris was the first circus in France) or traveling the English provinces, erecting amphitheatres along his route. Astley's chief rival, the equestrian Charles Hughes, who at one time had worked for Astley and later became a founder of the Royal Circus, also toured extensively and was responsible for establishing the first circus in Russia under the patronage of Catherine the Great. Thus the new entertainment begun by Astley quickly took root, and by the end of the eighteenth century a number of other managers had appeared whose circuses dotted the countries of Europe and even America. Artists attracted to these establishments, where language has always been a negligible consideration, already constituted an international fraternity. Their allegiances and persons were freely transferred to wherever they could work to their best advantage. Philip Astley and his equestrian son John were almost as well-known in France as they were in England. When they died there in 1814 and 1821, respectively—in the same bed, same room, and same house in the faubourg du Temple—both were interred at Paris.

*   *   *

Meanwhile, a multitude of circus artists had appeared, whose names and accomplishments are today but faint echoes down the corridors of time. Who now is familiar with the name of Porter, said to have been the first clown engaged by Philip Astley?[9] Of Richer, nearly always billed as the "inimitable" Richer, whose career spanned several decades and whom Strutt, the early chronicler of popular entertainments, praised for displaying "more ease and elegance of action, and much greater agility, upon the rope, than any other dancer that I ever saw"?[10] Of Ireland, the "Flying Phenomenon" from Yorkshire? Without benefit of the usual springboard, he appeared at the Royal Circus in 1799, leaping over nine horses with a rider on the middle one and kicking a bladder sixteen feet above the ground, and so overexerted himself during his initial season that he sprained a tendon and had to retire for two years.[11] Of the surprising equestrian George Smith, who while riding around the ring would leap through the body of a hackney coach suspended twelve feet in the air?[12] Or of the equally astonishing little equestrian Master Davis, billed at a

Glasgow circus in 1806 to exhibit the "Hornpipe renverse, his Feet being in the Air, his Head resting on a Quart Pot, placed on the Saddle," followed by the "Attitude a la Grotesque, in a compleat Circuit round the Amphitheatre, standing on one Foot, HIS TOE in HIS MOUTH, without the least Assistance from the Bridle Rein"?[13] The renown of these performers and most of their contemporaries is today faded or entirely forgotten. Were it not for a handful of advertisements, crumbling bills, and scattered references in accounts such as Strutt's, we might never know they existed.

How difficult it is to trace and reconstruct the careers of these early artists, the reader may readily imagine. They traveled prodigiously. Because they were generally held to be of low status in the hierarchy of entertainers and therefore did not merit the same consideration as their brethren in the dramatic profession, their activities frequently went unchronicled in local journals. While provincial newspapers such as those at Bath and Bristol regularly devoted paragraphs to the London theatres and the doings there of stars like Edmund Kean and William Charles Macready, more often than not they remained silent about circus performers who, at the same moment, were actually playing in their towns. Nor are the advertisements in these journals always an infallible source of information. Often circuses, particularly the smaller establishments, simply could not afford to advertise in this manner—or if they did, made a judicious selection from among several newspapers. Even then advertising was at best sporadic, as perhaps after receiving a favorable notice in a previous issue. To fully comprehend the significance of this last observation, one must consider the low state of journalism during the early nineteenth century. Frequently the proprietor, editor, and dramatic reviewer of a newspaper were one and the same, and the reception accorded an entertainment in print was directly proportional to the expense its manager was willing to incur in the matter of advertising, paid puffs, and free admissions. The rules of this game were understood by all, with managers, for their part, often withholding advertising from those journals that did not review their productions or, worse yet, lapsed into a too strict objectivity. The frankest and most succinct admission of the practice I have discovered occurs in the 16 August 1840 issue of the London newspaper the *Age*: "New Strand, Astley's, Surrey, and Victoria we believe are open, but cannot *afford* to *advertize*, consequently *we* cannot afford to *puff* them." It follows, then, that in any study making use of these early newspapers, failure to find something does not necessarily disprove its existence, and a distinction should be drawn between the genuine notice or review and the spurious puff. The latter soon becomes recognizable to anyone condemned to plod through a number of these journals, and even it is not without interest at times.

Even when newspapers did afford regular coverage of local circuses, however, there is no guarantee one will find in them the names and descriptions of every artist and act. Performers who had not yet attained sufficient eminence in the profession might be buried for an entire season or longer under the anonymity of the ubiquitous "&c." which customarily followed the names of better-known artists. Often, too, one finds them hiding under a maddening variety of sobriquets—*noms d'arena*, as Thomas Frost tells us they were termed —which might be changed from year to year or claimed by two or more artists at the same time. How many performers eventually aspired to the title the "Little Devil" I do not know, but certain it is that there were at least three vying for this distinction during the decade 1792–1802. One of them, the equestrian George Smith, sought to settle the matter by proclaiming himself "the real Little Devil."[14] More bewildering still is the host of "infants" appearing around this time, whose parents, like the itinerant manager Vincent Crummles in Dickens' *Nicholas Nickelby*, recognized only the broadest meaning of the word—i.e., anyone under twenty-one years of age. At almost every turn one encounters some "Infant Prodigy," "Infant Hero," "Infant Rossignol," "Infant Phenomenon," "Infant of Hope," "Infant Equestrian," "Infant Hercules," or, for variety, "Child of Promise." Again, the same titles were repeatedly bestowed on different children, whose identities can only be learned through scarce announcements that couple the titles with the children's real names. Another curious practice, posing no particular difficulty, that seems to have originated around the turn of the century was the italianizing of English names. This led to such absurdities as "Signor Woolfordini" and "Mademoiselle Clarkini." Commenting on the former's name in its issue of February 1809, the *Monthly Mirror* pointed out he might just as well have been called "Signor John Bullini." Both of these performers, incidentally, were ropedancers, and as a number of Italians had gained considerable reputations in the art by the mideighteenth century, it seems obvious the English artists were attempting to capitalize on this. Britain had already witnessed and applauded, for example, the feats of the celebrated Sieur Saxoni.

As with newspapers, so with playbills. They are, in any case, rare for provincial circuses and by no means common for the early years of Astley's and the Royal Circus. Occasionally one comes across a wretchedly spelled handwritten bill for some itinerant troupe performing at a local inn, meeting room, or barn; or perhaps a more pretentious printed bill turns up, advertising some out-of-the-way circus like the one at the "Nutshell Orchard, opposite Fisher's Hotel, Cheltenham" in 1822.[15] One is far more likely to discover bills of circus companies and artists whenever they appeared in local theatres —a common arrangement in the first half of the nineteenth century when so many theatrical managers were in financial straits—since these are often preserved in provincial libraries and the great collection of playbills at the British Museum. On the Continent such collections of ephemera are less frequently discovered.

It is therefore virtually impossible to follow the progress of these performers on anything like a day-to-day or, for that matter, month-to-month basis, and the person foolhardy enough to hazard a biography of one of them, in addition to becoming nearly as peripatetic as his subject, must be content with the few scraps of information that come his way. The problem, of course, is by no means unique to circus artists. To take but one outstanding example from the theatrical firmament—an example with some relevance to the present study— who among the many biographers of Edmund Kean can account for the first twenty years or more of that artist's life? His early biographers mention his at one time traveling with the circus company of Abraham Saunders, where he is said to have been a skillful tumbler and equestrian before falling and breaking both his legs against the ring enclosure.[16] Occasionally, too, one finds some brief reference to these youthful exploits in a contemporary source, as in the *Opera Glass* for 17 February 1827, where it is reported that Kean and the ropedancer Wilson, then performing in a Covent Garden pantomime, had been "tumbling chums" in their boyhood.[17] Even after he had turned actor and joined the traveling company of John Richardson, whose booth was a well-known attraction at all the English fairs, our knowledge of him is minimal. Indeed, so fragmentary is our information concerning the early career of England's most famous romantic actor that even the year of his birth is in doubt. As the Manchester barber Richard Wright Procter—whose remarks may with equal propriety be applied to circus performers—so eloquently put it, "An actor's career may be traced without difficulty through his provincial tours when starring from Theatre Royal to Theatre Royal; but when storming for his penny fee from booth to booth, or from barn to barn, all trace of him disappears. There is no theatrical critic to report the stroller's progress, —no one to tell us when he is living in clover, or dying through lack of food. True, when his end happens to be tragical,—when he perishes on his moorland circuit, and is discovered within a snow shroud, or beneath a snow monument, the reporter volunteers a suitable inscription, and the poet pens a touching elegy for the 'poet's pilgrim.'"[18]

* * *

Among the many circus artists who embarked upon careers at the end of the eighteenth century, none was destined to achieve greater fame than Andrew Ducrow. The name of England's most celebrated equestrian has long been familiar to historians of both the circus and the theatre, for in addition to managing Astley's Amphitheatre from 1825 to 1841, Ducrow was an accomplished mime and actor of mute roles in melodramas who regularly performed on the stages of legitimate theatres—Drury Lane, Covent Garden, and any number of provincial theatres royal included. He was also an animal trainer, contortionist, and equilibrist; a tightrope dancer, choreographer, and costume designer; an early exhibitor of tableaux vivants; and the director of most of the spectacles produced at Astley's during his tenure there. It was as an equestrian, however, that Ducrow made his most enduring impression, appearing in a brilliant series of pantomimes on horseback that revolutionized the art of circus riding and were recorded in numerous prints and the laudatory accounts of his astonished contemporaries. "Ducrow's Scenes in the Circle," as they came to be called, presented the artist in the activities of such diverse characters as a British Sailor, Page Troubadour, Indian Hunter, and Chinese Enchanter. By 1830 he had invented no less than thirty-eight such scenes, and one of them, "The Courier of St. Petersburg," in which he rode and managed as many as nine horses at once, may still be seen in the circus today. Variously styled in England the "Emperor of Horseflesh" and the "Kean of the Circle," and on the Continent, where he also performed, the "Vestris à Cheval" and the "Ecuyer Classique de l'Europe," Ducrow was universally acknowledged the finest rider of his day. His style, acts, and even the names he gave his horses were widely copied in other circuses. Nor was his name unknown in America, where artists who had once worked for him did not fail to add to their personal luster by trumpeting this fact in their announcements.

Although Ducrow stands as a pivotal figure in the history of the circus, his biography, remarkably, has never been written. Two short studies privately circulated among the members of the Union des Historiens du Cirque, several articles by the present writer, and a number of brief, often repetitious "memoirs" or biographical sketches published in the last century—this is virtually all we have that deals specifically with his life. Yet there can be no doubt he was a significant and influential artist in his time, or that his career, more than that of any other performer of his generation, epitomizes the Romantic Age of the English circus. He is often mentioned in contemporary journals, theatrical periodicals, and the memoirs of those who knew him; he was admired and patronized by persons from all ranks and walks of life, from the Duchess of Angoulême and the young Queen Victoria to Dickens, Walter Scott, Christopher North, and his friend and theatrical counterpart Edmund Kean; and descriptions of his acts, both written and pictorial, abound. It was with these facts and observations in mind, and having become curious to learn more about him while writing a previous book, that I decided to attempt his biography.

At the outset I may perhaps be permitted to remark that this task has been by no means so easy as I originally anticipated. For as I soon realized after beginning my research and checking a few well-known anecdotes, nearly everything that has been written to date about Ducrow is either inaccurate or totally false. Moreover, as this mass of misinformation has been perpetuated in any number of secondary and tertiary works, and since I knew many readers would be acquainted with these frequently amusing tales, I was immediately concerned with how to go about disabusing them as gently yet expeditiously as possible. The solution eventually determined upon, for better or worse, is the appendix "The Ducrow Apocrypha," to which readers with some prior knowledge of Ducrow may wish to turn in advance. As to what did or did not constitute reliable evidence, it rapidly became apparent that the only course here was to accept nothing at face value but, so far as was possible, to base everything on a firm foundation of one or more primary sources which might be subjected to further testing and interpretation themselves.[19] Whenever this procedure was not possible, the reader is clearly advised so that he can draw his own conclusions about the validity of the evidence and any suppositions advanced.

What follows, then, is neither fictionalized nor romanticized biography. The life of Ducrow is faithfully presented with all its moments of fleeting glory, together with its blemishes, sorrows, and contradictions, intact; and if the knowledgeable reader is disappointed to discover a number of his favorite tales have fallen by the wayside, I trust he nevertheless will admit that some equally good new ones—possessing the added inducement of truth—have been enlisted to take their place. Gibbon has somewhere remarked that diligence and accuracy are the only merits the historian can ascribe to himself. To this I would only add that he might also reasonably hope to provide his readers a few hours of interest and profitable amusement.

Westport, Connecticut
Easter Monday, 1977

FIG. 2. "Ducrow & the Dwarf Courier riding Five Horses."

SLACK WIRE-DANCING IN FULL SWING,
By Messrs. DUCROW and the INFANT HERCULES,
On which he will Balance a grand Pyrimid of WINE
GLASSES, embellished with LIGHTS, &c. &c.

—from a Liverpool playbill of 1799

1   *Infancy*

PETER DUCROW was a circus performer whose place of birth, according
to later memoirs of his more famous son, was the city of Bruges in
West Flanders. The inscription on his tomb in the churchyard of
St. Mary Lambeth (Old Lambeth Church), a few feet from the south
bank of the Thames, informs us he departed this life on 6 January
1815 at the age of forty-nine, so presumably he was born around
1765.[1] During his career he appeared as an equestrian, wire-dancer,
leaper, juggler, actor and dancer in circus pieces, and as a practitioner
of the fine art of "julking," by which was meant imitating the notes
of various birds, often with a full orchestra accompanying the whistler,
in which case a "Canary Bird Symphony" might be added to the
entertainment.[2] His chief pretension to fame, however, was as the
"Flemish Hercules," although it must be noted he was not the only
claimant to this title. Another Dutchman, Jan van Moritz, disputed
it with him and, to add to the confusion, traveled about Britain at the
same time as Peter exhibiting the same feats that he did.[3] These
included balancing two or three coach wheels on his chin or forehead,

31

sometimes with a child standing atop them, and supporting on his hands and feet a platform carrying ten or—especially on his benefit nights—as many as twelve people.

Less is known about Peter's wife Margaret, who managed to outlive her husband by nearly forty years. At the time of her death in 1854 she was officially declared nearly one hundred years old, but from other evidence I think it more likely she was then in her eighties and was born around 1768.[4] I have discovered a single clue to what her existence may have been before she retired from public view, apparently to look after a steadily increasing brood of children. On 2 November 1793 the New Sadler's Wells Theatre in Edinburgh was billed to open, with a troupe of actors and circus performers recruited from the London summer houses. An advertisement for the theatre in the Edinburgh *Evening Courant* for 28 October lists, besides Richer and Ducrow for ropedancing and tumbling, both Mr. and Mrs. Ducrow for the ballets and burlettas the company planned to give. How much longer Margaret continued in this line, and indeed whether she successfully fulfilled the Edinburgh engagement, is in doubt, for only three weeks before the theatre was scheduled to open she gave birth to her first son, Andrew.

The surviving children of Peter and Margaret Ducrow were at least six in number. A second son, John, born around 1796, eventually became a well-known clown at Astley's and is sometimes confused with his brother Andrew, especially in the earlier years. He died on 23 May 1834, aged thirty-eight, and was buried with his father. A third occupant of the family tomb is Hannah Cox, described thereon as a daughter of Peter deceased on 9 April 1834 at the age of thirty-one. I imagine it was this same Hannah who in September 1825 wrote to Robert William Elliston, then manager of Drury Lane, offering her services for the winter season as first figurante and as a "Pantomimicall Character." Her letter, signed "H. Ducrow" and giving her address as "Miss Ducrow / Amphitheatre / Westminster Bridge," makes it clear she had been working for her brother during the summer months, although she never attained any distinction.[5] I find scattered references to what I take to be her and her husband in bills dating from later seasons at Astley's, as well as to another daughter, Louisa, who married a person named Foi or Foy Wood and is mentioned in her brother Andrew's will of 1841. Louisa was probably the second eldest of the Ducrow sisters, and her daughter—also named Louisa—was destined to become a great favorite of her uncle Andrew.

FIG. 3. Watercolor portrait of Ducrow's mother Margaret, buried at Nunhead Cemetery.

A third daughter was born on 16 April 1811—or such, at least, is the information contained in a margin of the St. Mary Lambeth baptismal register for 1827, in which year Amelia, daughter of Peter and Margaret Ducrow, was "Received into the Church" on 21 September. Under her anglicized name she appears in other documents and playbills as "Emily" or "Miss E." Ducrow, a skillful equestrienne and herself an interpreter of pantomimes on horseback who began her career while still a child under the watchful eye of her brother. Finally, a fourth daughter, Margaret—who also became an accomplished equestrienne, especially in the elegant art of high-school riding—was probably the last of Peter Ducrow's children. Sometime after her mother's death in 1854 she married a Mr. Wallace and had at least one daughter of her own. Both Emily and Margaret are also mentioned in Andrew's will of 1841, by which time Emily had married the stage manager and actor William D. Broadfoot.

There need be no confusion over the family's most illustrious member's birthdate: 10 October 1793. It appears in bold figures on the fantastic mausoleum Andrew Ducrow erected to his own glory in the Kensal Green Cemetery and is confirmed in a letter he wrote to his brother-in-law Broadfoot on 10 October 1841: "I have to informe you that this is my Birth Day."[6] Moreover, in the baptismal register of the Parish of St. Saviour, Southwark, one finds the following entry under 3 November 1793: "Andrew, S. of Peter Ducreau, comedian, & Margaret." The misspelling of the family name is probably explained by the clergyman's or clerk's mistaking it for a French one; and Peter's listing himself as a "comedian" or actor, considering his wide-ranging activities, was not entirely without justification. Given the low status of circus performers during this period, it is not surprising to learn the artists were frequently sensitive about their position. Thus it is by no means unusual to find them describing themselves in official documents as Peter Ducrow did, or even (as Andrew was later to do) as "gentleman" or "esquire."[7] In any case, there can be no doubt this baptismal entry pertains to the equestrian Andrew Ducrow, for on 9 September 1815 he obtained an official copy of it which today is preserved in a scrapbook belonging to one of his descendants.[8] Why he desired a transcript of this document will be a matter for further speculation.

What is surprising, at first glance, is that the infant Andrew should have been christened to begin with. For despite Peter Ducrow's interment in the churchyard of St. Mary Lambeth (a final destination

FIG. 4. Watercolor portrait of Ducrow's sister, "Mrs. Wallace, late Miss Margaret Ducrow, Mrs. Robins's Mother."

to which all residents of the parish, whether or not they were members of the Church of England, were entitled[9]), the Ducrows, like many other members of the circus and theatrical professions of their day, do not seem to have been overly punctilious in the observance of such ceremonies. The family, originally, at least, appear to have been Dissenters—and it is in the unconsecrated section of Nunhead Cemetery, immediately behind the spot where used to stand the Dissenters' chapel, that Margaret Ducrow was herself eventually laid to rest.[10] Two of her daughters, Louisa and Margaret, were both belatedly baptized on 14 March 1817, some two years after their father's death;[11] and Amelia or Emily, as already noted, was received into the church some ten years later. To date I have discovered no baptismal certificate for John Ducrow. Delays in baptizing children are not unusual even among families belonging to the Church of England, of course, although children who are sickly or in danger of dying are baptized almost immediately. Possibly this last had something to do with the christening of Andrew so soon after birth (he was sometimes said to have been a weak child); or perhaps Margaret, taking advantage of her husband's absence while he was sojourning in the north, was simply testifying to her own belief in the efficacy of such sacraments.

Another thing we may be certain of—despite the misleading statement found in several contemporary and later accounts of his career—is that Andrew could hardly have been born on the very evening of his parents' arrival in England. For Peter Ducrow had been in London since at least as early as the previous June, having opened at the Royal Circus on the 24th of that month with a new company headed by the equestrian Thomas Franklin. A newspaper puff mentions a "Dutch Troop" forming part of this company,[12] and various other advertisements for the Circus around this time call for "Mr. Peter Ducrow" to leap over eight horses with four men upon them, jump through a "balloon" (i.e., a hoop or cylinder with its ends covered by paper) or hoop of fire fourteen feet above the ring, and to appear in the tilts, tournaments, and military exercises performed on horseback. Other artists appearing at the Royal Circus during this same period included the well-known equestrians George Smith and John Crossman, the clown John Porter, the dancer D'Egville (probably George, the younger brother of the choreographer James Harvey D'Egville), and the "Child of Promise," a seven-year-old pupil of Franklin whose real name was Master Meredith.[13] Interesting, too, is the presence of the ropedancer and occasional pyrotechnist Saxoni, who was advertised in this and other seasons sometimes as being from Rome, and sometimes from Berlin. On 9 September Saxoni and Ducrow, together with a third artist, were announced to dance simultaneously on two ropes, one above the other. Thereby were joined the names of two distinguished circus families whose paths would shortly diverge, but were fated to come together again at a later date.[14]

Franklin's company continued at the Royal Circus until its closing on 14 October. Then Ducrow and a band of performers from the other London summer theatres took the road north to the New Sadler's Wells Theatre in Edinburgh. This building, which housed Edinburgh's first circus, had been erected through subscription by the riding masters George Jones and William Parker in 1790.[15] At the time of Ducrow's engagement Jones was managing it—apparently not very well, for when he took his benefit on 28 December he informed the public he had had a very unsuccessful season and pathetically appealed for their support.[16] The brief season concluded on 31 December, and the only noteworthy thing about it I have to report is the presence in the company of the celebrated ropedancer Jack Richer, who had spent the previous summer at Sadler's Wells Theatre in London. At a gathering of titled spectators on the opening night he was described as the "grand phenomenon" of the evening and as receiving thunders of applause.[17] Ducrow was himself advertised in the "Rope-Dancing, Tumbling, &c." department, and the early association of these two artists was also not without future significance.

At the end of the year Jones immediately set out for Glasgow, where on 6 January 1794 he opened another circus building he managed. Ducrow, presumably, was still with him, for the majority of the artists who had appeared at Edinburgh continued in the company, but I find no mention of him in the Glasgow journals.[18] Nor, for that matter, do I find any specific reference to Peter Ducrow again until 1795, when no less than three circus troops were playing concurrently in London at the time of the Prince of Wales' nuptials. In May he was advertised for ground and lofty tumbling and equestrian exercises at the Royal Circus, and probably he was among the unnamed artists listed for similar feats at other times during this same season.[19] Jones was now one of the lessees of the Royal Circus, having entered upon this speculation the previous year. It therefore seems likely Ducrow remained with Jones following the season at Edinburgh in 1793, and for the next several years as well, since I find notices of him again at the Royal Circus in 1796—riding, julking, and exhibiting his "wonderful heavy Balances of a Coach-wheel, Ladder with a Child poised on it, surprising Equilibres on the Slack Wire, &c." [20] During the winter months Jones still took his company to the Glasgow and Edinburgh circuses, stopping at towns like Liverpool along the way. [21] Ducrow's colleagues during these years included the equestrians Smith and Crossman, Porter and Jenkinson as clowns, the father-and-son team of the Bolognas (with the former, Pietro, playing clown to his son's performances on the rope), and, in the dramatic and dance department, D'Egville and Mrs. Parker, the wife of Jones's partner at Edinburgh. If Peter was still with Jones toward the end of the 1796 season, his patience must have been sorely tested when the "celebrated Mynheer Jan van Moritz" showed up for a few nights at the Royal Circus to exhibit his equilibres on the slack rope, balance five persons while playing a drum, and support three coach wheels on his chin while surrounded by fireworks. Moritz's wife did "postures," and at this time neither he nor Peter appears to have put forth a claim to the "Flemish Hercules." [22]

Who was the child Peter Ducrow balanced at the top of a ladder during the 1796 season? Unfortunately, we are given no specific information concerning his identity, but in all likelihood it was Andrew himself, making his unofficial ring debut. At this point it becomes necessary to turn to the later memoirs of Andrew, the reliability and provenance of which are discussed in the appendix "The Ducrow Apocrypha." The majority were written during Andrew's lifetime, after he had returned to London from the Continent in 1823. A few of them were undoubtedly based on information supplied by Andrew himself; and while these accounts, coming thirty years or more after some of the events they describe, are occasionally off in a date or minor detail, in general I believe they may be accepted. One of the more satisfying characteristics of Andrew Ducrow is that he did not, as did many of his rivals, habitually exaggerate his abilities or engage in the deceptive publicity practices which even today are so widespread in the circus. He never, to my knowledge, paid to have puffs inserted in local newspapers (although he was, assuredly, sensitive to criticism); nor did he follow the practice so common during the period of Philip Astley of continually announcing the imminent departure of artists or withdrawal of productions, only to keep them on for weeks, or even months, longer. [23] In his public and professional life Andrew Ducrow prided himself on his truthfulness, and there is no reason to suspect he was any less candid when supplying biographical data to his early memorialists.

Thus a number of the memoirs inform us that Andrew was born at the appropriately named Nag's Head in Southwark, a carrier inn dating to the mid-sixteenth century which was located on Borough High Street near London Bridge. Considering that his initial engagement at the Royal Circus was for only a few months, Peter Ducrow may well have decided to stay there in the summer of 1793.[24] These same memoirs also inform us that from the age of three to fifteen Andrew regularly worked sixteen hours a day.[25] Besides the rigorous physical training required of every circus artist, this work must have included some grounding in the three R's, for Andrew was by no means illiterate or an ignorant person.[26] His contemporaries, in fact, often expressed their amazement at his knowledge of such subjects as mythology and the fine arts, as exhibited in his productions at Astley's and his representations of classic statuary. That he was also a passable artist is demonstrated by the published drawings he did of himself and the sketches and costume designs he made for these same productions. The precise manner in which he acquired all this knowledge remains in doubt, although Pierce Egan, in his sketch of Ducrow, grandiloquently declares that the "transcendant genius" of Andrew was discovered at an early age, and that his father, cherishing the hope that his son would someday shine as the "most brilliant star" of his profession, took care he should "gain a general knowledge of every thing that was useful for an aspirant to theatrical fame to acquire" and engaged masters in drawing, painting, music, fencing, and gymnastics.[27] There may be some truth in this flattering account, but from other reports it would seem Peter Ducrow did not look with favor upon all his son's accomplishments. These describe Andrew as at one time being more interested in drawing than in riding horses, and having to conceal his box of paints from the "prying and unartist-like eyes of his cruel father, who phlegmatically destroyed his pictorial efforts whenever he could lay his hands on them."[28]

We are on securer ground concerning Andrew's professional training. Circus children of Ducrow's day followed a carefully prescribed regimen of increasingly difficult exercises and acts—which is one reason they became proficient in so many different areas. An interesting description of the various steps in the training of equestriennes, for example, appears in the *Town* for 17 October 1840. Beginning with posturing at around five years of age and progressing through balancing, gymnastics, stilt walking, slack wire, tightrope, dancing, combat with broadsword, musical instruments, and riding in entrées—with a variety of exercises in the different steps—the pupil eventually arrived at a single act of horsemanship. The procedure did not differ much between the sexes, and Andrew himself, starting at the age of three, "at an early hour every morn...was to be seen with his face against a wall 'setting his feet,' i.e. getting into position heel to heel. Then began the business of the day—vaulting—tumbling— slack and tight rope—or by way of relief and recreation—balancing— riding, and boxing."[29] His teacher during this early period was his father. And although Egan paints him as a marvel of solicitude for Andrew's development in the "liberal arts and scientific acquire- ments," I have yet to run across a description of Peter Ducrow as anything but a cruel and tyrannical master. The most charitable account of his pedagogical methods occurs in the memoir published in *Oxberry's Dramatic Biography*, where he is said to have been a "most severe disciplinarian, a man who feared nothing himself, and would not permit any one belonging to him to use the words, 'I can't,' which as he most justly observed in ninety-nine cases out of a hundred means, 'I won't.' "[30] Earlier in this same account we are furnished a picture of the elder Ducrow becoming so out of humor at his son's taking two falls and "putting out" both an ankle and a wrist during an Edinburgh engagement that he returned to their lodgings in a drunken condition and accidentally set fire to them. Andrew, hopping about on a crutch, managed to extinguish the blaze; but the expenses resulting from this accident forced them to enter immediately upon another engagement at a small town in Wales, where Andrew—with his father's reassurance that "his falling was all idleness, and if it occurred again he'd break every bone in his skin"—danced the rope on one leg.[31]

There are other stories, too, possibly variations of the same account. One tells of their performing at a circus near Bathwick Fields on the outskirts of Bath, and of Andrew falling from a horse and breaking a leg. Peter ran to him and solicitously carried him out of the ring, but a few seconds later the spectators were startled to hear Andrew screaming behind the scenes. His father was horsewhipping him![32] Another describes a similar accident, this time a broken arm resulting from a fall from the rope, and how Andrew, upon returning home, received another severe thrashing for his clumsiness, his father shouting at him, "in his inimitable English, 'You break your dam arm again, you know what you catch.' "[33] On still another occasion, according to an anecdote that made the rounds during Andrew's later life, the famous clown Joe Grimaldi humanely interfered to stop one of these beatings—and the outcome was a pun. When Grimaldi chided Peter for his cruelty, the parent defended himself by pointing out that youth must be early trained and that it was "best to make an impression when the wax was soft." "Ay," Grimaldi replied, "but that don't hold here, for the *Whacks* were not *soft*."[34]

Most bitter of all is the memoir in the *Owl* for 24 September 1831, with its hint at Andrew's relations with his brother John and their sibling rivalry: "He was not the old man's pet; and received *divers* severe visitations from his bamboo, for *sundry* faults imagined or committed; and John Ducrow, the present clown of the ring, bore away his own and brother's share of Mynheer's affections." This last statement, however, is contradicted by the playwright and memoirist of Ducrow, William T. Moncrieff, who informs us it was Andrew who was actually "Old Crow's" favorite and that John was considered dull and unpromising by both his father and brother. Such partiality did not, of course, lessen the frequency or severity of Peter's habitual mode of instruction—in addition to which, Moncrieff continues, he had another odd way of showing his affection. He never went anywhere without Andrew, and "after performing at night he would take the boy with him to whatever public-house he might choose to spend the rest of the evening in, where he would make him crouch under his chair like a dog, that he might have him in readiness to lead him home at the conclusion of the revels—no very easy task sometimes, for the old Hercules generally got pretty *top-heavy* on these occasions —poking him down occasionally a bit of biscuit—and whistling for him to come out when he wanted to depart. Notwithstanding this brutal course of tuition, Ducrow always spoke of the old man with great affection."[35]

With Peter as his experienced but by no means gentle tutor, then, the infant Andrew Ducrow began his circusy career. I find no specific reference to them in the advertisements for the Royal Circus in 1797, although Jones's company was there again with many of the artists already noted; but in the fall of that year they were on the Continent, for a Portuguese playbill for 25 October announces the benefit of the English artists "Mr. Du Crow, e Mr. Smith, e o Infante Hercules," together with Richer, at the Theatre Royal of San Carlos, Lisbon. Peter himself was billed to leap through a barrel enveloped by exploding fireworks on this occasion. Smith, Ducrow, and the "Infant

Hercules" performed difficult "saltos" and "equilibrios," or balancing feats. Richer, who had spent the previous summer at Sadler's Wells, went through various exercises on the rope.[36] Their performance did not include any equestrian acts, and from the presence on the same program of a troupe of Italian actors who presented a farce and a pantomime, it seems Ducrow and his fellow artists had been engaged as a supplementary attraction. I imagine they must have formed their small company at the end of the London summer season for just this purpose, traveling light and picking up money wherever they could.

The next year Peter was back at the Royal Circus, where I find him listed as a member of the equestrian department for the opening on Easter Monday.[37] Jones was still in control, but his management ran into difficulty a few months later when a number of his performers defected to the rival establishment of Astley's. The trouble may have originated with his decision to merge his company during the 1798 season with the troop of Benjamin Handy, a well-known circus manager in the west of England who in previous years had brought his company up to London to perform at Astley's, the Royal Circus, and elsewhere. At other times he and his artists were to be seen in such towns as Oxford, Liverpool, Manchester, Bristol, and especially Bath, where Handy occupied an amphitheatre in Monmouth Street and sometimes engaged his colleagues from Astley's. An interesting figure, he has received scant mention in all the circus histories to date. Among his artists were the equestriennes Miss Simonet and Miss Marian, whom Handy at one time falsely advertised as the only female riders in England. The former, who was probably a member of the celebrated family of dancers, had begun her career as a juvenile performer at Hughes and Dibdin's Royal Circus in 1782; and the latter, sometimes billed as the "Original Child of Promise," was actually Handy's daughter. She later graduated to standing on her head atop an eleven-foot ladder which fell apart leaving her balancing on one half of it—surrounded by fireworks, of course. Handy himself usually took the part of the clown, but occasionally appeared as a "vaulting horseman" or voltige rider. He was obviously well thought of by his neighbors and patrons in Somerset, for upon his retirement from circus management he became a magistrate for that county.[38]

At the beginning of the 1798 season, however, Benjamin Handy could not have been in a very happy frame of mind. The previous December, in preparation for a Dublin engagement, he had seen his stud of horses and the majority of his performers, many of whom had children with them, aboard the packet *Viceroy*. Handy himself and a few other artists remained behind in Liverpool, intending to follow at a later date. But a storm blew up and the *Viceroy* sank, taking everyone, including the "Original Child of Promise," to the bottom of the sea.[39] There were others who suffered from this disaster, too. The brother and sister of Mrs. John Astley were aboard the vessel, and so were the wife and one of the children of William Davis, a former riding master at Astley's who had recently entered into partnership with Handy. The same Davis now showed up at the Royal Circus as manager of the horse department and was given a benefit, not without some touching references to his recent loss, on 23 April. A rare bill for this occasion preserved in the Theatre Museum of the Victoria and Albert Museum lists "Du Crow" as a slave in the spectacle *Black Beard, or The Captive Princess* and as Alderman O'Gobble in the pantomime afterpiece *Harlequin Mariner, or The Witch of the Oaks*. An advertisement in the *Times* for this same evening lists a "celebrated wire-dancer (from Portugal)," and I assume it is also Peter and Andrew who are meant in an earlier puff which mentions the "Modern Hercules and Infant Pierrot."[40] Later in the season, in an equestrian act titled the "Grand King Post," Smith was advertised to carry "Mr. Ducrow and the wonderful Infant, standing on one hand, round the Circle."[41]

At the beginning of June the equestrian company, which for weeks had been threatening to depart for Dublin, transferred instead to Astley's Amphitheatre, where a grand competition was trumpeted as about to take place for the reputed prize of 1,000 guineas. Originally scheduled for a few nights only and repeatedly announced as being in imminent danger of termination, the contest dragged on until early September, by which time the "double troop" had become three— Astley's, Handy's, and Smith and Crossman's—and no more was heard about the 1,000 guineas. The effect of these announcements on the fortunes of the Royal Circus may readily be imagined. The riders, it was stated in various publications, had "deserted the Circus," had "entirely quitted Jones's Royal Circus." Not all his artists had left Jones, however. Porter, D'Egville, the Bolognas, and the stage company stayed on, and with these and a new equestrian company hastily assembled he managed to limp through to the end of the season. He even came up with another rider named Smith, leading the company at Astley's to proclaim they had got the "genuine" one. Meanwhile, Peter Ducrow had at last gained entry to the ring of England's most prestigious amphitheatre, where on 4 September 1798 he was advertised to "throw a Somerset [i.e., somersault] through a Balloon of real Fire, and over Seven Horses; also over a Garter, Twelve Feet high."[42]

At the summer season's end the two companies went their separate ways, Handy's to Bath and that of Smith and Crossman to Birmingham. They did not remain long apart, however, for the following April they were again together at Liverpool, where they performed at the New Olympic Circus in Dale Street. The British Museum possesses a good run of playbills for this engagement, which commenced on 16 April and ended on 31 May.[43] Smith, Crossman, Davis, and Ducrow were billed for horsemanship, as well as "Miss Simmonet," who had obviously escaped the sinking of the *Viceroy* and was announced on her benefit night as the "first female performer in this kingdom."[44] Also present was a "little infant, only three years old," who performed the equestrian act the "Royal King Post" with Ducrow and Davis. Possibly this was a son of William Davis, for there was a William Jr. who offered Andrew stiff competition in the early years of the new century. In any case, Peter seems to have had Andrew with him, and in the grammatically interesting playbill for Peter's benefit on 30 May we find "*SLACK WIRE-DANCING* IN FULL SWING, By Messrs. DUCROW and the INFANT HERCULES, On which he will Balance a grand Pyrimid [*sic*] of WINE GLASSES, embellished with LIGHTS, &c. &c." The Infant Hercules was also advertised to be carried on the shoulder of the equestrian Lalouette who rode two horses at full speed in the attitude of Mercury, and Peter further demonstrated his own astonishing accomplishments on this festive occasion. The delightful cuts at the top of this bill are reproduced in figure 5, and it is interesting to note that Peter, following his recent trip to Portugal, was now describing himself as "from the Theatre-Royal, Lisbon."

There was a new recruit to the company at this time, Charles Dibdin the Younger, whose supplementary position as treasurer entitled him to a benefit of his own on the last night of the season. Dibdin writes of the company in his memoirs, although he did not remain with it very long. It was arranged, he tells us, on the sharing plan, with everyone expected to contribute in as many ways as he could. For his part Dibdin was treasurer, box money taker, addressed the audience, and wrote comic songs for another artist, Richard Johannot, which he sometimes attempted to sing himself. At the end

For the BENEFIT of

Mr. Ducrow.

Olympic Circus, Shaw's Brow.

Mr. DUCROW (from the Theatre-Royal, Lisbon) respectfully begs leave to inform the Ladies, Gentlemen, and Public in general of Liverpool and its Vicinity, that his *BENEFIT* is fixed for

THIS PRESENT,

Thursday, May the 30th, 1799.

Mr. DUCROW at a considerable Expence, has prepared an entire Change of Performances, which he hopes will excite general Approbation, and flatters himself to meet with that Support which the Inhabitants of Liverpool have generally bestowed on similar Occasions.

Mr. DUCROW will, in a surprising Manner, Exhibit his wonderful *Equilibriums and Balances*,

A LA TURQUE.

And for this Night only, will Balance on a Table several Persons ; and other Herculean Balances, With LADDERS, COACH WHEELS, &c. &c.

SLACK WIRE-DANCING

IN FULL SWING,

By Messrs. DUCROW and the INFANT HERCULES,
On which he will Balance a grand Pyramid of WINE GLASSES, embellished with LIGHTS, &c. &c.

TRIAL OF SKILL,

BY THE WHOLE TROOP.

Grand Trampoline Tricks,

By Mr. DUCROW,

Who will take several astonishing LEAPS, in particular, one over

EIGHTEEN

GRENADIERS,

AND OVER SIX HORSES,

AND THROUGH A

Hogshead of FIRE.

FIFTEEN FEET HIGH.

THE NOTES OF VARIOUS BIRDS

BY MR. DUCROW,

In which he will Accompany the Band in a favourite OVERTURE.

FIG. 5. Bill for Peter Ducrow's benefit on 30 May 1799 at the Olympic Circus, Liverpool. The cuts represent Peter in two of his celebrated feats, and the children at the top of the ladder are probably Andrew and his brother John.

of the Liverpool engagement the troop traveled to Bristol and a temporary circus in Union Place—a structure so flimsy that on the benefit night of Smith the gallery collapsed. From Bristol the company journeyed in July to Manchester. There they played alternately at the Circus and the Theatre (Dibdin produced a number of stage pieces at the latter) and were temporarily joined by the inimitable Richer. By this time, too, Peter Ducrow was being assisted by both his "infant" sons—billed, with the customary inattention to precise detail, as four and two and a half years old—for all three of them were announced in the 27 August issue of the Manchester *Mercury* to take their benefit at the Theatre Royal the following day. Prior to this, for the troop's opening at the Circus on 22 July, "Master Ducrow," also said to be from the Theatre Royal in Lisbon, had been advertised for "balancing feats of strength."[45] In Manchester Dibdin quarreled with William Parker, whose talented wife was also with the company, and left to take up a new position as manager of Sadler's Wells in London.[46]

The troop did not perform in London during the 1799 season. At the time of Dibdin's departure they were contemplating a trip to Dublin, and from other evidence it would seem they were again at the Liverpool circus toward the end of the year.[47] I have not attempted to trace their peregrinations in full. Meanwhile, at the end of the summer Philip Astley had formally resigned the management of his London amphitheatre to his son John, although he was to remain active in a number of other speculations until his death in 1814. On Easter Monday, 14 April 1800, Ducrow and his colleagues were back at Astley's, where the old ruse of advertising a limited engagement was again employed. Thus a puff and advertisement in the 3 and 5 May issues of the *Times* proclaimed the appearance, for six nights only, of the "Flemish Hercules," who was said to have recently arrived from the Continent. He was, of course, re-engaged for another six nights, and by the end of May, besides the other feats with which Peter Ducrow customarily regaled his audiences, was balancing a living horse.[48] That this was indeed Peter and not, say, his rival Moritz is proved by an account of a fête that took place before the Royal Family at Frogmore House, Windsor, a few weeks later. But here a digression becomes necessary on the "royal patronage" and "command performances" which artists traditionally find so very attractive.

Claims to such distinctions are often misleading but, in the case of the Ducrows, at least, were generally based on verifiable facts.

Upon reading in a bill or advertisement that an artist has performed before the "Royal Family" or the Emperor of Russia and King of Prussia, I confess that my own imagination instinctively conjures up visions of sceptered monarchs and romantic journeys to the nethermost regions of Europe. It often turns out, however, that such statements refer to nothing more than a performer's once having appeared before the junior members of the royal family in question, while the Emperor of Russia and the King of Prussia may have been entertained in no more distant a locale than London itself. Then, too, the vanity of those who "please to live" being what it is, many performers are constitutionally given to cherishing these memories until the very ends of their careers—perhaps, one might hazard, even beyond. Thus the command performance an artist takes care never to let his audiences forget may have occurred ten, twenty, or thirty years earlier, with the result that the proclaimed dates of these gala events are sometimes in error. Managers reacted in similar fashion. A single visit by the "Royal Family" to their establishments transformed them into "Royal Amphitheatres" or "Royal Circuses." On one occasion (it was during Andrew's own period of management) effigies of the distinguished visitors were actually installed in the plushly draped box where their models had once sat—perpetual reminders of the glorious past.

Not surprisingly, then, the troops with which Peter Ducrow was associated did not withhold such proof of preeminence from their appreciative public. When Jones and his company, with Peter Ducrow presumably among them, played at Frogmore in May 1795 to help celebrate the birthdays of the Queen and the Princess of Wales, the event led not only to some good advertising for the Circus, but also to the "re-creation" of the fête during the remainder of the season and part of the next.[49] During the 1799 season at Liverpool the company's bills boasted that they had performed, on unspecified occasions during the past twelve months, before the Royal Family at Windsor and in the Prince of Wales' riding school at Carlton House.[50] Since Andrew often listed himself in later years as having once performed at the last-named establishment, it may be he had this very engagement—when he was around five years old—in mind. There was also, for years afterward, considerable boasting about a performance before the Royal Family at Frogmore in 1800. The Frogmore Fêtes customarily took place in late spring or early summer and were often connected with royal birthday celebrations. They employed a medley of actors, singers, dancers, and popular entertainers whose performances, given outdoors in the gardens, at times took on an almost masque-like quality. For the fête held on 14 July 1800 I find no mention of any circus company's presence, but Peter Ducrow was certainly there, even eliciting his sovereign's personal attention. After encountering some actors dressed as gypsies who sang and recited verses, the Royal Family and their guests moved on to another part of the gardens where a stage had been erected and where "Mr. Du Crow, the Flemish Hercules, exhibited his inimitable performances on the slack wire; and afterwards on the stage his extraordinary feats of strength, such as balancing on his chin three large coach-wheels, also a ladder to which were affixed two chairs with two children on them, and bearing on his hands and feet a table in the form of a pyramid, with eight persons on different parts of its surface." His amazed Majesty afterward asked Peter some questions about the size of his muscles, to which the Flemish Hercules replied that surgeons had pronounced them to be one-fifth larger than those in men of much greater height and weight.[51] Such flattering attention led to an announcement in the *Times* of 17 July that the Flemish Hercules had been re-engaged at Astley's for four nights only and would go through the same program he had given at Frogmore, "when his MAJESTY condescended to honor the Flemish Hercules with his approbation on his superior strength."

Although Peter later boasted in his bills that his great hour at Frogmore had taken place in 1801,[52] it seems obvious it was this 1800 performance he had in mind. The mention of the stage and children in the newspaper descriptions also confirms my belief that on this occasion an incident reported in the later memoirs of Andrew occurred:

> Our young gentleman [Andrew] began his career in the upper circles, for his first bow was made to his late Majesty George III., at the fete of Frogmore, where his father and brother were engaged: a stage was erected for the exhibition, and in consequence of the weight upon it caused by some of Mr. D. sen.'s fetes [sic], part of the stage broke in, and our hero's brother, then a very little boy, fell through. His Majesty instantly rose and came in person to see if the little fellow was hurt. On being answered with the utmost simplicity by the child, "No, Sir, I am not hurt," the King asked him several questions; among others, whether he had any brothers and sisters? to which he replied, "Yes, Sir, I have a little brother Peter." The father of our hero was anxious to intimate to the

young gentleman that it was his Sovereign that he was address-
ing, but the King would suffer no interruption, and contented
himself with the title of plain Mister until the defect in the
stage was remedied.[53]

Strange to relate, at the conclusion of the "four nights only"
Peter Ducrow did indeed take leave of his companions at Astley's,
presumably, as the advertisement for 17 July promised, to exhibit
during the assizes at Yarmouth, Norwich, and elsewhere. By this date
Philip Astley had formed a company which he was taking around the
countryside, and at Stirbitch his troop of horsemen and the Flemish
Hercules were reported in late summer as meeting with great encouragement.[54] Later in the year, after John Astley had brought his
summer season to a close and taken his "dramatic" company (his
wife Hannah had some pretensions in this line) to the Royalty Theatre
for the winter months, "Mynheer Ducrow" showed up there, too.[55]
He was still with Astley when the Amphitheatre across the river
reopened on Easter Monday, 6 April 1801. Peter Ducrow's colleagues
now included the riders Sutton, Link, Bryson, and West—the last
in all probability James West, who became Andrew's partner in 1825.
At the same time the Royal Circus was billing such artists as Ireland
the leaper, now "perfectly reinstated in his health," the "surprising
Phenomenon, Master Davies (only seven years of age)" for exercises
on horseback, and the ropedancer and equestrian Master Saunders,
who had been the "Infant Equestrian Phenomenon" of the previous
season.[56] Young Saunders took his benefit on 6 June, and on this
occasion, as often happened when artists had reason to offer as
attractive a program as possible, he was assisted by performers drawn
from other establishments. This led to an interesting bill on which
"Ducroe" and Moritz both appeared, together with a Mr. Woolford

FIG. 6. Astley's.

who performed on the tightrope.[57] The last, I imagine, was Robert Woolford, whose daughter Louisa became Andrew's second wife. This is the first time I find the two families' names together. Also during this season Richer and "Master Carey" (the name by which Edmund Kean was presently going) were both performing at Sadler's Wells. The majority of these artists were to figure prominently in the later career of the Infant Hercules. But at this point I lose sight of Andrew and his family for the next four years.

This present MONDAY, Dec. 26,
will commence with *YOUNG DUCROW'S*
ASCENSION from the Stage to the Gallery, standing upon his Head
at the Top of A BALLOON, Carrying TWO PERSONS in the CAR.

—from a Bristol Theatre Royal playbill of 1814

2   *Youth*

IN LIEU OF ANY DEFINITE information on the whereabouts of the
Ducrows during the next few years, I can only offer a number of
speculations. One possibility is that they were touring on the Continent, although this does not seem likely on account of the Napoleonic
Wars. With the exception of the short-lived Peace of Amiens, which
lasted from March 1802 to May 1803, travel between England and
the Continent was severely curtailed during this period. Philip Astley
himself ventured to France in 1803 with the intention of reclaiming
his Parisian amphitheatre, but was detained as a prisoner of war after
the abortive Peace fell through and was even rumored in the English
newspapers to have died in Paris. He later showed up in London,
however, having made a daring escape while posing as an invalid.
Had the Ducrows been subjected to the same general detention, or
had they been performing abroad during this troublesome period,
one would expect to find some mention of it in the memoirs of Andrew.
Yet there is no evidence this was actually the case, and it is not until
the summer of 1814, following the first abdication of Napoleon, that

I find any reference to an English circus troop crossing the Channel in the new century.[1]

The more likely explanation, therefore, is that they continued performing in Britain during these "lost" years—if not in London, in the provinces. One town they must surely have visited was Bath, which at the time was still fashionable and an important theatrical and circus center. Benjamin Handy had his circus there in Monmouth Street, and Perry's New Circus in Frog Lane was flourishing at the turn of the century. It was at Bath, too, according to the memoirs, that Peter Ducrow whipped his son for perversely falling and breaking a leg during a performance at a temporary circus at the bottom of Grove Street near Bathwick Fields. The small company Peter had taken there included the equestrienne and ropedancer Miss Saunders, sister of the Master Saunders mentioned in the preceding chapter. The artists lodged at a small public house in Grove Street, where Andrew, for unspecified but easily imagined reasons, acquired the nickname the "little blackguard," prior to being engaged at Astley's and appearing there as "first rope-dancer and leading equestrian" under the more flattering appellation the "Little Devil."[2] Brief as they are, these statements agree with information gleaned from other sources and would seem to date the visit in question to sometime during 1802–1806, or possibly as late as 1808–12. Miss Saunders, for example, had made her debut at the Royal Circus in June 1802.[3] Both she and her brother performed at the Royal Circus, Astley's, and the Royalty Theatre in later years; and during the winter of 1803–1804 she was part of a company her father, Abraham Saunders, took to the last-named house. There she danced the slack wire and added to her accomplishments by descending into the pit to do a Spanish sword dance with the swords tied to her feet.[4] I find no reference to the Ducrows among this company, which departed for a brief tour of Scotland in February 1804, but possibly they and Miss Saunders were together for the Bath engagement. As to the "Little Devil," whose numerous claimants have already been remarked on (and there was yet another, the equestrian James West, during the 1802 season at Astley's), Andrew was indeed billed as the "Prussian Little Devil" during the 1807 season at Astley's and later, during 1812, as the "Equestrian Little Devil."

Around this time, too, Andrew graduated from his father's school of hard "whacks" and came under the influence of more specialized teachers. They were three in all, the first of whom—the English dancer and choreographer J. H. D'Egville—might initially strike one as a strange choice for a child being brought up in the circus. Strange, that is, until one recalls the eclectic nature of circus programs in Ducrow's day and the pantomimes, melodramas, and ballets d'action they traditionally included. James Harvey D'Egville was the eldest son of the ballet-master Peter D'Egville (or Daigueville), whose numerous family of sons and daughters seem to have performed at nearly all the London theatres during the last two decades of the eighteenth and early part of the nineteenth centuries. Unfortunately, it is not always easy to distinguish between them, and their careers— especially those of the junior members—have to date been imperfectly documented even for the more prestigious theatres in which they worked. James himself was born around 1770. After early training by his father, he was sent for final studies, known as "perfectionne-ment," to Dauberval of the Paris and Bordeaux Grand Operas. Back in England, he became ballet-master at the King's Theatre (Opera House) in 1799 and was active there and at Drury Lane and the Little Theatre in the Haymarket over the next decade. In the early 1820s he was associated with the Paris Opéra before returning for two final seasons at the King's Theatre in 1826 and 1827.[5] Thereafter he drops from sight, although it may have been he and his wife who were running a dancing school for boys and young ladies at 50 Frederick Street in Edinburgh in 1830.[6]

In his early years, beginning 1786, James often danced with his younger brother George at the Little Theatre in the Haymarket, Drury Lane, and elsewhere. "G." or George D'Egville is listed by Decastro (p. 158) among the performers at the Royal Circus around the turn of the century; and a "Master" or "Mr. D'Egville" is frequently mentioned as an actor, dancer, and choreographer in the bills and advertisements of the Circus from 1788 through the 1798 season, and occasionally in later years as well.[7] The family name, again without any distinguishing initials, also appears in the bills of provincial circuses around this time. Doubtless it is George who is meant in most of these announcements—even when the name is followed by the phrase "From the Opera House"[8]—but I am by no means certain James Harvey himself never deigned to perform with circus companies. Especially previous to becoming ballet-master at the King's Theatre in 1799, and during the summer months when the Opera and patent theatres closed their doors, he might well have worked at the Royal Circus and in the provinces; and these latter engagements, in particular, would help to explain some of the lacunae in his chronology. In any event, it was clearly the elder brother Pierce Egan had in mind when he wrote that "D'Egville, of the Opera, pronounced young Ducrow to be the most active in mind and body, and the most susceptible of all his pupils of becoming the *premier sujet* of the refined art of dancing. Nay, so much did the above distinguished teacher admire his abilities, that he expressed a strong wish to his friends to bind young Ducrow as an apprentice for seven years. His early talent as a dancer discovered itself when he was only eight years of age, in many of Mr. D'Egville's chorographic [sic] productions; in the foremost of which, whenever his master could, he placed his young favourite."[9]

Since Egan indicates these lessons commenced when Andrew was eight years old, I at one time thought it possible Andrew might have been dancing with D'Egville around the turn of the century, thereby accounting for the few years when I find no record of his appearing at the London circuses. D'Egville did like to feature his students in his ballets. For his benefit at the King's Theatre on 30 May 1805, for example, all of the characters in his *Paul et Virginie* were advertised to be performed by "Mr. D'Egville's Young Pupils";[10] and by 1809, as one gathers from a scathing review of his *Don Quichotte ou Les Noces de Gamache*, some members of the audience, at least, had seen enough of his "painted skeletons" and "numerous troop of infants."[11] In checking reviews and announcements for the King's Theatre and Drury Lane during this period, I find no proof that Andrew was ever among this emaciated crew. Yet he did certainly study with D'Egville, and later acknowledged his indebtedness to his master while performing in France, where critics frequently expressed their admiration for his gracefulness in dancing—on the back of a horse. Following a review in the *Mémorial Bordelais* for 21 April 1822, which reported he had received lessons in the dance from Vestris *fils*, Ducrow wrote to the editor to correct this statement: "Je n'ai reçu des leçons de danse que d'un seul professeur, M. d'Egville, de l'Opéra de Paris, et, à l'époque où j'étais son élève, directeur de l'école de danse et maître des ballets de l'Opéra de Londres."[12] These lessons Andrew eventually put to good use, not only in his performances on horseback, but in the dances and ballets he occasionally arranged for his own company at Astley's. His generally acknowledged ability as a mime no doubt also derived in part, at least, from this early instruction in the dance, and it is to James Harvey D'Egville that much of the credit for Ducrow's success in these areas must go.

Andrew's second teacher, the ropedancer Jack Richer, also had received training in the dance. In 1803 he was described as "one of the handsomest and best-made men in England. His skill therefore in dancing is aided by the most elegant motions, and his steps are infinitely more pleasing on the narrow diameter of a three inch rope, than nine tenths of our professed dancers are on the stage."[13] According to the memoirs, Andrew was for a time Richer's pupil, but later claimed he never had any "liking for the rope."[14] Like it or not, however (and no doubt Peter Ducrow had *his* say in the matter), he rapidly became proficient in the discipline and in his youth was often billed to dance the rope. After making his mark as an equestrian, his ropedancing appearances became infrequent, although his interest did revive in the 1830s, stimulated by the lovely Louisa Woolford, when he composed several duets which they danced together.

Andrew's third and final instructor during this period was an equestrian named Collett (or Collet), of whom so little mention is made in contemporary publications that I have been unable to determine his Christian name. A "T." Collett is listed by Decastro among the male performers at the Royal Circus around 1800, together with an "R." Collett in the technical department.[15] The family, again, appears to have been a numerous one, and in later years there was at least one "Master Collett" who appeared at Astley's in 1822 and 1823; a "J. Collett" who performed in the equestrianized musical *Cortez* at Covent Garden in 1823; while a Sarah Collett served as a witness to both weddings of Louisa Woolford. I imagine it was the T. Collett mentioned by Decastro who was Andrew's teacher, and that he is the one to whom I find various references at Astley's, the Royal Circus, and other establishments where he served as a rider, actor in hippodramas, clown to the pantomimes, and—less frequently—dancer and choreographer. Although never a star performer, he obviously had no little knowledge of equestrianism, for by 1812 he had risen to the position of riding master at Astley's.[16] And it was Collett who was Andrew's preceptor in horsemanship—the area in which he was destined to shine above all others.[17]

These three artists, then, were all instrumental in developing and refining the latent talents of Andrew during the first decade of the new century, with D'Egville's instruction presumably coming earliest, Richer's sometime around the middle of the decade, and Collett's commencing around the same time and conceivably extending to 1812, when he and Andrew were both riding at Astley's. Curiously, I find the names of at least two of them following in rapid succession when I next catch up with the Ducrows in 1805–1806, while they were performing with their old associates at various towns in the north. On 12 November 1805 the Olympic Circus in Edinburgh was advertised to open with a company that included Smith, Crossman, Davis, Parker, and Richer. Two weeks later, on 25 November, the managers announced they had engaged, at considerable expense and for three nights only, the "celebrated Flemish Hercules (being his First Appearance in this kingdom)," who was billed to go through the same program he had given before the Royal Family at Frogmore in "1801."[18] The feats of the Flemish Hercules were the same as before— and again, as various advertisements in the Edinburgh *Evening Courant* for December and January proclaimed, they were supplemented by the no less astonishing feats of his "Two Infant Sons." The more advanced of these prodigies, Master Ducrow, now said to be "only nine years of age," was announced on 28 November to exhibit the Polander's Equilibriums, which consisted of standing on his head on chairs, candlesticks, and a twelve-foot ladder that broke in half and left him balancing on one side, "where he will turn round several times."[19] Although the age given might suggest this was John, I have no doubt it was in fact Andrew; and John is usually distinguished as "Master J. Ducrow" in bills and advertisements around this time. Master Davis was announced to exhibit trick horsemanship on this same evening, and Richer to dance the rope. On 4 February 1806, during the company's final week at Edinburgh, the Ducrows were given a benefit night to themselves. On this occasion Master Ducrow was advertised to make his first appearance on the rope.[20]

Another oft-repeated anecdote of Andrew's youth probably dates from around the time of this engagement. One "Dr. Bartlett' of Edinburgh, it is said, used to recommend to his students that they go to see young Ducrow, "as they would then be able to form a judgment of what the human frame was capable of as regards position and distortion." They apparently took the good doctor at his word, visiting the circus to interview Andrew and feel his muscles, and causing an alarmed Peter to long for the day when he could get his son out of town, since he was convinced they only did this so they might "the more readily cut him up should he break his neck there."[21] My investigation of this incident did not turn up any "Dr. Bartlett," but there was a Dr. John Barclay who taught anatomy at the Edinburgh Medical School from 1797–1825 and who wrote several studies and left a museum to the school.[22] From the doctor's interest in "position and distortion," it is obvious he had something other than ropedancing and riding in mind—most likely these early "equilibriums," which did, in fact, involve posturing and a certain degree of contortionism. The act of the Serpentine Ladder, for example—which was also among Andrew's repertoire of feats at this time—required the artist to balance atop an upright ladder, then descend while weaving his body in and out among the rungs.

Following the Edinburgh engagement the company traveled to Glasgow, where on 15 February they opened at the new and elegantly fitted up Olympic Circus in Albion Street.[23] Collett was here billed as both an equestrian and clown to the pantomimes, and here, too, I find Master Ducrow taking his first tentative steps in the "dramatic" line. On 4 March he was billed to interpret the role of the Child in *Perouse* for the second time. *Perouse, or The Desolate Island,* a "pantomimical drama" in two parts adapted by John Fawcett from Kotzebue and originally performed at Covent Garden in 1801, was one in a long string of monkey-dramas popular during the first half of the nineteenth century. Their proven formula involved an interesting assortment of kindhearted apes, who served and protected—often at the expense of their own lives—their human friends, thereby assuring a copious flow of tears from equally sentimental spectators. There were a number of actors who made their reputations in such roles, of whom the most notable were the mime and dancer Mazurier in France, and in England a misshapen performer by the name of "Monsieur Gouffé," whose "singular and multiplied leaps... horizontal balancings...springing from tree to tree...dancing, inverted upon pint pots; and above all, his running round the auditory, upon the headings of box and gallery fronts," astonished spectators at the Surrey Theatre in 1825.[24] Since *Perouse* contains the first dramatic role I have discovered for Master Ducrow, and as Andrew later was to perform as a man-monkey himself, its plot is of some interest. The action begins when the shipwrecked Perouse swims to an island and begins assembling some useful items that have washed ashore. "Champanzee" appears to play with a chest and is on the verge of being devoured by a bear when Perouse returns and shoots the attacker. This earns for Perouse the undying loyalty of Champanzee, who shows Perouse where to find water and prevents him from eating some poisonous berries. Meanwhile, a hunting party of natives, led by the villainous Kanko, lands on the island. Both Champanzee and Perouse are wounded during encounters with them; but one of the savages, Umba, is smitten by Perouse and runs away from her companions to join him. Three years of this idyllic relationship are supposed to pass during the interval, and when Perouse appears in the second act he is dressed in skins and wearing a long beard. His wife and son arrive at the island in search of him, but are intercepted by the savages. There follows a series of rescues and recaptures, with Champanzee several times carrying off and saving the child. Umba, incensed by the presence of Madame Perouse, now sides with Kanko and lets down a drawbridge leading to Perouse's hut, hoping to see her inamorato and his wife murdered. While Perouse is being tortured by Kanko, however, Champanzee appears to untie one of his hands and slip him a pistol, with which Perouse promptly shoots his tormentor. In the ensuing melee the natives are about to discharge their bows upon Perouse and his family. At this crucial moment a party of marines comes rushing on, firing at and cutting down the savages, and the piece concludes with a triumphant tableau.[25]

After parting from the troop of Smith, Crossman, Davis, and Parker at the end of the Glasgow engagement, the Ducrows, together with Collett and a few other members of the company, moved on to Liverpool. Although they were probably present at the opening of the New Olympic Circus on Easter Monday, 7 April 1806, their names do not appear in the bills until two weeks later.[26] On 8 May a curious cut appeared at the top of one of these announcements depicting a strongman balancing two coach wheels on his face with a small boy atop them waving two flags (fig. 7). This particular feat was part of Peter's act, and there can be no doubt the illustration, however crude, is meant to represent him. The boy at the top is either Andrew or John—more likely the latter, who was assisting his father around this time under the sobriquet "Infant of Hope." Andrew's own performances at Liverpool were the same as before, including two appearances on the tightrope; and Peter now presented some "very curious feats with swords, plates, oranges, forks, bottles, hat, stick, hoop, glasses, pipes, &c." while in full swing on the slack wire.[27] The Ducrows took their Liverpool benefit on 15 May, Master Ducrow dancing a hornpipe on the occasion.

Meanwhile, the troop of Smith, Crossman, Davis, and Parker had gone elsewhere at the end of the Glasgow engagement, and I next encounter them in London, where they were billed to open the Olympic Pavilion in Wych Street on 18 September 1806. The Pavilion was a winter circus newly erected and managed by the restless Philip

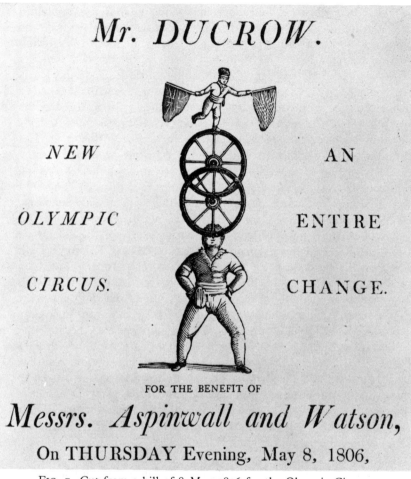

FIG. 7. Cut from a bill of 8 May 1806 for the Olympic Circus, Liverpool, showing Peter Ducrow balancing two coach wheels and one of his sons.

Astley; and from the fact that Mrs. Parker was now advertised to make her first appearance in London in three years, I gather that the company as a whole had not been there since the summer of 1803.[28] They remained at the Pavilion throughout the winter of 1806–1807, moved to the Amphitheatre across Westminster Bridge on Easter Monday, 30 March, and continued at the new location until 23 May. During this entire period I find no evidence of the Ducrows performing with their erstwhile colleagues, and it may be that, as is hinted in the later memoirs, the cause of their dissociating themselves from the company at the end of the 1806 Glasgow engagement was the growing friction between Peter and William Davis over the respective merits of their sons. For it was the "Astonishing Little Equestrian" Davis Jr. who at Glasgow had been given a benefit of his own and billed to dance the rope with Richer, and who continued to be featured as the "wonderful Phenomenon" in his acts on horseback at Astley's Pavilion.[29] By January 1807, in fact, there were *two* Master Davises simultaneously performing equestrian acts, while around the same time Richer, not to be outdone, mounted a "Junior" of his own on the tightrope.[30]

The Ducrows, then, were now traveling with new companions. In the fall of 1806 they were at the Circus at Manchester, where on 13 October Andrew was billed for equestrian exercises, the Polander's Equilibriums, and the Serpentine Ladder ("Master Ducrow...will stand on his head on a Ladder fifteen feet high; turn round, only holding by one hand, and drink a glass of wine; and afterwards will come down from the Top of the Ladder, in and out between every Spoke"). In the concluding pantomime of *Perouse* on this same evening, Mr. D'Egville—probably George—interpreted the title role, Collett played the part of Kanko, and Peter appeared as Umba's father.[31] On 23 October the Ducrows took their benefit, and Andrew, besides riding and performing on the tightrope, was advertised to make his first appearance in a new dance composed by D'Egville.[32] Toward the end of the season he was billed to leap over two garters and go through the six divisions of the broadsword on horseback, and Peter to play the part of the High Priest in *The Death of Captain Cook*.[33] The company then returned to the Olympic Circus at Liverpool, where on 8 December, in the ubiquitous *Perouse*, Master Ducrow— his histrionic abilities clearly on the rise—was billed for the role of Champanzee.[34] Other members of the troop now included the comic singer Richard Johannot and his daughter, the equestrians Port and Makeen, and Hicken as clown to the horsemanship.[35] D'Egville, as one might expect, got up a number of spectacles, pantomimes, and ballets d'action employing most of the company. On 8 December, for example, they performed the ballet *Little Red Riding Hood*; and on 15 December, in a "new Scotch ballet" of his own composition entitled *The Merry Highlanders, or Sawney's Whim*, D'Egville appeared as Sawney, Collett as Robin, and Peter Ducrow as an old man. In the course of this same ballet a *pas de trois* by Master Lasselles, Miss Johannot, and Master Ducrow was introduced.[36] Indeed, the histrionic and terpsichorean talents of both Andrew and Peter enjoyed a workout under D'Egville's direction during the Liverpool season, with the latter's contributions generally restricted to elderly roles.[37]

By this time, too, Andrew had obviously made progress under Collett's instruction, for I now find him often advertised for featured acts of equestrianism. On 19 March 1807, as "Master Ducrow, the infant Hero," he was billed to go through his "wonderful Feats of Agility on HORSEBACK"; and on 8 April, when he and his father took their benefit, he displayed "several new Feats on the Single Horse. With Whips and Handkerchiefs, and in particular will Leap over Four Garters, and go through the Six Divisions of the Broad Sword Exercise, the Horse in full-speed." At other times, as on 22 December, he danced the tightrope and was billed as "Pupil to the celebrated Richer," with Peter serving as clown to the rope. Apropos of Peter's role during these last performances, it should be noted that in nineteenth-century circuses "clowns to the rope" and "clowns to the ring" had several specific functions. Their hackneyed jokes with the master of the ring and acrobatic fooleries had a practical side, providing momentary rests for the artists in the midst of their strenuous exercises; and it was also they who traditionally held the banners (or garters) and balloons over and through which the riders leaped, handed up any props that might be required, and saw that the performers' feet were properly chalked. John Ducrow was also present during the Liverpool season and—as the "Infant of Hope"—assisted his father in his slack-wire act. At the family's benefit on 8 April, a "Grand Trial of Skill, by the Rival Brothers, Masters A. & J. Ducow" was billed to take place. On the same evening John also appeared as the Child in *Perouse*, Andrew having graduated to the more demanding role of Champanzee.

The season at Liverpool ended on 24 April 1807, and with it Andrew's protracted "infancy." If I have not succeeded entirely in rescuing him from oblivion during the preceding years, I nonetheless hazard the opinion that these past eighteen months constituted the most critical period in his development to date. Having mastered the early lessons of Peter Ducrow, Andrew now appeared in all three of his later teachers' specialties—taking his first tentative steps on the tightrope while in the same company as Richer; dancing and acting in the productions of George, if not James Harvey, D'Egville; and finally, under the watchful eye of Collett, performing his first single act of horsemanship. Moreover, by the time of the Liverpool engagement Andrew's growing reputation must have reached the ears of John Astley, for I next find the Ducrows and Makeen at the London Amphitheatre, beginning Monday, 25 May 1807 (Davis and his companions had departed on the previous Saturday), and continuing to the close of the season. The advertisements for Astley's during this year are sparing in the use of the performers' real names, but their descriptions of acts and sobriquets leave no doubt as to the precise dates when the Ducrows and Makeen were there. Andrew was now often billed as the "Young Prussian" or "Prussian Little Devil," while Peter's performances on the slack wire had somehow become "Turkish."[38] In a scoffing review that appeared in the *Monthly Mirror* for June 1807, a critic complained of the "parsimoniousness of entertainment" at Astley's, yet had a qualified word of praise for one of the latter's specialities:

> The only novelty which we have . . . is of a very elegant kind—
> "*Julking*," by Mynheer *Ducrow*. This term (the *unde derivatur*
> of which we know not) signifies, it seems, an imitation of
> birds, and, from the name of the imitator, it naturally strikes one
> that the *cock* would be the first on the list; but that is not the
> case, for the imitations consist entirely of *whistling*, which the
> good citizens, not knowing the note of a lark from that of an
> owl, gape at most wonderfully, whilst *Mr. Astley, Senior*, in
> the lobby, applauds it with ornithological rapture.

At the summer season's end the Ducrows accompanied John Astley to the Royalty Theatre. On account of a rise in the rent, however, Astley remained there only three nights until his lease expired on 29 September. Then, beginning 5 October, the company joined Philip Astley at the Olympic Pavilion. From cryptic advertisements in the newspapers and occasional comments in the *Monthly Mirror* it is apparent Peter and Andrew continued at the Pavilion until the close of the winter season on 9 April 1808. At the end of this engagement, however, I again lose track of them for several years, although I do find plenty of evidence for their former colleagues' presence in the capital. The troop of Smith, Crossman, Davis, and Parker performed at the Amphitheatre during the entire 1808, 1809, and 1810 seasons, and at the Pavilion during the intervening winters as well. During this same period there are many references to Collett,

Johannot, Richer, and the Makeens at both Astley's and the Royal Circus. Yet the Ducrows do not figure in any of the announcements I have seen for these years, and were it not for two scraps of information dating from 1811, my ignorance of their whereabouts would extend through that year as·well. The first of these clues is an advertisement for Davis's Equestrian Amphitheatre in Edgware Road, which was open every evening except Wednesday and Friday during the Lenten season, announcing "Mr. Ducrow, jun." for an act on a single horse;[39] and the second is a trio of rare bills for the Surrey Theatre, dated 26 and 31 July and 8 August 1811, in which "Ducrow" is listed as a Polish knight and "Ducrow Junr." as an English knight in the drama *Blood Will Have Blood, or The Battle of the Bridges.*[40] From other sources I learn that Davis's establishment in Edgware Road was in operation from 18 March until shortly before Easter Monday 1811, at which time Davis moved to the Surrey Theatre to take charge again of the equestrian department there.[41]

This evidence for the Ducrows' having renewed their association with William Davis is not without interest, for it naturally raises the question whether they had spent the previous seasons with him as well. There was, as already noted, some jealousy between the two families; and in time this rivalry with the son of Davis was to contribute to Andrew's decision to abandon his country and seek his fortune elsewhere. As reported in later years, "at the age of fifteen he was principal rope-dancer and equestrian at Astley's, enjoying a salary of £10 per week; but the father of Davies [*sic*], who was also an equestrian, being in partnership with Astley, was anxious alone for the success and popularity of his offspring, to which DUCROW was a decided bar; and D. finding himself rather unpleasantly situated, agreed to join a Mr. Blondell [*sic*] in an excursion to the continent, and he made his first appearance at Ghent."[42] Although this account would seem to explain the lack of information on Andrew during the period 1808–10, Ducrow's departure for the Continent and Davis's partnership with Astley do not occur until much later. In the meantime, however, the possibility exists that William Davis did his best to suppress or at least play down the rising genius of Andrew, which may account for the absence of his name in playbills and advertisements during this period.

The engagement at the Surrey, to be sure, was hardly an important one. Although ropedancing continued to be exhibited there and *Blood Will Have Blood*, besides the horses under Davis's direction, featured a living elephant, the house had ceased to be a proper circus at the start of the 1810 season, when Elliston converted the ring into a pit. The following Easter Monday, 30 March 1812, however, Andrew was back at Astley's Amphitheatre, where he was advertised under his real and arenic names until the last night of the season on 8 October. On 22 June, for example, spectators were promised "Mr. Ducrow (the Little Devil's) new and astonishing elevated Rope-Dancing, &c.: also, his extraordinary Equestrian Agility, on a single Horse."[43] Collett was listed as riding master during this season, and Peter and John were also with the company. The elder Ducrow seems to have passed his prime by this date, for I find no further references to the "Flemish Hercules" or to his feats. In a bill dating from mid-July he is listed for the role of a Spanish farmer in *The Siege of Badajoz*, with Collett as Wellington and the "Masters Ducrow" as children in the same spectacle. On the same program a "Ducrow" figured among the corps de ballet in the representation of *Voorn the Tiger*, following which Andrew performed on the rope and on horseback.[44] A Ducrow also appeared as a dancer in the equestrianized ballet pantomime *Oscar and Malvina* this season, but whether this was Andrew, Peter, or John is uncertain.[45]

The Davises were not at Astley's in 1812—which did not, however, prevent Andrew from competing on and off during the season with the riders Thomas, Avery, Collett, Link, Yates, and several others in a much heralded "Equestrian Trial of Skill."[46] This was undoubtedly the same competition Egan had in mind when he wrote that at the age of sixteen Andrew "acquired the palm at Astley's Amphitheatre, as the principal equestrian amongst upwards of a dozen aspiring young men, in whom consisted a fund of equestrian entertainments, highly interesting and instructive."[47] Of greater interest during this year is the first mention of Andrew's performing a mimetic act of horsemanship, even though the one in question was not original with him and had been around for some time. For that matter, "The Peasant's Frolic, or The Flying Wardrobe" may occasionally be seen in present-day circuses. The act traditionally begins with a drunken countryman rising from the audience, climbing over the ring enclosure, and noisily demanding that he be allowed to take a few turns on horseback. After trying to talk him out of this fool-

PLATE 1. "Mr. Ducrow as the Roman Gladiator." An early print possibly designed by Ducrow himself.

Mr DUCROW or the ROMAN GLADIATOR

hardy desire, the master of the ring finally gives in, and the peasant then goes on to amuse and horrify the spectators with his breakneck antics atop the rushing horse—only to suddenly shed his clothes (generally consisting of a good many layers) and stand revealed in a brilliant costume, leaving no doubt he is actually a star performer. It would seem Andrew perfected this scene during the summer of 1812, for I find him first advertised to perform it toward the end of the season—on 1 October for his teacher Collett's benefit and again on 5 October for that of John Astley.[48]

By 1812 Andrew had clearly progressed beyond his early training and the time when he was billed for the Polander's Equilibriums and Serpentine Ladder. His father Peter—either because of age or ill health—fades from the picture at this point, and henceforth Andrew appears as a featured tightrope dancer and equestrian. His growing reputation, particularly on the rope, now led to some provincial engagements of his own. When I next catch up with him a few weeks later at the Regency Theatre in Bristol, he is advertised, as the "Little Devil," to go through his "most extraordinary and wonderful performances on the Tight-Rope"—feats which, in the playbill's hyperbole, "require seeing to be believed, and Mr. Richer, and other celebrated performers in the same department, have candidly acknowledged his excellence and superiority."[49] The summer of 1813 seems to have been spent outside London as well (Davis and his son were back at Astley's this season), but the following autumn Andrew was again in the west of England, appearing at the obscure New Equestrian Circus in Prince's Street, Bristol. I find very few advertisements and no reviews whatever for this circus in the local papers, and from an announcement of reduced prices in the Bristol *Mercury* for 27 December it would seem the company was indifferently patronized.[50]

The trouble, in part at least, stemmed from the Bristol Theatre Royal, which at the time was offering some stiff competition. Not with Shakespeare or the legitimate drama, of course, but with a rival troop of equestrians headed by James West and Robert Woolford, whose horses were nightly prancing across the boards in such tested vehicles as *Timour the Tartar*, *Blue Beard*, and the musical romance *Lodoiska*. The same company had been at the Theatre Royal the previous summer. Their re-engagement during the winter of 1813–14, besides adding the traditional fillip to the lucrative holiday season, was probably calculated to prevent patrons from being drawn off by the

Prince's Street establishment. The two managers, as Kerim and Sanballat, were regularly billed for the famous equestrian combat in *Timour the Tartar*; a Master Woolford appeared as the young prince Agib; and the part of the heroine Zorilda was taken by Mrs. Vining, a regular performer at the Bath and Bristol theatres.[51] Ducrow and his rivals may have temporarily joined forces sometime in the new year, for in the summer of 1814 they were together in London, where on 4 July West and his troop, "from the Theatres Royal Bristol and Bath," were advertised to make their first appearance at the Royal Circus. The "Infant Equestrian" Master Woolford and "Mr. Ducrow, jun." were on the same bill for horsemanship, and were also listed— along with Woolford Sr., Mrs. West, and Collett—among the cast of a new hippodrama that opened on this date, William Barrymore's *The Tiger Horde*.[52]

The 1814 season at the Circus was a memorable one, leading to a number of claims and stories which Ducrow himself seems to have recalled in later years. One of these relates to his growing repute as a ropedancer. "At the Surrey, some years ago," begins an oft-repeated anecdote that later made the rounds,

> he wheeled a boy in a barrow on the rope, from the stage to the gallery, and (a much harder feat) back from the gallery to the stage! What the sensations of the gentleman were whilst in *transitu*, we can imagine better than describe, but on the second night he was *non est inventus*; this threw Ducrow into a fury, and he tried to persuade one of the supernumeries [*sic*] to take the boy's place; but he, having no taste for glory, declined; and Ducrow was obliged to ascend with an empty barrow, which he did, at the same time indulging in curses 'not loud but deep;' but judge of his amazement, when, on arriving at the gallery, he saw the aforesaid young gentleman, quietly seated, viewing the performances; vulture never pounced upon his prey as Andrew Ducrow did upon his victim. In vain did the urchin exclaim 'that he had paid his shilling,' and demand the courtesy due to an auditor. Ducrow seized him, as *Rolla* does the child, popped him into the barrow, and rolled him down at a brisk trot; the young gentle-man being, as Shakespeare says, 'distilled almost to jelly by the act of fear.' We have heard he left the country shortly after, but for this we do not vouch.[53]

The anecdote, considerably embellished by the journalist and with some predictable allusions to Ducrow's notorious temper and profanity, does appear to have some basis in fact. It was common at this time for tightrope artists to ascend on ropes strung from the stage to the uppermost gallery, and Andrew was advertised for this feat, wheeling a barrow before him, during the 1814 season at the Royal Circus.[54] Unfortunately, the newspaper notices I have seen do not specify the contents of this barrow. It does seem improbable that it would have been empty, however; and the less highly colored account in *Oxberry's* "Memoir" (p. 13), while making no mention of Ducrow's partner ever being "non est inventus," does state that it was occupied by a boy of fourteen, whom Ducrow carried on his shoulders on his benefit night.

During the same season Andrew also appeared in a famous French melodrama adapted by William Barrymore. Indeed, according to one of his memorialists (and one the most sparing in the use of hyperbole), it was Ducrow's acting in this play that first brought him some degree of attention: "Andrew's equestrian performances were at this period looked but lightly on; nor was it till 1814 that he brought himself into considerable notice, and shewed the germs of that talent, which has so richly ripened; by his excellent personation of Eloi, the Dumb Boy, in the Dog of Montargis."[55] Several later writers, having read either this account or, more likely, the plagiarized one in Pattie's *Actors by Daylight*—neither of which names the theatre at which the play was given—have been misled into believing Andrew was appearing at Covent Garden or even Drury Lane at this time.[56] Their confusion is possibly compounded by the fact that both Covent Garden and the Royal Circus mounted versions of Pixérécourt's *Le Chien de Montargis, ou La Forêt de Bondy* within a week of each other. The Covent Garden adaptation, the work of Henry Harris, was first presented on 30 September; while Barrymore's version, which the management of the patent theatre tried to suppress, opened at the Royal Circus on 6 October.[57] The action of Pixérécourt's play revolves around the discovery of a murder by a faithful dog and the attributing of this crime to a pathetic dumb boy, who unfortunately is found to have upon him the dead man's purse (nosed out by the amazing canine, naturally). The accused is tried and sentenced to death, but is saved at the last moment when new evidence comes to light; and the real murderer, who has been considerably harassed by the dog in the meantime, is shot while attempting to flee. Both Harris's and Barrymore's versions closely followed this outline, but there were a few subtle differences. In Harris's adaptation the dumb boy (played by Miss Booth at Covent Garden) was named Florio and his execution was threatened offstage. In Barrymore's *Dog of Montargis, or The Forest of Bondy* the same character was named Eloi (as in Pixérécourt's original play), the execution scene was played onstage, and the real murderer, Macaire, was at the head of the firing squad.[58] I have not succeeded in locating any review that makes specific reference to Andrew's acting in Barrymore's play, although he is listed in the Circus's announcements as one of the "Principal Characters." It therefore seems evident he did perform the role of Eloi during the 1814 season—neither the first nor the last in a long line of mute boys and men, idiots, and dumb animals that often engaged his peculiar talents.

One other event relating to this same London season concerns Ducrow's later claim that he had performed before the Emperor of Russia and King of Prussia and appeared at a fête given at Burlington House in 1814.[59] The sources of such statements are not always easy to trace; but in June 1814, following the defeat and abdication of Napoleon, London was ablaze with a continuous round of festivals and illuminations, and both monarchs did pay a visit to England at this time. A number of celebrations were scheduled at Burlington House. The most lavish of all was given by White's Club on 20 June and was attended by the Emperor, the King of Prussia, the Prince Regent, and some 2,500 other select guests. Aside from a Mr. Sadler, who was to terminate the festivities by ascending in a balloon (which must have occurred early the next morning, since the guests did not sit down to supper until 2 A.M.), I find no mention of variety or circus entertainments. However, it is entirely conceivable they were on the program, since a masquerade given at Burlington House on 1 July by Watier's Club made use of the same decorations, and the descriptions of this event refer to a stage in the gardens for ballets and a medley of other entertainments.[60] The Emperor and the King of Prussia, who had departed the metropolis by the time of the Watier's celebration, did not attend any of the minor theatres during their stay in London. Andrew must have been in town preparing for his opening at the Royal Circus when these events took place, and it would be strange if he did not participate in the general celebrations in some way or other—most likely as a ropedancer.

While monarchs and commanders of the victorious allied forces were hastening to England in the spring and summer of 1814, others were taking advantage of renewed intercourse with the Continent to sail in the opposite direction. Philip Astley returned to Paris, apparently with the intention of reopening his old circus in the faubourg du Temple, but died there in October before completing his plans. Davis took his troop of equestrians to Amsterdam over the summer, returned to Astley's at the beginning of September, and commenced preparations for a trip to Paris (perhaps at Astley's invitation) during the winter months. Ducrow himself did not join in this rush to the Continent, however. Having parted company with West and Woolford at the end of September, he later returned to the west of England and in December was billed for ropedancing and a curious stunt with a balloon at the Theatres Royal, Bath and Bristol. Balloon ascensions and experiments with early parachutes, generally attempted—for the results, especially in the case of the latter inventions, were not always successful—in parks and pleasure gardens such as Vauxhall, were highly popular diversions at this time. But the act Andrew now performed was an indoor one, featured at the start of the evening's program, no doubt on account of the advance preparations required. He was first advertised for it at the Bristol Theatre Royal on 19 December, but a delay in the arrival of some equipment from London forced a postponement until 26 December. Then he triumphantly ascended from the stage to the top of the gallery, standing on his head at the top of the balloon, while two persons rode in the car beneath.[61] Andrew was billed for the same act at the Bath Theatre Royal on 27 December—an arrangement that was not unusual, since the two theatres were often under the same management, and actors, as well as popular entertainers, alternated nightly between the two towns.[62]

I have little information concerning Andrew's whereabouts in 1815, but what I do know makes me suspect he must have spent at least part of the year in London. In January Peter Ducrow died and was buried in the churchyard of St. Mary Lambeth. As Andrew was the eldest of the children, the support of his family devolved upon him. He had probably been the family's mainstay for some time before Peter's death, however, since the "Flemish Hercules" had left off performing and was so little remembered at the time of his death that none of the newspapers or periodicals I have consulted mentions his demise. None of Andrew's four sisters appears to have been working by this date, and his brother John seems to have been equally inactive. It was probably his new responsibilities as head of the household and the necessity to have some proof that he was of legal age that led him to obtain—on 9 September 1815—the transcript of his baptismal certificate now in the Ducrow Album. Meanwhile,

Andrew appears to have returned to the Royal Circus following his engagement at Bath and Bristol, for a notice in the January 1815 issue of the *Theatrical Inquisitor* lists Makeen and "Ducrow" in the company there.

The following spring Andrew was again alternating between the Bath and Bristol Theatres Royal, where he continued to be featured as a ropedancer. At Bristol on 25 March 1816, previous to a performance of the opera *Artaxerxes*, he was announced to go through a five-part exercise on the rope and to imitate the specialities of three well-known rivals: Monsieur Godeau's celebrated French wooden-shoe dance, Mr. Richer's favorite polonaise, Mr. Wilson's garland dance, and Ducrow's own Scotch strathspey and "flag polacca."[63] On the same evening he appeared as Aesop, afterwards Harlequin ("with leaps"), in the concluding pantomime *Harlequin Aesop, or Hymen's Gift.* The same piece had previously been performed on 14 March at the Bath Theatre Royal, where Andrew, as one critic noted, after going through his "truly astonishing evolutions on the tight-rope . . . attempted to perform *Harlequin*, and was by no means successful."[64] The amazement of the Bath spectators at his agility on the rope was even greater on 28 March, when he was announced for an imitation of another rival, the famous Madame Saqui, who was then performing at Covent Garden. In an act entitled "L'Ascension au Vol des Oiseaux" Andrew repeatedly ran up a rope extending from the stage to the rear of the gallery and returned to the stage at full speed, pausing in the midst of one of these trips to add a few embellishments of his own. The performance was described two days later in a Bristol journal:

> BATH THEATRE—Thursday night an extraordinary degree of curiosity was excited by young Ducrow's announcement for his wonderful feat, the Ascension upon the rope from the stage to the back of the gallery. His performance of this daring exploit realised every expectation, and actually seemed to electrify the spectators. He sprang up to the tremendous height and returned again to the stage three successive times, with the same ease as an ordinary person would have walked upon the boards; and when he reached the central point exactly above the pit, he stood upon one leg alternately, and performed a double Somerset.—As far as *astonishment* is connected with amusement, the exhibition was unrivalled.[65]

The same act, presumably with the incredible double somersault thrown in, was announced for the Bristol Theatre Royal on 1 April.[66]

Back in London a few weeks later, Andrew resumed his equestrian career at Astley's. The Amphitheatre was now under the management of John Astley, Davis, and Parker; and it was Davis's son, William Jr., who was the featured rider at the Easter Monday opening. A week later, on 22 April, his name was replaced in the theatre's advertisements by that of Ducrow, which in turn gave way to Makeen's at the start of the third week. Both Ducrow and Makeen, predictably, were falsely announced as making their "first" appearances at the Amphitheatre. No doubt they had been present at the opening on 15 April, since for the next several months this three-week cycle—with each rider regularly taking his turn at the head of the equestrian department—was maintained. On 26 August Ducrow was finally announced for his "elegant equilibriums" on the tightrope. They were not of very long duration, however, for beginning 9 September Andrew was forced to take a back seat to the renowned Saqui herself. Having spent the summer at Vauxhall Gardens, where she mounted the rope at midnight amid a dazzling display of fireworks, she now appeared at Astley's to exhibit the same dizzying ascension to the gallery Andrew had performed a few months earlier at Bath and Bristol. On 14 October she and one of her brothers, Monsieur Lalanne, participated in a *pas de trois* on three ropes. The third dancer on this occasion was not Ducrow, however, but his rival Davis Jr.[67] Madame Saqui's last night and benefit occurred on 19 October, and four nights later Andrew received a shared benefit of his own with two other performers, one of whom, Brown, was clown to the ring. Besides riding and dancing the rope on this occasion, Ducrow repeated his headstand atop the rising balloon and performed a jockey hornpipe with Brown and Davis Jr. in the course of a ballet entitled—appropriately enough— *The Rival Brothers*.[68] On 24 October, the penultimate night of the season, he showed what he could do (and no doubt what some of his competitors could *not* do) by making the grand ascent from the stage to the gallery—backwards![69]

Although Andrew shared equal billing with Makeen and Davis Jr. in the ring this season, his performances on horseback were as yet ignored by the press. The only specific act for which I find him advertised was the old "Equestrian Booby" or "Peasant's Frolic," which might lead one to conclude he had made little progress as an equestrian over the past several years. That this was not the case, however—that Andrew had by now struck out in a new direction

FIG. 8. The celebrated ropedancer Madame Saqui as she appeared at Vauxhall Gardens in 1816.

FIG. 9. Ducrow in the role of "The Gladiator." One of the earliest depictions of him, published by William West on 27 September 1816.

which in a few short years would win him plaudits as Europe's most original rider—is attested by two prints issued around this time by the famous toy-theatre and theatrical-portrait publisher William West. The earlier of these (fig. 9), dated 27 September 1816 from West's establishment in Exeter Street, represents Andrew in the character of a Roman gladiator; and the second (fig. 10), published the following 21 January, is entitled "MR. DUCROW the Celebrated Equestrian at ASTLEY'S AMPHITHEATRE Performing his ROMAN DE- FENCE in the different attitudes of *THE GLADIATORS*: taken from Drawings made for NAPOLEON BUONAPARTE."[70] These are the earliest depictions of Andrew as an equestrian known to me. Aside from giving some idea of the nature of his "equestrian exercises" during the 1816 season, they are remarkable for portraying a type of act Ducrow is sometimes credited with inventing: the "poses plas-

Fig. 10. Ducrow in four different attitudes as "The Gladiators." Published by William West on 21 January 1817.

tiques" on horseback, wherein the artist rides round the ring while striking attitudes of various well-known subjects, often drawn from mythology and classic statuary. It should be noted that these representations—in effect tableaux vivants which, on account of the circling horse, could be viewed from all sides—were not the same as Ducrow's later, more celebrated creations such as "The Wild Indian Hunter" and "The Vicissitudes of a Tar," which were genuine pantomimes on horseback.

After spending the intervening winter at the Olympic Circus in Liverpool, where a company including Miss Saunders and the Makeens had been assembled from the London summer houses,[71] Andrew returned to Astley's for the 1817 season. The competition was considerably lightened this year by the absence of the Davises, who were now touring the Continent.[72] Consequently, the honors of the ring were divided evenly between Andrew and Makeen. On 1 September, after gathering fresh laurels at Vauxhall Gardens, Madame Saqui returned to the Amphitheatre for a brief engagement. At her benefit on 13 September the dance on three ropes was repeated, and this time she was joined by Ducrow and the slack-wire artist Il Diavolo Antonio.[73] For his own benefit on 1 October, now shared with the Harlequin Ridgway and comic singer Sloman, Andrew made his ascending and descending flight from the stage to the gallery doing a headstand on a "parachute" (presumably a rigid affair drawn up by ropes), exhibited equilibriums on the tightrope, and performed the "Equestrian Booby" and "Six characters on Horseback."[74] This last act, which Ducrow continued to perform for many years and which inspired several prints, was also in the burlesque tradition and consisted of the equestrian antics of such characters as a jockey, old woman, and butcher on the way to market. Also during the 1817 season Andrew seems to have been joined at Astley's by another member of his family. A bill for 6 September in the Victoria & Albert lists the Ducrow name twice in the concluding melodrama *The Sisters, or The Heroines of Switzerland*, both for the role of Michelli (which I assume Andrew to have played) and as one of a group of "Amazons." It is possible, of course, that either Andrew or his brother John may have made up as an Amazon; but it is more likely that Andrew's sister Hannah, who would have been around fourteen at the time, or perhaps his sister Louisa, performed the role.

During the winter Andrew was again at the Olympic Circus in Liverpool, performing on the rope and on horseback from 8 December

FIG. 11. Watercolor portrait of a young man thought to be Andrew
Ducrow around the time of his marriage to his first wife in 1818.

FIG. 12. Watercolor portrait of a young woman believed to be
Ducrow's first wife Margaret.

until the close of the season on 13 March 1818.[75] His visits to Liverpool
during these years are of particular interest, since presumably it was
here that he met his first wife, Margaret Griffith, who was later
described as a native of the city. She was, as one memorialist tanta-
lizingly puts it, "a lady of most prepossessing exterior, and amiable
unaffected manners."[76] Not much is known about Margaret, and she
is rarely mentioned in contemporary accounts of her husband.
Ducrow's machinist Matthew Mackintosh, who seems to have had
a soft spot for her, later reported that Andrew had met her while
performing at the Liverpool circus and married her at St. John's
Church in that city, and that "she was a fine-looking 'Lancashire
witch,' and a most valuable help-meet for Andrew. She had received
an excellent education, and was naturally a capital woman of business,
so she at once took the management of the financial department of the
concern into her own hands, and retained it through life to the profit
and satisfaction of her husband."[77] Unfortunately, Matthew Mackintosh, as is amply demonstrated in the first appendix to this work, was
notoriously inaccurate where facts are concerned, and not above
fantasizing when he had nothing better to offer—and the present
description is no exception. For there certainly was no "concern" to
manage in 1818, Ducrow and his partners employed a succession of
competent treasurers during their lesseeships of Astley's from 1825 on,
and the wedding itself, as I have learned to my cost, never took place
at St. John's Church or anywhere else in Liverpool. According to
the generally reliable memoir published in *Oxberry's Dramatic Biography* (p. 10), this event occurred on 24 May 1818. However, since
Ducrow was on this very day between engagements in Holland, the
possibility exists that he either married Margaret there or made a
flying visit to London to solemnize the nuptials among family and
friends. I have searched for the wedding certificate at Liverpool, The
Hague, and London for 1818 and other years—but without success.

Although Margaret Ducrow often rode in the stately entrées and
processions arranged by her husband, and occasionally performed in
the spectacles Andrew produced at Astley's and elsewhere, she was
obviously limited as an equestrienne. I find no mention of her performing at circuses in London or the provinces prior to her marriage,
and she appears to have acquired her knowledge of riding under
Andrew's tutelage while they were touring on the Continent. She
nonetheless seems to have come from a circus family, for in later years
a niece of hers, married to a member of the Bridges family of riders,

FIG. 13. "Mr. Davis, the Celebrated Rider at Ashley's [*sic*]."

was billed to dance the Cracovienne on horseback at Astley's.[78] The name "Griffiths" (as well as "Griffin") often appears in both circus and theatre announcements dating from as early as the 1770s.[79] Margaret was around twenty years old when she married Andrew (a tablet on the mausoleum at Kensal Green gives her age as thirty-nine at the time of her death in January 1837). There were no children from their union. The watercolor portraits reproduced in figures 11 and 12, from the collection of Mr. Antony D. Hippisley Coxe, are thought to be of Andrew and Margaret and were possibly executed shortly after their marriage while they were living and traveling in France.[80]

In the spring of 1818 Astley's reopened with the combined troops of John Astley and William Davis, but Andrew was not among them. Spurred on by his forthcoming marriage to Margaret and stories of the Davises' successful Continental tour during the previous season, he apparently had already made up his mind to try his own fortune across the Channel. Then, too, his attempts to develop a new style of circus riding—which to date had not progressed beyond the "poses plastiques" and attitudes of the Gladiators—had obviously failed to impress the majority of English spectators. As a later memoir (directly inspired by Ducrow, one suspects) caustically remarked, audiences still preferred the "senseless and attempted drollery of clowns and mummers, to the pure and classic chastity of Ducrow's efforts."[81] After fifty years of circus history, it was still burlesque scenes like "The Taylor Riding to Brentford" and "The Peasant's Frolic" that English spectators clamored for. With little encouragement in his own country, balked by the competition and envy of the Davises, Makeens, and a host of other indistinguishable riders, Andrew sailed for Holland in early April. He was twenty-four years old at the time. When he returned to England five years later, he would be at the head of his own troop of equestrians and would revolutionize the art of circus riding.

comme sa pantomime est expressive et
animée, comme ses poses sont belles!

—*L'Ami de la Charte*, 4 July 1823

3   The Years Abroad

FOR THE NEXT FIVE and a half years Ducrow roamed the Continent,
steadily adding to his repertoire and perfecting his skill as an equestrian. His travels during this period encompassed Holland, Belgium,
Switzerland, Italy, and Spain, but it was Paris and the provincial
cities of France that provided the more usual and most congenial
settings for his performances. Indeed, his enthusiastic reception
wherever he appeared, following so closely on the neglect by English
spectators and critics, undoubtedly contributed to his decision to
prolong his stay abroad and, in time, to hazard managing a company
of his own. For the first few months of this extended tour, however,
Andrew was content to accept an engagement as featured equestrian
with François Blondin, whose Cirque Olympique or Arena of the
Gods, together with a menagerie, was then traveling about the cities
and fairs of Holland. Blondin's circus was also well-known in Germany
—the manager regularly advertised both his establishment and
himself, in the capacity of riding master, as "geprivilegeerd" or
licensed by the King of Prussia—and to a lesser degree in Belgium

and France, where it was overshadowed by the famous Cirque Olympique of the Franconi family. The name is still remembered today, thanks to the ropewalker and "Hero of Niagara" Emile Gravelet, who served his apprenticeship with Blondin at a later date and, in the "père d'élève" tradition of the circus, was permitted to take his master's name.[1]

Another famous artist associated with Blondin's circus in his early years was Henri Martin, originally a trick rider who joined Blondin at Frankfurt. Born in 1793, the same year as Ducrow, he was later to make his mark as one of the first great lion trainers and to appear in a number of sensational melodramas specifically written to exhibit him with his big cats. In 1831 Martin appeared on the boards of Drury Lane in one such drama entitled *Hyder Ali, or The Lions of Mysore*, on a bill that included Ducrow in an act of his own, and afterward toured the British provinces with considerable success, joining forces with Andrew there as well. He retired from his hazardous profession in 1840 to become the curator of the Rotterdam zoo and lived to the advanced age of eighty-nine. In the spring of 1818, however, Martin, like Ducrow, was still a relatively unknown performer, and an equally restless one. He had recently deserted Blondin to set up a circus of his own—a venture his former master soon had the satisfaction of seeing end in failure, for the new troop, after experiencing numerous difficulties, was decisively routed during the August fair at Rotterdam, where Blondin had brought his circus also and Ducrow's "poses plastiques" created a furor. Unable to compete with so powerful an attraction, Martin nonetheless profited from the lesson and reapplied for his old position. Blondin was not reluctant to take him back, all the more so, one suspects, as Ducrow himself was by then about to depart for greener fields.[2]

Prior to this "contrecarre" at Rotterdam, Andrew had performed with Blondin in several Dutch cities, beginning at Ghent on 13 April in the pleasure gardens of Wauxhall. As one learns from a review in the *Journal de Gand* for 15 April, the circular "tent" or booth Blondin carried with him was open to the weather above the ring. This last, the critic promised, would in a few short days be encircled by a magnificent carpet of grass. During performances spectators were regaled by the spring songs of nightingales, accompanying the orchestra's raucous trumpet. As for Ducrow himself, in the opinion of the ornithologically minded reviewer he surpassed all riders past and present. "It seems impossible to assume on horseback such difficult attitudes with such equally incredible ease. This rider recognizes no difficulty, and his leaps possess the grace of a bird that hops about on a branch." The critic then went on to insist on a point he had made three days earlier in an issue containing the announcement of the circus's opening: while Ducrow was the "most celebrated" equestrian England had to offer, he was not an importation from that country, but was actually a native of Bruges! Had the writer, one wonders, some ancient recollection of the "Flemish Hercules," who had himself been born at Bruges? Or had Ducrow and Blondin themselves shrewdly furnished this piece of information in order to capitalize on Andrew's Flemish ancestry?

A week later the anonymous critic was pleased to report that his initial opinion of Ducrow had been confirmed by the majority of spectators who had visited the circus. The gracefulness of the artist belied the difficulty of his exercises, and in his attitudes of the Gladiator he stood out as though he were posing for an academy. The reviewer did find fault with one aspect of Andrew's costuming, however. Like all performers during the nineteenth century, Ducrow was limited by public mores in the degree to which he could expose the unadorned figure. Thus, while theatrical prints from the period often lead the viewer to believe limbs and chests were left bare, such was in fact rarely the case. To take but one outstanding example from much later in the century, the American actress Adah Isaacs Menken, who shocked her contemporaries on both sides of the Atlantic and was accorded the epithet the "Naked Lady" after making her debut in the title role of the hippodramatic version of Byron's *Mazeppa*, always discreetly augmented her trunks and scalloped top with silk fleshings. The same respect for propriety was required of male performers, and Ducrow was no exception. But the critic at Ghent apparently was, for he complained that "the Roman helmet ought to exclude ignoble tights." With a costume better affecting the nude, he argued, a chlamys or Greek cloak and some trifling accessories, Ducrow could reproduce with an elegant exactitude the antique statues of Apollo, Mercury, as well as the Gladiator. Such exhibitions would not please spectators avid for somersaults and cheap thrills, of course, but would have great appeal for true lovers of the arts and all those who prefer grace and beauty to feats of strength.[3] The critic's suggestions appear to have made an impression on Ducrow, for he shortly supplemented his attitudes of the Gladiator with representations of Apollo, Mercury, and other classic figures. In later years, too, the elastic body stocking he then wore for stage presentations was said to simulate nudity perfectly.

Meanwhile, at his benefit on 22 April Andrew reverted to a burlesque scene such as he had given in London, and on 26 April the Ghent engagement came to a close following a performance whose proceeds were donated by Blondin to a local charity.[4] Two weeks later the circus was at The Hague, setting up its booth in the Horse Market there and opening on 12 May in time for the annual city fair. Previous to this a number of advertisements had been inserted in the newspapers boasting of Blondin and Ducrow's reception at Ghent. The latter was described as a young Englishman only nineteen years of age. According to these same announcements, the company consisted of twenty-two artists and twenty trained horses, and the solidity of the "tent" was guaranteed.[5] Sometime around 16 May the circus was honored with a visit by the entire Royal Family. Blondin, naturally, did not let so momentous an event go unnoticed in his subsequent advertisements; and Ducrow himself, in a trilingual bill aimed at visitors to London on the occasion of Victoria's coronation, recalled it with satisfaction twenty years later.[6] On 24 May the manager drew up an announcement of his troop's imminent departure for the fairs at Antwerp and Utrecht which was published in the 's Gravenhaagsche Courant the following day. In the same announcement Ducrow thanked the spectators who had patronized him and who had expressed the desire that some of his exercises might be drawn and engraved. He was later to act on this suggestion also.

The date of composition for this announcement is of special interest, since it was on this very day that Andrew supposedly married his first wife Margaret. Assuming the reported date of the latter event to be correct, he must have either returned to England while the circus was on the move or celebrated the wedding in Holland, with Margaret coming over with Andrew in April or else joining him at The Hague after he had established himself with Blondin. Although she did not appear as a performer at this time, Margaret very likely had charge of another member of the Ducrow family, Andrew's little sister Emily, who also appeared before the Royal Family at The Hague. She was later billed during the August fair at Rotterdam to ride round the ring balancing on one foot on her brother's shoulder and for a character solo dance on horseback entitled "The Orphans of Waterloo."[7] The advertisements for the Rotterdam engagement describe her as being only three and a half years old—a figure just half her real age and no doubt incredible to the good burghers who came to see her, since in the following month's announcements she had already advanced to the age of four.

After performing at Rotterdam until the end of August, the circus spent most of September in Amsterdam. Ducrow continued as the star attraction. The attitudes of the Gladiator were repeated, and by now the act with Emily in which she balanced on his shoulder while Andrew himself posed on one foot on the back of a cantering horse had been given classical associations as well: "Mercury Being Led by Cupid." Another striking but as yet untitled pose now introduced by Andrew demonstrated his phenomenal sense of balance. Again standing on one foot (according to a later French writer, on one toe), he leaned far out over the side of the horse—an exercise, the advertisements proclaimed, never before seen and impossible to describe, "as [are] all other feats of this singular man."[8] There were also equestrian exercises of a more traditional nature. Between Ducrow's scenes the other members of the company appeared in acts involving trained horses, leaping, and pantomimes, and the performances generally concluded with fireworks and illuminations.

The itinerant troop of Blondin visited several other Dutch towns, and in time the fame of his rider reached the ears of his great French rivals, the Franconi family. The Cirque Olympique at Paris, the lineal descendant of Philip Astley's old Parisian establishment, was by now one of the most illustrious circuses in Europe. Owned and managed by Astley's successor Antonio Franconi—assisted by his two sons Laurent and Henri, the former an expert equestrian, the latter an actor, author, and *metteur en scène* of circus melodramas and pantomimes—the Cirque had recently moved back into Astley's original building in the faubourg du Temple, where it continued until the structure was destroyed by fire in 1826. The interior followed the English model, with a large scenic stage in addition to the ring.[9] After rejecting several offers to join this establishment, Andrew finally consented to an arrangement whereby he was to share in the profits of each evening's performance after the first 300 francs had been taken in.[10] The offer is indicative of Ducrow's growing reputation on the Continent, and doubtless the Franconis profited from the arrangement as well, although Pierce Egan's statement that Ducrow "in the course of six months, realized more money for the theatre than had been possessed by the treasury for as many years put together" must naturally be viewed with skepticism.[11] Nevertheless, the same writer's description of Ducrow's performances and enthusiastic reception in Holland and France is indeed borne out by contemporary press accounts. "The versatility of these performances," Egan writes,

> were already such as to furnish two hours and a half of recreation, and were attended by crowds in every place eager to get a sight of the ASTONISHING ENGLISHMAN, who, by his individual exertions could amuse an audience for so great a length of time. . . . His admirable method of obtaining rounds of applause by the simple and chaste execution of his different scenes, added to the grace which so distinguishes every movement, amounting to a seeming disregard for personal safety, while his horses, with their ardour and impetuosity, rent the very ground they trampled over, calling forth from the French critics and journalists the strongest expressions of their admiration and delight which words can express.[12]

Despite a near-calamitous fall that incapacitated him for several days, Andrew's debut at the Cirque Olympique on 16 December 1818 was a solid success. He performed, wrote a critic for the *Journal de Paris* (18 December), "with marvelous facility the most difficult feats of dance and gymnastics on horseback. . . . standing on the saddle, often on one foot in the most unnatural equilibrium, he maintains attitudes such as a dancer could hardly assume on a stage; but what distinguishes him above all else is that he shows himself always graceful in the midst of everything that is most difficult." The review in the *Quotidienne* (18 December) was equally lavish in its praise:

> The debut of M. Ducrow, the English equestrian, at the circus of MM. Franconi was most brilliant. It is impossible to unite to a higher degree grace and strength, elegance and temerity. His horse, launched forth as in a race at Newmarket, dashes round the ring with such speed that the eye can barely follow the rider's poses. In a pyrrhic dance M. Ducrow demonstrated that he had carefully studied all the attitudes of the gladiators; this part of his exercises received universal approbation, and the frequent applause he received during the evening must have consoled him for a fall which frightened the spectators much more than the rider himself.

The cause of the fall, together with the fullest and most interesting description of Ducrow's debut, appeared two days later in the *Camp-Volant*. That this particular review was highly gratifying to Andrew is proved by the presence of a handwritten translation in the Ducrow

Album, assembled, in part at least, from materials Andrew or Margaret gathered during their travels abroad. After recalling the appearance of young Davis at the Cirque Olympique during the previous season, the critic went on to remark that England had now sent over Ducrow and his horse:

> This is probably all we ought to expect, since it is doubtful a more airy horseman flys amid the fogs of the Thames. To grace which charms from the very first, M. Ducrow joins astonishing strength and boldness. Everything a good dancer does on a firm and solid floor, he performs on the saddle with extraordinary lightness and finish. Finally, to give some idea of the miracles he performs, I believe he actually flys beside his horse. This last experienced more than his master the anxiety of a debut: he committed several faults in "tempo," one of which came near to proving fatal to the cavalier. Thrown down into the arena, and almost trampled by the hoofs of his timid companion, the skillful equestrian adroitly disentangled himself and, with a leap, regained possession of his mobile stage, which he did not quit again. The bravos, the testimonies of concern and relief, burst forth from every part of the house; and when M. Ducrow returned as a Roman to assume, at a gallop, some attitudes imitated from antiquity, then finish with the "Grand Vol de Mercure," these marks of goodwill were redoubled—favorable omens of a great and legitimate success. With so fine a talent, this rider is worthy to have been born in the faubourg du Temple!
>
> M. Ducrow was not able to reappear on the day announced for his second debut. Wounded, although slightly, in the heel by a blow from one of his horse's hoofs, he will not "work" till tomorrow. This circumstance adds to the interest already inspired by his extraordinary merit; and one can take our word for it on this last article, for M. Ducrow is English.

There can be no doubt Ducrow was the undisputed star of the Cirque Olympique during the 1818–19 season. His gracefulness and daring, his "inconceivable skill," were frequently remarked on in the press; and the Franconis themselves, although they and the equestrians Bassin *père* and *fils* were also riding at the time, freely acknowledged and proclaimed his superiority.[13] During the Lenten season Andrew delighted his audiences with a burlesque scene entitled "Le Cocher de diligence," another version of "The Peasant's Frolic."[14] But in April he proved less successful in deserting his horse for the stage to perform the role of Lubin in the pantomime *Annette et Lubin*. "We advise him," wrote the critic for the *Quotidienne*, "to remount his horse, for there is his true 'terrain.'" The advice was taken and the pantomime speedily withdrawn.[15]

On 20 April 1819 the company left Paris for its annual summer tour, and for the next several months Andrew was on the road with the Franconis. Nancy, Metz, and Strasbourg were earliest on their itinerary. At the first of these cities Ducrow temporarily left his colleagues to exhibit his talent on the tightrope at the the local theatre, whose own artists were doing so badly that they deserted their home to appear as supernumeraries in the circus's pantomimes. As usual, too—in France as in Britain—whenever Ducrow or any other artist of less than "legitimate" status ventured to play in a regular theatre, there was an immediate outcry. "Whatever may be the talent he has displayed there," wrote an indignant correspondent to the *Courrier des Spectacles* (26 June) on the day following the exhibition, "I cannot help being astonished that the temple of Thalia and Melpomene should be turned into a home for a *mountebank*. For this is the only title M. Ducrow is able to merit in my opinion under the circumstances, despite all the bravos and applause showered upon him." In late August the troop again joined with local actors at the Cirque Olympique des Brotteaux in Lyons for a spectacular production of Cuvelier de Trie's hippodrama *La Mort de Kléber*. It was here that a fatal accident occurred which Ducrow or his memorialists later confused with the period when he was managing his own circus in France. On 29 August, while the enactment of an attack on a fort was in progress, a discharge of musketry mortally wounded a woman sitting in a box. The muskets had been loaded with blanks, of course, but one of the extras—a bona fide infantryman, no less, whose company had been hired for the production—forgot to remove the ramrod from his gun. The accident, understandably, occasioned a certain amount of unrest among the spectators, some of whom yelled "fire" and rushed from the circus. The performance was consequently halted for a time, but later resumed and "concluded in tranquillity."[16]

At summer's end Andrew returned to Paris with the Franconis and was announced to ride at the reopening of the Cirque on 2 October. His reception in the press was as favorable as before, although by this date he had a "happy" rival in the younger Bassin, who was beginning to claim his share of attention.[17] The critics' delight at the progress of this young and spirited French rider was no doubt stimulated by a sense of national pride, for while they were generally unstinting in their praise of Ducrow, there was one aspect of his character they could never forget: he was English. "One sees him again with pleasure," wrote a critic of Andrew's reappearance in the fall of 1819, "but his presence does produce one inconvenience, of which he is the innocent cause and one would be wrong not to pardon him for: on seeing him, one believes himself at London."[18] That Ducrow himself encouraged this impression of "English-ness" and thereby sought to add to audiences' curiosity about him seems certain enough, for in France, as in Holland, he was repeatedly advertised as the "écuyer anglais" and "premier écuyer du grand Cirque de Londres." A particularly ridiculous instance of the limits to which he sometimes pushed such nationalism after he had begun managing his own company was reported in the *Miroir des Spectacles* for 5 July 1821. During a performance at Nîmes, it was observed, two English spectators stood up and uncovered, while the orchestra struck up *God Save the King*! Once back in England, on the other hand, Ducrow for a good many years was to stress his *French* antecedents. He customarily billed himself and both his wives as "Monsieur" and "Madame," and his apprentices and the other female members of his family as "Mademoiselle." His equestrian acts, especially during the first few years following his return to England, often appeared under French titles. And he so thoroughly exploited the Napoleonic Legend in his spectacles at Astley's that a number of indignant critics and spectators genuinely believed England's foremost circus had fallen to a Frenchman. There is evidence, too, for his affecting a French pronunciation and trying to impress people with his knowledge of the language—which did not fool many of his English contemporaries, who laughed at his airs and ironically dubbed him "the Mounseer."

In the autumn of 1819, however, Andrew was becoming increasingly disenchanted with his fellow French riders, who were now, he observed, copying his style and the feats he had first exhibited.[19] He therefore decided to leave the Franconis, and at the start of November, after a final performance on the 1st, took to the road with a small company of his own. Their first stop upon leaving Paris was at Rouen, where Ducrow gave four performances on the tightrope at the Théâtre des Arts before taking his troop to the Cirque Olympique in the rue Duguay-Trouin.[20] At this point it may be well to consider the makeup of Ducrow's company over the next four years, especially those members of his family who were traveling with him. The last included his wife and young sister Emily; but despite the assertions of several later writers, I find no evidence that his brother John was

FIG. 14. "M. Ducrow's Equestrian Scene of the Indian & Wild Horses." An early English print, possibly for one of Ducrow's benefit nights, while the "Mounseer" was still giving himself out as French.

ever part of the company in France or anywhere else on the Continent.[21] At this time, in fact, John Ducrow had yet to enter upon the role in which he eventually gained a considerable reputation, and it is not until as late as 1825 that I first find mention of his appearing as clown to the ring. Meanwhile, in England he served in a number of useful capacities—as an acrobat, actor in pantomimes, member of the corps de ballet, and even as a rider in hippodramas—leading a few writers to confuse him with Andrew and to assume that the latter was performing in England when he was actually on the Continent. During the 1822 summer and winter seasons at Astley's, for example, a "Ducrow" was billed for secondary roles in afterpieces and among fourteen artists to do the Egyptian Pyramids, and a "Mr. Ducrow" for the part of St. Anthony in Charles Dibdin's hippodrama *St. George and the Dragon*; while during the 1823 season a "Ducrow" or "Mr. Ducrow" was repeatedly listed as a character or member of the ballet in a number of productions, and for the part of Sir Niel O'Niel in *The Siege of Londonderry*.[22] Although a few of these notices may refer to Ducrow's sisters Louisa and Hannah, I am certain none of them is to Andrew himself. Had he returned to Astley's during this period he would have been billed as a star attraction and doubtless for the same equestrian scenes he had developed in France, and in many cases the dates of these announcements correspond precisely to those of Andrew's appearances in various French cities. It therefore seems obvious that John—together with his sisters Louisa, Hannah, and Margaret—remained in England while Andrew was traveling abroad. The only other member of Andrew's "family" to accompany him to the Continent was the carefully trained horse on whose sturdy back Ducrow struck his poses and performed his pantomimes.

The newly formed company was quite small at the start—according to one account, only Andrew, his wife and sister, two boys, and ten horses[23]—but with increasing prosperity attained considerable size. By 1822 a Lyons correspondent, commenting on Ducrow's scouring the city with his artists, horses, and carriages, described his "cortège" as resembling that of a great ambassador; and in the following year, at the time of a visit to Nantes, the troop was reported to consist of thirty performers and thirty-six horses.[24] There were, of course, fluctuations in these numbers. The casts of Ducrow's pantomimes and spectacles were regularly augmented with actors and companies of soldiers from the towns in which they were given; various artists came and went; and on occasion Andrew entered into partnership with the head of some other troop. At the time of his return to England in 1823 he contracted to bring with him ten artists, fifteen horses, and a trained stag—which is probably a fair estimate of the size of the company's core of performers and stud.

As the troop grew and flourished over the next few years, so did Andrew's own reputation and publicity. Like many another artist before and since, he was never one to hide or depreciate his accomplishments. Tributes or souvenirs from reviewers, aristocratic patrons, and even his lowliest fans were carefully preserved and years later trotted out for inspection by his friends and memorialists in England. A telling epithet or especially picturesque description of his riding in a local journal might well be incorporated into the circus's advertisements in subsequent cities. Such honestly bestowed titles as "Le Vestris à Cheval" and "L'Ecuyer Classique de l'Europe" were, of course, too good to be permitted to lapse into oblivion, though on occasion Ducrow's vanity in these matters was bound to rub some people the wrong way. In 1821 one Parisian critic, who had obviously forgotten Ducrow's enthusiastic reception in the capital a few years before, sarcastically observed that "the Englishman Ducrow, celebrated more for his conceit than his agility, wishes to be styled the 'foremost rider of Europe.'"[25]

The years in France also saw the realization of the wish expressed by Ducrow's Dutch admirers that his poses and feats might be captured in prints. Of the several handsome depictions of him issued during this period, the earliest of all, dating from 1818–19 when he was with the Franconis at Paris, is a large hand-colored engraving of Andrew as the Gladiator, standing with one foot on the rump and the other on the neck of his galloping courser, a javelin in his right hand and shield over his upraised left arm.[26] An interesting feature of this naive print is that, as the title informs us, it was taken from a drawing by Ducrow himself ("dessiné par lui-même"). Possibly it was made to be given away on his benefit nights—an enticement Ducrow sometimes offered his English patrons. Andrew's artistry in this instance is not surprising; as pointed out in the initial chapter, he was fond of drawing horses during his boyhood and later designed costumes and properties for his productions at Astley's. Fortunately, there were other, more experienced artists who soon came to his aid, and their work is among the most expert and descriptive we have. The lithograph reproduced in figure 15, for example, dating from around 1821 and after the artist H. Reverchon, depicts Andrew and

Emily performing on the grounds of the Elisée Lyonnais, a pleasure garden at Lyons that featured the prototype of the roller coaster, the "montagnes russes" or "montagnes françaises," which loom faintly in the background. The act represented, apparently evolved from the 1818 "Mercury Being Led by Cupid," was titled "Le Bouquet de l'Amour, ou Les Jeux de Zéphyre et de Cupidon" and was one of the most frequently described and perhaps the most highly admired of all Ducrow's equestrian scenes on the Continent.[27] Two other poses from the same act were captured in lithographs after J. Bergmann published in 1820 at Geneva, where Ducrow performed in the fall of that year (figs. 16 and 17). These remarkable prints, with their balletic character and seemingly fantastic poses, all attest to the gracefulness and beauty of Andrew's performances and bear out the descriptions of him by his critics and fans. They also give a good idea of what these poses plastiques were like and the magnitude of his achievement in this type of entertainment. In all three prints Andrew appears in his winged Zephyr costume, while the bouquet itself, which figured in other poses, is visible in the ring. In figure 16 a birdcage with living doves has been placed on the horse, and the birds are released into the air while Andrew and Emily, having substituted a garland of flowers for the bow and dart of the first illustration, strike a new pose. Finally, the third lithograph shows Andrew alone on horseback holding the same garland and poised in the difficult equilibrium that had astonished the Dutch reviewers and now went by the name of the "Grand Vol de Zéphyre."[28] Upon viewing these prints, one is no longer inclined to wonder at those French reviewers who referred to Ducrow as the "aérien-voltigeur." Or that one of these critics, on seeing a similar pose while Andrew was impersonating Endymion— standing on a single toe and leaning far out to the sides of his rushing horse—should archly suggest that the explanation for this incredible feat must reside in some hidden magnet![29]

Stopping a few weeks to several months in each place they visited, Ducrow's troop crisscrossed the French provinces over the next four years and occasionally strayed across the borders into neighboring countries. Of the many cities visited during this period, Lyons served as a focal point, with the company settling there for extended engagements on several occasions. The Cirque Olympique des Brotteaux was the usual site of their performances, and it was to this location Andrew led his company in the spring of 1820. By now he had joined forces with the troop of an equestrian named Lalanne, a member of

FIG. 15. "Ducrow à l'Elisée Lyonnais," depicting Andrew and his sister Emily in their celebrated act "Le Bouquet de l'Amour, ou Les Jeux de Zéphyre et de Cupidon."

FIG. 16. Ducrow and his sister Emily in "Le Bouquet de l'Amour,
ou Les Jeux de Zéphyre et de Cupidon," 1820.

FIG. 17. "Le Bouquet de l'Amour, ou Les Jeux de Zéphyre et de Cupidon," showing Ducrow performing his famous feat of equilibrium in which he balanced on one toe, 1820.

the family to which the great Madame Saqui belonged. I imagine this must have been her brother Laurent, probably the same who had appeared with her at Astley's during the 1816 season and no doubt made Andrew's acquaintance at the time.[30] The two partners were for a while assisted at Lyons by the actors from the Théâtre des Célestins, a minor house where vaudevilles, pantomimes, and melodramas made up the usual bill. The company gave their first performance on 2 April, when Andrew's feats, according to the *Journal de Lyon* two days later, surpassed all reports and were greeted by continual applause. His Roman Gladiator and "Grand Vol de Mercure" left even those who had seen them doubting the possibility of their execution. The latter pose, as one learns from a later Astley's playbill, was based on the bronze statue by John of Bologna and involved balancing "upon the point of one Toe, with the Body in a *Horizontal* Situation, with the Horse put out at the very swiftest Pace."[31] On 10 April Ducrow took his benefit. In addition to his equestrian exercises he now played the human lead in a pantomime entitled *L'Ours et l'homme sauvage*. Another example of the early nineteenth century's fascination with the relationships between animals and men in a "natural" state—inspired in large part by the sensational reports of the "feral" twelve-year-old boy Victor discovered and captured in a French wood in 1800—the tale in this case involved a young man who as an infant had been lost in a forest and reared by a sympathetic bear.[32]

Notwithstanding he had already taken his benefit, Andrew's reception by the admiring Lyonnais led him to prolong his visit for another month, during which the critic for the *Journal de Lyon* waxed even more ecstatic in his reviews. "Not only does M. Ducrow deserve the title Foremost Equestrian of All the European Courts," he wrote in the issue of 28 April, "but foremost of all *equestrians*—past, present, and future." Especially remarkable, in the reviewer's opinion, was the fact that Andrew's perilous exercises, which normally might be expected to cause feelings of fright and anxiety in the spectators, never gave cause for alarm in Ducrow's case, so perfect were his grace and self-assurance. In his attitudes of Zephyr, Mercury, and the Gladiator it seemed as though the masterpieces of sculpture had come to life. On other occasions the critic commented on Andrew's act with his sister and the speed with which they circled the ring while holding their poses in the "Bouquet de l'Amour." By now Emily was reported to have reached the ripe age of six and was performing an act of her own on her brother's horse Zéphire. Lalanne, for his part, exhibited his trick horse Chéri; and a Mlle. Lalanne, also said to be aged six, performed on the tightrope. Andrew himself briefly returned to the rope around the middle of May before winding up the season at Lyons.[33] Previous to this he had received tangible if somewhat commonplace evidence of at least one spectator's appreciation on the evening of 16 April, when from the first tier of boxes a wreath came sailing into the ring. The equestrian, we are told in a delicately worded review, finally picked it up, "avec un transport de sensibilité qui couvrait le murmure de sa modestie."[34] It was at Lyons, also, toward the end of this or a later engagement, that Andrew received a signal tribute from his female admirers. On the morning previous to his departure he was surprised in his bedroom by a group of women who strewed the room with flowers and presented him with whips, silver spurs, and other mementos, "enough to fill a trunk."[35] The reaction of Margaret to this scene has not been recorded.

On 27 May 1820 Ducrow and Lalanne jointly signed a long letter, published three days later in the *Journal de Lyon*, thanking the citizens of Lyons for their patronage and promising that their troop, still in the process of forming, would be even better on their next visit. As an added inducement, Ducrow promised on his own to then perform exercises never before seen on one and two horses. One may be certain Andrew's fertile imagination was constantly at work on ideas for new scenes during this period, and that he was busily trying them out and rehearsing for long hours in private—a precaution he customarily observed in order to prevent, if only for a while, the theft of his scenes by imitators. There were a few persons, however, who most decidedly did not look forward to this promised return engagement or to any more of Andrew's scenes at Lyons.

The relations between Andrew and his erstwhile employers the Franconis are a matter of some interest during this period. There was bound to be a certain degree of rivalry between the managers, of course, although no overt competition ever took place: Ducrow did not attack the Franconis on their home territory, nor did the two troops, while the Parisian establishment was on its summer tours, confront each other in the provinces. Still, there is at least a hint of ill feeling in a letter addressed to the Minister of the Interior during April 1822 in which the Franconis, protesting a ruling that restricted their performances at Rouen to fifteen days only, complained that Ducrow, "un étranger encore," was permitted to exhibit everywhere in France with no limits set to the number of his performances.[36]

A potentially more serious breach occurred in the late summer of 1820, when the Franconis were at Lyons and Ducrow, still in partnership with Lalanne, was performing in Switzerland. Previous to this event a notice of the Franconis' activities at Marseilles had included a tantalizing hint that the celebrated English equestrian was about to rejoin the company.[37] Whether there was any actual cause for this rumor, Andrew most certainly did not return to his old employers; and when the Franconis moved into the Cirque Olympique des Brotteaux at the end of August, they brought with them the rider Constant Fabulet, then imitating Ducrow's "Vol de Mercure," as well as Ducrow's earlier competitor the younger Bassin, who by now was often described in the press as the "worthy rival of the English-man Ducrow."[38] On 21 September, shortly after the Franconis had concluded their engagement in the city, the *Journal de Lyon* published a long and highly indignant letter signed with the unlikely name of one "Fitz Patrick," who described himself as "régisseur du spectacle de MM. Ducrow et Lalanne."[39] The letter, dated at Lyons on 19 September, had been written with the object of putting down a calumnious rumor accusing Ducrow of ridiculing the French during his stay at Geneva the previous month; and Ducrow and Lalanne were reported as offering 100 louis to whoever could prove "that they have conducted themselves in a reprehensible manner toward the French nation on any occasion and in any way. The originators of this gossip, as untrue as it is criminal, have asserted that the afore-said equestrians, during their engagement at Geneva, performed—while in French uniform—some burlesque and indecent scenes with the object of insulting the French and turning them into ridicule. . . . One will readily understand that this outrageous gossip, sown with such active malice, can only have its source in a base jealousy which merits nothing but contempt." The letter went on to point out how improbable it was that Lalanne, a veteran of the Egyptian campaigns, would ever allow his country to be insulted, and—amazingly—even emphasized *Ducrow's* military prowess in the service of the French. "When M. Ducrow adorns himself with the French uniform in any of his exercises, this has always been to honor it with a victory—as is proved by the one he obtained in the Cirque des Brotteaux, while wearing the uniform of a French lancer, against three cossacks whom he fought with valor and completely routed." Certificates signed by the mayor and lieutenant of police at Geneva were duly produced, assuring the French public that the rumor was without any founda-tion. The letter from the former, dated 7 September, would seem to indicate the basis for the story was a fight Ducrow was supposed to have had with a Geneva spectator, presumably over Ducrow's interpretation of the French soldier. Even with such assurances, the matter did not die easily. As late as 1822, when Andrew was again at Lyons, the *Miroir des Spectacles* (2 April 1822) reverted to the subject and, commenting on Ducrow's mimic heroism, remarked that "we know plenty of warriors who call themselves French who have not done as much as this English rider."

Although at first sight their presence at Lyons might lead one to suspect the Franconis were behind it, neither they nor their riders were ever accused by Ducrow of circulating this rumor. And in later years, it is pleasant to relate, Ducrow and Laurent Franconi were on friendly terms, with the two directors exchanging letters and artists, and Franconi himself, together with his horses Blanche and Phoenix, performing at Astley's during the summer of 1835. The real broadcasters if not the fabricators of the story, curiously enough, were not from the circus world at all, but from the local theatre. Like most French provincial cities, Lyons possessed a "grand" or major theatre. It was here that operas, ballets, and legitimate drama were produced, as distinct from the vaudevilles, melodramas, and pantomimes performed at the secondary house of the Célestins and any other spectacle, like the Cirque Olympique des Brotteaux, that might flourish from time to time. Not surprisingly, the distinctions between the various genres of entertainment allotted to the different houses did not always work to the advantage of the Grand Théâtre, which was often hard pressed to compete with more popular fare. The problem was further aggravated when such itinerant troupes as the Franconis' and Ducrow's came to town. To alleviate the distress of the director of the legitimate house on these occasions, such companies were required, as in all French provincial cities, to pay one-fifth of their receipts to the Grand Théâtre as a form of tax or indemnity.[40]

At the time of Ducrow's initial visit to Lyons in 1820, however, the Grand Théâtre was in the midst of a three-month recess, and it would appear Andrew either used this as a pretext to evade payment of the tax or was genuinely ignorant of the law requiring him to pay it. The administration of the theatre, which began a new season of its own on 23 April, soon moved to put a stop to his performances, claiming they would otherwise have to "close their doors." Ducrow was forced to pay the twenty percent, and another ten percent to local charities—yet even then, as he later recalled, he retained the advantage over his rivals, and spectators who had formerly patronized the Grand Théâtre now flocked to his circus out of sympathy. This led to further hostilities, his opponents now claiming that "Mr. D. and his company had in other towns performed a piece lampooning the French soldiers." Meanwhile, the Grand Théâtre had discovered a counterattraction in the dancer Charles Mazurier. But "no sooner did the indefatigable Ducrow observe this than he advertized to do what Mazurier did on the stage on horseback, and after a fortnight's training accomplished this extraordinary feat. He gave his celebrated entertainment, The Carnival of Venice, in which his first character is Punchinello."[41]

While the above recollection is correct in its essentials, it is obvious from other evidence that Ducrow or his memorialist was confused in his chronology and ran two or more visits to Lyons together. For the ruckus over the "insult" occurred several months after Ducrow and Lalanne had left Lyons in the spring of 1820, and Ducrow's competition with Mazurier and the creation of his "Carnival of Venice" could not have taken place before 1821. It was after Andrew concluded his first season at Lyons that Mazurier made his debut there in Milon's two-act ballet *Le Carnaval de Venise*. His performance as Polichinelle in this piece catapulted him overnight into fame. And it was Mazurier, the remarkable comic dancer, mime, and acrobat whose creations were to make his name world famous in the few years remaining before his death at the age of thirty in 1828—not the Franconis, Constant, or Bassin *fils*—who was the real archrival of Ducrow in France. That this competition between two outstanding artists in ostensibly different fields should have ever occurred, that Andrew should have publicly announced to do on horseback everything Mazurier did onstage, is readily understandable, since Andrew's training was by no means dissimilar to Mazurier's. Their rivalry continued into 1825, when Mazurier added a new character to his repertoire: the monkey in Gabriel and Rochefort's *Jocko ou Le Singe de Brésil*. His phenomenal success in this role stimulated a host of man-monkeys and monkey dramas in England as well as on the Continent. The plot of *Jocko* was the familiar one of the "noble" animal serving and saving his human friends, and in this instance ended pathetically when the ape-hero was accidentally killed after rescuing his master's son. In November 1825 Mazurier appeared in an English version at Covent Garden, but was anticipated by his old rival from the French provinces. For his benefit at Astley's on 3

FIG. 18. The famous mime and dancer Charles Mazurier as Polichinelle.

October, Ducrow himself once again donned a monkey suit in an extravaganza on horseback, "The Death of General Jacko."[42]

In late May of 1820, however, Mazurier had just startled the Lyonnais with his first performance of Polichinelle in *Le Carnaval de Venise*, the simple plot of which dealt with two pairs of disguised lovers testing each other during carnival. Both the story and the other dancers were quickly forgotten when Mazurier came on as a Punch-puppet. "In this role," wrote an admiring critic, "he carries both the comic and the grotesque to their ultimate limits; and he plays the character in so natural a manner that one may truly take him for a puppet made to move, in a thousand different directions, by strings controlled by an unknown hand . . . from the flexibility of his movements, one can easily believe that his limbs are being operated by elastic springs."[43] When Ducrow returned to Lyons in the following year, Mazurier was still the toast of the town, dancing in grotesque ballets like *La Famille des innocens* and demonstrating his "inconceivable suppleness" in a revival of *Le Carnaval de Venise* and other Polichinelades. His name, reported the *Miroir des Spectacles* (10 March 1821), outshone all the other actors' in the theatres of Lyons and was billed in the biggest type; and his Polichinelle, which everyone was rushing to applaud, was danced "with a perfection worthy to be recorded in the annals of marionettes."

It must have been during this second engagement at Lyons in the spring and early summer of 1821 that Andrew first entered into rivalry with Mazurier. And the above descriptions of Mazurier interpreting Polichinelle as a marionette help to explain a curious cut in an Astley's bill dating from 1824.[44] The illustration (fig. 19) shows a clown on stilts holding two sticks from which dangle strings attached to the hands and feet of a Punch figure, complete with bells and humpback. Since the scene is obviously being played on the arena floor and no horse is in sight, the connection with Ducrow's famous equestrian act at first seems rather tenuous. But in fact the figure depicted is Ducrow, who early in the act imitated Mazurier *before* mounting his horse to undergo transformations into five other characters: Pierrot, Harlequin, Columbine, Bacchus, and Adonis or Endymion. Reviews in the *Mémorial Bordelais* and several descriptive accounts written after Andrew had returned to England permit us to reconstruct the scene in its entirety. As the act began, Ducrow was carried into the arena inside a toy box. Upon being taken out of the box, he assumed antic postures while some attendants tried to stand him on his feet. Then the clown, elevated on stilts, strode over, picked up the strings attached to his arms and legs, and made him walk around the ring. Still manipulated by the clown, Punch was next made to mount a horse on which he at first tottered and rolled about. "A

FIG. 19. Ducrow as Punch in the opening scene of "The Carnival of Venice," 1824.

mere torpid mass of deformity, and liker some dressed up image than anything animated," was how one Scots critic described the character in 1827; while a later writer recalled Ducrow's floundering and flinging his limbs about, once he had mounted the horse, "as if they were so many fly-flappers" and squeaking like a penny trumpet. After leaping up and kicking off his Punch costume, Andrew successively metamorphosed himself into the dreamy Pierrot and the sprightly Harlequin, performing, in the case of the latter, the peculiar type of dancing associated with the character and exhibiting "every *pas* and attitude of it . . . with a truth, a precision, and a force of *gusto*, not exhibited by any mere stage harlequin extant, and on a slippery stage a few inches square, that is all the while moving under his feet at the rate of twenty miles an hour!" Then came the character of Columbine, whom Ducrow interpreted as a delicate lady of "nervous sensibility." A few moments later, as Bacchus or Silenus, he pretended to drink and become gradually intoxicated, his legs, body, eyes, and expression progressively indicating the state he was in, until he rolled and staggered about the horse. Another Proteus-like change and another startling contrast—this time the athletic and graceful attitudes of Adonis or (as some French critics claimed) Endymion with his bow, including the amazing feat of equilibrium when Ducrow, on one toe, leaned out over the sides of the horse and seemed genuinely on the verge of flight. Finally, at the moment he let fly the arrow he assumed the pose of the *Apollo Belvedere*, while the applause from the ecstatic spectators came down like thunder. The changes of costume and accessories were made without Andrew's once quitting his horse, and the drama was heightened by an appropriate orchestral accompaniment.[45]

Spectators in Lyons and elsewhere in the provinces had plenty of opportunities to compare the interpretations of the two artists until the spring of 1823, when Mazurier made his Parisian debut at the Porte-St.-Martin Theatre. Meanwhile, Andrew had been touring other cities and countries, beginning with a visit to Switzerland where he and Lalanne performed at Geneva during August 1820. In September the company played at Berne,[46] then made their perilous way across the Alps and arrived at Milan on 27 November.[47] Not, however, before one of Ducrow's celebrated fits of temper took place while the troop was wending its way over the snow-covered passes. According to one account, the incident occurred after Andrew lost the way and stopped to engage some Italian guides. These, however, soon began rearranging the harnesses of the company's horses—an outrage which the Classic Equestrian of Europe refused to tolerate. A heated debate ensued in the snow, but as neither party could understand the language of the other, confusion reigned supreme. The guides eventually went their way, leaving the company stranded with night coming on, and Andrew was forced to ride back sixteen miles alone in search of new guides.[48] In Milan the troop performed at the Teatro Carcano, a house where operas and plays were usually given but which had the disadvantage of being removed from the center of town. Nevertheless, the theatre was daily crowded, especially on Sundays, during the circus's engagement, and Ducrow and his fellow artists were praised for their grace and skill.[49]

On 14 January 1821 Ducrow placed the usual notice thanking his patrons in the *Gazzetta di Milano* and announced that on the next day he would return to France. It seems he also parted company with Lalanne at this time, for the "famiglia Lalanne" stayed on to perform at the Teatro Carcano for some weeks after Andrew had left. For a while in 1821 Ducrow was also associated during his travels with a person named Dubost, the director of the Cirque Olympique at Lyons, whose own troop, when Ducrow or the Franconis were not in town, appears to have been indifferently supported. There is little point tracing in detail the itinerary of Andrew during his remaining years on the Continent. Such cities as Rouen, Clermont, Lyons, Gap, Nîmes, Marseilles, Limoges, Bordeaux, Toulouse, Tours, Nantes, La Rochelle, and Strasbourg were all visited at least once during this period, and on one occasion he even seems to have briefly visited Spain—a trip later referred to in his bills at Astley's—though not, to my knowledge, as a performer. Either Andrew or Margaret took care to collect a number of the more rhapsodic notices he received during these years, some of which were turned over to Leman Thomas Rede while he was working on his memoir of Ducrow for *Oxberry's Dramatic Biography*. "M. Ducrow shot forth into the circular lists; bravos exploded, applause rang out from all the tiers in the amphitheatre," begins one report of his performances at Marseilles in 1821:

> Lively, light, and graceful, the English rider beguiles and enchants with a pleasing variability. He sports with the laws of statics, and gravity has no center for him. Sometimes an aerial sylph, he appears to be about to take an easy flight; sometimes leaning out over the arena, he remains suspended in space by a marvel of equilibrium. His swift courser is the

pedestal on which he assumes every shape and takes every attitude—now the Mercury of Phidias on the verge of taking wing, now the Gladiator with admirable proportions, now the lover of Flora bearing Cupid in his arms, or disporting in a garland of flowers.[50]

In April of the following year at Bordeaux, whose Grand Théâtre had recently closed for lack of patronage, the Cirque Ségalier where Ducrow and his troop performed was so crowded with persons from all classes of society that seats were placed onstage to accommodate the overflow. It was during this engagement that the ecstatic reviewer for the *Mémorial Bordelais*—the same who mistakenly described Andrew as a pupil of Vestris *fils*—proclaimed Ducrow the "premier voltigeur de l'Europe" and assured his readers that

> a painter who should exactly delineate, without any exaggeration, all the attitudes, poses, and movements of this astonishing artist would be considered—in the opinion of those who have not seen him themselves—to have represented nothing but unreal fancies. To translate such fiction into reality would seem beyond any possibility. One would not believe, in fact, that it was possible to play in such a way with all the laws of gravity. After seeing M. Ducrow, one *still* cannot conceive the means by which he preserves his balance.
>
> To these prodigies of agility, address, and vigor is joined a grace which bestows on them the greatest merit they can have in the eyes of all who possess a feeling for the arts, and who realize that in the performance of games of skill and even of strength, the chief value does not reside in the mere mastering of difficulty.[51]

Similar tribute was paid in 1823 at Nantes, where Andrew was lauded repeatedly by the critic Victor Mangin. "The more one sees this extraordinary artist the more one admires him. He astonishes with his skill and his daring—I could almost say his recklessness."[52] A week later, by which time the usual complaints were being aired over the desertion of the Grand Théâtre in favor of the circus, Mangin paid another visit to Ducrow's crowded establishment and reported that the rider "surpassed himself, and was still more extraordinary, more graceful and skillful than usual. How expressive and animated is his pantomime, how beautiful are his poses! The more one sees M. Ducrow, the more one wishes to see him."[53]

Besides such tributes in the press, Andrew was the recipient of various epistles, petitions, and even poems from the more ardent of his French admirers. Fortunately, he also took care to preserve these items, which eventually came to be mounted in the album now in the possession of his great-great-grandson. In Nantes, during the same 1823 engagement, a number of spectators drew up a letter begging him to interpret three of his famous scenes—"Le Cuirassier français," "Le Carnaval de Venise," and "Le Chasseur indien"—which they had heard about but had yet to see Ducrow perform in their city. In Strasbourg he was presented with a handsomely inscribed petition from the "Amateurs des Beaux-Arts" asking him to prolong his engagement. At other times he was the recipient of less specific (and occasionally incoherent) effusions from anonymous fans with pretensions to poety. He was even, in May 1823, celebrated by an admirer signing himself the Comte de Cisté, "poète du département de la Vienne," in a madrigal addressed to "Monsieur Ducrow, Zéphyr-équestre":

> Du merveilleux Ducrow l'extrême agilité,
> Selon les amateurs, tient vraiment du prodige;
> L'oeil parait fasciné par l'effet d'un prestige,
> Et l'on croit voir agir une divinité!

There were also gifts of a more substantial nature; the traditional wreaths tossed into the ring which Andrew, playing his part in this ritual, always appeared reluctant to accept—"his modesty," as one reviewer noted, "that inseparable companion of true talent, not letting him believe these wreaths could be destined for him";[54] and visits from aristocratic patrons such as the popular Duchesse d'Angoulême, who presented the equestrian with a medal at Bordeaux in 1823.[55]

While not receiving such extensive coverage as Andrew, both Emily and Margaret were often noticed in the press during this period. The latter, in particular, seems to have made an impression on the critic for the *Mémorial Bordelais*, who referred to her beauty on several occasions and once even complained of the pantaloons she wore, since they prevented him and his fellow spectators from admiring her "formes les plus belles." My impression that Margaret must have received her instruction in riding from Andrew is confirmed by the same reviewer's statement that she had commenced riding under Ducrow's tutelage, and had made her debut in Italy only a short time before her appearances at Bordeaux in 1822. It is obvious, too, that at this date she was still noticeably unsure of herself, for in making her turns round the ring and executing such traditional exercises as leaping through "balloons," she was described as lacking in daring and confidence. "Her master and model never inspires anxiety when, in the midst of his most daring poses—poses truly aerial—he seems to soar above his horse rather than to support himself on it. One does not always have the same confidence in Mme. Ducrow."[56]

As pointed out in the preceding chapter, Margaret never did achieve much reputation as an equestrienne, although she was often billed to ride in the cavalcades and quadrilles on horseback which Ducrow termed "entrées." The claim that he was the inventor of this type of entertainment seems tenuous, however, since Philip Astley had himself presented equestrian cotillions at his Olympic Pavilion, while the allegorical character of Ducrow's entrées in many instances appears similar to that of the spectacular carrousels and horse ballets of the baroque era. Still, he does seem to have been the first to regularly feature them in the circus. A typical example called for four women (including "Madame" Ducrow) on horseback representing Europe, Asia, Africa, and America, each attended by two mounted cavaliers.[57] Andrew appears to have introduced these acts around the time Margaret was making her start as an equestrienne. At Bordeaux in 1822, for example, a grand entrée of eight horses with four knights and four "amazones" was repeatedly announced. Aside from their novelty and opportunities for spectacle, these entrées were useful in displaying members of the company—especially the artists' wives— who might otherwise have been left out of the equestrian department altogether.

If there were reservations about the talents of Margaret as a rider, no such doubts ever attached to the gifted Emily. While she continued to perform with her brother in "Le Bouquet de l'Amour" as late as 1823, by then she had developed into an expert solo rider herself—largely, or so the critic for the *Mémorial Bordelais* asserted, through observing other riders in the company and practicing on her own, since Andrew could not spend much time on her instruction. He must nonetheless have had a hand in devising the little scenes in which she appeared, the first in a long series of juvenile acts that he continued to create and feature, using sundry infants, for the remainder of his career. In "Le Chef de Lilliputiens et son cheval Pygmée," for example, Emily impersonated an old soldier, complete with moustache, first checking out her horse and equipment, then mounting and putting it through the various gaits, leaping it over barriers, and finishing by performing all the standard exercises of equitation, "rather as a master than as a young pupil."[58] By 1823, when she was around twelve years old, she was following even more closely in her brother's footsteps and was standing on the saddle to execute a character dance in "Le Petit Chaperon rouge."[59]

Both Margaret and Emily must have figured in another type of entertainment Andrew eventually produced, the spectacular plays on horseback, or hippodramas, such as the Astleys and Franconis had been presenting for the past two decades. Announcements in various periodicals indicate Andrew began giving these around the summer of 1823, by which time the company, now under his sole direction, consisted of no less than thirty artists and thirty-six horses.[60] The plays in which the troop appeared in France are listed in an agreement made in late summer 1823 between Andrew and the proprietors of Covent Garden and give firm evidence of his horses' histrionic progress during the intervening weeks: *La Mort de Kléber, Poniatowski, The Rape of the Sabines, Timour the Tartar, Aladdin, Blue Beard,* and *Cinderella.* Prior to undertaking these productions Andrew had emulated the Franconis in another way. Trained stags were one of the current novelties, and the Cirque Olympique possessed two—Coco and Azor—whose feats were commemorated in a number of prints. Accordingly, Ducrow acquired and began training a stag of his own during his 1822 visit to Bordeaux, where the "Cerf Sauvage," as he was billed, made his debut on 28 April.[61]

Other members and acts of the troop during its final years in France included a number of clowns and a "Chinese" buffoon and posturer (who was probably the English clown Charles Parsloe); a company of leapers and acrobats who were sometimes advertised as "Turkish" and at other times as "Chinese"; a comic scene entitled "Le Cheval gastronome"; and several trick horses exhibited by Andrew himself, among which the most famous was his Turkish mare Beda. Andrew continued to appear sporadically on the tightrope, usually reserving these exhibitions until the last one or two performances in a town. At Bordeaux he was announced, as "Pluton, dieu du feu," to make the grand ascension from the stage to the topmost gallery and to descend backwards while surrounded by flames and fireworks. One critic acclaimed him a worthy rival of Madame Saqui; another could not help wondering how the Master of Hell would be received upon reaching "paradis."[62]

Above all, however, it was Andrew's own riding that formed the heart of his programs and assured the company packed houses wherever they played. And it was now that his active imagination and phenomenal skill enabled him to progress beyond the earlier poses plastiques to the first in a long line of "scenes in the circle" with which his name would ever afterward be associated: Ducrow's famed pantomimes on horseback. Combining equestrianism with dance and mime, enhanced by appropriate costumes, properties, and music, these elegant and sophisticated creations were truly dramatic. In contrast to the static attitudes of such poses plastiques as the Gladiator, they presented continuous, often entire, actions played out on the backs of one or more rushing horses. Doubtless the seeds of this type of entertainment are to be found in the earlier burlesque equestrian interludes of Ducrow's predecessors in both France and England. But his own expressive scenes were of a completely different order and by no means confined to the comic. Many of them provided spectators with a mixture of emotions, and a number were downright tragic.

Precisely when Andrew evolved the first of his pantomimes is a matter for conjecture. I suspect that at first there was no clear line of demarcation between them and the earlier poses plastiques. The reviewer for the *Mémorial Bordelais*, for instance, who recognized the novelty of these scenes and on several occasions pronounced them "véritables pantomimes," in 1822 listed the "Bouquet de l'Amour" among them,[63] which leads me to believe that this scene, sometime around its 1820 representations, may have provided the transition. The character of the French soldier performed at Lyons and Geneva during 1820 was assuredly one of Andrew's earliest pantomimes and was very likely the same as "Le Cuirassier français" and "Le Soldat français et son cheval blessé" of later years. It therefore seems probable that 1820 marks the year in which Andrew struck out in this new genre; and there is evidence of several additional pantomimes in performance the following year. Among those I find mentioned by title during Andrew's sojourn in France are "Le Carnaval de Venise," "La Mort d'Othello ou Le Maure vaincu en défendant son drapeau," "La Grand Maman à cheval," "Le Cuirassier français" (probably the same as "Le Chasseur et son cheval"), "Le Moissonneur," "Le Retour du matelot," "Le Page troubadour," and "Le Chasseur indien." The first of these has already been described, and the last (fig. 14) featured the "grand écart" or split while Andrew rode and straddled two horses at once. I shall be referring in later chapters to several of these scenes under their English titles; but for the moment, to give some additional idea of the flavor and inventiveness of Ducrow's riding at this period, here are descriptions of two more scenes, the first of which—in the earlier burlesque tradition—was not original with Andrew but does serve to indicate the distance between his own creations and the "senseless and attempted drollery" of his predecessors.

"La Grand Maman à cheval" was another example of what was known as a "metamorphosis" act and, under such titles as "The Millers' Frolic, or The Arrival of My Grand Mother" and "The Humours of the Sack, or The Clown Deceived by a Woman," had been a staple in the repertoires of English and American circuses since the end of the eighteenth century. In Andrew's version the scene involved several performers and commenced with a group of millers trying to teach themselves to ride. They were shortly joined by two coal-men who began interfering with their pleasure and were punished when the millers seized one of them, put him into a sack, and tossed it onto their nag, which was then set going around the ring. But then a surprising thing occurred. Instead of falling off the galloping horse, the sack remained firmly in place. From the obvious skill of the person inside, spectators soon concluded this could be none other than Ducrow himself. It was indeed—and within the confines of his flying cocoon he underwent a strange metamorphosis. For when the sack suddenly fell, there stood revealed a little old woman, masked, and costumed and coiffed as though out of the period of the Frankish king Dagobert. Annoyed by the millers' laughter and shouts of derision, she urged on her mount in pursuit of them and, still standing on the saddle, attempted to go even faster by lunging ahead on two crutches which had somehow been concealed inside the sack![64]

An entirely original and far more poignant scene, presented as early as 1821, demonstrates more fully Andrew's pantomimical artistry and the emotional intensity he brought to his performances. "La Mort d'Othello ou Le Maure vaincu en défendant son drapeau" bore no relation to Shakespeare's play, but is of special interest as the subject of a superb French lithograph (fig. 20). Here one notes the extraordinary degree of realism Ducrow achieved through makeup, properties, and costuming, even to the leopard skin girding his galloping charger. The *Journal de Marseille* has left us an equally fine verbal description of Andrew in this role:

> We saw him, after quitting the transparent gauze [of the previous scene], re-costumed as an African, his face blackened by tropic suns, defying, his lance at rest, an imaginary rival.

FIG. 20. Ducrow performing "Le Maure des déserts" ("La Mort
d'Othello ou Le Maure vaincu en défendant son drapeau") at a
Continental circus, c. 1822. Compare the horse in this print with
that in fig. 17.

With what savage joy he dares to the combat! With what fury he attacks his enemy! With what art he seems to evade his blows! But Fortune has betrayed the courage of the gallant warrior—he is wounded, and the steel escapes from his failing hand. Summoning up all his remaining strength, he draws his scimitar. Rage discomposes his features and flashes in his eyes. Death, however, approaches, and his sabre is no longer swift; his final blows, feeble as Priam's spear, expire before reaching his enemy's bowels. The hero is dying; blood stains his armor; he falls—he rolls in the dust—and a cry of horror rings through the amphitheatre. Never has actor pushed so far the magic of illusion.[65]

A later account of the same act at Nantes in 1823 describes Andrew eventually dropping the flag, although the reviewer this time was curiously reminded of another catastrophic scene, played not in Africa but closer to home: "He is mortally wounded; one sees him growing weaker little by little, and by imperceptible gradations. His feeble arm still delivers some uncertain blows; his faltering hand reluctantly quits the flag the warrior has just pressed to his heart; his strength abandons him, but his courage outlives his life as French honor survives the glorious defeat of Waterloo!"[66]

In late summer of 1823, still relatively unknown in his own country, Ducrow received an offer to return to England and appear with his troop on the stage of Covent Garden. The agreement between Andrew and the theatre's proprietors, signed and dated at London on 3 September, called for Ducrow to bring with him six men and four women, together with fifteen horses and his trained stag, a variety of costumes, properties, music, and programs, and to perform and assist in the getting up of unspecified hippodramas under the direction of the regular stage managers. The engagement was to last a minimum of six weeks, preceded by a week of rehearsals beginning 15 October; and the troop was not to perform at any other theatre in London or the provinces until the expiration of the Covent Garden contract. The theatre, in return, agreed to find space within its walls for Ducrow's horses and to pay him twenty-five pounds for the week of rehearsals and forty-five pounds per week during actual performances. An indemnity of fifty pounds was promised in case the engagement should be shorter than anticipated.[67] Back in France a few days after signing the agreement, Andrew discovered it would not be so easy to move his company across the Channel after all. The French authorities, he complained in a letter to the theatre management dated at Caen on 13

September, would not permit him to take his stallions out of the country. This would necessarily reduce his stud to twelve or thirteen horses, and he would also require additional money to transport his company to London and maintain them there.[68] On 20 September a reply was addressed to him from Henry Robertson, informing him the proprietors had agreed to increase the amount of the indemnity to sixty pounds but wished him to understand "that not less than 15 horses will answer their purpose and of course they expect you will bring the stag."[69]

Before departing France for England, the company performed briefly in Rouen at the Théâtre des Arts, the same house in which Ducrow had first appeared after leaving the Franconis four years earlier. If any sentiment attached to this farewell engagement, it was sadly misplaced, for on the evening of 6 October, almost inexplicably, the troop failed to give satisfaction and precipitated a riot. As described by the journals and the historian Bouteiller, the evening was billed to conclude with special new exercises by Andrew himself. Accordingly, the theatre was crowded with spectators who waited patiently through the first half of the program and, following a short intermission, a tedious act by twelve "Chinese" acrobats who leaped interminably over a horse and finally went off with their backs to the audience. At the conclusion of this inept scene, which everyone assumed was a prelude to Ducrow's exercises, the footlights were extinguished and the spectators suddenly realized the performance had ended without the great equestrian appearing. The audience began yelling and demanding something else for their money. The director of the theatre tried to appease them with a comic opera, but this was greeted with hisses. Finally, the curtain was rung down and the spectators, after singing and dancing, took to fighting among themselves—until the police arrived and began making arrests.[70] It may be that Ducrow was ill on this occasion. Or perhaps, in view of the impending departure and necessary arrangements for the trip to England, he had taken leave of his company for a few days. Whatever the reason behind this debacle, it was a disappointing finale to what, until then, had been a prolonged period of unqualified success.

The next month Andrew made his debut at Covent Garden, and in the following year entered upon his long reign at Astley's Amphitheatre. His amazed compatriots, converted at last, now expressed their unbounded approval of his new style of riding; almost overnight he was acclaimed England's foremost equestrian; and dozens of imitators, making no pretense to any originality of their own, brazenly stole his scenes wholesale and performed them in circuses the length and breadth of the land. The years abroad spent in perfecting his revolutionary style of horsemanship and acquiring experience as a manager and director—years during which Andrew had been sustained in his efforts by a discerning and generous French public—now brought forth a golden harvest. The "Vestris à Cheval," shortly to be rechristened with more suitable English titles, had come home to stay.

FIG. 21. Box ticket, depicting "M. Ducrow" in his famous pantomime "Le Bouquet de l'Amour," probably dating from shortly after his return to England in 1823. Signed by Ducrow.

Wha the deevil was Castor, that the ancients
made a god o' for his horsemanship—a god o'
and a star—in comparison wi' yon Ducraw?

—Shepherd, in the "Noctes Ambrosianae"
of *Blackwood's Magazine*, January 1828

4   *Triumph*

Cortez, or The Conquest of Mexico, a three-act musical drama by James
Robinson Planché with music by Henry Bishop, opened at Covent
Garden on 5 November 1823. The legend of the Spanish conquistador
and the Mexicans' terror at the strange sight of his horses was admirably suited to the debut of Ducrow and his troop, and the cavalry was
conspicuously displayed in all three acts.[1] The horses, one critic wrote,
"seem to be 'instinct' with the knowledge of their duties, and curvet
and *caracole* with all the grace and confidence of Christians."[2] Between melodramatic scenes by the biped actors and bravura passages
by the theatre's singers, they were described as prancing, galloping,
capering, wheeling about, leaping over obstacles, and—despite the
restrictions of the stage—really seeming to *go.*[3] But the most sensational scene of all occurred in Act II when the Spaniards and Mexicans
engaged in battle and Ducrow, playing an Indian, unhorsed an opponent and mounted in his place. After furiously leaping and plunging
in an attempt to throw his "untutored" rider, the steed bolted up a
steep pathway to a tremendous height and raced across a bridge span-

116

ning a cataract. At this point the Indian was knocked from the horse by some projection and, falling over the bridge, plummeted down the cataract into a gulf below stage level. Nearly all the critics—even those who complained most bitterly about the presence of the horses in a "legitimate" theatre—professed their amazement at Andrew's skill in this terrifying scene. It was so good, in fact, that he retained part of the scene in his repertoire for some time afterward and performed it independently of the play itself.

Unfortunately, *Cortez* was not nearly so impressive as Ducrow's riding. To add to the disappointment of the patent theatre, the rival establishment of Drury Lane had prudently mounted a hippodramatic spectacle of its own, William T. Moncrieff's *The Cataract of the Ganges, or The Rajah's Daughter*, which had opened nine days previous to the Covent Garden production and was clearly superior to Planché's tepid concoction.[4] The result was that toward the end of November Ducrow's stud was employed in a revival of "Monk" Lewis's *Timour the Tartar*, and this favorite equestrian melodrama, together with an abridgement of *Cortez*, continued to figure in the theatre's programs up to the time of the Christmas pantomime and for a few weeks into the new year as well. The bills for the premieres of these productions are revealing, with that for *Cortez* providing the names of several equestrians Ducrow had either brought with him from France or recently added to his company. Among the Spanish cavalry, for instance, are listed Mr. J. Collett, either Ducrow's former teacher or some member of his family; Mr. J. Ducrow, Andrew's brother; "Mungo," who was actually the young mulatto rider Joseph Hillier, picked up by Ducrow while visiting Milan; and a number of other equestrians including Mackintosh and J. and G. Williams. Mr. Parsloe—who had probably been Ducrow's "Chinese" buffoon in France—was among the officers of Cortez. Interesting, too, is the presence of a woman named Griffiths among the dancing girls. Possibly she was a relation of Andrew's wife Margaret, if not Margaret herself, for Ducrow, as noted in the previous chapter, had promised to provide several females.[5] Another artist whose name appears in these bills—this time from the theatre, however—and with whom Ducrow was on friendly terms was T. P. Cooke, later to make his mark as the representative par excellence of the British tar after creating the role of William in Douglas Jerrold's famous nautical melodrama *Black-Ey'd Susan*. Although confined in *Cortez* to the pedestrian part of one of two Indian brothers in love with the same maiden, Cooke apparently knew something about riding, for in *Timour* he was billed for the part of the Tartar chieftain Kerim, who fought a spectacular equestrian combat with his rival Sanballat, played by Ducrow.[6]

Andrew himself, as already noted, had previously appeared in a number of stage pantomimes. During the engagement at Covent Garden he undertook the role of Squire Sap, afterwards Dandy Lover, in the Christmas production that opened on 26 December. Thomas Ellar was the Harlequin on this occasion, and Clown was interpreted by the younger Grimaldi, who was attempting to follow in the footsteps of his illustrious father.[7] The action of *Harlequin Poor Robin, or The House That Jack Built* included a scene in which Ducrow, as Squire Sap, arrived on a shooting pony with a plum pudding and tried to woo the heroine away from her lover, the miller Jack. Eventually these three characters were transformed respectively into Dandy Lover, Columbine, and Harlequin. Joined by Pantaloon and Clown, they participated in the traditional love chase, which included a scene on roller skates used to simulate skating in St. James Park and another in which a balloon trip from Vauxhall Gardens to Paris was represented using a vertically moving panorama painted with views encountered on the voyage.[8] Andrew, in his part, was described as comical and amusing, and his satirical jabs at the exquisites of the day obviously made a memorable impression. A year later one critic, commenting on the pantomimes of the 1824 Christmas season, still recalled his interpretation with enthusiasm: "How the Dandies—it was a moral lesson to behold them—used to turn pale, to a *thing*, last year when Mr. Ducrow appeared as the *Mock Lover*!"[9]

The company wound up their engagement at Covent Garden during the second week in February and a month later were at the Bristol Theatre Royal, performing a demanding repertory of hippodramas that included *Cortez* and *The Cataract of the Ganges* besides such older pieces as *Timour the Tartar, Blue Beard, The Secret Mine, Tekeli,* and the equestrianized musical romance *Lodoiska.*[10] The horses, which had numbered only thirteen at Covent Garden (Andrew apparently had been unable to overcome the objections of the French officials to his taking his stallions out of the country), were now augmented by those of the manager who had been competing with Ducrow at the London Theatres Royal over the past few months— none other than Andrew's old employer and the present lessee of Astley's, William Davis. The two men had previously toyed with the idea of combining their forces for a season at Astley's during the 1823–24 winter, a plan that fell through, however, no doubt on account of Andrew's commitment to Covent Garden.[11] By 15 March 1824, the commencement of the Bristol engagement, the two troops had merged under Ducrow's direction. The union of the companies, reported the critic for *Felix Farley's Bristol Journal* (20 March 1824), "produces the *grandest effect imaginable,* and when we have the example of the *Royal National Houses* receiving and patronizing these wonderful exhibitions, surely the prejudice of the most fastidious must be disarmed, particularly when we behold such surprizing feats interwoven with the Legitimate and Moral Drama. Monsieur Ducrow's exertions, while they *astonish, delight* the audience, and the curtain falls nightly accompanied by the *unanimous cheers of all present!*" The writer's admiration was echoed by the other Bristol reviewers, including that of the Bristol *Mercury,* who wrote of the opening spectacle that

> the very considerable expectation which the rumoured preparations for the *Secret Mine* had excited, was exceeded beyond all calculation by the splendid interest and effect of the performance. The beauty and extent of the scenery, the picturesque and strictly appropriate costume, the excellent acting, and, above all, the unprecedented equestrian display of Mr. Ducrow and his beautiful stud, left room for nothing to imagine, or for any expression but the tumultuous plaudits which lasted long after the fall of the curtain. . . . It has never been our lot to witness so unanimous an expression of approbation as on the present occasion.[12]

The same reviewer continued his panegyrics in later issues, and by the time *The Cataract of the Ganges* opened had so exhausted himself and his vocabulary that he confessed to being at a loss for words to describe the splendor of the production. "It exceeds every thing ever seen in the country," he wrote, and in its gorgeous scenery and trappings, beautiful effects, processions, and the "almost overwhelming clangour of the military instruments" supplementing the theatre's regular orchestra, formed an assemblage "never equalled upon the stage of this or any other theatre."[13]

Besides directing and acting in the Bristol productions, Andrew exhibited his horses and trained stag in a pantomime he had arranged entitled *The Persian Prince and Equestrian Genius.* A bill for "Monsieur" Ducrow's benefit on 7 April, for instance, describes his Turkish mare Beda and little horse Harlequin walking on their hind legs;

Marengo, a horse supposed to have formerly belonged to Napoleon's chief Mameluke, ridden by Ducrow in an exhibition of dressage; and the stag Salamander (the same "Cerf Sauvage" Andrew had trained in France) "Enveloped with a BODY OF REAL FIRE!"[14] The actors in the hippodramas were drawn from the two equestrian troops and the theatre's regular actors, with Sarah M'Cready, stepmother of the great tragedian William Charles Macready, often cast as heroine. Davis himself, aside from his ownership of some of the horses, seems to have had little to do with the Bristol season, which concluded on 9 April.

Upon completing the run at the Bristol Theatre Royal, the combined troop immediately headed back for London, where Ducrow had arranged to spend the summer with Davis at the foot of Westminster Bridge. In 1824 William Davis was sole lessee and manager of Astley's, having succeeded to this position in 1821 upon the death of his partner, John Astley. Following the will of the elder Astley, the property of the theatre, heavily encumbered with debts at the time of John's death, had been divided into sixteen shares, two of which were owned by Hannah Waldo Astley, the widow of John, and the others by the children of a sister of old Astley named Gill.[15] Davis was a creditor and the logical person to carry on with the enterprise, but for the past two years had been arguing with Hannah and the Gills over the theatre's license and his presumption in renaming the Amphitheatre after himself. By the time of Andrew's arrival he had nearly had enough and, upon being informed there would be a considerable increase in the rent for the 1825 season, gave up his lesseeship at the end of 1824 and eventually retired to Walworth.[16] His son, the same Master Davis who had given Andrew so much trouble at the start of his career, apparently did not live up to his youthful promise, for he drops from sight several seasons prior to Ducrow's return to England and I have no idea what eventually became of him.

Certainly Davis could not have wished for a better year to conclude his career in equestrian management at Astley's, for the production with which the Amphitheatre opened on Easter Monday, 19 April, was destined to run to packed houses the full season and to be repeatedly revived over the next several decades. J. H. Amherst's *The Battle of Waterloo*, with its clashing armies of supernumeraries, heroic charges and countercharges by foot and horse, exploding ammunition wagons and crackling musketry, was one of the most famous plays in the entire history of Astley's.[17] The spectacle was directed by William

H. Barrymore, the same who ten years earlier had made the adaptation of Pixérécourt's *The Dog of Montargis* in which Andrew appeared at the Royal Circus; the equestrian evolutions, employing as many as ninety horses onstage at one time, were superintended by Davis and "Monsieur" Ducrow; and the actor playing Napoleon, Edward A. Gomersal, was acclaimed so perfect a likeness of the Emperor that he spent a major portion of the remainder of his career wearing the famous grey greatcoat and re-creating the mannerisms of his model in this and assorted other Napoleonic productions (fig. 22). He was "such a counterpart of that illustrious hero he represents," wrote one

FIG. 22. The actor Edward Gomersal in his famous role of Napoleon in *The Battle of Waterloo*, 1824.

critic of him in a revival of *The Battle of Waterloo* several years later, "that we much doubt whether his appearance in St. Helena...in the full costume, would not cause some *little* riot, were he to insist that Bonaparte's death was but rumour, *himself* being secretly exiled."[18] A perennial subject for jokes by the editors of *Punch* and other periodicals, the object of the amazed admiration of Colonel Newcome in Thackeray's novel *The Newcomes*, Gomersal's Napoleon also figures amusingly in one of the ballads of Bon Gaultier, where the Lord of Castlereagh is depicted as brooding in his room over the news of Napoleon's escape from St. Helena.

'Twas midnight! all the lamps were dim, and dull as death the street,
It might be that the watchman slept that night upon his beat;
When, lo! a heavy foot was heard to creak upon the stair,
The door revolved upon its hinge,—Great Heaven!—What enters
there?

A little man, of stately mien, with slow and solemn stride;
His hands are crossed upon his back, his coat is opened wide:
And on his vest of green he wears an eagle and a star,—
Saint George! protect us! 'tis THE MAN—the thunderbolt of war!

Is that the famous hat that waved along Marengo's ridge?
Are these the spurs of Austerlitz—the boots of Lodi's bridge?
Leads he the conscript swarm again from France's hornet hive?
What seeks the fell usurper here, in Britain, and alive?

Pale grew the Lord of Castlereagh, his tongue was parched and dry,
As in his brain he felt the glare of that tremendous eye;
What wonder if he shrunk in fear, for who could meet the glance
Of him who reared, 'mid Russian snows, the gonfalon of France?

The Emperor, after reaching into his vest for a pinch of snuff and delivering some Surrey-side threats about launching an attack on London the following day, finally throws down a piece of paper and strides from the room as mysteriously as he came.

With trembling hands, Lord Castlereagh undid the mystic scroll,
With glassy eye essayed to read, for fear was on his soul—
"What's here?—'At Astley's, every night, the play of MOSCOW'S
FALL!
NAPOLEON, for the thousandth time, by MR. GOMERSAL!'"[19]

Ducrow himself, in addition to directing the "Foreign Equestrian Evolutions" in the production (Davis presumably superintended the "English" ones), performed the role of the Duke of Brunswick and died heroically at the Battle of Quatre Bras. Both he and his troop figured prominently in the other entertainments as well. The nightly program began with a Grand Amazonian Entrée by eight members of the company riding Ducrow's Turkish and Hanoverian horses; and following the spectacle onstage the ring was turned over entirely to Andrew for his scenes in the circle. Beginning on 19 April with three of the ones he had invented in France—"Le Page troubadour," "Cupid and Zephyr," and "Le Chasseur indien" on two horses—he later went on to perform "Le Retour du matelot, or Sailor's Return," "The Death of the Moor Defending His Flag," "Le Jockeis anglais, aux courses de Newmarket," "Le Pasteur, or Shepherd Boy," "The Reaper," "The Roman Gladiator," "The Flight of Mercury," "The Irish Lilt," "Le Carnaval de Venise," and "The Wild Horse and the Savage," based on his performance at Covent Garden the previous fall. The confused status of Ducrow's nationality at this time (and the "w" in his name certainly caused some people to wonder!) is reflected in the titles of these scenes and those he assigned himself and the members of his troop—an absurdity that culminated on 13 September, the evening of his benefit, when the bills were actually bilingual.[20] Yet there can be no doubt his electrifying horsemanship had an instantaneous effect on the majority of spectators. Ducrow's performance, wrote the critic for the *Times* of 20 April, "certainly outruns imagination. His first entry could be compared to nothing but the swiftness of the wind, and he seems as little to need the saddle to support his feet. He is the most expert, graceful, and surprising performer yet seen in the ring." Nor was the freshness of Andrew's pantomimes lost on the astute critic for the *London Magazine* (August 1824), who commented on several of them and pointed out to his readers how innovative the rider's style was:

> There is a rider in the ring, worth going miles to see—a Mons. Ducrow, the king of horsemanship, one whose genius clearly that way tends. He is the first true horseman that ever gave a meaning to the display of fine riding. He shows the attitudes of the ancient statues;—represents a peasant going to the fields to reap—getting weary—remembering an appointment with his mistress—and hastening to see her, until he seems breathless with his flight!—All this you see distinctly, although he

is standing on a horse at full speed, the whole time. The savage horse which he catches in the ring, and then rides, at first awkwardly and at last skilfully, without saddle or bridle, is a fine picture. We advise all those who like to see a genius, be his line what it may, to hasten to Ducrow. He looks like a handsome enthusiast, when he is well on the horse.

There was the usual fee exacted for such tributes, however, and at least twice during the season Andrew experienced unsettling accidents. The last occurred on the night of Davis's benefit when the horse, suddenly slackening its pace, caused him to take a severe fall on his back.[21] The history of the circus is replete with such events, and Ducrow, although suffering his fair share of them, was luckier than many of his contemporaries. The "Northern Wonder" Makeen, for example, who with his wife appeared in *The Battle of Waterloo* during the 1824 season, was later to die at a provincial circus as the result of a fall from his horse; and in 1825, during a performance of *The Invasion of Russia* at Astley's, the equestrian William Smith fell off his mount, broke his back, and was buried a few days later.[22] Funambulists, of course, were even more likely to be killed or seriously injured when something went wrong with their performances, as in 1823 when the slack-rope artist Blackmore fell and was killed at a circus in Cheltenham; or in 1837 when Mlle. Irvine, attempting the perilous ascension from the stage to the gallery at Covent Garden, fell to the stage and caused considerable anxiety among the spectators —until they were assured by the management she had only landed on her head and no other part of her anatomy was damaged.[23]

Well before the close of the season at Astley's on 2 October, Andrew had arranged to spend the forthcoming winter in London again, this time at Drury Lane. His plans were doomed to disappointment, however, for George Croly's Arabian-Nights entertainment *The Enchanted Courser, or The Sultan of Curdistan*—despite the tramplings of Ducrow's stud and a flying horse ridden by a villainous sultan— was a dismal failure. Condemned as "one of the most expensive, and at the same time the most inefficient dramas which we have for years witnessed," and cited as evidence for the sinking of the English into a state of "second childishness," the play survived but eleven performances from its premiere on 28 October.[24] Yet the short-lived venture did give rise to an amusing anecdote that soon began making the rounds concerning Andrew's sharp dealing with the theatre's lessee, Robert William Elliston, who had entertained fond hopes

Ducrow and his horses might somehow save his faltering management. As reported in a contemporary journal, after signing the agreement with Elliston for the appearance of his troop at Drury Lane, Ducrow stopped at a legal friend's to show him his copy of the document. The sharp-eyed lawyer declared it to be in perfect order, especially since there was not a word in it respecting Ducrow's own performance. The hint was quickly taken, and on the day rehearsals of the piece were due to begin, Elliston soon discovered his star performer was not in the theatre,

> but that the horses were there, under the care of Mr. D.'s people, one of whom was immediately summoned before Mr. E., who asked him, "Where is your master?" "I think he is gone to call upon Mr. F. [John Fawcett, stage manager at Covent Garden], Sir." "Mr. F.—Tell him to come to me immediately." Mr. D. appeared. "How comes it, Mr. D., that you have not attended the Rehearsals?"—"Because I have nothing to do with the performance." "Nothing to do! Have I not engaged you and your troop." "My *troop* you have engaged and the horses are now here; you shall have more if necessary; but my own performance you have not engaged; I am thinking of going to *the Garden*, and am looking out for horses for them." Mr. E. was astonished; referred to the article, and found that although he contemplated the services of Mr. D. with his *troop*, he had neglected to stipulate for them. He was in consequence obliged to enter into a new arrangement with the Equestrian, by which he bound himself to pay that capital performer fifteen pounds a week in addition to the sum specified in the original article.[25]

The agreements and correspondence pertaining to Ducrow's engagement at Drury Lane, now in the Folger Shakespeare Library, bear out the above story with a few minor variations. In the original agreement, signed by Ducrow and Elliston on 24 May 1824, the former promises to provide a maximum of twelve competent riders and twenty horses, together with trappings and ornaments, for a period of seven weeks beginning 27 September. The weekly payment is set at sixty pounds, and Ducrow's own services are nowhere mentioned in the document.[26] That Elliston had indeed committed an oversight is attested by a second agreement signed by the two men on the following 5 July. The sole purpose of this hastily scrawled document is to insure the presence of Ducrow in the troop already contracted for, at an additional salary of four pounds ten shillings per week.[27]

The original agreement had also optimistically specified a second engagement to begin on 15 February 1825 and run to the Saturday preceding Passion Week; and Ducrow, in addition to the rate of payment mentioned above, was promised one-third of the clear receipts of a benefit night to be chosen by Elliston on twenty-one days' notice. There was no second engagement of the troop during the 1824–25 season, and the disappointing results of the first one, coupled with Ducrow's surprising maneuver over the terms of the agreement, undoubtedly led to some hard thinking on Elliston's part as to how he might get out of this last promise. The plan settled upon was to wait until Ducrow was in the midst of his own season at Astley's and then to fix the night at short notice. Or so it would seem from an indignant letter to James Winston, Elliston's acting manager, signed by Ducrow on 15 July 1825:

> Sir,
> By my Agreement with Mr. Elliston of the 24th May 1824 I am entitled to a third part of the Clear Receipts of Drury Lane Theatre as a Benefit, and previous to the fixation of such Benefit night I was to have received a notice of *Twenty one days*. I have repeatedly requested that such Notice should be forwarded to me in writing but have either obtained an evasive answer or none at all, until now, when I find that instead of 21 days you apprize me of your intentions under six days. Now Sir, you are well aware as must be Mr. Elliston, that it is entirely at my option to accept or to refuse such deficient notice and indeed I should be strongly inclined to the latter were it not for the desire I have of getting rid of the anxiety to which such irregularities give rise. I therefore Consent to the night you have fix'd upon in your Note although the worst of the Week, and am agreeable that my Benefit shall be announced for Saturday next 23[d] July & although such treatment on the part of Mr. Elliston is as misplac'd as it is unmerited.[28]

As it turned out, Elliston ran out of money and was forced to shut down the theatre two days before the projected date of Ducrow's benefit. Winston noted in his diary on 16 July that Ducrow had come to the theatre and agreed to put off his night until sometime before Christmas in the following season.[29] Before this ever occurred, however, Elliston—in difficulties again—resigned from the theatre, and the agreement never seems to have been fulfilled.

Ducrow had arranged to take his troop to the Dublin Theatre Royal during the interval between the two anticipated engagements at

Drury Lane. After encountering some stiff weather that delayed the shipping of his horses from Holyhead,[30] he opened with his company there on 30 December in *The Battle of Waterloo*. "Mons. Ducrow"— "perhaps it should be *Ducros*," speculated one Dublin critic—billed for his first appearance in Ireland, performed the role of Bonaparte's favorite Mameluke riding Marengo, his previous role of the Duke of Brunswick now being assumed by the equestrian Mackintosh. The troop was considerably augmented by soldiers drawn from several companies stationed in Dublin;[31] and Gomersal, predictably, received commendation for his "wonderful likeness" to Napoleon. Spectators wishing to see a facsimile of the Emperor were urged to see him.[32] *The Cataract of the Ganges* also appeared on the company's programs, and Andrew, since there was no ring in which to perform his scenes in the circle, again exhibited Beda and Harlequin in the pantomime he had arranged at the Bristol Theatre Royal the previous winter, now retitled *The Persian Prince and Equestrian Talisman*.[33] The scene did not make much impression on the critic for the *Dramatic Argus* (17 January 1825), who soon tired of seeing the horses at the Theatre Royal:

> After the play, we had an *entertainment* called the *Persian Prince*, (but why so called, we cannot tell; except from the circumstance of a hero with a pipe in his mouth about two yards long, having overseen the classic display,) which was the most silly attempt at any thing like dramatic, or any other *effect*, we have ever seen. Perhaps our feeling of disappointment would not have been so great, had we not seen the piece announced as "the fruit of (M. Ducrow's) *indefatigable search* after novelty!" There were two horses that walked on their hind legs, and a poney that was raised to the dignity of regaling at the same table with two of the biped race. This little animal conducted himself with real *Chesterfieldian politesse*, and really munched his share of an apple-pye with great propriety. This was the wonderful result of the *indefatigable* search after *novelty*! The whole thing reminded us strongly of the *Mountain in Labour*.

Because the troop originally had been scheduled to rejoin Elliston at Drury Lane on 15 February, the engagement at the Theatre Royal terminated at the end of January. But as Andrew had no reason to hasten back to London after all, he took his company instead to a regular amphitheatre in Dublin, where the same critic who had scoffed at *The Persian Prince* experienced a change of heart and professed himself much satisfied with Ducrow's "Roman Gladiator" and "Flight of Mercury" performed in the ring: "The equestrian performers evidently had not an opportunity for the full display of their powers at the Theatre-Royal."[34]

Meanwhile, William Davis had departed Astley's on a tour of his own and had refused to renew his lease for the coming season.[35] The opportunity was too good to pass up, and in early February it was announced Ducrow and the equestrian manager James West had taken a lease on the Amphitheatre for seven years.[36] The latter I assume to be the same West who was riding at Astley's in 1801 and 1802 and who later was in partnership with Robert Woolford in the west of England and at the Royal Circus during the summer of 1814. He had recently returned from the United States, a country many English and French circus managers of the early nineteenth century found both hospitable and profitable. From 1816 to 1822 West's troop had toured the Atlantic seaboard, Midwest, and Canada, performing in amphitheatres and regular theatres, including New York City's famed Park Theatre. West himself had a curious act in which he exhibited sleight-of-hand feats on horseback, and his wife was sometimes billed to sing and accompany herself on the pianoforte while balancing on a double tightrope. By 1822 his young son William was also assisting in the circus's pantomimes. At the time he sold out to Price and Simpson, the proprietors of the Park Theatre, in 1822, James West possessed considerable holdings in leases and property in several American cities and was accounted a major competitor of the Park when playing New York.[37] He realized a handsome fortune from the transaction and thus, in terms of both wealth and experience, was an excellent partner for Ducrow.

The two men seem to have got along well together. The only instance of any difference between them I have discovered occurred during the 1826 season, when Ducrow, exercising his managerial authority, fined Mrs. West for missing a rehearsal. This led to high words between West and Ducrow and culminated with Ducrow's writing his partner a letter in which he precipitously declared that for a thousand pounds he would give up his share of the lease. West immediately took the letter to Somerset House where he got some functionary to stamp it, then sent an attorney to inform Ducrow he

---

PLATE 2. "Mr. Ducrow as Rob Roy McGregor."

MR DUCROW *as* ROB ROY M^C GREGOR

Pub. by J. DYER, 53, Bath Street, Old Street.

was now bound by this "legal" document and that West was prepared to accept his terms. In the words of the journalist who reported the flare-up, "Ducrow stared with all his eyes, kicked and strained, but found to his cost, that his partner, as well as he, knew how to hold a strong curb on a restive horse. At length, after a vast deal of conversation fore and aft, in which anger subsided into recrimination, recrimination into altercation, and altercation into accommodation; the legal, illegal, bit of paper was resigned into the hands of its hasty scribe, on the understanding that, in after-times, he was to resign all ensigns of authority behind the curtain, to his ingenuous [*sic*] partner, and no longer be omnipotent, but in that circle in which his skill most fits him to move."[38] In fact, however, as the bills for the theatre demonstrate, Ducrow continued to function both before and behind the curtain, while West, who had given up riding by the time of his association with Ducrow, contented himself with contributing his stud of Andalusians and Canadians to the establishment, helping Andrew with the training of the horses and riders and in the perfecting of his pantomimes, and sometimes superintending the scenery and machinery. Mrs. West continued to act in the theatre's productions until around 1830, and Master William West was frequently in the bills as well. The latter succeeded his father as Ducrow's partner when the original lease expired at the end of the 1831 season. The Wests also had a daughter named Sophia, who married the American equestrian Levi North in 1842.[39]

The new lessees were off to a rousing start with the Easter production of 1825. On 4 April J. H. Amherst's latest contribution to the Napoleonic Legend, *Bonaparte's Invasion of Russia, or The Conflagration of Moscow*, opened with the redoubtable Gomersal in the lead.[40] He was joined at this time by another actor destined to achieve fame in the annals of Astley's, the earsplitting John Cartlitch (fig. 23). Cartlitch's shouting in the role of Petrowitz, the leader of the Russian patriots, wrote the stunned critic for the *Weekly Dramatic Register* (20 August 1825), "is beyond all bounds. We would, likewise, beg leave to hint to Mr. C. that no man, however brave, would enter into the presence of so renowned a man as *Napoleon*, in so arrogant a manner—we might almost say insolent, as he does; a slight tinge of respectful awe would, in our opinion, add greatly to the effect of the scene, without diminishing the interest of his own character." Many were the tales about the amazing vocal powers of Cartlitch, whose former master, the traveling showman Richardson, left him a bequest

FIG. 23. "Mr. Cartlitch as Tippoo Saib."

of a thousand pounds because he was "such a bould speaker and might be heard from one end of the fear [*sic*] to the other when the trumpets were going."[41] It was said that his "fine anti-whispering tones" made night hideous and could be heard on the opposite side of the Thames, and that on one of his benefit nights he actually fitted up seats for his friends *outside* the theatre.[42] His greatest moment arrived in 1831 when he created the title role in *Mazeppa*. Several years later he emigrated to America and died at Philadelphia in 1875, aged eighty-two.

Both Ducrow brothers had roles in the spectacle (Andrew doubling as the Hetman Platoff and Rousteau, Napoleon's Mameluke, John as General Ney), and Mrs. West, "of the Theatres New York & Philadelphia," was billed for the role of Catherine. And there was another performer in the part of General Schomaloff who, along with Gomersal and Cartlitch, completed the triumvirate of Astley's best known, not to say most eccentric, actors under the management of Ducrow and West. John Esdaile Widdicombe (1787–1854) often figured as an actor in the spectacles and afterpieces at Astley's. Together with Gomersal he had been at the Amphitheatre for some time prior to Ducrow's arrival, and before this he had acted in pantomimes and melodramas at Sadler's Wells during the seasons from 1816 to 1820.[43] But it was in his capacity as master of the ring that Widdicombe found his true niche in life, and surely he was the most frequently commented upon ringmaster in the history of Astley's or any other circus. His fame rested entirely on his appearance and carefully contrived manner (fig. 24), with the former, in particular, eliciting much speculation on the part of his beholders. Years after Ducrow had passed from the scene, Widdicombe was still being hailed as "the immortal," "the mysterious, the undying one," "Widdicombe the cool!"

> There, whip in hand, in the circle's very centre, will that great man stand and pursue his striking calling, not only unwarmed by the inspiration of the scene around, but with a look that might freeze the sun in the tropics. His eyes are black diamonds dug out of icebergs—nothing else. He is immoveable—no emotion stirs him. Hundreds around him applaud the beautiful results of his whipping, and yet he whips as though the mysteries of the thong were to him no more than snowballs. So he acts. Genius is with him so much a thing of course, and its developments have become so familiar to him that he refuses to be either excited or amazed. He exerts his power with quies-

FIG. 24. John Esdaile Widdicombe, the famous ringmaster at Astley's.

cent grace, with proud impenetrability of demeanour, which must be admired, if only for its matchless self-possession and *sang-froid*. Widdicombe is a being *per se*. His popularity is great, and he bows with silent approval of the public taste. He is devoured with rapture, but, while the world is boiling over, he simmers down into the mildest complacency of respectful gratitude.[44]

"Ever *point-device*—from the scented curl on his southern brow, to the elaborated splendour of his French-polished boot—self-possessed with an extensive feeling of Lotharioism and dignified dandyism," he was hailed by another writer as "the very Brummel and D'Orsay of the ring."[45] Dickens, too, in his *Sketches by Boz*, has left us a pleasant picture of him turned out in his quasi-military uniform, engaging in polite badinage with the clown and assisting Miss Woolford in her equestrian exercises.[46]

Widdicombe's perpetual youth and dandified appearance were the subjects of more than one joke, and a few individuals hinted that he had achieved the former by unfair means. The actor Fred Belton, in fact, insisted he wore stays and a wig and painted his cheeks, lips, and eyebrows—"the vainest man I ever saw—or ever shall see."[47] There were suspicions, too, it would seem, concerning his "peculiarly effeminate expression of features," although these were quickly laid to rest by his "constant attentions to the opposite sex."[48] Perhaps the strangest tale of all was the one related by a writer for the *Squib* (30 July 1842) concerning how Widdicombe managed to keep himself in his state of "ever-greenness." The writer claimed he had received the story from an obliging informant over a draught of porter following a performance at Astley's.

> "He is a strange man, sir. I ought to know, sir; I've known him upwards of forty years!"
> "Indeed! Did he look as well then as now?"
> "Oh, bless you, nothink like."
> "That's very odd!"
> "Why, yes it is; but you see he was a sight bigger then."
> "Bigger!"
> "Yes, bigger. He's lost a deal o' height. I wonder where it's gone?"
> We suggested a retreat into his chest.
> "Nothink o' the sort; *that's* reduced too. Now, don't you see he's growed less altogether, and *that's where it is.*"
> "Where what is?"
> "The whole secret. I have seen it wisably. I don't know how he does it, but he's *a-growing younger.* And, mark my words, if you lives to see this day fifty years hence, that 'ere gen'leman will be a little boy about four years and a half old!"

It all made for excellent fun, even among Widdicombe's closest friends, who nonetheless insisted he was a man of sound sense and that his dandyism and affectation, both on and off the stage, were the stock-in-trade by which he retained his position at Astley's.[49] If so, it must have been the longest sustained role in history, as another friend, the picaresque journalist Renton "Lord Chief Baron" Nicholson, alluded to in the concluding lines of a poem he wrote on the subject of Widdicombe's eventual destination:

> Perhaps a grand Egyptian grave
> Is made for him across the wave.
> If so, in pyramidic pride,
> He'll sleep with mummies side by side.
> There mummy maids may chance discover
> In Widdicomb a long-lost lover;
> And Widdicomb, from other zones,
> At last lie with his fathers' bones.[50]

While not so long-running as its predecessor, *Bonaparte's Invasion of Russia* did trigger the wrath of at least one good Englishman, who in a letter to the Tory journal *John Bull* (6 June 1825) complained that such spectacles had gone on long enough. The writer, posing as a family man who was accustomed to take his children on an annual outing to Astley's, began his tirade by expressing the belief the theatre was now under the management of a Frenchman. As evidence he cited the highly favorable depiction of Napoleon in both the last and present productions. The Russians and Wellington were being slandered and belittled in order to build up the heroic character of the Emperor; even Napoleon's desertion of his troops during the retreat from Moscow, in the Astleian version of which he was shown sharing his provisions with his men and taking the wounded into his sledge, had been introduced "for the purpose of adding fresh laurels to HIS glory."[51] And these spectacularly realistic productions were obviously having a bad effect on the impressionable lower classes who composed most of the audience and who now, for the first time, were nightly shouting "bravo" at the sentiments expressed by the "bitterest and most rancorous enemy this country ever had." The letter, which went on at some length, concluded on a political note: "The policy, indeed, is such as a Frenchman would pursue—but it is, alas, too much impressed with the character of English apostasy, to lead us to the necessary conclusion that it must be foreign. . . . we may easily believe the manager of the riding-shop over Westminster-bridge, to be either a Jacobin, or a thorough-paced Whig." In keeping with his usual policy on such occasions, Ducrow did not engage directly in battle with his anonymous critic. Instead, he answered through the theatre's resident writer, whose duties traditionally included those of amanuensis and all-around rhetorician. The stinging reply signed "J. H. Amherst" did not find space in *John Bull*, of course, but was published a few days later in the *Weekly Dispatch*. No Frenchman was employed at Astley's, the letter insisted, and the theatre's proprietors were good family men—loyal and of unblemished character. As to the charge that the Russians were depicted as base in the latest production, they were nevertheless shown driving the French before them.[52]

There was no pleasing everyone, however, and when later in the season Ducrow produced a showy new piece whose outline he had devised and given to Amherst to write out—built around the recent coronation of Charles X of France and interspersed with comic scenes involving some English tourists—the *Weekly Dramatic Register* now stepped in to assail the play for abounding in "the most sickening apostrophes to British valor, humanity, generosity, hospitality; and in fact, to every virtue, to the exclusion of all other nations. We never remember to have seen, even during the hottest of the war, any piece that teemed so much with illiberality, or national prejudice."[53] Ducrow and Amherst had obviously taken at least part of the complaints of the writer in *John Bull* to heart. The bill for the premiere of *Sights in England, and Fetes in France*, lest anyone should think otherwise, was headed by the cautionary statement that the managers' intentions were not "directed towards the endeavour to interest British Audiences with the Ceremony of CROWNING A FOREIGN MONARCH, but to surprise and delight by a Variety of Views and Objects they are unaccustomed to behold." With this same bill, in fact, "Monsieur" himself put by his French pretensions for a while and descended to plain "Mr. Ducrow."[54]

It is beyond the scope of this work to discuss in detail all of the spectacles produced at Astley's and elsewhere under Ducrow's direction. Rather, I am providing a broad outline, in general pausing only at those pieces which possess some peculiar relevance to Ducrow's career. Throughout his management the programs at Astley's continued to follow the tripartite structure previously described.[55] Occasionally preceded by an entrée of Ducrow's invention, the hippo-dramatic stage spectacle would comprise the first part. There were several of these produced each year, with the second usually falling on Whit Monday, a holiday second in importance during the "summer" season to Easter Monday. The ring acts in the second part of the program, lasting some forty-five minutes, also continued as before, only now highlighted by Andrew's own performances—"Ducrow's Scenes in the Circle"—and those of his pupils. Meanwhile, the stage would be cleared and reset for the afterpiece that formed the program's final section—a burletta, melodrama, pantomime, or extrava-ganza. Sometimes an earlier hippodrama, abridged or *in toto*, would be substituted for the last. During the 1825 season, for example, *The Battle of Waterloo* was revived and served as the afterpiece to *Sights in England, and Fetes in France*.

During the same season Andrew performed a number of his earlier equestrian scenes. These included "The Shepherd," billed as exhibiting at full speed "a Variety of the chaste Designs of GESSNER, and pourtraying the Descriptions of ALLAN RAMSAY and other

FIG. 25. Bill for Ducrow's benefit at Astley's on 26 September 1836.

Pastoral Writers, in a faithful Delineation of the tender Wishes, anxious Thoughts, awakened Jealousies, deep Despair, and ultimate Joys of an amorous Rustic."[56] In *Sights in England* he made use of his earlier training under D'Egville, choreographing and dancing in a *pas de huit* termed a "characteristic military ballet," and also performing the role of a noted tambour major, Jean Henri, whose living model had been at Drury Lane the previous winter. The bill for this production provides us with a reminder of another of his varied talents: the carriage of Charles X was executed from a drawing made by Andrew, who had witnessed the King's entry into Paris from a balcony opposite the Porte-St.-Martin Theatre. He must have taken time out from Astley's to do this, for the coronation had taken place at Reims the preceding 29 May, and Ducrow's outline for the piece itself was no doubt also from firsthand knowledge. Other artists of interest appearing during this season were Charles Parsloe, the "Chinese Buffoon to the Circle," and George Woolford "of great Provincial Renown," who was billed to make his London debut in the circle on 22 August. By this time, too, Andrew's young sister Margaret had begun her career as an equestrienne and was riding in entrées and cavalcades along with Ducrow's wife and a "Miss Emile." The latter was in all likelihood Emily. Hannah Ducrow, judging from her letter to Elliston asking for employment over the forthcoming winter, was at the Amphitheatre this season.[57] Andrew's fourth sister, Louisa, also seems to have been working for her brother by this time, for it is she, I take it, who is meant by the "Mlle. Louise" billed to ride in Ducrow's entrées the previous season.[58] John Ducrow continued his career as an equestrian and leaper, but had not yet become clown to the ring, Parsloe and Buckley both serving in this capacity.

I believe it must have been during the fall of 1825, while the troop was performing at Bristol in a new amphitheatre erected by Ducrow in the riding school there, that John made his first essay in the role of Clown. Andrew had actually hired Dicky Usher and Bell as clowns to the ring for his provincial tour this season, but at the former's benefit on 19 November it was John and Usher who were billed as clowns.[59] Since artists traditionally claimed the privilege of making up their own programs on their benefit nights and were always on the lookout for some novelty to bring in the crowds, it is likely Usher had recognized some comic potential in John and perhaps even coached him in advance of the occasion. He obviously proved successful in his new role, for by the time the company reached Liverpool at year's end he had stepped into Parsloe's shoes as the Chinese buffoon.[60] Thereafter, until shortly before his death in 1834, John regularly appeared as ring clown at Astley's, where he was sometimes billed as "Prime Grinner, and Joculator General to the Ring, whose Circumgyrations and Facetiae extraordinary will occupy the Intervals between the Acts."[61] One of his more celebrated fooleries was a scene in which he and two dwarf ponies participated in a tea and supper party, descended from the "Cheval gastronome" which Andrew himself had exhibited in France. In a famous print of the act (fig. 26) John appears in the grotesque, rather frightening whiteface and tufted hairpiece favored by so many nineteenth-century clowns, perversely stirring his tea with one toe, while the ponies— bonneted, bewigged, and with napkins around their necks—politely sup at their separate tables. The act was billed in 1827 as "Darby & Joan Supping with the Clown," and the ponies were probably the same Andrew had trained to take the places of the lion and unicorn in a humorous representation of the King's Arms at the opening of

MR J. DUCROW,
THE CELEBRATED CLOWN TO THE CIRCLE
IN THE GROTESQUE SCENE, THE TEA AND SUPPER PARTY.

FIG. 26. John Ducrow and his ponies in their famous scene "Darby & Joan Supping with the Clown."

the Amphitheatre in 1826.[62] It is certain John did not abandon his earlier equestrianism at this turning point in his career. A print entitled "Mr. J. Ducrow, as Clown in the Comic Act of the Fairy Steeds," published by R. Lloyd in 1832, shows him in the same costume bestriding two horses at full gallop, while his brother, whip in hand, stands nonchalantly in the ring (fig. 63). We see him again in the print of Andrew and Louisa Woolford as "The Tyrolean Shepherd and Swiss Milkmaid" behind the ring at the left (plate 4). John also frequently appeared opposite his brother in the comic ring scenes of the latter's invention. Thus, in 1831 he was Pan to Andrew's Apollo; in 1832, in a representation of a Spanish bullfight, Gracioso to Andrew's Leon; and in 1833 he was Mr. Kill'emwrong to his brother's Mr. Jenkins in "The First of September, or The Cockney Sportsman." Although a few people hinted he had been somewhat lazy in his youth, the evidence from his later years indicates John Ducrow was a gifted and versatile performer.

The winter of 1825–26 was spent at Bristol, Bath, Birmingham, and Liverpool. The size of the touring troop is indicated by a bill for the Theatre Royal at Bath, where it was announced twenty-four equestrian artists of the first celebrity and twenty-nine horses would appear on the boards of the theatre.[63] Also at Bath, Andrew renewed his competition with Mazurier, who had recently been engaged by Covent Garden. For two nights he appeared as the hero in *The Brazilian Ape, or Jocko*. "Mr. DUCROW is the only rival of M. MAZURIER," the bills proclaimed.[64] Mazurier's fame as Jocko had by now penetrated to the English provinces, and the same play was repeated at Liverpool the following March, but with John Ducrow in the title role.[65] Andrew's equestrian scenes and colleagues were much the same as before, and Beda and Harlequin now shared their laurels with Arabe and Phoenix. The last received some incredible publicity at the Liverpool Olympic Circus, where the company played for nearly three months prior to the opening of Astley's on Easter Monday. According to the Circus's bills during this engagement, "the indescribable performances of this noble Animal acquired him at the Theatres Royal, Covent Garden, and Drury Lane, the appellation of the ENCHANTED HORSE, particularly at the latter theatre, after his appearance in the Grand Eastern Spectacle, to which he gave the above title."[66]

Amherst's *The Burmese War, or Our Victories in the East*, with a final scene showing "Britons Triumphant and England Revenged," began the 1826 season at Astley's on an appropriately patriotic note. "Mr. Ducrow" himself, in the role of Ziam, portrayed a dumb pariah boy protected by an Indian widow.[67] Despite the play's appeal to chauvinism, it was not so successful as Amherst's Napoleonic epics and on Whit Monday gave way to a comic equestrian piece by William T. Moncrieff, *Paul Pry on Horseback, or A Peep at the Election.* In July Ducrow directed a new spectacle by Amherst based on recent developments in Greece, *The Siege of Missolonghi, or The Massacre of the Greeks,* which in turn made room at the end of August for another piece by Moncrieff, a "sporting, equestrian, pedestrian burletta" entitled *Shooter's Hill, or The First of September.*[68] Andrew appeared in three new scenes in the circle this season. The first, "The Grecian Cataphract, or Armed Horseman," was also tenuously related to the struggle in Greece. Costumed as a Greek warrior, he successively mounted four different horses to demonstrate the virtues of the light squadron charger, pack horse, war horse, and Arabian charger used for parade.[69] His second and by far most sensational new scene, which he seems to have tried out at Liverpool the previous March, involved the riding of three horses at once in the character of "The Chinese Enchanter" (fig. 45).[70] The third had its premiere at Andrew's benefit on 11 September, when as "The English Sportsman" he straddled the bare backs of two hunters and leaped them over a five-bar gate. Also on this evening Ducrow's stag Salamander appeared enveloped in fireworks, and Emily Ducrow, who earlier in the season had given "academical demonstrations" in the art of riding, performed an allemande on horseback with Master Brown.[71] A further novelty was provided on the same occasion when Andrew, for the first time at Astley's since 1817, performed on the tightrope. His decision to return there may have been catalyzed by the performances of another funambulist, albeit one of his own employees. Herr Cline, who had been dancing on the elastic cord since early in the season and who occasionally varied his performances by doing a jig in wooden shoes, had begun on 19 June to conclude his exhibitions with the "Grand Flight of Pluto from the Stage to the Gallery," the same act Andrew had performed in France.[72] It was Cline's preparations for this last feat that led to an oft-repeated story concerning Ducrow's own intrepidity on the rope. On first viewing the rope stretching from the stage to the gallery, Herr Cline was reported to have "declined" making the ascension. "'What, Sir,' said Ducrow, 'afraid of hurting yourself, I suppose. I'm not pretty, and have nothing to hurt: give *me* the pole.'

And, in his duffel dressing-gown and *slippers*, he ascended and descended—an attempt amounting almost to madness, and at which even the practised performers of that theatre shuddered."[73]

At the conclusion of the 1826 season the troop again took the road west to appear on the boards of the Theatres Royal, Bath and Bristol. The bills for the former city contain several interesting items. Herr Cline, for instance, was now cast for a number of roles in the company's spectacles and afterpieces, and there was also a Mr. Griffith or Griffiths in the same productions. Ducrow himself, in a comic pantomime he directed entitled *The Daemon's Forest, or Harlequin and Oberon*, undertook the role of Clown and was joined by a "Miss Louise" in the role of Columbine.[74] I very much doubt, as certain writers have inferred, that this could have been the twelve-year-old Louisa Woolford making her debut at this time, although her brother George was still with Ducrow and played a recruiting sergeant in the same piece.[75] Louisa Woolford had for at least the two previous years been performing elsewhere under her proper surname, and if one must identify the "Louise" of these bills then I propose Andrew's sister Louisa as a more likely candidate. Woolford himself had performed a burlesque equestrian scene known as "The Drunken Hussar" at the Amphitheatre during the previous season. Some idea of its action may be had from a bit of doggerel commemorating his performances at the New Olympic Circus at Newcastle in 1824:

> Young Woolford will ride without saddle or bridle,
> His grace and his merit, 'tis superfluous to sing them,
> He's by judges considered the first in the kingdom:
> As a
> DRUNKEN HUSSAR
> He will finish this act,
> And seem actually drunk for a positive fact;
> Though not able to stand, yet to ride will persist in,
> And on horseback he keeps, th[r]ough cork-screw like
>   twisting;
> Tho' reeling and staggering, head foremost, ne'er down,
> Hat lost, bottle broke,—rare fun for the Clown.[76]

The provincial tour this winter also provided Andrew an opportunity to rehearse and try out what was to become his most celebrated pantomime on horseback. And as the announcements during the following season at Astley's abundantly make clear, he himself had no doubts whatever about the historical significance of his most daring creation. "The Courier of St. Petersburg" had been "invented," the bills proudly proclaimed, the previous 15 February at Manchester. Having perfected "The Indian Hunter" on two horses while touring France and "The Chinese Enchanter" with three during the 1826 season, Andrew had obviously been wondering to what limits he might extend his command of his quadrupedal supporting cast. By the time of his benefit at his Fashionable Arena in Manchester on 19 March, he was announced, as "The Courier of St. Petersburg," to ride "Four Ramping Horses at once, put out at their fleetest speed."[77] At Astley's, where he first performed the scene on 7 May 1827, he incredibly pushed the number of horses simultaneously ridden to five. The bills for this season, with their various woodcuts and lengthy descriptions, permit us to follow the evolution of the "Courier" through its stages of development—and no doubt about it, Andrew did at one point gather up the reins and, in a pose worthy the legendary Colossus of Rhodes, actually straddle the backs of five rushing horses (fig. 27)! A bill for the week of 28 May, for instance, shortly after he had added the fifth horse, describes the picturesque action as follows:

> The Courier receives his Dispatches, and is prepared to proceed on his journey.—His Four Horses are in readiness, on their backs are surmounted Banners bearing the names of the Four great Countries through which he has to pass, viz. *Russia, Austria, France,* and *England*, but otherwise having no covering nor trappings whatever, whereby to assist the Rider; anxious to depart, they are soon urged forward by the Courier with characteristic zeal, and measure the Ground at their Swiftest Speed; the striking of the Clock distantly heard, announces his near approach to the place of relay, where he refreshes, and starts with renewed vigour.—In the Second & Third Part of the Scene, he shews the mastery in the management of the rein, by impelling his Horses through all the changes & paces of equal & unequal galloping, distancing them in all directions, putting them apart, bringing them up again, placing them in all possible situations, disposing them angularly, diagonally, extending them in a parallel line, circuitously, &c. &c.—And lastly, by playing with the manifest difficulty of such a Feat, HE MAKES A COLOSSAL STRIDE over the Five Backs of his Steeds, without breaking from their Speed; he reposes on their backs when he becomes fatigued, and finally arrives at his supposed destination within the time his exertions would bespeak him to be limited.[78]

FIG. 27. Ducrow doing the "grand écart" or split over the backs of five horses in "The Courier of St. Petersburg," 1827.

From other descriptions one learns that additional horses were gradually introduced as the act progressed. In July first one and eventually as many as four more horses were let into the ring—bringing the total to no less than nine—with Andrew snatching up the reins of the new arrivals as they passed between his legs and managing them as well.[79] The scene was accompanied by specially composed music by Chevalier Lorentio, and on 9 July Ducrow tacked on, as a sort of afterpiece, a comic scene performed by one of his infant pipils, "The Pygmean Messenger, or Dispatches from Lilliput."

"The Courier of St. Petersburg" was an exhausting pantomime to perform—so exhausting, in fact, that Andrew could not exhibit it every night—and the effort to describe it seems to have taxed some of the reviewers as well. "It is of a complexion altogether too poetical to be rendered intelligible by ever so minute and faithful a summary of items," wrote one critic. "To be sufficiently appreciated it must be seen."[80] Ducrow's memorialist Leman Thomas Rede referred his readers to the "Courier" as proof of Andrew's unsurpassed histrionic talents. "No actor on the stage (not even Kean)," he wrote, "could exceed his powerful expression in this assumption. *His* pantomime, indeed, reminds us of that celebrated eulogy on the mimes of old. Their very nods speak—their hands talk, their fingers have voices."[81] The act was quickly immortalized in a number of prints showing Andrew in the Courier's various poses and the horses in their different positions (fig. 28). It became so famous, in fact, that one of these same prints served as a pattern for a representation of Ducrow as the Courier on the base of a handsome brass-inlaid mantle clock (figs. 86 and 87).

Considering the labor that had gone into the "Courier" and its phenomenal appeal, it is understandable that Andrew should trumpet his accomplishments in the theatre's bills. It was a "daring Feat and an Act of most uncommon hardihood for which the annals of Horsemanship offer no parallel. All that has hitherto been accounted *Wonderful* in the bold and manly Attainment of Equitation, becomes, by the incredible Feats of the COURIER, outstripped and immeasurably surpassed."[82] Moreover, as the bills grandiloquently announced, the "Courier" was a product of the "NEW SCHOOL OF EQUITATION As Invented and introduced into this Country by Mr. DUCROW, in 1824, and which has since that period, been improved and diversified to the utmost, by the research, experience, and assistance of his Co-partner, Mr. WEST."[83] In truth, the 1827

FIG. 28. "Mr. Ducrow as the Courier of St. Petersburgh." The same print served as pattern for the Ducrow Clock.

season at Astley's was a banner year for equitation. Released from some but not all of his duties as stage manager thanks to the return of William Barrymore (did the argument with West the previous season have something to do with this?), Andrew was now able to devote more of his time to riding and exhibiting his highly trained horses. One of these, Pegasus, "surnamed the Hippogriffe," with a pair of wings strapped to its back, had been trained by Ducrow to mount a pedestal in the center of the ring and dance to the air "We're a'Noddin" (fig. 29).[84] More ambitious, still, was a hippodramatic extravaganza composed, directed, and acted in by Andrew entitled *The British Artist, or The Hundred Arabian Steeds*. The avowed purpose of this strange mélange was to answer the wish of the public that all of the theatre's horses might be seen at once; and by joining the stage to the ring with "ponderous platforms," upwards of one hundred horses were presented at the same time. As the chieftain Helal Ebn Rachid, Ducrow presided over equestrian evolutions and a wrestling match by his warriors. The hunting of a stag, with Ducrow's red deer Coco in the lead, the throwing of the discus and javelin, the walking of the mare Beda on her hind legs, the impersonation of a tiger by a dog named Neptune—all these and more were thrown

FIG. 29. Ducrow's horse Pegasus dancing on a pedestal.

together, and the hodgepodge concluded with a "Grand Composed Pyramidical Picture of MEN AND HORSES." Prior to this stirring finale, however, Andrew exhibited several of his horses and appeared in a scene in which he was advertised to "make his ARABIAN PACK HORSE Fetch the Wild Fowl which he destroys in the Chase, and Climb the Side of a Tree for Coco Nuts. The Horse will likewise form a Resting Place and Chair for his Master, share his Meal with him, place himself as a Couch for his Master's Repose." As the season progressed, Ducrow added to the piece a live elephant, which he also rode and exercised.[85] As more than one visitor to the Amphitheatre pointed out, only a fool would expect logic at Astley's!

For his benfit on 10 September, Andrew again turned "author." This time his eclectic imagination ran riot in a piece entitled *The Taming of Bucephalus, the Wild Horse of Scythia, or The Youthful Days of Alexander the Great*. The authorities cited were Plutarch and Herodotus, and the action commenced with the priests of Jupiter Ammon offering prayers for Philip's army before the walls of Macedon. The climax and finale arrived when Alexander, played by Ducrow, met the wild steed Bucephalus and after a terrific struggle succeeded in taming him.[86] Meanwhile, J. H. Amherst had been making his own contributions to dramatic history, beginning with the opening Easter Monday spectacle, another piece of patriotic claptrap entitled *Spain and Portugal, or Rebels and Guerillas*, and later in the season, from an outline furnished by Ducrow, *England's King! or A Soldier's Gratitude*.[87] Andrew himself directed but did not act in one of the afterpieces this year, a melodrama entitled *The Frozen Cliff, or The Exiles of Siberia*, which included a poignant scene portraying "the awful effects of Frost and Snow, which deprives a *Banished Lady of her Sight in the midst of her Family*." His wife and sister Emily were also riding this season, as were two of his equestrian infants. One of them, the same who came on at the end of the "Courier," was advertised as only nine years old and had an act in which he managed twelve horses while standing on two of the hind ones.[88] The name of this child is nowhere given, but I suspect he may have been the young Reuben Bridges, a member of a well-known circus family, who together with his father was named in the Amphitheatre's announcements in 1829 and later seasons.[89] Ducrow's other equestrian prodigy at this time was a Miss DeLille, said to be only four years of age, with whom he now performed the scene of "Cupid and Zephyr."[90] Another of Andrew's pupils, the mulatto Joseph Hillier, had by now worked up a spirited equestrian act of his own which in present-day circuses is sometimes billed as "Cossack" riding or "Voltige Infernale": he "rode with a most extraordinary power of retaining his hold on the horse, he went at full gallop, tumbling, reeling, under and over, and all about the animal, yet never coming to the ground, with really frightful celerity and cleverness."[91]

In the fall of 1827 Andrew first took his troop to Edinburgh, where from 6 November until 31 January 1828 they performed at Ducrow's Arena and Royal Amphitheatre in Nicolson Street. The stone building the company occupied did not have a stage; consequently the spectators' attention was focused entirely on the ring. And what a reception the Scots gave them, and above all their leader, Ducrow! "Wha the deevil was Castor," asked Shepherd in the January episode of "Christopher North's" *Noctes Ambrosianae,*

> that the ancients made a god o' for his horsemanship—a god o' and a star—in comparison wi' yon Ducraw? A silly thocht is a Centaur—a man and a horse in ane—in which the dominion o' the man is lost, and the superior incorpsed wi' the inferior natur! Ducraw "rides on the whirlwind, and directs the storm." And oh, sir! how saftly, gently, tenderly, and like the deein awa o' fast fairy music in a dream, is the subsidin o' the motion o' a' the creturs aneath his feet, his ain gestures, and his ain attitudes, and his ain actions, a' correspondin and congenial wi' the ebbin flicht; even like some great master o' music wha disna leave aff when the soun' is at its heicht, but gradually leads on the sowls o' the listeners to a far profounder hush o' silence than reigned even before he woke to ecstasy his livin lyre.[92]

In more staid terms the Edinburgh *Evening Courant* (8 November 1827) proclaimed that "the stud is the finest ever exhibited in Edinburgh, and several of the horses show a tractability perfectly astonishing; they seem to understand the words, and perform the commands, of their master, in a manner most surprising. The riders exhibited great address; but the horsemanship of Mr. Ducrow surpasses that of all his compeers; he is unquestionably the most skilful and graceful rider that has appeared in our metropolis." As invariably happened when Ducrow and his troop appeared in the provinces, there was an immediate rush to the circus by all classes of society, from the lowliest burgher to the magistrates and Lord Provost. By the time of Ducrow's benefit night, in fact, there was such a "dreadful crush" that even the critic for the *Evening Courant* failed to get into the Amphitheatre and was forced to mingle his disappointment with that of the crowds returning through the streets.[93] As was also usually true on such occasions, the management of the local Theatre Royal suddenly saw its attendance drop off and was shortly faced with imminent ruin, leading to several denunciations and expostulations from local diehards on the depraved taste of their fellow citizens.[94]

Such complaints had little effect on the majority of Edinburgh's inhabitants, however, and for nearly three months Andrew continued to 'witch these cheering spectators with noble feats of horsemanship. There were even, on 8 December and 1 January, supplementary "morning" performances (which actually commenced at 1 P.M.) to accommodate children from the town and outlying areas who could not come to the circus at the regular hour.[95] Besides repeating his older poses plastiques and pantomimes, Andrew now performed a number known as "The Peruvian Chasseur," which may have been the same as "The Indian Hunter," and added a transformation to his scene "The Shepherd" that was peculiarly pleasing to his Scottish audiences. As "Andrew the Mountain Shepherd," wrote the reviewer for the *Evening Courant* (2 February 1828), he appeared on a rapid courser "imitating the manner and peculiarities of the Scottish rustic, and dancing a Scotch jig on his narrow and slippery stage, with as much ease and agility as if he had been tripping it on a green. When the band played the 'Gathering of the Clans,' he assumed the character of Rob Roy. This was an imposing scene. After exhibiting a variety of beautiful and warlike attitudes, he concluded with the representation of a combat, and displayed all the ardour and excitation incident to mortal strife" (plate 2). The winged steed Pegasus by this time had been incorporated into a dramatic scene with his master entitled "Apollo and Pegasus"; Ducrow amused his audiences with his burlesque scene showing the various "modes" of riding practiced by such diverse characters as a butcher, a shop boy on a hired hack, and a riding master; and the "Infant Equestrian Prodigy," Miss DeLille, now performed "The Lilliputian Bonaparte and His War Horse."

Most interesting of all, however, was a new type of entertainment Andrew got up and which he seems to have first exhibited at his benefit on 28 January 1828. Originally titled "The Living Statue, or Model of Antiques," it was to experience many changes in title and content over the forthcoming years and was even to acquire, after being transformed into a quasi-dramatic piece, the status of a regular stage entertainment. It was also an act which those who thought lightly of circuses and trick equestrianism felt they could safely let themselves admire, possessing as it did pretensions to both "art" and "instruction." The new note of appreciation was already being sounded at Edinburgh, where the critic for the *Evening Courant* (2 February 1828), despite his enthusiastic reviews of Andrew's horsemanship over the past several weeks, concluded that

> the most interesting part of the whole, and that which places Mr. Ducrow in a higher point of view as a man of talents and taste than any of his former achievements, was the classical scene of the living statue, or "Model of Antiques," being a representation of some of the finest ancient statues, which he has copied with the most astonishing exactness and fidelity. His figure was a most perfect model for the sculptors art, and rendered the illusion almost complete. Nothing could surpass the effect produced by the representation of the Slave Remoleur (the grinder) overhearing the Conspirators. The attitude is taken at the moment when he has suspended his operation of grinding, under the magical effect of the Conspirators words, as they fall upon his ear, and enchain his countenance, attention, and awe. The three dying positions of the Gladiator were equally striking.

The same sentiments were echoed by the reviewer for the Aberdeen *Journal* (17 November 1830) when Ducrow performed at that city:

FIG. 30. Ducrow performing "The Dying Gladiator" on a pedestal at his Royal Olympic Arena in Aberdeen, 1838.

"The elegance, the spirit, the truth, of his various attitudes, were models for the chissel [*sic*] of Phidias; and far too fine to be contrasted with the feats and drolleries of the Equestrian circle."

Ducrow's representations of classical figures, modeled on well-known statues and paintings, were related to his earlier poses plastiques on horseback. The difference was that the horse was now dispensed with and the artist assumed his attitudes, initially, at least, on a pedestal in the center of the circle (fig. 30).[96] Such tableaux vivants became increasingly popular in circuses and theatres as the century progressed. And while Ducrow cannot be credited with having introduced the new genre of entertainment to England—for that distinction would seem to be reserved to the notorious Emma Hart, Lady Hamilton, who appears to have given some private exhibitions in London around the end of the preceding century, previous to which she had exhibited her "attitudes" in her husband's art gallery at Naples[97]—he was certainly one of the very first to exhibit them publicly and was to exert far-reaching influence on other performers. It seems certain, for instance, that he was indirectly responsible for the introduction of tableaux vivants to America, where in the autumn of 1831 at least three artists recently arrived from England performed his "Living" or "Venetian Statue."[98]

The bills for the 1828 season at Astley's provide us with a catalogue of Andrew's early attitudes, although the act was now being advertised as "The Venetian Statue! or Living Model of Antiquity!" There were nineteen poses in all, listed as follows:

> 1. Hercules struggling with the Nemean Lion, in the 6 well known attitudes. 7. Cincinnatus, the Roman, fastening his Sandals. 8. Hercules throwing Lysimachus into the sea, from Canova's chissel. 9. The Slave Remoleur (the Grinder), sharpening his knife while overhearing the Conspirators. 10. Three of the beautiful Poses of the Fighting Gladiator. 11. The African alarmed at the Thunder. 12. Ajax defying the Lightning. 13. Romulus, from David's Picture of the Sabines. 14. Remus's Defence, from the same. This Representation will conclude with three of the celebrated Positions of the Dying Gladiator.[99]

Modifications were continually being made, and by the time of Andrew's benefit a year later the act included "Achilles, throwing the Discus or Quoit" and "Horatius Shielding his prostrate Brother from the uplifted Weapons of the opposing Curiatii, the eldest of whom is afterwards pourtrayed in the act of aiming a deadly thrust at his Adversary."[100] The last scene, based on the painting by Vernet in the Louvre, had been added several months earlier at the express request of a local artist while the company was performing at the Dublin Theatre Royal.[101] It was during this same engagement at Dublin in 1828 that the German traveler Prince Pückler-Muskau, who had visited Astley's in the summer of 1827 and expressed his wonder at Pegasus and Ducrow as the "Courier," wrote a glowing account of Andrew's tableaux:

> I went to the theatre, where Ducrow, the English Franconi, ennobles his art by his admirable representation of animated statues. This is a high enjoyment to a lover of art, and far surpasses the 'Tableaux' which are in such favor on the continent. When the curtain draws up, you see a motionless statue on a lofty pedestal in the centre of the stage. This is Ducrow; and it is hardly credible how an elastic dress can fit so exquisitely and so perfectly represent marble, only here and there broken by a bluish vein. He appeared first as the Hercules Farnese. With the greatest skill and precision he then gradually quitted his attitude from one gradation to another, of display of strength; but at the moment in which he presented a perfect copy of the most celebrated statues of antiquity, he suddenly became fixed as if changed to marble. Helmet, sword, and shield, were now given to him, and transformed him in a moment into the wrathful Achilles, Ajax, and other Homeric heroes. Then came the Discobolus and others, all equally perfect and true. The last was the attitude of the fighting Gladiator, succeeded by a masterly representation of the dying Gladiator. This man must be an admirable model for painters and sculptors: his form is faultless, and he can throw himself into any attitude with the utmost ease and grace. It struck me how greatly our unmeaning dancing might be ennobled, if something like what I have described were introduced, instead of the absurd and vulgar hopping and jumping with which we are now entertained. It gave me pain to see this fine artist (for he certainly merits no less a name) ride nine horses at once, in the character of a Chinese sorcerer [sic]; drive twelve at once in that of a Russian courier; and lastly, go to bed with a poney dressed as an old woman.[102]

As Prince Pückler-Muskau's description makes clear, the act could be given on the stage as well as in the circle. The trouble was, Andrew eventually sought to improve upon these chaste representations by incorporating them into "dramatic" pieces written by his hacks (the two-legged ones) at Astley's. The result was the usual gallimaufry, treading a thin line between the sublime and the ridiculous. Ducrow obviously did this in order to have something that might stand on its own, independent of his usual setting, for he often entered into solitary engagements, generally for a few nights only, with theatres in London and the provinces while his troop was plodding from one town to another. At the conclusion of the Edinburgh season on 31 January 1828, for instance, he stayed on in the city for one additional night to "volunteer" himself and his "Living Statue" for service at the Theatre Royal. The manager of this distressed establishment, needless to say, was more than willing to accept this gesture of good-will and billed him on a program that included the two-act melodrama *Mary Stuart*.[103]

Meanwhile, the company had left Edinburgh for Glasgow, where Frank Seymour, manager of the Theatre Royal, had torn up the pit of his house and made it into a regular arena. As the editor of the Glasgow *Herald* (11 February 1828) sourly noted, he had "adapted the theatre to the present performances in a style of the purest taste." Two months later the Amphitheatre in London opened, having received some renovations of its own in Ducrow's purest taste. Over the winter the house had been repainted, and the fronts of the boxes were now ornamented with classical scenes of chariots and processions on a scarlet ground highlighted by gold. The walls and lobbies of the theatre had also been freshly painted with the figures of numerous mythological characters. Yet, as a puzzled reviewer remarked at the opening of the theatre on 7 April, "the artist has been evidently a Frenchman; for, although the proprietors had very properly deemed it prudent, for the benefit of their visitors, to have the names given under each figure, they are all given with the French terminations, as *Apollon*, &c."[104] The new season began with the latest absurdity by Amherst, a hippodramatic melodrama entitled *The Death of the Race Horse, or The North Steamer* whose hero and villain were played respectively by Gomersal and Cartlitch. Included were a stag hunt with full pack of hounds and a spectacular fire in which the villain and his henchman were burned to a crisp. Prior to this satisfying denouement, the hero and heroine were reunited in a snowdrift.[105] On the same evening an equestrienne named Woolford made her debut at Astley's, performing the scene of "The Flower Girl" while being gently borne round the ring by her cantering horse. She was, the reviewer for the *Morning Chronicle* laconically observed the next day, a "very attractive and promising young lady."

FIG. 31. Louisa Woolford in her act "The Flower Girl." Small colored cutout from a juvenile drama sheet.

In 1828 Louisa Woolford was barely fourteen years old. She had been born, as the census of 1841 was later to record, somewhere in Ireland, presumably while her father, the equestrian and sometime circus manager Robert Woolford, was on tour. The Woolfords were a prolific and far-flung family of circus artists in the nineteenth century, and Andrew had been in contact with them since his early years. It is in connection with an 1824 engagement at the New Olympic Circus in Newcastle, where Woolford senior was functioning as conductor of the ring, that I first find mention of Louisa. On 15 November "Master and Miss Woolford" were billed to do a waltz on stilts, and later on the same program Miss Woolford, "the greatest Wonder of the present Age," performed on the tightrope. A later bill for the same engagement announced the "Second appearance of the Celebrated Young Woolford on the Tight Rope, Assisted by Miss Woolford."[106] This slender catalogue of Louisa's acts—stilts, tightrope, and a single act of horsemanship—up to the time of her arrival at

Astley's bears out the progressive scheme of education for circus children described in an 1840 issue of the *Town*; and the writer of this article (probably Renton Nicholson, who was on friendly terms with several artists at Astley's) seems to have consulted Louisa on the subject, for he concludes with some flattering statements about her and her father and assures us that Louisa was "graduated in every particular department we have laid down."[107] The same writer, in a later article on tightrope dancers, reverted to Louisa and proclaimed her the "most chaste and elegant *artiste* in this department" as well. Moreover, he proudly pointed out, "she is entirely our own, without a single drop of foreign blood in her veins."[108]

During the 1828 season and later years Louisa Woolford regularly alternated between the arena and the rope. On 28 July, for example, she was first announced at Astley's to do her "Elegant Operatic Dancing & other Astonishing Feats" on the tightrope. Previous to this she had performed another exercise circus children were expected to master—namely, the divisions of the broadsword, which Louisa performed on horseback.[109] I have no doubt her arrival at Astley's tempted Andrew to conquer his "dislike" for the rope and to bring himself to appear there on a more regular basis, for by the end of the year they were already dancing on the double tightrope together—the first in a number of highly ornamental duets that delighted audiences for many years to come.[110] But I regretfully must report—despite the romantic fantasizing of several authors who have touched on Louisa's life in their popular works—that there is no evidence whatever for Andrew's being smitten by his fourteen-year-old employee or of his lusting after Louisa at any time while his wife Margaret was alive. There can be little doubt she was a beautiful creature to behold. More importantly, however, she was the most talented and promising of the female artists Ducrow had hired to date, a worthy partner for him on the tightrope and, as time was to prove, in the elegant duets on horseback he created with her in mind.

At the peak of her career in the 1830s Louisa Woolford was second only to Ducrow in popularity with audiences at Astley's and was often noticed in the writings of journalists and authors who visited the establishment. Her own repertory of single acts of horsemanship, besides "The Flower Girl" or "La Rosière" with which she made her debut, included such pantomimes as "The Fair Circassian," "Helen Macgregor," "The Amazonian Maid," "The Dashing White Sergeant," "The Nymph of the Floating Veil," and "Poverty and

Abundance." In addition, she often did a shawl dance on horseback and performed the "Jeux des drapeaux," a standard equestrian act in which the rider manipulated two flags while making his circuits.[111] To her contemporaries Louisa was sometimes known as the "Sylph of the Circle"—at other times, following the lead of the reviewer for the *Examiner* (13 April 1834), as the "Taglioni of Horsewomen." Her shapely, pretty figure was not unappreciated as she cantered round the ring, for reasons which—in contrast to the sentimental twaddle one must usually suffer through when reading descriptions of equestriennes and ballerinas—are candidly set forth by the writer for the *Town*, whose remarks were meant to apply to equestriennes in general:

> Their natural beauty heightened by every ornament with which the most tasteful arrangement of art can adorn and set off feminine graces; the expression of their eyes rendered brilliant by the artificial light through which they are beheld, and gathering a yet greater intensity of interest from the fixed regard developed by these fine organs, when brought to perform their office in maintaining the balance or equilibrium of the body under aspects of apparent difficulty and danger; their limbs rounded by muscular development—acquired by habitual exercise in the various departments of the gymnasium assigned to females—displayed in all the voluptuous witchery of elastic stockings which mimic the reality of nature; their elegant and agile movements, governed by the most refined art, though assumed with an apparently natural ease; their dress, too, generally composed of a slip of white muslin, profusely ornamented with Lama work, and rather serving as a transparent veil to betray the various movements of the limbs, than to afford such concealment as modesty calls for and decency demands—then the richly-spangled vest and fly catching innumerable refractions of light, occasioned by the abruption of millions of rays from the various chandeliers and candelabra, and exhibiting, while giddily whirling round the ring, the fitful resplendency of moonlit waters—now gleaming with light—now quenched by a ripling [*sic*] undulation of the sea; and, above all, the sanction accorded to a display so repugnant to our customary notions of female propriety, by the plaudits of thousands of spectators, all tend to excite emotions of admiration in the one sex and of envy in the other.[112]

My own favorite description of Woolford occurs in another of Bon Gaultier's ballads, which gives what I take to be a fair representation of the lady and her admirers:

Donna Inez Woolfordinez!
    Saw ye ever such a maid,
With the feathers swaling o'er her,
    And her spangled rich brocade?
In her fairy hand a horsewhip,
    On her foot a buskin small;
So she stepped, the stately damsel,
    Through the scarlet grooms and all.

And she beckoned for her courser,
    And they brought a milk-white mare;
Proud, I ween, was that Arabian,
    Such a gentle freight to bear;
And the Master moved towards her,
    With a proud and stately walk;
And, in reverential homage,
    Rubbed her soles with virgin chalk.

Round she flew, as Flora flying
    Spans the circle of the year;
And the youth of London sighing,
    Half forgot the ginger beer—
Quite forgot the maids beside them;
    As they surely well might do,
When she raised two Roman candles,
    Shooting fireballs red and blue!

Swifter than the Tartar's arrow,
    Lighter than the lark in flight,
On the left foot now she bounded,
    Now she stood upon the right.
Like a beautiful Bacchante,
    Here she soars, and there she kneels;
While amid her floating tresses,
    Flash two whirling Catherine wheels![113]

During the 1828 season Andrew performed a "metamorphosical Olio" entitled "Septem in Uno" which he had first given on his benefit night the previous September. This was another variation of the act wherein he changed costumes and impersonated several characters without quitting his horse and whose ancestry, running through the "Carnival of Venice," can be traced to the burlesque "Peasant's Frolic" performed by Ducrow and others at the beginning of the century. The characters in this case were listed as a Sailor returning from the sea; Paul Pry in a rainstorm; a Dutch Broom

Girl; Vanderdecken, the "Flying Dutchman," entreating a conveyance for his letters to his wife and friend (fig. 59); Dusty Bob, with
characteristic dance; Tom at boxing school; and Fame "bearing the
semblance [on his shield] of our BELOVED SOVEREIGN, in rapid
Circuit ROUND THE WORLD" (fig. 32).[114] In July, to introduce
a Persian steed he had recently acquired and trained, Ducrow got
up a showy scene entitled "Regee Pâk, or The Omrah's Charger"
(fig. 33), in which the pampered animal was escorted and waited on
by a numerous train of grooms, guards, and footmen in oriental costumes, with Andrew himself among them as Meerza-Beg, Meer-
Akhoor, or Master of the Horse.[115] At his benefit on 25 August he
rode and leaped a troop of blood horses in the first representation of
"The Windsor Post Boy" (fig. 35); exhibited his "Venetian Statue";
and for the first time in London gave the "Modes of Riding" previously tried out at Edinburgh. The bill for the occasion informs us
these last comprised

> 1. The Start and Coming-in at the Winning Post of the
> JOCKEY at the RACES. 2. The untutor'd, negligent, and
> perilous Style of the DANDY. 3. The rough and re-acting
> motion of the BUTCHER, which will change to 4. The easy,
> light, and graceful mode of Cantering observable in an ELE-
> GANTE.—LADIES in Hyde Park; next comes, the SHOP-
> MAN on a Hired Hackney. 5 [sic]. The DUSTMAN, shewing
> off his bit of *Bone*. 6. The DRUNKEN GAMBLER, returning
> home from the Races late at Night; and 7. And Lastly, the
> RIDING-MASTER putting a well managed Horse through
> his Movements of *Piaffe, Passage, Curvet, Terre-a-Terre,
> Cabriole,* &c.[116]

There was a near riot in the Amphitheatre this season on the
night of the benefit of Mrs. West, who had decided to engage the
elephant from Cross's Menagerie for the spectacle *Blue Beard*. The
pachyderm performed admirably in the play itself, but afterwards
suffered a delayed case of stage fright upon being taken into the circle
to perform some tricks there. In its determination to make its exit as
quickly as possible, the terrified animal got its trunk and forelegs
over the barrier and showed every intention of taking a gallop through
the pit. At this there was a mad scrambling among the spectators for
the nearest exits, while the women in the audience added to the
confusion with "terrific" screams. Several ladies were injured by the
elephant's trunk—one so severely that she had to be taken to a sur-

FIG. 32. "Mr. Ducrow as the God of Fame." The original drawing for the famous print.

geon and immediately bled. After the animal was finally got under control and led from the arena, it was announced it would be brought in again. The spectators shouted "No" for all they were worth![117] As previously noted, Andrew himself had exercised and ridden an elephant during the 1827 season. Possibly it was an incident dating from this earlier performance that gave rise to another tale of his

FIG. 33. "Mr. Ducrow as the Omrah, with his Charger," 1828.

fearlessness. The elephant—a male, we are told—had entered the frenzied period of "must," broke out of its stable, and was rampaging in the yard outside the Amphitheatre. Andrew, who was ill at the time, struggled up from his couch and into the yard, where he grabbed the elephant by the trunk and somehow managed to fasten a cable round its leg. This done, he returned to his quarters and promptly fainted.[118]

Three other events during the 1828 season illustrate Ducrow's growing prestige among London society and his colleagues. On two evenings the theatre was patronized by members of the Royal Family,[119] and in June he was engaged to direct a mammoth representation of the Battle of Waterloo at Vauxhall Gardens. The Battle, which was fought on 18 and 20 June, required several acres and 20,000 lamps in addition to those already in the Gardens (the performances took place at night after Astley's had closed); and Andrew, who took his entire company and stud with him, assumed the role of Napoleon.[120]

Meanwhile, he had made arrangements to take his troop to Dublin again, whose Theatre Royal was now under the management of Alfred Bunn. Bunn already had some firsthand knowledge of Ducrow's business dealings. He had been Elliston's stage manager during the 1824 season when Andrew brought his stud to Drury Lane and had served as witness to the notorious agreement concerning *The Enchanted Courser*. He nonetheless seems to have been favorably impressed by Andrew, for the two men were the best of friends in later years, and he now offered to convert the Dublin Theatre Royal into a circus for the company Ducrow planned on bringing to Ireland.[121] The proposal augured well for Bunn's future career as manager of Drury Lane, where he frequently was excoriated for featuring Ducrow and the lion trainers Martin and Van Amburgh with their quadrupedal pupils to the "detriment" of the legitimate drama. His present decision—which included rechristening the house the "Theatre Royal and Olympic Circus"—infuriated a number of Dublin's citizens. The troop played at Dublin from 25 September until 15 November, all the while, however, receiving stiff competition from another circus company headed by the equestrian Henry Adams. The renowned Madame Saqui was currently numbered among the performers at Adams's Royal Hibernian Arena, and the manager himself was imitating some of Ducrow's creations, including "The Russian Courier."[122] Andrew obviously harbored no ill feelings toward his competitor, for a few years later he engaged him at Astley's and freely turned over to Adams a number of his scenes. On looking over the bills and reviews for the early 1830s, in fact, I am led to conclude Henry Adams was probably the most outstanding of all the disciples of Ducrow's new school of equitation. This impression is corroborated by the clown William Frederick Wallett, who wrote of him that he was the "only real rival" Ducrow ever had.[123] In addition to Adams there was, of course, the great Saqui to contend with. Ducrow countered with his usual "flight" from the stage to the gallery, a grand ascension of two hundred feet.[124] The Infant Equestrian Prodigy, Miss DeLille, was still playing Cupid to Andrew's Zephyr; and on 14 October "Ducrow's little Boy" of the previous season, now said to be ten years of age, first appeared riding and managing nine horses at once.[125] Emily Ducrow and Master Brown performed a scene on two horses entitled "Jockey and Jenny," and Louisa Woolford had also come along with the troop. On the final night and benefit for Madame Ducrow, the honor of speaking the farewell address was conferred on the stentorian Cartlitch.

In December the company was again at the Glasgow Theatre Royal, where Ducrow and Woolford were announced to perform together on the double tightrope—an act they soon repeated at the Edinburgh Theatre Royal, to whose stage Andrew, "Mademoiselle" Woolford, and the "Infant Bonaparte" paid a flying visit, for two nights only, on 22 and 23 December.[126] Seymour had previously closed the Glasgow theatre for a few days in order to convert it into a circus again. Predictably, he succeeded in arousing the ire of some of the city's inhabitants as he had the season before, and within a few days a rumor began circulating that the amphitheatre was unsafe. This led to an offical court inspection which found it safe after all, although a few minor alterations were ordered. If the "evil disposed persons" responsible for the rumor were chagrined by the finding, they must have rejoiced at an event that occurred a few weeks later. Shortly after Ducrow's troop had departed for Liverpool, the theatre burned to the ground.[127]

Although the engagement at Glasgow was not scheduled to terminate until 30 December, Andrew and part of his troop left the city several days earlier, presumably in order to have two companies in the field over the lucrative holiday season, which customarily began on Boxing Day, 26 December. Such, at least, seems to have been the plan from advertisements in the Liverpool papers, where it was announced the troop would commence operations on that date at the New Royal Amphitheatre.[128] The last had been built in 1825 and first occupied by the Cooke circus family, and Andrew had just taken a lease on it for the next several winters. He obviously considered it an important investment, for despite the building's comparative newness he immediately set about altering and redecorating it, both inside and out, to the extent that one critic judged it "both for extent and beauty, superior to any theatre of the kind out of the metropolis."[129] When the first season closed the following April and Ducrow came forward to speak the farewell address, he not only boasted of the 7,000 pounds he had already "paid and discharged to the different employments of this establishment," but mentioned a sum set aside for the completion of the theatre's renovation following his departure for London.[130] At the time of the company's return in the winter of 1829–30, the Amphitheatre was described as able to accommodate between three and four thousand spectators and as possessing a stage fifty-one feet deep and nearly forty-two feet wide at the proscenium opening, three tiers of boxes and galleries whose fronts were painted crimson and gold, gas chandeliers at the center and sides, and busts and paintings scattered about the house—an "Oriental palace" in glow and radiance.[131]

The stage was put to good use over the next few seasons, beginning on 29 December 1828 (the circus had not opened on Boxing Day after all) when a melodrama entitled *False Accusation* and the harlequinade *The Yellow Dwarf* were given before and after the scenes in the circle.[132] Here, too, Ducrow occasionally tried out his big hippodramatic spectacles in advance of their London premieres. Amherst's *The Storming of Seringapatam! or The Death of Tippoo-Saib*, for example, with which Astley's opened on Easter Monday 1829, was first presented at Liverpool some five weeks earlier. The stage spectacles, one critic opined, "have never been surpassed in any place of amusement in the kingdom."[133] The performers in the ring received their share of praise, too, with Woolford and Ducrow nightly drawing down thunders of applause. The latter was described as "the *nonpareil*, the very *ne plus ultra* of equestrian perfection. We never saw combined so much fearlessness, perfect ease, and still so many beautiful and appropriate attitudes as he evinced on the backs of his four highly-managed and beautiful chargers. Never did a Miss, upon the floor of a ball-room, foot it with greater confidence and ease than did he, whilst going through his elegant and expressive attitudes, changing his steeds, and guiding these beautiful and docile animals, which attended to their master's will as if there had been some stronger community of feeling between them than that of the bit and the rein."[134] By the time the long season concluded on 10 April, Ducrow and his artists had insured themselves a warm welcome to Liverpool in future years.

It was during this same season at Liverpool that John Ducrow finally decided to chance the rough seas of matrimony. The wedding was announced in the Liverpool *Mercury* of 6 March 1829 as follows: "On Saturday last, at St. Nicholas's Church, Mr. John Ducrow, brother to Andrew Ducrow, Esq., the celebrated equestrian, to Eleanor, third daughter of Mr. Charles Minter, late First Lieutenant of the 21st Regiment of Foot, or Royal North British Fusileers." At least two of the Minter sisters and probably their mother had been working at Astley's during the 1828 season, afterwards leaving on tour with the company in the fall of that year. The family, as the newspaper announcement indicates, was not originally a circus one, and the women performed as actresses in the spectacles and after-pieces. According to Moncrieff, Eleanor was much younger than her husband, "extremely pretty and extremely gay," and the marriage was not a happy one. Already secretly envious of his brother's success, John now became suspicious and jealous of his wife and "fell at last into a state bordering, or very nearly so, on hypochondriacism."[135] There do not appear to have been any children from their union; and Eleanor, following John's death in 1834, later married the American equestrian Benjamin Stickney Jr.

The 1829 season at Astley's commenced on 20 April with Amherst's *The Storming of Seringapatam*, produced, as usual, by Ducrow himself. Cartlitch, as the murderous Tippoo Saib, "looked very fierce, and roared as loud as any of the tigers of the royal sultan ever did" (fig.23), while the part of Colonel Wellesley was played by the noble Gomersal.[136] The Liverpool tryout of the play, which required no less than thirty-seven settings, had given the initial London per-formances a greater degree of polish than usual; and the prediction of one critic that the piece was destined to make big profits for Ducrow and West was quickly fulfilled, leading to a boast in the bill for 27 April that 22,864 people had visited the theatre the past week and thousands had been turned away.[137] Most of the other new pieces during the season were also due to the prolific Amherst. In May, for instance, his *Massaniello, or The Revolt at Naples*, an operatic historical drama with equestrian scenes and forty dancers, music by Auber (the spectacle was adapted from his opera *La Muette de Portici*, produced in Paris the year before), and concluding eruption of Vesuvius, was also directed by Ducrow.[138] In June, beginning Whit Monday, it would appear a goodly portion of the females in the Ducrow clan performed in his *The North West Indians and Canadians Near the Falls of Niagara*. The spectacle had been written by Amherst from an outline provided by West—having toured in America, West presumably knew something about the subject—but the Falls were disappointingly painted on canvas that silently traveled over rollers. Among the squaws in the play were Mesdames Cox, Wood, M. Ducrow, Minter, E. Minter, and J. Ducrow. The first three I assume to have been Andrew's sisters Hannah, Louisa, and Margaret; and the last three to have been the mother- and sister-in-law and wife of John. Mrs. West was a "Wild Squaw" in this production, and Master West appeared as a Young Chief.[139] Amherst's *Battle of Waterloo* experienced its customary revival; and in September, for Ducrow's benefit, he again turned his hand to the Napoleonic Legend in *Bonaparte's Passage of the Great St. Bernard*.[140] Meanwhile, in July a comic pantomime by him entitled *The Seven Champions of Christendom, or Harlequin St. George* had also appeared.[141] Amherst's impressive output, it should be noted, was by no means unusual for an "author to the establishment" of this time. Charles Dibdin the Younger describes in his memoirs the many tasks he had to fulfill, often on extremely short notice, while serving as author to the Amphitheatre under Philip Astley's management and later in the touring company of Smith, Crossman, Handy, et al.; and Ducrow expected his money's worth from his playwrights as well. Thus, in addition to turning out a steady stream of plays and adaptations, drawing up bills and announcements for the press, and acting as Ducrow's secretary and treasurer in the provinces, Amherst was frequently cast for minor roles in his own creations, beginning with the comic Monsieur Maladroit in the 1824 production of *The Battle of Waterloo*. In his earlier years, before coming to Ducrow, he had aspired to an acting career and therefore was not totally averse to treading the boards at Astley's. His very slender talents in this area, however, elicited nothing but scorn and ridicule from the London critics, so it is not difficult to imagine his reasons for switching to playwriting.[142]

Another revival during the 1829 season was *The Cataract of the Ganges*, originally produced at Drury Lane in the fall of 1823 while

Ducrow and his horses were competing at Covent Garden. The piece was spruced up with new scenes by its author, William T. Moncrieff, and presented by permission of the current Drury Lane manager, the American Stephen Price.[143] Whether it was in return for this favor or because he hoped to profit from his generosity in some other way, Andrew "kindly volunteered" his services to the patent theatre for eight nights beginning 2 October, when he performed his "Living Model of Antiques" on bills that included such standard fare as *Hamlet* and the romantic opera *Der Freischütz*.[144] A second favorite hippodrama, *Timour the Tartar*, was also revived at Astley's and directed by Ducrow the night of Mrs. West's benefit on 14 September. Miss Woolford was cast (and no doubt fetchingly attired) as Agib, the young prince of Mingrelia.[145] Louisa Woolford again appeared on the rope and in the circle as "La Rosière" this season, and on 8 June she and Andrew made their London debut on the double tightrope. The title of their act—described in the bills as a "mariner's aerial ballet," doubtless the one they had given over the previous winter in the provinces—was "Steer Straight Young Pilots While Crossing the Line!" Andrew himself had arranged the ballet, and as the title suggests, even in this unusual environment his inventive faculty for pantomime was brought into play. For this was hardly tightrope dancing such as one sees above the rings of present-day circuses, but involved two parallel lines rigged above the stage at Astley's. Enhanced and accompanied by specially made scenery and music, the exercises consisted of "elegant and characteristic dancing to the Movements of *Tempo Giusto*, *Staccato*, *Maestoso*, *Forte*, and the last accelerated *Fortissimo*, preceded by Graceful, Picturesque, and Complex Positions, Attitudes and Figures, maintained upon the quivering and tremulous Cords."[146] It was, in fact, a ballet d'action transferred to the ropes, with Andrew and Louisa in appropriate costumes. There were to be several other such ballets by the two artists in future years.

In the ring Ducrow revived many of his earlier poses and pantomimes and added three new titles to his repertoire. "The Ascot Heath Jockey," I suspect, was his "Jockeis anglais" all over again; but in "The Conspiracy of Horses Against Mr. Ducrow" he presented a comic scene supposedly depicting his tribulations and triumphs at a rehearsal of his stud. Here were exhibited the horse with the toothache, the horse contumacious, the horse found in his master's bed, the horse drunk as a beast, and the horse that waits upon his master, brings him chair, plates, wine, fire and boiling kettle.[147] Ducrow's final new act this season, "Make Way for Liberty! or The Flight of the Saracens," first performed at his benefit on 7 September, was again related to the struggle in Greece. Aside from providing Andrew the opportunity to display his command over a troop of fleet horses while standing on their bare backs, the scene introduced several of his pupils in a battle episode. On this same bill he first enacted St. George in a ring spectacle he had been busy devising over the past several months. Not only was Andrew responsible for the plot of *St. George and the Dragon*, but he also, in a field that was frequently to engage his talents in forthcoming years, designed all the costumes. The dragon's den was modeled and presented by Andrew's friend the dancer and ballet-master Oscar Byrne; and the dragon itself was guaranteed in the bill to possess "enough of verisimility to convey proportionate Illusion of ideal nature, and to identify it with the looker-on, as the Fabulous Animal itself; its Mechanism and Automatous Serpentine Movements being so ably calculated and put into play, as to stamp the Action-Scene with the character of TRUTH

Fig. 34. Ducrow as St. George combating the Dragon in the ring at Astley's, c. 1829. Note the ring enclosure and clown in the background.

throughout its progress, and thereby constituting the principal merit of the whole Performance."[148]

Meanwhile, toward the end of June he had left London for a brief "theatrical foray" in Paris. Ducrow often made excursions to the French capital in search of ideas and talent, but he never, to my knowledge, actually performed there during his years of management at Astley's. The departure for Covent Garden in the fall of 1823 signaled an end to his appearances on the Continent, and his competitors in France were doubtless glad to be rid of him. As late as 1837, for instance, when he applied to the Minister of the Interior for permission to bring his company to Paris over the winter months, he was refused without explanation.[149] Yet he continued to maintain cordial relations with his great French rivals the Franconis, visiting them and the Cirque Olympique whenever he was in Paris; and it was shortly after the 1829 trip that a friendly letter signed "M. & A. Ducrow," in what appears to be Margaret's hand, was directed to Laurent Franconi at the Cirque Olympique, inquiring after his health, introducing to his notice the "celebrated artist" Tomkins, and asking for news of himself and his son.[150] Tomkins was in fact one of Ducrow's stage designers, who must have been traveling to Paris to pick up some ideas for the coming season at Astley's. The son referred to was Victor Franconi, who had been riding since the age of six and was around nineteen years old at this time. Andrew was probably hoping to engage him for his own establishment. Instead, he got a "Mademoiselle Lucie de Franconi" who made her London debut on 28 September and remained with the company during its winter tour.[151]

The rider Adolphe Berg was new to the Amphitheatre this season. Master Bridges was now billed by name for equestrianism and ropedancing; Master Brown, who previously had danced a duet on horseback with Emily, graduated to Ducrow's act "The British Sportsman" while his employer was visiting Paris; and Master West, who in the past had occasionally been entrusted with minor roles in the theatre's spectacles, now performed Ducrow's "Venetian Statue" at his mother's benefit on 14 September. Andrew was never one to jealously hold back his creations from his pupils and friends, and such generosity—though sometimes out of necessity—was to become even more common over the next decade. Emily and Madame Ducrow were also riding this year and participated in a dance on four horses with Ducrow and Hillier.

On 2 October, the penultimate night of the season, Andrew inaugurated what he termed an "Annual Fete of the Closure Eve." The program included several artists from other theatres, among whom were Mr. Lee in his celebrated combat with a boa constrictor. But the real novelty was Andrew's preparations to receive his patrons as they rode or strolled across Westminster Bridge. The arrival of company, the bills announced, would be greeted by "Discharges of Flying Artillery" from the Thames.[152] As the fireworks boomed forth their welcome on the evening air, Ducrow could take satisfaction in his progress to date.

Ducrow was of all masters of the horse the greatest;
it was his genius and enterprise that erected the modern
circus. He found it, as has been happily said, a mere
ring for ground and lofty tumbling, for buffoonery and
rough riding; and he made it a scene of picturesque,
rational, and chivalric entertainment, full of dramatic
and olympian attraction.

—William T. Moncrieff, "Dramatic Feuilletons,"
Sunday Times, 2 March 1851

5   *The Emperor of Horseflesh*

HAVING DEVELOPED MY TALE chronologically to this point, in these few
pages I propose to leap with abandon from one year to another in
order to examine in more concentrated detail both the personal
attributes and professional accomplishments of Ducrow. For the
moment, therefore, the reader may wish to imagine the writer an
ancient *desultor* of the library, a veritable "Courier of the Note Cards,"
shuffling, permuting, impelling his sources through their various
paces, disposing them across his desk angularly, diagonally, circu-
itously, &c. &c., now putting them apart, now bringing them together
again—even bestriding as many as a dozen at one time—and hopefully
managing all to a grand conclusion.

In the few years since his return to London in the fall of 1823,
Andrew had rapidly ascended from obscurity to the position of
England's most celebrated equestrian and circus manager. His inde-
fatigable labor as lessee and principal director of Astley's, his visits
to the boards of legitimate theatres and far-ranging tours of the
British Isles, and above all the remarkable character of his own per-

FIG. 35. "Mr. Ducrow as the Windsor Post Boy."

formances—on the tightrope, in the center of a pedestal while exhibiting his attitudes, but especially on horseback—won him the widest recognition among his contemporaries, many of whom refreshed their memories by decorating their walls with the thousands of theatrical portraits that were struck showing him in his poses and pantomimes. By the 1830s his fame was so great that Disraeli had no fear of losing his audience when he drew a parallel to Ducrow's riding six horses at once in a humorous speech on the Reform Ministry made before his constituents at High Wycombe;[1] and Dickens, always an enthusiast where Astley's was concerned, could assure his timorous fiancée in one of his letters that she need not worry about his mode of travel in the countryside, since he had arranged to go by four-wheeled chaise and would attempt nothing "in the Ducrow way."[2] Nor was such recognition confined to the more humble classes of spectators to which Surrey-side theatres traditionally appealed. Among his patrons Ducrow proudly listed the noblest families in the land, and as early as 1827 he was described as being "popular with all classes— 'ladies of high degree and low-born lasses'—nobs from the West, and 'burgomasters and great moneyers' from the East." Like the famous clown Grimaldi, the same writer continued, he was "at once beloved by boys and admired by men."[3]

With such popularity there was bound to be curiosity about the man himself, and in 1827 there also appeared the two earliest and best memoirs of Ducrow, those by Pierce Egan and Leman Thomas Rede, both of whom—unlike the majority of their successors—seem to have gone directly to their subject. Several other sketches were published in the thirties and later. Meanwhile, the inevitable anecdotes, bons mots, and apocryphal tales began making the rounds, the general tenor of which was that Ducrow had a hair-trigger temper and a tongue that could stand curbing. He was, in fact, judged by many to be a "character," and as such was considered fair game by journalists in his own day and the fantasizers who have written about him in more recent times. When he temporarily went insane after the fiery destruction of Astley's in 1841, there were some who wagged their heads and pointed to these earlier manifestations of eccentricity as being but the prelude to the final overthrow of reason! I do not mean to gloss over any defects in our hero, but merely to separate the genuine from the spurious and to place the former in proper perspective.

At this point, however, some physical data is in order. In connection with his performance of "The Living Statue," the remarks of Prince Pückler-Muskau and the reviewer for the Edinburgh *Evening Courant* about Andrew's "faultless" form and how perfectly his figure was adapted to the sculptor's art have already been noted. Around this time he was described as being about five feet eight inches in height, fair-complexioned, and of a singularly muscular build, the result of his rigorous training since early childhood.[4] And although we have what is reputedly Andrew's own remark—made on the occasion of Herr Cline's "declining" to make the grand ascension— about his not being "pretty," the many extant prints of him attest at least to his not being ugly. The small lithograph by J. Rogers after Wageman in which he strikes a romantic pose as a Spanish bullfighter (fig. 36), executed when Andrew was around thirty-three years old, gives what I take to be a fair likeness, although the moustache may be the result of makeup. The gracefulness of his appearance is conveyed in any number of other prints, and confirmed by written descriptions.

What did not always meet with his contemporaries' approval,

Mr DUCROW.

FIG. 36. Ducrow in the costume of a Spanish bullfighter.

although to many a source of amusement, were his brusque manner and unbridled tongue, with the last in particular often exercised on his hapless employees whenever any of them had provoked him to an outburst of rage. For Ducrow was hardly what one would term a "patient" man, and indeed was notorious for his displays of temper. His memorialists tactfully contented themselves with the briefest references to these eruptions—"possessed of a very impetuous temper," "unites the *best* heart to the *worst* temper of any man in the world"[5]—while other journalists made light of it. In a facetious article in the *Columbine* (25 September 1830), giving "recipes" to the performers at Astley's, the writer prescribed for the manager himself "anti-metaphor to be taken when the *bilious* manias appear, together with a small portion of good nature; a moderate draught to be swallowed when regulating the theatrical movement—this will check any sudden bursts of passion; the horsewhip only to be used to the quadruped race, and not too brutally to them." Yet against this general impression of ungovernable rage must be set the surprising claim by William T. Moncrieff, who sometimes wrote for Astley's and knew Ducrow personally, that Andrew was not naturally a passionate man, but got up these shows of temper with the express purpose of keeping his actors and equestrians in check. "A man more mild and gentle never . . . existed; his blow high, blow low voice must still dwell in the memory of every one who heard him while moving among us, but its mixture of *con furore* and *sotto voce* was not natural."[6] To support this assertion Moncrieff tells a funny story concerning an employee named Jem, a seemingly superfluous lout of a fellow whose position at the Amphitheatre was for some time a source of puzzlement to him. The mystery was finally cleared up when Moncrieff realized this character was the instrument by which Ducrow commanded the respect of his company:

> Finding it necessary at any time to put himself in a rage when on the stage, while he seemed almost bursting to select some one on whom to vent his indignation, the accommodating Jem would invariably make his appearance at one of the sides in the most *apropos* manner. "Oh, *you* are there, are you, sir!" Ducrow would roar out on seeing him, and suddenly opening his book of hard words, which, like many other books of hard words, really meant nothing—"I'll pay *you* off at all events; I've long threatened I'd give it you, and now you shall have it." Then suddenly seizing a horsewhip from some one of the subdued and abashed company, he would, as if worked up to

the highest pitch of fury, make his way after the apparently affrighted Jem, who retreated at the dreadful sight, as the saying is, in double quick time, hallooing out all the way he went "Murder! mercy! Oh lord!"—followed by Ducrow with well-feigned manifestations of foaming at the mouth with rage, &c. These cries would be heard long after both parties had disappeared till they at length died away in the distance, but not before innumerable horrid sounds had been heard by the trembling company on the stage, caused by Ducrow making a most furious onslaught with the whip on some convenient water-butt, or what not that happened to present itself in his path. Ducrow would then suddenly re-appear panting for breath, as if completely exhausted with his flagellating exertions, exclaiming—"There, I've given it to that fellow at all events; I've long threatened it, and now he's got it he won't forget it for one while; and that's the way I'll serve all negligent beggars," looking fiercely at any one of his company who might happen to have offended him by inattention, insufficiency, or otherwise. It is, perhaps, needless to say Jem never had been touched; the whole scene was an understood thing to keep the company in order by apprehension. Amongst others, even the great Nestor of the masters of the ring, the illustrious Methuselah himself, though vaulted high in his saddle would often shake in his magnificent pantaloons. This *terrorem* had the desired effect; Jem, exclusive of his standing salary, was extremely well paid after each of these make-believe exhibitions—his place was in some respects no sinecure, though it really was so in others.[7]

Another trick Andrew had for enforcing attention is related by the actor Fred Belton, who writes that it was Ducrow's custom to show up at the theatre on the last day of rehearsing a new piece with a new hat, to whose beauties and costliness he would craftily call the company's notice. Then, "when he came to his grand effects and anything went wrong, he would deliberately give his hat a crushing blow, and cry, 'There goes 7s. 6d.!' 'Try again.' They generally did it better the second time. Failing in another effect, he takes off his hat, and rubbing it furiously, growls, 'There goes 15s., darn it; try again.' But when the climax came, and all went wrong, he would dash the remnants down, and vigorously jumping on them, yell, 'There goes 1l. 1s.; try again, and do it, or darn ye I'll smash the lot!'—and they did try, and did it well."[8]

To be sure, such tactics did not endear Ducrow to the majority of his employees. If they did not exactly fear him, many of them thoroughly disliked him and did not hesitate to malign him behind his back. While he was conceded to be honorable and punctual in his business dealings with his artists, in many cases paying salaries well above the going rate elsewhere, it was also reported that his performers would rather serve at half-pay with less secure but more genial managers than work for the terrible "Mounseer."[9] Andrew's good friend Alfred Bunn (who had sufficient tribulations of his own at Drury Lane) narrates a conversation in which Ducrow once complained about the conduct of his employees toward the end of the season, when the carpenters and supernumeraries would begin pilfering from the theatre and the riders themselves would "come into rehearsal gallows grand, 'cause they've had all the season a precious deal better salary than they were worth; and at night they come in gallows drunk, from having had a good dinner for once in their lives; and forgetting that they may want to come back another year, they are as saucy as a bit of Billingsgate."[10] The problem was not restricted to Astley's, of course, but the message seems clear enough: there was no love lost between the master and his retainers.

Nor was the billingsgate all that one-sided. If there were suspicions concerning the genuineness of Ducrow's tantrums, there were never any doubts about the foulness of his language, which even his staunchest defenders were forced to acknowledge. The American clown Joe Blackburn, who together with the equestrian Levi North performed at Astley's during the summer of 1838, writes in his diary of attending a rehearsal and being amused by Ducrow's swearing at his men—"I hardly think a set of Yankees would stand it." Two days later he was back at the Amphitheatre for another rehearsal, and "Ducrow swore at his men, as usual."[11] Again, there were the expected witticisms in the theatrical journals. Having grown "hoarse" from constant swearing, one punster averred, Ducrow had engaged a stand-in to curse the supernumeraries.[12] Another *on dit* had it that the frost was so severe "Mr. Ducrow could not even d——n the weather."[13] Even Andrew's pet parrot had picked up the habit, to the delight or consternation of those who came calling at Amphitheatre House.[14]

What might be tolerated and even laughed at on the Surrey-side of Westminster Bridge, however, became an entirely different matter when transferred to the fashionable West End. In the fall of 1838 Andrew was again involved in a production at Drury Lane and on this occasion seems to have genuinely offended some of his auditors. A pathetic note in the *Age* for 2 December, after politely suggesting Ducrow should "moderate" his language, told of a noble duke and

noble baron somehow finding themselves behind the scenes one evening and becoming disgusted at the language they heard there. The
noble gentlemen were doubtless in quest of the fair game that traditionally dwells in such regions, and it was with the preservation of
this fauna in mind that a writer for the *Sunday Times* (21 October
1838) had earlier expressed his outrage at Ducrow's conduct. Unlike
the actresses who had the green room to escape to, the poor defenseless
girls in the corps de ballet were compelled to remain onstage throughout rehearsals, and morning after morning were being assaulted with
language too disgusting even for the ears of men. "Is there a MAN
in Drury-lane Theatre?" the writer thundered. "We hope so; we
believe so. Does he wait until *his* wife is insulted, or until *his* child's
ears are polluted?—and can he not feel for the wives, sisters, daughters, and infants of others? The language of Ducrow may be congenial
to the saw-dust in which he was bred, but it cannot and shall not be
suffered at Drury. Obscene language and disgusting oaths form an
offence at common law, and if Mr. Ducrow will indulge in slang
common amid costermongers, but untolerated elsewhere, he must
pay the penalty of exposure." The tirade continued with the observation that Ducrow's language had been within "decent, though
never within grammatical bounds, some years since, cre fortune had
been lavish of her smiles" and concluded by calling for the suppression of the theatre as a nuisance.

It must have been in connection with this well-publicized visit
to Drury Lane in 1838 that Moncrieff later felt called upon to refute
a rumor that Ducrow had been coarse and harsh in his conduct toward
women. Such gossip, he swore, was totally false, although it was true
Andrew had never been very select in his choice of words before the
females of his company. But then, as Moncrieff pointed out, he had
never "particularly hurt their feelings," besides which the standards
of ladies of the arena in Ducrow's day were not nearly so decorous
as those of their Victorian successors. As proof of the esteem in which
Andrew held the female sex, Moncrieff noted that his personal
dressers were invariably women, "whose delicacy was never for a
moment put to the blush by any act of his."[15] An interesting conclusion that emerges from this scholarly investigation into Ducrow's
profanity, confirmed by the writer for the *Sunday Times*, is that it
seems to have got worse with the passing of time. Why older men
should swear more than young ones is a mystery the writer has only
begun to fathom—possibly it has something to do with experience at

life. In any event, Andrew was hardly unique among his contemporaries where foul language was concerned. His brother-in-law William D. Broadfoot was himself widely known as "the great swearer"; and the author and stage manager William Barrymore, whenever something went wrong with one of his productions, was said to curse until even "the scene-shifters' ears curled up."[16]

Aside from its undeniable profanity (of which more anon), Ducrow's speech poses several problems which are difficult to resolve at this distant date. Here again Moncrieff's "Dramatic Feuilletons" published in the *Sunday Times* are our best source of information, although, as stated in the appendix "The Ducrow Apocrypha," I believe he deliberately exaggerates in the few tales where he has Ducrow speak like a cockney. What is certain is that Andrew's language—with its frequent expletives, foreign words and phrases, malapropisms and "dogberryisms"—was a continuing source of aural delectation to his contemporaries, many of whom have left us examples of his colorful use of the King's English. His great foible, according to Moncrieff, was his mock refinement, which led him to style himself and his lady "Monsieur" and "Madame" (and his colleagues to laughingly dub him "the Mounseer"), to delight in "hard" or high-sounding words and foreign terms in his bills and public pronouncements, and to show off the vulgar *patois* of French and Italian he had picked up on his tour of the Continent, "very often quite as much to the mystification and perplexity of the *natives* of those countries as to the wonder and admiration of the uneducated bumpkins of his own."[17] In the course of his professional duties Andrew sometimes gave riding lessons, and a clipping in the Harvard Theatre Collection furnishes us an additional example of these ludicrous attempts at gentility: "Why, Marm," said Ducrow while instructing a noble pupil, "if you want him to jump, you must hold on behind and *insinivate* the *persuaders* into his sides."[18] There are some hints by Moncrieff as to what his French sounded like—"cord leg-air" for *corde légère*, "pitty vere" for *petit verre*, "waultyjews" for *voltigeurs*—and whenever faced with a word difficult to pronounce or remember, Andrew unhesitatingly barged ahead with whatever nonsense first came into his head: "puffing" for piaffing, "currycomb" for caracole, "crackwhack" or "kittywhack" for *caoutchouc*, "funny man" for phenomenon, "summer assaults" for somersaults, "buffalo" for buffo, and so on. He was once reported to have asked a lady to take a glass of "Bucephalus" (Bucellas) with him, and his most famous malapropism of all—

"dialect" for dialogue—led to a statement that became proverbial. Precisely what moment in history Andrew delivered his immortal direction to "cut out the dialect and come to the 'osses" is unknown to me, but judging from the comments of journalists it would appear to have been sometime during the fall of 1838, when Ducrow took his troop to Drury Lane to perform in the spectacle *Charlemagne*. And despite the assumption by a few later writers that this *cri de coeur* was uttered while Ducrow was impatiently watching a rehearsal of *Hamlet* from the wings,[19] I do not think we need attribute so total a lack of appreciation for fine poetry to one who, whatever his own linguistic failings may have been, was himself a patron of the legitimate theatre and English Opera House, and who by this date was well able to dispense with the horses in some of his own performances. No—as the reviewer for the *Morning Chronicle* more plausibly informs us, the admonition was delivered to the equestrian's own "poet"; and as *Charlemagne* was billed as having been got up and produced under the exclusive direction of Ducrow, who also, interestingly, played the part of a Moor named Hamet in the piece, I am inclined to believe the phrase must have originated in connection with this very production.[20] Like most good things, Ducrow's famous dictum suffered with the passing of time, with the most common corruption being the substitution of the word "cackle" for "dialect." Thus, in chapter 25 of George Moore's *A Mummer's Wife*, Dick, forced to listen to the tales of his wealthy patroness Mrs. Forest, says to himself, "If I can only get her to cut the cackle and get to the 'osses." The reader is solemnly assured the correct word is "dialect" and that the quotation I have given reproduces the statement in its pristine condition.

As with his language, so with his actions. The peremptory way in which Ducrow managed his artists also gave rise to many jokes and well-known stories, but here it is necessary to recognize the nature of the material he had to work with. They were mainly a rough and outspoken breed, these riders, acrobats, ropedancers, and clowns— the women no less than the men—and one must beware of idealizing them, of confusing, say, the ethereal and demure appearance of the equestrienne in the ring with what she may have been like when out of the saddle. Likewise, the "Reaper" or "Shepherd" so eloquently pleading his silent love on horseback could in the next moment turn into a cursing tyrant behind the scenes. In regard to the actors who appeared on the boards of Astley's, there were never any illusions about their capabilities. With the exception of Gomersal and one or two temporary accessions like Mrs. Pope and the comic singer Herring (who, the critics almost invariably felt called upon to remark, were "too good" for the house), they were of the most indifferent kind. "People do not care about fine acting at Astley's," wrote William Clarke in his 1827 guide to London amusements. "The horses are esteemed to be the principal performers, and if they do their parts well, the whole house—'pit, boxes, and gallery, egad'—is content."[21] So long as they were able to run up and down lofty precipices, keep out of the way of the horses, kill and be killed and rise again in a later scene, scowl and menace, look wicked or jealous, and swear "revenge," "murder" and other bloody oaths with Cartlitchian fury, the biped actors' histrionic talents were rarely of more than passing interest to the majority of spectators, who were hard pressed enough to follow the logic and incidents of the plays themselves. The real pleasure of attending a stage production at Astley's—and it *was* a treat in the eyes of most every beholder—lay not in the human acting or the incomprehensible plots with their wretched dialogue, but in the glittering spectacle and massive groupings, the swift-paced action and profusion of gorgeous settings, the crashing music and pyrotechnical displays, and above all the thundering hoofs of the real stars of the establishment, Ducrow and West's mighty troop of horses. And it was here, as elsewhere, that Andrew's genius blazed forth, since the majority of these productions, until a few years before his death, were got up under his personal direction. No one, not even those who most objected to his merciless cutting of the "dialect," could deny he was a masterful producer. "Ducrow—as we have often said—has the finest eye in the world for stage effect," wrote one critic after seeing the Easter spectacle, *The Siege of Jerusalem*, in 1835.[22] "In his profession he was without an equal," wrote another in an obituary notice several years later, "and it was often a theme of surprise how a man whose whole life had been devoted to the circle, could form such grand ideas of the picturesque and the beautiful. We do not use the latter term as significant of what alone attracts the eye, but in its true meaning—its attestation of mind in the manager, its appeal *to* mind with respect to the spectator. Ducrow's groupings were things of life, and purpose."[23] The reviewers were continually amazed by the effectiveness of Andrew's staging, and especially by his handling of crowds and movement. Consequently, while they rarely found anything to praise in the actors or plays themselves, they generally urged their readers to attend all the same, if for no other reason than the brilliance of the spectacle.

We have several descriptions of Ducrow at rehearsal, most of which, like the stories surrounding his temper, bear out his reputation for dictatorial behavior. In attempting to review the 1838 Drury Lane production of *Charlemagne*, for example, the critic for the *Era* (28 October) complained that his job had been made difficult, since Ducrow had made so many cuts in the script during rehearsals that the author could no longer be held responsible for the play's deficiencies. "Mr. Ducrow seems to think with the orator, that there are but three things necessary; the first is *action*, the second is *action*, and the third is *action,—action—action—action*. Accordingly, he limits the dialogue between what he calls the effective scenes, by a kind of Procrastean [*sic*] law, exactly to the time that it may take to set the said scenes, crying out, 'There, there's enough of that are d——d nonsense—the scene is set.'" Commenting on Ducrow's earlier visit to Drury Lane to direct and perform in *St. George and the Dragon* during the 1833–34 season, Alfred Bunn—who also admired Andrew's extensive knowledge of stage management—described his handling of a scene in that play. The second act commenced with a wedding celebration, which was rudely interrupted by the entrance of a neatherd who announced the reappearance of the dragon.

> Ducrow had told the supernumeraries to rush, on hearing the intelligence, to the feet of their Monarch, for advice—then to the Chancellor, to whom the Monarch was to refer them, and from him to the altar of their gods, then burning on the stage, as advised by the said Chancellor. He might as well have spoken as much Greek to them: they set off in a smart trot to one party, then to the other, without betraying the slightest indication of the alarm they were supposed to be suffering. Ducrow got into a positive fever, and acting it for them, exclaimed, "Look here, you d——d fools! you should rush up to the King—that chap there, and say 'Old fellow, the Dragon is come, and we're in a mess, and you must get us out of it.' The King says, 'Go to Brougham,'—then you all go up to Brougham; and he says, 'What the d——l do I know about a Dragon? Go to your gods—' and your gods is that lump of tow burning on that bit of timber there." He accompanied all this with splendid pantomime action and the effect was altogether perfect.[24]

There were lighter, more relaxed moments as well, especially when Andrew was among his usual associates and on the familiar territory of Astley's. In an amusing series of sketches by Henry Valentine, purporting to show various actors and directors at rehearsal, I find the following one of Ducrow. How the writer came by his information is unknown to me, but I should not be surprised to learn he had actually sat in on the rehearsal he describes, so credibly has he captured the tone and content of Ducrow's speech:

Clear the stage, sir; clear the stage—"let me have no intruders; above all, keep"—There's the bull loose again—all ready, eh? —coming to come, eh?—I always find myself first—that's for the honour, I suppose. Now, sir, where's Mr. Prettycome [Widdicombe], Mr. Brown, Mr. Jones, Mr. Robinson, Mr. Smith, Mr. Snooks, all ready? Come, my bell—my stick— now we're just going to begin the rehearsal of a rehearsal. Where are the supernumeraries? Where's the man that hangs by his nose from the top of the castle?—"He's ill, sir."—Oh, he's frightened, is he? Now, then, where's the brave no-kill militia?—Get ready for the Battle of Squirt—nobody wounded —nobody hurt. First twelve of the red-cross shields—the pot-lid smiters—come on, come on, come on! Now for this grand march—altogether—some one way, some another. I don't want a trample, nor a shuffle, nor a trot; I want a slow march— don't get in tangle, there—left foot first. Beautiful—anything's good enough for Ashley's—look at that flying pieman!—See! there's exactly five men in the first six. "Please, sir, this here oss won't go up the rake." Eh?—did he tell you so—you're frightened of him, eh?—Go home and go to bed, sir—cover over your head with the sheet. Now, sir, music when convenient—ah!—tweedle-dum-de-dee, de dar, fal-lal-la. Won't do, sir—that music won't do—waste paper bought; give us the old march again—anything's good enough for Ashley's. Mrs. Toddle, you're sitting on that horse doubled up like a big salmon in a little sarcepan. Are you frightened, too? "Heroic Conduct of a Female" (Walker)—anything's good enough for Ashley's. I'll keep you here all night, gentlemen, and settle with you to-morrow—good entertainment for man and beast. Fine weather to go a fishing—suppose we "hook" it, and give the treasurer a holiday on Saturday, eh? Who'll make one to put up the shutters, eh? Now, my misters, suppose I try to play master, eh? Where's the bull—the goats—the zebra—all over again from the beginning. Is the boy in the camel's chitterlings, or is he coming on by steam. A steam camel, eh?—anything's good enough for Ashley's. Sweep away all this sawdust, sir—half over the gentlemen in the orchestra, and half into the prompter's box. That's it, sir—anything's good enough for Ashley's.[25]

There is another sketch in the same collection, this time dealing with the "undying one" himself, "Methuselah" Widdicombe. Besides providing some interesting insight into the diction of actors at minor theatres (confirmed by other writers on the subject), it contains evidence for a slightly malicious humor on the part of Ducrow. Here, too, the sketch has the ring of authenticity, for all of the characters introduced are actual circus personalities, either living or dead. Broadfoot, who married Ducrow's sister Emily around 1836, sometimes acted as stage manager at Astley's; Barnabas Rayner was one of the house authors; the call boy John Avery was the son of one of Andrew's early competitors; Jacob Decastro and Richard Johannot, actor and comic singer respectively, flourished around the turn of the century; *Cat*lich is, of course, the bawling actor John Cartlitch. It is Widdicombe who speaks:

Will you allow me ladies, thank you. Johnny, please to call Mr. R. Glindon, he enters with me. Coming, sir. I'm here, Mr. Ducrow, but I have no opponent. The call-boy has gone for Mr. Glindon, sir; he is painting a new scene, sir. Go on to the next scene? very good, sir. I—I—I presume I address Mr. *Cat*lich. Sir, do you enact Saladin, Mr. *Cat*lich? Very good, sir; I await the cue. Be kind enough to enlighten me. A—a—a Mr. Palmer is the King of England? just so. I thank you. The fact is, Mr. D—— is so impetuous, and I am so nervous, unwell, indeed—taken away forcibly to the Duke of Richmond's last evening; brilliant assemblage, lovely women, maddening champagne—in fact, Mr. *Cat*lich, I may exclaim, "Heaven save us from our friends." I am suffering all the torments of a most excruciating head-ache. Go on? Yes, sir. Now, Mr. *Cat*lich, if you please, what is the cue?
"—attack these walls."
"Trimble! a Neat of Osstria noose not hoo to trimble; and as faw thy bosted wolls, our trups would foss aw scale thim, as they would a shid faw kettle!" Chopping up the author, Mr. Ducrow? I deny it, sir; I am perfect, letter perfect, sir. Have the kindness to read the manuscript, Mr. Rayner. Mr. Broadfoot, I will guarantee I have not omitted a word. Read, sir; this is most unjust. (*Broadfoot reads.*) "Tremble! a Knight of Austria knows not how to tremble; and as for thy boasted walls, our troops would force or scale them as they would a shed for cattle!" Just so. I was quite correct; chopped up the words, sir? I deny it, sir. I am no spokesman. Perhaps you had better give the part to a *clever* man, sir. I cannot brawl, I do my best, Mr. D——. "Can't act and got no tact," sir? I am quite undeserving of this, sir; I have not the *tact* of giving a very superficial knowledge the appearance of profundity, sir.

I do my best; do not let us quarrel, Mr. D——; you well know I am one of the pillars of the theatre, sir; or if you doubt it, suspend me for a week. Nice middle-aged man, sir? Philip Astley, sir? 60 years old when Philip Astley died, sir? I deny it, I never did wear his left-off white waistcoats, sir; I never said I was handsomer than his son; Mr. D——, this is exceeding *un*handsome. No, sir, you have not hurt the *old* gentleman's feelings, the *old* gentleman may see your lease expire yet, sir. Well, sir, if even I was a man when Jemmy De Castro was a boy, and before Johannot was born, what has that to do with it? Mr. Herring, discontinue your practical jokes, sir. Mr. John Ducrow, you had better fetch the whole of the family to ridicule me. Shall we go on with the Siege of Jerusalem, Mr. D——, or continue this farce? No, sir, my mouth is not full of plums, sir; I shall leave the theatre, sir, and when you have learnt the treatment due to a gentleman—an unassuming gentleman, sir—you may send the call-boy over to Lomas's Hotel, and you will find me ready both to forget and forgive. I am rarely taxed with a want of courtesy, but I will not be made a laughing-stock before the whole company, sir. Go and commit my shoes aside? Oh, dear no, sir, I shall not commit suicide. Do as I like? No, sir, I will do what you require, in reason. Do, pray, let us go on, sir; many of these poor gentlemen supernumeraries have got very wet feet. This may be sport to you, but it is death to them, sir. Oh, here is Mr. Glindon; if we have concluded our "pretty little quarrel," I will commence the fight with him. "Whose hair dye do I use?" What has hair dye to do with the question? Will you allow me to thrash you before the company, sir? Are you in jest or earnest? "Why?" Why, sir, when you have learnt how to behave yourself you may send for me. John Avery, you will find me at Lomas's Hotel. Gud monning, Mr. D——. Gud monning, ladies and gentlemen all. Mr. John Ducrow, fools are privileged persons; my hat is bought and paid for, sir; pass off your practical jokes on somebody who will not resent them. I trust I always behave as a gentleman—but I am wasting my breath. Fined! you may fine me five pounds, sir; I will not go on until you apologise. I am to be found at Lomas's Hotel. Gud monning, sir; gud monning, ladies and gentlemen. *Exit*.[26]

One suspects poor Widdicombe must have had a good deal to endure from his fun-loving colleagues, despite his elevated position as master of the ring. His delicate feelings and the respect due his office were again violated at the end of one summer season when Ducrow called his troop together to discuss their forthcoming route to Derby and Leicester. As was customary while on their provincial tours, those performers who could ride were expected to travel aboard the company's horses; but on this occasion there were more horses than equestrians available, so that it would be necessary for some to take charge of more than one animal. The affront to one's dignity under such an arrangement is amply demonstrated by the following discussion, which Andrew terminated in his usual resolute manner. "What say you, Widdy," said Ducrow, after outlining the problem. "Will you condescend to *lead* on the present occasion?"

> *Mr. Widdicomb.*—I beg pardon, Monsieur; but I was not engaged for the *leading* business.
> *Sloane.*—Nor I, and riding's entirely out of the question.
> *Bland.*—I'll be d——d if I can or will ride double.
> *Ducrow.*—*Widdy*, you know my *way*—shew these refractory people a taste of your quality.
> *Widdicomb.*—But consider propriety, Monsieur!
> *Ducrow.*—Damn propriety, Sir; can't you clap on a red wig and ride in the character of a countryman, leading two osses? You may have their tails straw'd, or any other gammon, to save appearance; there are plenty of dresses in the wardrobe. Ladies and gentlemen, I expect you all to take part in the progress. Mr. Widdicomb, I hate unnecessary pride; you know my way, and I'll have it, by G——!
> The company then retired.[27]

Mention has already been made of Ducrow's other connections with the many stage spectacles produced at Astley's. Pierce Egan, in his 1827 memoir, writes of his uniting in one person the talents of stage manager, ballet-master, and designer of all the costumes for his company;[28] and Moncrieff also, in regard to this last employment, tells of his possessing "no small skill in costume, particularly in female costume, though he did sometimes cut the ladies' petticoats a little too short."[29] Andrew was certainly handy with a pencil, whether portraying himself on horseback as the "Roman Gladiator," sketching the carriage of the King of France for eventual duplication at Astley's, or, in time for the Easter opening in 1832, designing all the interior decorations during a total renovation of the Amphitheatre.[30] He was often, particularly during the thirties, credited with designing the "dresses" for the company—for the opening spectacles and more modest entertainments at the end of the evening's program, as well as for the entrées and his own scenes in the circle—and doubtless he was active in this area on many other occasions which went unnoticed in the theatre's bills. I have located a design by him for a headdress pasted into a letter he wrote to William Broadfoot in the fall of 1841

FIG. 37. Sketch of a headdress made by Ducrow for the 1838 production of *The Passage of the Deserts, or The French in Egypt and Siege of Acre.*

(fig. 37). Broadfoot obviously thought it worth preserving as a memento of his brother-in-law, who died some two months after writing the letter, and below the sketch he has noted that it was done by Ducrow for an 1838 production of *The Siege of Acre*. Even in the field of scene design there is evidence for his interest and direct participation. One writer describes how, whenever he wished to suggest something to his painters, Andrew would fling himself upon the stage boards and begin sketching with a piece of chalk, "always cleverly—often beautifully."[31] There were plenty of competent professional designers and technicians at Astley's, of course. Minor theatres of the nineteenth century, with their heavy reliance on spectacle and sensational melodrama, rarely stinted where the magnificence of the stage was concerned and regularly employed armies of scene painters, machinists, and property men. At Astley's the changing roster of designers under Ducrow's management included Walker, William Stanfield, Charles Tomkins, Parker, Danson, F. C. Turner, Cuthbert, Gordon, and William Telbin —several of whom also made their mark in the legitimate theatre.

Egan's 1827 remark also reminds us that Andrew, the former pupil of D'Egville, was an accomplished dancer whose steps were by no means restricted to the back of a horse. Although the theatre kept a ballet-master on the payroll, Ducrow himself sometimes arranged dances for the company. These were not, of course, the spiritualized creations one associates with the Romantic Period, but were often described in the bills as being of a "military" character. Most likely they were in the earlier pantomimical tradition of the ballet d'action, in which Andrew had received his own early training.[32] Combats and equestrian evolutions in the spectacles also fell to his province, and on rare occasions he displayed his own terpsichorean talents on the stage. More often, after the arrival of Louisa Woolford at Astley's, he was seen dancing the tightrope, where many of the steps done onstage were also exhibited. In this specialty, too, Andrew's superiority was widely acknowledged by his contemporaries. The opera singer Paul Bedford wrote of him that "he was by many degrees the most elegant rope-dancer I ever beheld. In fact, every movement of this wonder was the poetry of motion."[33]

In virtually every area of stage production, then, did Ducrow busy himself—again illustrating the interdependence of circus and theatre in the first half of the nineteenth century. The extent of his achievements is all the more remarkable when we add to the above his own exhibitions of tableaux vivants, his performances as a mute actor or equestrian in so many Astleian dramas, and the claim, at least, that he was the author of several of these last. I do not think we can go so far as to say Ducrow was actually a dramatist, although a few pieces, like *The Taming of Bucephalus*, seem peculiarly his own. Rather, he frequently functioned as a scenarist, suggesting translations and adaptations, supplying topics and situations to his house authors, who often went unrecognized in the theatre's bills. His tableaux and scenes in the circle, however, do attest to a highly original and fertile dramatic imagination, for these were entirely of his own creation.

One of the more winning aspects of Andrew's personality was his fondness for children. "In the torrent of his rages, which were awful," reported the anonymous writer of the obituary in the *Sunday Times* for 30 January 1842, "a child could always tame him. We do not remember to have noticed...this peculiarity developed so fully in any other man." Audiences at Astley's and in the provinces included a large number of children, and it was for this particular segment that Andrew regularly got up scenes in the ring which he billed as "Juvenile Fêtes" or "Entertainments." *Puss in Boots*; *The Little Old Maid, or Duchess Fiddlefaddle and Count Pompolorum*; *The Emperor, Mameluke, and Roguish Drummer*; and *The Marquis of Lilliput and Court Countess* were the titles of a few such pieces, whose leading actors, to the delight and envy of youthful spectators, were themselves children. As noted in a previous chapter, it is not always easy to arrive at the identities of these talented infants, but among those whose names I have discovered were Ducrow's sister Emily; Miss DeLille, the miniature impersonator of Napoleon, who seems to have been the first of Ducrow's juvenile performers after he succeeded to the management of Astley's; Master Reuben Bridges; Master Jean Frederick Ginnett and, in time, his sister; and during the thirties such performers as Masters John Avery and Charles Adams (both sons of earlier competitors of Ducrow); Master Cottrell and the Misses James, Rosina Lee, and Caroline Avery; Master Andrew Chaffé, who was known as "Le Petit Ducrow"; and Louisa Wood, Ducrow's niece. The majority of these children went on to win laurels as adult performers, and all of them were personally instructed by Andrew. Several of them, in fact, were apprenticed to and lived with him in his lodgings at the theatre. In the national census made on the evening of 7 June 1841, for instance, both Andrew Chaffé and Caroline Avery, aged respectively ten and fifteen, were listed as apprentice equestrians living with Ducrow at Amphitheatre House. A third apprentice named Susan Beechdale, aged sixteen—who I believe must have been the "Miss Susan Leroux" who appeared at Astley's as early as 1836 and in later years, beginning 1837, performed a single act of horsemanship entitled "The Indian Hunting Girl" under her more usual appellation, "Miss Susanne"—was also present.[34] Both Chaffé and Beechdale were also listed as apprentices and left bequests in Ducrow's will written a few months after the census.[35]

Preeminent among all Andrew's pupils, however—whether in the adult or juvenile category—were the spirited four-footed creatures whose movements he carefully choreographed for the spectacles onstage and whose more talented members were the privileged companions of his own exploits in the ring. As more than one commentator of the period makes clear, it was not the quality of the plays or the actors that caused spectators to flock to the theatre at the foot of Westminster Bridge, but above all the horses, whose well-ordered stalls with their individual occupants' names attached were as much a part of the theatre as the crowded dressing rooms of their less fortunate human colleagues.[36] The reviewer for the *Times* (2 September 1834), while professing to admire Ducrow's biped actors, could not help expressing his preference for the quadrupeds. With the exception of Swift's erudite Houyhnhnms, he could conceive nothing finer: Ducrow's horses did everything but talk! Predictably, when not exercising their wit at the expense of the theatre's playwrights, critics found plenty to joke about concerning the real "stars" of the establishment. "There are great and beautiful actors and actresses at this popular theatre," began one writer, "but then, shame to biped and flesh and blood-devouring humanity! they *all* move on four legs and

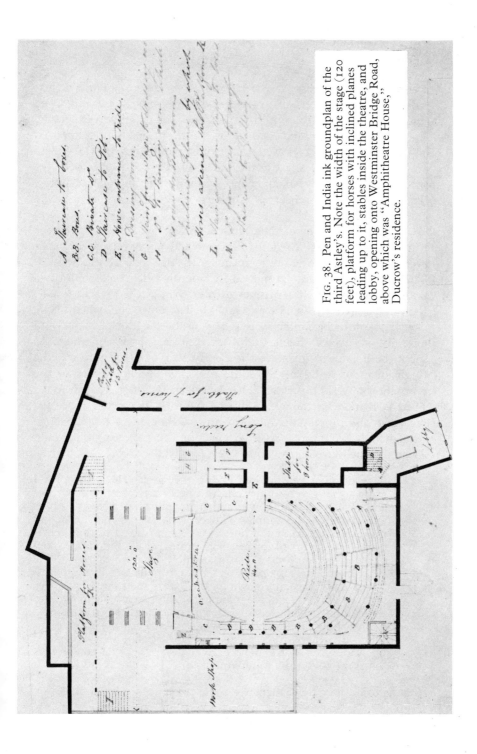

Fig. 38. Pen and India ink groundplan of the third Astley's. Note the width of the stage (120 feet), platform for horses with inclined planes leading up to it, stables inside the theatre, and lobby, opening onto Westminster Bridge Road, above which was "Amphitheatre House," above which was "Amphitheatre House," Ducrow's residence.

are granivorous merely."[37] At Astley's, it was stated, a horse of histrionic ability was certain to "meet with encouragement and to be engaged on as liberal terms as any quadruped can reasonably expect."[38] Another sortie of the kind claimed to set forth the list of fines imposed on performers when they were guilty of infracting the theatre's rules: one peck of oats for any "scenic indecorum," one quarter peck for snorting during rehearsal, and conscription for life into Her Majesty's army for coming to rehearsal with dirty shoes or lying down in the green room.[39]

The satirical tone of these notices in no way detracted from the widespread admiration felt for Ducrow and his pupils, as becomes even more evident when one considers the age in which they lived. The horse population of England in Ducrow's day was around two million, approximately ten times greater than at the present time.[40] Railroads were only then beginning to be laid down and, whether one liked it or not, the animal was indispensable to transportation and mobility—as well as being useful for pleasure, show, and sport. As such, the horse was of interest to nearly everyone, and rare was the Englishman who did not at some period in his life aspire to the reputation of a skillful rider. The American Calvin Colton, who resided in Britain for four years during the early 1830s and afterward recorded his impressions of the country, thought it a fault and a "melancholy picture of perverted affection" that the English should lavish so much love on the horse. The English, he wrote,

> have peculiar reasons for loving the horse. He is the proud animal that gives dignity, show, and ease to the public airings and resorts of their town, and that ministers to the pleasures and sports of the country. There is no city in the world that makes such a display of horses, either in respect to the superiority of their breed, or to their number, as London. One can never cease to wonder at this exhibition, for nearly half the year, in the western parts of the metropolis and in the parks. It is a daily pageant, at which the actors themselves, at every renewal of the scene, are filled with admiration. One could not doubt that they suffer a sort of mental intoxication by gazing at the show, as they roll or gallop along in the midst of it, themselves a part. Nor can they forget that it is the noble horse reduced to the most perfect discipline, that contributes so essentially to their enjoyment.[41]

How natural, then, that Ducrow—the most famous rider of his day—should be "at once beloved by boys and admired by men." Or that his horses, the visible evidence of his superb skill as trainer, should elicit such universal interest and applause.

They were not all of star calibre, of course. As in any theatre, the majority were merely walking ladies and gentlemen, sufficiently competent to be entrusted with bit parts in a spectacle, but hardly able to sustain leading roles. Nor, for that matter, were these secondary players all that remarkable for their beauty. The Hanoverians, pie-balds, and roans did not impress William Clarke as having the form and visible breeding of some of the other horses in the stud, although he conceded they were showy and good enough for the spectacles. Many of them, in fact, attempted to improve upon nature by trotting over to the makeup department, but not invariably with success, it would appear, since the tail-pieces attached to their stumps did not always match and sometimes seemed in danger of coming off.[42] On the other hand, those favored few who performed in the ring with Ducrow or were ridden by the master himself were of the choicest appearance and intelligence. Frequently they inspired outbursts of lyricism that—to the ears of the uninitiated in this remote, mechanical age—can only sound extravagant. Referring to the steed Taglioni that Andrew first exhibited in 1834, an enraptured critic proclaimed the beautiful *pas seul* of this wondrous animal to be "more truly fine in art than any human dancing we ever witnessed—that of M. Laporte's [i.e., Covent Garden's] Taglioni excepted. We had intended to have written a curious essay here, showing how tuition and knowledge can elevate brutes into things soul-inspired, whilst for the lack of them men live and go down into graves, gross, drunken and every-way bestial—we had intended, we say; but will not: our readers may become very learned in the matter by indulging themselves with a night's study in the Circle at Astley's."[43] And here is how Shepherd, in *Blackwood's* "Noctes Ambrosianae," glowingly described the horses ridden by Ducrow a few years earlier at Edinburgh:

> Yon's a beautifu' sicht, sir—at ance music, dancin, statuary, painting, and poetry! The creturs aneath him soon cease to seem horses, as they accelerate round the circus, wi' a motion a' their ain, unlike to that o' ony ither four-footed quadrupeds on the face o' this earth, mair gracefu' in their easy swiftness than the flight of Arabian coursers ower the desert, and to the eye o' imagination some rare and new-created animals, fit for the wild and wondrous pastimes o' that greatest o' a' magicians —Man.[44]

Fig. 39. "Mr. Ducrow's Feats of Horsemanship at Astley's Theatre." *Fairburn's Scraps*, plate 12.

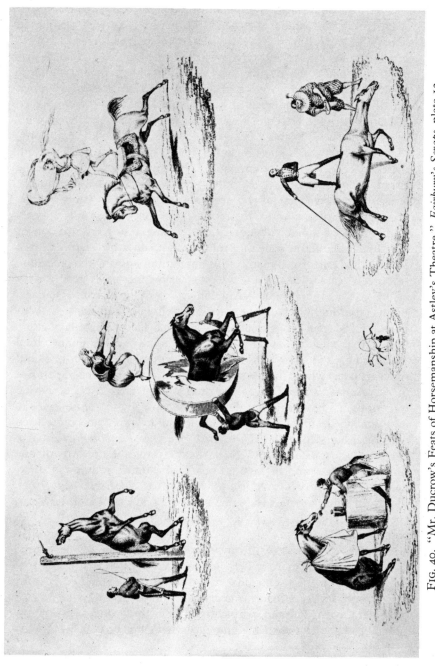

Fig. 40. "Mr. Ducrow's Feats of Horsemanship at Astley's Theatre." *Fairburn's Scraps*, plate 13.

The exotic names of these handsome performers are often listed in Ducrow's bills, and as they—no less than the names of the human actors who worked with Andrew—deserve to be remembered, I herewith inscribe them for posterity, without making any guarantee that in a few instances two or more may not refer to the same individual:[45] Zéphir and Beda, who were both with Andrew in France; Marengo and the pony Harlequin; Arabe, Phoenix, Vienna, Aboukir, Regee Pâk, and the winged steed Pegasus; Danzatore, Unica, and the diminutive ponies Butterfly and Ferret; Chingering Merrybell, Pretty Pony, Marsette, and the miniature horse Fire Fly; Brigand, Champion, Alfred, Gray, Taglioni, Commander, Bucephalus, and Beauty—the last of whom, according to the bills, "steps with grace, has the courage of a lion, the swiftness of the deer, and as docile as a lamb."[46] The prosaic name of one horse, the most serviceable of all, rarely appears in the theatre's announcements and became generally known only at the time of Ducrow's death. John Lump, on whose sturdy back Andrew had performed many of his pantomimes during the preceding seventeen years, died but a few days after his master. A good variety of breeds was represented—Arabians, Barbs, Turkomans, Persians, English thoroughbreds and hunters, Neapolitans, Calabrians, Andalusians, plus several types of ponies—and one can estimate how many they were in all from several of the theatre's bills. The combined total of Ducrow's and West's horses in 1827 was given as forty-one, and six years later, when Andrew took his troop to Drury Lane to perform in *St. George and the Dragon*, the stud was advertised as numbering forty-four.[47] The strength of the resident company therefore seems to have remained fairly stable, although it could certainly be augmented when occasion demanded. *The British Artist, or The Hundred Arabian Steeds*, for instance, produced in 1827, boasted of upwards of one hundred horses; and in 1836 a remarkably similar sounding extravaganza, *The One Hundred Battle Steeds, or The Enchanted Arabs*, displayed approximately the same number.[48] The supernumeraries in these productions were probably recruited from local livery stables and paid a daily wage.

Famed as he was for his incisive directing of his human actors, Andrew was even more widely acclaimed for his superb training of his horses. The "best schoolmaster for horses in the kingdom," whose pupils were said to attend his every nod and to lack only the accomplishments of reading and writing to complete their education, Ducrow never ceased to astonish his audiences with his mastery over four-

Fig. 41. "Mr. Ducrow's Feats of Horsemanship at Astley's Theatre." *Fairburn's Scraps*, plate 14.

footed creation. Since many descriptions of the tricks he taught his horses are given elsewhere, I shall here limit myself to but two additional examples, the first pertaining to a group of Shetland ponies, known for their obstinate temperament, trained by Andrew to leap through burning hoops, play tricks on the clown, "die" in the ring, and "appear in the character of old ladies sitting at the breakfast table, while the third reads the Newspapers for their edification."[49] On another occasion, in the course of one of his pantomimes, Ducrow was described as fairly "inhabiting" his horse: he "sits on his houghs, leans against his knees as in a chair, reclines on his back as on a sofa, makes his body a seat and his head a footstool, and employs his hoof to hold his paper while he pens a letter to his mistress. His horse, like a Houhynhym [sic] servant, follows his steps, comes at his beck, stops at his nod, and is perfect in its obedience."[50] There were other challenges, too, that must have required considerable patience, such as the stag Salamander trained in France and, at the beginning of the 1832 season, four or five zebras—declared by naturalists of the time to be untameable.

Besides the scenes in which his horses either performed at liberty or supported him as he posed and danced atop them in his pantomimes, there were "academical" demonstrations in which Andrew, seated in the saddle for a change, exhibited the precise movements of dressage and haute école. In this more traditional field of equitation he was also conceded to be an expert, and there can be no doubt he took the art seriously, as indeed he did everything having to do with horsemanship. Throughout his career he delighted in references to the horse and riding in literature and the fine arts, incorporating them whenever he could into the scenes and hippodramas at Astley's, and often displayed his knowledge of such sources in the theatre's announcements. In the late 1830s he sometimes headed his bills with an effusion he had culled from the Dauphin's speeches in Shakespeare's *Henry V*. The same piece, entitled "Le Cheval Volant," appears at the top of a lithograph depicting Ducrow as Charles II on his white steed Bucephalus (fig. 42):

Le Cheval Volant

When I bestride him, I soar! I am a Hawk! He trots the air! The Earth sings when he touches it! The basest Horn of his Hoof is more musical than the pipe of Hermes! he is the colour of Nutmeg, and of the heat of Ginger the Prince of Palfreys!

FIG. 42. Detail from "Mr. Ducrow as Charles the Second on His White Steed Bucephalus." The poetic effusion "Le Cheval Volant" is at the top of this print.

his Neigh is like the bidding of a Monarch, and his Countenance enforces homage; turn the sands into Eloquent Tongues, and my Horse is argument for them all. "He is a subject for a Sovereign to reason on, and for a Sovereign's Sovereign to ride on."

The voluble Dauphin's passion for his mount was obviously something Andrew could sympathize with, for I find him quoting other lines from the same play in an autograph written for a fan at Liverpool in early 1840: "I will not change my Horse with any that treads upon four Pasterns. He bounds from the earth, as if his entrails were Hairs."[51] It is also certain he was not content to be thought of merely as a circus equestrian, for he often called attention to the dignity, utility, and manliness of his art, bolstering these claims with literary allusions and citing his illustrious predecessors in the history of equitation. In an erudite essay Andrew himself apparently wrote for his benefit bill of 1838, there are references to classical mythology, Homer, Virgil, Darius, Caligula, and Rousseau, as well as to such famous riders and teachers as C. B. Pignatelli of the academy at Naples and the seventeenth-century Duke of Newcastle. Among all peoples and in all ages, the bill continues, "HORSEMANSHIP Has been considered one of the most brilliant, most noble, and most useful exercises, to which man can apply himself," and Ducrow, who flatters himself that in his scenes and exercises he has illustrated the various schools of riding in different periods, takes pride in the fact that "he has found himself enabled to associate the *Equestrian Art* with the *highest order of Literature.*"[52]

I have already stated that Ducrow, through his poses plastiques and especially his pantomimes on horseback, revolutionized the art of circus riding. If any reader suspect I exaggerate on this point, there are plenty of testimonies to convince him otherwise, from the early observation of the reviewer for the *London Magazine* (August 1824) that Ducrow was "the first true horseman that ever gave a meaning to the display of fine riding" to the words of a French critic, writing two years after Andrew's death, who recalled that twenty years earlier Ducrow had been responsible for "a complete revolution in equestrian exercises. A skillful designer and graceful dancer, Ducrow diffused an artistic coloring over a profession which until then had been exploited only by more or less energetic tumblers."[53] As these and numerous other writers pointed out, previous to Andrew's time, with the exception of a handful of burlesques like "The Taylor Riding to

Brentford" and "The Peasant's Frolic," circus equestrianism had consisted of isolated mechanical feats such as exhibiting various equilibriums while going full speed on horseback, maneuvering two flags, juggling, and leaping over banners, boards, and through hoops and flaming "balloons" held up by grooms and clowns.[54] The newness of Ducrow's riding was due to the dramatic and *continuous* nature of his performances, and to the elegance, taste, and intellect he consistently brought to them. "He found theatrical equestrianism a knack," was the comment of one memorialist on his pantomimes. "He made it an art; he brought to it grace and meaning; he *told histories on horseback.*"[55]

The astonishment and incredulity everywhere inspired by Ducrow's performances—which one feels even today upon gazing at the ephemeral prints that captured his acts—are documented in any number of sources. Again and again the reviewers confessed their inability to do justice to their subject, insisting that Ducrow, who seemed to become one with his horse the moment he touched its back, must be seen to be believed—and how even then one could hardly trust his senses. "Were his pantomimic exhibitions confined to a fixed stage," wrote one English observer several years after Andrew's return from France, "they would be beautiful, and far surpass all of this or any previous era; but, when we see them performed on the unstable and rapid movements of a heated animal, admiration is increased by wonder, almost amounting to discredit of our vision."[56] How Andrew managed to retain his balance in his various poses was an insoluble mystery to most spectators. Even those who knew something about centrifugal and centripetal force and realized he was making use of them while seeming to hover in the air—leaning out over the sides of his rushing horse, his only contact with the animal the tip of one toe—were quick to concede him miraculous skill. As one knowledgeable writer put it after analyzing the problem, in Ducrow's case "seeing is *not* believing."[57]

But it was not simply his expert equestrianism and amazing sense of balance that led to such enthusiasm among critics and audiences. More than anything else, it was the inventiveness and daring, the poetry and dramatic expressiveness of Andrew's pantomimical creations that captured the imagination of his contemporaries. To these last he epitomized the Romantic Age of the circus as surely as Edmund Kean and Marie Taglioni (both of whom, incidentally, attended Ducrow's performances) epitomized the romantic theatre and ballet. Not

FIG. 43. "Mr. Ducrow as Harlequin," one of the characters in the pantomime "The Carnival of Venice."

surprisingly, he was sometimes compared to the former and was hailed, shortly after his return to England, as the "Kean of the Circle." Among other titles bestowed upon him by his admiring English viewers were the "Roscius of the Ring," the "Napoleon of the Circus," the "Emperor of Horseflesh," and the superlative "Shakspere of the Sawdust Ring." From his early years in France, Ducrow was acknowledged to be a supremely talented actor. His pantomime, a memorialist reported, was so expressive that "we understand all he does and means to imply, and find it all tend to one grand point. His riding is a little melo drama."[58] It would be a mistake, as one Edinburgh critic pointed out, to class Ducrow with the general run of circus equestrians, for his creations were to a great degree dramatic:

> They consist in the display of character; of humour and pathos, and of all the various emotions of the mind, in which Mr. Ducrow shews himself a great master. The positions which he takes on horseback are truly amazing; at times they seem to go

counter to the fixed laws of gravitation; yet they are only a subordinate part of the performance, the main purpose of which seems to be to display the character which Mr. Ducrow is for the time representing. The basis of the whole is no doubt equestrian skill; on which, however, Ducrow has raised a super-structure of the most amusing representations; insomuch that the skilful rider is frequently lost in the fine performer; and we almost forget that we are witnessing feats of horsemanship, so deeply are we interested in the dramatic illusion, equally novel and surprising, which we see engrafted on it. He is so much at his ease while he is on his horse, that it seems to impose no restraint on him; he possesses the same freedom in all his attitudes as if he were on *terra firma*; and it is this which enables him to give character to his equestrian exhibitions.[59]

While Andrew's vivid pantomimes naturally engaged the lion's share of the critics' attention, his poses plastiques on horseback—an interesting extension of classicism into the romantic period—were thought no less wonderful by his audiences, as one sees from Tickler's lyrical description of "The Flight of Mercury," revived during a visit to Edinburgh in the winter of 1830–31: "The glory of Ducrow lies in his Poetical Impersonations. Why, the horse is but the air, as it were, on which he flies! What godlike grace in that volant motion, fresh from Olympus, ere yet 'new-lighted on some heaven-kissing hill!' What seems 'the feathered Mercury' to care for the horse, whose side his toe but touches, as if it were a cloud in the ether? As the flight accelerates, the animal absolutely disappears, if not from the sight of our bodily eye, certainly from that of our imagination, and we behold but the messenger of Jove, worthy to be joined in marriage with Iris."[60]

Elsewhere I have described Andrew's acting in several of his pantomimes: "Le Carnaval de Venise," "La Grand Maman à cheval," "La Mort d'Othello," "The Courier of St. Petersburg," and "Andrew the Mountain Shepherd." How many they were in all I cannot vouch for with certainty (the same pantomime would sometimes be given under two or more different names), although I have attempted to include at least the titles of all of them in the text. An Astley's bill for 13 September 1830, in which Ducrow is announced to appear in his latest creation, "The Guerilla's Steed, or The Death of the Brigand," asserts this to be the "38th Equestrian Scene invented by him," a claim that does not seem exaggerated.[61] Since Andrew was principally celebrated for his scenes on horseback, some additional information on a few of the better-known ones may be apropos at this time. The pantomimes that had been invented in France were revived in English arenas, leading to a number of reviews that supplement the observations of French critics. "Le Moissonneur" or "Reaper," for instance, which the critic for the *Mémorial Bordelais* had declared a "véritable pantomime" and praised for its grace and expressive power, was briefly described in the *London Magazine* in 1824 and more fully three years later while Ducrow's troop was at Edinburgh. From the last two descriptions in particular one gathers that Andrew, mounted on one of his swiftest steeds, first appeared with a hook and bundle of wheat in his hands, miming the action of a reaper at work. He later took out a letter supposed to be from his sweetheart and, reading it while standing on one foot, exhibited the emotions of hope, jealousy, despair, and joy. The scene concluded with his then rushing to his imaginary beloved, "until he seems breathless with his flight," and clasping her in his arms.[62]

Next to "The Courier of St. Petersburg," the most widely acclaimed of Ducrow's pantomimes was his representation of nautical life, "The Vicissitudes of a Tar." Although this too, under the title "Le Retour du matelot," had been previously exhibited in France, it was destined for obvious reasons to become a favorite with British audiences. Consequently, our documentation of this pantomime is fairly extensive, and there are several prints showing Andrew at different moments in the scene's action. At the opening Ducrow represented the sailor merrily taking leave of his friends on shore, parting with his wife, making his way to his ship with his belongings in a bundle at the end of a stick, and meeting with his shipmates. He then rocked from side to side and imitated the motion of a vessel going gaily along, smoked his pipe, and danced a naval hornpipe. The action then shifted to the return voyage, with the tar pulling out a picture of his wife and summoning up recollections of home. In the midst of these pleasant reveries, however, a terrific storm arose, at which point the horse was urged to its full speed and flew "like lightning" around the ring. Ducrow's countenance assumed a wild and horrific look as he struggled against the storm—vainly, as it turned out, for the ship was wrecked and he was cast into the deep to battle with the waves. Upon reaching shore he collapsed from exhaustion, but revived to a joyous reunion with his wife and friends.[63] A graphic description of portions of the pantomime and Andrew's swimming once he had been swept overboard appears in the Edinburgh *Evening Courant* for 15 December 1827:

When he enters in the habit of a sailor, with his stick and his little bundle tied to the end of it, how expressive are his attitudes and whole deportment of the character of a real Jack Tar! On horseback the scene commences with the poor sailor plodding his weary way to his ship, in which he is to encounter the perils of the deep. Having embarked, he is represented as having parted from his native shore, his friends, his sacred home, and casting many a lingering look behind. The ship is then on its return, as we may suppose, after a prosperous voyage, and the sailor's imagination wandering to his distant home, he takes out a picture of his wife, which he kisses with ardent affection; he then pulls out two dresses for his children, one for a little boy, and another for a girl, on which he gazes with delight; and, lastly, he draws forth a purse of gold, which he chinks, laughing all the while, with infinite glee [plate 3]. Every thing seems to be going on well with him—a spanking breeze, and good sea room, and all that a seaman can desire—when his hopes are suddenly baffled by the treacherous winds. A dreadful storm

FIG. 44. Ducrow hauling on the ropes during the "storm" scene in "The Vicissitudes of a Tar."

arises; and it is astonishing with what effect Ducrow contrives to represent this conflict of the sailor with the elements. He doffs his jacket, pulls up his sleeves, hauls the ropes [fig. 44], mounts the shrouds, displaying all the bustle and anxiety of a seaman amid the perils of a storm. The ship is lost, and he is then seen swimming amid the stormy waves. The position necessary to convey this idea is most perilous, one foot only being on the horse, which is at full speed, while the body is thrown forward in a very daring manner; yet it was executed with the most perfect ease, and the exertions and anxiety of the seaman most naturally depicted. The loudest plaudits followed.

Andrew's horse in this scene, as we learn from contemporary prints, was decorated with a cloth to represent a man-of-war with cannons protruding from its sides. According to one viewer, the story was made as palpable "as though it were written by a poet and recited by a Smart or a Young."[64] Others tell of the spectators' attention remaining riveted throughout and of their being struck dumb with fright during the representation of the storm.[65] The clown William Frederick Wallett, who in his youth worked as a scene painter at Hull, recalled seeing Ducrow perform the scene on his first visit to any circus and how, upon returning to the theatre, he was inspired to try something similar on a long ladder being used as a scaffold for painting the theatre's interior. Unfortunately, while he was bounding up and down on this improvised mount the ladder broke, precipitating the aspiring equestrian into the pit and costing him his job.[66]

Those fortunate enough to see these representations always insisted Ducrow's pantomime was perfectly understandable, but I cannot help feeling the story of "The Chinese Enchanter," first performed at Astley's in 1826, must have been beyond the comprehension of at least some spectators. The bills and reviews tell of the scene's commencing with Andrew, in a splendid oriental costume, riding three horses abreast, standing with a foot on each of the outside ones. He then shifted his footing as he repeatedly made the animals change places, eventually relinquished one of them, and continued the performance on the remaining two, "terminating with the GRAND ECART."[67] As always, however, this was no mere exhibition of trick horsemanship, but was another of Andrew's "histories on horseback." In this case the story involved the flight of the Enchanter from the Fiends of Vengeance, who had some mysterious claim on him and were pursuing him for retribution. The three horses that bore him were emblematic of the emotions he alternately felt as he made his escape—Despair, Terror, and Hatred—and as the Enchanter succeeded in putting distance between himself and the Fiends, he surrendered the first and then the second, finishing, upon attaining his goal, on Hatred alone. Such, at least, is the abstruse plot contained in some verses at the bottom of a large engraving titled "Mr. Ducrow as the Chinese Enchanter, Flying from the Fiends of Vengeance On his three Wild Coursers Terror, Despair, & Hatred" (fig. 45):

Forth from the burning Wilds of far Cathay
The Enchanter comes, forcing his daring way;
Into the wide arena see him dart,
Fire in his eyes and fury in his heart!
To foil the Fiends of Vengeance! tis, he flies,
They claim their due, and he escapes, or dies!
Too long has the dread forfeit been delay'd
Of violated vows, and rights [sic] unpaid;
And from their maddening tortures, now, he speeds,
Seizing with desperate hand three desert steeds,
Terror, Despair, and Hate! to aid his flight
From retribution's stings, to realms of night.
All uncaparison'd each fiery horse,
His snake entwined wand impels their course;
In vain would they escape his daring stride,
His skill reigns [sic] in their power, and curbs their pride.
Hatred upholds him now with glaring eyes!
Now Terror bears, now he on both relies!
While stream their manes like meteors, in the air!
Anon, he yields himself to fierce Despair!
Faster and faster urging on their speed,
Making their strength obedient to his need;
Round the arena's space like lightning hurl'd
Twou'd seem they made a circuit of the world.
Swift as the winds, he goads them on their way,
Not more impetuous ocean's flow than they!
The fix'd eye dizzies at their wild career,
And all are slaves of wonder and of fear!
As on they fly, his eye with triumph shines,
The goal's half won! Despair he now resigns,
Terror and Hatred then, the sister[s] twain
He trusts to, safety and repose to gain.
On, on, they rush, they wheel, they stream, they dart,
They fly, impell'd by more than human art,
Joy! Joy! the prize is won! and foiling fate,
He terror yields, and gives himself to Hate![68]

FIG. 45. Ducrow riding three steeds as "The Chinese Enchanter." Verses explaining the pantomime appear at the bottom of this print.

The phenomenal popularity of Andrew's pantomimes is reflected in the dozens of inexpensive theatrical portraits of him sold by the publishers of juvenile drama, as well as the finer quality engravings and lithographs available to more discriminating purchasers. On occasion Ducrow would commission prints of himself for distribution on his benefit nights. William West, the original and most famous publisher of juvenile drama, once told the social historian Henry Mayhew of sending one of his artists at Ducrow's request to do a drawing of him in "The Indian and the Wild Horse": "You see, sir, Mr. Ducrow paid for it being done by my man, and guv it away on his benefit night, and I had the plate of him afterwards."[69] The large engraving of "The Chinese Enchanter" with its explanatory verses is probably another example of such publicity material, as are perhaps the print of Ducrow as Charles II on Bucephalus and the earlier print of "The Gladiator" issued while Andrew was riding at the Cirque Olympique in Paris. As in France, too, Andrew was regularly eulogized by his adoring fans in poetic effusions, several of which are preserved in the Ducrow Album. Most of these—or so one would think from the quality of the verse—appear to have come from adolescent admirers, including one Andrew Campbell who wrote an acrostic on Ducrow's name. Another unsigned poem praises Andrew's performance in his tableau piece *Raphael's Dream* and suggests that not all his ecstatic viewers were earthly:

> 'Tis sure some Vision that I see
> That rises thus so gracefully;—
> . . . .
> Ducrow!—if really it is thee—
> That thus appears some God to be—
> Your pow'rs are far beyond, what I
> Should have conceiv'd below the Sky;
> And Angels surely must attend
> And whilst you act—their Graces Lend.

These pleasant reminders of Ducrow's favor with younger spectators were matched in more substantial terms by his adult friends and admirers, who at various times presented him with such traditional testimonials as silver snuff boxes and vases. During the winter of 1833–34, while Andrew was performing at Drury Lane in *St. George and the Dragon*, the "Prince of Dandies" Count D'Orsay went these one better with a brace of pistols and a handsome dirk mounted in gold and ivory, once the possession of Lord Byron. The gifts were kept on permanent display at Andrew's home, in what Bunn terms his "celebrated Cabinet of Art."[70]

But the ultimate tribute to Ducrow's popularity and superiority was the countless imitations of his acts that shortly sprang up, not only in virtually every British circus, but in those on the Continent and even in distant America. "All the troops in England copy his performances," remarked Pierce Egan as early as 1827—an observation that was echoed over forty years later, some thirty years after Ducrow's death, by William Frederick Wallett, who complained that "all the riders of the present day have been living upon their inferior imitations of his great and glorious conceptions."[71] In truth, one need only glance through the bills and newspaper advertisements of Andrew's competitors to realize how extensive this influence was. Many of these announcements are almost word-for-word copies of Ducrow's programs, even to the names of the horses. Thus, in two bills dating from early 1836 for Cooke's Circus in Aberdeen, I find various members of the Cooke family listed for "The Chinese Enchanter," "Rob Roy," "The Tar's Vicissitudes," "The British Fox Hunter," "The Roman Gladiator," and "The Flight of Mercury," while George Woolford, who was then with the Cookes, was billed to do "The Page Troubadour," William and James Cooke to exhibit "The Living Statues," and a Miss Barlow to perform with James Cooke the act of "Cupid and Zephyr." The stud included the winged horse Pegasus and even Regee Pâk![72] Such wholesale copying was not unusual, and rare indeed was the British or American circus rider who did not attempt at least one of Ducrow's scenes. Meanwhile, in Paris the celebrated François, better known as "Paul" Laribeau began presenting several of Ducrow's creations at the Cirque Olympique. These included "Le Moissonneur" and "Le Relais à six chevaux, ou La Poste royale," the title by which "The Courier of St. Petersburg" went in France.[73] To be sure, one must concede Andrew's competitors some degree of originality. The equestrian James Cooke was famed for his impersonations on horseback of Falstaff, Shylock, and Richard III (and one wonders why Ducrow himself never added Shakespearean characters to his repertoire); while Henry Adams, whom Andrew employed in the early thirties, invented several fine scenes of his own. Still, so many bills of the period read in whole or in part like those of Ducrow that one can readily understand his precaution, reported by Rede, of rehearsing in secret until his pantomimes were ready for the ring.[74]

Once he had introduced his scenes, however, Ducrow rarely objected to others copying them or imitating his style, although on occasion he did—when sufficiently provoked for other reasons— refer scathingly to his rivals' lack of originality. His own artists, especially after age and ill health had begun taking their toll on him, were increasingly entrusted with his creations. It was inevitable, of course, that the "new school of equitation" should attract disciples. That the public appreciated and responded to the change from the hackneyed feats and buffooneries of an earlier age is evident from a notice of George Woolford's riding at Astley's in 1832. The reviewer singled out for special commendation a " 'rapid act in character,' and rapid it was certainly as well as characteristic. These things have as much as any other caught the march of improvement, and we now see them mixed with mind, where once they were only calculated to astonish— they now are adapted to please and astonish. They have assumed a classical complexion—while they make the ignorant stare they afford study for the artist. They are really poetry of the highest school of poetry of motion. The applause bestowed upon them, which was immense, said much for the taste of the audience."[75] Nor were all Andrew's imitators the outright plagiarists the Cookes seem to have been. Many artists, either because they were more honest or less certain of their abilities, or simply because they recognized the magic of his name, proudly listed "Ducrow's Popular Scenes in the Circle" in their bills. So it is that one often finds his pantomimes headed in the announcements of provincial and American circuses, although Andrew himself never crossed the Atlantic. Similarly, his exhibitions of tableaux vivants—in particular "The Venetian Statue" and *Raphael's Dream*—were widely copied pose for pose, with some imitators, like the tightrope dancer Wilson, omitting to credit Ducrow with their creation,[76] and others, like the Mr. Rae who toured Scotland and the north of England, advertising their performances as "Same as Exhibited by Mr. Ducrow."[77] In America, where Andrew's statues were first performed in 1831, the infant Joseph Jefferson III saw the English actor John Fletcher exhibit them and became "so statue-struck that I could do nothing but strike attitudes, now posing before the greenroom glass as 'Ajax Defying the Lightning,' or falling down in dark corners as the 'Dying Gladiator.' "[78]

Ducrow's fame among his contemporaries was as widespread as his *grand écart* on horseback. Everyone who knew anything about the circus and riding knew who he was. Consequently, it is not unusual to find his name, used as an endorsement by artists who at one time had worked for him, in bills from cities as far-flung as Prague and New Orleans.[79] The titles of his acts persist in the bills of Astley's and other circuses for decades following his death. Yet, with the exception of an occasional feeble imitation of his "Courier of St. Petersburg"—which today goes by the title "La Poste" in French circuses and was announced, during a recent season at Ringling Bros., as "Roman Post Riding"—his pantomimes on horseback are no longer seen. For in the second half of the nineteenth century the "meaning" and intellectual quality of Ducrow's elegant pantomimical school of equitation were eventually lost, acrobatic riding became the new furor, and circus equestrians, led by such riders as the American Levi North, who was one of the first to turn somersaults on horseback, reverted to the mechanical feats of an earlier age. By that time, too, the long-standing association between the circus and the theatre had begun to break down. As scenic stages came to be omitted from newer circus buildings and the equestrian and dramatic companies of such establishments as the Cirque Olympique went their separate ways, it was inevitable that circus artists should no longer receive the training or opportunity to perfect themselves in so many theatrical areas as Ducrow and his fellow riders had. Today, when even acrobatic riding has few expert practitioners and the horse and rider are no longer preeminent in the circus, one sees but a pale reflection of the glorious era when Ducrow, flying round the arena on his proud coursers, was the reigning star. If he was not for all time, he was certainly of his age.

FIG. 46. "Ducrow riding Five Horses" as "The Courier of St. Petersburg."

Astley's, the delight of our childhood, the joy of our boyhood, the admiration of our manhood. Astley's, redolent of red fire, gunpowder, cannonading, prancing palfreys, tight-roping, and saw dust. Who that has witnessed thy wonders can ever forget thee? . . .

Oh, 'tis a glorious sight to see,
Ducrow with all his chivalry!

—*The Era*, 12 July 1840

6 *Provinces and Provocations*

GLORIOUS INDEED WERE THE SIGHTS to see during the seventeen seasons Ducrow held the managerial reins at Astley's. Not the least fascinating part of this spectacle was the audience itself. The most truly English theatre in the metropolis—"splendid and uproarious beyond all that an experience of other places of public amusement would lead the play-goer to imagine"—Astley's was the playhouse where John Bull felt most sincerely at home. What matter if its strutting actors and their bellowing declamation were most outrageous. Were not the lionhearted deeds of generous Englishmen, decked out in overpowering scenic splendor and awesome tableaux of foot and horse such as Bonaparte himself might have envied, chronicled on its stage for all to see? Did not the unparalleled feats of Ducrow and his prancing pupils nightly ornament its sawdust ring? The public flocked to Astley's in their merriest mood, shedding their cares and inhibitions as easily as the steaming galleryites took off their coats and rolled up their sleeves, and at no time was this universal sense of fun more apparent than on the traditional holidays following Easter

FIG. 47. The interior of Astley's in the early nineteenth century.

and Whitsunday. Then the stage dialogue was mercifully obliterated by the antics of the crowd—shouting, joking, singing, laughing, and, especially in the gallery, engaging in brawls—to a running accompaniment of nut-cracking, orange-sucking, and the popping of ginger beer bottles. Those in need of more substantial refreshment stripped the neighboring cook shops of their viands; more potent beverages were freely imbibed from receptacles ranging in size from the handy pocket-pistol to the satisfying three-gallon stone jar. If the majority of such spectators could not lay claim to much elegance or refinement, this was all to the better, in the opinion of some observers, who rejoiced in the knowledge that fashion had not yet laid its withering finger on Astley's: none of its patrons was too well-bred to join in a hearty laugh. It was all good-natured, wholesome fun. Nor did these boisterous spectators ever engage in the shameful and destructive riots visited upon so many English theatres of the early nineteenth century.[1]

It would be erroneous to assume, however, as is so commonly done in discussions of nineteenth-century minor theatres, that the appeal of Astley's was restricted to any particular social class or neighborhood. From its earliest days under the management of

Philip Astley the theatre had drawn its patrons from all strata of society, with carriages nightly arriving via Westminster Bridge to deposit aristocrats and well-to-do burghers before the portico outside the principal entrance in Bridge Road, coaches and omnibuses setting down suburbanites from the east and the south, and artisans and laborers from Lambeth itself crowding through the gallery entrance farther down the street.[2] And always, or so it would seem, with children in tow, from babes in arms to young exquisites just down from school who pretended to disdain what their younger sisters and brothers were so indecorously shrieking at. Astley's was London's preeminent theatre of family entertainment. "It is pleasant to look around this theatre, and see hundreds of youthful countenances glowing with delight," commented the social historian James Grant in his description of the house published in 1837,[3] a short time after Dickens had written his humorous account of a family outing at the Amphitheatre: "pa and ma, and nine or ten children, varying from five foot six to two foot eleven: from fourteen years of age to four," not to mention a timorous governess, stuck behind a pillar in the box the family had taken, who occasionally peeped out to ingratiate herself "with a look expressive of her high admiration of the whole family."[4] A frequent visitor to Astley's himself, Dickens later set a scene in *The Old Curiosity Shop* in the same locale. This time the less grand families of Kit and Barbara made a rush for the best seats in the gallery, prior to which little Jacob had been squeezed flat and the baby had received "divers concussions" at the gallery door. "Dear, dear, what a place it looked, that Astley's," he continues,

> with all the paint, gilding, and looking-glass; the vague smell of horses suggestive of coming wonders; the curtain that hid such gorgeous mysteries; the clean white sawdust down in the circus; the company coming in and taking their places; the fiddlers looking carelessly up at them while they tuned their instruments, as if they didn't want the play to begin, and knew it all beforehand! What a glow was that, which burst upon them all, when that long, clear, brilliant row of lights came slowly up; and what the feverish excitement when the little bell rang and the music began in good earnest, with strong parts for the drums, and sweet effects for the triangles! Well might Barbara's mother say to Kit's mother that the gallery was the place to see from, and wonder it wasn't much dearer than the boxes: well might Barbara feel doubtful whether to laugh or cry, in her flutter of delight.[5]

All, for the moment, were children at Astley's, and many a writer other than Dickens—besieged by memories of being taken there in childhood—returned in later years to recapture the same unabashed feeling of excitement.

It all meant excellent business for Ducrow and West, of course. At a time of severe economic recession when other managers were reducing prices and going bankrupt, Astley's remained one of the most profitable establishments in town. During the 1834 summer season alone, its lessees were reported to have cleared some 5,000 pounds.[6] Ducrow was rapidly becoming a wealthy man. The annual forays into the provinces during the fall and winter months, when the equestrian company was under Andrew's exclusive direction (the "dramatic" performers were usually left behind to fend for themselves), were generally lucrative as well, often at the expense of the legitimate theatres in the towns the troop visited. By the 1830s provincial managers were in a precarious position. The circuits established in the eighteenth century had begun to shrink, and many theatres remained closed for half the year or longer. To make matters worse, Ducrow's winter tours, which followed no set schedule

Fig. 48. The exterior of Astley's in Ducrow's day, showing the portico in Westminster Bridge Road with the entrances to the pit and boxes and Ducrow's residence, "Amphitheatre House," above.

or round of places, came at the height of the regular theatrical season and offered devastating competition. Thus the descent of the famous London troop could easily spell the difference between success and disaster for the hapless manager of a provincial theatre royal, and nowhere was this more apparent than at Newcastle upon Tyne in 1829. After an abortive plan to spend the winter in London at the Pantheon Theatre,[7] the company instead headed north and opened for the first time at Newcastle in a new circus located in the Nun's Field. The Royal Amphitheatre or Olympian Arena, as this building was called, had been erected to accommodate Ducrow's troop of twenty-seven artists and forty-three horses for a modest run of fifteen performances, beginning 26 November. Although the structure did not possess a stage, such was the enthusiasm of the Newcastle public for the ring attractions that the engagement was easily extended for an additional four weeks.[8] This kept the company in Newcastle through the Christmas holiday week, a cause of no small concern to Nicholson, the manager of the local Theatre Royal, who had already been forced to close his house for three weeks in December owing to the "unprecedented opposition." In a poignant notice announcing the reopening of the Theatre on 26 December, he begged for at least "a portion" of the public's patronage and complained that he had suffered a loss of two hundred pounds during the three weeks preceding his decision to close the theatre.[9]

The event occasioned considerable comment in the press. Some writers attributed the difficulties of Nicholson and provincial managers in general to the baleful influence of Methodism—others to the decreasing quality of theatrical talent. In the present instance, however, there was no doubt in anyone's mind that Ducrow's company had been the precipitating factor. The critic for the short-lived Newcastle *Theatrical Critique* (10 December 1829) dutifully lamented the decay of taste in the town, observing that it "certainly reflects no honour upon our gentry, that so refined an amusement as the drama should give way before, comparatively speaking, such a vulgar exhibition as horsemanship." A lengthy account—signed, curiously, with the initials "A. D."—published in the London periodical the *Dramatic Magazine* (1 February 1830) related, in rather jubilant fashion, the misfortunes and thin houses of the Theatre during the early part of December and how "finally, the management were, for a space of three weeks together, reduced to the necessity of shutting up their shop, totally driven out of the field by the attraction of the

Equestrian Circus, recently opened by Mr. Ducrow, and to which the fickle public, ever on the hunt after novelty, without ceremony, deserting the old banner hoisted at the Theatre Royal, walked over to them 'of the opposite faction,' whose attractive entertainments on a scale never before witnessed in this town, proved a 'tower of strength' quite irresistible." Meanwhile, the more objective critic for the *Tyne Mercury*, while admitting the astonishing feats of Ducrow fully deserved all the support and applause they received, could not help regretting the "pro-amphitheatrical" feeling in the town. Might not Ducrow and Nicholson, he suggested, arrive at some compromise which would be beneficial to both—with Ducrow, say, taking his horses to the Theatre to perform in such surefire attractions as *Blue Beard, Timour the Tartar*, and *The Cataract of the Ganges*?[10] Strangely enough, some sort of accommodation was reached by the two men the following October when Andrew stopped off at the Theatre Royal for four nights only to perform his latest tableau act, *Raphael's Dream*. By then, however, Nicholson's affairs had reached a critical state, and when the manager, hoping to capitalize on his rival's popularity, rushed in to take his own benefit on the first evening after Ducrow's engagement, he was rudely interrupted by the arrival of the bailiffs. Riot and confusion broke out behind the scenes, the audience was abruptly dismissed, and on this ignominious note Nicholson's management came to a close.[11]

In early 1830 the company was again at the Liverpool Amphitheatre, where they remained until traveling back to London for the opening of Astley's on Easter Monday. Meanwhile, a new star of impressive magnitude had arisen in the theatrical firmament, the renowned elephant Mlle. Djeck (fig. 49). Trained by the menagerie proprietor Huguet de Massilia, she had made her debut at the Cirque Olympique the previous July in a drama especially written for her, Ferdinand Laloue's *L'Eléphant du roi de Siam*. To be sure, elephants were nothing new to circuses or even the stages of legitimate theatres by this date. In 1811 the young male elephant Chuny—Chuny who in 1826 became ungovernable during a period of "must" and had to be destroyed by the militia—had been hired from Cross's Menagerie in Exeter Change to appear in the Covent Garden pantomime *Harlequin and Padmanaba*.[12] Even earlier than this elephants had occasionally been employed in stage processions, as at the Park Theatre, New York, for a production of *Blue Beard* in 1808.[13] Astley's, too, had sometimes exhibited them during Ducrow's early years of

FIG. 49. "The Gallopade; or The Grand Theatrical Constellation," caricature of the celebrated elephant Mlle. Djeck at the time of her debut at the Adelphi Theatre in 1829. "Ducrow may now go to Bartlemy Fair," says the Monsieur Mallet perched on her tail.

management. Other houses, which either could or would not engage the genuine article, relied on their machinists for this part of their casting—an expedient not without certain advantages, since these ponderous animals, besides eliciting symptoms of uneasiness from spectators and their fellow actors, were capable of committing *faux pas* of mammoth proportions. Unless kept from the water butt until after performances, they were likely to deluge both stage and orchestra pit, to the no small discomfort of actors and musicians and the general hilarity of those fortunate enough to be a safe distance away, while curtains were hastily rung down and sawdust was liberally distributed. Mademoiselle was herself guilty of at least one such breach of manners during her London debuts, and was credited with brazening it out like the best demirep.[14]

Fortunately, Mademoiselle possessed other talents as well and was given ample opportunity to display them in the exotic vehicle Laloue had created for her. Appearing in a succession of scenes in which she defended the hereditary prince of Siam against the machinations of a usurper, she was seen carrying her master into battle, rescuing him from the inevitable prison, snatching the royal diadem from the villain to place it upon the brows of its rightful owner, and sharing in the triumph at the end of the piece. Prior to this she sat in the midst of a splendid banqueting hall with an immense napkin around her neck, ringing a bell to signal her wishes to her attendant slaves and courtiers.[15] The play had an enormous success at the Cirque Olympique and the following December was transferred to London's Adelphi Theatre. The result was a rage for elephant drama over the next several years, with playwrights either dishing up new pieces or rehashing old ones to accommodate pachydermatous performers, and managers reinforcing their stages and scrambling to obtain the services of Djeck or one of her reasonable facsimiles. Ducrow himself, always abreast of developments at the Cirque Olympique, brought out *The Elephant of Siam* at the Liverpool circus toward the end of February and the following season at Astley's, beginning 13 September, produced an adaptation he and his ballet-master Leclercq had made entitled *The Royal Elephant of Siam and the Fire-Fiend*.[16] Neither production featured the redoubtable Mademoiselle, who was not destined to make her debut at Astley's until late in the 1831 season. Meanwhile, billed as "of the Theatre Royal, Adelphi," she toured the English provinces and Ireland; added to her repertoire a reworking of the old hippodrama *Timour the Tartar*, now retitled *The Triumph of Zorilda, or The Elephant of the Black Sea*, whose climax arrived when Mademoiselle—improving upon a feat formerly reserved to a star horse—plunged between painted waves to rescue the heroine and her son; and delighted her audiences by distributing flowers to the ladies in the boxes.[17] In late summer of 1830 she appeared at Newcastle and Birmingham and then, seized by lust for greater fame, embarked for New York aboard the packet *Ontario*. For a while it was feared her ambition had been her undoing, as a rumor circulated that Djeck had been thrown overboard in the midst of a storm (another had it that she had saved herself by wrapping her trunk around the mast). The story was shortly denied, however, and Mademoiselle, after establishing her reputation at the Bowery and Chatham theatres, triumphantly returned to England in 1831.[18]

Deprived for the moment of the talented Djeck, Astley's nevertheless mounted an oriental fantasy of its own, *The Spectre Monarch and His Phantom Steed, or The Genii Horsemen of the Air*, first performed on Easter Monday, 12 April 1830. Written by the prolific Amherst from an outline supplied by Ducrow, the action in this case was set in China, whose rightful prince was assailed by a Tartar usurper. The latter, played by the bawling Cartlitch, entered into a pact with and received from the Spectre Monarch a magic ring, by aid of which his unlawful desires were instantly gratified. Virtue, predictably, won out in the end, and the discomfited villain, in a final settling of accounts with his dread master, was borne off through the air in a car of fire, "pursued by Daemon Horsemen above THE GREAT WALL OF CHINA." The profusion and beauty of Danson's romantic settings were much applauded, as were the stunning special effects, which enhanced one scene in which the Spectre Monarch (Gomersal) mysteriously appeared in the Temple of Death and ascended on his skeleton horse and another depicting the "SINKING OF THE EARTH, And Celestial Vision, with the Advance of the ARMY of the CLOUDS And Cortege of Genii, Maidens on their Aerial Coursers, &c."[19] On the same evening Louisa Woolford, by now firmly enrolled in Ducrow's "new school of equitation," appeared on a single horse in a new transformation scene, beginning in the character of a Dutch broom girl and finishing as Diana, Goddess of the Chase. Her family was becoming increasingly well represented at Astley's. In addition to her brother George, Messrs. E. and H. Woolford were now listed among the company.

Another artist new to the Amphitheatre was the American rider Benjamin Stickney Jr., who eventually married John Ducrow's widow.

Undoubtedly the finest equestrian pantomime created by Andrew during the 1830 season was the double act with Louisa entitled "The Swiss Milk Maid and Tyrolean Shepherd." First performed on 10 May,[20] the number was captured the following year in a fine theatrical portrait by Lloyd (plate 4), where we also see Widdicombe in the ring and John Ducrow watching in the background. The irate character climbing over the ring enclosure with a cane in his hand also played a prominent part in the action, as may be gathered from a description written several years later when Andrew was performing the scene with one of his sisters:

> The beauty and elegance of the fair peasant (Miss Ducrow) and the symmetry and strength of her horse, win the hearts of the spectators at the opening of the piece, and their admiration is enhanced every moment by the agility with which she and her lover (Mr. Ducrow) manage their horses, and perform their parts. First comes the pursuit of the coy fair one, who, however, is soon overtaken. Then follows the suit of the swain, and the gradual assent of the maiden, testified by her accepting his offering of a bouquet, and returning a scarf. This harmony, however, is not of long duration. The lover lays violent hands upon a letter from another suitor, and a quarrel ensues. Next comes the gradual return of a more amicable feeling, and then the kiss of reconciliation. The pair then execute an exquisite *pas de deux* standing on their saddles, and the horses galloping round the circus. They are interrupted by the entrance of the angry father, who separates the lovers, and pursues his daughter with fury.

Unfortunately, at this point the reviewer breaks off his description, advising his readers he will not spoil their pleasure by revealing the end of the piece. The act, he assured them, was "*worthy alone*, the cost of admittance."[21]

Andrew and Louisa also returned to the double tightrope this season, and both of them performed several of the solo equestrian acts they had previously exhibited. The death of George IV in June and the elevation of the Duke of Clarence, who had earlier attended the Amphitheatre, now permitted Ducrow to boast in his bills that several of these scenes had been performed "before and under the Patronage of HIS PRESENT MAJESTY," William IV;[22] and at his benefit on 13 September he appeared in his latest pantomime, "The Guerilla's Steed, or the Death of the Brigand" (figs. 50 and 51)—based on the popular "banditti" pictures, recently engraved, by Charles Eastlake—which was advertised as "his Last and Thirty-eighth Scenic Invention of the Arena."[23]

Another major event during the summer of 1830 was the farewell benefit of the great Edmund Kean, previous to his departure for America. This occurred at the King's Theatre on 19 July, when Kean performed separate acts from five different plays in order to display himself in his most celebrated characters, and was attended by the largest concourse of people the critic for the *Times* (20 July) had ever seen on such an occasion. Because of the arduous nature of the program, it was necessary for Kean to rest between the acts, and a number of performers volunteered their services to fill the intervals. Among them was Andrew with his "Grecian Statue, or Living Model of Antiques."[24] This led to a meeting with Walter Scott, who complimented the artist on his classical representations—a tribute Andrew did not fail to mention in his later billing in Scotland, of course.[25] It was only natural that Kean and Ducrow, the greatest practitioners of their respective arts in their day, should have felt an affinity for each other, and the actor Paul Bedford informs us their friendship was a sincere and lasting one.[26] The two had probably met at an early age, for Kean was reported not only to have spent part of his youth as a tumbler and equestrian, but also to have received lessons in the dance from Andrew's teacher, D'Egville.[27] It is certain he attended Andrew's performances, as at Liverpool in early 1829 when, on the way to his estate on the Isle of Bute, he stopped off at the Amphitheatre and was observed sitting in Ducrow's private box.[28] Bedford also furnishes descriptions of two dinner parties at which both men were present. The first was an intimate affair at Kean's house in Richmond, to which Ducrow, Bedford, the actress Mrs. Glover, and the surgeon Carpue (who was later to dissect his host's brain) had been invited. During the evening Mrs. Glover prevailed upon Kean to recite the Litany and Lord's Prayer—a strangely Victorian request of one who was best known for his volcanic personations of Sir Giles Overreach, Othello, and Richard the Third, and whose own life was hardly a model of restraint and decorum. No doubt it was an entertainment his fellow artists greatly relished, if for no other reason than its novelty.[29]

The other dinner was on a far grander scale, given by Andrew

FIG. 50. "Mr. Ducrow as the Brigand," a scene from the pantomime based on the "banditti" pictures of Charles Lock Eastlake,
1830.

FIG. 51. Ducrow in the death scene of his pantomime "The Brigand," 1830.

at his residence adjoining Astley's, and was attended by, besides Kean and others, Count D'Orsay, Lord Adolphus Fitzclarence, and Sir George Wombwell. The last two, in particular, were often in Ducrow's company. Fitzclarence was one of the numerous illegitimate offspring of the Duke of Clarence, later William IV, by the actress Mrs. Jordan. A noted gambler, lover of horseflesh, and wine-bibber, after taking on a goodly cargo of the last he would appear behind the scenes of the London theatres, where he engaged the actresses in small talk and discreetly alluded to his distinguished parentage. His constant companion and "Siamese twin" on these rambles was the fashionably dressed Wombwell—said to look "remarkably imposing by candle-light"—who also had an eye for the actresses and was seldom heard to utter any word but "ya."[30] Count D'Orsay, variously described as the "Prince of Dandies" and the "handsomest man and the greatest *beau* of the present day," was also known for his gambling and "girlantry" and in time would be forced to flee London to escape his creditors.[31] On the present occasion he was being helped to some roast pig by Madame Ducrow, who somehow got the carving knife stuck in the ribs. Andrew, dressed in the *robe de chambre* he customarily wore after performances, asked her what she was trying to do. "My dear Andrew," Madame answered, "I am endeavouring to help the Count to a slice of the pig." "My love," Ducrow said, "you have got in the wrong place. What's the use to fiddle away at the ribs? Why don't you cut him on the hind part; that's where the meat lies." A bit later in the evening Andrew requested the composer Nathan, the arranger of Byron's *Hebrew Melodies*, to sing the pretty song he so much admired. Upon being asked which one he meant, he replied the one about "Jaffier's Fair Daughter." When Nathan politely pointed out he must mean "Jephtha's Fair Daughter," Ducrow casually told him to "never mind her name. I am told she was a very nice girl. So pray chant."[32] It was another story that soon made the rounds, and one which Andrew himself apparently was not above improving on, for Bunn describes a later dinner party where the host made the same request of Nathan, this time baiting him with a well-trained parrot. No sooner had the composer sat down and begun to sing than the parrot, perched on the pianoforte, screamed out "Damned stuff, damned stuff, Polly Ducrow."[33]

PLATE 3. "Mr. Ducrow in the Vicissitude[s] of a Tar."

Among Andrew's other close friends the names of Oscar Byrne, Alfred Bunn, and Charles Molloy Westmacott are especially prominent. Byrne, a well-known choreographer, solo dancer, and supervisor of crowd scenes for such managers as Madame Vestris and Charles Kean, was most likely another childhood friend, having begun his career around the same time as Andrew and performed at the Royal Circus in the early 1800s. He occasionally helped out at the Amphitheatre—modeling, for instance, the dragon's den in the production of *St. George and the Dragon* for Ducrow's benefit in 1829—and was one of the executors of Ducrow's will. His son Andrew was a favorite with Ducrow and may even have been named after him, for Ducrow left him a handsome bequest of two hundred pounds. Bunn, poet manqué, journalist, and manager of several provincial and London theatres during his lifetime, had known Ducrow since at least the time of Elliston's ill-fated production of *The Enchanted Courser*. An amused and approving witness to many of Andrew's exploits, he later engaged him to produce three highly profitable spectacles at Drury Lane and in his memoirs had nothing but praise for the equestrian and his four-footed actors. Despite ample precedent established by Sheridan, the Kembles, and other managers of legitimate theatres, Bunn was frequently attacked by critics for relying so heavily upon the quadrupeds and "desecrating" the stage of a theatre royal; and in 1836 he suffered an attack of another kind when the irascible tragedian William Charles Macready, enraged at being forced to appear in a truncated performance of *Richard III* so that the same program might include two of Bunn's latest spectacles, burst into the manager's office and felled him with a blow.[34] Thereafter Bunn and everyone associated with him came in for an even greater share of abuse in "Boxing Mac's" diary and the loaded criticism of his journalist friends. Bunn and his supporters in the press, to be sure, gave as good as they got.

One person who was always certain to arouse the wrath of the sweet-tempered Macready—"filth," "reptile," "beast," as he alternately termed him in his diary and, when half-loaded, even to his face—was the notorious journalist and editor of the *Age*, Charles Molloy Westmacott. The sometime friend and ally of the perfidious Bunn,[35] Westmacott was generally accounted to be a merciless blackmailer—not excepting of the Royal Family—and was characterized by his enemies in the press as "Sweep" (an allusion to his illustrious ancestry: his father was said to be a London chimney

sweep) and in Bulwer's *England and the English* as "Sneak."[36] His
stinging attacks on Macready and his friends the playwright Thomas
Noon Talfourd and John Forster, theatre critic for the *Examiner*,
led to threats of chastisement and libel suits; and on one occasion,
after humorously referring to the popular actress Fanny Kemble as
a "doxie" in one of his poems, he received a public thrashing from
Fanny's father, Charles Kemble, at Covent Garden. The spectators
at this celebrated event, we are told, hooted their approval, and
many seemed inclined to join in the attack.[37] Fat, ruddy of countenance, and standing around five feet five, in later years, after
realizing considerable profits from his conduct of the *Age* (which
Bunn eventually took over), Westmacott attempted to get into
society and politics and was once nominated by the Tories as M.P.
for Lewes. I confess to finding him a strange companion for Ducrow,
since hardly anyone, as may readily be imagined, had a good word
to say about him. Yet friends the two men certainly were, possibly
through Westmacott's own early association with the theatre, for
he had once been a property man and scene painter at Liverpool,
Manchester, Birmingham, and Bristol, and in 1820 was the principal
designer and author of comic pantomimes at Sadler's Wells Theatre,
then under the management of John Howard Payne.[38] He later
dabbled in and wrote several works dealing with the fine arts, including
his *British Galleries of Painting and Sculpture* (1824), and it would
seem his knowledge of these subjects made some impression on
Andrew as well. In his reviews of Astley's and Ducrow's performances
he was, of course, unstinting in his praise.

Painting and sculpture were very much to the fore at Ducrow's
benefit at the end of the 1830 season, when on 13 September he
introduced his most celebrated exhibition of tableaux vivants,
Raphael's Dream, or The Mummy and Study of Living Pictures. Like
the earlier "Living Statue," from which it was descended, the act
was to experience minor changes in content and title over the next
several years. It was *Raphael's Dream* that convinced Christopher
North, upon witnessing it at Edinburgh during the winter of 1830–31,
that Ducrow was a man of genius. "Thus to convert his frame into
such forms—shapes—attitudes—postures—as the Greek imagination moulded into perfect expression of the highest states of the soul,"
he wrote, "shows that Ducrow has a spirit kindred to those who in
marble made their mythology immortal."[39] Dickens, likewise, in a
review of the act five years later at the Colosseum, wrote admiringly

of Ducrow's wonderful skill and taste "in a department of his art peculiarly his own," although he did not care for the lengthy and "melancholy" introductory descriptions by Raphael himself.[40] As the complaint indicates, Andrew's classic poses were no longer the unadorned affairs of "The Living Statue," but were now encased within a dramatic framework—elaborated, moreover, by scenery and dioramic views from the pencil of Danson, properties and machinery by Woodyer, Kelly, and Shaw, and lyric background music by Astley's house composer William Callcott. The dialogue to this hodgepodge (the credit for the overall "inventing" of which, however, Ducrow reserved to himself) was the work of C. A. Somerset, whose "nautical panoramic spectacle" *The Fall of Algiers by Sea and Land* had been produced at Astley's earlier in the season.[41] Somerset's absurdities may still be relished, for upon performing *Raphael's Dream* several years later at Drury Lane, Andrew was required to deposit a copy of the piece with the Lord Chamberlain for licensing purposes, and the manuscript is today at the British Museum.[42] Together with descriptive bills and the comments of reviewers, it enables us to arrive at a fair reconstruction. All of the statues and pictures were personated by Ducrow, and the speaking part of Raphael, in the original production, was taken by Gomersal.[43]

The scene opens in the studio of Raphael at Urbino, where the artist pauses in his painting to comment on some statues in an alcove at the rear of the stage:

> Thus far the Work goes well—the Colors blend most lovingly!
> —(*Business*). Thanks to my noble Patron Duke D'Urbino,
> I live and study in his stately Palace as freely as at home—last
> night, methought I saw these statues performing all the
> functions of life—Giving to Art, that which it only needs to
> make the works of Man the works of Heaven.

Here Raphael goes to a statue representing the "Mummy or Idol"— it is, in fact, Ducrow—and the series of "Rude Specimens of Ancient Art," based on the Egyptian sculpture in Belzoni's collection, commences:

> This rudely chisl'd mass of Egyptian art, conceals as I am
> informed a secret spring, that changes its positions, with as
> rude a motion—This must be the bolt, which touched will
> instantly awaken those sounds [*sic*] that give to it apparent

> Life—What says the Program? (*reads it*) "First—The Idol bearing the Book of Fate"—but I forget the Spring (*Business*).

True to the "program," apparently a copy of the theatre's bill, Ducrow now assumes the pose of "A Figure bearing the Book of Fate"—then, as Raphael continues reading aloud the titles and playing with the secret spring, those of "An Egyptian Prophet administering an Oath to the People" and "An Egyptian Warrior launching his Arrows at the Enemy." Becoming displeased with these ungraceful attitudes, Raphael longs for a "magic pencil / To catch the glories of the Setting Sun." He is interrupted in this passionate outburst by the arrival of a group of minstrels, sent by the Duke to enliven the tedium of the artist's work (and also to allow Ducrow the necessary time to disappear, change costume, and get into position for the next series of poses). After listening to the music for a while, Raphael remembers he should be at work, and at this point the "Stone Statues of the Grecian & Italian Schools" are displayed. These include "Jupiter sending Mercury to the Earth" from a statue in the Louvre, "Brutus condemning his Son to Death" from a statue at Florence, and conclude with the representation of "Prometheus on the Rock, with the Vulture" based on the statue at the Colosseum in Regent's Park. The last—acclaimed by Christopher North "the very Prometheus of Aeschylus"[44]—furnishes a nice opportunity for some pointed moralizing, which the appalled artist does not fail to do:

> ere
> This Monument of Misery I remove,
> Let me this Lesson learn—Avoid Presumption,
> Nor dare blasphem [*sic*] the sacred powers above!

The music resumes, and Raphael, possibly owing to the verse he is now speaking, is overcome by sleep. Even in his sleep, however, he continues talking and provides a running commentary on the "Imaginary Moving Forms of Sculpture" which he sees in his dream. These incorporated some of Andrew's earlier attitudes, and the new note introduced at this point in the program was the intermittent movement of the characters portrayed from one pose to another. "The resemblance is so correct, so true to Nature," wrote an enraptured critic of a performance two years later, "that when the figure moves the effect is magical, and we see with a surprise which it is difficult to describe a statue start into life." The same reviewer—who considered the entire exhibition so fraught with mind, feeling, and taste that he despaired of adequately describing it—singled out for particular praise Ducrow's representation of the "Dying Gladiator" (fig. 30): "His fierce and desperate contest, his anguish on receiving his death wound, his subsequent effort to rally and resume the combat, and the despair with which he feels his powers forsake him, and sinks dejected to the earth to yield and to expire, are models not less for the artist than for the classical student, to whom they [reveal] the visions of antiquity, and the sanguinary scenes of the Circus or the Colosseum."[45] Other moving figures in this part of the program were "Hercules' Combat with the Lion" in four positions, "Discus Throwing the Quoit" (later clarified as "Elatreus throwing the Discus or Quoit"), "The Fighting Gladiator" in three positions, and "Romulus and Tatius" from David's painting of the Sabines.

Awakening from his dream upon the death of the Gladiator, Raphael returns to his easel ("Still hath the Canvass charms for Raphael") but is once more interrupted by the kindness of his noble patron, who now sends a servant with a letter which Raphael considerately reads aloud in its entirety:

> Dear Raphael. The beautiful Frame which is to contain the Tableau's of the Dutchess [sic] is arrived—The artisans of my household have placed it for your inspection in the centre alcove of your Study, from whence I have ordered the Statues to be removed—Bologna August the 17th signed *1505*.
>
> D'Urbino

This introduces the final and most elaborate part of the program, the "Coloured Specimens of Art in a series of Living Pictures," featuring the dioramic paintings of Danson "illuminated on a novel principle." From the text of the play and the comments of reviewers, one gathers these "specimens" were successively displayed within an enormous frame (the one mentioned in the letter) at the rear of the stage, over which a curtain was drawn while the settings were shifted and Ducrow changed costumes. Music, Raphael's rambling narrative, and "business" filled the intervals, with the last apparently consisting of Raphael's opening and closing the curtain. The unadorned setting and classic whiteness of the earlier statues now gave way to pictorial foregrounds and backgrounds richly lit in various hues, and in the midst of these striking settings Andrew appeared in a series of animated paintings.[46] The first represented "Mercury fastening on his Wings to take his Flight" in a sacred copse near the summit of Mount Ida; and the second, after the figure by John of Bologna, was of Mercury again, this time standing atop the colossal Fountain of the Oracle in the grove at Delphos, preparatory to rising from the earth at the call of Jupiter. Meanwhile, Raphael went on with his prosy commentary, providing transitions between the different settings:

Hail Mercury! thou light & airy god!
From thy fair form let me withdraw the veil,
That doth conceal thy beauties!

Business [opens the curtain]

See he stops,
To bind his Sandals round his graceful feet
Obedient to the call of Jupiter!

Business [closes the curtain]

What activity and grace
Are united in that form!
He's now preparing,
Homeward-bound to pierce the skies,
Shewing Man that noble daring
Ev'ry Obstacle defies.
Yet that attitude
Of nimble Mercury is not so striking,
As were he on the Mountain summit seen
Ready to take his flight—

Music & Business [opens the curtain]

See him standing on the Mountain,
Light as air in Beauty bright;
Aided by the gushing fountain,
To commence his heavenly flight!

In the third setting, "The REGION of the FIRMAMENT, with the luminous Celestial Bodies," Atlas appeared struggling beneath the weight of the world; and in the fourth, "The TEMPLE of the MUSES, on an Eminence at Parnassus, with the Pierian Spring, all shewn in a rich glow of Sunset," Apollo struck up a melancholy air on his lyre. Then followed the "Laughing Satyr or Merry Pan" in a picturesque setting "exemplifying all the charms and beauties of a Grecian Paysage"—a spirited depiction that moved Raphael to some rollicking verses about Bacchus and the pleasures of drunkenness. Following this jovial scene classicism and pagan mythology were abandoned for the solid pleasures of the Old Testament, and the last two tableaux were devoted to the edifying spectacle of Sampson escaping from Gaza and punishing the uncircumcised Philistines. In the first setting the gateless city of Gaza was viewed in the distance, and in the foreground Sampson came marching up the hill before Hebron:

> Sampson
> He who upon his Shoulders bore away
> The Massy Gates, and having reach'd the height
> Even in defiance of his Enemies,
> Then hurl'd them down with a tremendous Crash.

Then came the climactic scene in the great Temple of Dagon, where the Philistines' "Sounds of Joy and Gladness" soon changed to cries of terror and despair as the hero, his supernatural powers returning, shook the "Ponderous Architecture to its foundation, till reeling at his resistless force, the spacious Edifice totters and falls in one tremendous RUIN." The moral of the horrifying spectacle was again obligingly underscored by the loquacious Raphael:

> Let the Tyrants in that Picture read their fate
> Who spurn a people's love and court their hate.

The artist then advanced to the footlights to optimistically address the audience in more immediate terms:

> From your silence so profound
> And the smiling looks around,
> May I then most humbly deem
> That you're content with *Raphael's Dream*?

While the spectators were presumably obeying their cue to applaud, the curtain covering the frame was drawn a final time, revealing Ducrow, *in propria persona*, in the midst of an "Equestrian Group . . . surrounded by the Attributes of his Profession, and supported by his Faithful Steed; accompanied by a Grand Chorus Finale."

So ended Ducrow's most daring tableau creation, an act which in the hands of a lesser artist might easily have led to much unsolicited merriment, or worse, on the part of its viewers. Ridiculous as a bare outline of its scenes must make it appear, the piece almost universally delighted and awed both spectators and critics, despite the general condemnation of Raphael's banal monologue and a complaint by one reviewer concerning Ducrow's final appearance "supported by his Faithful Steed"—a stuffed one, it turns out.[47] The concluding representations of Sampson were especially fraught with danger of degenerating into the ludicrous. As one skeptical Scots reviewer later observed, the natural impression was "that no human skill could in this manner render any semblance to the wonderful narrative." Yet the same critic was convinced otherwise upon actually viewing these scenes, in which he reported that Ducrow, "by his astonishing attitudes, the general boldness of his execution, and his strict ideas of dramatic propriety, contrives to keep all in subordination to the sublimity of the theme, and thus present a spectacle of a grand and imposing character—where the slightest shortcoming or incongruity would in a moment dissolve the charm."[48] Andrew's extensive knowledge of art and discriminating eye for the pictorially striking and beautiful, his graceful movements and superbly trained body, his expert skill at mime acquired through long years of performing his poses plastiques and pantomimes on horseback—all combined in the mute eloquence and faultless execution of *Raphael's Dream*.

At the close of the 1830 season the company again set out for Scotland, while Ducrow himself stopped over at Newcastle to exhibit *Raphael's Dream* at Nicholson's rapidly failing Theatre Royal. When he caught up with the troop they were deep into Scotland, where on 19 October they opened Ducrow's Royal Amphitheatre and Olympic Arena in Aberdeen. This marked the first visit of the company to the Granite City, and according to the bills and newspapers the new circus they occupied was itself a fairly substantial affair. Securely tiled and "perfectly impervious to the weather," its brilliantly lighted interior consisted of pit, gallery, and a row of boxes; and the solidity of the structure was vouched for in the second night's bill, which boasted that 2,015 spectators had been present at the opening. The performances were confined to the circle. Louisa Woolford appeared as "La Belle Rosière" and her brother George in Ducrow's act "The Yorkshire Sportsman, or British Fox-Hunter";

Madame Ducrow headed the cavalcade "The Conquest of the Amazons" and performed a minuet and gavotte on horseback with Hillier and Emily; and Andrew himself, besides exhibiting his Persian horse Regee Pâk, performed his "Roman Gladiator," "Games of Cupid and Zephyr," "Chinese Enchanter," and his earlier tableau act "The Grecian" or "Venetian Statue," again on a pedestal in the center of the ring.[49] Following an ill-attended benefit performance for the local Poor's Hospital on 13 November, the troop headed south to Edinburgh, where on 22 November they commenced operations at Ducrow's New Royal Amphitheatre in Nicolson Street. The deposed Charles X had recently taken up residence in Edinburgh —that gloomy St. Helena of legitimate French monarchs—and honored the circus with a visit on 30 November. Unfortunately, it was also on this distinguished visitor's account that Andrew had to abandon his plans to bring out a new spectacle based on French history which included a moving panorama depicting "all the principal scenes of the revolution." Advised by the civic authorities of the impropriety of the intended piece, he willingly agreed to suppress it.[50] When the troop left Edinburgh in early December, Andrew again temporarily deserted and remained behind to perform *Raphael's Dream*, for six nights beginning 14 December, at the Theatre Royal.[51] The winter tour concluded with the usual engagement at the Liverpool Amphitheatre. In a bill for the opening there on 27 December one finds impressive evidence of the extent to which Ducrow was now relying upon the talents of the Woolford family. Besides Louisa, her brother George, and the Messrs. E. and H. Woolford of the previous season, a Mrs. Woolford (probably George's wife) and Miss E. Woolford are listed among the members of the equestrian department. By this time, too, Andrew was advertising an "entirely new Prodigy," a "baby" only three and a half years old, styled the "Infant Nonpareil, or Lilliputian Bacchus."[52] He was elsewhere identified as Master Jean Frederick Ginnett, no doubt the same "Lilliputian Bacchus" who had made his ring debut the evening of Ducrow's benefit at Astley's the previous September, whose immigrant father, Jean Pierre Ginnett or Ginet, had been listed among the riders at Astley's as early as 1827. The family name was destined to become prominent in the annals of British circus artists and managers, and Jean Pierre himself, when he died in 1861, was laid to rest only a short distance from Ducrow's tomb.

On 4 April 1831 the new season at Astley's commenced with a

spectacle whose success rivaled and in time even eclipsed that of the legendary *Battle of Waterloo*. *Mazeppa and the Wild Horse of Tartary*, loosely based on the poem by Byron, presented the tale of a youth who dared love above his station and was condemned by his sweetheart's father to be lashed naked to the back of a wild horse that was then set galloping over the Polish countryside. He nonetheless managed to survive this terrifying journey, was proclaimed rightful heir to the throne of Tartary, and, in a gratifying scene of retribution, returned with an army to rescue his beloved from marriage to a detested suitor and trounce the troops of his future father-in-law.[53] Although Ducrow claimed credit for arranging and producing it, the play was the work of Henry M. Milner, who replaced Amherst as company author this season. The lavish scenery by Danson and his assistants included spectacular views of practicable mountains up and down which the fiery steed bearing Mazeppa was seen to rush, and in one scene a moving panorama representing the course of the Dnieper slowly unwound as the agonizing hero, still bound to the horse, was assailed by a mechanical vulture. It was melodrama at its best, and it was also the making of Cartlitch who—departing from his usual round of villains, tyrants, and interesting lunatics—created the role of Mazeppa. Upon the play's attaining its one-hundredth representation on 27 July, Ducrow and West presented him with an elegant gold medal. All of the other employees of the theatre, including the stagehands, received half a sovereign on the same occasion, and the event was also commemorated with a banquet.[54]

Another star of the establishment this season was Andrew's old Dublin rival, the equestrian Henry Adams, who not only performed many of Ducrow's pantomimes on horseback but created several notable examples of his own. Among these last, over the next several years, were "The Spanish Don," "Obi, or Three-Fingered Jack," "The Deserter," "The Lover's Dream" (accompanied by Adams's two infant sons, one of whom by 1836 was performing on his own as "The German Jockey"), "The Mexican Lasso Thrower," and a number arranged for him by Ducrow with the self-explanatory title "The Trumpeter and Bottle of Burgundy." Perhaps the finest scene of all was his "Shaw, the Life Guardsman," which the reviewer for the *Times* (27 May 1831) praised for its eloquence. Beginning with the enlisting, drilling, and arrival of Shaw in London, the pantomime went on to depict his pugilistic exploits and finally his desperate fighting and death at Waterloo. Like the majority of

FIG. 52. The famous cut of Mazeppa lashed to the fiery steed, from an Astley's bill for 8 August 1831. The same cut continued in the bills of Astley's for many years and was frequently copied for other circuses.

Ducrow's own scenes, it was copied and continued in circus bills for many years afterward, and a later description of the act's final moments tells of a shot being fired outside the ring, while the rider simulated the fatal wound by pressing to his forehead a sponge soaked with red dye.[55] Benjamin Stickney, Reuben Bridges, Louisa Woolford and her brother George (now performing a scene of his own entitled "The Slave") were also featured riders this season; and the diminutive Jean Ginnett, billed as "the second astonishing Child Reared and Tutored in this Establishment," now appeared with Andrew in his Cupid and Zephyr number and in several other scenes specially arranged for him, including "The Fairy King on His Winged Pegasus." Among foreign artists were the Longuemaro family of tightrope dancers; the two "minicans" of Il Diavolo Antonio, who were billed as being tutored in their acrobatic evolutions by their famous father; and, having safely returned from her tour of America, the immensely talented Mlle. Djeck, who by now had attained the weight of 9,000 pounds. She was first exhibited in the ring on 15 August, on which occasion it was announced that "One of the most pleasing features of this Performance is, that should any of the Spectators, Male, Female, or even Children, present it with the Smallest Sweetmeat, this GIGANTIC QUADRUPED Will Receive the Gift with the utmost Amenity, and apparent symptoms of Gratitude. She will Conclude her Performance with Raising from the Ground and Carrying on the extremity of her Back, the BUFFO, Playing with him as with a Ball, evincing at once her tremendous *POWER AND WONDERFUL GENTLENESS.*"[56] On 29 August Mademoiselle was joined by a new pupil of Huguet, and the two pachyderms first appeared onstage together in an afterpiece expressly written for them, *The Grot of the Jungle, or The Elephant Chase.* The action included a scene in which the young elephant Carascamaquinta was pursued and captured by some hunters riding in a palanquin atop Djeck, and another in which the latter displayed her "surprising instinct" by snatching a nabob's daughter from a rushing stream.[57]

Andrew himself did not introduce any new equestrian pantomimes this season, although he did appear in several of his earlier scenes and with Louisa Woolford—now acclaimed the "Sylph of the Circle"—on horseback and the double tightrope. For his benefit on 12 September he essayed a new tableau act entitled *The Fall of Athens, or The Son of the Sage,* a "MIRROR OF HISTORY & Science, shewing Scenes of the PAST, the PRESENT, & the FUTURE," which was an obvious attempt to improve upon the success of *Raphael's Dream.* The piece was invented, arranged, and produced by Ducrow at a cost of nearly 1,000 pounds; the poetry, songs, and choruses were again the work of Somerset; the scenery, dioramas, and "aerial tableaus" were by Danson and Tomkins; and such intriguing accessories as a peacock, silver swan, flying dove, fish, monsters of the deep, the body of a centaur, vultures, serpents, birds of prey, decorative emblems of the seasons, etc. also graced the concoction. It was as preposterous and—judging by what the reviewers had to say about it—mystifying a creation as ever issued from Ducrow's brain. The format appears to have been roughly the same as in *Raphael's Dream.* This time Gomersal, again acting as commentator on Ducrow's poses, was Albinos, a sage of Athens; and Andrew personated Zelikos, his son. There was also a black slave named Orgo (played by the equestrian Fillingham) who functioned as a sort of clown; and Mrs. John Ducrow, Emily Ducrow, and a Miss Tuft represented the allegorical characters Terpsichore, Industry, and Hope. Andrew's poses now included those of the Triton and Spirit of the Ocean; the Olympian encounter and poses of the Grecian warrior as Mars; the passions—wonder, hope, anger, revenge, despair, and madness—exhibited during a scene in which Albinos instructed his son in the expressing of the emotions; the Spirit of the Starry Night on his aerial cloud; Morning, the golden sylph of early day; Mercury's descent to Earth at the command of Terpsichore; the seasons—spring, summer, autumn, and winter; the combat and encounter of the centaur with the lion, and death of both (fig. 53); the fall of Phaeton with the car of the skies and horses of the sun; the last man, or the overwhelming waters of the Deluge; and finally the champion of Olympus in his war chariot, drawn by the offspring of Pegasus—stuffed horses again![58] While appreciative of Ducrow's skill and the picturesqueness of his attitudes, the reviewers confessed their inability to make sense out of the jumble. As one of them complained when the piece was revived two months

FIG. 53. Ducrow as the centaur combating the lion in his tableau drama *The Fall of Athens*, 1831.

later at Drury Lane under a slightly different title, Andrew "might just as reasonably have termed it the days of Queen Bess, the days of King Charles, the seven days of the week, the three days of Paris, the two Deys of Algiers and Tunis, or any other day, as *The Days of Athens*. Nothing, in our humble judgment, could be more flat and stupid; it would really have been utterly unendurable, but that it was now and then so ridiculous." The piece, the same critic informs us, was abundantly hissed; and Somerset's "exquisitely nonsensical" verses did not help matters.[59] The reception of *The Fall of Athens* must have been a keen disappointment to Andrew after his triumph in *Raphael's Dream* the previous year. He did not often perform it.

In early October the company departed for the west of England. Beginning 31 October they were scheduled to give a few performances at the Bristol Theatre Royal before going on to Ireland.[60] Here too, however, Andrew received an unexpected setback, in this instance occasioned by the frequently violent Reform Movement that was then sweeping the country. The troop had barely arrived at the theatre on Saturday, the 29th, when an appalling riot broke out. Over the next two days the Bristol prison was liberated and the Mansion House, Bishop's palace, and custom house were sacked and burned. Not content with visiting their wrath upon the government, the mob looted and set fire to private homes, whose occupants were in several cases deliberately prevented from escaping. To many it looked like the French Revolution all over again, and matters were not made any better by the paralysis of the civil and military authorities. Order was not restored until the 31st (a second riot broke out at Bath on Sunday night), and in the meantime many an uneasy moment was experienced by travelers unfortunate enough to be trapped in the city. Madame Tussaud, who had recently arrived to exhibit her wax figures, trembled at the thought of what might happen to her celebrated collection. Ducrow, made of sterner stuff, upon being warned the rioters were approaching the theatre, commanded his employees to "go on; I pay you for rehearsing, not listening to firing." When it seemed the theatre would indeed come under attack, he took the precaution of arming his people and, going to the door with a pistol in hand, swore he would shoot the first man who dared lay a finger on his property. The threat proved effective, the theatre was spared the mob's violence, and an admiring journalist, reporting the incident a few days later in the Bristol *Mirror* (5 November 1831), could not help regretting that such resolution and *esprit de corps* were "so lamentably wanted in other quarters."[61] There was, of course, no chance the theatre would open on the scheduled date; and the troop—whose determined stand undoubtedly would have earned them some displeasure among the galleryites—made a strategic retreat from the city during the night of the 30th.

In November Andrew returned briefly to London, where he encountered another rival from former years. Henri Martin, having abandoned equestrianism and married the daughter of a menagerie proprietor, for the past decade had been touring the Continent with an extensive collection of exotic animals, many of which he had personally trained. Not content with being a mere showman, he had made a serious study of zoology—particularly ornithology—and the considerable reputation he had acquired in this field had earned him the approval and friendship of such notables as Friedrich Wilhelm III of Prussia, the great French naturalist Baron Cuvier, the Archduke of Saxe-Weimar, and the Duchesse de Berri. In 1830, under the patronage of the last, he installed his menagerie at Paris, and on 21 April of the following year, at a performance attended by Louis-Philippe, made his debut on the stage of the venerable Cirque Olympique in a drama written to exhibit him and his animals. *Les Lions de Mysore*, the first of the sensational "lion dramas" to be produced with such trainers as Martin, Isaac Van Amburgh, and John Carter as their heroes, followed the usual melodramatic formula. As was typical in these pieces, Martin acted in dumbshow, playing the role of the nabob Sadhusing, forced to seek refuge in the forest of Mysore to escape the persecution of the sultan Hyder Ali. The latter is in love with Delhi, Sadhusing's daughter, a *faiblesse* which does not abate his hatred for her father, whom he eventually captures and consigns to his fate in a large cage containing a "ferocious" lion.

Before this much heralded combat took place, however, Martin was provided numerous opportunities to display his mastery over his four-footed pupils, beginning with a scene in the forest where he was discovered asleep on a lion. The novel stage arrangements for this and several of the following scenes included a strong wire net, ingeniously masked by the jungle scenery and so disposed as to give the illusion that the other actors were within the same area as Martin and his animals. Upon awaking and rising from his comfortable divan, Sadhusing was called upon to rescue his two sons from the menacing embraces of a pair of boa constrictors—an excellent excuse

FIG. 54. Henri Martin engaging his boa constrictors in a scene from *The Lions of Mysore*, as produced at Drury Lane in 1831.

to strike the attitude of the *Laocoön*—and in the following scene was defended against the troops of the Sultan by two of his lions. In the second act a comic scene occurred when a pelican waddled onstage to steal the dinner of Hyder Ali's jester. Llamas and a buffalo traversed the forest, a monkey sat chattering and scratching itself atop a tree, even a kangaroo came hopping on! The stage, one reviewer reported, "seems alive with almost every variety of bird and beast." Hyder Ali then entered the forest on his state elephant to take part in a tiger hunt, and several of these felines were seen running about. The same hunt served as pretext for Sadhusing and his allies to launch an unsuccessful attack upon Hyder Ali. Defeated and taken prisoner by his implacable enemy, the nabob was given one last chance to save himself: vanquish in single combat the untamed lion in the "arena" of Mysore. This, of course, he proceeded to do, belaboring and subduing the King of the Beasts with a spear. In the final tableau, by which time Sadhusing and Hyder Ali had made up their differences, the hero appeared in a triumphal procession with the conquered lion at his feet, while Hyder Ali and Delhi entered on the elephant, accompanied by standard bearers, bodies of troops, dancing girls, and military bands.[62]

News of the immensely successful production was not long in reaching the ears of London managers. Accordingly, on 17 October 1831 *Hyder Ali, or The Lions of Mysore*, featuring Martin and his menagerie, opened at Drury Lane. The superfluous curtain-raiser on this occasion was *Jane Shore*, with the part of Hastings by the genial William Charles Macready, whose reaction to the real stars of the evening may readily be imagined. Over the succeeding weeks the "Eminent Tragedian," in such plays as *Richard III, William Tell, Macbeth, King John, Virginius*, and *The Stranger*, continued to take a back seat to Martin and his beasts. He was certainly in no better frame of mind on 14 November when, after performing the part of Daran in *The Exile*, he was followed on by Ducrow in his *Days of Athens*, which in turn served as prelude to *Hyder Ali*.[63] Yet Andrew's engagement at Drury Lane, as previously noted, was a dismal failure—partly, or so the critic for the *Times* (15 November) suggests, because of the spectators' impatience to see the lions. Despite some puffery in the bill for the 15th to the effect that the piece, having been received with "great enthusiasm" on its first representation, would be given three more times that week, *Days of Athens* was withdrawn after its second performance. Ducrow's trip to London was not without some profit, however, for at this time he seems to have entered into an agreement with Martin whereby the latter, after finishing at Drury Lane on 23 December and paying a brief visit to Dublin, contracted to appear with his lions at the Liverpool Amphitheatre. Meanwhile, the troop had proceeded to the Manchester Theatre Royal and opened in *Mazeppa* on 28 November. The engagement extended up until Christmas, and so thoroughly did Ducrow and his artists drain the playgoing portion of the town of its money (or such, at least, was the explanation later offered) that when the regular season at the Royal commenced on 26 December with a performance of *Macbeth*, the house was virtually deserted.[64]

Things were not going all that well for Andrew, however. By

FIG. 55. Henri Martin subduing the lion in *The Lions of Mysore*, as produced at Drury Lane in 1831.

the end of the year, after suffering the disappointments of Bristol and Drury Lane, he was beginning to have second thoughts about Liverpool, where his lease on the Royal Amphitheatre in Great Charlotte Street would soon be up for renewal. The company was again scheduled to commence operations there on Boxing Night, but competition from the town's half-dozen theatres—not to mention two visiting menageries, a diorama, and a series of concerts by the great Paganini—promised to prove formidable this winter. In addition, Ducrow had already committed himself to pay Martin 1,000 pounds and to lay out extra sums to engage Huguet and Djeck and a troupe of musicians known as the "Russian Horn Band." His uneasiness over the situation was openly communicated in the Amphitheatre's announcements, wherein interested readers were informed of the status of the lease and repeatedly admonished that "should the expences [*sic*] exceed the returns, this will probably be the last Season, in which the Company will appear in Liverpool, Mr. D. having so many advantageous prospects in other places."[65] The new season began with *The Battle of Waterloo* and the afterpiece *The Witch and the White Horse*; *Mazeppa*, *Timour the Tartar*, *The Spectre Monarch*; *Raphael's Dream*, and *The Fall of Athens* followed during the ensuing weeks. Djeck and Huguet arrived at the Amphitheatre in early January; Martin and his menagerie made their debut on 13 February in a production of *Hyder Ali* directed by Ducrow, who extended the stage twenty feet into the ring for the occasion, with Djeck herself now a part of the colossal spectacle. In mid-March, by which time the usual round of benefits had begun, Andrew sent the production and a portion of his artists on the road. They were billed to perform for the first of three nights at the Theatre Royal, Chester, on 12 March, but were back in Liverpool by the beginning of April. Meanwhile, Andrew managed to keep the Amphitheatre going with a reduced company. Henry Adams, the Woolfords, the prodigy Ginnett, and John Ducrow were among the artists in the ring, where Andrew—besides exhibiting several of his earlier scenes such as "The Vicissitudes of a Tar" and "The Carnival of Venice"—performed his elegant duet "The Tyrolean Shepherd and Swiss Milk Maid" with Louisa Woolford.[66] A curious entr'acte entertainment was the Russian Horn Band, which consisted of twenty-five members playing airs on single-note conical tubes ranging up to six feet in length. "They are all dressed in a very becoming uniform," one reviewer wrote, "and are of various ages. There is a great sadness of expression in their features, and they look as if they never laughed."[67]

The critics of the Liverpool newspapers were again unanimous in their praise—unanimous, that is, until one of them disobligingly bolted from the pack and precipitated what was to become the first, but by no means the last, of Ducrow's protracted rows with the press. To fully unravel the causes and involved history of this comic interlude—to understand how a critic who had once hailed Ducrow as the "great enchanter" and "prince of equestrians" could only a few weeks later be excoriating him as the "prince of mountebanks"— is no hard task, since the battle was fought in full view of the public. On his side Ducrow answered his antagonist in rival journals and even in red ink at the tops of his bills. Only it was not Andrew himself who joined directly in this literary fray, of course, but rather his "champion" and spokesman Henry M. Milner, then serving as company author, treasurer, and secretary in the provinces. This strategy did not deceive the editor of the *Albion*, who in turn unconvincingly claimed to be someone other than the offending reviewer for his paper.

It all began innocently enough with a review in which the critic, after praising Ducrow and Woolford for their beautiful duet on two horses, complained that an afterpiece entitled *The Assassin Labourer* was not, as the bills stated, a play new to Liverpool, but "merely an old piece with a new name."[68] This led to instant retaliation, and when the critic returned to the subject of the Amphitheatre two weeks later, his tone and opinion of Ducrow and his establishment gave evidence of having undergone a wondrous change. After prefacing his remarks with the ominous observation that "it were well if the great body of exhibitors, who, by contributing to the amusement of society, exist under the shadow of its patronage, could be brought to profit by the truths which a candid and impartial criticism from time to time unfolds to them," he now extended the charge of staleness to *Raphael's Dream*. Not content with attacking one of Andrew's most cherished creations ("as dull as an oft-repeated tale"), he then went after the artist himself in a devastating—and to Ducrow perfectly infuriating—critique of the final scene in which Andrew, "surrounded by the Attributes of his Profession," posed with the stuffed horse:

We cannot help thinking, that there is something almost childish in thus so openly courting the plaudits of an audience. After a picture so superb as *Samson*, to produce Ducrow as a climax is too much. Within the very frame, where we have viewed such a succession of classical subjects, to see Ducrow carressing a canvass horse, and acting pantomime as *Ducrow*, is startling! Would it not be thought strange, if Kean, after playing Richard, were to have the curtain again drawn up, and to exhibit himself as Kean, carressing a folio of Shakspeare? We are sorry to see an individual, who has earned so much fame as Mr. Ducrow has done, laying himself open to the imputation of weak and effeminate vanity.

The critic did not let up in the following paragraphs. In his comments on the scenes in the circle the "Roscius of the Ring" was barely mentioned while Adams and George Woolford received generous praise; the management (i.e., direction) of *Timour the Tartar* was condemned as "common-place and defective"; Ducrow was accused of selling his hard-sounding playbills within the house; and, as a final warning to those who might be contemplating a visit to the Amphitheatre, the promenade at the back of the pit was declared a rendezvous for prostitutes, who "spread their lures for the inexperienced and unwary."[69]

On the following day Milner, signing himself "Treasurer to Mr. Ducrow," sat down to compose a long letter to the editor of the Liverpool *Mercury* in which he patiently refuted one by one the aspersions cast upon his employer's establishment (the prostitutes, he pointed out, never appeared except in the pit, "and there but at a late hour"). As the result of "some misunderstanding about the situation of our advertisements" and the false assertion by the critic for the *Albion* that *The Assassin Labourer*, "a piece peculiar to this establishment, and never before performed here, was an old piece with a new name," the editor's complimentary card of admission had been withdrawn.[70] This explanation prompted a double blast in the 20 February issue of the *Albion*, with both reviewer and editor (who were doubtless, as Milner claimed in another letter published a few days later, one and the same) continuing the battle. The latter, since Milner had brought up the subject in his letter to the *Mercury*, addressed himself mainly to the complimentary card of admission. Far from being "withdrawn," it had actually been stopped at the door—"and stopped, too, under circumstances which amounted, as they were, no doubt, intended to be, to *a gross personal insult*, an

insult which one gentleman would not have dared to offer to another."
Had Ducrow dared offer this affront in his own person, in fact, it
"would have called from the individual insulted an expression of
opinion which would have made Mr. Ducrow sensible of the impropriety of his conduct." Thus the public, the editor continued,
could see "the rage into which our remarks have thrown this clever,
but vain and egotistical, *artiste*," and all because the critic of the
Albion had not joined others in feeding his "insatiable passion for
popular applause." Needless to say, the review of the Amphitheatre
in the same issue, in which *The Lions of Mysore* came in for a major
share of attention, was hardly any better. The best actors in the piece
were decidedly the monkeys and lions—"the latter are a pair of fine
spiphlicating, apparently toothless, old creatures"—and it was all
good enough for those who preferred spectacle to food for the mind.
As for Ducrow himself, he "presented his thousand-and-first edition
of the Sailor in a Storm. When will he present us with something
novel in horsemanship? He should take care, that the Adamses
and the Woolfords do not rob him of his well-earned equestrian
laurels." These comments in turn elicited another letter from the
erudite Milner, who sarcastically suggested the critic might wish
to test the lions' teeth with one of his fingers and pointedly inquired
where he had got the word "spiphlicating."[71]

By now the conflict had assumed mock-heroic proportions and
Ducrow, besides unleashing Milner's mighty pen in the public
press, had begun castigating his foe in his daily bills. A sample of
one of these lengthy diatribes, printed in red ink, runs as follows:

> Death of two Monkeys and the Editor of the Albion. It is with
> regret that the Public is informed, that Two Monkeys of
> M. Martin's collection have reached the termination of their
> career, and departed this life: to which doleful intelligence
> may be added, that of the *Editor of the Albion*, having, in
> desperation, perpetrated an act of suicide; and, as a critic at
> least, become *felo de se*. This was effected by a mortal stab
> given to his critical pretensions, in an article in his last
> Monday's paper, excited, it is presumed, by the temperate
> but decisive exposure emanating from this establishment, of
> his want of candour, good feeling, and information. By which
> demise society has sustained the greater loss, we leave to the
> Public to decide. Certain it is, that no effort of an antagonist
> could so completely have written him down, as in that article,
> he has written down himself. *De mortuis nil nisi bonum ...*
> *Vale infelix.*[72]

Notwithstanding such funereal announcements, the editor-critic of the *Albion* was hardly ready to give up the ghost. Having unsuccessfully called upon his fellow editors to publish his lucubrations as well as Milner's in their journals, he now accused his silent (and no doubt amused) colleagues of having sold their opinions for cards of admission and Ducrow's seven-shilling advertisements. And with the stopping of his own card and the insult he had received from the "*sanguinary fellow*" Ducrow still very much on his mind, he also published a letter Milner had written to him on 3 February in response to a note in which he had originally complained of his treatment at the Amphitheatre. The card had been withdrawn not simply on account of the critic's statement about *The Assassin Labourer*, but because, in Milner's words, "the advertisement sent for insertion in your paper has been made a secondary consideration to an establishment of inferior pretensions, instead of occupying the situation he [Ducrow] conceives it ought to do, namely, immediately after the Theatre Royal, or in the place of it. This apparent intention to degrade the establishment induced Mr. Ducrow to believe, that the card was a compliment to which no further value was attached. Notice to this effect was intended to be sent, but was anticipated by the presentation of the card."[73]

Despite such crushing revelations, the battle dragged on for another week. Milner and the editor continued quibbling over each other's grammar and vocabulary, and the Amphitheatre's redlettered bills now began suggesting the editor would have to answer to his insulted colleagues. By early March the editor obviously had been worn down by the struggle and, in a temperate article containing some general reflections on the qualifications, duties, and value of dramatic critics, attempted to make a dignified end of it.[74] Significantly, he avoided any direct reference to Ducrow or the Amphitheatre in his valedictory—nor did he mention them in any other issue while the troop was still at Liverpool. By this time, too, Andrew had had his fill of Liverpool and the fractious editor of the *Albion*. As early as February he had decided not to renew his lease.[75] When the doors of the Amphitheatre opened for the final performance on 7 April, it was the last opportunity Liverpool audiences would have for a while to see Ducrow and his company.

Meanwhile, the lease on Astley's itself had come up for renewal, providing James West, Ducrow's partner of the past seven years, an excuse to retire from circus management. He was succeeded by his son William, who had acted in many of the Amphitheatre's spectacles and who now assumed responsibility for the "Front of the Theatre." Along with the lease the interior of the Amphitheatre was completely renewed from designs by Ducrow, who also supervised their execution. An advance bill for the opening on Easter Monday 1832 was devoted entirely to describing these wonders, which included flying horses of burnished gold and looking-glass columns in the dress tier of boxes, a "beautiful hippodramatic panorama" by Danson running around the second tier and depicting Alexander's triumphal entry into Babylon, a series of ceiling paintings representing the "birth, training, passions and death of the horse," and, ornamenting the proscenium frame, the figure of Apollo lancing forth Pegasus from the sun. The ring was illuminated by a novel "double variegated revolving chrystal [sic] expanding chandelier" whose eighty brilliant gas jets were screened from the eyes of the spectators by a gigantic "medium" or shade bearing the emblems of different nations.[76]

The season began with a new spectacle by Milner, *Chevy Chase, or The Battle of Otterbourne*, based on the ballad.[77] Despite the picturesque settings by Danson, F. C. Turner, Telbin, and Lear, and a scene in which real deer were chased over mountains by mounted hunters, the play was indifferently received; and beginning in May the remainder of the season was largely taken up by revivals of such spectacles as *Mazeppa, The Battle of Waterloo, The Invasion of Russia, The Blood Red Knight*, and *The High-Mettled Racer*. The last, founded on the poem of the same title by Charles Dibdin the Elder, had been a huge success during the 1815 and 1816 seasons and had earned for the then lessees of the Amphitheatre, John Astley and William Davis, profits in excess of 10,000 pounds.[78] It had last been revived during Davis's penultimate season in 1823, and Andrew was probably set thinking about it by a new edition of Dibdin's poem, illustrated with engravings after Robert Cruikshank, issued in 1831. According to the publisher's preface, the "star" of the original production, the Hanoverian horse Brigand, had passed into the possession of Ducrow, who gave Cruikshank access to the stables and ring at Astley's so that he might sketch the horse from life.[79] Andrew now obtained the original manuscript from Davis and revived the play on 11 June. It, too, experienced only a modest run. Clearly, things were not going well in the playwriting department, and Milner—notwithstanding his success of the previous year—was proving to be no J. H. Amherst.

Spectators' attention this season must have been focused to a greater degree than usual on the ring, where for his benefit on 24 September Andrew introduced two novel productions of his own. The first of these, a spectacle "from the best authorities" entitled *The Wild Zebra Hunt*, once more demonstrated his superb skill as a trainer. Having purchased several zebras for the sum of six hundred guineas from the captain of an East India Company ship, he had spent the summer patiently tutoring these animals—previously declared by naturalists to be untameable—and they now made their debut in a scene in which Ducrow, personating Hatman Danfodio, the Negro Sultan of Fellatah, made a grand entrance with two of them. Prior to this the Sultan's black Mamelukes were shown engaging in a hunt and capturing a "wild" zebra; and when Madame Ducrow, as the Queen Adumissa, Princess of Dahomey, accompanied by female slaves carrying "living birds of the country," arrived in her state chariot drawn by two more of the zebras, the captive was presented to her in a "brilliant PARHELION, formed of PYROTECHNICAL FOUNTAINS OF REAL FIRE."[80] Despite the fact that five zebras are individually named in the bills, I confess to being in the dark about their precise number, for the same bills also refer to their total number as four. The ambiguous nature of the fifth animal— no doubt the "wild" zebra hunted by the Mamelukes and later so precariously enveloped by fireworks—is perhaps explained by the other new ring scene presented on the same occasion, *The Correo, or Spanish Bull Fight*. Founded on the visit Andrew had made to Madrid in 1823, the action involved the opening of the arena by the

FIG. 56. "Ducrow riding Six Horses" as "The Courier of St. Petersburg." Note the spectators who sometimes occupied the stage while the scenes in the circle were in progress.

Governor and civil authorities of Madrid; the filing in of caballeros and their ladies; the entry of banderilleros, picadores, and muleteers; and the challenge of the royal bull by the champion matador Leon, played by Ducrow. There followed a careful reconstruction of an actual bullfight, with the banderilleros and picadores joining in, and the scene concluded on a comic note with a burlesque combat between the gracioso or privileged clown (John Ducrow) and the city bull. It seems obvious Andrew's enactment of the battle aroused genuine alarm, possibly even resentment, among some of his tender-hearted countrymen. When the scene was revived the following season (by which time the zebras had been incorporated into it), the bills were careful to point out that "to prevent any Misconception on the part of the Visitors of the Arena, & at the same time add to the surprising Nature of this Performance, Ladies & others are informed that the Bull is personated by one of Mr. DUCROW's broke Horses, tutored by him for the purpose,—enveloped in an Elastic Skin,—and so managed as to deceive even the nicest eye; some apprehension having been originally expressed by those who had not witnessed this Exhibition, that the Bull was a REAL ONE, this announcement is made to obviate any mistake of the kind; this interesting and highly Romantic and Chivalrous Pageant may be witnessed by the Spectator with the utmost delight." [81]

Again there were no new pantomimes on horseback by Andrew this year, although he and his pupils did revive many of his earlier scenes. On 21 May, for example, George Woolford made his first appearance of the season, personating seven characters on horseback— Ducrow's old "Septem in Uno." He was later entrusted with "The Death of the Crescent Bearer" ("Le Maure vaincu"), and meanwhile Hillier had taken over "The Yorkshire Fox Hunter." Henry Adams, the finest of all Ducrow's pupils, performed "The Reaper," "The Chinese Sorcerer," "The Page Troubadour," and "The Courier of St. Petersburg." Louisa Woolford revived her "La Rosière" and together with Andrew performed "The Tyrolean Shepherd and Swiss Milk Maid." More sensational than any of the above, one suspects, was the "infant" Jean Ginnett, now said to be six years old, who toward the end of the season leaped his two "pigmy coursers" over a five-barred gate as "The Miniature Fox Hunter" and then did a transformation act based on and titled "Shakespeare's Seven Ages." There was an entirely new prodigy this season, too. On 14 May she was introduced in a humorous ring scene Andrew had created entitled "The Emperor, the Mameluke, and Roguish Drummer." The role of Bonaparte was assumed by Ginnett; the Emperor's Mameluke by "La Petite Lee," another of Ducrow's juvenile performers; and the character of a thieving drummer was performed by the "Infant Eloise Ducrow," billed as only two and a half years old. Eloise was in fact the daughter of Andrew's sister Louisa Wood, who had consented—in the "père d'élève" tradition of the circus—to this renaming of her offspring. In later seasons she was usually billed as "La Petite Ducrow," but the wretched spelling of the company's announcements so often transformed her gender into that of the opposite sex or consigned it to a puzzling limbo somewhere in between that she has frequently been confused with Ducrow's somewhat later and more famous pupil, his apprentice Andrew Chaffé, who went by the name of "Le Petit Ducrow." Other artists of interest this season were the ropedancer Cline, who returned to the Amphitheatre after an absence of five years, the German rider Philip Lendemann, the Russian Horn Band, and a new lion trainer from Atkins' Menagerie named Winney. The last appeared in a pageant got up to display the participants in and offspring of a wondrous mating whose progeny George IV had imaginatively dubbed "lion-tigers."[82]

Undoubtedly one of the most beautiful numbers of the entire 1832 season was the double tightrope ballet, first exhibited during the previous spring at Liverpool, which Andrew and Louisa Woolford introduced to London spectators on 21 May. Invented by Ducrow and titled "The Hungarian Wood Cutters, or The Ascent of Zephyr in the Temple of Flora," the act was heightened by appropriate music, scenery, properties, and "travestiment"—the last being Ducrow's (or Milner's) "hard-sounding" term for trick costume changes. Once again the two performers combined their tightrope artistry with a mimetic action, starting out as the young rustics Gatz and Ida and later transforming themselves into the deities of the subtitle. The latter part of the ballet was captured in a fine theatrical portrait by Lloyd (frontispiece), where we see Woolford posing in her scallop-shell "temple" balanced on the two parallel ropes and Ducrow in his winged Zephyr costume flying high above her, trailing garlands whose ends are held by members of the corps de ballet on the stage below. The whole is backed by a handsome décor of arches, clouds, and painted stars. That the artist's rendering is not as fanciful as it first appears—that Ducrow did indeed "ascend" into the air in the second part of the act—is attested by a notice dating from later in

FIG. 57. Pencil portrait of a young girl, possibly Ducrow's niece
Louisa Margaret Foy Wood, "La Petite Ducrow."

the season. The review also bears witness to the considerable risk such scenes involved:

> There was some spell upon the house this evening. A mass of clouds, or rather a quantity of canvas and a large beam, fell from aloft while Mr. Ducrow was flying in the air, and Miss Woolford supporting herself on the tight rope. The escape of each was astonishing, but more especially that of the lady, who saved herself by some masterly balancing. Had the beam either struck her, or caused her to fall off the rope, she must inevitably have been maimed if not killed. The curtain was instantly huddled down, and the performance, in just consideration of the lady, not resumed.[83]

Following the closure of the Amphitheatre on 6 October, Andrew took his company for the first time to Brighton, where they opened at the Theatre Royal on 22 October. The programs consisted of several of the spectacles staged during the past season at Astley's and beginning 5 November included *Raphael's Dream*. This last was enthusiastically reviewed by the critic for the Brighton *Guardian* (7 November), who nonetheless reported Ducrow had not assisted the illusion by giving "audible directions" to the stagehands. Even these largely static acts were not without hazard, for the same writer tells of Andrew taking a severe fall in the course of the piece. Possibly on account of the absence of a ring in the theatre, the engagement at the Royal appears to have been disappointing, and by the third week another reviewer was expressing his regret at the indifferent support the company was receiving.[84] Ducrow had little reason to complain, however, for on 19 November he was privileged to give a command performance before William IV, his old patron the Duke of Clarence, who had ordered the Royal Carpenter to convert the great indoor riding school behind the Pavilion into a circus, complete with a ring and gas-lit stage. To add to the illusion the windows of the school were darkened (the performance began at two-thirty in the afternoon and lasted until six), and the company's own orchestra was supplemented by the band of the 3rd Dragoon Guards. The King and his family were attended by an extensive suite, and the gentry then at Brighton and pupils from a local boys' school were also let in for the occasion. The ring acts were the same as at Astley's—an Amazonian entrée and cavalcade, a minuet and gavotte on horseback, scenes involving the establishment's infant prodigies, Ducrow as Apollo tutoring Pegasus and later with Woolford in "The Tyrolean

Shepherd and Swiss Milk Maid," the pageant of *The Wild Zebra Hunt*—and the program concluded with a full-scale performance of *Raphael's Dream*, which "elicited repeated approbation from the Royal Box." On the following day Ducrow was summoned to the palace by the Earl of Erroll, who conveyed the King's pleasure at the performance and stated he was commanded to give Ducrow His Majesty's authority to "exercise his profession in all towns in His Majesty's dominions." It was an honor Andrew was not likely to forget, of course, and two of the trophies he preserved from this occasion—a copy of the printed program and the letter from the Earl of Erroll setting the date and time of performance—eventually wound up in the Ducrow Album.[85]

On the evening of 20 November the troop gave a final performance at the Brighton Theatre Royal, then moved on to Portsmouth for a brief engagement. Since Andrew was no longer committed to an extended winter season at Liverpool, the weeks leading up to the opening of the London Amphitheatre were now spent at Birmingham, where on 20 February 1833 the company opened Ducrow's Royal Arena in Worcester Street. The interior of this building was declared to be both elegant and comfortable (Andrew had taken the precaution of installing eleven stoves), the house was nightly crowded with eager spectators, and the reviewers for the local newspapers were no less appreciative.[86] Ducrow, wrote the critic for the Birmingham *Journal* (16 March), was "incomparable; tripping on the 'light fantastic toe,' he seems rather to be accompanied by the horse in his evolutions round the ring, than as receiving aid or support from the creature's back"; while his pretty partner Louisa Woolford was hailed as a "paragon—her smile, her self-possession, her skill, are winning and delightful." Toward the end of March the artists took their benefits, then departed for London and Astley's, which opened on 8 April. As events turned out, however, they were hardly finished with Birmingham this season. On 27 May an enraged Ducrow was back in town, reopening the Arena for an additional three weeks and thundering forth threats and pronouncements that occupied considerable space in his bills and the local newspapers:

A Clue having at length been obtained to the assassin-like Authors of the foul and secret slander, for the discovery of which Mr. DUCROW has offered a REWARD of ONE HUNDRED POUNDS, and the falsity of which he has come to Birmingham expressly from Town to prove by

AFFIDAVIT, measures are now in progress to bring the guilty parties to their merited punishment; and, in direct contradiction to the insinuations held out, that Mr. DUCROW would close his Season without contributing his customary tribute to the Benefit of the Charitable Institutions of the Town, the arrangements made for that purpose will be duly announced early in the ensuing week, an example which he trusts, for the sake of the Poor of Birmingham, will be followed by all those competitors in the paths of Public Amusement, who have sought to shift the duty from their own shoulders, by their mock show of ultra benevolence, and ridiculous affectation of a charitable feeling, which, however they may have bandied it about in their mouths, has never yet found its way to their hearts. . . . [87]

As may readily be gathered from this scathing announcement, at issue was a charity performance for the Birmingham poor which Andrew had somehow neglected to give before departing for London. To comprehend the significance of this momentous event, another digression here becomes necessary, focusing on an important aspect of eighteenth- and nineteenth-century entertainments that has frequently been touched on in earlier pages—namely, the benefit.

The benefit performance took many forms in the English theatre, and the reader curious about its history and modus operandi is referred to the comprehensive study by St. Vincent Troubridge.[88] Briefly stated, such performances were given for individuals (generally the performers themselves, who were often dependent on them for a major portion of their seasonal earnings), groups of individuals, or institutions, with the receipts of the evening, usually less the expenses of the house, turned over to the beneficiary. The other performers and employees of the theatre were expected to donate their services on these occasions, although it was not unusual for a beneficiary— since the planning of the program was often his responsibility and it was in his interest to make this as attractive as possible—to hire a star or curiosity from outside his own establishment. Beginning in the eighteenth century actors appearing in the provinces were also expected to give benefits for local charities. This was one way of insuring the goodwill of the authorities, whose approval, like that of provincial spectators in general, had to be courted and, during the length of one's stay, assiduously sustained.[89] Actors were not the only ones subject to this polite form of extortion, of course; nor were the officials and local magistrates alone in taking an interest in per-

FIG. 58. Ticket for Ducrow's benefit, signed by the equestrian.

formers' charitable intentions. Circuses and other nondramatic entertainments were expected to contribute their fair share as well, and citizens kept a watchful eye on these proceedings. When, for example, Paganini appeared at the Liverpool Theatre Royal in 1832 and announced a benefit for the public charities of that town, a number of visitors to the theatre on the evening in question speculated on the amount the charities were to realize; and one of them, indignant upon learning the actual proceeds were considerably below these amateur estimates, complained of the "deception" in a local news-paper.[90]

Ducrow's own contributions to various charities, while never so spectacular as those of a Paganini, were nonetheless regular and over the years amounted to a considerable sum. The importance he attached to these public relations is evidenced by the contents of the Ducrow Album, the bulk of which consists of letters to him from various officials, nearly all of them relating to benefit performances for provincial charities. Together with information gleaned from other sources, the letters permit us to follow several of these transactions, which were not without definite advantages for the benefactor himself. One of these advantages, quite obviously, was the support of the local authorities, an especially important consideration whenever Andrew planned on exhibiting his troop in an establishment of his own. From several of the letters it appears he customarily secured their approval by writing several weeks, or even months, ahead of time, coupling the announcement of his intended arrival with an expression of willingness to aid the local charities. A letter from the Lord Mayor of Dublin's secretary, for example, written some three months prior to Ducrow's opening there in the fall of 1828, acknowledges the receipt of one such letter and, in addition to assuring Ducrow of the Lord Mayor's patronage, thanks him for his recollection of the city's charities.[91]

Once the company had arrived in town, there were inducements held out to the officials themselves, such as the granting of free admission. In addition, the selection of the charities to be benefited and the actual conveying of the receipts were generally delegated to the town officials—a diplomatic maneuver followed by other circus managers of the century.[92] Of the many letters in the Album testifying to this practice, those addressed to Andrew during his stay at Leeds over the winter of 1835–36 are perhaps the most revealing. In two separate letters dated 22 and 28 January 1836 the mayor suggests the House of Recovery (otherwise known as the Fever Hospital) as a worthy object of Ducrow's "liberal proposal" and mentions that Lord Arthur Hill and the officers of the 4th Dragoon Guards will be attending a performance. A third letter from both the mayor and treasurer of the House of Recovery, dated 11 February after the benefit had taken place, thanks Ducrow for the £31.10s.6d. realized and concludes with the reassuring statement that "should Mr. Ducrow ever want to recommend anyone to receive the benefits of the institution, the Mayor believes this contribution would entitle him to avail himself thereof." Of more immediate concern to Ducrow himself was the publicity given such performances in the local papers. The receipts were often reported, at times with the beneficiaries themselves publicizing the results. Following a benefit at Manchester in 1827, a letter from the treasurer of the House of Recovery in that city promised Ducrow's contribution of £20 would "be acknowledged thro the Manchester Newspapers at a future day." Of course, there was always the chance that the results of a benefit might prove embarrassing. On occasion such events were poorly attended, as at Aberdeen in 1830 when the receipts of a performance for the Poor's Hospital did not cover expenses and Andrew dug into his pocket and gave the hospital £10 anyway.[93]

Nor did Ducrow's contributions necessarily cease with a single charity benefit. Extraordinary circumstances called for extraordinary liberality, and thus only a few days after a benefit during the winter of 1835–36 which netted £25 for the Dispensary at Hull, Andrew announced another grand spectacle "for the benefit of the distressed wives and families of the mariners blockaded in the ice."[94] The arrival of the Christmas holidays traditionally called for an added display of philanthropy as well. An advertisement in the Edinburgh *Advertiser* for 19 December 1837 announced Ducrow's intention to distribute on the following Saturday "150 cards to the out-doors poor, which will entitle the bearer of each, to a 150 [*sic*] Christmas dinners"; and a representative of the Edinburgh Society for the Relief of the Destitute Sick, which had already received £20 as the result of a benefit given the previous November, wrote on 25 December 1837 to thank him for 100 dinner cards sent for those under the charge of that society. On 24 December 1836 the debtors in the Newcastle upon Tyne gaol wrote to thank Ducrow for a donation of £5. The letter went on to mention, rather pathetically, that "through your benevolence and that of others they have been enabled to restore (this morning) to the bosom of their families 2 of the small debtors and are in hopes of being able to release 2 or 3 more this day."

The above examples are representative of Andrew's charitable contributions in the provinces and are typical of what was expected of circus and theatrical managers in general. Such contributions, while not, of course, enforced by law, were looked upon as moral obligations; and regardless of what Ducrow's real thoughts on the subject may have been, he discharged his duty with commendable regularity. On two occasions, however, either through misunderstandings or, in one case, perhaps outright rebellion, he was in danger of running afoul of the system. The first of these took place in Dublin during the fall of 1828 when the company was appearing at the Theatre Royal. On 11 October Ducrow signaled his intention to give a benefit for the Mendicity Association, which at the time was in such dire straits that the governing committee had taken to parading 1,600 beggars through the streets "to excite the commiseration of the public." The date eventually settled on was 31 October—an unfortunate choice, as it turned out, for on the following day the *Evening Packet and Correspondent* complained that because the benefit had been assigned to Halloween, the house was empty and the charity *lost* money, and blasted the proceedings as a hoax. Three days later, in what was ostensibly a letter to the editor of the same paper from someone signing himself "D. H.," the attack was renewed; and

Ducrow, now referred to as the "leader of those stableboys" who were nightly desecrating the "temple of Shakspeare," was accused of knowing full well that the night he had selected would not bring a good house. The writer went on to embellish his account with a description of a meeting that purportedly took place between Andrew and a representative of the Association. As the description is so colorful, I give it here in full:

> When the Committee of the aforesaid Charity understood that this tender-hearted Groom of the Stables had fixed on Holy-eve for the accomplishment of his magnificent promise, instead of spurning with indignation both the giver and the gift, they deputed (for the purpose of expostulation) one of their number, Mr. W.—a Gentleman well known for his zealous and persevering endeavours in the cause of charity—a Gentleman of high professional reputation, and universally esteemed and respected by his fellow citizens—a Gentleman as far superior to this Lord of curry-combs, as the Duke of Wellington is to Jack Lawless; but who, nevertheless, in the sacred cause of charity, condescended to hold a communication with him, and for that purpose went to his lodgings in Westmorland-street. After considerable delay, and having sent up his name, he was graciously admitted to the mighty potentate, whom he found at breakfast, lolling on a sofa in a silk morning gown, feeding himself with one hand and a pet parrot in the other; without any manner of salutation, without the usual courtesy of asking his visitor to be seated, without scarcely deigning to look at Mr. W., he abruptly opened the conversation by addressing that Gentleman thus—"Well, Mister"—"Sir," said Mr. W., "I have been requested to wait on you by the Noblemen and Gentlemen who are interested in conducting the Mendicity Association, to take the liberty of stating that"—here he was rudely interrupted by "Oh aye—yes—I recollect—the beggars—yes—that's all settled—I have sent to Mr. Latouche about that—you need not wait—there—that will do—you may go."—And this, Sir, was the manner in which one of the most respectable of the citizens of Dublin was treated by a tumbling show-man—a horse-riding rope-dancer—equally devoid of intellect and good manners, and who, after having *humbugged* the good people of Dublin out of a thousand pounds of their money, wishes to *humbug* them into a belief that he is very charitable, and that, if the Mendicity Benefit produced nothing, it was not his fault, but their own. Let the Jack-pudding be told that his character is known; and, if ever he inflicts his mountebanks upon us hereafter, let the citizens of Dublin shew, by their neglect of his mummery, that they are not to be insulted with impunity.[95]

How much of the above is truth and how much pure fantasy is impossible to determine, although Andrew's penchant for luxury and abruptness of manner (not to mention his celebrated swearing parrot) are amply documented elsewhere. What is certain is that the benefit did not *lose* money for the charity, for on 1 November 1828 the secretary to the Mendicity Association, W. Abbott (the "Mr. W." in the above account?), wrote to Ducrow "on behalf of the Managing Committee of the Mendicity Association to return you their best thanks for your very liberal donation of twenty four pounds eight shillings being the amount of the receipts of a benefit given by you for the above Institution." No doubt the amount realized could have been greater, and no doubt the choice of Halloween was ill-advised. Yet the receipts for this benefit compare favorably with those taken at other major cities around the same time,[96] and the likelihood exists that "D. H." was more incensed by Ducrow's presence in the "temple of Shakspeare" than he was by anything else.

The second and more revealing incident was the one that now brought Ducrow charging back to Birmingham, fulminating against the "competitors" who had been slandering him in his absence. One may safely infer he had left the city at the end of March without the slightest intention of returning as soon as he did, since his re-appearance there, following the opening of Astley's for the summer season, was both costly and troublesome and was, moreover, an unprecedented event. In all probability, fed up with the incessant demands on his time and money, he had simply decided to bolt from town without giving the customary benefit for the poor. He might have succeeded in this dangerous experiment had it not been for the presence of a dangerous rival. Andrew's anger at being exposed by this person and forced to return is patently evident in his bills and announcements, which for once—judging from their style and vehement language—were of his own uninhibited composition. His descent upon Birmingham toward the end of May, besides vindicating his honorable intentions toward the Birmingham poor, was planned as a severe chastisement for the offending party.

James Ryan (1799–1875), an accomplished equestrian, tumbler, and tightrope dancer who in his youth had frequently performed at Astley's, was the one-eyed manager of several amphitheatres, of which the best known were those at Bristol, Sheffield, and Birmingham. He eventually went bankrupt as the result of erecting a brick circus at the last city and in later life was notable for his eccentric behavior.[97]

In 1833, however, Ryan was still in his prime and a regular visitor to Birmingham. The city, in fact, was at this time pretty much what might be termed his "territory," which may also have figured in the decision of Ducrow, who did not appear there as frequently as in other towns, to run out without giving the benefit. On 23 March, while Andrew's company was performing at the Arena, an advertisement appeared in the Birmingham *Journal* announcing that Ryan would open his Royal Circus and Equestrian Arena on 27 May (Whit Monday) and assuring readers that his company would be "superior to any Equestrian Establishment ever witnessed in Birmingham." To add insult to injury, the list of acts included in the announcement was almost word-for-word a copy of Ducrow's program, even to the names of the performing horses.[98] It was Ryan who eventually broadcast Ducrow's failure to perform for the benefit of the Birmingham charities, and who also, judging from an announcement in the Birmingham *Journal* of 25 May, circulated a sarcastic rumor bearing on Ducrow's reasons for not doing so:

> To the inhabitants of Birmingham.—Mr. Ducrow entreats the attention of all classes to a wicked and virulent report, set afloat with great industry by some professional persons, taking advantage of his absence in London, and fearful of the superior strength of his large establishment, who have affirmed that he (Mr. Ducrow,) has caused a representation to be made to His Majesty in particular, and to both Houses of Parliament in general, that no distress whatever exists in the city of Birmingham. Mr. Ducrow declares by all the solemn affirmations that bind a christian and gentleman to his fellow-men, that this is a gross and most daring falsehood. Mr. Ducrow had he the inclination which he has not, could command no time for politics, as the arduous duties of his profession employ him wholly ... Mr. Ducrow hopes and trusts, the bare assertions of ignorance and malice will not find entrance in the minds of his hitherto warm supporters, for whose enjoyment he has incurred an expense seldom equalled and certainly never surpassed.

To be sure, the maligning of one's competitors was nothing new among circus managers. Since the early days of the circus in the eighteenth century managers like Philip Astley had joyfully seized upon similar opportunities to blacken the reputations of troublesome rivals. Ducrow, to his credit, rarely engaged in these polemics; but Ryan had obviously gone too far. One can imagine the surprise of the latter when Ducrow decided not only to return to Birmingham but, in a superb countermove, announced the reopening of his own arena for the same day as Ryan's. On 1 June, in a long advertisement in the Birmingham *Journal*, Andrew boasted of the good houses of the past few performances and pointed to them as proof of the falseness of the stories circulated against him and the "pleasure felt by all classes at the triumphant way in which he has unmasked the miscreants, and justified himself in the eyes of the public." The precise nature of this unmasking was never specified, of course, and presumably extended no further than allusions and name-calling in playbills and newspapers. The same advertisement then went on to describe the preparations for the all-important benefit night, scheduled for Saturday the 8th, and offered a rather lame explanation for its omission during Ducrow's earlier visit: "The short stay of the company on their last visit here, and the peremptory necessity of their departure at Easter, to open Astley's, precluded Mr. Ducrow from yielding, at the moment, that assistance to the poor of Birmingham, which it is one of the greatest pleasures of his profession to afford; he, however, gave his promise to appoint a benefit for the charitable institutions of the town on his next visit, and has now come to redeem his pledge." As further proof of Ducrow's solicitude for the poor of Birmingham, the advertisement continued, on the following Monday cards for one hundred "festival dinners" would be distributed to the private poor, entitling each recipient to one pound of best beef, two pounds of potatoes, a twopenny loaf, twopence for beer, and one penny for snuff or tobacco. "In paying this just tribute to the distressed of the town of Birmingham, Mr. Ducrow hopes, as all his efforts are so closely followed by his competitors, they will not omit to *copy* him in this laudable particular, and prove, by his example, that they have charity and benevolence in their hearts as well as in their mouths."

The final blow in this vindictive campaign was struck a week later in another advertisement, in which Ducrow announced that the promised benefit would not take place on Saturday after all, since he had been informed that Monday the 10th would be a better night (there would be no complaints about his choosing a bad date this time). As further testimony to this noble sincerity, the Arena would be closed the preceding Saturday in order that the company might rehearse an entirely new spectacle for the benefit. Despite—or perhaps because of—this unparalleled display of magnanimity, Andrew could not resist the opportunity to refer once more to his hated rival. This time he did not hesitate to name him:

Mr. RYAN having very pompously announced that he would close his Circus on the evening of Mr. DUCROW's Benefit for the Poor, it is hoped he will prove that he is not, as is suspected, all talk, but that he will, for once, keep his word, especially as it will afford him and his troop a chance of witnessing the performances, and receiving a lesson in their profession.—Mr. R. would, no doubt, have closed his Circus had the Benefit taken place, as announced, this evening, well knowing he would have no one under his canvas, and that, while affecting to aid the poor, he would have been aiding himself, by picking up a little knowledge of his art.

This Mr. RYAN ... through the means of the needy scribbler he has hired to do his dirty work for him ... has questioned the extent of Mr. DUCROW's previous contribution to "*charitable* and *benevolent*" purposes. The following list of sums, which might be multiplied *ad infinitum*, are pointed out for Mr. Ryan's conviction and example.[99]

The published list of sums, complete to the shilling (e.g., Edinburgh, £182.6s; Bristol, £85.11s.), cannot be vouched for with certainty. But on the basis of the fragmentary evidence in the Album, the amounts do not seem inflated, especially when one considers Andrew and his troop had been touring the provinces for the past ten years.

With this notice the saga of the Birmingham benefit came to an end. The proceeds of the benefit went to the General Hospital, whose chairman wrote on 14 June 1833 to thank Ducrow for a donation of £15 "arising from his Public Benefit on Monday Evening last." Shortly after the performance Andrew hastened back to London, leaving his company behind to perform for a few more days at the Arena. If he took with him any lesson from this costly experience, it must have been that charity—in the case of public performers—most certainly did not begin at home, and that in future he would have to guard against similar slips, since Ryan and others would no doubt be watching and would be quick to call them to public attention.

Meanwhile, Astley's itself had been kept going during Ducrow's three-week absence by a reduced company that included Adams, Stickney, and Louisa Woolford. By 1833 the economic health of the nation was in critical condition and theatrical managers were experiencing lean times. Andrew was better off than most of his colleagues; he even boasted, in fact, that he and West were "not among the Complainants of the decrease of Theatrical Patronage."[100] There was no doubt a certain amount of bravado in his stance, and for his own benefit in late September he added a pointed postscript to the bills:

"The immense Sums of Money which are regularly paid to Tradesmen and others serving this Establishment, obliges Mr. D. to state that he feels himself entitled to their support; and it being so often practised to obtain a number of Tickets, which are afterwards sent to be Sold at the Doors of the THEATRE, or disposed of at a lower Price, Mr. DUCROW again requests that those Persons with whom he expends his money, will not take more Tickets than they want, as their Names will be placed on the backs."[101] Certainly Andrew was doing everything possible to maintain the credit of the Amphitheatre. Having been disappointed in his expectations for the stage productions the previous year, he had succeeded in luring back the redoubtable J. H. Amherst, whose latest hippodramatic extravaganza, *The Giant Horse, or The Siege of Troy*, got the season off to a rousing start. The spectacle included a gorgeous scene in which the stage and circle were joined to represent the interior of the "Trojan Circus" with the latter converted into a painted water arena where galleys and barges spread their sails; and another in which a novel diorama with a "treble countermovement"—advancing, ascending, and passing— depicted the entry of the giant horse into the doomed city. It was an Astleian production in the most approved tradition, complete with zebras trotting through the streets of Troy, Egyptian "Grotesques" and a dance of mummies, and such authentic characters as Menelaus of Troy (played by Gomersal), Paris of Greece (Cartlitch), and Helen, daughter of Queen Hecuba![102]

Dressed in a splendid costume presented to him by the Greek ambassador at Paris, Andrew got up in the ring this season a scene entitled "The Horse Tamer of Corfu and His Pet Steeds," which featured a small Spanish palfrey and some beautiful creams he had recently obtained from the Royal Stables. One of these last had been trained by Jean Pierre Ginnett and christened Alfred. He later starred in an eastern tale, "The Horse of 10,000, or The Bedouin Merchant and Arab Chief," in which Ginnett and Ducrow played the two human characters of the title. Together with his brother John, who personated Mr. Kill'emwrong, Andrew also appeared in the comic ring interlude "The First of September, or The Cockney Sportsman." The only indication of his performing any new solo equestrian pantomime this season occurred at his benefit on 23 September when he was billed for the mythological scene "Love Among the Roses." This was probably his old "Bouquet de l'Amour" or "Games of Cupid and Zephyr," however, for earlier in the season he had been announced to do the last with both the Infant Prodigy Ginnett and the "Petit" Louise Ducrow. There were a number of other scenes featuring the establishment's juvenile performers— "Jack the Giant Killer," "The Night Guard and Frederick, King of Prussia"—and on 22 April Andrew and Louisa Woolford introduced to London a new duet on horseback which they had previously tried out at the Birmingham Arena: "The Fisherman of Naples and the Market Girl of Portici," with music culled from Auber's opera. Even Herr Cline's evolutions were now fitted into a dramatic format bearing the title "Frederick the Great, or The Artists and the Royal Rope Dancer." For his benefit night on 23 September Andrew invented, designed, and directed a chivalric pageant entitled *The Blacksmith of Kenilworth, or The Days of Good Queen Bess*, in which Louisa Woolford and her brother George were entrusted with the title roles.[103]

In addition to his woes at Birmingham and any financial worries he may have been experiencing around this time, Andrew had to contend with the continuing onslaught, begun the previous year, by one of his most relentless and virulent critics, the reviewer and editor of the *Figaro in London*. The anonymous mover behind this satiric periodical was the young Gilbert Abbott à Beckett (1811–56), who at various times in the course of his career was a playwright, journalist, theatrical manager, barrister, police magistrate, and one of the original writers on the staff of *Punch*. His colleagues in this last enterprise were later to praise him for his "genial, manly spirit"; another writer has described him as "one of the shyest and most nervous men that ever lived."[104] They conveniently fail to mention he was also one of the most vicious and perverse figures in the annals of dramatic criticism. For three years, during his conducting of the *Figaro* from 1831 to 1834, à Beckett spewed forth a steady stream of abuse directed at managers, performers, and even their audiences; and he frequently boasted of "driving" from the stage actors like the Negro tragedian Ira Aldridge. It seems incredible this waspish individual should have lasted as long as he did, and he was often taken to task for his "severity" even by his professional brethren, to whom he sharply replied that "we never attack any one without desiring to cure him of some objectionable property. It is in mercy that we wound."[105] By the time he relinquished his editorship of the *Figaro* he had been the object of several law suits. He had even—as he triumphantly announced in the issue of 22 November 1834—been publicly assaulted by an actor named Edwin in the saloon of the Royal Victoria Theatre.

By this date, too, out of increasing paranoia, well-founded precaution, or most likely a combination of the two, he had taken to carrying a gun to protect himself from some half-dozen "ruffians" who were out to waylay him and "break our editorial bones." He was prepared, he blustered, to give "satisfaction" to anyone who felt injured by his criticism—a threat he did not stay around long enough to make good on, however, for a month later he suddenly announced his retirement from the periodical, not without some characteristic reflections on the "many imbeciles who will rejoice at losing the wholesome correction of our most healthful criticism."[106]

It was at the start of the 1832 season that Ducrow originally incurred à Beckett's wrath. Had he known what he was in for, he no doubt would have thought better of it. In an article preceding the opening of the Amphitheatre on Easter Monday, the reviewer had expressed his eagerness to exercise his profession again at Astley's, where Ducrow "rides five horses with a leg upon each," Cartlitch was certain to be heard above all the cannons, Gomersal, in the role of Napoleon, would be taking snuff and wiping his fingers on his "inexpressibles," and the clown would be cracking his jokes of twenty years standing. It was a mildly funny piece, and à Beckett himself apparently had some second thoughts about it, for he tempered his remarks with the concluding statement that "by what we have said we do not mean to detract from Astley's Amphitheatre, where we seldom go without finding some amusement."[107] Ducrow and his partner West did not find it funny, however, and, in a repetition of the incident at Liverpool only a few months earlier, the latter immediately wrote to inform the reviewer that his privilege of free admission had been revoked.[108] This had the not unexpected effect of provoking the critic, who made a point of staying away from the Amphitheatre throughout most of the season. He nonetheless did not hesitate to report the opinions of "friends" about the "pristine vulgarity" of the performers and to shudder in print at the thought of the "chaos of filth, which in the dog days must be encountered by any one coming in contact with an Astley's audience."[109]

At the beginning of the 1833 season à Beckett informed his readers that he still lacked sufficient courage to visit the "region of brutality and bestiality" across the water, where the "Astley gang" was scheduled to commence its "horrors" on Easter Monday. He had, he now recalled, mistakenly gone there early in the past season, but "our pockets were rifled, and we were also personally insulted by the frightful ejaculations of the pit and the galleries. The state of rabid fury on the part of the audience was excited by the simple incident of our making use of an opera glass, an optical luxury which being the produce of science, was scouted as an insulting introduction by the wretched and ignorant barbarians into whose propinquity we had so injudiciously trusted ourselves."[110] But he did go to the Amphitheatre after all this season—and fairly regularly at that—fuming over the ignorance of those who nightly packed the house and on one occasion receiving so severe a shock from an exclamation by one of these plebeians that "we literally swooned, and found ourselves under the hand of a medical man, who was resorting to sharp restoratives."[111] His delicate constitution in order once more, à Beckett ventured forth again to the Amphitheatre a few months later, this time to dutifully report he had found the pit "strewed with drunken men, and orange peel, while the performances in the ring comprised the torture of some half dozen little children."[112]

Malicious as these reviews patently were, Ducrow could not afford to shrug them off altogether as the work of a crank, for on a number of occasions—especially after other, more objective journals had pointed the way—they touched on matters close to home. During the 1832 season, for example, at a performance on Whit Monday (a holiday when spirits were traditionally at their most ebullient and there was always danger of things getting out of hand) one of the clowns was reported by the *Morning Chronicle* (12 June) to have insulted the audience by blowing out a candle "not with his mouth." Predictably, this led the absent critic for the *Figaro* (16 June) to proclaim the culprit "an egregious beast, and his grossness ... of a grade unequalled in the annals of vulgarity" and to threaten chastisement in future issues. True to his word, early the next season he reverted to the "indecencies nightly perpetrated by the clown at Astley's" and called for the intervention of the Society for the Suppression of Vice. He had naturally not been to the Amphitheatre himself, but had received a letter on the subject from a "most respectable individual residing in Lambeth," and he now proceeded to describe the scene with his usual embellishments:

> The filthy biped who wallows in the saw-dust of this establishment in all the luxury of manure and orange peel, is, we are told, in the habit of committing indecent assaults on the persons of respectable females, who imprudently mix in the ruffianly gang constituting the pit portion of the audience at the place we have alluded to. His filthy ribaldry is objectionable even when unaccompanied by violence, but when

the act of a ruffian is united with the language of a blackguard, the performance of the clown ceases to be amenable to a critical tribunal, and positively becomes a matter for the interference of the authorities. Our correspondent complains also of being spit at, but this he must expect at Astley's, where a discharge of rheum into a neighbour's face, seems to be regarded merely as an act of pleasantry.[113]

The matter, whether real or imagined, might have gone no further, were it not that on 17 May the normally staid *Times* itself published a letter from a correspondent signing himself "C" who complained of the indecency of one of the equestrians! The vagabond, according to the writer, had positively taken off his breeches, "exposing his bare posteriors to the house," while riding round the circle. Having conducted an investigation of his own, the editor reported in an appended note that the rider had not "positively" exposed his nakedness, although he was forced to agree there was sufficient obscenity in the performance to justify the writer's complaint: "The integuments in which the accused party had invested his person were just sufficient to cover his nakedness without concealing it, and it certainly did require considerable accuracy of vision to discover in the rapidity of his movements whether or not he was in the situation described. There can be no excuse for resorting to such disgusting and vulgar indecency, which we should have expected even the lowest audience to hoot from the stage. If the manager persist in such filthy exhibitions, the police should interfere and take Mr. Ducrow and his mountebank before a magistrate." This, of course, was all grist to the mill of à Beckett, who in his next issue of the *Figaro* (25 May) congratulated the *Times* for following "our acknowledged leadership in the dramatic department" and jubilantly prophesied the season at Astley's would be cut short by an involuntary engagement at the Brixton prison: "Instead of capering on the back of a beast to the smackings of Widdicomb's whip, Ducrow and his equestrian ragamuffins will, if they do not take care, wind up the summer in a Sisyphian walk up the perpetually revolving wheel, to the smart accompaniment of the overseer's cane, and amid the oaths of the irritated governor." The "mountebank" in question was not identified, but very likely he was George Woolford, who in another publication around this time was said to have offended a portion of the audience by donning a bustle during one of his transformation scenes.[114]

FIG. 59. Ducrow as Vanderdecken, the "Flying Dutchman," entreating a conveyance for his letters, 1828.

Infuriated as he was by these notices and complaints, Andrew had other, more pressing problems on his mind during the spring of 1833. At almost precisely the same time as they were appearing, Louisa Woolford fell seriously ill[115] and he was forced to rush back to Birmingham to administer some well-deserved "chastisement" of his own. As if this were not enough, his old friend Edmund Kean, worn out by his drinking and fornicating, collapsed onstage at the end of March and died at his Richmond home on 15 May.[116] And there was a second funeral to attend before the season was over, when James Yates, an equestrian and riding master at Astley's for the past twenty-five years, went home after directing Louisa Woolford through a rehearsal and hanged himself.[117] After the ease with which he had established himself following his return from the Continent ten years earlier, Ducrow's road to the Temple of Fame had grown unexpectedly rocky. No wonder he was acquiring the reputation of being "terrible-tempered."

7 *Losses and Gains*

WHEN THE 1833 SEASON concluded on 12 October, Andrew was in
no mood for another extended tour of the provinces. Fortunately,
he was to be spared any quarrels or tribulations there this winter,
thanks to an invitation from his friend Alfred Bunn, now in control
of both Drury Lane and Covent Garden, to take his troop to the
former house for a new spectacle billed to open on Boxing Night.
During the few weeks preceding the commencement of rehearsals
at the Theatre Royal the company paid a visit to Norwich, where
on 30 October they first performed at Ducrow's National Arena and
Equestrian Studio, a temporary wooden structure on the Castle
Meadow.[1] *St. George and the Dragon, or The Seven Champions of
Christendom* opened at Drury Lane on 26 December. The play was
initially the work of William Bayle Bernard, who in a letter post-
marked 22 November 1833 acknowledged Bunn had assigned him
the topic, but boasted "the writing is entirely mine."[2] He was not,
of course, mentioned in the theatre's bills; and poor Bernard's
opinion of his dramaturgical talents was destined to receive a severe

shock once Andrew arrived on the scene—slashing and rearranging the piece to best display himself, his riders, and his entire stud of zebras, ponies, and forty-four horses. As Bunn admiringly reports on this surgery in his memoirs, the "outline" of the play was submitted to Ducrow's experienced judgment and "under his guidance was eventually moulded into a most effective piece of pageantry."[3] It was Ducrow, too, the bills proclaimed, who was exclusively responsible for directing the spectacle and who performed the role of the valorous St. George. Among the gorgeous settings designed for the production was a "diorama" or moving panorama by Clarkson Stanfield, the theatre's chief decorator, who received equal billing with Andrew. The huge length of painted canvas, unwinding from one vertical roller and taken up by another at the opposite side of the stage, was set in motion midway through the second act to depict the Cataracts of the Nile, the Dragon's Haunt by Moonlight, the Excavated Temples of Ghirsheh, the Caverns of Abou Samboul, the Ascent of a Pyramid, a Distant View of the City of Memphis, and finally the Interior of the City and Temple of Memphis.[4]

The action begins in the "Cabalistic Cavern" of the enchantress Kalyba, who years before carried off the infant St. George when his nurse stepped out for a cup of milk.[5] Kalyba now wakens her grown captive and promises him dominion over earth, air, and water if he will promise to marry her. While preparing for this unholy event, she exhibits a dragon to George and mysteriously hints that his fate is somehow linked to this creature. She also takes him to see the other six champions of Europe, all of whom are in her power; gives the hero his magic armor, charmed sword, and horse Bayard; and provides him with a mortal she has recently captured to serve as his squire. The last, Tom of Coventry (played by the comic actor Harley), immediately senses his new master's danger and, snatching up Kalyba's wand, entombs her in the hell to which she would have led St. George. As fiends are heard laughing and tearing Kalyba apart, George and Tom release the imprisoned knights and "all ride off" to Coventry. There some comic relief occurs between Tom and his sweetheart, to whom the squire interestingly confides that his master is "yclep'd the Silent Knight, being under a vow till he hath reached the holy Sepulchre, to let his deeds speak for him." At the end of the act George is recognized by his aged nurse, a grand cavalcade takes place, and the seven champions go riding off to pagan lands to "plant the Cross and rid the world of tyranny."

In the second act the scene is transferred to Egypt, where King Ptolemy, at the wedding of his daughter Sabra, regales his prospective son-in-law with the story of a devouring monster—a flying dragon with poisonous breath—whose fury can only be appeased by pure young maidens. Fortunately, Osiris drove the creature out of Egypt twelve months ago. No sooner do the nuptials begin in earnest, however, than news is brought to the startled guests that the dragon has just flown back to the Nile and is again filling the air with his pestiferous breath. Ptolemy realizes he must find a sacrificial victim, but where to look? His question is neatly answered when Sabra steps forward to declare she will be the offering that will free her country. Meanwhile, George and Tom have been shipwrecked off the coast of Egypt and rescued by a group of herdsmen. King Ptolemy himself arrives at the hut of these last and informs them the oracles have revealed his daughter can only be delivered by some unnamed "native of a distant shore." A thousand swift horsemen have been sent about the country to proclaim the King's offer of the throne of Egypt to any such person who will contend for Sabra. George, who has been listening to this story, presents himself as the lady's champion—a scene calling for some more interpretation by the garrulous Tom, who again explains the reason for the hero's muteness. This leads to the climactic struggle at the dragon's haunt in the Desolate Valley (Stanfield's panorama now slowly traversed the stage at the rear) where Sabra has been bound to the rock of sacrifice. The maiden cheerfully wishes George good luck as he rides on to defend her. A moment later the dragon rushes out of his den to attack the champion and his steed. In the ensuing battle George and Bayard are at one point precipitated into a cataract. After climbing out of the water and renewing the terrible struggle, Bayard—rearing, furiously pawing at his awful antagonist, tottering and falling motionless to the ground—is lamed and then killed by the dragon. St. George, however, finally conquers and slays the monster, and the fight concludes with a victorious tableau. In the final scenes the other six champions arrive at Memphis and then ride out to meet St. George, who enters in the midst of a splendid procession.

The reviewers' opinions of *St. George and the Dragon*, as was true for just about everything Bunn attempted during his ill-starred management of Drury Lane, were strongly colored by the personalities involved. Perhaps the most balanced account appeared in the 27 December issue of the *Times*, whose critic, while acknowledging he had been impressed by the gorgeous scenery and Ducrow's spirited combat with the dragon, complained he had "never sat out a production which the God of dulness could more justly claim as his undoubted offspring." It was well Ducrow performed in dumbshow, for the dialogue was "beneath even nursery intelligence." The *Age*, run by Andrew's friend Westmacott, predictably assured its readers the spectacle was an unqualified success and that Ducrow, in all his "long and brilliant career," had "never done any thing to surpass his representation of *St. George*."[6] Less enthusiastic were the comments of John Forster, whose friend Macready was condemned to appear in his star role of Werner on several of the same evenings Ducrow performed. In all his recollections of theatrical productions, Forster declared, he had never seen so worthless a play as *St. George*. It was a "sad piece of trumpery, utterly unworthy the attention of any child who has passed his seventh year—long, dull, witless, no good dancing, no good music, an eternal braying of trumpets, a little prancing of steeds, and no superior horsemanship, even from DUCROW."[7] There was also, of course, the vitriolic Gilbert Abbott à Beckett of the *Figaro in London*, whose vilification of "Alfred the Little" and his managerial policies at times exceeded even his contempt for "Andrew the Great." The highpoint in his present campaign of character assassination was achieved on 22 March, when the periodical published a caricature of Ducrow as St. George thrusting his sword into the mouth of a two-legged dragon, played— or so à Beckett claimed—by Bunn himself (fig. 60). In the written description accompanying this pleasantry, the critic depicted Ducrow, "the director of living dog's-meat," as "blustering about the boards, flushed with gin, and excited by the yelps of the greasy gods, fancying himself the veritable champion of Christendom." Elsewhere in the same issue, in an obvious reference to Ducrow's benefit bills of the past season at Astley's, the equestrian director was accused of forcing his tradesmen to "take out what he owes them in benefit tickets, and victimises those with whom he deals by causing them to witness his mountebank performances. It is we understand a fact, that many tradesmen have been threatened with a loss of custom in case they refused to take the nauseous documents known by the name of Ducrow's benefit tickets, and they have been forced either to sell the filthy things for half price, or what is still worse, undergo the martyrdom of being present at the benefit." This time even à Beckett had gone too far, and a few days later a letter from Ducrow's lawyer,

FIG. 60. The infamous caricature of Ducrow, "flushed with gin," supposedly thrusting his sword down the throat of his friend Alfred Bunn in the 1833–34 Drury Lane production of *St. George and the Dragon*.

threatening a suit for libel, was delivered to the periodical's publisher. In the next issue (29 March) the editor diplomatically retracted his statement about Ducrow compelling his tradesmen to take benefit tickets "in *lieu* of his debts," but could not resist hinting to his avid readers that the equestrian was using the threat of an action to pay off a grudge *"on some other grounds."* Nor did he repent his attack on Andrew's four-footed companions: "cat's-meat in *embryo* is the very highest rank we can award to the stud at the Astley establishment."

There was clearly no doubt in the public's mind, however, as to the merits of *St. George and the Dragon*. For fifty nights it ran almost uninterruptedly until the first of March; by the time of its final representation on 22 March it had achieved no less than sixty-two performances. Bunn joyfully declared the receipts from the production had exceeded those of any pantomime in the history of Drury Lane. So sure had he been of success, in fact, and so overwhelmed by the generosity of his friend, who refused any emolument for conducting the rehearsals of the piece, that he commissioned in advance of the opening a splendid silver vase, surmounted by a gold cast of St. George slaying the dragon, as a "very inadequate token" of his regard for Ducrow.[8] Andrew himself threw a banquet on the stage of Astley's to commemorate the success of *St. George*. Although Bunn writes this occurred on the fiftieth night, it would seem it—or possibly another banquet—was held somewhat earlier, for Macready comments exasperatedly on one such festivity in his diary for 5 February: "At Garrick Club, dined ... Heard of Mr. Westmacott's speech at Mr. Ducrow's dinner—that his 'unspotted character had raised him to his present eminence'!!! Oh! Virtue!"[9]

Andrew certainly was not idle during the winter of 1833–34. Beginning 26 December he also operated a new amphitheatre in the Whitechapel district of London, where he and his artists nightly performed before rushing over to Drury Lane to appear in *St. George* (which was always preceded by a full-length play and thus did not come until fairly late in the evening). Ducrow's New Royal National and Olympic Arena, described as a comfortable and gaily decorated building capable of holding only 800 persons, was devoted primarily to equestrian acts.[10] But it also possessed a small scenic stage which was put to good use during the Lenten season when, on the Wednesdays and Fridays Drury Lane was presenting the customary oratorios, Andrew borrowed the dragon, costumes, and other paraphernalia and performed a reduced version of *St. George* at his own establishment.[11] On 17 March, for his benefit at Drury Lane, he appeared in his favorite tableau act, *Raphael's Dream*.[12] Two weeks later the company was back at Astley's for the annual opening.

The Wars of Wellington, with which the summer season began on 31 March 1834, was another attempt to recapture the glories of past years when J. H. Amherst had been the reigning playwright at the Amphitheatre. Alas, the creator of *The Battle of Waterloo*, following his spectacular *Siege of Troy* the previous season, had again departed the scene of his triumphs—eventually to travel with the circus company of Thomas Taplin Cooke to distant America, where he died, diseased and destitute, at a Philadelphia almshouse in 1851.[13] His loss was sorely felt at the Amphitheatre, for never again was there a playwright so magically possessed of the Astleian touch. Thenceforth Andrew himself was forced to meddle increasingly with his authors' works. In the present instance he was billed as having arranged and "compiled" all the incidents in the spectacle. From its four-part structure—India and the Capture of Seringapatam, Spain and the Death of Sir John Moore, the War of the Peninsula and the Storming of Badajoz, France and the Battle of Waterloo—it seems obvious he simply strung together some of the best scenes from earlier pieces. Even Gomersal was absent this year, and the role of Bonaparte now fell to Cartlitch.[14] The most ambitious spectacle during the season was Andrew's revival of *St. George and the Dragon*, now got up with new scenery by Danson, Telbin, Tomkins, and Gordon and making good use of the "Triple Diorama" introduced the previous year. Andrew also improved on the fight with the dragon, for the bills now tell of the combat at one point taking to the air and St. George being "raised from his Steed in the Gripe of the GREEN MONSTER."[15] Several woodcuts depict this intriguing maneuver (fig. 61). A number of other plays were revived this summer, and on 4 August there was a new but short-lived spectacle by Milner entitled *The Tournament of London*.[16]

It was at best a mediocre season for drama, and what novelty there was occurred primarily in the ring. There Ducrow produced several cavalcades and mimetic pageants, beginning with "The Historical Union and Cavalcade of Henry VIII and Francis I" in which he and George Woolford, assisted by some twenty "Cavaliers and Dames," performed the title roles.[17] His biggest and most spectac-

FIG. 61. Ducrow as St. George being "raised from his Steed in the Gripe of the GREEN MONSTER." Cut from a bill relating to the revival of *St. George and the Dragon* at Astley's in 1834.

ular creation along these lines was his "Gustavus' Masked Ball," featuring no less than "50 Horses & 20 Quadrupeds" (the distinction was apparently between the horses and the ponies, zebras, and other animals), inspired by the recent Covent Garden production of the Scribe-Auber opera *Gustave III*. The arena itself was decorated with draperies of flowers, heads, and "masques of mirth." At the commencement of the pageant Harlequin and Columbine guided the "Motley Train to the SCENE of MIRTH"—a riotous scene on foot that included, besides the traditional characters from the harlequinade, Punch and Judy on hobby horses, the Devil and baker on a double-headed steed, Swedish nobles, dominoes, Hercules, a dancing bear and his pony, a monkey, dogs, Beelzebub, and even (according to the wording of the bills, at least) a Miss Lane as "Europa, the Bull"! There followed a grotesque dance by Punch and Judy and several of the other characters, after which Ducrow, as the Soldan of Persia, entered on horseback with eight mounted body-guards and purchased a fair slave (Mrs. John Ducrow) from a Greek merchant played by Adams. Also in this part of the spectacle Emily and Madame Ducrow appeared as attendants, and Andrew introduced his wonderful horse Taglioni, who executed a beautiful *pas seul*. In the fourth part there was a "Dance of Folies on Horseback" leading up to a grand quadrille by twenty-four dames and their cavaliers. Miss Margaret Ducrow, Mrs. George Woolford, and Louisa Woolford were among the Folies. The fifth part of the pageant took place at Gustavus's court and somehow involved a sorceress and band of conspirators; and the sixth and last part featured a grand gallopade by all the characters and horses, terminating with a "Chorus Finale" and grouping titled "God Bless the King." It was a strange yet splendidly characteristic production, and spectators testified their approbation by "shouts of applause."[18]

For the first time in several seasons Andrew performed an entirely new pantomime on horseback, "Giromio and His Wife, or The Flight of Hymen,"[19] and at his benefit on 1 September a new Caledonian ballet of action on a single horse with Woolford, "The Lost Hunter, or The Sylph and Enchanted Piper." The last— as with the name of Andrew's new horse this year—was undoubtedly inspired by Marie Taglioni, whose interpretation of the ethereal title character in the ballet *La Sylphide* had bewitched Parisian spectators barely two years before. On the same evening, in another pageant presenting a "Classical Picturesque History of Ancient and

Modern Equitation," Andrew appeared as five different characters riding and instructing their various mounts, including Xenophon with his war steed and the celebrated Duke of Newcastle, training his horse in the presence of Louis XIV.[20] Ducrow's infant pupils also made good progress in the circle this season. By this time, too, still another had appeared who was destined to win a special place in his master's affections.

The origins of Andrew Chaffé (or Chaffe, as the name is more often spelled in earlier years before the process of frenchification had been completed) are a mystery to me; and apparently Andrew himself was not very sure about them. In the census returns of 1841— where he is listed as one of Ducrow's apprentices living with his master at Amphitheatre House—his place of birth is left in doubt ("N.K.": not known).[21] The only clue to his parentage I have located occurs in one of the anecdotal accounts of Ducrow by William T. Moncrieff, who mentions a groom at Astley's named Joe Chaffy, known to his familiars as "Chaffing Joe."[22] The June 1841 census lists Andrew Chaffé as ten years old, a figure that accords well with his published age in the theatre's announcements. In the bills for 1 June 1835, for instance, he is advertised, under the sobriquet "Petit Andrea," as under four years of age. He must therefore have made his ring debut when he was barely two, for he is billed among the other infants in Andrew's production of "The Night Guard and Frederick, King of Prussia," first performed on 23 September 1833. By 1834 he had replaced Ginnett as Bonaparte in "The Emperor, Mameluke, and Roguish Drummer."[23] In later years, as "Le Petit Ducrow" he was often taken for Andrew's adopted or (especially in France) legitimate son—mistakenly in both cases, it turns out, since Ducrow had simply granted him his name in the long-standing "père d'élève" tradition and did not refer to him as other than his "apprentice" in his will of 1841. Still, the conferring of his name was a powerful testimony to the promise Andrew saw in his infant pupil, and it may be, too, that the advent of this prodigy whom he took into his home filled some long-standing need in his personal life. His marriage to Margaret had been a barren one—a keen disappointment to one who, even his severest critics were quick to acknowledge, was extraordinarily fond of children.

All was not joy during the 1834 season, however. On 9 April Ducrow's sister Hannah Cox died at the age of thirty-one and was laid to rest beside Peter Ducrow in the yard of Old Lambeth Church.

FIG. 62. "Ascension of the Infant Favorite [Andrew Chaffé] on his Little Fairy Pony from the Stage to the Gallery in a Beautiful Variegated Horse Balloon." Astley's bill for 29 September 1835.

Less than two months later John Ducrow followed her to the same tomb. As late as the week of 21 April he was still performing nightly as clown to the circle. Then, unable to struggle any longer against the relentless consumption that gradually had wasted his life away, he finally took to his bed, where he died on 23 May. When his body was conveyed to the churchyard a few days later, it was preceded, as he had requested, by his two favorite ponies who had joined him so often in his ring fooleries. An immense crowd attended the funeral, and for a week afterward the Amphitheatre's bills were bordered in black—a final tribute to the artist many considered the best ring clown of his day and whose comedy, some thought, was equal to the great Grimaldi's.[24] Whatever the feelings between John and Andrew may have been during the years they were under the rough tutelage of their martinet father, the two brothers seem to have got along well in later life. Each also appears to have been proud of the other: John's marriage announcement and now the inscription on the tomb bore witness to their relationship.

FIG. 63. "Mr. J. Ducrow as Clown in the Comic Act of the Fairy Steeds." Andrew serves as ringmaster.

Adding to Andrew's afflictions at this time was a fresh outburst by the spiteful à Beckett of the *Figaro in London*. Earlier in the season the critic had again been crying up the "vulgarity and ribaldry . . . at the celebrated cat's-meat establishment." On one evening, he claimed, the program was so disgusting that a "sweep" (a patent reference to Ducrow's friend Westmacott) had been seen fainting into the arms of "an adjacent scavenger."[25] Now, in what was his most outrageous and gratuitous attack of all, he focused on an announcement in the *Morning Herald* which mentioned Andrew's bearing the expenses of John's funeral, and sarcastically complimented his "dog's meat friend Ducrow" on his businesslike manner in taking out a seven-shilling advertisement to puff himself and "his acting in the character of chief mourner for his brother John, and defrayer of the expenses of burial."[26] Regrettably, there is no evidence Andrew ever horsewhipped this individual.

Upon the closure of the Amphitheatre on 20 September the troop rode off to the provinces again. At Manchester they enjoyed a prosperous run at the Theatre Royal beginning 27 September, but were opposed by another of Andrew's professional brethren, the circus proprietor Thomas Taplin Cooke, whose company was then performing in Stevenson's Square. The two managers traded some choice words in their announcements, with Ducrow, to be sure, giving as good as he got and characterizing Cooke's establishment as a "roundabout."[27] On 24 November the troop commenced a seven-week engagement at Liverpool. Since their old quarters in Great Charlotte Street were now occupied by the circus company of William Batty, they performed at the Theatre Royal in that city also.[28] Meanwhile, determined to repeat his success of the previous year, Bunn had begun preparations for a new Christmas spectacle at Drury Lane, Isaac Pocock's *King Arthur and the Knights of the Round Table*. Again the splendid scenery of Clarkson Stanfield was to be featured, and again Ducrow—"whose genius alone," as Westmacott promised in the *Age* for 14 December, "is enough to be the making of any piece"—was enlisted to direct the spectacle. As it turned out, however, Ducrow was suffering from ill health at the time and informed Bunn he could not fulfill his commitment after all, other than allowing several of his horses and riders to travel down from Liverpool to appear in the play. This unexpected development had a chilling effect on the plans of Bunn, who pleaded with his friend to reconsider his decision and argued that the success of the piece depended on his at least directing the spectacle scenes. Moved by these eloquent appeals, Andrew finally consented to return to London the week *King Arthur* was billed to open, and in the brief course of two days arranged all the equestrian evolutions, combats, and tableaux. This done, he immediately returned to Liverpool.[29] It was also during this flying visit that Andrew ran afoul of Stanfield, who had painted a beautiful scene for the triumphal entry of the Knights of the Round Table into the City of Carlisle. As Bunn tells the story, at the final rehearsal Ducrow decreed that when the setting was revealed it should already be crowded with knights, squires, and a host of characters to give "life and animation to the scene." Stanfield indignantly objected that the scene had "life and animation" enough without any of Ducrow's assistance and threatened to leave the theatre "unless the said scene was first discovered for the audience to gaze on and admire, and the multitude sent on afterwards." When Bunn sided with Ducrow, the enraged artist made good on his threat and instantly quit the theatre.[30]

Among the riders appearing in the production were Adams, Wood (probably the father of Ducrow's niece "La Petite Ducrow"), Hillier, Southby, and Clarke. The last was a member of a long line of British circus artists and managers, one of whom Dickens is said to have used as the model for Sleary in his novel *Hard Times*. Either his sister or daughter had been dancing the rope at Astley's for the past two years and during the 1834 season was actually billed as "Mademoiselle Clarkini." Southby, married to another tightrope dancer of some repute, became excessively jealous of his wife as the result of a fall she once took during a performance at Lisbon. She was able to save herself by catching the rope with one of her legs, and was rescued from this awkward position by the ropedancer Wilson—who daringly clasped her knee in the process.[31] There was evidently a good deal of confusion over the riding abilities of T. P. Cooke, who played Sir Roland, the hero of the piece. In his review of the production in the *Age* for 28 December, Westmacott took it upon himself to correct a story in the *Morning Herald* that Ducrow had served as Cooke's equestrian double. The latter, Westmacott claimed, in addition to giving a perfect idea of what ancient knighthood was like, was "one of the best melo-dramatic actors and horsemen we ever had." Even he was in error, however, for in a letter to the *Times* (1 January 1835) a few days later Ducrow revealed that neither he nor Cooke had performed Sir Roland's equestrian scenes, which were actually done by Hillier. As to the horses themselves, they were, wrote the diarist Henry Crabb Robinson, "admirable whatever the Christians may be—They perform all the feats usual at Astley's—indeed it is a transfer of Astley's to the regular theatre."[32]

Like its predecessor the year before, *King Arthur* did not disappoint the expectations of Alfred Bunn. The production ran uninterruptedly until 7 March, on which date it achieved its fifty-ninth representation, then intermittently until 11 April, after which Ducrow's riders and horses left the theatre to begin preparations for the opening of Astley's. Meanwhile, they had also found time to trample across the boards of the Theatre Royal in a few older hippodramas, as on 9 March when *Timour the Tartar* was presented with Hillier and Adams in the featured roles of Kerim and Sanballat, and 17 March when *Tekeli, or The Siege of Montgatz* was revived.[33] Bunn again expressed his appreciation of Ducrow's help with a gold and silver vase; and Queen Adelaide, who had witnessed *St. George* the previous season, now testified her approbation of the theatre's continued service in the cause of British history by ordering one hundred pounds distributed among the performers.[34]

Following a brief holiday at Brighton in the company of Bunn and a few other friends,[35] Ducrow commenced operations at Astley's on 20 April. He was obviously feeling better after his recent illness at Liverpool, for on opening night he appeared in the circle doing his "Hibernian Lilt" and pose plastique "The Flight of Mercury." Both acts had been in his repertory since his early days, the former apparently invented in France, where it was advertised as "Le Pas irlandais." The reviewer for the *Times* (21 April 1835), who dubbed Ducrow the "Napoleon of the Circus" on this occasion, admiringly described him as dancing his jig "to the tune of 'Judy Callaghan,' on the back of a big gray horse in a hand-gallop, and he did 'cover the buckle,' 'right and left,' 'heel and toe,' as truly and more vigorously than any one of the Irish representatives could do these national steps on the firm floor of 'a mud edifice' and the outside of a trencher." Despite such apparent vigor, however, Andrew's performances of his famed pantomimes on horseback had been steadily tapering off since the early thirties. To be sure, he continued to create the beautiful duets which he danced and mimed with the blossoming Louisa Woolford, the many novel acts for the other artists of his establishment, and the equestrian pageants and dramatic ring scenes in which he frequently rode and exhibited his steeds in a more conventional manner. But his more strenuous roles, such as "The Courier of St. Petersburg" and "The Chinese Enchanter," were increasingly assigned to his able disciples. By 1830, in fact, the majority of his pantomimes had already been invented. That the "Kean of the Circle" was growing older and no longer had so much time to devote to the rehearsing of such scenes only partially explains this decreasing activity. A more urgent consideration was the state of his health. By the late 1830s it was common knowledge Ducrow suffered from severe attacks of asthma. Harsh weather aggravated the condition, which may account for his illness at Liverpool during the winter of 1834–35. The disease was most likely the intrinsic, nonallergenic type that generally commences in later life, for I find no indication of Andrew's being afflicted with it in his boyhood or youth. And while it is always risky to attempt a diagnosis at so distant a time, it also seems likely the onset of his breathing difficulties dated from the early thirties, when he began surrendering his more arduous roles. At any rate, there is what I take to be a curious reference to the problem in the "Answers to Correspondents" column of the *Owl* for 15 October 1831. In reply to someone who had written in to report that Andrew had fainted after a recent performance, the editor stated that "Ducrow always *faints* when he has done riding. . . . There is something extraordinary in Ducrow's *fainting*; others can endure greater hardships without that effect." Extraordinary or not, the tremendous energy and stamina required for some of these scenes was painfully brought home at the end of the 1835 season, when on 9 October spectators were horrified to see a stream of blood spurt from the mouth of Henry Adams while he was in the midst of his equestrian performances. He was carried out of the ring and taken home in a dangerous condition, after a surgeon had examined him and determined he had broken a vessel through overexertion.[36] When he reappeared as "The Courier of St. Petersburg" the following season, it was obvious he had still not recovered fully from this accident, leading one fearful reviewer to advise him to abstain from such strenuous activity a little longer.[37]

There was an improvement in the dramaturgic department this season, beginning with the opening hippodrama, *The Siege of Jerusalem, or The Camp of the Wilderness*. Based largely on Scott's *The Crusaders*, the action began with Saladin's sacking and burning Jerusalem and ended with his reception of the victorious Richard Coeur de Lion at a magnificent feast. The *Times* (21 April 1835) reported the opening night audience was so enthusiastic that the dialogue could not be heard, but concluded this was hardly a matter of consequence, since at Astley's "the necessity of suiting every word to an appropriate action being so fully felt by the performers, the spectator is left at liberty to enjoy his conversation with his friends, while he at the same time observes each successive step in the progress of the work even unto its conclusion." According to the bills, Andrew himself had "composed, got up, and arranged" the piece, which on 8 August was scheduled for its one hundredth and final performance.[38] In the meantime, on 8 June, barely two months after the original's premiere in Paris, a harlequinade version of the Scribe-Auber opera *Le Cheval de bronze* was presented under the title *The Bronze Horse, or The Flying Palfrey of China*. The production included a representation of a steeplechase and the traditional characters from the commedia dell'arte; and the dialogue was credited to Milner's pen, although Ducrow himself claimed to have "arranged" and "brought over" the piece from Paris.[39] Another free adaptation this season was *The White and Red Rose, or The Battle of Bosworth Field*, based mainly on Shakespeare and commencing with the insurrection of Buckingham. Andrew's first incursion into the Shakespearean canon had actually taken place on his benefit night the previous 1 September, when a hippodrama with the intriguing title *The Life and Death of King Richard II, or Wat Tyler and Jack Straw* had been given. The *Times* (2 September 1834), which termed the "new" parts of the spectacle execrably bad, reported that the "good" parts were from *Richard II* mixed with copious extracts from *Henry VI*, whose dialogue for Cade (Part 2) had been transferred to the characters of Straw and Tyler. The adaptation now offered seems to have been the work of Dibdin Pitt, who added several new scenes for "comic relief." Henry Mayhew, the new editor and critic for the *Figaro in London*, indignantly protested that the author should not cut and maim such plays.[40] Among the actors taking part in the spectacle were Henry Widdicombe —son of the resplendent ringmaster—in the part of Leonard Luckless, a thin trumpeter, and Hillier's wife as the Princess Elizabeth. Cartlitch played Richmond, and Richard was interpreted by the actor S. Palmer, formerly of the Sadler's Wells Theatre, who had made his debut at the Amphitheatre at the start of the 1834 season.

In the circle Ducrow's pupils and disciples turned in their usual fine performances. The most prominent among them continued to be Henry Adams, who prior to his accident at the end of the season interpreted several of Ducrow's pantomimes such as "The Reaper" and "The Chinese Enchanter." More often he now appeared in his own creations. Benjamin Stickney was entrusted with "The Reaper" as well, and Hillier with "The British Fox Hunter"—which in his hands, at least, became a spirited voltige act sometimes billed as "The Flying Huntsman." George Woolford was gone from the Amphitheatre this season. After joining Andrew's rival Thomas Taplin Cooke, he traveled with the latter's company to America, where in 1836 and 1837 he was billed to perform the role of Mazeppa and several of Ducrow's pantomimes on horseback. Mr. Clarke was still with the company, and the infant contingent was also out in full force. Jean Frederick Ginnett, who by this time was said to have reached the advanced age of nine, performed a new act titled "The Union of the Nations, or England, Ireland & Scotland" and his diminutive version of "The British Fox Hunter." On 5 October his sister was billed to make her ring debut with him in "The King and Queen of Fairy Land." The infant Louisa Ducrow was now advertised as three years old, while Andrew Chaffé, under the sobriquets "Petit Andrea" and "Mons. Andree," was billed as being under four. Together they appeared in several numbers arranged by Ducrow, including an act on a single horse titled "The Little Old Maid, or Duchess Fiddlefaddle and Count Pompolorum" and an equestrian version of "Punch and Judy."[41]

New to the Amphitheatre this season was the Chiarini family of ropedancers—Felix, Joseph, and the eight-year-old Vergunir—who performed simultaneously on a single rope.[42] The greatest novelty of all, however, was the first appearance in England of Laurent Franconi, Andrew's former employer at the Cirque Olympique and currently the leading member of the great French dynasty. On 29 June he made his debut at the Amphitheatre with his highly trained steed Blanche. In order to set off this stellar attraction, it was decided Franconi and his horse would have the stage to themselves, accompanied by specially painted décors and music from (what else?) *La Dame blanche*. After performing with her master the formal maneuvers of the high school of riding, in which Franconi directed her without recourse to the bridle or stirrup, Blanche went on to fence, smoke, defend her master, waltz, perform "academic poses," fire a cannon, ascend a flight of stairs backwards and, in the time-honored "salamander" act, remain unperturbed amid a dazzling shower of fireworks.[43] "What a beautiful creature is Franconi's horse Blanche," rhapsodized Henry Mayhew in the *Figaro in London* for 11 July. "How gentle, how tractable, how graceful, and really clever. It is a pleasure to see this horse, because we know that no torture, no flogging, could have trained it to such exploits. It must have been a superior instinct and natural cleverness in the animal." A month later Franconi introduced Phoenix, another horse he had brought with him, and on this occasion descended for the first time to the circle.[44]

Andrew himself did not appear very often in his solo pantomimes this season, although he continued to perform with Louisa Woolford and at his benefit on 28 September introduced an entirely new equestrian duet, "Polly of Portsmouth, or The Commodore and Man of War's Man." Louisa on her own exhibited her "Chase of Diana" and a new pantomime arranged for her by Ducrow entitled "The Nymph of the Floating Veil."[45] For his benefit, also, Andrew got up a splendid ring pageant, "The Royal Cotillon of Days Gone By, or The Court Beauties of Charles II," featuring costumes of

FIG. 64. Laurent Franconi and one of his trick horses in three different scenes.

real gold, silver, and rich embroidery which he had ordered from Lyons. Louisa Woolford personated the Queen in this spectacle, Mrs. Hillier took the part of Nell Gwynne, and Emily and Margaret Ducrow appeared respectively as Susan Armine and "La Belle Stuart." Ducrow interpreted the part of the Merry Monarch—a role that remained a great favorite with him until the end of his career. The large lithograph by Clutterbuck with the poetic effusion "Le Cheval Volant" depicts him in this character on his white steed Bucephalus (fig. 42).[46] The plumed Cavalier hat and long gloves he wore in the role are perpetuated in marble at the side of his tomb.

After closing the Amphitheatre on Saturday, 10 October, Andrew spent the following week at the Colosseum. Originally built to house an immense panorama of London as viewed from the top of St. Paul's, this great domed building in Regent's Park had later added other exhibits, amusements, and a scenic stage. It was for the last that the new proprietors, John Braham and Frederick Yates, engaged Ducrow for six representations of *Raphael's Dream*.[47] While Andrew was performing at this establishment, the troop itself proceeded to Bristol for a special engagement at the Theatre Royal, now under the direction of Sarah M'Cready, stepmother of the great William Charles. Their season there, extending from 19 October to 13 November, enabled Mrs. M'Cready to keep the theatre open a month beyond the usual closing time—a "solitary instance" of such longevity during her period of management, according to the chronicler of the Bristol Theatre Royal.[48]

Following the Bristol engagement the company traveled to Hull, where they opened at the new National Olympic Arena of Arts in Queen Street. This was one in a series of buildings Andrew was now erecting in the north of England with a view toward expanding his tours into new territory. A letter of 6 August 1835 to Westmacott confirms these ambitious plans:

> I have just received a letter from Mr. Atkins my architect in the country, wherein he desires my presence to visit some spots of grounds [sic] in different parts of the country in the North, intending to build there this winter. As I am compelled to start in a few days, it will deprive me of the pleasure of going with you on our intended excursion, as Business must be minded before Pleasure.[49]

A large bill for the Hull season describes the Arena as "one of the most SPLENDID and COMMODIOUS ever erected out of London" and as possessing a dress circle of private boxes, second tier of boxes suitable for school children (who were admitted in groups for half-price), gallery and pit, and mirrored saloon with "Crystal Columns." Referring to the grand spectacles which had been the making of Astley's and the means of "renovating the Equestrian Profession," the bill goes on to boast of these "restoring the Theatres Royal in London from a sinking state, to that of a crowded and profitable Seasons [sic]"—a claim Ducrow's friend Bunn would no doubt have endorsed. The same bill contains evidence for the only instance I have discovered of Andrew's ever deliberately parading his establishment out-of-doors. This event—a rare occurrence at such an early date in English circus history—was scheduled to take place (weather permitting) at 12 noon on Tuesday next and was to serve as an answer to those critics who had complained the advertised number of the stud and company had been greatly exaggerated. The order of the impending procession is described in detail and mentions such interesting features as Ducrow's van with his private wardrobe drawn by two hacks; two "hired" chaises and pairs with the treasurer and other members of the company; four mounted jockeys leading four trained horses; Alfred and the Flying Horse (Pegasus); Adams on Bonaparte's white charger Marengo; the "Baby" or Horse in Miniature, the "smallest ever seen"; Messrs. Clarke and Needham on John Lump and Gray; Miss Ducrow and Miss Woolford on their hobbies; three of the infant actors and Hillier in a pony chaise drawn by four Lilliputian horses; Madame Ducrow's phaeton drawn by two Hanoverian creams; Mazeppa's wild horse and Beda; and Ducrow's private carriage drawn by four of his milk-white steeds.[50] Besides presenting the same stage spectacles and ring acts previously given at Astley's, the troop was augmented at Hull by the "Russian" ropedancers Fanny and Carl Ivan de Vintner (also spelled Winther and Winter). At the end of the first week in January the company moved on to Leeds, another new town on Ducrow's unofficial circuit, and at the beginning of March to York, prior to returning to London.[51]

The new season commenced on 4 April 1836 with a spectacular production of Barnabas Rayner's *The Great Fire of London and the Plague of 1665*. Following a royal cavalcade of fifty mounted knights and twelve emblematic chariots, a wild boar hunt, and a scene depicting the looting of the red-crossed houses of plague victims, the climax of this potpourri arrived when Charles and his courtiers were interrupted during a banquet at Whitehall by the news that London was in flames. The firing of the city, according to the *Times* (5 April), was done under the eyes of the audience by a disgruntled regicide, Hubert de Gray, played by the blustering Cartlitch. This furnished an opportunity for Charles and his followers to rush about in the attempt to extinguish the fire, rescue people, and discover the incendiaries. The *Figaro in London* (16 April) humorously described Palmer as Charles II strutting around in a gold dressing gown and Cartlitch setting the fire with a sixteen-a-shilling bundle of firewood, but despite such absurdities had high praise for "the admirable arrangement of the groups, the splendid nature of the properties, and the gorgeousness of the whole getting up." The stage was extended into the ring by two "terraces" or platforms; among the settings was a built replica of the towers and gates of London Bridge.[52] Other plays of interest this season were a harlequinade entitled *The Devil on Two Sticks, or The Miracles in the Moon,* based on—and presumably burlesquing—the startling "discoveries" Herschel and other astronomers were then supposedly making with their telescopes, and a dramatization of Moore's *Lalla Rookh* (13 June). In the latter the redoubtable Gomersal made his long-anticipated return to the Amphitheatre. He had not been a regular member of the company since the summer of 1833, although he had condescended to perform his cherished role of Napoleon in *The Battle of Waterloo* for Ducrow's benefit the previous September.[53]

Andrew appears to have been in better health this year. Besides performing with Louisa Woolford in their duet "Polly of Portsmouth" and reviving his "Vicissitudes of a Tar" and "The Court Beauties of Charles II," he now introduced a mythological ballet of action on foot and horseback entitled "The Evening Star, or Rosebud and the Mischievous Sprite," in which his niece appeared as Cupid, the "Infant Phenomenon" Chaffé as Puck, another pupil, Miss James, as Rosebud, and Ducrow in his old role of Zephyr.[54] The following month he and Louisa Woolford performed a romantic ballet on two rapid horses with the title "The Sylph of the Hollow Oak, or The Mountain Shepherd and Little Boggle"—a "Caledonian scene" complete with metamorphoses and a mechanical fairy temple—which seems to have been a revival or variation of their "The Lost Hunter, or The Sylph and Enchanted Piper" of the 1834 season. Ducrow interpreted the part of Reuben the shepherd and Woolford figured as the Sylphide.[55] At his benefit on 26 September he introduced a new pantomime, "The Persian Tiger Hunter," and a new equestrian tale, "The Alpine Driver with His Spanish Palfrey, or The Horse of a Lady's Drawing Room." In the former, accompanied by his pupil Chaffé, Andrew drove and managed as many as nine horses at once; while in the latter, an adaptation of Mrs. Fitzwilliams' ballad "The Muleteer," Ducrow, his sister Margaret, and Chaffé appeared respectively as Alphonso the driver, Alphonso's wife and "Shepherdess of the Wild Horses," and the little muleteer boy.[56] Ducrow's sister Emily, still single during the previous winter's tour, had married sometime around the beginning of the season, for she now was billed as "Mrs. W. Broadfoot."[57] Her husband William and, later, his brother the actor A. Y. Broadfoot were both in Ducrow's employ, the former eventually becoming stage manager and serving in Andrew's place whenever he was ill or otherwise absent from the establishment.

Both Chaffé and Louisa Ducrow were featured in several juvenile equestrian scenes this season; and for Ducrow's benefit a new pupil, Miss Susan Leroux, was billed to perform for the first time a pantomime entitled "The Turkish Maid." The real name of this apprentice, I suspect, was Susan Beechdale—the same who is named in Ducrow's will and the census returns of 1841, in which latter document she is listed as then being fifteen years old and a native of the county of Surrey. As in the case of Chaffe, Chaffé, or "Le Petit André," the process of frenchification had already begun. Master Adams was also riding this season (at the opening on 4 April he fell twice while performing "The German Jockey and His Leaping Hobbies"), but the two Ginnett children were no longer with the company. Possibly feeling pressure from more junior "infants," they had left Andrew at the end of the 1835 season. The following winter they were at the Liverpool Amphitheatre, where on 8 March 1836 they rode together at Master Ginnett's benefit.[58]

Foreign artists were well represented at Astley's this year. Alfred Petreus, one of the stars of Franconi's establishment, posed and danced atop a barebacked steed and at Ducrow's benefit performed "The Carnival of Venice." Massotta, also from the Cirque Olympique, performed a voltige act, and Mlle. Caroline Loyo appeared with her mount Emperor. Loyo, who had ridden at the Cirque Olympique since 1833 and whose education included such illustrious masters as Laurent Franconi, Jules-Charles Pellier, and François Baucher, is generally believed to have been the first and one of the greatest equestriennes to exhibit haute école in the ring. She was also a trainer of some repute, though not known for the gentleness of her methods.[59] The brother-and-sister act of the de Vintners was still with Ducrow, and on 22 August a sensational new ropedancer, Joseph Plège, made his debut. Alternately billed as the "Acrobatic Fury" and "Wonder of the World," Plège was equally at home on the tight and bounding rope, the latter being especially suited to his "Wonderful Tourbillons & Somersets, with Fire Arms, &c."[60] At Ducrow's benefit he was advertised to dance the rope with two persons fastened to his legs and a third on his shoulders. Plège is a curious figure in the history of the circus. He was not born into the profession, and before coming to England from France he had received a medal for heroism from the Académie Française after rescuing several persons from various fires. As the mayor of one town where he had saved some property enigmatically put it, "partout où le danger se trouve, on est sûr de le rencontrer." The "Acrobatic Fury" was a familiar sight to English audiences over the next decade. His son Victor eventually joined him at Astley's, and his son Antoine (b. 1831) became a well-known circus director.[61]

Not so foreign were a troupe of "Arab Bedouins." The gymnastic feats of these "Sauteurs, Antipodeans, Elastic Negroes, Tumblers, and Equilibrists" led to some comic rivalry with Braham of the Colosseum, who claimed to be exhibiting four of the genuine article. Feeling Ducrow was encroaching on his rightful domain, the indignant manager applied at Bow Street for a warrant to stop Ducrow's proceedings. Andrew, of course, was not one to take such an attack lying down and, according to Bunn, issued the following challenge in one of his bills:

> Extraordinary Equestrian and Gymnastic Arab Feats! surpasses anything of the kind ever produced. The public are respectfully informed that these are not the four black men who play without their shoes and stockings at the west end of the town, but upwards of forty British artists, that challenge all Europe for talent, variety, extraordinary feats of manly skill and activity, and who nightly receive thunders of applause from crowded audiences, and do not play to a dozen of daily loungers. The union of talent and Arab spectacles of this establishment does not confine itself to the tumbling of four great ugly blacks, who have been refused an engagement at Astley's, because there are so many superior and more extraordinary men of our own country nearly starving, and com-

FIG. 65. Ducrow's "Bedouin Arabs" as they appeared in 1836.

pelled to perform on an open race-course for a penny, whilst those four men can get one hundred pounds per week, because they are black, and foreigners.

The reader no doubt has witnessed boys running alongside of a coach, doing what is termed CAT-IN-WHEEL, and turning foresprings with one hand and then the other; or throwing summersets from a sand-bank. Such is the grand performances of these Sauteurs, consisting of three or four blacks, who walk on their hands, with their NAKED FEET IN THE AIR, LIKE TWO BLACK FRYING-PANS, (of course no lady or respectable person can sit and see this.) . . . [62]

I have not located an original of this document, although there is a clear reference to the rivalry in the Astley's bills for 25 July. Following a description of the feats to be performed, the bill goes on to inform spectators that "the above Outline may convince the Reader that it is not the mere Tumbling of Four Arabs; and the Proprietors can positively assert, that none but BRITISH ARTISTES are in the above Entertainments, they being much superior." [63]

On a more genial note, Andrew seems to have been on excellent terms with the members of his company this season. On 30 July a delegation headed by Broadfoot, Gomersal, Widdicombe, Cartlitch, Adams, and Hillier presented him with a magnificent silver snuff box bearing a suitable inscription: "To Andrew Ducrow, Esq., whose transcendent talent has stamped him the Brightest Star of the Equestrian Profession, and the most eminent Pantomimic Artiste that ever graced the British Stage: this Testimonial of respect is presented to him (July 30th, 1836) by the Ladies and Gentlemen of the Royal Amphitheatre, as a slight memento of their esteem and admiration of his unparalleled energies and genius." [64] The immediate cause of this testimonial was probably an event that took place the following day, when Andrew threw another of his famous banquets on the stage of Astley's. These annual affairs, which began with the dinner commemorating the success of *Mazeppa*, were eagerly anticipated by members of the company and green room habitués fortunate enough to be invited to them, and were frequently commented on by London journalists. A dialect-filled notice of the original 1831 *Mazeppa* banquet, for example, in a humorous allusion to Andrew's traditional muteness onstage, relates that when the manager's health was proposed, "Disney Frosty [Sidney Foster, Ducrow's secretary at the time] returned thanks in a very neat speech, M. Duckrow [sic] always doing such things by deputy." [65]

Another account of one of these banquets tells a quite different story. According to this source, when his health was drunk Andrew himself returned thanks in a long speech on the "history of life," interlarded with many rich bits of slang from the "horseriding community." He finished this remarkable tour de force by observing that of all the delicacies on the table before him, "give me a baked shoulder of mutton and taters."[66] Bunn, too, in his account of Ducrow's banquet upon the success of *St. George and the Dragon*, remarks that he would "sooner by far hear any one of Ducrow's very shortest speeches, than listen to all [the] harangues of at least eleven-twelfths of the enlightened British Parliament; and there is many a member of the senate who has heard both, and will say the same."[67]

Most hilarious of all, however, appears to have been the dinner of 31 July 1836, whose combined menu and guest list has survived in several copies (fig. 66). Andrew's guests obviously thought it worth preserving—although a later collector, puzzled by several of the items under the heading "The Repast," learnedly annotated the example that came into his possession with the statement that "the above Bill was done as a skit on the meanness of Ducrow, it caused great amusement at the time."[68] But the banquet in question did indeed take place, and the inclusion of such delicacies as "horses leg and head of a young donkey with sweets" and "little snuff between and saw dust if wanted" is simply another expression of Ducrow's fund of humor—half of which, his friend Bunn declared, would be the making of any professional comedian.[69] Nor was there anything "mean" about Ducrow. Indeed, the profusion of dishes (not to mention the beverages) seems almost Lucullan. The list of "visitors" bears witness to Andrew's association with the *bon ton*. Besides his friends Sir George Wombwell and Lord Adolphus Fitzclarence, Lord Castlereagh, Lord Allen, and the Honorables Fitzroy Stanhope and T. Duncombe were among the guests, and letters of acceptance from several of these individuals have been preserved in the Ducrow Album. Ducrow's mother was also present, and so was, apparently, the eccentric playwright and actor Sheridan Knowles. Judging from the penned-in names on one copy I have seen, a few last-minute additions were made to the printed guest list.

Upon closing Astley's on 8 October, Andrew again took his troop to the north of England and another new building at Sheffield. The negotiations over this arena had begun the previous winter while Ducrow was playing at Leeds. An announcement in the Sheffield

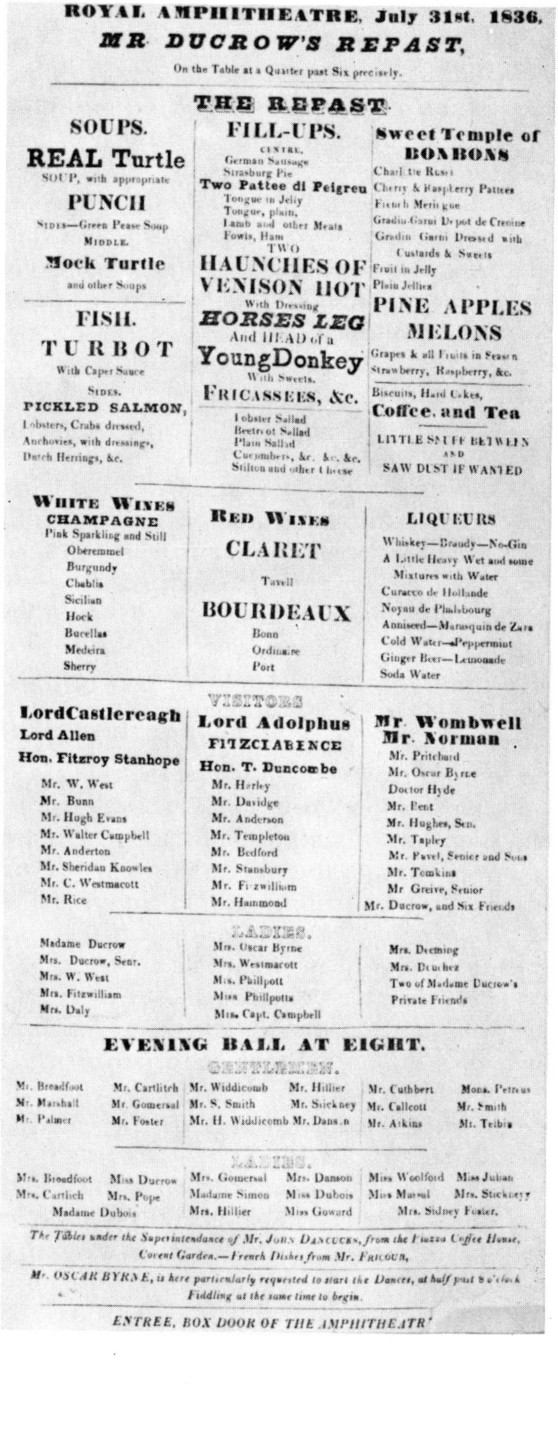

ROYAL AMPHITHEATRE, July 31st, 1836.

MR. DUCROW'S REPAST,

On the Table at a Quarter past Six precisely.

THE REPAST.

SOUPS.

REAL Turtle
SOUP, with appropriate

PUNCH

SIDES.—Green Pease Soup
MIDDLE.

Mock Turtle
and other Soups

FISH.

TURBOT
With Caper Sauce

SIDES.

PICKLED SALMON,
Lobsters, Crabs dressed,
Anchovies, with dressings,
Dutch Herrings, &c.

FILL-UPS.

CENTRE.
German Sausage
Strasburg Pie
Two Pattee di Peigreu
Tongue in Jelly
Tongue, plain,
Lamb and other Meats
Fowls, Ham
TWO
**HAUNCHES OF
VENISON HOT**
With Dressing
HORSES LEG
And HEAD of a
YoungDonkey
With Sweets.
FRICASSEES, &c.
Lobster Sallad
Beetroot Sallad
Plain Sallad
Cucumbers, &c. &c. &c.
Stilton and other Cheese

**Sweet Temple of
BONBONS**

Charlotte Russe
Cherry & Raspberry Patties
French Meringue
Gradin Garni Depot de Creine
Gradin Garni Dressed with
Custards & Sweets
Fruit in Jelly
Plain Jellies

PINE APPLES

MELONS

Grapes & all Fruits in Season
Strawberry, Raspberry, &c.

Biscuits, Hard Cakes,

Coffee, and Tea

LITTLE SNUFF BETWEEN
AND
SAW DUST IF WANTED

**WHITE WINES
CHAMPAGNE**
Pink Sparkling and Still
Oberemmel
Burgundy
Chablis
Sicilian
Hock
Bucellas
Medeira
Sherry

RED WINES

CLARET

Tavell

BOURDEAUX

Bonn
Ordinaire
Port

LIQUEURS

Whiskey—Brandy—No Gin
A Little Heavy Wet and some
Mixtures with Water
Curacoa de Hollande
Noyau de Plaisbourg
Anniseed—Marasquin de Zara
Cold Water—Peppermint
Ginger Beer—Lemonade
Soda Water

VISITORS

LordCastlereagh
Lord Allen
Hon. Fitzroy Stanhope

Mr. W. West
Mr. Bunn
Mr. Hugh Evans
Mr. Walter Campbell
Mr. Anderton
Mr. Sheridan Knowles
Mr. C. Westmacott
Mr. Rice

**Lord Adolphus
FITZCLARENCE**
Hon. T. Duncombe

Mr. Horley
Mr. Davidge
Mr. Anderson
Mr. Templeton
Mr. Bedford
Mr. Stansbury
Mr. Fitzwilliam
Mr. Hammond

Mr. Wombwell
Mr. Norman
Mr. Pritchard
Mr. Oscar Byrne
Doctor Hyde
Mr. Bent
Mr. Hughes, Sen.
Mr. Tapley
Mr. Pavel, Senior and Sons
Mr. Tomkins
Mr Greive, Senior
Mr. Ducrow, and Six Friends

LADIES.

Madame Ducrow
Mrs. Ducrow, Senr.
Mrs. W. West
Mrs. Fitzwilliam
Mrs. Daly

Mrs. Oscar Byrne
Mrs. Westmacott
Mrs. Phillpott
Miss Phillpotts
Miss Capt. Campbell

Mrs. Deeming
Mrs. Deucher
Two of Madame Ducrow's
Private Friends

EVENING BALL AT EIGHT.

GENTLEMEN.

Mr. Breadfoot	Mr. Cartlitch	Mr. Widdicomb	Mr. Hillier	Mr. Cuthbert	Mons. Petreus
Mr. Marshall	Mr. Gomersal	Mr. S. Smith	Mr. Stickney	Mr. Callcott	Mr. Smith
Mr. Palmer	Mr. Foster	Mr. H. Widdicomb	Mr. Dans n	Mr. Atkins	Mr. Tribis

LADIES.

Mrs. Breadfoot	Miss Ducrow	Mrs. Gomersal	Mrs. Danson	Miss Woolford	Miss Julian
Mrs. Cartlich	Mrs. Pope	Madame Simon	Miss Dubois	Miss Marval	Mrs. Stickney
	Madame Dubois	Mrs. Hillier	Miss Goward	Mrs. Sidney Foster.	

The Tables under the Superintendance of Mr. JOHN DANCOCKS, from the Piazza Coffee House,
Covent Garden.—French Dishes from Mr. FRICOUR,

Mr. OSCAR BYRNE, is here particularly requested to start the Dances, at half past 8 o'clock
Fiddling at the same time to begin.

ENTREE, BOX DOOR OF THE AMPHITHEATRE

FIG. 66. Charles Molloy Westmacott's copy of the menu and guest list for Ducrow's banquet on the stage of Astley's in 1836.

Independent for 30 January 1836 throws light on its financing. Having received an offer from "some Gentlemen of Sheffield, stating it to be their intention to erect a permanent amphitheatre; and also wishing Mr. Ducrow to open the Establishment with his splendid London Company," Ducrow declared his willingness to enter into such an arrangement and designated his architect Atkins to oversee the immediate construction of the arena. Apparently the work did not get under way as early as expected, for a notice in the 18 October issue of the Sheffield *Iris* reported that a crew of two hundred had been laboring the past six days to complete the arena in time for the troop's arrival. The substantial, even opulent nature of the building is attested by a large, attractive red and green advance bill in the British Museum. The National Olympic Arena of Arts, according to this announcement, was offered to the public "as one of the most novel and beautiful erections of splendour and comfort ever formed out of the Metropolis." Its artistic embellishments were themselves "sufficient to repay the Visitors without the addition of the Spectacle." Erected at immense expense, it was not a temporary structure of wood and canvas, but was firmly built, slated, and possessed a stage and ring, dress tier of boxes (to which only ladies in "full costume" would be admitted), second tier of public boxes, two galleries, commodious pit, cloak room, lobbies, a mirrored saloon with couches, separate entrances, and carriage halt. The decorations consisted of emblematic devices, flags and standards of various nations, medallions and draperies, a painted French ceiling above the arena, a gold-embossed chandelier, a drop curtain by Danson representing the "Poet of Harmony in his aerial flight on the Music-Footed Steed," flower vases and statues, alcoves with dioramic views of history and "heathen mythology," and paintings by Telbin and Cuthbert depicting the taming of Bucephalus, Mazeppa and the wild horse, Neptune and his sea coursers, etc. The exterior of the building, illuminated by Greek lamps, had a portico and arcade; and the location in South Street, the bill ambitiously proclaimed, had been chosen as the "most appropriate and select place for the NOBILITY, and approach of CARRIAGES."[70]

Ducrow's occupancy of this splendid edifice, extending from 19 October to 2 December, marked the first and last appearance of his establishment at Sheffield while it was directly under his management. The brief visit there—despite an oft-repeated tale about Andrew's ruining his season by insulting the Master Cutler[71]—

appears to have been highly successful. The newspaper reviewers were unanimous in their praise of the company; and apparently the appeal to the "nobility" paid off, for the house was frequently described as both "crowded" and "fashionable." Aside from Andrew himself, the critics were especially delighted by the feats of "Le Petit Ducrow." "This beautiful little thing," wrote the reviewer for the *Iris* (15 November), "whilst in the act of jumping, standing on one foot, at the same time putting the toe of the other foot to its mouth, riding backward, &c., displays all the ease and agility of the most experienced rider, and such is the independence and courage evinced in his performances, that the most pleasing emotion occupies the minds of the audience in place of the painful fear that his infantine appearance first calls forth." The same account provides an interesting description of Hillier in his voltige version of "The British Fox Hunter":

> After throwing himself off the horse, and afterwards running by its side with the speed of a deer, he would bound on the saddle in an instant, down again in a moment, and planks being placed during the time he was going round, probably 5 feet high, the horse and its late rider leapt side by side over two or three obstructions placed near together, several times repeating this most astonishing feat of activity.

Plège, Petreus, Adams, Stickney, and Ducrow's niece and sister Margaret were among the artists touring this winter, but Louisa Woolford appears to have been elsewhere. Consequently, when Andrew revived "The Mountain Maid and Tyrolean Shepherd," his partner on this occasion, "Miss Ducrow," was in all probability his sister Margaret.[72] For his benefit on 25 November Andrew performed both his *Raphael's Dream* and *St. George and the Dragon*.[73]

From Sheffield the company proceeded to Newcastle upon Tyne, where at the beginning of the new year Andrew received his severest blow to date. On 15 January 1837, "after a short but painful illness," his wife Margaret died at the age of thirty-nine. I have been unable to ascertain the precise nature of this illness, but most likely it was related to the influenza epidemic that was then devastating England. In the London parishes alone the disease accounted for no less than a thousand burials on the following Sunday.[74] The newspapers were appropriately sympathetic and told of Ducrow's inconsolable affliction at the loss of his wife and the sorrow of all who knew her.[75] Early on the following Thursday morning, having seen the body encased in a series of expensive coffins, Andrew set out in his private carriage to accompany the hearse on its long journey to London. Hillier, Broadfoot, and several other members of the company formed a mounted escort to the edge of town, then turned back to finish the engagement which still had two days to run. It was their last opportunity to pay their respects to one who—whatever her limitations in the ring—seems to have been liked and honored by all.[76]

When the body finally arrived at Amphitheatre House, Andrew, weeping like a child, was met and comforted by his mother and friends to whom Broadfoot had solicitously written in advance.[77] But the climactic scene in this funereal drama was yet to come. On Thursday, 26 January, the procession again formed for Kensal Green Cemetery. Ducrow's machinist Matthew Mackintosh—who despite his usual inaccuracy over dates for once seems to have had a clear recollection of the event—tells what happened next. After traveling the four miles to the cemetery in a downpour of rain and sleet, the body was taken into the chapel for the service. While this was going on, Mackintosh stepped outside to check the grave site and vault Ducrow had purchased a few days before and discovered some two to three feet of water in the latter. When Ducrow was apprised of this he broke into a towering rage, called the minister a "swindling old humbug," and demanded his money back.[78] He also called the minister a few other things, which contemporary journalists all deemed "unprintable." There exists, however, a more candid manuscript account of Ducrow's language on this occasion—although even M. Willson Disher, whose possession it once was, seems to have been somewhat appalled by the swearing and added a few more dashes in his description of the flare-up than the original calls for. We of a more enlightened age need feel no such inhibitions. According to this source, upon seeing the water in the grave, Ducrow "began in the presence of the clergyman with bug——y [buggery—more accurately, bugger] the bloody thieves &c. &c. and swore that his wife should not lie there. The parson remonstrated on his manner and told him he could not think of remaining there if he used such language—he said he did not care for the blasted parsons."[79] After being dissuaded by his friends from taking the body home again, Andrew agreed to leave it overnight in the chapel provided he could take the key with him. There followed, according to Mackintosh, a frenzied round of inquiries at St. Paul's and Westminster Abbey, into one of which Andrew now insisted he would get his wife. However, he was finally persuaded to deposit the body in the catacombs beneath the chapel while a fitting mausoleum was erected from designs by his scene painter Danson.

While these stormy scenes were being played out in London, the troop, under Broadfoot's management, had moved on to Liverpool. Andrew was shortly there as well,[80] but was often absent from the company over the next several months. On 10 March he wrote from Paris to Broadfoot at the arena in York, informing him he had received his letter of the 4th from Liverpool and had just spent three days in Brussels. He had sent some outlines of plays to Foster at Astley's and, should Broadfoot be planning to write to him also, wished to have the front curtain taken down and sent out for brushing and mending. Plège was engaged for the summer again but, since he would not be needed at the start of the season, could be let out to someone for one to three weeks.[81] If anyone at York inquired about his absence, Broadfoot was instructed to reply that "you expect me *every day.*" He was also to "take a full acount [*sic*] of all persons that neglect their Duty in my absence."[82] That Andrew's visits to the Continent this year had objectives other than his usual picking up of ideas, plays, artists, and costumes is evidenced by letters he wrote over the next several months. Eager to break from the routine of touring the British provinces each winter, in May he addressed a letter to Edmond Duponchel, director of the Paris Opéra, informing him of his intention to bring his establishment to Paris at the close of the London season and suggesting *St. George and the Dragon* would make a "magnificent Ballet Spectacle" for the Académie Royale de Musique. The part of St. George would be interpreted by Ducrow, and the piece, with "some trifling addition of dancing," would no doubt do.[83] The next month Ducrow was in Paris again, attempting to win approval for his ambitious plans. In a petition to the Minister of the Interior, in which he took care to point out that French managers were annually permitted to bring their entertainments to London, he solicited the same privilege for his troop of equestrians, whom he planned on bringing to Paris for four months beginning in October. The spectacles and mimodramas presented by the company would be in English, and such was the special nature of these entertainments that they would not operate to the prejudice of any other theatre in the capital. Andrew's convenient forgetting of the Cirque Olympique, now under the direction of Louis Dejean, obviously did not take in the Minister or one of his subordinates. On 8 July a reply was addressed to Ducrow's residence in the rue Montmartre refusing his request without explanation.[84]

Meanwhile, Astley's had opened on 27 March with a new spectacle taken from Scott, *The Lists of Ashby, or The Conquests of Ivanhoe*. The adaptation, apparently the work of Broadfoot, was praised as being far superior to the usual Astleian fare, and Ducrow received equally flattering notices for his staging of the piece.[85] The director had returned from the Continent in time for the Easter Monday opening, but instead of appearing in any of his pantomimes contented himself with serving as master of the circle to the more energetic exertions of his juvenile pupils. In addition to Louisa Ducrow and Andrew Chaffé, by now these included Miss Rosina Lee, an "infant" Cottrell, and a "petit" Avery—probably the child of Andrew's old fellow rider, whose daughter Caroline was listed as one of Ducrow's apprentices in the 1841 census. By this time, too, Chaffé had been accorded the sobriquet "Le Petit Ducrow," leading at least one reviewer to identify him (falsely, if not illogically) as Ducrow's son. The *Times* (28 March 1837) admiringly described him in the pantomime "The Royal Post-Boy" as galloping round the circle standing on and leaping two diminutive ponies "with as much ease and confidence as if he had grown up in the position." Later in the season he graduated to riding and managing as many as four "pigmy" horses at once in the character of "The Fairy Huntsman" and appeared with Hillier in Ducrow's pantomime of the previous year, "The Perisian Tiger Hunter."[86] Following the death of his wife Andrew lavished even more attention than formerly upon his infant riders (in his letter of 10 March to Broadfoot he refers to them as "my dear children"). Under the new title "The Enchanted Woodman, or Good and Evil" he revived his equestrian ballet of action "The Evening Star" with Chaffé, Louisa, and Miss Avery as his partners;[87] and on 15 May he performed with his pupils in a new scene, "The Golden Age." Other junior members of the company this season included Master H. Adams, who appeared on his leaping palfries as "The German Jockey" and toward the end of the summer with Miss Susanne in a duet entitled "The Jingling Jumpers of Pekin."[88] The latter performed a new pantomime of her own, "The Indian Hunting Girl";[89] and by the time of Ducrow's benefit on 25 September even the petite Louisa Ducrow was entrusted with a solo act, "The Terrace

Girl of Madrid," in which she danced a cachucha on horseback.

Among the adult members of the troop this year Adams senior was conspicuous by his absence. His place was filled by a new rider of note, Edward Hicken, whom Ducrow tried to pass off as German but who, the *Times* stoutly maintained, was an English rider whose real name was Hicks.[90] Whatever his origin, he obviously enjoyed the confidence of Ducrow, who assigned his "Carnival of Venice" to him and later in the season, under the title "A Tale of the Sea," his famous "Vicissitudes of a Tar."[91] Alfred Petreus was still with the company and on opening night performed a new pantomime, "The Young Mahometan," on a single horse. Hillier, not to be outdone, worked up a new act of his own on six barebacked steeds entitled "The Polish Patriot."[92] Even Andrew's partner West seems to have been infected with the riding fever this season, for he now replaced Cartlitch as Mazeppa, a role he had sampled and apparently found to his liking the previous September on the night of his benefit.[93] Other noteworthy artists were the Chiarini family of ropedancers and—if one can believe the bills—a troop of "Philistines" and "real" Sahara Arabs imported from "Suez on the Atlas Mountains"![94]

A recherché spectacle presented at West's benefit was *The Renegade, or The Siege of Alcazar and Struggles of the Moors*—an

FIG. 67. Ducrow and his Infant Pupils in the ring scene "The Evening Star, or Rosebud and the Mischievous Sprite," 1838.

adaptation of Dryden's *Don Sebastian*—while earlier in the season Harrison Ainsworth's popular novel *Crichton* received the full hippodramatic treatment.[95] French grand opera received its share of attention this season, too, when for his own benefit Andrew produced a "Melo-Dramatic Pageant" employing 100 horses, 75 performers, 180 supernumeraries, and armor and coats of mail he had recently purchased in Rouen entitled *The Council of Constance, or The Doom of Rachael* [*sic*] *the Jewess*. Based on Halévy's *La Juive*, the piece had been tried out the previous winter in the provinces, where Andrew was billed for the role of Eleazar and his sister Margaret for Rachael.[96] More characteristic was Andrew's production of *The Wars in Spain*, whose patriotic claptrap involving a bold British tar one critic hailed as a return to the old-fashioned plan that "would have charmed an audience some thirty or forty years back." Another commended it for being "replete with every kind of horror—Cartlitch as a Carlist, and Palmer as a Christino, both go at it with fearful ferocity, and tumble one another about with all the enthusiastic butchery of a brace of bloodhounds—First Cartlitch plants his dagger in the side of Palmer, then Palmer gives a dig at the ribs of Cartlitch, then they scuffle and struggle, and pitch and heave, and turn somersets, and gasp, and start, and scream, and the Queen of Spain is victorious."[97]

Ducrow's own mimetic exhibitions were fairly limited this year. Toward the end of the season he did, however, introduce a new equestrian duet with Woolford, "Jenny Jones, the Pride of Llangollen," and a new solo scene with music by Rossini, "Figaro, the Barber of Seville," in which he interpreted both the intriguing barber and the music teacher Don Basilio.[98] For his benefit he also got up a ring scene entitled "The Royal Riding Master of Berlin" in which his sister Margaret—not to be outdone by Caroline Loyo of the previous season—exhibited haute école exercises in the character of the Countess of Cologne. In the same scene Andrew, as the Court Tutor, successively introduced Beauty, a Horse for a Lady's Drawing Room; Pegasus, a Horse for a Lady to Dance with; Alfred, a Horse for a Poet; and Marengo, a Horse for his Master only.[99] Louisa Woolford, to be sure, continued as a worthy complement to the "Roscius of the Ring" and displayed her pantomimical expertise in such solo scenes as "The Standard of Liberty," "Poverty and Abundance," and "The Female Hussar."

The most interesting event of the 1837 season, however, did not occur in the ring or on horseback, but on the stage in a strictly pedestrian melodrama Andrew had brought back from Paris. *The Factory Assassin, or The Dumb Man of Manchester* (the play soon went by the subtitle alone), translated by Rayner from *Une Cause célèbre*, offered Ducrow another extended opportunity to display his famed skill as a mime. First performed at his benefit on 25 September, it was repeated during the week of 9 October at the Adelphi Theatre and thereafter remained one of his best known vehicles. The action of the play—despite what one might expect from the original English title—has nothing to do with social unrest or anarchism. Rather, it revolves around the machinations of a middle-class wastrel named Edward Wilton. Having stolen from his adoptive aunt and been turned out of doors five years ago, this unsavory character has profitably spent the intervening years becoming an accomplished forger, gambler, murderer, and escaped convict. Meanwhile, Jane, the wife he abandoned at the time of his flight, has been staying with the unsuspecting Mrs. Wilton as a companion and friend, and her mute brother Tom has also managed to insert himself into the old lady's affections. Wilton now returns to his aunt's house in the guise of a beggar, determined to be revenged on her for her "hard-heartedness" and gain for himself his rich inheritance. After craftily donning the role of a penitent and making up to his long-suffering wife, he gains entrance to the house in the dead of night, drugs Jane during a love feast, and enters his aunt's bedroom with murderous intent. Mrs. Wilton's screams and the noise of overturning furniture arouse Tom who is sleeping in the attic above. He climbs down on a rope and has barely entered the room where his sister is sleeping when Wilton comes rushing out of his aunt's bedroom with a bloody knife, triumphantly exclaiming "All is over! the inheritance is mine!" Tom quickly hides behind the sofa on which Jane is lying, but springs to her defense when Wilton, having decided there must be no witness, prepares to stab her also. In the ensuing struggle the villain is disarmed but makes his escape over a balcony. Tom rings the alarm bell and all the other characters rush in. But Mrs. Wilton, unfortunately, is not quite dead after all. Wounded and bleeding, she staggers into the room and with her last breath points an accusing finger at Tom: "Behold—behold my assassin!"

The remainder of the plot need concern us only briefly. Wilton—as is obvious from his change into "fashionable attire"—comes into his "inheritance"; and Jane, who now recognizes him for what he is, nonetheless remains silent out of consideration for their absent "son," even though Tom is threatened with imminent execution. Justice prevails all the same, of course, and she is rescued from her dilemma by an enterprising lawyer named Palmerston who connects Wilton with a murder at Dieppe. Faced with conclusive evidence of his criminal past, Wilton conveniently commits suicide by throwing himself out a window. As the curtain descends to the sound of a tolling bell, "Tom falls on his knees, thanking Heaven for his deliverance; at the same time embracing the fainting form of his sister." [100]

A bare reading of the play gives but the faintest impression of Ducrow's interpretation of Tom. Yet the reviewers were unanimous in their praise and considered it one of the high points in his long career as a mime. The *Times* (10 October 1837), commenting on the production at the Adelphi, acclaimed Ducrow's acting "the finest piece of dumb show that has been exhibited on the stage for many seasons." Another critic wrote of one of his initial performances at Astley's that it was "nature itself; it is the mind acting and conveying its feelings with quicksilver velocity to the body; as a pantomimic actor he is the first in the world";[101] while a few months later, after Andrew had taken his troop north again, an enthusiastic Scots critic described his scenes as being given "with a fidelity and vividness of expression and an energy of action we have never seen excelled by any other actor or pantomimist whatever." There was a "terrific grandeur," the reviewer continued, in the scene where Ducrow recapitulated the circumstances of the murder before the Chief Justice. "Nothing could surpass the feelings of gratitude he gave vent to when his Lordship expressed a conviction of his innocence. It was touching in the extreme, and fearfully true to nature, and caused a tear to start in many an eye." [102] An unsigned letter from one of Andrew's fans shows to what extent he affected the less sophisticated portion of his audiences—and also, one suspects, the impression he made on many of his female admirers:

> However singular it may appear to you to be thus addressed I cannot refrain from writing to you to thank you for the inexpressible gratification you afforded me by your performance of The Dumb Man of Manchester—I never in my life witnessed anything so powerful—The expression of your affection towards your [sister?] was so beautiful so tender as to melt me into tears—And in the scene with Edward Wilson [*sic*] your acting was so agonising the attempts to scream so terrible and when you were accused by Mrs. Wilson as her assasin [*sic*] your agony your horror were so dreadful as

nearly to cause me to go into a fit—And when you were at
last acquitted I felt as delighted as if it had all been real—Your
expression of pain from the chain having hurt your wrists
was so interesting your appeal to your sister by giving her
your mother's ring so affecting—And when Edward Wilson
asks who saw him commit the murder your pointing up to
heaven so impressive—Altogether I never saw anything to be
at all compared to your acting throughout the whole piece—
The talent of an actor is shewn by his power over the feelings
and you are triumphant over them—I hope you will not be
displeased at this sincere tribute of admiration from one you
do not know but who does not think she does wrong in expressing in this manner her admiration of the talents of
Mr. Ducrow.[103]

After reading such tributes, one is almost certain to feel disappointed upon turning to the directions in the play itself—all the
more so since the speaking characters are often called upon to interpret
what Tom has just mimed! Here, for instance, is a passage from the
obligatory scene in which Tom explains the reason for his muteness:

> *Mrs. Wilton.* . . . But I think you told me your brother was
> not always dumb?
>
> *Jane.* Relate to the lady in what manner your misfortune
> occurred to you.
>
> *(Music—rustic air, to commence with pipe. Tom, by a
> series of picturesque representations, relates that at the age
> of ten years he was tending sheep on the mountain; (change)
> while asleep one escapes; he follows it, and falls into a deep
> ravine; (start drum) catching branch as he fell, he hung
> by the hands until he was released, and that the fright
> deprived him of the faculty of speech.)*
>
> *Mrs. Wilton.* If I understand him right, terror deprived him
> of the power of utterance?
>
> *Jane.* Yes, madam; while tending his flocks, some of them
> strayed and fell over a precipice. He pursued them.
>
> *Mrs. Wilton.* Poor youth!

And here the crucial scene where Tom mimes the circumstances of
the murder before the Chief Justice:

Chief Justice. His eye sparkles with gratitude as he listens to you. Let him repeat the manner in which he described the fatal event to his judge. (*Consults the depositions.*)

(*Music. Tom eagerly signifies that he will; then, in animated pantomime, relates that he saw a man (imitating beggar) sharpening a knife on a stone; he came to warn Mrs. Wilton of her danger, who made him remain in the house.*)

Chief Justice. If I understand him rightly, he saw a man who had asked alms, sharpening a knife on a stone. He flew to warn Mrs. Wilton of her danger, who wished him to sleep in the attic above.

(*Music.—Tom signs "Yes, yes," and continues—that at bed time he heard a noise; that he descended by a rope into the chamber, saw his sister asleep, and an ill-looking fellow come out of Mrs. Wilton's room; that he hid himself behind the sofa; the man offered to strike his sister, but he (Tom) wrested the knife from his hand; that they wrestled together; Tom was thrown down, and the man escaped through the window; that he rang the alarm bell, opened the door, when Mr. Palmerston entered; Mrs. Wilton was led from her chamber bleeding, and accused him of the murder.*)

Chief Justice. You further say. . . .

The imitations inevitably followed. James Ryan, who copied everything Ducrow did, was advertising a play called *The Dumb Man of Birmingham*, with Mr. T. Thompson in the lead, at his Sheffield circus in the spring of 1838;[104] and a lighter touch was introduced the following winter when the Theatre Royal, Glasgow, promised its audiences a "laughable farce," *Shocking Events, or The Dumb Man of Dunkirk*.[105] Dumb beings of one sort or another, in fact, were soon quite the rage. Only a short while before the appearance of the Dunkirk mute the Glasgow theatre had presented a melodrama with the interesting title *The Dumb Girl of Genoa, or The Bandit Merchant*. Apparently this bore no resemblance to Ducrow's play, for the bills mention a "celebrated drunken combat" in the second act.[106]

Denied permission to take his equestrians to France, Andrew spent the winter of 1837–38 in Scotland. At the conclusion of his performances at the Adelphi in October, he caught up with the troop in Edinburgh, where they played at Ducrow's Royal Arena until

23 December. In mid-November he entered into an engagement with W. H. Murray, manager of the Theatre Royal, to give seven representations of *The Dumb Man of Manchester* after finishing each evening at his own establishment.[107] The artists and ring acts were essentially the same as during the previous summer at London. Plège and his son Victor astonished the burghers, and Ducrow and Woolford delighted them with their ballets on horseback. Andrew was obviously in fine fettle this season. The reviewer for the Edinburgh *Advertiser*, commenting on his duet with Woolford in "The Maid of the Mountain and the Swiss Boy" ("The Swiss Milk Maid and Tyrolean Shepherd"), could not make up his mind whether he excelled more as an actor or an equestrian. "His exquisite skill in telling a story in dumb show, and his address in executing his movements on horseback are still unrivalled."[108] The critic for the *Evening Courant* (28 October 1837), on the other hand, while allowing Andrew to be the "most accomplished horseman that ever appeared in this country," professed his preference for Ducrow's skill as a "dramatist." "He seems to have studied effect deeply and skilfully, and is a perfect master of every variety of appropriate and picturesque attitude." In all Ducrow's exhibitions, the reviewer continued, "we trace the master-mind of the contriver, in the taste, the design, and in the appropriate devices and costumes which give effect to the whole." New during the Edinburgh season was an act Andrew worked up for himself and his pupils in which they posed, without benefit of horses, in a series of "living statues." Beginning with the Life of Bonaparte "in bronze," they went on to represent the marble figures of *Evening Prayer, Cupid with His Lyre*, Belzoni's *Egyptian Slave*, the new *Gladiator* from the Tuileries, and various figures from Canova's chisel. From the announcements one gathers a costume change was involved, most likely from bronze-colored body stockings and makeup to stark white for the marmoreal figures that followed. The two pupils performing these scenes with Ducrow were later identified as "Le Petit Ducrow" and "Mlle. Susanne."[109]

At the end of the year the company traveled to Ducrow's New Royal Arena in Glasgow, where they played until 14 February 1838.[110] Around this same time a curious rumor began circulating to the effect that Ducrow had purchased the splendid estate of Castle Rossie in Forfarshire from an ex-M.P. named Horatio Ross. A newspaper account of the supposed transaction reported that "Ducrow's accession to the castle and estates of Rossie . . . has induced a slight panic among the good people in the North lest he should make that county his hippodrome, and the castle itself an arena for Spanish bull-fights."[111] In the attempt to run down this rumor I have consulted the Forfar Sasines and Search Sheet for Rossie at the Scottish Record Office. But as is so often the case with tales about Ducrow, this too must fall by the wayside, for the latter document conclusively proves Horatio Ross was sole possessor of the property from 1827–45. The most likely explanation is that someone was out to embarrass not Ducrow, but Horatio Ross, who was a controversial political figure in his day. The Aberdeen *Herald* frequently attacked him in its 1838 issues, and the reputed sale of his ancestral estate to a circus performer would no doubt have been looked on as a particular instance of depravity.

The final weeks of the winter season were spent at Aberdeen. A severe storm delayed the troop on their route from Glasgow, and the horses arrived in a fatigued condition, with the result that their opening at Ducrow's Royal Olympic Arena had to be postponed until 1 March.[112] When the company left the Granite City at the end of the month, they were spared the usual drudgery of an overland trek and were treated to the luxury of traveling to London by steamer. Andrew himself, having recovered from his grief of the previous winter, was about to embark on a new and final chapter in his eventful career.

Ducrow riding Nine Horses.

FIG. 68. "Ducrow riding Nine Horses" as "The Courier of St. Petersburg."

Let Lions, & Leopards to the Desert go,
Give us thy riders, & thy stud, Ducrow!

—"To Mr. Ducrow," manuscript poem
    by "E. K." in the Ducrow Album

8   Decline

IN 1838 LOUISA WOOLFORD was a desirable young woman of twenty-three. As lead equestrienne and ropedancer at Astley's, where she floated demurely above spectators' heads in her gossamer costumes, she inflamed the imagination of more than one would-be swain. Such—or so I suspect—was the underlying cause of a curious disturbance the previous July, when a Richard Glynn from fashionable Pall Mall attended the Amphitheatre and loudly hissed her from a private box while the other spectators were enthusiastically applauding. So strident was his disapprobation, in fact, that the startled equestrienne fell off her horse. An indignant box-keeper burst in upon Glynn and unceremoniously dragged him by his collar into the theatre's saloon, knocking off his spectacles and hat and tearing his coat in the process. The dispute was continued before a magistrate, who upheld the right of spectators to express their disapproval and fined the offending box-keeper.[1] The widowed Andrew himself had obviously come to look upon his partner's charms with an increasingly unprofessional eye. Matters took a serious turn during the winter tour of 1837–38. On 10 June 1838 the couple were married at St. George's Church in Camberwell, following which, Bunn writes, the "matrimonial honours" were celebrated at Topham's New Hotel in Richmond.[2] Their first child, Peter Andrew John, was born the following 28 November.[3]

Celebrations of one sort or another were very much a part of the new year. On 29 April, shortly after the Amphitheatre had opened for the season, the pretty widow of John Ducrow married the American equestrian Benjamin Stickney Jr.[4] Two months later London was crowded with tourists and visiting dignitaries who had arrived to witness Victoria's coronation. A distantly mournful note in the midst of these rejoicings was Andrew's concern over the mausoleum, erected after Danson's fantastic designs to receive the body of Margaret, which was finally nearing completion at Kensal Green. On 3 May he wrote to his friend Westmacott, who had recently given up the editorship of the *Age*, to inform him his name was still on the "free list" and ask him to ride out to the cemetery with him "to instruct respecting the plants best durable for weather, evergreens &c. being quite ignorant of anything in that way, & your taste & judgment being so superior in this I have told the gardener to delay marking the ground till I had seen you."[5] Meanwhile, the Amphitheatre itself had sustained another loss in the person of Henry M. Milner, the author of *Mazeppa* and Ducrow's former secretary and treasurer in the provinces. According to his fellow playwright Edward Fitzball, it was while answering a summons to Covent Garden to translate a new play from the French that he fell down ill and died.[6] All the same, the theatre opened on 16 April with a new piece by its "late" author, *The Passage of the Deserts, or The French in Egypt and Siege of Acre*, in which the Battle of the Pyramids, revolt of Cairo, and death of Kléber were enacted and the French were shown finally destroyed at the Siege of Acre. Gomersal strode about once more in the Emperor's famous gray coat, took snuff and discreetly wiped his fingers on his trousers, and exhorted his troops from the back of a camel (a llama and one of Ducrow's zebras appeared in a scene showing an encampment in the desert). At one point in the action he had a particularly narrow escape when two soldiers, standing on each side of him, were killed by the same cannon ball.[7] The audience was kept in a roar by the antics of Widdicombe's son Henry who played the part of a black cook named Julius Caesar, although at least one critic regretted the loss of the "luxurious lungs"

FIG. 69. Pencil drawing of Ducrow's mausoleum at Kensal Green Cemetery around the time of its erection. The Anglican chapel is the large building in the left background.

of Cartlitch, "whose voice mocked the thunder of Jove." Alas, the original Mazeppa had departed the Amphitheatre in 1837—a few months after receiving a bequest from his former master John Richardson, who so admired his penetrating voice—and was shortly to turn up in America, where he eventually kept a saloon in Philadelphia and died in 1875.[8] Nevertheless, the consensus was that the opening spectacle was one of Ducrow's most magnificent. At the conclusion of the initial performance the equestrian director came forward amidst a storm of applause and personally gave it out for repetition.

An interesting advance bill for the 1838 season lists the members of the company and theatre personnel and points up the doubling that was still expected of some circus employees. Sidney Foster, Barnabas Rayner, and the dancer Leclercq all figured among the "Candidates of the Company," but were also listed as, respectively, treasurer, house author, and ballet-master. Among the equestrians judged worthy to appear in the circle were Hillier, who also held the important position of master of the horse; the German riders Otti Mottie and Ludovic, who had been with Ducrow since the 1837 season; Hicken, Stickney, and Clarke (whose name was misspelled "Clarkson"); and the perennial master of the ring "Methuselah" Widdicombe. The composer and leader of the orchestra was still William Callcott, who had provided many of the musical accompaniments for Andrew's equestrian pantomimes. Wives often supplemented their families' incomes by appearing in the spectacles and afterpieces when the opportunity arose, and these included those of Gomersal, Leclercq, Hillier, and Stickney. Louisa Woolford headed the roster of "Female Equestrians," followed by Ducrow's sisters Margaret and Emily (Mrs. Broadfoot) and his pupils and apprentices Mlles. Susanne, Lee, King, and Avery. The father of the last was also with the company as a rider. The names of Ducrow's "Infant Pupils and Equestrian Prodigies" were left unspecified, but these continued to include Master Adams, Andrew's niece Louisa Wood, and his apprentice Andrew Chaffé. New to the company this year were the pantomime actor John Bologna and the "Antipodean Wonder" Mr. Price, whose talents as a gymnast were to shine forth in a patriotic competition later in the season.[9]

The female members of the troop were especially strong in the ring this year. Woolford presented her "Standard of Liberty," "Poverty and Abundance," "Chase of Diana," and "Female Hussar," and for her triumphant debut as the new "Madame" Ducrow appeared with her husband in their celebrated duet "The Swiss Milk Maid and Tyrolean Shepherd." Mlle. Susanne impersonated "The Indian Hunting Girl" and "The Turkish Maid"; Miss Lee "The Greek Maid"; and the petite Louisa Ducrow "The Spanish Girl." Andrew again restricted his own ring performances to his less strenuous roles, leaving such demanding numbers as "The Courier of St. Petersburg" to Hillier and others. Besides reviving such older acts as his "Alpine Driver," "Figaro," "Cockney Sportsman," and the ring pageant "Gustavus' Masked Ball," for his benefit on 8 October he created a new scene for himself and his pupils entitled "The Magic Bell and the Enchanted Flute, or The Toad in a Hole"—an entertaining "Equestrian Metamorphosis, interspersed with Mechanical Tricks, Changes and New Attire"—which seems to have been akin to his earlier "Evening Star."[10] On the same evening, as in the previous year when he first mimed the title character in *The Dumb Man of Manchester*, he made his debut in an ambitious three-act drama based on the French play *Le Pauvre Idiot*—which Ducrow was personally credited with arranging and adding to—*The Poor Idiot, or The Souterain of Heidelburg* [sic] *Castle*. The plot of this strange "romantic" drama concerns the villainies of the widowed Duchess of Heidelberg. Determined to insure the succession of her own son to the estate and title, she has ordered the secret imprisonment of Edgar, the infant son of her murdered brother-in-law (the former Duke) within the crumbling walls of Heidelberg Castle. This poor youth—played by Ducrow—has been kept in a gloomy dungeon for the past sixteen years, tended by the caretaker of the deserted castle. Deprived of any education or human intercourse, his sole companions a picture of the Madonna and a solitary flower that has somehow managed to grow inside a piece of broken crockery, he has grown up in a state of inarticulate idiocy. Adding to his misery is an addiction to opium, which his jailer has regularly fed him to keep him pacified.

As the action begins, Frederick, the good-natured son of the heartless Duchess, pays a visit to the ancient castle in the company of some noble friends and his tutor Dr. Athanasius (another dignified role for Gomersal). While there, they discover and liberate the Idiot, whose true identity Athanasius learns while listening to the caretaker's deathbed confession. Back in Nuremberg, the Doctor attempts to inculcate some rudimentary lessons upon the mind of his savage pupil, but is torn between his loyalty to Frederick and the knowledge that Edgar is the rightful heir to the Heidelberg title. While Athanasius is wavering on this nice point of conscience, the Duchess learns what has happened and, aided by the son of the Idiot's former keeper, lays plans to murder him. A further complication arises when the Idiot's mother, forced to flee Germany following the mysterious murder of her husband, returns in answer to a summons from Athanasius and is introduced to the son she has long believed dead. This leads to a heated meeting between the two women, while Athanasius finally reveals the truth to Frederick—who takes the news of his disinheritance amazingly well. Unfortunately, the Duchess has managed to poison the Idiot with a lethal dose of opium (to which even the good Athanasius has not been above resorting as one of his novel pedagogical methods), but nonetheless receives justice at the hand of her victim. The final scene takes place in a chamber with an alcove bed whose curtains are initially closed. Here Athanasius and the Idiot's mother engage in a frantic search for some crucial documents which the Idiot has hidden in the vase containing his cherished flower. No sooner do they find them, however, than news is brought that the Duchess's accomplice has been found murdered in her chamber—a fact that has not prevented him from somehow confessing he has poisoned the Idiot at the Duchess's instigation. "My son poisoned!" shrieks the distracted mother as the Idiot collapses at her feet in the pangs of death. "Oh, Heaven! let her not escape; but hurl thy retributive lightning to strike with death the assassin of my husband—the destroyer of my child!" The final directions are an answer to her prayer:

> The Idiot utters a shriek, and starts up—suddenly he runs to the alcove, C., and opens curtains.—A general cry of horror at the sight of the Duchess, dead.—The body lays across the bed—the head, arm, and hair are bloody.—Idiot points to the corpse, laughs convulsively, and then falls dead.—Tableau.—The last action is done in an instant to very rapid music.[11]

For once Andrew was not entirely mute. Throughout the play he was called upon to scream, shriek, sob, utter strange cries, laugh wildly, and at one point—thanks to the tutelage of Athanasius—even call indistinctly the word "friend" through a closed door. In contrast to the text of *The Dumb Man of Manchester*, the published play contains many descriptions of his expert pantomime. Here, for instance, are the directions for the scene in which the Idiot first appears, dressed in his rags and crouching in his cell with his flower beside him and picture of the Madonna affixed to a nearby pillar (fig. 70):

> Music.—The *IDIOT* is cramped up under straw on the matting, his eyes turned towards the window as if watching for some one's arrival—all his movements express anxiety and eagerness.—Music changes.—He places beside him a flower, the companion of his solitude—the flower has grown in the remains of a broken earthen vase—he seems to pity and caress the poor flower.—A glimpse of light is seen through the bars of the window, as if day were breaking—he shivers with cold—his teeth chatter in his head—his whole body trembles—the rays of the sun finally penetrate through the bars of his dungeon—he rises joyfully as the obscurity disappears—bounds about, making strange noises and inarticulate sounds of "*Ah—ah—ah!*"—He places himself in a gleam of sunshine, and by pantomime expresses that he feels its genial warmth—he takes his flower, and places it in the light of day—he regards it with affection, and seems to say that, like himself, the sun will give the plant fresh vigour.—In a reverie, he demands from whence come the light and day—then, by a movement of pious resignation, he points to the holy picture affixed to the pillar—he approaches it, kneels, and seems to indicate the revelation comes from holy source. As he bends the music changes to an "*Ave Marie.*"—Music again changes.—Suddenly the Idiot starts as if he heard a sound—he places his ear to the earth, rises quickly, takes his flower, hides it behind pillar, and signifies his food is being brought.—A hand appears through the wicket of the door, *L.*, and presents to the Idiot, who seizes it with avidity, a phial—the hand is then withdrawn, the wicket closed, and all again silence.—The Idiot regards the phial, then swallows the opium it contains, and falls by degrees asleep, first placing the flower by his side, as if serving for a companion in his slumbers. —A storm rises, the clouds become dark, the beams of light no longer penetrate the dungeon, where reigns obscurity the most profound.

While by no means a failure, *The Poor Idiot* never received the same acclaim as did its predecessor of the previous year. The reason lay in the starkly tragic and—to many viewers—highly unsatisfactory ending of the piece.

More characteristic was the mélange of fifty mounted Olympians, battling Amazons, colossal hall of sphinxes, and galleys floating down the Euphrates River in the new spectacle produced on Whit Monday, *The Oracle, or The Olympic Conquest of Babylon.*[12] The

FIG. 70. Ducrow in the title role of *The Poor Idiot, or The Souterain of Heidelburg Castle*, 1838.

coronation of Victoria on 28 June called for more than the usual infusion of patriotism into the Amphitheatre's productions this year. In June Andrew got up a "Musical Burletta Pageant" on the subject;[13] a few weeks later he mounted another, more ambitious spectacle in which Mrs. Hillier impersonated the Queen. Seated on a richly caparisoned living horse, both she and her steed were borne in on a platform supported on the shoulders of "her devoted Subjects."[14] In deference to the princes, ambassadors, and tourists who were thronging London, the theatre's bills were sometimes printed in foreign languages, and Ducrow proudly listed in them the names of all the crowned heads who had witnessed his performances.[15] Beginning 2 July a widely publicized vaulting contest was nightly held between Price and the American gymnast and equestrian Levi J. North, who together with his friend the clown Joe Blackburn had recently arrived in England. The colonial party, to the chagrin of the English, generally emerged victorious during this three-week round of somersaults.

Blackburn himself kept a diary of his trip to Europe and jotted down many candid observations on Astley's and its figures.[16] On 5 June, having just arrived in London, he spent the evening at the Amphitheatre and was favorably impressed by *The Oracle*—"one of the most gorgeous and best got-up pieces I ever witnessed; I never saw anything in that way half so magnificent." He goes on to describe, in generally unflattering terms, the various artists of the establishment, including Ducrow's little niece who "rode very well with a catgut string attached to her waist, run down through the pommel, and so on to the ringmaster's [Hillier's] hand, *who by-the-by, was a nigger.*" Clarke, who performed "The Indian" this evening, was "the worst man-rider I ever saw; it would have been a disgrace to old Sizer's Steamboat Circus on the Mississippi." As for Price, with whom North would shortly be competing, Blackburn concluded with satisfaction that "he would be rather bad-shaped among the Yankees." Next came Ducrow's turn to bear the sharp scrutiny of the American visitor:

> Last of all came the renowned Mr. Ducrow, the great, the wonderful; rode an act called 'Figaro;' he pantomimed well, first-rate, but he has been overrated unmercifully as a rider. He never was the rider that North is. He tried to make a finish to his act, his attitudes were all incorrect, and in throwing off he pointed his heel as much as any rider I ever saw come

from the mill at Somers town, where they make 'em. In fact, he in his time has stuck a horse well—all dash and splash, but he never was a Herr Cline for grace. So much for my first impression of Mr. D. as a rider.

In subsequent entries Blackburn expressed his admiration for the riding of Ducrow's pupil Rosina Lee (whom he thought better than Woolford) and for Hicken in Ducrow's pantomime "The Sailor," and on 26 June acknowledged that Ducrow and his new wife's duet "The Mountain Maid and Tyrolean Shepherd" was "one of their best—it was a very pretty one."

More interesting are the descriptions of Ducrow behind the scenes—directing rehearsals, swearing at his men—and of the spectators who showed up for the contest between North and Price: "Yankee Hill, J. Wallack, and Taglioni the great dancer also in front, with a great number of foreign ambassadors, nobility, etc." On 15 July the two Americans were obviously nettled when a note they had sent to Ducrow was returned by a servant with the message that it could not be received "until it came in a proper manner—that is sealed." When Broadfoot called a few minutes later and asked them their terms for a renewed engagement, they refused to give him an immediate answer. They continued to defer their decision over the coming week, with the result that Ducrow now sent them a note to inform them they had been dropped from the next week's bill. This abruptly put an end to their stay at Astley's. Returning to the Amphitheatre as spectators on the night of 23 July, upon leaving the house they were told by the doorkeeper that West, whom they had just seen as Mazeppa, was insulted by their not coming to terms and had ordered their free admission stopped. "Did not care a d——," was Blackburn's heated reaction. Notwithstanding these petty misunderstandings, the two men were treated well by Ducrow, who received them at Amphitheatre House, invited them into his private box at Astley's, told them his theatre was "always open to us for any time and any length of time" and, prior to their departure for the provinces and an engagement at Ryan's circus, accompanied them to the Italian Opera House, where they "drank champagne, ate ice-cream, and

---

PLATE 4. "Mr. Ducrow and Miss Woolford as the Tyrolean Sheppard [sic] and Swiss Milkmaid." John Ducrow stands watching behind the ring enclosure, and Widdicombe serves as master of the ring.

ogled the ladies through a double-barreled spyglass." Earlier in his account Blackburn furnishes a comic description of the "great Monsieur" at home—which confirms other reports of Andrew's penchant for luxurious living. Arriving at Amphitheatre House for their initial interview, after ringing the bell and sending up their letter of introduction Blackburn and North were ushered into "his great Mogulship's presence, had a talk with him, and arranged to come and try the board in the afternoon. Well, you may talk about circus-riders living, but if he don't live like a prince I'm a dog-fish. He lays back in the shade, with his morning-gown on; biggest kind of an arm-chair, more mahogany side-boards, silver plates and marble statues. He took us into his best room. I expect he thought he would scare us at the start."

Another American making his London debut at Astley's this year was the lion trainer Isaac Van Amburgh, shortly to be immortalized in the large painting by Landseer (fig. 71). After starting out as a keeper in the traveling menageries of Rufus Welch and the New York Zoological Institute, around 1833 he first publicly entered a cage with his pupils and overnight became one of America's most celebrated figures. In 1837, inspired by the example of Henri Martin, he began appearing in a series of lion dramas whose climactic moments invariably arrived when the hero found himself in a cage, "den," pit, or forest of wild felines which he usually (but not always) succeeded in mastering.[17] It was Van Amburgh who was popularly credited with being the first to stick his head into a lion's mouth, a feat that was later described in the following memorable lines in the song "The Menagerie":

> He sticks his head in the lion's mouth,
> And holds it there a while;
> And when he takes it out again,
> He greets you with a smile.

As may be gathered from a notice by the new editor of the *Age* on 26 August 1838, not everyone approved of this last "piece of gratuitous impertinence." Aside from being a "highly hazardous proceeding for the exhibitor," the writer warned, "there have already been several cases in which lions have snapped off the heads of persons persisting in this sort of foolish experiment."

Following a private performance for members of the press and friends of the house, Van Amburgh and his animals made their first

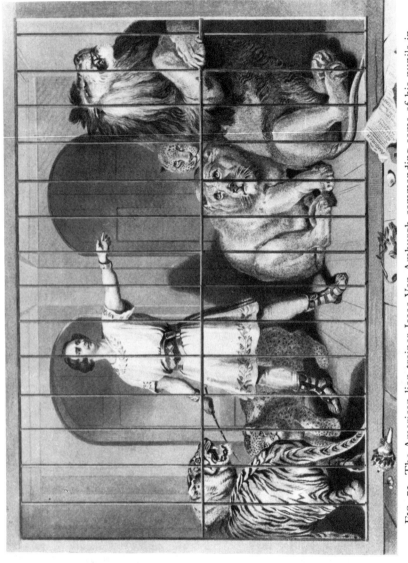

FIG. 71. The American lion trainer Isaac Van Amburgh commanding some of his pupils in their "den" at Drury Lane. The actor William Charles Macready's name appears in the playbill littering the stage.

public appearance at Astley's on 27 August. The vehicle in this instance was *The Brute Tamer of Pompeii, or The Living Lions of the Jungle*, in which the trainer played a Roman renegade named Malerius who is condemned to be thrown to a mixed group of lions, tigers, and leopards in the arena at Pompeii. Thanks to his knowledge of wild animals acquired in the course of his travels, instead of being torn to pieces Malerius is fondled and caressed by these beasts— with the result that the Emperor becomes convinced he is witnessing a miracle and orders him released. The actual "arena" consisted of two separate cages, into both of which the hero was successively cast. The spectators at this fearless display of man's dominion over the beasts of creation echoed the actors in it by roaring their approval, and the reactions of the press were hardly less enthusiastic. One reviewer went so far as to cryptically claim that "in subduing entirely to his will these furious natives of the torrid zone," Van Amburgh had "opened a new field of inquiry for the philosopher and the meta-physician, whilst the naturalist may regard the whole as a task of supererogation, which not Hercules himself could have surpassed."[18] What was deemed unexceptionable at Astley's, however, was bound to cause outrage in some quarters when transferred to the boards of a "national" theatre. Upon the closure of the Amphitheatre on 20 October (on which occasion, the *Age* for 21 October gaily reported, Van Amburgh was scheduled to deliver the farewell address, but was drowned out by a lion's roar, leading Ducrow to observe it was the "best speech of the season") both the trainer and the manager im-mediately proceeded to Drury Lane, where Bunn was awaiting them with open arms. The following Monday, 22 October, they and their charges opened in a new spectacle produced by Andrew, a grand chivalric entertainment entitled *Charlemagne*, whose hapless author Bernard was once more destined to see his work mangled by the equestrian director. According to one source, the "dramatic Pro-crustes" Ducrow tore whole handfuls of leaves from the manuscript in his determination to "cut out the dialect and come to the 'osses," with the result that even critics favorably disposed to the piece were incapable of giving their readers a clear outline of its action.[19] But the scenery by the Grieves, all agreed, was magnificent to look at; the music and trumpet movements by Eliason were fine to listen to; and the plot—so far as anyone could make out—dealt with true and false knights, the abduction and rescue of a fair maiden, charges and tableaux of foot and horse, and, as a grand finale, the condemning of a character played by Van Amburgh to the two cages of big cats in a repetition of his recent exploits at Astley's.[20] In addition to leading his riders in the equestrian evolutions, Ducrow impersonated a mute Moor named Hamet; and "Le Petit Ducrow," also mahogany-colored, appeared as his brother Sadi. Together they at one point rode up a precipice and tumbled down a waterfall, and later they performed a *pas de trois* with Andrew's trick horse Pegasus (fig. 72). All was not well between the two stars of the piece, however, and in early November Ducrow and Van Amburgh had a violent falling-out behind the scenes. Voices were raised and blows were given, and the actor John Hatton, who unwisely attempted to separate the two brawling men, received a black eye for his trouble. The incident was alluded to in several periodicals. As one journalist humorously de-scribed the fracas, "Jack fell, the Monsieur galloped off, while Van Amburgh, master of the well-fought field, was received with one universal *roar* of approbation from the Menagerie."[21]

Whether or not the fight had anything to do with it, the "Mon-sieur" and his cavalry did indeed gallop off following the performance on 1 December, leaving Van Amburgh and his animals to get on as best they could. Bunn temporarily resorted to exhibiting them inde-pendently of any dramatic action, but somehow managed to work them into the Christmas pantomime, *Harlequin and Jack Frost, or Old Goody Hearty*.[22] The beasts and their trainer remained at Drury Lane, in fact, until 23 March, the last night of playing before Passion Week. It was during this later period that Bunn incurred the most stinging censure of all for turning Old Drury into a menagerie—although the real reason for these onslaughts was the royal patronage that was suddenly bestowed on the theatre. The young Queen was evidently fascinated by Van Amburgh. From 10 January to 12 February 1839 she paid no less than six visits to Drury Lane for the express purpose of seeing him and his charges, and on the evening of the 24th even stayed behind after the other spectators had left so she might go upon the stage herself and watch the animals being fed. According to Bunn, who naturally makes the most of these visits in his memoirs, they had been kept from food for the preceding thirty-six hours—a device for the royal gratification that was not without hazard for one of the menagerie's star performers, a snowy white lamb which Van Amburgh, in the course of his exhibitions, used to introduce to his less civilized pupils in order to demonstrate his control over them. On the present evening both a lion and a panther

FIG. 72. Ducrow, "Le Petit Ducrow," and Pegasus performing a *pas de trois* in *Charlemagne*, produced at Drury Lane in 1838.

simultaneously made a rush for this tasty morsel, and the trainer was forced to whip his fractious subjects into abject submission.[23] The Queen was highly pleased at seeing the animals gorge themselves, and Bunn himself was so overjoyed that he decided to grant the British public the same privilege following the performance on 4 February (on which night Victoria was again in attendance).

Further rejoicings were in order on 14 February when Van Amburgh threw a dinner for seventy persons in the Drury Lane saloon. Bunn presided, and the Queen and her patronage were fulsomely toasted.[24] The howls of protest from some members of the press that greeted these royal visits were as much a matter of political partisanship as they were of artistic priorities.[25] The Queen had already lost favor with many of her subjects, and Bunn and his managerial policies had been a source of contention for many years. In his memoirs the manager attempted to justify his importation of Ducrow and Van Amburgh by recounting the similar expedients of his predecessors at both Drury Lane and Covent Garden. In answer to those who had raised the perennial cry that Shakespeare was being trampled underhoof, he took perverse delight in claiming these persons had forgotten "we had no Shakspearian actors alive, and that an attempt at the representation of any of the bard's immortalities would disgrace the theatre far more than any other performance."[26] It was Macready, of course, whom the wily manager was baiting with such outrageous statements. In 1838 "Boxing Mac" was himself in theatrical management and valiantly attempting to keep the legitimate drama alive at Covent Garden. As always, his diary during this dark period is revealing. On 22 October he recorded his premature rejoicing over some news concerning Bunn's production—only to be immediately deflated upon learning there was adverse criticism of his own latest effort: "Bartley brought the news of the failure of the 'horse and beast' piece at Drury Lane. I do *feel thankful* for this defeat of a bad man's attempt to debase still lower the art and artists he has so long and brutally oppressed. Serle came into my room; told me that Mr. G. Smith—in the *John Bull*—had violently abused the *Tempest* !!!"[27] The next few days were no better for the embittered manager as the reviews of *Charlemagne* came pouring in. "For the last two days, having been excited by the base unmanly conduct of the papers, the *Times*, *Post*, and *Herald*, who have been lauding the trash of Ducrow and Van Amburgh and depreciating the business of Covent-Garden theatre, I have suffered from internal throes of passion and indignation until life has felt painful to me. In my prayers I have failed to tranquillize myself; my sufferings have been most acute . . . I lift my heart to God—but in vain. I must hope for repose and comfort, or I shall sink under the torture of mind I undergo."[28] In his entries for January and February he repeatedly expressed his indignation at the Queen's going to Drury Lane to patronize Van Amburgh and his beasts—conveniently forgetting that the monarch was then often paying the same compliment to his own rapidly failing theatre.

Meanwhile, Ducrow and his troop were again scouring the provinces, opening at Norwich over the Christmas holidays and finishing at Birmingham around mid-March. The lease on the Amphitheatre was renewed for another seven-year term, and during the winter the interior was again entirely remodeled.[29] Among the renovations appears to have been a new second gallery, for beginning with the 1839 bills this location is mentioned for the first time in the list of admission charges. The last remained reassuringly constant throughout Ducrow's seventeen-year period of management: 4s. to the dress boxes, 2s. to the pit, and 1s. to the original gallery. The new addition cost a mere 6d. On 1 April the season commenced with a new spectacle produced by Ducrow, *The Victories of Edward, the Black Prince, or The Battlefield*, a typical mélange which included such interesting features as the "Ambush of the War Hag!—Union of the Kings of France, Spain, and Bohemia. Battle of Crecy!! Explosion of the Mill, and Death of the Blind King of Bohemia. *ICH DIEN!* . . . Friar Tuck, Maid Marian, Hobby Horse and Green Griffin." By this date, too, Andrew had made up his difference with Van Amburgh, who appeared on the same bill with a new group of lions. The evening concluded with a revival of *St. George and the Dragon* in which Ducrow re-created his role of the British champion.[30]

Then, unexpectedly, activities at the Amphitheatre were thrown into turmoil when Andrew, on his way to Paris at the end of April, experienced a severe accident. As reports reached London and rumors of an amputation began circulating, Louisa Ducrow hurriedly left to join her husband, who a few days later had recovered sufficiently to send back his own account of what happened. While the crowded diligence in which he was riding was entering St. Denis, he had opened the window and rested his arm on the ledge in order to permit another passenger to move. At that moment the wheel of a huge timber wagon crashed into the coach, tearing the lower part of his arm and breaking it between the elbow and shoulder. His fellow passengers had rendered him every assistance, and his friend Laurent Franconi had done his best to ease his sufferings in Paris. A skillful surgeon had managed to save and set the arm. "I have borne the affliction better than I could have expected," Andrew concluded, "and, although still in bed, yet am I so far improved as to hope the worst is over."[31] By mid-May he was back in London, "much better than could have been expected," reported the *Age* (12 May), but the accident placed a strict check on his riding for the rest of the season. On 15 July he was well enough to return to the circle in an equestrian minuet and gavotte with his wife, Hillier, and Mlle. Susanne; in later weeks he performed his burlesque scene "The Cockney Sportsman" and his "Modes of Riding."[32] Other than this, however, his activities were mainly restricted to directing and occasionally riding in the spectacles. Attendance at the Amphitheatre began falling off, and the season did not promise to be a good one.[33]

A number of older pieces were revived this year, including Ducrow and Leclercq's 1830 adaptation *The Elephant and the Fire Fiend*, whose current star was a "stupendous" elephant from Van Amburgh's menagerie.[34] The perennial *Mazeppa* achieved its four hundredth representation on 15 July with Mr. Shepherd in Cartlitch's old role. Gomersal was gone again from the Amphitheatre, although the "evergreen" Widdicombe remained as conspicuous as always. Among the new spectacles were a hippodramatic féerie entitled *The Enchanted Horse of the Fairy Lake, or The Bright Gold Rider of the Mystic Waters* (20 May) and *Joan d'Arc, or The Siege of Orleans* (4 November). Both pieces were produced by West, who out of necessity had begun to take an increasingly active role in the theatre's directing chores. In honor of a re-creation of a medieval tournament in which the British aristocracy had just disported themselves at Eglintoun Castle, beginning 2 September the Amphitheatre, in a variation of the 1837 production *The Lists of Ashby*, presented the tournament scene from *Ivanhoe*, proudly billed as "From the Pen of Sir WALTER SCOTT." The lists were again extended by connecting the stage to the circle, stuffed knights were violently knocked from their horses while real ones were unhorsed in a gentler manner, and Ducrow and West appeared respectively as the Knights of Sicily and Love.[35]

But the principal event of the 1839 season was the arrival from America (although he was by birth an Englishman) of a sensational new animal trainer. As an advance notice described this prodigy, he would "take the Untamed Lion by the Throat! do Battle with the Wild Hyena, and make the Fierce and Ravenous Tiger crouch at his feet like a beaten Hound." These stirring words, be it noted, did not originate with Ducrow or his publicist-secretary, but were drawn from the dialogue of the play in which the handsome six-foot-two John Carter and his animals made their debut on 14 October. *The Miracle, or Afghar the Lion King* offered more dramatic possibilities than had Van Amburgh's vehicle of the previous year. Besides participating in the obligatory struggle in a "den" containing a mixed group of lions, tigers, leopards, and panthers, in earlier scenes the trainer was rudely startled from his sleep by a leaping leopard, drove a lion harnessed to a car up a mimic mountain, and paraded an assortment of horses, ponies, zebras, ostriches, crocodiles, and other animals —"natural and unnatural"—up and down the stage.[36] There were also increased opportunities for disaster, especially since the other human actors in the drama were not—as were the spectators on the opposite side of the footlights—protected from the animals by a strong wire curtain. The actor Fred Belton, who later performed with the "Lion King" at Sheffield, tells of his horror upon learning he was required in one scene to take the paw of a leopard in his hand and in another to make certain a lion did not gobble up a young lady standing on its back. Another dangerous moment occurred when Carter drove the harnessed lion up the mountain. At Sheffield, Belton reports, Carter once struck the beast when it refused to go. The lion turned and seized him by the thigh, and for two weeks the trainer's life hung in the balance.[37] At Astley's, to which he returned during the 1840 season, the same scene led to another accident when Carter, the lion, and car all fell off the practicable mountain and hit the stage with a tremendous crash. The actors went flying in every direction, and the spectators evidently were anxious as well. On this occasion it was the lion who was severely injured.[38]

Thanks to Carter and his menagerie, when the Amphitheatre finally closed on 16 November Ducrow and West were reported to have had a tolerably good season after all. Meanwhile, during July and August, anticipating a type of exhibition Laurent Franconi and his son Victor were to place on a permanent footing at Paris in 1845, Andrew had got up a species of hippodrome entertainment presented twice-weekly during the early afternoon at Vauxhall Gardens. The part of the Gardens used for fireworks and Ducrow's earlier represen-

Fig. 73. The lion trainer John Carter riding in his perilous lion chariot.

tation of the Battle of Waterloo was laid out as a race course; spectators, for an extra consideration, were encouraged to attend on horseback and promenade around the course during intermissions; the military band of the Surrey Yeomanry was engaged; and Andrew himself, dressed in a glittering gold costume, presided over the festivities as "Grand Constable & Master of the Ceremonies." The "Curriculum, or Olympic Games," as this entertainment was called, sought to re-create the games of the ancients and other nations. Included in the program were a grand cavalcade by the entire company and stud of over fifty horses and ponies, a contest of female jockies (Mme. Ducrow among them), a scene of English racing between the juvenile members of the troop on twelve pygmy ponies, Greek chariot racing, and a race between six unmounted horses in the manner of those run on the Roman corso during Carnival Week. Especially acclaimed was the race between Hillier and Hicken as the "French Courier" and "English Post Boy." Bestriding two horses apiece and driving two others before them, they went tearing around the course for a total of three laps in their determination to win the imaginary prize. Although the performers in this novel entertainment were advertised as having just arrived from the Continent, the majority if not all of them were from the Amphitheatre, which now included a mixed troop of French, German, and Italian riders led by Baptiste Loisset. An exotic note was added by the chariots' being driven by some of "Africa's sons"—in this case not the result of makeup, but the genuine article.[39]

Apropos of black performers, a surprising number of them flourished during the early nineteenth century, and several rose to prominent artistic and managerial positions. Thanks to its interna-tional character and emphasis on physical skill, the circus—in Europe, at least—was always open to them. Reviewers and spectators seem to have considered their presence natural enough; nor did they take any undue interest in their personal lives. Ducrow's pupil Joseph Hillier, who joined Andrew around 1820 and remained with him to the end, was a Negro or mulatto. He eventually became riding master at Astley's and Ducrow's successor.[40] His wife, I assume, was white, since she was chosen to represent the Queen during the Coronation pageant of 1838. Widdicombe's own wife—mother of the well-known comic actor Henry—was described by Belton as a "celebrated black equestrienne," although I have found no confirmation for this lady's race either.[41] Indeed, in many instances it is only the occasional

FIG. 74. Joseph Hillier, Ducrow's black protégé, as "The Courier of St. Petersburg" at Vauxhall Gardens in 1842.

illustration or joke ("Hillier is looking as black as ever," Hillier "has ridden until he has become black in the face") that enables one to determine the race of these performers at this distant date, so little was thought of the matter then.[42] Andrew himself, beginning with his pantomime "La Mort d'Othello ou Le Maure vaincu," was fond of making up in blackface, and certainly no burlesque was intended in such serious scenes. He also created several acts for his infant pupils in which they appeared as Negroes and eventually numbered at least one bona fide black among his juvenile performers. This was the "Infant Pablo," who during the 1839 season performed on the tight-rope and as the title character in the acrobatic interlude *The Witch's Son, or The Minikin Sprite of China*.[43] His father, who also joined Ducrow for the first time in 1839, was the Negro equestrian, gymnast, and slackrope artist who went by the exotic name Pablo Fanque—variously styled the "Flying Indian" and "Jumping Jean of the Jungle"—but whose real name was William Darby. A native of Norwich, before coming to Ducrow he had been apprenticed to the circus manager William Batty and also had served time in Ryan's circus, where in 1836 he was billed as "the loftiest Jumper in England." At his benefit on 4 July of that year he promised that "though a dark subject himself, by borrowing the LIGHT of the remainder part of the Company, as the MOON from the SUN, he will shine forth like a STAR."[44] In 1841 Fanque founded a circus company of his own, and in later years occasionally returned to Astley's with his black mare Beda to demonstrate the difficult exercises of haute école.[45]

Andrew had hoped to remain in London over the winter of 1839–40 and had entered into negotiations with Madame Vestris for the leasing of her theatre, the Olympic. When these plans fell through,[46] he kept the company on at the Amphitheatre until mid-November, then took them east to Norwich again, where they opened at Ranelagh Gardens on 23 November.[47] In early December, temporarily leaving his equestrians behind, he proceeded to Edinburgh to fulfill a brief engagement at the Theatre Royal. There he appeared in *Raphael's Dream*, *The Dumb Man of Manchester*, and *The Idiot of Heidelburg Castle* and received the usual praise for his pantomimic skill, although the reviewer for the *Caledonian Mercury* (12 December) took strong exception to the last piece on account of its violating "the fundamental principles of poetic justice." Here, too, he interpreted the title role in the play *The Conscript*. His juvenile pupils had accompanied him and performed their gymnastic fairy tale *The Witch's Son*. The Infant Pablo danced the tightrope, and the petite Louisa did a cachucha. Together with some of the regular actors from the Theatre Royal, they also assisted Andrew in a series of living pictures—apparently an elaboration of those he and his pupils had exhibited in the same city two years previously—which went by the collective title *The Artist's Mirror*. These included "New Classical Studies from the Groups of Canova" and the "Brazen Timepiece, portraying Vernet's celebrated Pictures of the Life of Bonaparte."[48]

It was during this same engagement, which lasted from 9 to 20 December, that Andrew was honored at a banquet given by the Shakespeare Club of Scotland. The card inviting him to this affair, held on 18 December at the Waterloo Hotel, is preserved in the Ducrow Album, as is a letter from the official clothiers to the Club who offered to supply him with the Club uniform. The *Caledonian Mercury* for 23 December reported the event, and so did at least one of the other Edinburgh newspapers, whose lengthy account of the festivities was also saved by the delighted equestrian. In the early nineteenth century several British cities boasted Shakespeare Clubs, the general object of which was the bringing together of artists, literati, prominent actors and musicians, and others interested in the arts for the reading of papers and selections from Shakespeare and, of course, a generous amount of pure conviviality. The London Club —which numbered among its members such distinguished figures as Dickens, Thackeray, Sheridan Knowles, Clarkson Stanfield, Macready, and the composer Balfe—for obvious reasons has received most attention in the present day, although its term of existence was barely two years.[49] As one would expect from the presence of Macready and his friends in this illustrious body, Ducrow was not a member of the London society. Yet a humorous account in the *Age* for 12 August 1838 does suggest that, as a "non-Clubbite," he once attended a meeting at which Bunn and the theatrical managers William Davidge and Benjamin Webster were also present. The writer is so satirical that it seems likely he invented the whole story. At the Edinburgh banquet, however, Ducrow was referred to as having long been "honorarily associated" with the Scottish Club; and in response to a toast he expressed his happiness at "having been so long a member of the Club" and recalled that on a former occasion in the same room he had "had the honour of receiving the flattering encomiums of Sir Walter Scott, Mr. Sheridan Knowles, and a large assemblage of the *literati* of Scotland." The chairman of the evening, R. W. Jameson, lauded his "mastering the instincts of, and developing almost human intelligence, in the horse" and had even more flattering things to say about his tableaux and pantomimes. In his own person Ducrow had animated the masterpieces of Phidias, Raphael, and Canova; while through his extraordinary pantomimic efforts "he had at once acquired what the labour of a lifetime could scarcely be expected to bestow, the power of conveying his thoughts and feelings, mutely but most expressively, to universal man." Jameson concluded his eloquent testimonial with a tribute to the "personal virtues and gentlemanly demeanour of their celebrated guest," pointing out that they were as familiar to the members of the Club as Andrew's talents were to the admiring crowds who nightly applauded him.[50] High praise indeed for one who only a few years before had been characterized as "prince of mountebanks" and "director of living dog's meat"!

The euphoria at Edinburgh was destined soon to wear off as Andrew caught up with the troop at Liverpool in time for the traditional opening on Boxing Night. For the first time since giving up his lease there in 1832, he had arranged for a season at the Amphitheatre, whose character had steadily been sinking under a succession of less expert managers. The newspapers—even Ducrow's former antagonist the *Albion*—rejoiced in the restoring of the house to its former pristine glory, and the crowds were so great that the ferry boats plying the Mersey scheduled extra runs to accommodate spectators living on the other side of the water.[51] At the end of January, however, Andrew's luck ran out again. His little niece, fatigued after an evening performance, fell asleep before a kitchen fire in a house adjacent to the Amphitheatre. A spark or cinder ignited her clothing, and she was immediately enveloped in flames. As the child screamed for help, the wife of a company member rushed in and threw her down to extinguish the flames, but Louisa was so horribly burned that she could not be moved. Consequently, when the Liverpool engagement concluded on 14 March and the troop moved on to Birmingham, Andrew was forced to leave her behind. On 26 March, after lingering for two months in pain, "La Petite Ducrow" slipped away. It was only then that the majority of spectators learned the real name of the eleven-year-old prodigy whose performances had so delighted them was not Ducrow at all, but Louisa Margaret Foy Wood. Her parents, Ducrow's sister Louisa Wood and her husband, were still in the profession and had been at Liverpool when the accident occurred.[52]

The death of this little favorite had a crushing effect on Andrew, who fell ill himself and was reported to be suffering intensely while the company was at Birmingham.[53] His asthma was also giving him serious trouble, with the result that he was forced to abandon almost all his equestrian pantomimes and increasingly had to restrict his other activities. When the London Amphitheatre commenced operations on 20 April 1840, it was West and not Ducrow who directed the opening spectacle. As the new season wore on and his absences from the ring became more and more prolonged, business fell off and reviewers began commenting elegiacally on the great loss sustained by the lovers of horseflesh.[54] His concerned friends suggested various remedies and physicians, and in the fall of 1840 he wrote to thank one of them for recommending a new doctor whom he promised to consult on his next trip to London. "My health," he acknowledged laconically, "is such that requires other advice."[55] To make matters worse this season, his wife Louisa, pregnant again, was also forced to curtail her ring activities. And toward the end of May there was another bad scare when Ducrow's other favorite, Master Andrew Chaffé, fell off

FIG. 75. Ducrow at the height of his fame. Photograph of the destroyed oil portrait, once the property of "Lord" George Sanger, depicting the equestrian when he was around forty-five years old.

ACTORS BY DAYLIGHT,

AND PENCILINGS IN THE PIT.

REPUTATION IS AN IDLE AND MOST FALSE IMPOSITION, OFT GOT WITHOUT MERIT
AND LOST WITHOUT DESERVING.—*Shakspeare*.

No. 20.   SATURDAY, JULY 14, 1838.   **Price 1d**

FIG. 76. The cut of Ducrow that appears on the cover of *Actors by Daylight* for 14 July 1838, based on the destroyed oil portrait once the property of "Lord" George Sanger.

and became entangled in the trappings of a horse he was riding and was dragged some dozen yards round the ring. Several doctors in the house rushed to his assistance, but a few minutes later he was able to return and—in the best tradition of the circus—gallantly take a bow "as if nothing had happened."[56]

The other members of the troop carried on as best they could. The actor A. Y. Broadfoot, brother of William, was now with the company and was additionally listed as "Bill Inspector" (i.e., of tradesmen's accounts). In the ring Stickney, Hillier, and Hicken rode under the watchful eye of the impeccably turned out Widdicombe, while the juvenile members continued their romps. By now "Le Petit Ducrow" had graduated to a miniature version of Ducrow's famous "Vicissitudes of a Tar," and Miss Rosina Lee galloped round the ring as Psyche with two tiny wings attached to her shoulders.[57] The Fanques were no longer with the company, but Signor Cincelli (or Cinicelli, as the name was occasionally spelled) and his wife, who had been with Ducrow since the 1838 season, returned to the circle. It was generally an indifferent season onstage as well. The opening hippodrama, *The Merchant's Steed of Syracuse, or The Flight of Damon*, received generous praise from the critics,[58] as did *The Tower of London, or England in the Dark Ages*, based on Harrison Ainsworth's popular novel. The latter was got up by Ducrow for Whit Monday (8 June) using some costumes and materials he had bought at a recent auction of the trappings for the Eglintoun Tournament.[59] Terming the costumes, scenery, and appointments correct in every detail and the concluding tableau a "triumph of dramatic skill," the reviewer for the *Era* (28 June) lauded the manager for again proving himself "the master spirit of the stage in this department." Mercifully, there was no evaluation of the dialogue in the piece, which was the work of the "author" of *Raphael's Dream*, C. A. Somerset.[60] Aside from these, the season was made up of revivals of previous productions: *Mazeppa*, which on 11 September reached its 474th representation with Shepherd in the lead; *Lalla Rookh*, *The Wars of Wellington*, and *The Battle of Waterloo* (in which Ducrow's treasurer Sidney Foster was now the admired representative of Napoleon); *The Siege of Troy*, with all its absurdities—plus the Rape of the Sabines and some cannonading—intact; and Bunn's big hit of the 1834–35 Drury Lane season, *King Arthur and the Knights of the Round Table*. Even Van Amburgh's "sagacious" elephant and Carter returned to the Amphitheatre, the latter to perform in a new drama entitled *The*

Lion of the Desert.[61] The two trainers had been battling it out in Paris over the previous winter and now continued their rivalry in London as Van Amburgh took up quarters at the nearby Surrey Theatre.[62] By July the "Lion King" was nightly ascending in a balloon accompanied by one of his leopards—a feat which, the reviewer for the *Theatrical Journal* (1 August 1840) declared with admirable understatement, created "emotions of mingled astonishment and fear" in the spectators below. Besides the *contretemps* with the lion-drawn chariot, Carter sustained at least two attacks by his animals this season, which led to his absence from the house at different periods.[63] Meanwhile, one spectator, no doubt echoing the sentiments of a sizable number of Ducrow's patrons, addressed a poetic missive to the manager calling for a return to the traditional entertainments. Fed up with seeing

> . . . a Leopard acting the Buffoon,
> Ascending in a puppet show Balloon,

the writer urged him to

> Let Lions, & Leopards to the Desert go,
> Give us thy riders, & thy stud, Ducrow!
> Nor let a scene, once famed for graceful Men,
> Be longer turned into a Lion's Den![64]

The one bright note in this lackluster season was a private performance before Victoria and Albert on the afternoon of 20 May. It was the first and only time during his management that a reigning British monarch honored the Amphitheatre with a visit, and Andrew naturally made the most of it. Both he and West were on hand in full dress to receive the royal couple and their suite at the portico and conduct them to a box specially fitted up for the occasion. The band meanwhile struck up the national anthem, and in the ring scenes that followed, Ducrow, his wife, and "Le Petit Ducrow" all participated.[65] For some time afterward the theatre's announcements were headed "Under the Special Patronage of her Most Gracious Majesty the QUEEN"; while the *Theatrical Journal* (30 May)—which only a few weeks earlier had been lamenting the fact that one of the Amphitheatre's pretty actresses, Miss Daly, was worthy of a position at a better house—now changed its tune and informed its readers that Astley's was "attended by the first classes of society . . . there being a very talented company for the performances of spectacles on a very superior scale to those got up at other houses." The entertainments, the writer concluded, evidently carried away by the subject, were "very intellectual." The pride Ducrow and West understandably felt over this momentous event was ludicrously communicated by their decision to preserve the royal box, conspicuously situated in the center of the dress tier, as a kind of permanent shrine reserved for the "nobility" alone. In lieu of the distinguished couple themselves, gilt effigies of the Queen and Prince Consort were set up to beam down upon the actors and dazzled spectators. A number of reviewers protested the "childishness" of this Tussaud-like display, which remained on exhibit until the theatre burned the following year.[66]

On 17 October the company finished at the Amphitheatre and again rode off to the provinces. Leicester, Manchester, Derby, Nottingham, Edinburgh, and Glasgow were all visited during the winter tour; both Carter and Van Amburgh teamed up with Ducrow at various times during this restless progress. Having given birth to a daughter named Louisa sometime around the close of the London season,[67] Ducrow's wife was back with the troop by the time they reached Edinburgh, where on 21 December she and Andrew appeared on their beautifully managed horses at Ducrow's Amphitheatre of Arts.[68] Aside from an occasional pageant, cavalcade, or equestrian ballet, however, the manager continued to absent himself from the ring—with a noticeable effect on the nightly attendance and receipts. With the coming of winter Andrew's asthma grew worse, and he experienced several severe attacks.[69] "We hardly ever even see him," lamented the critic for the Edinburgh *Opera-Glass* (15 January 1841). There was some improvement by the time the company reached Glasgow, where Alexander, the manager of the Theatre Royal, had engaged them for a brief season commencing 8 February. For his benefit night on 22 February Andrew hazarded his celebrated role in *The Dumb Man of Manchester* and, despite some telltale signs of the state of his health, acted "with all his wonted fire."[70] He was loudly applauded by the Glasgow citizens, although the usual complaints were voiced concerning Alexander's turning the Royal into a stable for such other productions as *Mazeppa* and *The Siege of Jerusalem.*[71]

By the time Astley's reopened on Easter Monday, 12 April 1841, Ducrow's asthma had subsided to the point where he could safely promise his appearances would be more regular than during the previous year. But the "Kean of the Circle" was no longer capable of performing his pantomimes on horseback and instead had to content himself with less demanding roles, such as those of Charles II in a revival of "The Royal Cotillon of Days Gone By" and the Grand Master of the Horse opposite his wife in the pageant "Catherine of Russia," or riding in stately processions and exhibiting the tricks of his pet palfrey Beauty, "the Horse of the LADY'S DRAWING ROOM."[72] Hillier, Hicken, and Stickney were left to carry the torch, aided during the present season by Mme. Seraphine Bassin from the Cirque Olympique and, of course, the infant pupils. Among the last, Miss Lee, it seems, had done some developing, for one critic could not resist remarking on her well-formed leg ("and she knows it," he piquantly added).[73] "Le Petit Ducrow" continued to prove himself a worthy disciple. Together with Hicken and several other members of the juvenile corps, he performed in a revival of Ducrow's lyric equestrian scene "The Evening Star," which now went by the title "The Golden Axe, or The Enchanted Woodman."[74]

Onstage the season commenced with a tolerable success, T. Wilks' *The Conqueror's Steed, or The Prophet of the Caucasus*. Reviewers waxed ecstatic over its picturesque costumes and groupings, its gorgeous processions and "spirit-stirring scenes by flood and field," and at least one of them—so strong was force of habit—automatically credited Ducrow with its admirable getting up.[75] But in fact it was West who again took charge of the opening spectacle, and who also arranged and produced the second new hippodrama of the season, *The Wars of Oliver Cromwell, or The Royal Oak*, for the Whitsun festivities on 31 May. The latter piece, which began with the Battle of Worcester and carried spectators through a series of episodes leading up to the restoration of Charles and his procession through the streets of London, was followed by a revival of Ducrow's "Correo, or Spanish Bull Fight" in which—audiences were again assured—the bull was personated by one of Ducrow's horses wearing an elastic skin.[76] Unfortunately, neither *The Conqueror's Steed* nor the best efforts of Ducrow's disciples in the ring could satisfy spectators indefinitely, and when only a few weeks into the season West revived *The Merchant's Steed of Syracuse* of the previous year, a number of critics began complaining about worn-out dramas and stale scenes in the circle and speculating on how long it would be before *Mazeppa* was brought back. "Mr. Ducrow is an able manager," wrote one of them, "but he appears to be tired of holding the reins, and having already galloped up the road to Fame, he is content to put up while his coachman and guard have omitted to remove the drag which clogs the vehicle from going rapidly down hill."[77]

Downhill it did go in the early hours of 8 June. For the third time in its history Astley's caught fire and burned to the ground, leaving only a few blackened walls behind. In retrospect, what seemed a premonition of the dread event had occurred in early March, when a gas line running beneath the pit had sprung a leak and a fire had started in some overhead beams. At that time a German groom named York had distinguished himself by calling some nearby workmen to his aid and putting out the flames before the arrival of the fire brigade.[78] He again proved himself a hero on the present occasion, but without such happy results for the Amphitheatre. From a variety of eyewitness reports and depositions that appeared in the newspapers, it seems clear the second fire began under the stage, although whether from gas or some sparks from the pyrotechnics in the previous evening's representation of *The Wars of Cromwell* was never established with certainty. A constable making his rounds at half past four had first smelled and then spotted smoke issuing from the back of the theatre and, after giving the alarm, had rushed to the stage door to knock up the watchman. In the inquest that followed there were some sharp questions put to the latter individual, who eventually was charged with neglect of duty. He swore, however, that he had noticed nothing suspicious upon making his last round at 3:30 A.M. and that he could have kept the fire under control if he had had another to help him. Both he and the constable had run to the stage, which they found completely enveloped in smoke. The watchman had seized a fire hose and plunged ahead, but the constable, instead of manning the pump, had gone back to get assistance.[79] By then it was probably too late anyway. Within eight minutes of the initial alarm flames were shooting through the Amphitheatre's windows, lighting the London sky for miles around. As cries of "fire" rang out and police and fire brigades dashed to the scene, the neighborhood's terrified inhabitants were additionally startled by the fierce clatter of hoofs. York and the other grooms had rushed to the stables and were releasing Ducrow's stud of over fifty horses, ponies, and zebras into the streets. Their task was made difficult by the fact that the stables on the south side of the theatre could only be reached by crossing the arena and by the animals automatically wanting to turn into the ring. Four times the intrepid York himself chanced this awful journey, while flames raged and burning beams fell about him, leading out one of Ducrow's prize horses each trip. By the fourth crossing the heat was so intense that the horse he was leading collapsed and died in the ring, and attempts to rescue the remaining animals had to be abandoned. The toll was nevertheless surprisingly low: only two horses and a jackass named Moke. Ducrow's employees had served him well.

The loss in human terms, however, was much greater. As the flames continued their inexorable advance, the inhabitants of the over forty houses and shops abutting Astley's began scrambling to save themselves and their possessions. Ducrow himself, sleeping in Amphitheatre House, his residence above the pit and box entrances, was aroused by Louisa, who noticed their bedroom filling with smoke. He immediately ran to a back window opening onto the Amphitheatre and, sizing up the situation in an instant, snatched up one of the children and led the rest of his family, his apprentices and servants, down a staircase leading to a door opening onto Westminster Bridge Road. By a curious coincidence, only a few hours earlier on the evening of 7 June the first British census to list names had been taken, and we therefore have a fairly good idea of those accompanying him.[80] Besides his wife and children Peter and Louisa, they included Ducrow's apprentices Andrew Chaffé, Caroline Avery, and Susan Beechdale, together with at least three servants and a cook. Others may have been present, too, since Ducrow was later reported as saying eleven "females" had been under his roof at the time of the fire. When Andrew and this cortege arrived at the door, however, they found it so securely fastened that they could not open it. Their only hope was to retrace their steps to the smoke-filled living quarters above and descend by an intricate staircase leading to a courtyard. They were nearly suffocated by fumes and hot clouds of dust, but finally made it into Stangate Street, where they took refuge in Hillier's house. The nightclothes they wore were all they had managed to bring with them. "Let me only see my horses out," Ducrow was heard to say upon arriving with his family, "and I shall be satisfied. My private loss I am able to bear, but for God's sake preserve everybody about me."

He did not notice that one of his servants, Elizabeth Britton, had slipped back into the building to retrieve her bank book or some other trifle. Her body, charred almost beyond recognition, was later discovered in a crouching position behind one of the locked theatre entrances. Meanwhile, the police and firemen had forced their way into the Amphitheatre, but had quickly given up any idea of saving

FIG. 77. "The Destruction of Astley's Theatre" in 1841, drawn "on the spot" by J. W. Gunthorp.

it when they saw that the whole of the interior—stage, pit, boxes, and galleries—was a solid mass of flames (fig. 77). They had barely retreated and taken up positions on the roofs of neighboring buildings when an ominous grumbling noise was heard and the theatre's walls began giving way. A moment later the roof fell in with a tremendous crash, sending a huge fiery cloud into the air. Philip Astley's crazy structure of ship masts and spars, canvas, rope and tenpenny nails had been reduced to rubble within forty-five minutes.

The newspapers over the next several days were full of reports detailing the losses sustained by Ducrow and West, their employees and neighbors. The buildings surrounding the Amphitheatre were extensively damaged, and Ducrow's own residence, the property of West, was completely destroyed. The thin partition separating it from the theatre had been barely adequate to allow Andrew enough time to lead his family to safety, and the flames, upon bursting through, had consumed the large collection of objets d'art and presents he had accumulated over the years.[81] West, at least, had possessed sufficient foresight to insure his property, which also included the theatre's machinery and scenery; and John Chevalier Cobbold of Ipswich, the owner of the theatre, was insured to the amount of £7,500. But Andrew himself was totally uninsured and was reported to have lost at least £10,000 by the fire. His costumes alone were valued at several thousand pounds. Among the other losses were all of the instruments belonging to the members of the orchestra and a beautiful chandelier, valued at £500, which the Duke of York had presented to Philip Astley. Sidney Foster, whose treasury office in Stangate Street was still standing, had somehow managed to enter the theatre and save the previous evening's receipts; but West's writing desk, containing some £1,000 in bank notes, had gone up in flames.

The dispossessed managers bore their losses bravely enough. On 10 June Ducrow was sufficiently recovered to visit the ruins and give his version of the fire to a reporter from the *Times* who met him there. He appeared deeply moved by the death of his servant, who had been with him many years, but was already involved in plans for the future. A few days later he and West authorized Foster to pay half-salaries to all the actors and full salaries to the stage carpenters, grooms, and other members of the company for the remainder of what would have been the regular season—a welcome relief to the nearly 250 persons who so unexpectedly had been thrown out of work. Almost immediately, too, plans were laid to erect a temporary amphitheatre elsewhere in the city and to rebuild Astley's itself, which was to rise, phoenix-like from its ashes, in time for the traditional opening on the next Easter Monday.[82] While these ambitious plans were being formed, there was a gratifying outpouring of sympathy for the performers and managers. A public subscription, headed by the Queen Dowager and the Duke of Northumberland, was soon got up for the relief of the artists, and a committee was formed to sit daily at Foster's office to receive and disburse the funds. From a published circular reporting the progress of the subscription a few days later, it is obvious John Chevalier Cobbold was holding his own following the loss of his theatre, for he was announced as having made two donations of £50 each. Ducrow's colleagues in the profession also contributed—even Macready sent in 10 guineas.[83] As was traditional on such occasions, the managers and performers at other theatres tendered their services for benefit performances. So many offered, in fact, that Andrew was forced to turn some of them down.[84] Bunn, predictably, was first on the scene, offering Drury Lane for the night of 22 June. The bill for this star-studded evening included Mme. Vestris and her husband Charles Mathews, who appeared in *The Loan of a Lover* and *Two O'Clock in the Morning*; the French dancer and mime artist Mlle. Céleste; Giulia Grisi, the great opera singer; and the comic actors Robert Keeley and Benjamin Webster. The evening concluded with a performance of *Charlemagne*, in which Ducrow and "Le Petit Ducrow" re-created their roles of Hamet and Sadi and performed their *pas de trois* with Marengo. The receipts amounted to nearly £800.[85] Sadler's Wells gave a benefit for the sufferers by the fire on 26 June.[86] The Strand Theatre and the Eagle Tavern got up benefits as well. The magician James Anderson, the "Wizard of the North," donated the receipts from his performance at the Adelphi Theatre on 14 June; Macready was said to be thinking about lending his aid to a similar plan.[87]

By early July the riders and horses were back in action, divorced from their half-pay dramatic brethren, some of whom had gone off on their own for a two-month season of horseless pieces at the Olympic Theatre.[88] For three weeks the stud appeared on alternate nights at Sadler's Wells Theatre, where Hillier and "Le Petit Ducrow" acted the leads in a hippodrama entitled *The Horse of the Pyrenees*.[89] Meanwhile, Andrew had also entered into a new engagement with his excellent friend Bunn, who recently had become one of the lessees of Vauxhall Gardens. The Rotunda there was converted into a "spacious amphitheatre" with a ring in its center, and the company, when not performing in Islington, exhibited their entrées, cavalcade of Amazons, and scenes in the circle up until the second week in August.[90] The prancing and leaping horses, wrote the reviewer for the *Theatrical Journal* (10 July 1841), actually seemed to enjoy the applause that for the past few weeks had been denied them. Both these engagements were only stopgaps, however, while Andrew was busy making preparations to place his establishment on a more permanent footing. On 24 July, in a letter to the *Times* from his new residence at 19 Albany Place in York Road, he announced what those plans were. He had arranged with William Davidge and Willis Jones to take his troop to their theatre, the Surrey (*olim* the Royal Circus), which was to be restored to its original form. In subsequent announcements the details of this restoration were more precisely described. Following a final performance by the theatre's regular company on Friday, 6 August, a gang of machinists and carpenters immediately set to work, taking up the pit floor and reconstructing what was termed in the bills the largest circle in the world. Notwithstanding this sizable addition, the pit was somehow enlarged to accommodate an additional 350 persons. By an ingenious mechanism the front of the stage, together with the footlights and orchestra pit, could now advance and recede to cover or uncover a portion of the ring, depending on whether a stage spectacle or the scenes in the circle were being given at the moment. All of this work was achieved in less than three days' time for the opening on 9 August.[91]

In his letter to the *Times* Andrew had actually announced that his season at the Surrey would commence on 2 August. There was, however, some delay; and on the day in question his family and friends were unexpectedly thrown into confusion by a new and even more terrifying catastrophe than the recent one at Astley's. The troubled equestrian—unable to bear up any longer—had suddenly gone mad and attempted to kill himself. As reports of Ducrow's illness appeared over the next several months, there was much speculation on the cause of his breakdown. A number of persons suggested, somewhat ungenerously, that his recent losses at the Amphitheatre were at the root of it. But as a writer for the *Age* (30 January 1842) astutely observed, it was more likely the steady accumulation of disasters—the death of his beloved first wife Margaret in 1837, the accident to his arm that had so severely curtailed his professional activities, the tragic death by burning of his niece, "La Petite Ducrow," and the death, again by fire, of his faithful servant—besides financial reverses that had finally brought him to the breaking point. "Mr. Ducrow's health," the writer added, was "at all times most powerfully operated upon by his mind," and signs of his present illness had been evident for nearly twelve months before the burning of Astley's.

Whatever the cause, there was no mistaking the symptoms. Upon returning to his home in York Road from his daily ride, Ducrow had appeared extremely agitated, although no particular notice was taken of it. A short time later, however, he was discovered preparing to fling himself from an upstairs window and was only prevented by the timely intervention of some of his family. They did their best to calm him, and thought they had succeeded, when he suddenly broke from them and ran outside to the swimming baths on the opposite side of the road. There he demanded to be given a lodging, since his own, he insisted, was on fire. It was only with the assistance of several neighbors that the family finally succeeded in dragging him back to the house, where a physician advised placing him under immediate restraint.[92] A "residence" (i.e., madhouse) at Clapham Common was proposed, but Andrew himself put up such a struggle that a compromise was finally reached and he was taken instead to a private cottage in suburban Norwood. There he was constantly watched over by an attendant and received daily visits from his physician, Dr. Sutherland, whose course of treatment seems to have been both humane and effective. Within a few weeks he was reported as recovering (there was, however, a relapse around the beginning of September) and as receiving frequent visits from his wife and friends.

Meanwhile, Louisa and the troop had opened at the Surrey with the old chestnut *Mazeppa*, splendidly got up and featuring a new lead actor, N. T. Hicks, whose cast-iron lungs and "energy of voice and action" brought back fond memories of Cartlitch.[93] Hillier, Hicken, Stickney, and "Le Petit Ducrow" carried on with Ducrow's famed scenes in the circle, and Madame Ducrow, despite her pressing troubles, bravely appeared at the head of a cavalcade of Amazons and warriors. She later took to presenting Ducrow's trick steeds Beauty, Pegasus, and Bucephalus as well. A new hippodrama entitled *The Battle of Blenheim, or The Horse of the Disinherited Son*, with Hicks again in the lead, eventually appeared in the bills. Ducrow's brother-in-law W. D. Broadfoot climbed back into the saddle to impersonate the notorious highwayman Turpin; and *Charlemagne*, with Hillier now in Andrew's role of Hamet, was also revived. The performances by the company extended to mid-November, and from early September on—or so the bills claimed—were "under the immediate Superintendence of Mr. DUCROW."[94]

In fact, Ducrow was hardly in condition to superintend anything during the first weeks of September, although a month later he had improved to the point where he could contemplate a visit to London and again busy himself with the affairs of his company. On 10 October, in a shaky but nonetheless legible hand, he wrote to Broadfoot, acknowledging some letters he had received and informing him that "this is my Birth Day, and thank god my health is much better." In an apparent reference to the course of treatment prescribed by Sutherland, he added that he had just returned from his shower bath. His wife had informed him the members of his establishment were anxious to learn what arrangements he had made for the winter, and he would be better able to decide on these after traveling to London on Sunday or Monday and seeing whether the management of the Surrey agreed to his terms for another engagement.[95] By November he was back at his London residence and for a time, at least, appeared intent on starting up at Astley's again. The previous month Cobbold and Hannah Waldo Astley had succeeded in getting the theatre's annual license renewed, arguing that while it was true no such theatre as Astley's existed at the moment, a new building would be up in time for Easter Monday (it was, but for the 1843, not the 1842, season).[96] Ducrow was said to be involved in this scheme, but a few weeks later announced his retirement from the establishment in favor of William Batty, who had just brought his company to town and opened at the converted National Baths in Westminster Road.[97]

Under Broadfoot's leadership the troop in the meantime had again taken to the road. Andrew had been unable to come to terms with the Surrey managers (Batty was to replace him there too in the coming season), and in a note appended to a letter he addressed to his brother-in-law on 22 November, Louisa complained that there was also "a bother about the things at Astley's."[98] By now the handwriting was on the wall. When the troop opened at Leicester on 22 November, a melancholy note crept into the bills with the announcement that they were "on their last provincial tour."[99] Andrew himself, his mental powers restored, continued to direct the company's activities from London. His leisure moments were spent visiting friends and attending the theatre, as on 27 December when he was observed with his wife in a box at Covent Garden, "apparently in the enjoyment of excellent health and spirits."[100] According to one account, he even decided to rejoin the troop at Liverpool, where they had opened at the Amphitheatre over the Christmas holidays, to perform his celebrated role in *The Dumb Man of Manchester.*[101] He was persuaded to abandon this idea and agreed to ride in a grand Russian entrée instead, and had even packed his costumes for the journey, intending to make his debut on 7 February, when the final blow fell. On Saturday, 22 January, he was stricken with paralysis and lost his speech and the use of one of his sides. A second stroke occurred on the following Tuesday. Two days later, at half past eight on the evening of the 27th, in the forty-eighth year of his life, the great equestrian breathed his last.[102]

FIG. 78. "Ducrow & his Horse Pegasus."

Poor Ducrow—thy Race is o'er,
Thy passing knell has struck;
From memory's page, alas, no more
Thy virtues can we pluck.

—from a manuscript monody
in the Ducrow Album

9   *Aftermath*

THE FUNERAL WAS NOT UNWORTHY of the former equestrian director
and principal lessee of Astley's. In fact, the bill for this curious
mixture of the lugubrious and the ludicrous might have been drawn
up by Ducrow himself. His will, dated the previous 10 November,
had left specific instructions for its staging, preceded by the morbid
injunction (was Andrew recalling the early interest of the Edinburgh
anatomy students, or the curiosity of the medical profession over the
brain of his friend Edmund Kean?) that his body not upon any account
be subjected to postmortem examination. After lying in state for "an
entire week at the least," it was to be encased in three coffins, the
middle one of carefully soldered lead, and transported to the mausoleum at Kensal Green in a "fitting and proper manner." The retinue
was to include not only all the members of Andrew's family and
household, but also his former employees and grooms at Astley's,
together with his favorite horse and trained steeds, suitably adorned
with crape and funeral feathers. The munificent sum of 500 pounds
was set aside for this spectacle.[1]

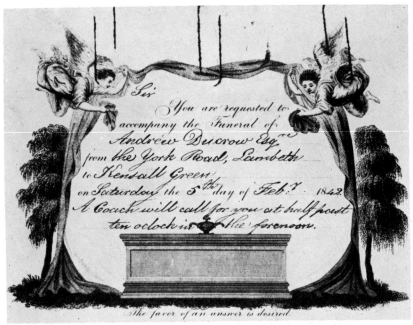

Sir

You are requested to accompany the Funeral of Andrew Ducrow Esq from the York Road, Lambeth to Kensall Green on Saturday the 5th day of Feby 1842. A Coach will call for you at half past ten oclock in the forenoon.

The favor of an answer is desired

FIG. 79. Invitation to Ducrow's funeral.

Accordingly, at half past noon on 5 February 1842, Andrew Ducrow set out on his final journey. For several hours previous the streets in the vicinity of his residence in York Road had been crowded with eager spectators, while six mutes stood conspicuously before the house door. Some among this vast throng were accommodated in temporary booths erected for the occasion; others occupied windows or jammed into coaches and stood on carts to obtain a better view. Nor did the great press of people diminish much along the long route to Kensal Green, with traffic consequently brought to a halt in all the adjacent streets and thoroughfares through which the procession passed. The *Age*, in its awed description of the event, characterized it as "an occurrence that may not take place again in the next half century."[2] Preceded by a vanguard of policemen to clear the way, the procession was led by the undertaker on horseback, followed by mounted porters and pages on foot carrying plumes of sable ostrich feathers. Then came three of Ducrow's highly trained steeds—Vienna, Pegasus, and Beauty—each led by two grooms and costumed in velvet, feathers, and crape headdresses. Beauty, incidentally, was said to be the last horse Ducrow rode in the ring. But the "favorite horse" mentioned in the will was lamentably absent: John Lump, whose sturdy back had supported his master's dazzling impersonations for the past seventeen years, had died of old age a few days before the funeral. The hearse, drawn by six horses with postilions and accompanied by pages, came next. The outer coffin was of oak, covered with purple velvet and studded with silver gilt nails, and bearing an allegorical plate showing Genius weeping over the ashes of her favorite son. This in turn was followed by eleven mourning coaches, also accompanied by pages, bearing Ducrow's family, close friends, and colleagues. Additional mourners on horseback and in private carriages brought up the rear.

A note of levity was inadvertently injected into these solemn proceedings at the opposite end of Westminster Bridge, where the Speaker and Members of Parliament were just getting into their carriages to travel to Buckingham Palace with the Address. These fell in immediately behind the funeral train, leading some spectators to believe the Speaker's ornate state carriage was one of the vehicles from Ducrow's establishment. Shortly after one o'clock the procession turned up Regent Street, where the pickpockets were out in full force to take advantage of the crowd assembled there.[3] The number of mourners swelled along the route as actors and others on horseback joined the procession. One person who was not present, however— although he had been invited by Ducrow's executors and was reported to have attended by at least one newspaper—was the self-righteous William Charles Macready, as unforgiving toward Ducrow and his friends now as he had been while the equestrian was alive. In his diary entry for 6 February, the tragedian wrote that he "rejoiced in my absence from Mr. Ducrow's funeral, which was attended by a fearful set—Messrs. Bunn, etc. When will my funeral come?" he piously mused. "Let it be as simple as the return of dust to dust should be, and somewhere where those that love me may come to think of me."[4] At the cemetery Louisa Ducrow, supported by Ducrow's old friend Alfred Bunn and William D. Broadfoot, entered the mausoleum to spend a few final moments with her husband and to strew his casket with immortelles. Their second son, Andrew Jr., would be born the following June. Then the iron door clanged shut and Ducrow's last great spectacle was over.

It soon became evident to all that Ducrow—despite his heavy losses the previous June—had died anything but poor. His will, running to fourteen sheets and proved on 17 February, named Louisa Ducrow, Oscar Byrne, the Lambeth boat-builder George Searle, and James Anderton of the West of England Fire Office as executors. Besides the 500 pounds for the funeral and money designated for the improvement and upkeep of the mausoleum, it provided 200 pounds for Louisa's immediate expenses; 200 pounds each for Andrew's sisters Margaret Ducrow and Mrs. Louisa Wood; and 150 pounds for his third surviving sister, Emily, whose husband Broadfoot received the same amount. Andrew Byrne, son of Oscar, and Tissey [*sic*] Avery—the latter apparently of age—received 200 and 25 pounds respectively. One hundred pounds was left in trust for Ducrow's apprentice Susan Beechdale (the "Mlle. Susanne" in the Astley's bills) until she should reach the age of twenty-one; while 200 pounds was to be similarly invested for "Le Petit Ducrow," who is nowhere in the will referred to as Andrew's adopted son, but simply as "my Apprentice Andrew Chaffé." Byrne, Searle, and Anderton were each left 100 pounds for their services as executors. Joseph Hillier received the handsome sum of 300 pounds. The residue of Andrew's property, including monies in the public stocks and government securities, was left in trust for his wife and children. Half of this was bequeathed to Louisa, together with Ducrow's personal effects. The remainder was to be equally apportioned to Peter Andrew John and Louisa and to any other children who might follow. As remarked in a number of newspaper accounts, it was curious that Ducrow, in this long and carefully prepared document so tedious in its endless repetitions and legal jargon, should have forgotten to mention his aged mother, whom he had generously provided for up to the time of his death. Louisa, however, immediately agreed to continue her allowance. She could well afford to do so, since the fortune Andrew left was eventually determined to amount to no less than 47,560 pounds in securities alone. Together with the value of his stud, paraphernalia, furniture, articles of vertu, etc., and the bequests noted above, the grand total came to nearly 60,000 pounds.[5] Whatever else one might say of him, Ducrow was hardly improvident.

Meanwhile, the company had continued to perform at the Liverpool Amphitheatre, where "Le Petit Ducrow" took his benefit on 31 January and Madame Ducrow received a final benefit of her own on 21 February.[6] It would be a mistake to assume, however, as several writers have, that Louisa Ducrow continued in the ring following her husband's death. She did not personally perform during the Liverpool engagement, and in fact now renounced the circus forever, shortly to enter upon an entirely different kind of life. The management of the troop now devolved upon Hillier, who eventually bought the stud for himself,[7] although Ducrow's name continued to figure prominently in the announcements and the personnel remained much the same as before. Over the Easter holidays the company performed at Worcester, then returned to London to open on Whit Monday, 16 May, at Sadler's Wells Theatre, whose dramatic company joined with the equestrians in the production of a new hippodrama by William T. Moncrieff, *Harry of England, or The Trumpeter's Horse and the Conquest of Harfleur*. Following the spectacle the stage floor was raised mechanically to reveal a ring beneath for "Ducrow's Unequalled Productions and Historical Scenes in the Circle." Andrew Chaffé, by now also billed as "The Living Ducrow," performed the equestrian scene "The African Springers" with the Masters C. and H. Adams and later appeared as "The Drunken Drummer of 1747," and Hillier interpreted "The Courier of St. Petersburg." Other ring artists included Hicken, the Venetian rider Signor Allard, Stickney, and Widdicombe, while the distaff side was composed of Mesdames Hillier, Adams, Stickney, and Susanne.[8] In June *The Battle of Waterloo* was revived with Gomersal returning to re-create his famous role of Napoleon; *Mazeppa*, with Broadfoot in the title part, achieved its 800th representation on 18 July; *Timour the Tartar*, *The Conqueror's Steed*, *St. George and the Dragon* (again with Broadfoot in the title role), and *Lalla Rookh* were also produced anew. The scenes in the circle were in time augmented with Hillier as the muleteer in Ducrow's "Spanish Bull Fight," Mlle. Susanne as "The Maid of Corfu," Stickney as "The Troubadour of Naples," and Chaffé as "The Little Briton," "The Irish Boy, or Hibernia's Son," and "The Lilliputian Fox Hunter." Beginning 22 August, in a melodramatic afterpiece entitled *The Dumb Norwegian and His Pony, Iceland*, "Le Petit Ducrow" also undertook the role of Carl, the mute Norwegian boy of the title— thereby following his namesake in another area. On 15 August Hillier took his benefit, Broadfoot took his on the 22nd, and the engagement came to a close on 27 August.[9] But not, it would seem, with the success which the theatre's lessee, Robert W. Honner, had hoped for. The season of equestrian pieces proved so unprofitable, in fact, that he was forced to secede from the management in early August, an event that led one critic predictably to declare that "it must, indeed, be vastly gratifying to all well wishes [*sic*] to the stage, to perceive animal spectacles thus declining with the public."[10]

During July and August Hillier also arranged to take the troop to Vauxhall Gardens, then as during the previous summer under the management of Alfred Bunn. Here, in the ring set up in the Rotunda, the company confined themselves to gymnastic and equestrian exhibitions.[11] An amusing illustrated article published in the *Squib* at this time depicts a dark-complexioned Hillier riding four horses as "The Courier of St. Petersburg" (fig. 74) and describes "the little wonder, Andrew Ducrow, who dances a hornpipe on the back of a horse at full speed, with all the saucy audacity of a reckless Jack Tar, and hops backwards and forwards over his whip, and balances himself upon one leg, as if he could dispense with the other without incurring any serious inconvenience; ever and anon laying the silk across the shoulders of his galloping ball-room, and shouting at the top of his small voice, to the delight and admiration of all beholders."[12] Widdicombe, as riding master, came in for his share of attention, with the expected jokes about his "ever-greenness." At the end of August the company left London and performed for a week at the Theatre, Cambridge. On 13 September they opened in Norwich, whose Theatre Royal, rechristened the "Grand Olympic Amphitheatre of Arts," had undergone a transformation similar to that of Sadler's Wells.[13] The engagement here lasted through 8 October and appears to have been successful. Both Hillier and "Le Petit Ducrow" received

FIG. 80. Widdicombe at Vauxhall Gardens in 1842.

abundant notices in the press, and the company in general was praised for its skill, talent, and daring and for presenting "the most gorgeous spectacles with a rapidity, superiority, and grandeur, that is perfectly imposing."[14] While it was agreed Ducrow's memory was being faithfully preserved by his disciples, the master's absence was regretted by many. The horses and the pageantry, one critic remarked, "tend, in mournful association with the past, to remind us of that unwearied spirit in enterprising exertion, of that refined taste in conception and consummate tact in arrangement, by which this metropolitan establishment was raised to the highest attainable perfection, under the master-mind, and eagle-eye, and vigorous activity of HIM who is now, alas! no more."[15]

There is no need to chronicle the further travels of the company in detail. Following Norwich they appeared in a succession of provincial towns and cities—including Lynn, Hull, and Sheffield—and eventually arrived in Liverpool to play for two nights at the Royal Amphitheatre before going on to Dublin, where they opened at the Theatre Royal on 18 February 1843 and remained until 20 March. By this time a number of changes had taken place in the company's roster. The equestrian Mosely took over Ducrow's scenes of "The Vicissitudes of a Tar," "The Wild Indian Hunter," and, in conjunction with a Mrs. Fuller, "The Tyrolean Shepherd and Swiss Milk Maid," while Harcourt Bland replaced Broadfoot in *Mazeppa*.[16] Joseph Plège returned to the company with his sons. The breakup of the troop was imminent, especially since William Batty, the circus manager who had moved into London at the time of the burning of Astley's, was about to open the fourth and final building of that name. There was no chance Ducrow's establishment would ever return intact to its old home, although many of its members—Hicken, Widdicombe, Stickney, even the resurrected Gomersal—were shortly to enter Batty's employ. By the time of the Dublin season William D. Broadfoot had already deserted Hillier to act and assist in the production of *The Affghanistan War*, the spectacle with which the new Astley's was to open on Easter Monday, 17 April.[17]

At the conclusion of the Dublin engagement—whose results were reported to have been unsatisfactory[18]—the troop returned to the Liverpool Amphitheatre. The bills were still headed with Ducrow's name, as were the scenes in the circle, even though the company, as the announcements also proclaimed, was under Hillier's sole management. And it was Hillier who in April was prosecuted by the proprietors of the Liverpool Theatre Royal, who objected that one of his productions, *The Horse of the Rialto*, was a "play and entertainment of the stage" and therefore in violation of the law since it had been given without the permission of the Lord Chamberlain, the licensing authority for all such entertainments. The real issue, of course, was not Hillier's failure to obtain a license, but his drawing off patrons from the Theatre Royal. The result of this action was that the manager was convicted and fined the nominal sum of twenty shillings, while the play itself was withdrawn.[19] However, the precarious position of the Theatre Royal was hardly improved by this decision, and the following month, after receipts had fallen to the level where they were barely sufficient to cover the expense of lighting, the theatre was forced to close its doors. Hillier then magnanimously stepped forward to offer the Amphitheatre and services of his company for two benefit performances in support of the actors who had been thrown out of work.[20]

The Liverpool season, ending in June, was the last opportunity Britons had to view the "Grand National Establishment" of Andrew Ducrow. For over a year Hillier had striven valiantly to keep the company together, traveling the roads of England and Ireland, arranging for appearances in converted theatres when no circus buildings were available to him. With the approach of summer, however, the lack of a permanent base in the metropolis was beginning to tell. Batty was firmly in control of London and was luring the more prestigious artists to the elegant new Astley's. In a last desperate move Hillier embarked his troop for the Continent. In July and August they were at Hamburg, performing in the Circus-Gymnasticus in the suburb of St. Pauli. In July *Der Ritter St. Georg und der Drache* was presented with Hillier as St. George, Stickney as St. Anthony, and "der kleine A. Ducrow" as Sycorax, a devil. A month later "Herr A. Ducrow" was billed to appear as "Cupido in Reiterstiefeln."[21] But at this point disaster struck and the company was unexpectedly, and definitively, dissolved. Hillier went broke, and the horses—those epitomes of their race that had once belonged to Andrew Ducrow— were sold to pay for the company's board and lodging![22]

Not all of the troop, as one journalist foretold, returned to England minus their property and with less money in their pockets than when they had left. Stickney, it is true, was riding for Batty a few weeks after the breakup; but Hillier and Chaffé had no intention of returning. Almost immediately they set out for Paris, where they made their debut at the summer home of the Cirque Olympique, the Cirque des Champs-Elysées, on 19 September. The advent of "Le Petit Ducrow" was of keen interest to French spectators, many of whom still remembered his illustrious "father." The *Theatrical Journal* provides a good description of the event and Chaffé's reception by the Parisian public:

> A highly fashionable and very numerous audience congregated on Tuesday evening at the Cirque Olympique, in the Champs Elysees, to witness the *debut* of Master Ducrow, who bids fair to tread in the steps of his late lamented father. The little fellow, who appears not yet to be twelve years of age, gave a vivid delineation, on a fleet steed, of the vicissitudes of a tar's life, and the ease and elegance which he displayed, coupled with the rapidity of his movements, and the perfect *aplomb* he maintains whilst executing the most difficult manoeuvres, elicited the wonder and admiration of all present. At the close of the performance, Master Ducrow was rewarded with three distinct rounds of the most enthusiastic applause ever witnessed in the amphitheatre, and having made his bow, withdrew, highly gratified at the reception he had experienced from a Parisian public. Mr. Hillier officiated as master of the ring; Le Petit Ducrow being, we hear, under his tuition.[23]

"Le Petit Ducrow" was back at the Cirque des Champs-Elysées in the spring of 1844, at which time *L'Illustration* for 4 May, in addition to publishing a gravure of him in "The Vicissitudes of a Tar" (fig. 81), described him as no disgrace to his ancestors: "Nous n'avons point affaire à un Ducrow dégéneré." The ardent reviewer of popular entertainments Théophile Gautier has also left a vivid account of "Le Petit Ducrow's" interpretation of the same act on the occasion of his benefit the following 7 October: "The little Ducrow is already a rider full of spirit, daring, and composure. He has a charming fair-complexioned face, and yet is possessed of singular audacity and energy; beneath that feminine daintiness one senses a virile resolution. How masterful he is on his horse! How he is at his ease on that undulating croup, that moving deck on which he executes, with a pantomimic art that is really remarkable, all the phases in a sailor's life!"[24] In 1845, too, there are notices of Chaffé's activities at the same establishment, and in the following winter at the Cirque Olympique, where he interpreted the role of Djelmi in the drama by Vilain de Saint-Hilaire and Anicet Bourgeois, *Les Eléphants de la pagode*, first performed on 9 December. Set in India

FIG. 81. "Le Petit Ducrow," Andrew Chaffé, in "The Vicissitudes of a Tar" at the Cirque des Champs-Elysées in 1844.

in 1740, the play's action involves the overthrow of the usurper of the Nagpour throne and the triumph of Djelmi, the former monarch's infant son, through the efforts of a sacred elephant improbably named Kelly. There is melodramatic intrigue in abundance. The plot often calls for Djelmi to appear with his mother, advisers, and others; but in all these scenes he remains mute, with an explanation for this convenient loss of speech written into the play. The climactic moment arrives when Djelmi, rescued from a river by the sagacious Kelly, recovers his voice and utters the only two words he speaks in the drama: "Ma mère!"[25]

The scenes in the circle, mute roles in melodramas, prolonged status as an "infant," even the Cirque Olympique itself—all a repetition of Ducrow's own youth. The circle had come full round in the person of Andrew Chaffé, whether billed as "Le Petit Ducrow," "The Living Ducrow,". "Master Ducrow," or—as he was soon styled in France—"André Ducrow." My records of his later life are only of the most cursory nature and in part are indebted to the patient research of my colleague M. Tristan Rémy. As Zamba in Vilain de Saint-Hilaire's *Le Cheval du Diable*, which opened at the Cirque

Olympique on 3 February 1846, André was captured in a Galerie Dramatique print (no. 226). There one sees him on foot in a red and yellow quasi-medieval costume, a poised and well-formed young man with moustache, short beard, and receding hairline—no doubt the results of makeup—whose overall appearance gives sufficient evidence that he has at last outgrown his "infancy." In the summer of 1846 he was again riding at the Cirque des Champs-Elysées and during this and the following year was listed as residing at 109 Quai Valmy. By July 1850 he was at Vienna in the troop of Gaètano Ciniselli; and in July 1854, according to M. Rémy, was director of a circus in Christiania, Norway. The last position was probably related to André's eventual association with the circus manager Carl Magnus Hinné, whose sister Adelheid he married around 1850. André and

FIG. 82. "La Voltige de l'Ecuyer Ducrow," plate of French manufacture depicting "Le Petit Ducrow" and the Negro equestrian and riding master Joseph Hillier, c. 1848.

Adelheid must have met at the Cirque Olympique, where in 1846 she was listed at the head of the equestriennes and was often compared to a cat on account of her grace.[26] Both Saltarino and Halperson tell of the brothers-in-law entering into partnership and of the Zirkus Hinné & Ducrow touring Germany and Scandinavia in the 1850s.[27] Thereafter I lose track of the career of "Le Petit Ducrow." Nor have I attempted to trace Joseph Hillier, Ducrow's black protégé and successor, after his initial appearance at the Cirque des Champs-Elysées.[28]

*   *   *

In the meantime Ducrow's aged mother continued to live on in the London suburb of Norwood. A small portrait of her (fig. 3) in the collection of Mr. Antony D. Hippisley Coxe shows a pleasant looking woman in a voluminous black dress and ruffled white bonnet that barely allows her face to peek out, holding a small Bible in her right hand. She died of "natural decay" on 8 December 1854 and was buried behind the Dissenters' chapel in Nunhead Cemetery. Her death certificate, however, poses a problem, for her age is therein given with great precision as no less than 99 years, 5 months, and 8 days.[29] If the officially recorded age is correct, this would make her some ten years older than her husband Peter, who died in 1815 at the age of 49.[30] It would also raise questions concerning her phenomenal childbearing abilities, since Andrew, her eldest child, was born in 1793; her daughter Hannah died in 1834 at the age of 31; Emily was born in 1811; and Margaret, whom I believe to have been the youngest child, was probably born within a year or two of her father's death, when her mother would have been around 60 years old. In the accounts of Andrew's funeral published in 1842 his mother is described as then being 74 years old, a figure which leads to the more plausible age of 86 at the time of her demise. Also of interest in the certificate is the statement that her daughter Margaret —still single—was present at the death. She, too, has been captured in a small portrait in Mr. Coxe's collection (fig. 4). The portrait, unfortunately, is undated; but an inscription at the bottom, obviously a later addition, informs us the subject is "(Mrs. Wallace) Late Miss Margaret Ducrow / Mrs. Robins's Mother." Margaret's marriage to Wallace presumably took place sometime following her mother's death in 1854, and the birth of a child after this date provides additional reason to believe her own birth must have occurred sometime close to her father's decease in 1815.

As for Emily Ducrow, who married William D. Broadfoot sometime in 1835–36, I have little to report. The nineteenth century was not particularly interested in preserving the histories of its women— especially married women—always barring notoriety, of course. A number of writers, by what authority I know not, have stated she was eventually abandoned by her husband.[31] Broadfoot did have a reputation for playing the tyrant with his subordinates and, like his former master, was celebrated for his swearing. The clown William Frederick Wallett, who worked at Astley's while Broadfoot was directing spectacles for Batty, tells an anecdote about an actor who became so exasperated at being required to rehearse a piece over and over again that he finally floored the director with a stuffed cannonball.[32] For a time he was in management elsewhere, as in 1845 at the New Standard Theatre in Shoreditch, another house specializing in equestrian drama, although he afterward returned to Astley's and continued to direct for Batty until 1849, when he was succeeded by Ducrow's partner William West.[33] He died on 5 January 1852 at Edinburgh, where he had gone to work for another of Ducrow's old artists, the Negro Pablo Fanque. The age recorded on his death certificate is only thirty-six; if the figure is correct, he must have been some five years younger than Emily.[34] The later career of Ducrow's third surviving sister, the Mrs. Louisa Wood mentioned in his will, is also an enigma to me.

We are on securer ground regarding Andrew's widow and children. Louisa Woolford Ducrow retired from the circus at the time of her husband's death and shortly afterward sold out to Hillier. On 18 June 1842, still residing at 19 York Road, she gave birth to a second son, whose name, quite simply, was Andrew.[35] A few writers in the present century, letting their romantic fantasies becloud their judgment, have expressed wonder at her quitting the circus. One even goes so far as to imagine she had been "loathing and despising it all the time."[36] But in fact Louisa now had three fatherless children to look after; she had been left a considerable fortune and consequently was not obliged to continue working; besides which, at twenty-eight she had reached an age when—even with the most willing suspension of disbelief—she could hardly expect to be much longer termed the "Sylph of the Circle." On 28 February 1844, by which date she had moved to Park Road in Marylebone, she was

364 / THE LIFE & ART OF DUCROW

married to John Hay of Conduit Street, who is described in the marriage certificate as a bachelor and estate agent. The witnesses included Alfred Bunn and the same Sarah Collet (or Collett) who had been present at Louisa's marriage to Ducrow in 1838.[37] There were no children by this second marriage; and Hay, when he died in 1873 at the age of sixty-six, was interred by Louisa in the mausoleum at Kensal Green. She herself lived on quietly for another twenty-seven years until her death of bronchitis and heart failure on 25 January 1900, when she followed her two husbands to the same tomb.[38]

A number of descendants have furnished recollections of Louisa in her old age. One great-granddaughter, drawing upon her mother's memories of Louisa's visits to the family of her son, Peter Andrew John, describes her as a "prim old lady in a black velvet dress with a white cap" who presented something of a mystery to her later descendants, since "none of them had any idea where she came from, except that they guessed she was of humble origin as she hadn't an 'h' in her vocabulary. But she looked as though she would swoon if anyone suggested her entering a theatre—and as for a circus!"[39] The reticence regarding her background, however, was apparently the result of the superior airs assumed by her son, who spelled the family name "Ducrôt" and also—according to the same informant in a letter written to me in the summer of 1971—"liked to be thought of some grand French family and forbade anyone to mention 'Circus' even though 'Grandma' Hay lived with them for ages. *She* was only too eager to tell of the Circus and her husband." Another great-granddaughter, descended through Louisa's daughter, tells of her mother and aunts being taken to Louisa's home in Maida Vale to sing hymns to her. This was after the death of Hay, when she was living with a companion and stuffed pet dog.[40] Through the kindness of a third descendant I possess a faded photograph of Louisa in old age, showing her seated outdoors with two of her grown grandchildren (fig. 83). There she sits, wearing the black dress, white cap and a shawl, her feet comfortably resting on a pillow, next which there lies a small dog (the one that was immortalized?). She stares at the camera through bespectacled eyes; the wrinkles in her face are plainly evident; and her lips, drawn back in an unconvincing smile, reveal—unless I am mistaken—the absence of a few teeth. *Sic transit venustas mundi!*

Strangest and most uncharitable of all, however, is the account of the aged Louisa by the journalist Robert James Cruikshank. In

FIG. 83. Detail of a photograph of Louisa Woolford in old age.

his book *Charles Dickens and Early Victorian England*, following a fantastic, deliberately hallucinogenic conjuring up of Ducrow and his acts—subjects about which the writer obviously had little, if any, rational knowledge—he portrays her as a "gruff, grim and snobbish old woman" and as "the forbidding old lady who hated the thought of the circus . . . and would not talk of it."[41] One might almost think he had been to see her and become angry over her refusal to unclose her memories to him. But as Cruikshank was born in 1898, it is obvious he was simply letting his imagination run wild, lashing himself into a vicarious indignation over Louisa's leaving the circus after Andrew's death. Poor Louisa Woolford Ducrow Hay! She was served no better by Cruikshank than she had been some eighty years earlier by the slanderous Matthew Mackintosh, who did his best to make her out a heartless creature who imprisoned her husband in a madhouse.[42] It was her fate to be either extravagantly adored or vilified by those claiming to know her. What she was really like remains, in large part, a mystery.

As already noted, the Woolfords were a prolific and far-flung circus family whose name continued to figure prominently in bills long after Louisa's retirement from the ring. On 11 March 1845 at Cooke's Amphitheatre, Manchester, a Mrs. Woolford was advertised to dance the rope and to appear with Alfred Cooke in Ducrow's equestrian scene "The Tyrolean Lovers." On the same program a Miss Woolford, the "Precocious Equestrian, and Graceful Juvenile Artist," appeared as the young prince Agib in the hippodrama *Timour the Tartar*—a role Louisa herself had performed in her youth.[43] The mother and daughter are very likely the same "Madame" and "Petite Woodford" [*sic*] who figure so tragically in an anecdote told by Peter Paterson. While performing at a circus in Hull, they rode an act in which the daughter, then nine or ten years old, used to pose on her mother's shoulder and head. One evening the horse stumbled while they were in the midst of their number, and "La Petite Woodford" was dashed against a large beam. She was already dead when she hit the arena floor, and the despair of her mother was terrible.[44] When Louisa Ducrow Hay died, she left bequests to several generations of Woolfords, although the bulk of her estate, valued at 7,127 pounds, was divided between her nephew Reuben C. Parish and the husband of her daughter Louisa.[45]

None of Andrew and Louisa's children ever performed in the circus. The youngest and shortest-lived of them, the posthumous

Andrew, entered the Army and, as an ensign in the 40th Regiment, died of wounds received in the Maori War on 23 December 1863, shortly after his twenty-first birthday and coming into the handsome fortune provided for him in Ducrow's will. He was buried in the Auckland cemetery and is commemorated on the same tablet as his father on the Kensal Green mausoleum. Two newspaper clippings reporting his death and funeral, and another detailing his gallant conduct during a Maori attack the previous September, comprise the final items in the Ducrow Album—pasted in, no doubt, by Louisa herself. In a photograph of him in my possession he appears fair and slender, dressed in his ensign's uniform. Ducrow's other son, Peter Andrew John, seems to have inherited some of his father's reputed temper, as well as the French predilection which led him to change the spelling of the family name to "Ducrôt." From information gleaned from his descendants it appears he too served in the Army, but somehow managed to retire as a captain while still in his early twenties. He married a Sarah Carroll and set up in a house called "Windsor" in the village of Douglas outside Cork, where he obviously lived in handsome style, since he there began to keep race horses. One of them, Empress, won the Grand National in 1880; and the following year another of his horses, Fair Wind, was entered in the same race but fell and did not finish.[46] He once became enraged upon learning a race in which he had entered a horse had been fixed, and in the course of four weeks sold his thoroughbreds, leased his house, and moved his wife and seven children to Germany.[47] The family later returned to "Windsor," however, and "Peter A. J. Ducrôt, J.P." is buried in the Protestant cemetery at Douglas. He died on 25 January 1885 aged forty-six, and the motto on his tombstone might, with some degree of appropriateness, be similarly incised on the tomb of his father's biographer: "Patient in Tribulation."

None of Peter's three sons married, and as his brother Andrew did not marry either, the male line of the family is extinct. One of Peter's sons, Louis Hay Ducrôt, adopted the name of Louisa's second husband at her urging and was clearly a great favorite with his grandmother, who left him 1,000 pounds in her will. Louis died in 1939, around eighty years of age—after selling off, one relative complains, some souvenirs of his grandfather. A great-nephew of Peter Andrew John recalls with some amusement being taken to the Kensal Green mausoleum by his "Uncle" Louis, who took some measurements there in the futile hope of getting himself in.

The most interesting line of descent, however, is that through Ducrow's daughter Louisa. She married Henry R. Wilson, an army surgeon major who served during the Indian Mutiny, died in October 1900 at the age of seventy-seven, and was also interred in the Ducrow mausoleum. His wife, the last member of the family to be admitted there, died on 17 April 1917. In Louisa's case, however, the death certificate is clearly in error, since her age is therein given as seventy, which would make her a posthumous child by some five years. As previously mentioned, she was most likely born in the fall of 1840, and certainly before the census of June 1841, in which she is listed as eight months old.[48] Louisa's four daughters were all on the stage, and two of them, Alice (who with her sister Dora went by the name "de Winton") and Lucy, gained considerable reputations. Both are written up in the 1912 and 1916 editions of *Who's Who in the Theatre*, as is Lucy's husband, the actor Gordon Bailey, in the 1914 edition. George Moore is said to have dramatized his *Esther Waters* for Lucy; she was a friend of George Bernard Shaw; and Gordon Craig, as one learns from his memoirs and his son's biography of him, acted with her on provincial tours in the 1890s and—in addition to instructing her in the role of Ophelia—became thoroughly infatuated with her.[49] Lucy's son Peter, deceased in 1976, was an actor who took the name Peter Ducrow, worked for the BBC and in the West End theatre, and did much television. He was recently with the Pitlochry Festival Theatre in Scotland. The daughter of Lucy is the actress and director who goes by the name "Joan Shore." She is married to a Cambridge don, and their daughter acts under the name of Sally Ducrow. Thus, after five generations and nearly two hundred years, the name "Ducrow" may still be encountered in bills, reviews, and advertisements—if not of the ring, at least of the stage, to which both the original Peter and especially his illustrious son made contributions of their own.

Finally, a few words about those "Ducrows" who did continue in the circus and related entertainments until well into the present century. Whether they were actually entitled to the name or not, of one thing we may be certain: none of them was a legitimate descendant of Andrew Ducrow. Nor, for that matter, can I conceive of any of them being Andrew's bastards. In researching his life I have never come upon the slightest hint of sexual indiscretions. As Rede admiringly testified in his 1827 memoir of Andrew, he had "turned his ear from the syren voice of pleasure" and "lived like an Hercules in a continued series of labours."[50] Nor is there any evidence that Andrew's brother John ever fathered any children, although, as previously explained, Andrew's niece by his sister Louisa Wood went by the sobriquet "La Petite Ducrow," and the possibility does exist that other children of his four sisters may have assumed the Ducrow name. In such manner, at any rate, did Andrew Chaffé take the name of his former master—an assumption that was not without some justification, surely, since Ducrow himself had for so long billed him as "Le Petit Ducrow." And it is to this same Andrew or André Ducrow that one must look when attempting to explain at least some of the Ducrows who later appeared in the circus. In his *Circus Life and Circus Celebrities*, for example, Thomas Frost reports that Charles and Andrew Ducrow, "descendants of the great equestrian of that name," performed with the circus of Charles Hengler in 1873.[51] Elsewhere in his book Frost quotes the reminiscences of a gymnast who traveled with James Newsome's circus and who tells of this same "Charley Ducrow" emulating his ancestor in an equestrian act with six horses and performing subordinate characters in the ballets d'action included in the programs.[52] Moreover, in a large bill in the collection of Mr. Coxe for an appearance of Newsome's circus at Middlesborough on Saturday, 4 November (and therefore most likely in 1871 or 1876), I find listed among the riders a Mr. Charles Ducrow and a Master Andrew Ducrow, "Grandsons of the celebrated ANDREW DUCROW." As related above, "Le Petit Ducrow" eventually married a sister of Carl Magnus Hinné. Another of Hinné's sisters, Pauline, married the equestrian and manager James Newsome.[53] It therefore seems evident that these two "grandsons" were the children of André Ducrow, engaged by their uncle when they were both, I imagine, around twenty years old.

There was an equestrian named William J. Ducrow who as early as 1861 was billed as a hurdle rider and leaper with the American circus of Lewis B. Lent, whose company alternated between Philadelphia and New York City. By 1865 he was exhibiting an educated horse and performing upon two steeds as one of the "Olympian Brothers" at Lent's New York establishment. A year or two later he was joined by the infant rider "Le Petit Ducrow," subsequently identified as "Little Georgie Ducrow, the Baby Hurdle Rider." In later years they were both with Stone and Murray's Circus.[54] It was doubtless this same William Ducrow who figures so prominently in the programs and route books of the Barnum and Bailey Circus from the late 1880s into the first decade of the twentieth century. Besides exhibiting performing stallions and ponies, he presented an act in which he directed, in a single ring, no less than seventy horses at the same time. This phenomenal feat was accomplished, as one learns from program illustrations, by using a series of concentric platforms of increasing height, with the horses traveling on them in opposite directions while the mounted director, brandishing his *chambrière* or long riding whip, occupied the highest tier, like the decoration atop a wedding cake.[55] Despite this singular achievement which might lead one to expect some connection with the great Andrew, there is no evidence for any such relationship. William Ducrow died at Bedford City, Virginia, on 25 September 1909, aged sixty-four.[56] If the age given is correct, he was born well after the deaths of Andrew and his brother John, and presumably too early to have been the offspring of André Ducrow, who would have been around fourteen at the time of William's birth.

There were also two brothers named Tote and Dan Ducrow who at one time had a famous clown act with Ringling Bros. and Barnum & Bailey Circus but who later broke up when Tote went to Hollywood. In a letter published in the *Billboard* for 10 February 1923 Mrs. Tote Ducrow writes of her husband appearing most recently as Pablo in the movie *The Pride of Palomar*. She also informs her readers that she is the daughter of R. H. Dockrill, who was an equestrian director with Barnum and Bailey during the same period as William Ducrow. Dan Ducrow, the last surviving brother, died in harness at Pittsburgh on 11 August 1930. In his obituary notices he is said to have been born in California in 1855 and to have toured extensively with the Great World Circus and with Sells Brothers, beginning as a trick–mule rider at nine years of age and later taking up the profession of clown. At the time of his death he still walked the Pittsburgh streets in his "rube" makeup on various advertising jobs and was busily working on a monkey suit. His landlady described him as a "very peculiar character."[57] Tote and Dan were conceivably the brothers of William Ducrow. But again, there is nothing to connect them with Andrew Ducrow.

* * *

On a drizzly day in early December, accompanied by my friend the circus bibliographer Mr. Raymond Toole Stott, I again traveled to Kensal Green Cemetery in northwestern London. Fortunately, there was no difficulty locating Ducrow's mausoleum this time. On my first trip there the previous October, with no help forthcoming from two lounging gatekeepers, I had been forced to strike out on my own —a veritable safari through the weeds and dense underbrush that have taken possession of the older section of what was once London's most fashionable middle-class cemetery. The remains of Thackeray, Trollope, and Leigh Hunt are here. So, too, are those of the actors Liston, Charles Kemble, Charles Mathews the Younger, the composer Balfe, and the artist whose quarrel with Ducrow led to his abrupt departure from Drury Lane, Clarkson Stanfield. Macready himself rests comfortably in the perpetual gloom of the catacombs. Once found, there is no mistaking the tomb of Andrew Ducrow (fig. 84). It stands at an intersection of a main avenue, with the decrepit chapel in which the body of Andrew's first wife was temporarily deposited several hundred feet to the west. Nearby are the monuments of the Cooke and Ginnett circus families, both of which furnished Ducrow with numerous artists and rivals.

In winter, at least, one has a much better view of the tomb, for at that time of year the leaves are gone from the trees, seedlings, and bushes that so densely screen it during the summer months. On the south side, especially, a thick growth of ivy covers everything, even to the weed-encrusted roof. The tomb's architecture, the work of Danson, Ducrow's stage designer, is basically Egyptian but might better be described as "Astleian." Cited as an example of vulgarity even in its own day, it is actually a rather fine representation of the "eclecticism" so popular in the nineteenth century. Two low walls with sphinxes atop them lead obliquely to the front of the tomb, at the corners of which are Egyptian columns. Over the entrance a phoenix supports a tablet bearing the inscription "The Family Tomb of Andrew Ducrow. Erected Anno Domini 1837." In fact, the mausoleum's construction extended several years beyond the death of Andrew's first wife, and Ducrow left 800 pounds in his will for additional alterations, improvements, and inscriptions. The will also provided for a fund of 200 pounds for the perpetual upkeep of the monument and for shrubs and flowers, although there is certainly no evidence for the continuance of any such attention today. Unless it be the bricking up of the entrance, whose original iron door, until several years ago, was broken and off the hinges, affording the casual passerby a view of the interior. Above the architrave and entablature,

FIG. 84. Ducrow's mausoleum at Kensal Green Cemetery as it appeared in the winter of 1971.

incorporated into what is obviously a Greek pediment, is an allegorical high relief depicting a dejected figure seated on a cloud and holding an urn, while in the background a riderless Pegasus mounts to heaven. Again, it is the familiar Genius weeping over the ashes of her favorite son. The structure is curiously continued above the pediment by a square base, upon which is a pedestal supporting a large stone vase with sculptured horses' heads. All that is lacking is a "Paris the Greek" or "Jupiter Ammon" to top the whole thing off.

The pediments on the north and south sides of the tomb contain their bits of allegory, too: beehives, testifying to the indefatigable industry of the person who could afford to erect such an extravaganza. On these sides, also, are the tablets commemorating the mausoleum's occupants. Those on the south are dedicated to Margaret, Ducrow's first wife, to John Hay and Louisa Ducrow Hay, and to Louisa Wilson and her husband. The single tablet on the north is dedicated to Ducrow and his posthumous son Andrew. The former's epitaph, as one learns from a letter in the Victoria and Albert Enthoven Collection, was originally composed by C. A. Somerset—he who had so distinguished himself with *Raphael's Dream* and *Days of Athens*—at the express request of Ducrow. Writing to the actor T. P. Cooke on 22 September 1842, Somerset enclosed a copy of his composition, which had not yet been inscribed on the tomb since the latter was still undergoing alterations. According to Somerset, Andrew had sent for him to write his epitaph in October 1841. In the course of their discussion the author tactfully remarked that it seemed unfashionable to allude to the religion of the interred. "Somerset," replied Ducrow, "whatever may have been my Errors—whenever called away—*I die a Christian.*" There was obviously some discussion about the propriety of appending the usual "Esq." to the name, for Somerset also reports Ducrow as sententiously observing "*there are no Esquires in the Grave.*" Yet the original epitaph—with its reference to Andrew as a "Boon Companion" and uninspired verses about "Death on the Pale Horse" striking down the "Tamer of the Wild Steed" tacked on at the end—did not earn the unqualified approval of Louisa Ducrow, whose revised version of Somerset's lucubration is carefully copied out in the Ducrow Album. It is this modified version that actually appears on the tomb tablet:

WITHIN THIS TOMB
ERECTED BY GENIUS FOR THE RECEPTION
OF ITS OWN REMAINS ARE DEPOSITED THOSE OF
ANDREW DUCROW,
MANY YEARS LESSEE OF THE ROYAL AMPHITHEATRE,
LONDON,
WHOSE DEATH DEPRIVED THE ARTS AND SCIENCES
OF AN EMINENT PROFESSOR AND LIBERAL PATRON,
HIS FAMILY OF AN AFFECTIONATE HUSBAND
AND FATHER,
AND THE WORLD OF AN UPRIGHT MAN.
HE WAS BORN IN LONDON 10th OCT. 1793,
AND DIED 27th JAN. 1842:
AND TO COMMEMORATE SUCH VIRTUES
HIS AFFLICTED WIDOW HAS ERECTED
THIS TRIBUTE.[58]

In his will Andrew left instructions for a final embellishment: "two Marble truncated or broken Obelisks or Columns ... by the side of my said Monument one to the right and the other to the left ... the column to the right ... dedicated to me and that to the left to my dear deceased Wife Margaret Ducrow." The broken columns are there, and the one dedicated to Andrew—which I discovered only after climbing the rusty iron fence and forcing my way through the underbrush—is an edifying sight in itself. Its four pieces, including a fallen Corinthian capital, are artistically arranged on a heavy base. A marble wreath hangs from an upright section; and resting on the side of another fallen piece, carved with startling realism, are a plumed broad-brimmed hat and pair of riding gloves—exact replicas, or so I suspect, of those worn by Ducrow in one of the last ring pageants in which he appeared: "The Royal Cotillon of Days Gone By, or The Court Beauties of Charles II."

Thus in death as in life the career of Andrew Ducrow is not without its contradictions and absurdities. The phoenix rising with outspread wings, the disconsolate Pegasus mounting riderless through the clouds, the medley of Egyptian and Grecian architectural motifs, the plumed Cavalier hat—all are expressive of the original, unfettered imagination whose manifold creations were for years the delight and amazement of thousands. "We shall not look upon his like again," was the general cry at the time of Ducrow's death. Nor shall we, in this tired and wonderless age.

FIG. 85. The hat and gloves worn by Ducrow as Charles II, carved in marble on a segment of the broken column at the side of his mausoleum.

Of no one, perhaps, has so much been said,
and so little truly known, as of Ducrow.

—William T. Moncrieff

APPENDIX I *The Ducrow Apocrypha*

ᴀꜱ ᴡᴀꜱ ᴏɴʟʏ to be expected with so colorful a figure as Ducrow, a sizable body of apocryphal anecdotes, deliberate distortions, and downright lies accumulated around him during his lifetime and the years immediately following his death. Many of these tales, gaining undeserved credence with the passing of time and their embellishment and repetition in numerous memoirs and popular histories, remain current to the present day. In organizing my materials I was consequently faced with a dilemma: such is the extent of the misconceptions surrounding Ducrow that I knew many of my readers would expect to encounter these stories and might reasonably conclude I had not done my "homework" were they omitted. Yet to include all this material, only to have to repeatedly interrupt my narrative to correct or disprove it, seemed equally unsatisfactory, and I have therefore settled on the present arrangement as the best for satisfying the curiosity of those with some prior knowledge of Ducrow.

For the benefit of those who pay little attention to such matters as documentation, it should be pointed out that the present biography is based almost entirely on primary sources—archival materials, letters and manuscripts, playbills, iconographic records, memoirs of persons who personally knew Ducrow and wrote of their experiences with him, reviews and notices in contemporary newspapers and theatrical periodicals—although even these sources, as will become apparent from what follows, present no ironclad guarantees of accuracy and must sometimes be interpreted with considerable caution. The numerous, often repetitious "memoirs" or biographical sketches of Ducrow published during and after his lifetime, together with obituary notices, have also been consulted, but here I have admitted only such information as seems to have originated with Ducrow himself or those who had direct knowledge of him. Of these accounts the best and the source of most subsequent sketches is the fifteen-page "Memoir of Andrew Ducrow" published in 1827 in *Oxberry's Dramatic Biography*, then being conducted by Leman Thomas Rede, who had married Oxberry's widow. That Rede based his account on data supplied him by Ducrow is established in a letter dated 22 June 1836, pasted into the Ducrow Album, to Ducrow from Rede's brother William Leman Rede: "In looking over the papers of my late brother, Mr. Leman Thomas Rede [d. 1832], I find some letters, the tributes of admiration to your talents that have been paid you abroad." Rede enclosed the materials he had discovered, and these must have included the letters, petitions, and poems from Ducrow's French fans that are also pasted into the Album. Leman Thomas Rede's "Memoir," incidentally, does not make use of any of these encomiums (possibly the writer considered them excessive), but does include literal translations of reviews from the *Courrier des Spectacles* and the provincial newspapers the *Echo du Midi*, *Ami de la Charte*, and *Mémorial Bordelais*—the originals or translations of which were no doubt also provided Rede by Ducrow, since he could not easily have come by them otherwise. Presumably these materials were lost or destroyed in the process of publication, for they are not in the Album, although there is present a translation of a review published in the *Camp-Volant* for 20 December 1818 which Rede did not use.

Further proof of Rede's personal acquaintance with Ducrow and the latter's assistance in the preparation of the "Memoir" occurs in a note on page 9 where the writer remarks, after describing Ducrow's career in France, that "among other momentos [*sic*], we were favoured by a sight of a medal, presented to this unrivalled horseman, by the Duchess d'Angouleme." Rede's account may therefore be accepted as authentic—for both Andrew's English and French careers—and the chief objection that can be made to it is that it came fifteen years too soon. None of the memoirs that followed is of even remotely comparable quality. Yet even here one must remain on guard against occasional slips of memory, as when the fatal accident to a woman spectator at Lyons in 1819, while Ducrow was still employed by the Franconis, is attributed to a later period in that city when he was managing his own company.

Two other memoirs are also worthy of mention: the three-page "Theatrical Sketch of Mr. A. Ducrow, the Unparalleled Equestrian" in Pierce Egan's *Anecdotes*, published in the same year as Rede's account; and the even briefer "Memoir of Mr. Ducrow" in the 24 September 1831 issue of the *Owl*. Egan, a well-known figure on the sporting scene, also appears to have personally known Ducrow. It is he, for instance, who relates the story of Andrew's early training under the choreographer James Harvey D'Egville, whose tutelage is confirmed by Ducrow's letter to the editor of the *Mémorial Bordelais* in 1822. The anonymous memoir in the *Owl* contains little information that is new, but is nonetheless interesting for its hint of sibling rivalry between Andrew and his brother John—an intimate detail that very likely originated with Andrew himself, although Moncrieff later claimed it was Andrew, rather than John, who was the old man's favorite. It is this last writer who now engages our attention, with his

"DRAMATIC FEUILLETONS

OR,

LEAVES FROM THE COMMON-PLACE-BOOK OF AN OLD STAGER"

These anecdotal accounts of Ducrow consist of four articles (part of a longer series) that appeared in the *Sunday Times* for 16 and 23 February, 2 March, and 22 June 1851. It would seem the second article was meant to precede the others. "Old Stager," as the *Theatrical Journal* for 12 January 1853 and scattered references in the articles themselves inform us, was William T. Moncrieff, the prolific melodramatist and stage adapter of Dickens, author of the highly successful *Tom and Jerry* and *Cataract of the Ganges*, who claimed to have had a "close private intimacy of many years' duration" with Ducrow. There is no reason to dispute this statement, and Moncrieff did occasionally write for Ducrow, as during the 1826 season at Astley's when both his *Paul Pry on Horseback* and *Shooter's Hill* were produced. The epigraph at the head of this appendix is taken from the second article by Moncrieff, who ought to have known.

Ducrow, the "Champignion," and the Coronation of William IV in 1831

In all fairness to Moncrieff, it should be noted that in the "Introduction" to his "Feuilletons" series, published in the 5 January 1851 issue of the *Sunday Times*, he candidly declares that his primary aim is to amuse his readers and that some of the anecdotes he tells are based on hearsay. The present oft-repeated tale is a case in point. It was received "from those who profess to have been present at the greater part of the incidents it details," reports the writer, who cautions that it is "believed to be as authentic and correct as most relations of this nature generally are." The story is a long one, occupying the whole of the 16 February article and around half that of 2 March. Briefly, it tells how Ducrow boasted of having trained the King's "Champignion" (Champion), whose duty it was to ride his horse into Westminster Abbey and challenge anyone to battle who disputed the new monarch's right to rule. The ceremony traditionally called for the Champion to back his horse out of the Abbey after the challenge had been delivered for the third and final time—a maneuver that presumably called for the expert tutelage of Ducrow. As a reward for this service, Moncrieff writes, Ducrow and his wife received tickets to attend the coronation of William IV. Dressed in some splendid costumes borrowed from the wardrobe at Astley's, and driven to the Abbey in a fantastic carriage requisitioned from the same establishment, they were taken for persons of rank and given good seats in the gallery. The following extracts will give some idea of the humorous speeches attributed to Ducrow on this august occasion:

> They're a plaguy long time beginning. I suppose they have got no prompter. I don't think our audience vould be quite so patient. I vonder who's the stage-manager here!... Oh! that's the first music striking up, I suppose, so I dare say the spectacle will soon commence. Eh! here comes the Lord High Chamberlain, I suppose, with his vand. I'm sure Viddicomb vould make a much better master of the ceremonies than that

ere chap. There's calves! vhy, Viddy's is tvice as good. . . .
Oh! that chap with the feathers is the Markiss of Derrydown,
is he? Vell, all I can say is, if he don't mind and keep that ere
long sword of his from getting between his legs, it will be
soon all derry down with him!

Meanwhile, Madame Ducrow, looking, as Ducrow termed her, "remarkably distinky," is nudging her husband trying to get him to
keep quiet, since the noble spectators on either side are listening to
this running commentary. Her husband continues, however, and
after comparing the King to the actor Robert William Elliston, is at
last given the opportunity to express his opinion of his pupil.

> Does he call that keeping his seat properly? . . . There's a
> fellow for you!—he'll be heels over head in no time!—jist
> sarve him right! only folks vould vonder as I had the edicating
> of him. Why isn't he *puffing*? . . . What's he standing still
> for? I taught him the grand salam proper enough. . . . A
> pretty harticle he is to be Champignion of all England!—Vhy
> any of my grooms vould do it better. Oh! I'm d——d if he
> von't be down! If I ain't ashamed of ever having given him
> a single lesson my name ain't Andrew! He's not fit to ride a
> drayhorse, and has backed out in a most dunghill manner.

Again Madame tries unsuccessfully to hush her husband, who then
begins speculating the rider may have ruined the "hanimal's" mouth.

> If he has, he'll have to pay a pretty penny for it . . . That's
> vone of the best performing osses ve're got in the whole stud;
> that's our *Mazeppa mare*! Mr. Champignion will find himself
> in a fine pickle if he's spoiled her . . . I can't say much for
> the pomp of the thing, in spite of all their fine *paperphanalia*.
> Blamire vould have turned out a crownation a precious sight
> more gorgeous, if he'd only tin foil and Dutch metal enough.
> But I'm getting plaguy peckish. I suppose you hadn't the
> sense to put any sandvidges in your pocket, though ve've
> got that real German Bologna sassage that Old Bent brought
> us from the Borough. . . .

It all makes for very funny reading, of course. And there is only one
thing the matter with it. There was no Ceremony of the Champion
at the coronation of William IV. The ceremony had been discontinued following the coronation of George IV ten years earlier, while
Andrew was touring the Continent.[1]

Ducrow and the Blacksmith's Shop

Another tale Moncrieff relates secondhand and offers as an example of Ducrow's penchant for repeating any striking effect that originated with him concerns the setting of a blacksmith's shop by moonlight. Here Moncrieff provides us with another amusing dialogue, this time between Andrew and one of his playwrights, in which the latter—reading his new play to the manager—is continually interrupted with the suggestion that *here* might be a capital place to insert the favorite setting. The author in turn puts up a spirited defense against all these proposed intrusions ("What! a blacksmith's shop in the countess's bed-chamber, my dear sir!") and eventually goes off convinced he is to be spared the infliction of this hackneyed setting ("Why, it's been seen in every piece you have brought out since you were a manager"). But upon attending a rehearsal of his piece a few days later, he is startled to hear a terrible clanging of hammers and to see the familiar blacksmith's setting onstage for the opening of his play. In fact, Ducrow has decided to insert the setting at *two* places in the play.

This is so obviously an exaggeration that it hardly deserves comment. However, as a simple matter of curiosity, I have made an examination of 120 playbills carrying descriptions of settings during the seasons 1824–41. A blacksmith's setting occurs in five of the productions described in these bills, and two of them—*St. George and the Dragon* (1833) and *Charlemagne* (1838)—were got up by Andrew for Drury Lane.

Ducrow's Cockneyism and Speech

It is virtually impossible to reconstruct Ducrow's speech at this date, of course, yet I think we may safely assume it was hardly so cockney as Moncrieff's derivative tale about the coronation would have us believe. Ducrow was not, in fact, a cockney; and Moncrieff, we must remember, was the dramatizer of *The Pickwick Papers* and Sam Weller. It is only in Moncrieff's accounts that I find this substituting of "v" for "w" and vice versa and some of the other peculiarities popularly associated with cockney speech. Curiously, when he wrote the story about the blacksmith's shop, the author contented himself with only an infrequent "wery vell" and "wary" (vary) in the dialogue; and when he came to write up the tale of

"Ducrow's Scarecrow" (see above, pp. 174–75)—a stratagem with which Moncrieff was personally acquainted—he dropped the cockney altogether ("There, I've given it to that fellow at all events; I've long threatened it, and now he's got it he won't forget it for one while; and that's the way I'll serve all negligent beggars"). The dropping and adding of "h's" is not peculiar to cockney, of course, and here Ducrow and many of his circle, including his second wife Louisa Woolford, seem to have frequently transgressed.

There was undoubtedly a certain amount of affectation and bluff in his speech, with Andrew framing it to meet varying circumstances. Moncrieff, for example, writes that "his blow high, blow low voice must still dwell in the memory of every one who heard him while moving among us, but its mixture of *con furore* and *sotto voce* was not natural." His use of such pronunciations as "champignion" (if indeed he did use it) Moncrieff similarly attributes to his affectation of French airs, which earned Ducrow among his contemporaries the telling appellation "the Mounseer." And there were also what Moncrieff terms his "dogberryisms," such as the well-publicized substitution of "dialect" for "dialogue," "currycomb" for "caracole," and so on. Here, too, I believe we should view these *cum grano salis* and can safely infer they were often deliberately used to achieve some desired effect. No such absurdities appear in any of Ducrow's letters I have seen.

THE *Stage Reminiscences* OF MATTHEW MACKINTOSH

By far the memoir that has given me the greatest trouble, and which is also the most widely known account of Ducrow's life, is that occurring in Matthew Mackintosh's *Stage Reminiscences*. Would that they had never been written! Matthew Mackintosh, or "Old Stager" as he too preferred to call himself on the title page of his recollections, was a stage machinist who commenced his career in Scotland and later worked at several London theatres. In 1866, possibly in collaboration with a journalist, he felt compelled to issue his reminiscences of (and perhaps revenge himself on) the various theatrical celebrities with whom he had come into contact. It has long been recognized by scholars that Mackintosh is notoriously inaccurate where dates are concerned, and that he is frequently unreliable on other matters as well. Yet unfortunately it is he who provides the most extended memoir of Ducrow's life—a chapter running to twenty-eight pages—

and it is this mass of misinformation that has supplied the needs of popularizers and hacks ever since. The most recent example of the perpetuating of these fairy tales occurs in an undocumented article by John M. East, published in the autumn 1971 issue of the British periodical *Theatre Quarterly*.

One might expect at least part of Mackintosh's narrative to contain a kernel of truth, since he did work for Ducrow for some nine seasons. According to Mackintosh, he was engaged by Ducrow around the beginning of 1829, after having made Andrew's acquaintance the previous year in Glasgow, and assisted in the preparations for *The Storming of Seringapatam*, produced at Astley's on Easter Monday 1829. This statement seems to square with the facts, and the absence of Mackintosh's name in the playbills at this time is probably attributable to his starting out in a subordinate position. By 1833 he was listed in the bills as the theatre's machinist and continued to be so designated through the 1837 season. His name does not appear in the advance bill for the 1838 season which lists the personnel at Astley's. Nor do I find him in any subsequent bill. It would therefore appear that he left Ducrow's employ around the end of the 1837 season, although Mackintosh himself is characteristically confused on this point and states that almost immediately following Andrew's marriage to Louisa Woolford "early in 1839" (in fact, June 1838), he and Ducrow "had a disagreement, on a matter of comparatively little moment, and I left the amphitheatre, never to return to it again."

For these nine seasons, then, Mackintosh was in Ducrow's service; although one might never suspect it from his recollections, since his tales concerning this period in Andrew's life are no less fantastic than what he has to say about the rest of it. The unexplained "disagreement" is a point of interest, particularly since it is so closely associated with Andrew's marriage to Louisa Woolford—a marriage which, Mackintosh writes, "was in no way a good or desirable union." At other places in his narrative he does not withhold his praise of Andrew's first wife: "one of the best of wives," "a fine-looking 'Lancashire witch,' and a most valuable help-meet," "a capital woman of business." In view of his malicious account of Ducrow's final days and the part Louisa Woolford Ducrow supposedly played in them, I believe he may have been paying off an old score. It would require a book in itself to examine and expose all the inaccuracies and lies of Matthew Mackintosh. The following are only a few of the more egregious examples.

Parentage and Birth (pp. 137–38)

A story wholly originating with Mackintosh is that Peter Ducrow was a native of the German state of Mecklenburg-Strelitz and was brought to England by Queen Charlotte as her court jester. In this capacity, "for about twenty years," he amused the Queen and the young princes, instructed the latter in riding and gymnastics, and in 1795, with the Queen's approval, married one of the ladies' maids at Buckingham House. A short time later Ducrow and his wife "removed back to his native place in Germany," but the Royal Family were so desolated by his absence that he was summoned to return. On the night of their arrival back in England they put up at the "Three Nags' Heads" in Southwark, and it was on this same night of 12 May 1796 that Andrew Ducrow was born.

Aside from the fact that Mackintosh is a mere thirty-one months off on Ducrow's birthdate, there is not a shred of evidence to support this absurd story. If, as Mackintosh states, Peter Ducrow was a great favorite with the Princess Charlotte prior to her marriage to George III and her removal to England, he must have commenced his career as "court jester" at a very tender age indeed, for the royal wedding took place in 1761 and Peter Ducrow died in 1815 at the age of forty-nine. Following the birth of Andrew, Mackintosh somehow maneuvers the family into a series of engagements at English and French circuses, and the court connection, inexplicably, is forever dropped. The disappointment of the Royal Family at this second decamping of their favorite jester may readily be imagined.

Ducrow's Career in France (pp. 138–42)

Here Mackintosh introduces the character of "Fabian Franconi" who, after seeing Andrew perform at Astley's in the summer of 1812, engaged the entire Ducrow family for a period of five years for his Parisian "Winter Amphitheatre on the Boulevard de Temp [*sic*] and the Summer Circus in the Champs-Elysées." At Paris Andrew was tutored in riding by Franconi himself, began exhibiting equestrian scenes such as "The Death of the Moor" at the circus in the Champs-Elysées in 1813, entertained his compatriots there following the Battle of Waterloo in 1815, was promoted to the position of riding master while his brother John was engaged as a talking clown, and finally, as the result of an accident which incapacitated his employer, rose to become "sole manager of the business," much to the annoyance of Franconi's two sons, Fabian and Sebastian. The sons eventually succeeded in turning the Ducrows out of the circus, and Andrew then erected a Parisian circus of his own and began touring the French provinces. With time out for an occasional flying visit to England, he continued in this manner until his troop was engaged to appear at Covent Garden in 1823.

In this hopelessly confused passage Mackintosh would appear to be referring to Antonio Franconi, the founder of the French circus dynasty, and to his sons Henri and Laurent, who succeeded their father in the direction of the Cirque Olympique in the boulevard du Temple. The Cirque des Champs-Elysées, the summer home of the Cirque Olympique, was first opened by Louis Dejean and Adolphe Franconi, son of Henri, in 1836, prior to which the company customarily spent the summers on tour. As related above in chapter 3, Andrew made his debut at the Cirque Olympique in December 1818 and remained with the Franconis only until the fall of 1819. He was not tutored by any member of the Franconi family and was already a star equestrian at the time of his arrival. He was never "sole manager of the business" or even riding master at the Cirque Olympique. Nor did he ever erect a circus of his own in Paris. It is probably useless to speculate on any reason behind the above fabrication, but it may be that Mackintosh was able to justify (to himself, at least) his habitual carelessness in this instance with the thought that such an account would appear compatible with the generally remarked French airs of "Mounseer" Ducrow.

Ducrow's Later Visit to Paris (pp. 148–53)

I now skip ahead to the period when Mackintosh was working for Ducrow and presumably had his wits about him and to a story which —more than anything else in his wretched account—has cost me considerable time and trouble. Following the opening of *The Storming of Seringapatam* (i.e., in 1829), Mackintosh writes, Ducrow decided to pay a solo visit to Paris and took Mackintosh along as his assistant. After spending a week at Boulogne, the two men traveled to Paris, where Andrew devoted three days to practice (the horse was a "stranger to him") before appearing at the Champs-Elysées circus in the equestrian pantomime "The British Sailor."

After the performance inside the circus, there was a display of fire-works in the gardens, at which he hit them harder even than in the ring. A tight-rope was stretched from the ground to the flagstaff on the top of the building, an elevation of about eighty feet, up which Andrew walked, amid the burning of blue fire and other pyrotechnic effects, and to the enthusiastically-expressed admiration of an immense crowd of spectators. At the end of the ascent there was a little platform prepared, where I was in waiting to receive him, and held the balance-pole while he turned round and rested before descending. When he arrived here I saw he was in high spirits at the great reception he had experienced, and, as he wiped the perspiration from his brow, he said—"I wonder what they think of the young English 'stripling' now?" This was said with reference to the Franconis junior, and to their former disparagement of him when he had been made manager of the place by their father. "But stop a bit—I'll tickle them going down." With this resolve he tripped lightly down until getting to the "belly" of the rope, where he suddenly halted and sat down. He then went through a variety of posturing feats, finishing by standing on his head—after which he nimbly recovered his position, and ran down the rope to the ground.

This startling exhibition led to Andrew's being carried on the shoulders of the rapturous spectators to the Café Royal, "where he might have had champagne and cognac enough to drown him, and was nearly like to be killed with kindness." Here Ducrow favored his admirers with a "short, characteristic speech" in which he made several remarks about his old rival Franconi, who had hired him for twelve nights, and promised a treat for his benefit. The whole affair, Mackintosh writes, was "reported next day in *Galignani*."

There follows a circumstantial account of the preparations for and actual evening of the benefit—not without some appropriate details concerning Matthew Mackintosh's own contributions to this event, of course—and a touching tale of a reunion with a horse trained by Andrew seven years ago, but which "remembered its old instructor's voice at once, and immediately came up and licked his hand." Besides his equestrian scenes, Andrew went through an exhibition of the "Grecian Statues," but became so infuriated by the bad timing of the Frenchman who provided the commentary that "the moment they were out of the ring he caught hold of the stout stuffed club used by him in the representation of Hercules, and, mistaking the poor describer for the Nemean lion, belaboured him with it until the unlucky Frenchman thought it was all over with him." Even more curious is Mackintosh's description of the "out-door display" that followed,

> an effective but also a somewhat hazardous one, entitled "The Mission of Mercury." In place of the tight-rope a strong iron wire, 300 feet in length, was this time stretched from the flag-staff to the ground. Suspended from this wire, or rather from a hardwood "traveller" working easily along it, was a small platform on which stood Ducrow made up as the winged god. To the bottom of this platform was attached a sufficient counterweight to prevent it turning over with the movements of the performer, the whole apparatus being disguised with painted canvas and "profile" to resemble a white cloud. While Ducrow stood on this cloud, poised on one toe, I worked certain tackle which pulled it up, and thus was achieved what was supposed to represent the upward flight of "the herald Mercury." The sensation part of the performance was in the coming down again, however, which was done "with a run," and which, in addition to nerve and steadiness on Andrew's part, required perfect promptitude on mine. It may be easily imagined that on a decline of 80 feet in the 300, a weight such as that of the performer and the apparatus would descend with great velocity. So it did, and was immensely effective; but the success or failure of the affair depended upon the velocity of the descent being stopped at the precise instant necessary to avoid the shock that would be experienced by coming down to mother earth at such a rapid rate, and also to make an artistic landing. This was the part of the business which I had to work, and it was done by means of suddenly slackening the tension of the wire considerably, just when the performer had attained a certain stage in his downward journey. I was pretty nervous over this portion of the business previous to its coming off; but our tackle was the best that could be procured, and, you may be sure, I had seen beforehand that it was all in working order, and everything went off well. I was very glad, however, when it was all over.

Upon leaving Paris, Ducrow and Mackintosh proceeded to Belgium, where Andrew studied the field at Waterloo in preparation for the representation of the battle he was scheduled to produce at Vauxhall Gardens the following 18 June. They arrived back in London on 27 May 1829; and Mackintosh then goes on to briefly describe the spectacle at the Gardens the following month, mentioning, among other things, that "we had three companies of the Grenadier Guards nightly assisting in the performance" and that "Mr. Sotheby, the celebrated pyrotechnist, made his reputation through his judicious administration of the 'villanous [sic] saltpetre' department."

The elaboration of detail in the above account lends a strong note of authenticity, of course, but unfortunately this impression rapidly fades once one begins searching for confirmation of Mackintosh's story. The departure for Paris following the opening of *The Storming of Seringapatam* would seem to accord with Mackintosh's statement that they returned to London in May 1829, for the play itself was indeed produced in the spring of that year. But Andrew's re-creation of the Battle of Waterloo was presented at Vauxhall Gardens in 1828—the only year in which he produced this spectacle there, the year before Mackintosh supposedly entered his service—and there was no Battle by anyone at the Gardens during the 1829 season.[2] Mackintosh's description of the Vauxhall Gardens gala and what "we" had there is probably only one more instance of the heights to which his poetic fancy propelled him, unless we are willing to concede that his term of employment with Ducrow (and in truth, dates, as we have seen, were never his forte to begin with) commenced a year earlier than the memoir would lead one to believe. What, then, can we say of the Parisian engagement itself, described by our observant guide in even greater detail? Here the problem is complicated by the fact that Ducrow was indeed in Paris during the 1829 season, for an Astley's bill for the week of 6 July mentions him as having "returned from Paris, from his Theatrical Foray, in the French Capital." From the absence of his name in earlier bills it would seem, moreover, that he left on this trip sometime around the end of the third week in June.[3] Mackintosh claims that the initial performance at Paris was "reported next day in *Galignani*," by which he presumably means the English-language publication *Galignani's Messenger*. I have not been able to locate any issues of this journal for the period in question. I have, however, made a thorough search of the advertisements and reviews of all Parisian places of entertainment in the *Journal des Débats* and the daily theatrical journals the *Corsaire* and *Courrier des Théâtres*. The Cirque Olympique, managed by Adolphe Franconi and Ferdinand Laloue, was open during the early summer of 1829, as was also the Tivoli pleasure garden, with the latter featuring a ropedancer known as Diavolo Roberto. But there is no notice of Ducrow performing at either of these establishments or anywhere else in Paris during the period in question. Additional inquiry, on the off chance that the visit Mackintosh describes might have occurred in the spring of 1828, has proved equally fruitless; and my colleague M. Tristan Rémy, who has done extensive research on the history of the Franconi family and Parisian circuses, assures me there is no evidence for Ducrow performing at the Cirque Olympique from the opening of the third house to bear that name in 1827 to its bankruptcy in 1830.

But the most telling argument of all against Mackintosh's story is not the lack of confirming evidence, but the story itself. Despite all the technical details and jargon we are regaled with, the outdoor exhibition of the "Mission of Mercury" is totally uncharacteristic of Ducrow and his tightrope performances. In no other place—either in Britain or on the Continent—do I find him performing this sensational feat, although the act was an old one and there were other artists around who did perform it. It also seems strange that the triumph Mackintosh waxes so rhapsodic over should have gone unreported in the English newspapers, let alone the bills and advertisements of Ducrow's own establishment, since Andrew was never one to hide his light under a bushel and would certainly have managed some good publicity out of it. Yet during neither the 1829 nor any other season following his return to England in 1823 did Andrew ever boast of such foreign exploits; and on this topic all other sources —with the one notable exception of Matthew Mackintosh—are equally dumb. To be sure, Ducrow was often on the Continent traveling for recreation and searching for novelties and artists for his London circus. It is in connection with these last pursuits that the term "theatrical foray" must be understood.

I daresay I might have spared both myself and the reader this laborious explanation, for Mackintosh, as we shall shortly see, was quite capable of making up the whole thing. The possibility also exists, of course, that at a distance of thirty-five years he confused Ducrow with some other performer he had once worked for. There was, for instance, during the winter of 1828–29 and following spring, a slack-rope artist at the Cirque Olympique known as "Il Diavolo Antonio," whom the traveler Prince Pückler-Muskau saw in January 1829 and likened to "the flying Mercury descended again on earth in human shape."[4] His namesake, probably the same individual, was to be seen in England around this time. It would be curious indeed—but not, I think, entirely unexpected—if Mackintosh had in the preparation of his memoirs confused this artist or some other like him with the equestrian Andrew Ducrow.

Brighton and the Princess Victoria (pp. 155–60)

Another beautifully circumstantial story told by Mackintosh—a story that has taken in everyone to date and which even inspired the title "Queen Victoria Rides in the Ring" for a chapter in M. Willson Disher's *Greatest Show on Earth*—concerns a command performance by Ducrow and his troop at the Brighton Pavilion. Mackintosh is deservedly proud of the part he played on this momentous occasion and consequently spares us none of the details. In 1833, he writes, when the commission for the performance was received, he was immediately dispatched from London to Brighton to see what would be needed to fit up the Riding School behind the Pavilion as a temporary circus. Having been informed by the Royal Architect that the performance was to take place "this day week," Mackintosh took his measurements and an hour later was in a "fast coach, *en route* for town again." That same evening, after conferring with Ducrow and receiving *carte blanche* to carry out the necessary arrangements, he rounded up thirty-five workmen and, "at the cost of 15 pounds," hired a large van to depart from the Harlequin in Drury Lane on the following morning. At his final meeting with his employer that night, Ducrow "clapped me on the shoulder, and said, 'Well, we astonished them a bit in Paris—let us do the same at Brighton.'"

But this was not to be the only instance of Ducrow's bonhomie on the same occasion, for the next morning, while the van with Mackintosh and his men was passing over Waterloo Bridge, Ducrow hailed them, climbed up beside Mackintosh on the box, and rode with his crew as far as the Elephant and Castle.

> When Ducrow got down off the box, he went at once round to the door of the van behind, and, when he saw the men all comfortably seated on either side, with a long narrow table running up the centre, he said, "Ah, you look all very snug here; I wish I was going with you. You've got a very nice table here, but you want something to put on it, don't you? What'll you take?" Every one sat mute, but I replied for them that they had had a good breakfast, but would be none the worse of a drop of "jacky" (gin). The cordial was quickly produced, and he filled out a glass to each of them with his own hand. He then took his leave, the men giving him three cheers for his kindness. I mounted the box again, and off we started.

The astonishing memory of Matthew Mackintosh provides us with a wealth of similar details concerning this historic journey, and on the following day, after the men had commenced their work at Brighton, goes on to inform us that

> at about 11 o'clock a young lady, mounted on a white cob pony, and with a groom in attendance, entered the Riding School, and took two or three turns round our newly-made ring, while glancing at what was going on. The noise of thirty hammers and saws hard at work, however, was rather too much for her, and she soon left. Immediately afterwards the groom returned alone, and, coming up to me, said that if I was superintendent here, I was to come outside for a minute, as her Royal Highness wanted to see me. I obeyed, and approached the lady, hat in hand. Her first words were— "Are you the Master of Works here?" I replied that I was. "Have your men got any refreshment yet this forenoon?" she said. "Not yet, your Highness," was my answer. "Oh then, I'll look to that," said the lady, and immediately set off at a canter up the walk. About half-an-hour later, four servants in livery came into where we were at work with a couple of large trays filled with cold beef, mutton, and bread, and also with two large flagons of Windsor home-brewed ale. Through one of these servants, I soon discovered that the kind young lady who had visited us was the Princess Victoria, daughter of the Duke of Kent, and now, need I say, her most gracious Majesty the Queen of England. She paid us a visit at least once a-day while we were engaged there, and seemed to take a lively interest in the progress of the work. She always took a turn or two round the ring when she came, and I may mention that on these occasions she never would have the ring door opened, but made her pony leap into the circle, and leap out again when leaving.

Our favored "Master of Works" then describes the actual performance, not omitting to tell how Queen Adelaide had to administer a cup of coffee to the King to keep him awake, and mentions that on the following day Ducrow had a private audience with the King, who complimented the equestrian and offered to be of service to him.

Unfortunately for "Old Stager," we must now look at some facts. There was indeed a command performance in the Riding House behind the Brighton Pavilion, but, as might be expected, it did not take place in 1833 as Mackintosh relates, but on 19 November 1832.

A copy of the bill for this occasion is in the Ducrow Album, together with a letter from the Earl of Erroll setting the date and time of performance; and descriptions of the program were carried in the three Brighton journals, the *Gazette* for 22 November, *Guardian* for 21 November, and *Herald* for 24 November. But it is also evident from perusing these journals that there was no necessity for Ducrow and his company to make a special journey to Brighton: they had been performing at the Brighton Theatre Royal since 22 October and continued there until 20 November, the day after the command performance, before moving on to Portsmouth. Mackintosh's rushing back and forth between London and Brighton a week before the performance was to take place, his meetings with Ducrow in London, Ducrow's wishing he might be going to Brighton with Mackintosh and his men when in fact he was already there, and all the other minutiae of this narration are highly improbable to say the least. But where Mackintosh can unequivocally be given the lie is in his puffed-up account of his meeting with Princess Victoria. The above journals regularly carried columns detailing the daily movements of the Court at Brighton, and neither Victoria nor her mother the Duchess of Kent is mentioned during the entire period under discussion. Nor, for that matter, are they anywhere mentioned as visiting Brighton in the November issues of the *Court Journal*, which also ran a brief account of the fête and listed the guests attending in its issue of 24 November. However, on the ridiculous assumption Mackintosh might be correct after all, and recalling it was around this same time that Victoria began keeping her famous Journal, I dispatched an inquiry to the Royal Archives at Windsor Castle. The answer I received from the Registrar there should put an end to this story once and for all: "It is clear from her Journal that Princess Victoria was at Kensington Palace in November 1832 and never left London on 19th November or during the previous week."[5]

It may also be worth mentioning that the Brighton *Guardian* for 21 November, in its account of the command performance, states that "the Riding School was fitted up with great care and ability by Mr. Fabian, Carpenter to His Majesty," and that on the following day Ducrow was summoned to the Pavilion for an audience with the Earl of Erroll, "who stated that he was commanded by His Majesty to express the gratification which Mr. Ducrow's performance had afforded to the Court, and to give Mr. Ducrow His Majesty's authority to exercise his profession in all towns in His Majesty's dominions."

Ducrow's Final Days, or Matthew Mackintosh to the Rescue
(pp. 163–65)

By far the wildest story told by Mackintosh is his account of Ducrow's last days and death. Following his "disagreement" with Ducrow, Mackintosh writes, he spent most of the next three years in America. On returning to England he found Astley's in ruins and "Ducrow himself in a private madhouse at Peckham Rye, where, with the advice of Dr. Sutherland, he had been placed by his *kind* wife." Despite their argument and Mackintosh's absence of three years, it is obvious Ducrow had not forgotten his old friend and faithful retainer, for we have Mackintosh's own word that "he had frequently sent for me, but always before his messages had been intercepted." One of these messages finally got through and Mackintosh paid a visit to the madhouse:

> When I was introduced to him now, he caught hold of my hand with both his, and the big tears rolled down his cheeks, while he deplored to me his situation.
> "They call me mad," he said; "do you think I am?"
> I replied that I did not.
> "Then you will not let me stop here," he entreated.
> "Not if I can get you out."

The resourceful Matthew Mackintosh did indeed get Ducrow out, after summoning the trembling proprietor of the madhouse and lecturing him on the illegality of Andrew's confinement. This accomplished, he immediately conveyed Ducrow to his home in York Road:

> His wife was not at home when we arrived, and as I did not particularly care about meeting the lady, I soon took my leave.
> Next morning I received a letter asking me to come to the house in York-road at once, as Mr. Ducrow had taken suddenly ill, and was anxious to see me. When I got to the house, I found Dr. Brooks in attendance, who said that his patient was suffering from severe internal inflammation. His mind, too, was now wandering in earnest, and I found that what he wanted to speak to me about was the plans for a new theatre, which he insisted I should see about at once. In this state he lingered for only a few days longer. On Monday the 4th of February 1842, I went up to see him, and he recognised me. Partly speaking and partly by signs, he signified his desire

that I should raise him a bit in the bed. When I had so done, he breathed very heavily for a few minutes, then his head dropped forward towards his breast—and it was all over!

At this point we must concede Mackintosh a long overdue compliment: he was off by only eight days on Ducrow's death date. The veracity of the rest of his fable may easily be ascertained by referring to the facts related above in chapter 8, where it is pointed out that by the autumn of 1841 Ducrow had sufficiently recovered from his mental breakdown to return to his home in York Road and resume, at least on a limited basis, the management of his company. He was seen attending the theatre and opera in the company of his wife during these final weeks. At the time of his death from a series of strokes he was rumored to be preparing to rejoin his troop, then performing at Liverpool.

Matthew Mackintosh was a distinctly secondary character who claimed for himself a far larger part on life's stage than in fact he had ever played. On rare occasions—as in his relation of Ducrow's conduct at his first wife's funeral—his narrative does seem to impinge on the truth; and in these few instances, where confirmation is forthcoming from other sources, I have cautiously admitted his testimony. In later years he was not above using his former employer's name to advance his career, as in a bill for the Prince of Wales Arena and Saloon of Arts, Yorkshire Stingo, for 21 August 1843, where I find him listed as "late of A. Ducrow, Esq.'s Amphitheatre."[6] Were it not for the appearance of his name in a few playbills, one would hardly believe from his sorry *Reminiscences* that he had once known and been associated with Andrew Ducrow.

MISCELLANEOUS

Ducrow and the Sheffield Cutlers

The following story, so far as I can tell, was first published in *The Public Life* of William Frederick Wallett, the noted "Shakespearean Jester," and is another familiar tale about the "terrible-tempered Mr. Ducrow." Wallett does not give the dates for either Ducrow's or his own appearances at Sheffield:

> My next engagement was with Holloway's Amphitheatre at Sheffield. This was an enormous temporary building erected by Mr. Ducrow for a circus. Mr. Ducrow had ruined his own season, and brought the building into disrepute by his hasty temper. The Master Cutler, and most of the *élite* of the neighbourhood came to patronize the performance one night. Some forty or fifty carriages were drawn up in front of the circus, headed by the Master Cutler, who sent in his card to Ducrow, whom he expected to do the honours of his establishment by welcoming his patrons. But Ducrow returned a message saying that Ducrow only waited upon the Queen of England and not upon a set of dirty knife-grinders. They were so indignant that they turned their horses' heads round, proceeded to the Town Hall, improvised a band, and spent the evening with a ball instead of the circus entertainment.[7]

In the effort to run this chimera to the ground, I have made a thorough search of the Sheffield *Courant and Advertiser*, *Independent*, *Iris*, and *Mercury* for all the years of Ducrow's management in England. Neither they nor any other source I have consulted lends the slightest credence to Wallett's story. Nor has the tale become part of Sheffield local legend.[8] Ducrow's troop first visited Sheffield in the fall of 1836, settling in at the sumptuous National Olympic Arena of Arts that had been erected in anticipation of their coming. They opened on 19 October and remained in Sheffield until the beginning of December. The reviews in the local newspapers were almost uniformly laudatory and tell of the company playing to crowded houses; there is not the least hint that Ducrow offended any member of the Sheffield public. The only return visit during Andrew's lifetime occurred in December 1841, by which time he himself was no longer traveling with the company. To anyone familiar with the capricious, often destructive temper of nineteenth-century English audiences, Wallett's tale is bound to appear suspicious. No manager with half a grain of sense would have dared do such a thing. I have uncovered no evidence of Ducrow ever deliberately insulting a spectator in any place he performed.

Ducrow Confused with Philip Astley

Circus figures have always provided good "copy" for journalists, and among these latter gentlemen the founder of the circus, Philip Astley, has been the inspiration for probably more stories and anecdotes than Ducrow himself. Occasionally one finds Ducrow confused with Astley in these accounts, or an anecdote originally told of Astley transferred to Ducrow. Two examples will suffice.

W. P. Frith, in his *Further Reminiscences* (pp. 109–10), tells of Ducrow treating the members of his company to boat excursions down the Thames on the anniversaries of his birthday (which Frith places in August). A short time before one of these trips "several of the banners so essential to the story of the plays were either lost or stolen" from the Amphitheatre. On the day of the voyage the members of the troop who were rowing took off their coats, but one refused, saying he was not hot. Ducrow finally commanded him to remove his coat, and it was then seen that this person had made a waistcoat out of one of the missing banners, whose line "She Dies at Sunrise" was clearly written across the back.

The banners Frith refers to were used in stage entertainments given toward the end of the eighteenth century at Astley's and the Royal Circus, whose licenses did not permit them to use prose or "speaking" dialogue. In order to conform to the licensing regulations, whenever a line of dialogue was considered absolutely essential, it was customary for someone to walk on with a banner on which the line had been printed ("Lead Her to the Bridle Halter" is an example often cited). The use of such banners went out around the turn of the century, and Ducrow, of course, never used them in his productions.

Another anecdote concerning Ducrow's much publicized banquet of 1836 appears in the *Satirist and the Censor of the Time* for 7 August 1836:

> Ducrow gave a grand dinner party the other day to a number who lounge behind the scenes of theatres, and did the honours of the table after his usual fashion. He had a full band on the occasion, and was very anxious that they should gratify his company. At one time he observed the horn players not using their instruments, whereupon he started up, and asked them the reason. "We have twenty bars rest," was the reply of one. "Rest!" exclaimed Ducrow, "I'll have nobody rest in my company. Damn it, go on playing." They did so, and pretty confusion they made.

This story was originally told of Astley, whose supposed ignorance of music was a continual source of fun to his contemporaries. That Ducrow himself was so ignorant is patently preposterous, since his own acts—both on horseback and the stage—were almost invariably cued to music.

Ducrow's "Illiteracy"

Finally, it is sometimes stated by those who know least about the subject that Ducrow was "illiterate." If the word were meant in its broader context—that is, as of one lacking in formal education—then one could hardly argue the point, although Andrew's contemporaries often expressed their amazement at his familiarity with classical mythology and the fine arts and wondered where he had acquired such knowledge. More often, however, such statements are made in reference to his ability to read and write, and Moncrieff himself, in his fourth article in the *Sunday Times*, relates that Andrew possessed "a bare knowledge of reading and writing, which he had chiefly taught himself." Ducrow generally employed an amanuensis (who was often, like J. H. Amherst and Henry M. Milner, the "author to the establishment") for his business correspondence and publicity, but there are extant a fair number of letters in his own hand to friends and acquaintances such as Charles Molloy Westmacott and William D. Broadfoot, invitations to his famous banquets, and verses inscribed for a Liverpool fan. The letters, written in fine, medium-size characters, are legible and give the impression of having been easily tossed off. Misspellings ("wright" for write, "informe," e.g.) are rarely encountered and are certainly less frequent than in the letters of many of his supposedly better educated contemporaries, of whom Mrs. Siddons may be cited as a fair example.[9] Capitalization, by nineteenth-century standards, is sometimes erratic, although occasionally it is used for emphasis. Commas (dots below the line) are generally indistinguishable from periods. A letter to Broadfoot, written on 10 October 1841 while Andrew was recovering from his bout of insanity, is in a bolder but less steady script and is probably indicative of the strain he was undergoing at the time.[10]

I might add that I have seen letters and other writings by both of Ducrow's wives, and that these ladies also possessed good hands. Nor need this be considered a cause for surprise. Although it is frequently stated and generally credited that many, if not most, circus performers of the nineteenth century were unable to write, I have found exactly the opposite to be true. Even the man-monkey Gouffé—in some accounts depicted as little more than a savage— could manage a comprehensible, if not altogether orthographically and grammatically correct, letter when occasion demanded, as is demonstrated by a bona fide communication in my own collection.

Nor was Philip Astley the "illiterate" person he is often made out to be. When one considers the sporadic opportunities for education among children of itinerant performers around the beginning of the nineteenth century—performers who were generally of quite limited means but who managed to scrape together the money to send their offspring to various schools for a few weeks or months at a time— this accomplishment is not to be taken lightly. For all I know, it may even provide a telling comparison between the quality of instruction in that day and our own, when educators, laboring under far more favorable conditions, have such difficulty turning out literate pupils. In the nineteenth century illiteracy was still considered a sign of ignorance. Consequently, even children with limited time to devote to study were encouraged to make the most of their opportunity to escape this stigma.

The above examples by no means constitute an exhaustive catalogue of the Ducrow Apocrypha, but do include those myths with which knowledgeable readers are most apt to be acquainted. A number of other tales and anecdotes—for which, however, there does appear to be some factual basis—are related in the main body of the text.

APPENDIX II *The Ducrow Iconography*

DURING HIS LIFETIME DUCROW was the subject of numerous portraits, prints, and other representations. My research has led me to well over a hundred such items, yet I am certain I have not seen all of them. Even today Ducrow occasionally turns up in the most surprising places—most recently, as I discovered during a visit to a local gift shop, on the covers of some matchboxes manufactured in Japan, where an imaginative designer obviously had access to some crude bill cuts depicting the equestrian in his characters of Rob Roy and the Flying Dutchman. The following is therefore not meant to be a definitive catalogue of these various objects, but only a broad categorical outline.

Original Portraits & Drawings

At least one full-length oil portrait of Ducrow painted during his lifetime might have been seen until the present century. In the second half of the nineteenth century it was somehow acquired by

"Lord" George Sanger, the famous circus director and last proprietor of Astley's, who bequeathed it to his nephew George Sanger.[1] In a letter of 13 October 1976 to me, Mr. Robert Dick, married to a descendant of "Lord" George, writes that the portrait depicted Ducrow as "a man of approximately 45 years of age sitting in an armchair, but unfortunately some twenty years ago, when the family were on tour, the painting was destroyed in a fire in the Winter Quarters at Horley." The Sanger family, incidentally, appear to have acquired quite a few relics of Ducrow. Many of the superb Astley's bills for the years of Andrew's management in the Theatre Museum of the Victoria and Albert Museum were donated by "Lord" John Sanger & Sons. "Lord" John was another nephew of "Lord" George.

Notwithstanding the destruction of this portrait, we can still appreciate what it looked like, since it served as model for a print of Ducrow on the cover of the 14 July 1838 issue of *Actors by Daylight* (fig. 76). When I first encountered this print several years ago, I was immediately struck by the fact that it depicts Ducrow in mufti (the bill under his arm announces "The Courier of St. Petersburg"). That the print, as I later reasoned, was indeed based on the portrait is confirmed by Mr. Dick's letter and by an extant photograph of what appears to be the actual painting in the collection of Mr. Richard W. Flint (fig. 75), to whom I am also indebted for calling my attention to the reference to the portrait in Sanger's will. The photograph came to Mr. Flint in a collection of memorabilia once belonging to the Howes circus family, two of whose members, twins Egbert and Elbert, toured in England and married two English sisters. It is likely the photograph dates from around the end of the century. The only substantive differences between it and the print in *Actors by Daylight* are that the figure in the print is the reverse of that in the photograph—strong evidence, of course, that the engraver worked from the portrait—while several horses, partially depicted behind the drapery in back of Ducrow in the photograph, are absent in the print. The artist's name is unknown to me.

Mr. R. Toole Stott informs me that another oil portrait, depicting only Ducrow's head and shoulders, hung in a dark corner of M. Willson Disher's London home some years ago. From another photograph that has recently come to my attention I should not be surprised to learn this was actually a salvaged, perhaps extant, portion of the picture mentioned above. Another likely candidate would be the original for the fine print of "Mr. Ducrow in the Dress of a Spanish Bull Fighter" by J. Rogers after Wageman (fig. 36).

In the Antony D. Hippisley Coxe Circus Collection there is a small group of original works relating to Ducrow and his family. Included are the two watercolor portraits of a young man and woman (figs. 11 and 12), obviously by the same artist, which I assume to be of Andrew and his first wife Margaret around the time of their marriage in 1818.[2] The same collection contains two other watercolor portraits identified as "Mr. Andrew Ducrow's Mother, Buried at Nun H^d [Nunhead] Cemetery" (fig. 3) and "Mrs. Wallace, Late Miss Margaret Ducrow, Mrs. Robins's Mother" (fig. 4); a pencil drawing of Andrew's newly erected mausoleum at Kensal Green (fig. 69); and an unidentified pencil portrait of a young girl (fig. 57), possibly executed around the same time as the drawing of the mausoleum. The last subject is very likely Ducrow's niece Louisa Margaret Foy Wood, "La Petite Ducrow," who would have been around ten years old at the time of the mausoleum's erection.

Mr. Peter Ducrow, the great-grandson of Andrew, in addition to two later photographs of Ducrow's daughter Louisa and posthumous son Andrew, possessed an interesting oval portrait, supposed to be of "family," depicting two small children in mourning dresses. I suspect this must represent Louisa and Ducrow's first son, Peter Andrew John, at the time of their father's death. I have discovered no daguerreotypes of Ducrow.

Bust

In 1842 a cabinet bust of Ducrow, "taken from the life two months previous to his death," was exhibited at the Royal Academy by the sculptor J. Howe.[3] To date I have been unable to ascertain its whereabouts or whether it is still in existence. Nor have I located any illustration of it.

Prints

Among the finest and rarest are the two superb large lithographs by G. Charton of Geneva after J. Bergmann, showing Ducrow in his act "Le Bouquet de l'Amour" (figs. 16 and 17). Only the one in which Andrew appears with his sister Emily is dated, but both were undoubtedly published around the same time—i.e., in 1820. Two other fine lithographs dating from the period of Ducrow's travels on the Continent are the smaller and somewhat more common "Ducrow à l'Elisée Lyonnais," representing Andrew and Emily in the same act, published by Villain after the artist Reverchon (fig. 15); and the large dramatic portrait of Ducrow and his horse in "Le Maure des déserts" (fig. 20). The only copy of this last I have discovered is in the Harvard Theatre Collection and does not contain any information as to the artist or publisher. A final but much cruder print relating to Ducrow's Continental period is the large colored engraving of him as "The Gladiator," reproduced opposite page 168 in Marian Hannah Winter's *Le Théatre du Merveilleux*. Published at Paris by Badoureau while Andrew was performing at the Cirque Olympique, its naïveté is attributable to Ducrow's having been the artist himself.

Among English prints the finest of all is the large one of Andrew straddling five horses as "The Courier of St. Petersburg," printed by Engelmann after the artist E. F. Lambert and published by George Hunt in May 1827 (fig. 27). Two examples, one colored, are in the Harvard Theatre Collection. Other noteworthy prints are "The Celebrated Pas de Trois, as danced by MR. DUCROW, 'Le Petit Ducrow,' and his beautiful Steed Pegasus . . . in the Grand Spectacle of 'Charlemagne'" lithographed by Madeley (fig. 72); the small portrait of Ducrow in the costume of a Spanish bullfighter by J. Rogers after Wageman (fig. 36); and the large lithograph by C. Clutterbuck of "Mr. Ducrow as Charles the Second on His White Steed Bucephalus" with the passage entitled "Le Cheval Volant" at its top (fig. 42). What appears to be a fine lithograph of Ducrow as Apollo managing his winged horse Pegasus and a variety of other horses, zebras, and ponies—all in the ring at once—is reproduced on page 27 of M. Willson Disher's *Fairs, Circuses and Music Halls* (London, 1942). I have not seen the original, and Disher characteristically gives no source or publication information, although the print must date from no earlier than 1832, when Andrew began exhibiting his trained zebras.[4]

As noted elsewhere, Ducrow sometimes commissioned prints of himself to be given away on his benefit nights, and several of the above probably fall into this category. Other examples of the practice, I suspect, are the print "Mr. Ducrow as the Chinese Enchanter" (fig. 45) with its appended verses explaining the pantomime; and the large print entitled "M. Ducrow's Equestrian Scene of the Indian & Wild Horses" (fig. 14), not to be confused with other, smaller prints of the same scene. The second of these prints is probably the one the publisher William West meant by "The Ingun and the Vild Oss" in his interview with Henry Mayhew published in the *Morning Chronicle* for 25 February 1850: "You see, sir, Mr. Ducrow paid for it being done by my man, and guv it away on his benefit night, and I had the plate of him afterwards."

Far more common are the dozens of popular prints of Ducrow in his equestrian scenes issued by the publishers of toy-theatre or juvenile-drama sheets. Although a few of these figures (sometimes of Andrew with Louisa Woolford) are small enough to have been cut out, mounted on cardboard, and manipulated on the stages of model theatres, nearly all of them are of the larger theatrical-portrait format: one scene or figure to the sheet, meant to be framed and, if so desired, colored and even tinseled. The exact provenance of some of these portraits is not always obvious, since it was common for later publishers to take over the stock of their predecessors and continue issuing the same prints over their own imprints, with the result that several were issued and reissued by at least three different publishers. The reader interested in the subject is referred to the authoritative study by George Speaight, *The History of the English Toy Theatre* (London, 1969), which contains a thorough explanation of these conversions. Here the finest portraits are those by the original publisher of juvenile drama, William West, who employed a number of talented and eventually well-known artists to do his work, closely followed by the series of equestrian pantomimes published by Robert Lloyd after the artist W. Cocking. The Lloyd portraits, in particular, were frequently reissued by the firms of M. and M. Skelt and, later, G. Skelt; and several of them are still being printed and sold today by Benjamin Pollock Ltd., which acquired the stock of G. Skelt following his death in 1956 and possesses many of the original lithographic stones. Other firms publishing theatrical portraits of Ducrow and his family were J. Dyer, O. Hodgson, A. Park, J. Fairburn, Dyer ("Miss Ducrow as the Spanish Girl as Companion to Rob Roy McGregor"), and J. L. Marks.

I think it must have been West who was the first to publish and sell a theatrical portrait of Ducrow, and that this was of the earliest of his famous representations, "The Roman Gladiator." Besides the fairly common print of 1817 showing Andrew in four different poses as "The Gladiators" (fig. 10), there is, as discussed in chapter 2, the extremely rare print of him in the same character dating from the previous year (fig. 9). Another early and, to my knowledge, unique colored print of Ducrow in the same character is in the Stone Collection of the Theatre Museum at the Victoria and Albert (plate 1). Smaller than the West portrait, it bears no publication information and is simply titled "Mr. Ducrow as the Roman Gladiator." The poses of both horse and rider (though not the costumes and trappings) are similar to those in the French print by Badoureau, which leads me to suspect that this, too, may have been designed by Andrew himself.

Nearly all of these portraits represent the equestrian with one or more of his steeds. The few exceptions include prints by Lloyd showing Andrew as the "Courier," standing and triumphantly flourishing his dispatches; "Mr. Ducrow as Zephyr," in which he dances with an infant Cupid; and "Mr. Ducrow and Miss Woolford as Flora & Zephyr on the Double Ropes" (frontispiece), the only print I have discovered relating to his exploits as a ropedancer. A portrait of Ducrow as a dismounted St. George was published by A. Park. I have discovered no theatrical portraits depicting him in his mime roles the Dumb Man of Manchester or the Idiot of Heidelberg; nor have I seen any of him in his famous tableau act, *Raphael's Dream*.

While not conforming to the usual format of portraits issued by publishers of juvenile drama, three prints (plates 12–14) in the series *Fairburn's Scraps* published by J. Fairburn are of special interest (figs. 39, 40, 41). Each depicts Ducrow in five or six of his "Feats of Horsemanship" at Astley's and gives what I take to be an excellent idea of how these scenes actually looked. Stripped of the usual rhetorical gestures and stances associated with theatrical portraits, they exhibit a careful attention to detail and equine anatomy which is often lacking in other prints of Andrew and his horses. Interesting, too, is a scarce series of colored miniature prints, each measuring a little over two by four inches, after the artist Robert Cruikshank. How many there were in all I am not certain. The circus collection of Lord Bernstein contains five different prints— "Ducrow & his Horse Pegasus" and four others depicting him riding five, six, and nine horses in "The Courier of St. Petersburg"—and Thétard, besides reproducing two of these in his *Merveilleuse Histoire du cirque* (I, 47), includes a sixth print showing Andrew and his brother John with the latter's two ponies supping at their separate tables (II, 245). All of them give a lively notion of the spectators who watched these acts and sometimes, as one sees in fig. 56, moved between the ring and stage in the course of the evening's program if the house was crowded. Another fine colored print showing this practice, and Andrew bestriding two horses in the character of "The Wild Indian Hunter," was designed and etched by Theodore Lane to accompany the memoir in Pierce Egan's *Anecdotes*. I have already reproduced this print in my *Enter Foot and Horse*.

Several other memoirs of Ducrow include portraits as well. The fine one of him as the Spanish bullfighter, previously mentioned, figures as frontispiece to the memoir by Leman Thomas Rede published in *Oxberry's Dramatic Biography*. The memoir in *Actors by Gaslight* (27 October 1838) is headed by a rather crude depiction of Ducrow as Hamet in the chivalric spectacle *Charlemagne*; the memoir in the *Owl* (24 September 1831) includes a colored print of him as Zelikos in his tableau drama *The Fall of Athens*; and the account in *Actors by Daylight* (14 July 1838) is accompanied by the highly unusual portrait of him in civilian dress (fig. 76).

Finally, there are the innumerable illustrations found in playbills, of which several of the more outstanding examples are reproduced in the text. These generally bear a strong resemblance to Andrew, and I have no doubt they were specially commissioned to depict him in his various roles, since even lesser-known performers during the early nineteenth century often had cuts of themselves made which they carried about for use in the bills of the circuses and theatres employing them. Whether portraying the valorous St. George lifted into the air by his pestilential-breathed adversary, the wretched inmate of Heidelberg Castle, the "authentic" costume worn by Andrew as the centaur in *The Fall of Athens*, or Peter Ducrow himself performing his amazing feats of strength and equilibrium—here one finds a rich iconographic source for scenes and characters often represented nowhere else.

The Ducrow Clock

Further testifying to the popularity and renown of Ducrow is his appearance on the base of an elegant rosewood and brass inlaid Regency mantle clock (figs. 86 and 87), whose approximate dimensions are 17 inches high and, at the base, 14 inches wide and 6 inches deep. As my colleague Antony D. Hippisley Coxe has pointed out, the representation of Ducrow riding and driving five horses in his most famous pantomime, "The Courier of St. Petersburg," corresponds exactly to one of the many prints of him in this role (fig. 28). It is therefore obvious that the print served as a pattern for the clock design. How appropriate that this particular scene, in which the Courier impels his swift coursers under the necessity of arriving at his destination within an appointed time, should have been chosen to illuminate the clockmaker's art!

Of the three examples of the clock personally known to me, one is in the collection of Mr. Coxe, another is in the British Theatre Museum, and the third is in my own collection.[5] In the first two the figures of Ducrow and his horses are executed in brass inlaid on wood, but in my own the exact opposite is the case—that is, wood on brass, with the eyes, buttons, and harness trappings of Andrew and his horses highlighted by brass and copper nails set into the wood—and the figures are depicted traveling in the opposite direction. This last fact leads me to conclude the cabinetmaker was economical with his materials. After cutting out the brass inlay for one clock, he then went on to use the rectangular plate from which this was cut for a second clock, filling in the cut-out area with wood. But as the plate had probably been scratched on the one side while cutting out the inlay for the first clock, it was turned over for use in the second, with the result that the direction taken by Andrew and his horses became reversed. In theory, then, there should be a wood-on-brass for each brass-on-wood clock.

There seems to have been more freedom of design in the inlays for the rest of the clock, although here too one would expect economy to prevail and each "positive" design to possess its "negative" counterpart. The clock is usually said to date from 1820–30, but the upper figure is the more reliable since Andrew did not invent his "Courier" until 1827. None of the clocks I have seen possesses its original clockwork.

Pottery

A number of untitled Staffordshire figures have eagerly been identified by dealers and owners as Ducrow and Woolford performing their duets on horseback, Woolford alone dancing the rope, and even—in the case of a pair of figures representing a boy and girl standing atop their individual horses—the "Ducrow Children."[6] I am not so certain. As Gordon Pugh and other authorities on the subject have demonstrated, the potters occasionally took as their models popular prints of actors, singers, and other entertainers, and

FIG. 86. The Ducrow Clock, depicting the equestrian in his most famous pantomime, "The Courier of St. Petersburg." Wood-on-brass version.

FIG. 87. The Ducrow Clock, brass-on-wood version.

positive identifications are sometimes possible through the discovery of the prints upon which particular figures were based. Unfortunately, none of the sources I have consulted provides any such evidence for the figures supposedly relating to Ducrow and his family; nor have I personally discovered any such corresponding prints. The figure reproduced in fig. 88, an example of which was offered to me in 1974 for the modest price of $350, is a case in point. Commonly believed to be of Ducrow and Woolford, it does not resemble any print I have seen of them in their famous duets. The colors and patterns of the costumes do not provide any clues either, for these are not always consistent in other examples of the same figure, and in any case the potters were limited in their range of colors.[7] Green and red plaid dresses are especially prevalent among females in Staffordshire figures.

Another problem in assigning these crude figures to Ducrow and Woolford is that most if not all of them were produced after 1840, by which time Ducrow had given up his pantomimes on horseback and duets with Woolford. This does not rule out the possibility that the potters may have used earlier prints, of course; but in view of the failure to discover any such evidence, it seems to me that if the potters did model these works on living persons, other artists—any number of whom had taken to imitating Ducrow and Woolford and performing their acts by mid-century—are more likely candidates. The Cooke, Ginnett, Woolford, Clarke, Bridges, and Adams families all produced their share of expert equestrians and ropedancers during this period, and there were many celebrated individual performers as well. The trouble is, collectors and dealers generally have a minimal acquaintance with the nineteenth-century circus and its artists. In their attempts at identification they dip into one or two books on the subject which take little notice of these other performers, but where they quickly discover Ducrow and Woolford were the most famous artists of the day. Ergo, their figures must represent Ducrow and Woolford! Pugh's suggestion (p. 28) that such figures were often inspired by, but not meant to be exact likenesses of the persons in the prints the potters worked from is another point to be kept in mind. Their primary purpose, as he observes, was a decorative one, which accounts for the lack of titles on so many figures. Thus, while it may be comforting to believe one or more of these figures represent Ducrow and Woolford in their celebrated roles, the most that can be said of them with certainty is that they give an idea of what such acts were like.

FIG. 88. Staffordshire figure sometimes said to depict Ducrow and Louisa Woolford in one of their equestrian duets.

We are on firmer ground in the case of an interesting French plate depicting "La Voltige de l'Ecuyer Ducrow" (fig. 82). But it does not—as collectors have assumed until now—represent the famous Andrew. This is one of a set of pictorial plates having the circus for its subject; other plates in the same series, representing such artists as the clown Auriol, the high-school rider Baucher, and the Loisset family of equestrians, are on exhibit in the Musée des Arts Traditionnels et Populaires in Paris. The plates were manufactured between 1844 and 1848, and the present item is from the collection of Dr. Alain Frère. Its subject is actually "Le Petit Ducrow" and Andrew's former pupil the Negro equestrian and riding master Joseph Hillier, who found their way to the Cirque des Champs-Elysées in the fall of 1843 and for several years afterwards performed in Paris. As noted elsewhere, Ducrow's apprentice Andrew Chaffé eventually went by the name André Ducrow and in France was commonly believed to be Ducrow's son. He was probably in his late teens at the time he was depicted on the plate. A colored print of him entitled "Ducrow, rôle de Zamba, dans *Le Cheval du Diable*," no. 226 in the Galerie Dramatique series of theatrical portraits, is also often mistakenly identified as being of his former master.

Notes

While this work was in progress the library of the British Museum officially became known as the British Library. I have nonetheless retained the designations "British Museum" and "BM" in my text and documentation, since most readers will be more familiar with the earlier name and its abbreviation and since I wished the present book to be consistent with my earlier publications.

Frequently Used Abbreviations

"BM" refers to the British Museum (British Library) and is used specifically in connection with the three Astley's scrapbooks and the great collection of bound playbills catalogued in the "Register of Playbills, Programmes, and Theatre Cuttings" available at the information desk in the main reading room. Individual volumes of the last are referred to as "BM Playbills ____."

"Disher Scrapbooks" refers to the three Astley's scrapbooks formerly the property of M. Willson Disher, now in the Kenneth Spencer Research Library at the University of Kansas.

"Dramatic Feuilletons," followed by date, refers to the series of articles by William T. Moncrieff ("Old Stager") in the *Sunday Times* for 1851.

"Ducrow Album" refers to the album of Ducrow memorabilia, assembled by Andrew and his two wives, formerly the property of Mr. Peter Ducrow and now in the possession of his son, Mr. Simon R. Bailey.

"Harvard," followed by volume and page numbers, refers exclusively to the four Astley's scrapbooks in the Harvard Theatre Collection.

"*Oxberry's* 'Memoir'" refers to the biographical sketch of Ducrow by Leman Thomas Rede published in the 4 August 1827 issue of *Oxberry's Dramatic Biography and Green Room Spy*.

"V&A" refers to materials in the Theatre Museum of the Victoria and Albert Museum. In general, no distinction is made between the Enthoven and Stone Collections, both of which are neatly organized by subject and chronology. Playbills are almost always from the former collection, and illustrative materials often from the latter.

Prologue

1. The name itself, it should be noted, does not derive from the Roman structures, but from the ring or circle in which Astley and his competitors gave their performances. Astley himself always referred to his establishment as a riding school or, later, amphitheatre, and the latter term was commonly used in Britain and America until well into the nineteenth century. The rival name was first employed in 1782 when the equestrian Charles Hughes, in association with Charles Dibdin the Elder, opened the Royal Circus (later the Surrey Theatre) in St. George's Fields, a few hundred yards south of Westminster Bridge.

2. See, e.g., John Britton and A. Pugin, *Illustrations of the Public Buildings of London* (London, 1825–28), which contains, in vol. 1, the "Account of the Royal Amphitheatre, Westminster Bridge" by Charles Dibdin the Younger; Edward Wedlake Brayley, *Historical and Descriptive Accounts of the Theatres of London* (London, 1826), containing essentially the same account, plus a history of the Surrey (Royal Circus) Theatre; Jacob Decastro, *The Memoirs of J. Decastro, Comedian* (London, 1824), which includes Decastro's "History of the Royal Circus"; M. Willson Disher, *Greatest Show on Earth* (London, 1937), a history of Astley's and its artists; A. H. Saxon, *Enter Foot and Horse: A History of Hippodrama in England and France* (New Haven, 1968), concerned mainly with Astley's and the analogous Cirque Olympique in Paris; George Palliser Tuttle, "The History of the Royal Circus, Equestrian and Philharmonic Academy, 1782–1816," Diss. Tufts, 1972.

3. *The Microcosm of London* (London: R. Ackermann, 1808–10), I, 19.

4. Saxon, *Enter Foot and Horse*, pp. 13–14.

5. On the licensing of the minor theatres and their types of entertainment, see *Enter Foot and Horse*, pp. 1–6.

6. George C. D. Odell, *Annals of the New York Stage* (New York, 1927–49), II, 469–70.

7. Advertisements for 17 August 1772 and for the months of June and August 1775 in I, 19–20 of the Astley's Scrapbooks in the Harvard Theatre Collection. (Note that in all subsequent references to these scrapbooks they will be designated "Harvard.") There were, in fact, two celebrated apiarists by the name of Wildman, and the other—Thomas—also performed with his bees. In a future work I shall elucidate their histories and "training" methods.

8. *Enter Foot and Horse*, pp. 30–31. Before adding a clown to his establishment, Astley himself interpreted the first of these comic characters.

9. *Londina Illustrata* (London, 1819–25), II, 183.

10. Joseph Strutt, *The Sports and Pastimes of the People of England* (London, 1834), p. 221. Dibdin the Younger, who worked with him around 1800, also described Richer as "the best Rope Dancer then known, and—in my opinion—*always* the most elegant"—*Professional and Literary Memoirs of Charles Dibdin the Younger*, ed. George Speaight (London, 1956), p. 41.

11. Fully restored by 1801, he then leaped over forty men with a pole three feet above their heads, over ten horses, and kicked an object eighteen feet in the air—see the advertisements in the *Times* for 2 May 1799, 6 April 1801, and 11 August 1801. Cf. Strutt, who describes Ireland at length, pp. 230–31.

12. Advertisement in the *Times*, 26 September 1808.

13. Bill for the Olympic Circus, Glasgow, 15 March 1806, in the Library of the University of Glasgow.

14. Advertisement in the *Times*, 13 October 1794. The two other contenders were the equestrian Giles Sutton and the ropedancer and Harlequin Paul Redigé. The latter seems to have had the most valid claim.

15. Bill for 3 August 1822, in the Guildhall (London) Collection of Circus and Menagerie Playbills.

16. See, e.g., F. W. Hawkins, *The Life of Edmund Kean* (London, 1869), I, 38–41; J. Fitzgerald Molloy, *The Life and Adventures of Edmund Kean, Tragedian, 1787–1833* (London, 1888), I, 38–40.

17. On Kean's own ability as a ropedancer, see Molloy, I, 86–87.

18. *Our Turf, Our Stage, and Our Ring* (Manchester and London, 1862), pp. 26–27.

19. For additional comments on the methodology of this study—together with several examples of the problems and false leads the writer encountered —see A. H. Saxon, "Adventures in Nineteenth-Century Biography: Some Problems and Principles, with Examples from the Life of Andrew Ducrow," *Theatre Survey*, XVII (1976), 92–105.

1. Infancy

1. Here, however, we are already faced with the first of many contradictions, for in the burial register of St. Mary Lambeth—where his full name is entered as John Peter Andrew—Peter Ducrow's age at death is recorded as fifty-seven. While I have discovered no confirmation for either of these figures, I tend to favor the one on the tomb itself. Otherwise, the family would have easily detected the error (always assuming, of course, they themselves knew Peter's birthdate) and probably had it corrected. (Note that all parish registers mentioned in this study, unless otherwise stated, are currently stored in the Archives of the Greater London Council.)

2. See, e.g., the advertisements in the *Times* for 28 July 1796 and 25 May 1807 and the *Monthly Mirror* for June 1807; and cf. Strutt, p. 255. "Julking" (the word does not appear in the *O.E.D.*) was a fairly common act in the circuses of Peter Ducrow's day. An unidentified advertisement dated 5 February 1807 in Harvard I, 74, for instance, lists Mr. H. Bryson for "Whistling, Warbling, and Julking, in imitation of the notes of the different Song Birds . . . with a canary bird symphony, accompanied by a full orchestra" at Astley's Olympic Pavilion in Wych Street. The act was sometimes designated "à la Rossignol" after a Signor Rossignol, supposedly from Naples, who appeared at Sadler's Wells and elsewhere in the 1770s, imitating the notes of birds and exhibiting a troupe of twelve or fourteen linnets and canaries which marched about a

table carrying muskets and wearing paper caps. According to Frost, he later disgraced himself and dropped from sight after being detected using a hidden instrument at Covent Garden, where he had promised to imitate a violin with his mouth—Thomas Frost, *The Old Showmen and the Old London Fairs* (London, 1881), pp. 188–89, 193–94.

3. It was Moritz, I believe, whom Strutt (pp. 233–34) had in mind when describing the Dutchman he had seen at Sadler's Wells around 1799, for Moritz did perform there that year. He was also, at times, a conjuror; and it is probably his booth that appears in the background of Rowlandson's print "Brook Green Fair."

4. See below, p. 362.

5. Letter dated 6 September 1825 in the Folger Shakespeare Library, Y.d.23 (134).

6. Letter in the Theatre Museum of the Victoria and Albert Museum. (Note that in subsequent references this collection will be designated "V&A.")

7. Nor, one might add, did the situation improve much in the nineteenth century. At the time of the founding of the General Theatrical Fund Association, an early attempt to establish a pension plan for actors, there was considerable debate over whether circus equestrians should be admitted. The riders from Astley's argued that they were respectable members of the profession and no greater risk than ballet dancers, but were opposed by those who feared that to admit them would be to throw open the doors to "all the mountebank equestrians in England . . . to the great injury of the Association." A compromise was eventually reached whereby only riders who worked in amphitheatres possessing stages were admitted, since under these circumstances —such is the perennial vanity, and logic, of actors—their respectability would be assured. See *Actors by Daylight*, 2 February 1839. But the stage itself, as anyone familiar with the theatrical history of the first half of the century is well aware, was as yet hardly considered a respectable institution. The "Eminent Tragedian" William Charles Macready, a model of righteousness and self-approval in everything he did, literally hated his profession and was overjoyed at finally being able to leave it. If circus artists were considered inferior to members of the acting profession during this period, their status must have been low indeed.

8. The Ducrow scrapbook or album, bound in contemporary green leather with the name "A. Ducrow" stamped in gold on its front, was until recently in the possession of Mr. Peter Ducrow, the great-grandson of Andrew, who kindly permitted me to examine and make use of its contents. From some handwritten notes and newspaper accounts published after Andrew's death pasted into it, it appears Louisa Woolford, Ducrow's second wife, at one time had charge of it; although a number of items, dating from much earlier in Ducrow's career, must have been assembled by Andrew himself and possibly his first wife, Margaret. (Note that in all future references this scrapbook will be designated "Ducrow Album.")

9. I am indebted to the Reverend Harold Lockyer of Hartland, Devon, for information concerning the rites and customs of the Church of England.

10. She is buried in Square 130 on a map of the cemetery; but Nunhead Cemetery is now in such a ruinous state that I was unable to locate her grave on a recent expedition there.

11. St. Mary Lambeth Baptismal Register.

12. Unidentified clipping, hand-dated 23 June 1793, in the folder of clippings relating to the Royal Circus at the Theatre Collection of the Performing Arts Library (New York Public Library), Lincoln Center.

13. Notices and advertisements in the *Times* for 22 June, 2 July, 15 and 21 August, 18 and 30 September, and 14 October 1793. In his *Circus Life and Circus Celebrities* (London, 1875), Thomas Frost reproduces a bill of the Royal Circus from the same period on pp. 42–44. Additional mention of a number of these performers may be found in Decastro's *Memoirs*, pp. 147–48.

14. Unidentified advertisement, dated 9 September, in the first of three scrapbooks for Hughes' Royal Circus at the Theatre Collection, Lincoln Center. Sometimes billed without the "i" in his name, Saxoni was probably a member of the famous Italian family of dancers and equestrians, other members of which also appeared in England.

15. The Edinburgh Public Library possesses an interesting volume of manuscripts, pamphlets, etc. relating to this establishment. Among them are Jones and Parker's original proposals for the circus.

16. Advertisement in the Edinburgh *Evening Courant*, 26 December 1793.

17. Edinburgh *Evening Courant*, 4 November 1793.

18. Richer himself, a star artist who often traveled on his own, seems to have left Jones before the conclusion of the Edinburgh season. On 16 December 1793 I find him billed for the Theatre Royal, Dublin, where he danced the rope following a performance by Mrs. Siddons in *The Grecian Daughter*—playbill in the Trinity College Library, Dublin. The mingling of such acts with legitimate drama was quite common in theatres during the first half of the nineteenth century.

19. See, e.g., the advertisements in the *Times* for 7, 9, and 12 May 1795.

20. Advertisements in the *Times* for 25 and 28 July 1796.

21. See the *Times* for 29 October 1796; and cf., for the end of the 1795 season, *Londina Illustrata*, II, 192.

22. Advertisement in the *Times* for 24 October 1796.

23. Ducrow was of so strong an opinion on this latter point that he made it a policy during his management of Astley's "never to announce the breaking up of any passing Novelty, until its departure is really intended"—see, e.g., the Astley's playbill for 8 June 1829, V&A.

24. See, e.g., the "Memoir of Andrew Ducrow" in *Oxberry's Dramatic Biography and Green Room Spy*, N.S. (1827), II, 4. For a description of the Nag's Head, see William Rendle and Philip Norman, *The Inns of Old Southwark and Their Associations* (London and New York, 1888), pp. 221–25. A watercolor of the Nag's Head by T. H. Shepherd, painted in 1855, is in the Crace Collection of the British Museum.

25. See the biographical sketch "Mr. Andrew Ducrow" in the Edinburgh *Opera-Glass* for 4 September 1840; cf. *Oxberry's* "Memoir," pp. 10–11.

26. On Ducrow's handwriting and the charge that he was illiterate, see the appendix "The Ducrow Apocrypha."

27. "Theatrical Sketch of Mr. A. Ducrow, the Unparalleled Equestrian," in *Pierce Egan's Anecdotes of the Turf, the Chase, the Ring, and the Stage* (London, 1827), p. 266.

28. "Memoir of Mr. Ducrow" in the *Owl* for 24 September 1831.

29. *Oxberry's* "Memoir," p. 11.

30. Ibid., p. 12.

31. Ibid., pp. 11-12.

32. See "The Late Mr. Ducrow" in the *Sunday Times* for 30 January 1842.

33. "Mr. Andrew Ducrow," Edinburgh *Opera-Glass.*

34. *Theatrical Journal*, 12 September 1840. No doubt Grimaldi had some vivid recollections of his own on this occasion, for his father, who was a pantomime actor and ballet-master, was a great thrasher also and actually beat his son on the stage. When the elder Grimaldi was employed at the Royal Circus during the early days of Hughes and Dibdin, he used to punish his juvenile charges there by putting them into a tiny cage, which was then hoisted up into the fly area and left aloft for several hours. For this and less savoury reasons, criminal charges were eventually brought against him—see Charles Dickens, *Memoirs of Joseph Grimaldi*, ed. Richard Findlater (New York, [1968]), pp. 34-36, 295.

35. "Dramatic Feuilletons," *Sunday Times*, 22 June 1851, n.

36. The bill is reproduced among the "Scarce Advertisements" in Decastro's *Memoirs*, pp. 248-49. The subscribers to this work included Ducrow, who perhaps furnished Decastro this very bill.

37. Advertisement in the *Times*, 9 April 1798.

38. Most of this information is gleaned from various advertisements in the *Times, Morning Post*, and Bath *Journal*. The Circus World Museum at Baraboo, Wisconsin, possesses a rare bill for "Handy's Royal Troop" at Liverpool on 24 October 1797; additional details concerning his life may be found in Richard Wright Procter's *Manchester in Holiday Dress* (London and Manchester, 1866), pp. 46-47, and in Dibdin the Younger's *Professional and Literary Memoirs* (where his Christian name is given as Robert), p. 34. An amusing poem celebrating Handy's company—no doubt commissioned by the manager himself—appears in the *Thespian Magazine and Literary Repository* for September 1794:

> Handy, go on, thy feats are nobly done:
> Ye *Bucks* and *Bloods*, who love a little fun,
> This is the place to which you must resort;
> Sheer off to Handy, and he'll shew you sport.
> *Keep it up*, Handy! *bravo! that's your sort!*

39. For the names of the passengers lost in this accident, see the *Morning Herald* for 12 January 1798. Decastro, p. 141, also comments on the disaster.

40. *Times*, 18 April 1798.

41. Advertisement in the *Times*, 17 May 1798.

42. Unidentified advertisement in the second of three Astley's scrapbooks in the British Museum; cf. the advertisement in the *Times* for 4 September 1798. (Note that in all future references to these scrapbooks they will be designated "BM Astley's Scrapbooks," with the volume number following. Only the third volume is paginated.)

43. British Museum Playbills Collection, vol. 244. Note, however, that the printed date on the first of these bills, for Tuesday, 16 April 1798, is

NOTES TO PAGES 44–50 / 419

obviously wrong. A check with a perpetual calendar and comparison with the other bills show that it belongs in fact to the 1799 engagement. (In all subsequent references to bills from this collection, note that they will be designated as—for the above—"BM Playbills 244.")

44. Bill for Tuesday, 28 May [1799]. The spelling (and misspelling) of performers' names was subject to considerable variation, of course. Thus, Miss Simonet sometimes appears as "Simmonet" or "Simonett," and Peter Ducrow's name, as already observed, was sometimes spelled "Ducreau," "Du Crow," or even, as in the *Times* for 11 June 1798 and 6 June 1801, "Ducross" and "Ducroe." In most cases I shall adhere, without further comment, to what seem to have been the most common spellings. While on this topic, I should perhaps point out that my use of the word "troop" is deliberate. Circus companies of Astley's and Ducrow's periods customarily billed themselves this way—possibly in the desire to stress their equestrianism, although even bands of pedestrian actors might follow the same spelling.

45. Advertisement in the Manchester *Mercury*, 16 July 1799.

46. *Professional and Literary Memoirs*, pp. 34–38. Cf., on the Manchester engagement, Procter, *Manchester in Holiday Dress*, pp. 47–49; J. L. Hodgkinson and Rex Pogson, *The Early Manchester Theatre* (London, 1960), p. 154, where Peter is confused with his son John.

47. Dibdin, editor's note, p. 38; R. J. Broadbent, *Annals of the Liverpool Stage from the Earliest Period to the Present Time* (Liverpool, 1908), pp. 180–81.

48. *Times*, 27 May 1800.

49. See, e.g., the *Times* for 20, 21, and 23 May 1795 and later.

50. Bill for 17 April 1799, BM Playbills 244.

51. *Morning Chronicle*, 16 July 1800; cf. the description in the *Times* for the same date.

52. See, e.g., the Liverpool bill for 22 April 1806, BM Playbills 244.

53. *Oxberry's* "Memoir," pp. 3–4. A few later sketches, largely plagiarized from *Oxberry's* to begin with, become tangled and assign the accident to Andrew himself—see, e.g., the account "Andrew Ducrow" in *All the Year Round* for 3 February 1872, p. 223.

54. *Monthly Mirror*, September 1800.

55. See the various advertisements in the *Times* from 27 October 1800 to 28 March 1801.

56. *Times* advertisements beginning 6 April 1801. Saunders was the son of the showman Abraham Saunders, and both he and his sister were billed to ride and dance the rope in later years. A bill of 25 January 1793 for Astley's Dublin amphitheatre—reproduced in Decastro, p. 54—lists a Master George Pinto Saunders, only six years old, for his "second appearance on any Stage" in the pantomimic sketch *La Foret Noire, or The Natural Son*. The "Gothic" novelist William Beckford became enamoured of young Saunders in 1807, and Mr. George Speaight, drawing upon Beckford's letters and other materials, has written about this sordid episode in a privately circulated study ("Master Saunders," 1961) for the Union des Historiens du Cirque.

57. Advertisement in the *Times* for 6 June 1801, where Peter is awarded the distinction of being termed the "Flemish Hercules." A garbled advertisement for the same event in the 4 June issue, however, would seem to assign Woolford the same honor.

2. Youth

1. A note in the *Times* for 11 June 1814 tells of the troop of Astley, Davis, and Parker having been engaged for the Amsterdam Theatre; and see the advertisement for Astley's in the issue of 5 September, where it is stated Davis and his horses have just returned from Amsterdam and are scheduled to go to Paris over the winter. Mr. Ben Albach, vice-president of the Amsterdam Toneelmuseum, has researched this interesting bit of circus history and has kindly provided me with a copy of a paper he read on the subject during a recent conference at the University of Manchester. The troop was at the Hollandsche Schouwburg from 22 June until 6 August, performing—for the first time in a Dutch theatre—equestrian divertissements and two hippodramas previously produced in London, *The Secret Mine* and *Timour the Tartar*. The famous actor Johannes Jelgerhuis recorded his impressions of these productions in a notebook he kept, and was ashamed and indignant at being forced to appear in the first of them. Richer was also with the troop and took his benefit on 4 August.

2. See "The Late Mr. Ducrow" in the *Sunday Times*, 30 January 1842.

3. See the puff for the Royal Circus in the 14 June 1802 issue of the *Times*.

4. Advertisements in the *Times* for 19 and 23 December 1803.

5. For information on the various members of the D'Egville family, see Philip H. Highfill, Jr., Kalman A. Burnim, and Edward A. Langhans, comps., *A Biographical Dictionary of Actors, Actresses, Musicians, Dancers, Managers & Other Stage Personnel in London, 1660–1800*, IV (Carbondale, 1975), 266–76. For James Harvey D'Egville, see the brief biography in the *Monthly Mirror* for March 1809; Ivor Guest, *The Romantic Ballet in England: Its Development, Fulfilment and Decline* (Middletown, 1972), pp. 22–24, 36; Marian Hannah Winter, *The Pre-Romantic Ballet* (London, 1974), pp. 199–200 and passim. I am especially indebted to Dr. Winter for much expert advice and additional information on the D'Egvilles and their careers.

6. Advertisement in the Edinburgh *Evening Courant*, 30 October 1830.

7. This information is largely gleaned from materials in the V&A. "Mr. D'Egville" also appears among the cast lists for several pieces in J. C. Cross's *Circusiana, or A Collection of the Most Favourite Ballets, Spectacles, Melo-Drames, &c. Performed at the Royal Circus, St. George's Fields*, 2 vols. (London, 1809). It is likely Peter D'Egville was also associated with the Royal Circus. An advertisement dated Saturday, 23 August [1788], in the V&A lists, besides "Master D'Egville" for a minuet and gavotte, a comic divertissement entitled *The Impressed Recruits* with dances composed by "Mons. D'Egville."

8. Where George also worked—see the bill for the Liverpool New Olympic Circus for 8 December 1806, BM Playbills 244.

9. "Theatrical Sketch of Mr. A. Ducrow," p. 266.

10. Advertisement in the *Times*, 27 May 1805.

11. See the *Examiner* for 26 February 1809.

12. Letter dated 24 April, published in the issue of 25 April.

13. James Peller Malcolm, *Londinium Redivivum; or, an Ancient History and Modern Description of London* (London, 1802–1807), III, 235. Richer's "exquisite ease, and unaffected natural grace" were also recalled by Hazlitt, many years after he had seen him, in his essay "The Indian Jugglers" included

in *Table Talk*. His father Jacques, a theatrical dancer in the company of the Grands Danseurs du Roi in 1778, had also appeared at Sadler's Wells in the eighteenth century. Like the D'Egvilles, the family were originally French. Campardon, in his *Les Spectacles de la foire* (II, 323), lists several artists by the name of Richer, one of whom, Charles-Toussaint Richer, a ropedancer and vaulter with the troupe of Jean Restier in 1753–62, may have been Jack's grandfather.

14. See, e.g., *Oxberry's* "Memoir," p. 3. The biographical sketch published in the Edinburgh *Opera-Glass* for 4 September 1840 states Andrew was actually "articled" or apprenticed to Richer.

15. *Memoirs*, pp. 158–59.

16. See, e.g., the Astley's bill for 3 August 1812 in the V&A and the advertisement for Collett's benefit in the *Times* for 1 October 1812. The riding master in nineteenth-century circuses was responsible for superintending the "horse department" and ring acts; the stage manager directed the plays and spectacles.

17. *Oxberry's* "Memoir," p. 4, n.; Edinburgh *Opera-Glass*, 4 September 1840; "The Late Mr. Ducrow," *Sunday Times*, 30 January 1842.

18. Advertisement in the Edinburgh *Evening Courant*, 25 November 1805.

19. Advertisement in the Edinburgh *Evening Courant*, 28 November 1805. The "Polander" was an acrobat and equilibrist who had performed at Sadler's Wells at the end of the eighteenth century. His various feats, including the breakaway-ladder trick, are captured in a colored print of twenty-four panels, reproduced (from a copy at the British Museum) at the end of the third volume of R. Toole Stott's *Circus and Allied Arts*. All twenty-four illustrations, interestingly, show him head downward on an assortment of chairs, candlesticks, bottles, wheels, etc., at the same time holding chairs and flags in his free hand (the other is always helping him retain his balance) or dangling them from his feet. He was, to use the contemporary designation, "antipodean."

20. Advertisement in the Edinburgh *Evening Courant*, 1 February 1806. The family also assisted in other areas, of course, as on 10 January when Peter played the part of the landlord in a pantomime entitled *The Prophecy, or The Mountain in Labour*—bill in the Edinburgh Public Library.

21. *Oxberry's* "Memoir," p. 13. In the plagiarized account in *All the Year Round* (p. 288) and in Pichot's *Mémoirs d'un dompteur* (p. 24), which is obviously based on the former, the doctor's name becomes "Barker."

22. On the chance that Barclay or his students might have left a few notes on Ducrow, or that Barclay might have engaged Andrew as a living model (a practice that continued in the School until the 1960s), I at one time visited the University of Edinburgh and its Anatomy Department, but found no trace of Andrew.

23. The Library of the University of Glasgow possesses a *rara avis* for the period, a separately bound volume of playbills for this engagement titled "Glasgow—Olympic Circus Bills—1806."

24. *Weekly Dramatic Register*, 16 July 1825. Mazurier, who will be discussed in chapter 3, was also in London in 1825, earning fifty pounds a night as a man-monkey at Covent Garden and leading one critic to remark sulkily that

"monkeys swarm in the theatres just now. Gentlemen with ugly faces, and unshaved arms and legs, are grinning to music at heavy salaries, on almost every great stage in London. Apes are looking up"—*London Magazine*, December 1825. Notwithstanding such complaints, the actors did appear in costumes.

25. John Fawcett, *Perouse, or The Desolate Island* (London: J. Barker, 1801).

26. Bill for 22 April 1806, BM Playbills 244. Information concerning the remainder of this engagement is derived mainly from bills in the same volume.

27. Bill for 14 May 1806.

28. Advertisement in the *Times*, 16 September 1806. For the history of the Olympic Pavilion as a circus, see *Enter Foot and Horse*, pp. 16–17. Converted into a theatre, this same building was to house the celebrated Madame Vestris in the 1830s.

29. See, e.g., the bill for 15 March 1806 and the undated bill for Friday and Saturday in "Olympic Circus Bills," University of Glasgow; advertisement for Astley's in the *Times*, 13 October 1806.

30. See the advertisements for the Olympic Pavilion in the *Times* for 12 and 26 January 1807. The other Master Davis is sometimes identified in later advertisements as Master J. Davis, raising the possibility that he may in fact have been the younger brother or nephew of Davis Sr. Dibdin the Younger in his memoirs (pp. 133–34) mentions a brother John who later became the proprietor of an equestrian concern near Belgrave Place. Andrew's rival—if we may believe the bills and other announcements dating from the beginning of the century—was around the same age as he.

31. Bill for 13 October 1806 in the Manchester Central Library.

32. Advertisement in the Manchester *Mercury*, 21 October 1806.

33. Bill for 10 November 1806 in the Manchester Central Library. Cf. Procter, *Manchester in Holiday Dress*, p. 50.

34. Bill for 8 December 1806, BM Playbills 244.

35. Makeen, who had performed at the Royal Circus the previous summer, was one of the better-known equestrians of the day and was billed during his early career as the "Youthful" or "Flying Highlander." His wife—who could also ride—and he frequently appeared in dramatic pieces, as during Elliston's initial season managing the Royal Circus in 1809, when Mrs. Makeen performed the roles of Jenny Diver in *The Beggar's Opera* and Lady Macbeth in Elliston's notorious burletta version of Shakespeare's play. Makeen himself appeared as Banquo during this season and, for his benefit on 23 October, undertook the part of Macbeth for the first time, later on the same program riding and taking a leap through a hackney coach. Their later histrionic careers at Astley's are commented on by Dibdin the Younger (*Memoirs*, pp. 131–35), who obviously found Mrs. Makeen an asset in the plays he was then writing, since she "fought a Combat, with the spirit of a Man" and was a "fine Woman, stout, active, and vigorous." Dibdin also reports that Makeen eventually lost his life as the result of a fall at a provincial circus. The Hickens were a fairly well-known circus family in the nineteenth century, and the one who appeared at Liverpool, I suspect, was the father of the rider who later performed with Ducrow at Astley's.

36. Bill for 15 December 1806, BM Playbills 244.

37. As on 22 December, when Peter was billed for the role of an old Spaniard in D'Egville's grand spectacle *The Conquest of Buenos Ayres, or Bad News for Boney*; on 13 January as an old shepherd in *The Tartarian Robbers, or The Rival Brothers* (which was obviously an adaptation of Schiller, with D'Egville himself as Charles Moor, captain of the robbers and son to Count Moor); on 20 January as Pantaloon in *The Brazen Head, or Harlequin's Rainbow* (with Master Ducrow as Punch's wife and D'Egville as Clown); and on 16 March as an old man in the pantomime *The Devil in a Bottle* (with Master Ducrow as Dwarf). Andrew himself, besides performing in several of these productions, was billed to appear on 9 February as a page in a spectacle entitled *The Wild Girl*; on 3 March as a cottage boy in *The False Friend, or Assassin of the Rocks*; and on 14 April as a page again in the serious pantomime *Valentine and Orson* (with D'Egville as Orson, the wild man, and Makeen as Valentine, a foundling). At other times he was advertised to dance, as on 3 April in a ballet entitled *Highland Sports, or Blind Man's Buff*, and on 8 April with Miss Johannot in a double hornpipe—see the announcements in BM Playbills 244.

38. Advertisements in the *Times* for 25 May and 13 July 1807. The real names of the performers were finally given in an advertisement which appeared in the 27 July issue of the *Times* ("Tight-Rope Dancing, by the celebrated Master Ducrow . . . Turkish Performances on the Slack-Wire, by Mr. Ducrow. Horsemanship by Mr. Makeen"); and in an advertisement in the same paper for the benefit of Mr. and Master Ducrow on 22 September the identity of the "Young Prussian" becomes even more evident. Andrew, of course, was no more "Prussian" than Peter was "Turkish." Circuses have always tried to impress their audiences with exotic acts, and in this instance the "nationalities" probably referred to the Ducrows' costumes, with Andrew in some kind of military dress.

39. Unidentified advertisement, hand-dated March 1811, in the first of three Astley's scrapbooks formerly the property of Maurice Willson Disher and now in the Kenneth Spencer Research Library at the University of Kansas. (Note that in subsequent references these volumes will be designated "Disher Scrapbooks.")

40. BM Playbills 310. *Blood Will Have Blood* was one of several productions at the London theatres this season parodying the fare then being offered by John Philip Kemble at Covent Garden, which on 18 February 1811 had gone "illegitimate" with an equestrianized revival of George Colman's eighteenth-century melodrama *Blue Beard, or Female Curiosity*. For further information on this phase in the history of the patent theatres, see *Enter Foot and Horse*, pp. 83 ff.

41. See, e.g., the advertisements in the *Times* for 14 March and 15 April and the puff in the issue of 3 April.

42. *Oxberry's* "Memoir," p. 4.

43. Advertisement in the *Times*, 22 June 1812.

44. Single bill for 16–18 July 1812, Disher Scrapbooks I.

45. See, e.g., the bill for 3 August 1812, V&A.

46. See, e.g., the single bill for 27–29 July 1812 in BM Playbills 170 and the bill for 3 August 1812 in the V&A.

47. "Theatrical Sketch of Mr. A. Ducrow," p. 266.

48. Advertisements in the *Times* for these dates. A famous description of the act occurs in chapter 22 of Mark Twain's *The Adventures of Huckleberry Finn.*

49. Bill for 27 November 1812 in the first scrapbook of the Richard Smith Collection, "Bristol Theatre," in the Bristol Central Library. Cf. the bills for 2, 3, and 4 December 1812 in the same volume.

50. See the loose bill for this circus in the Bristol Central Library. A few advertisements also appear in the Bristol *Mercury* for 20 December 1813 and Bristol *Mirror* for 1 January 1814.

51. Bills for the summer engagement, for 26 and 27 July 1813, are in vols. 1 and 3 of the Richard Smith Collection, "Bristol Theatre." For the winter season, see vol. 3 and BM Playbills 203. Prior to appearing at Bristol over the holiday season, West and Woolford's troop had spent several weeks at the Bath Theatre Royal, to which they returned for a few nights following the Bristol engagement—bills for the Bath season in BM Playbills 178.

52. Advertisements in the *Times* and *Morning Chronicle* for 4 July 1814. Cf. the bill for 2 August 1814, in which the cast of the play is also given, among the loose Surrey bills in the Harvard Theatre Collection. Elliston had given up his lease of the Surrey at the end of March, and under the management of Dunn, Branscomb, and Heywood, which lasted until 1816, the ring was restored and the building rechristened with its original name. It may also be worth pointing out, for the benefit of those familiar with what I have termed the "Ducrow Apocrypha," that there is no evidence for Peter Ducrow's having leased the Royal Circus during this or any other season.

53. "Mr. Andrew Ducrow," Edinburgh *Opera-Glass*, 4 September 1840. Cf. "The Late Mr. Ducrow," *Sunday Times*, 30 January 1842.

54. See, e.g., the advertisements in the *Times* and *Morning Chronicle* for 6 October 1814.

55. "Memoir of Mr. Ducrow," the *Owl*, 24 September 1831.

56. See, e.g., Disher, *Greatest Show on Earth*, p. 98; Ruth Manning-Sanders, *The English Circus* (London, 1952), p. 47.

57. On Harris's authorship, see the review of the Covent Garden production in the *Theatrical Inquisitor and Monthly Mirror* for October 1814 ("the piece is a translation from the French by Mr. Harris," etc.). The Royal Circus version is attributed to Barrymore in contemporary advertisements—e.g., the *Morning Chronicle* for 7 October and the *Times* for 8 October—which is what one would expect, since Barrymore was house author at the time.

58. The differences between the two versions are commented on in the October 1814 issue of the *Theatrical Inquisitor*, which clearly preferred Barrymore's adaptation and termed it "infinitely superior to the piece of the same name represented at Covent Garden Theatre."

59. See, e.g., the Astley's bill for 9 July 1838, BM Playbills 170.

60. Descriptions of the White's fête were carried in both the *Times* and *Morning Chronicle* for 22 June. The *Times* for 13 June promises Sadler's ascension, and mention of the gardens and stage for the Watier's festival (to honor the Duke of Wellington) is in the issue of 1 July. The *Morning Chronicle* for 4 July devotes an extensive article to the later fête, at which ropedancers, jugglers, dancers, singers, actors, and the clowns Grimaldi and Bologna performed.

61. Bill for 26 December [1814] in the Richard Smith Collection, "Bristol Theatre," vol. 3. Cf. the bills for 19 and 28 December in this same volume and the advertisement in the Bristol *Gazette* for 15 December, which announces the first appearance of "Young Ducrow" from the Royal Circus for Monday, the 19th.

62. Bills for Ducrow's appearances at Bath during December 1814 are in BM Playbills 178. Andrew was also billed for ropedancing at both the Bath and Bristol theatres.

63. BM Playbills 203.

64. Bath *Journal*, 18 March 1816.

65. *Felix Farley's Bristol Journal*, 30 March 1816. Cf. the advertisement for Ducrow's performance on the 28th in the 25 March 1816 issue of the Bath *Journal*.

66. Bill for 1 April 1816 in the Richard Smith Collection, "Bristol Theatre," vol. 3.

67. See the advertisement in the *Times*, 14 October 1816.

68. Advertisements in the *Times* and *Morning Chronicle*, 23 October 1816.

69. Advertisement in the *Morning Chronicle*, 24 October 1816.

70. The second of these engravings is not infrequently encountered in collections of theatricalia and circusiana; but the first, to my knowledge, exists only in a single copy in the Lysons Collection at the British Museum. Unfortunately, the imprint of this particular engraving has been somewhat cropped, but through a comparison of what remains with the imprint of the later engraving, both the date and publisher's identity are easily established.

71. See the *Theatrical Inquisitor* for February 1817.

72. Beginning 3 April they were at the Cirque Olympique for a month in Paris, where young Davis, to give him his due, appears to have been well received: "Il a exécuté sur son cheval des pas de danse anglaise avec autant de précision que s'il eût dansé dans un salon; il y a joint plusieurs exercices d'agilité avec des cerceaux et le tambour de basque"—*Mémorial Dramatique ou Almanach Théatral pour l'An 1818*.

73. Advertisement in the *Times*, 13 September 1817. Il Diavolo Antonio, sometimes described as a Venetian but more often as of Portuguese origin, had also performed at Astley's during the 1816 season. His real name, as one learns from an autographed print of him in the British Museum Perceval Collection IV, 91 (the same collection contains several letters from him in IV and XIV), was Antonio Blitz. Here again, however, we are faced with a "nom d'arena" that seems to have been shared by two or more artists.

74. Advertisements in the *Times* and *Morning Chronicle*, 1 October 1817.

75. Advertisements in the Liverpool *Mercury*, 5 December 1817 to 13 March 1818.

76. *Oxberry's* "Memoir," p. 10.

77. *Stage Reminiscences* (Glasgow, 1866), pp. 141–42.

78. An unidentified clipping with an engraving of Mrs. Bridges performing at Astley's, hand-dated 1848, is in Harvard III, 92. The clipping states that she is the niece of the late Madame Ducrow and acquired her skill as an equestrienne under the tutelage of Signor Chiarini.

79. Frost, for example, quotes an advertisement for Astley's dating from 1772 in which a Mrs. Griffiths is scheduled for equestrian feats and a

role in a French piece—*Circus Life and Circus Celebrities*, p. 19 (and see, on pp. 20 and 22, the references to "Griffin" at Astley's in 1775 and 1780). A Mrs. Stewart, formerly Miss Griffiths, was singing and playing in pantomimes at the Royal Circus in 1805—advertisement dated 16 April 1805 in vol. 2 of the Hughes' Royal Circus Scrapbooks at Lincoln Center. And two illustrations of a Mr. Griffiths riding at Hughes' Royal Circus appear in the borders of an engraved sheet of paper, published in 1789, for children's writing exercises. The last interesting bit of ephemera is in the collection of Dr. Marian Hannah Winter and is reproduced in her article "La Prise de la Bastille, pantomime de cirque de 1789," *Vieux Papier*, fascicule no. 247 (janvier 1973), p. 14. The same engraving is also reproduced and discussed further in an article of my own, "Capon, the Royal Circus, and *The Destruction of the Bastille*," *Theatre Notebook*, XXVIII (1974), 133–35. There were also a number of Griffiths associated with the Bath Theatre Royal around 1830. Margaret's own name, incidentally, is spelled without the "s" in *Oxberry's* "Memoir," though this may be a typographical error.

80. The provenance of these portraits remains unclear, and the identification of the woman as Margaret is solely my own. Both portraits, along with several other illustrations pertaining to Ducrow—two watercolors clearly identified as being of his mother and sister Margaret, an engraving of Andrew as Charles II on his white steed Bucephalus, a pencil sketch of the Ducrow mausoleum at Kensal Green shortly after its erection, and an unidentified pencil drawing of a young girl who may be the "Petite Ducrow" discussed in a later chapter—were purchased by Mr. Coxe from a family whose ancestry includes a mysterious ill-tempered grandfather, or rather step-grandfather, who is believed to have brought the portraits into the family together with himself under an assumed name. This leads to all sorts of interesting speculations, none easily verifiable. The important thing is that all of the items in this small collection seem to have some association with Ducrow, and the man in the watercolor does bear a resemblance to him. The woman's portrait is obviously by the same artist and intended as a companion piece. From this and the apparent closeness in age of the two sitters (Andrew was around four years older than Margaret), I believe, and Mr. Coxe concurs in my opinion, that the portraits are of Andrew and Margaret. The reader will perhaps pardon my desperation in this matter when he learns that no other depiction of Margaret is known to exist.

81. "Memoir of Mr. Ducrow," the *Owl*, 24 September 1831.

3. The Years Abroad

1. Blondin's own real name was Frans Erasmus, as he acknowledged in his announcements, which in 1818 often begin by naming him "De heer Erasmus, genaamd" or "gezegd Blondel." In his younger years, while performing as a leaper, he also went by the name "de kleine Blondel"—see Marja Keyser, *Komt dat Zien! De Amsterdamse Kermis in de negentiende eeuw* (Amsterdam and Rottendam, [1976]), pp. 76, 79.

2. See Pierre-Amédée Pichot, *Les Mémoires d'un dompteur rédigés d'après les souvenirs personnels du célèbre Martin* (Paris, 1877), pp. 17–28.

3. *Journal de Gand*, 21 April 1818.

4. Ibid., 22, 23, 24, and 26 April 1818.

5. *'S Gravenhaagsche Courant*, 1 and 11 May 1818.

6. Ibid., 18 and 25 May 1818; Astley's bill for 9 July 1838, BM Playbills 170.

7. See, e.g., the *Rotterdamsche Courant* for 11 August 1818.

8. *Amsterdamsche Courant*, 23 September 1818.

9. For additional information on the history of the Cirque Olympique and descriptions of the different buildings it occupied in Paris, see *Enter Foot and Horse*, pp. 18–27.

10. *Oxberry's* "Memoir," pp. 4–5.

11. "Theatrical Sketch of Mr. A. Ducrow," p. 267.

12. Ibid. "At Paris," according to the "Memoir of Mr. Ducrow" published in the *Owl* for 24 September 1831, "he was the rage, and the enthusiastic Parisians worshipped Ducrow, as the first horseman in the world."

13. See, e.g., the *Journal des Débats* for 21 December 1818 and the *Courrier des Spectacles* for 2 January 1819.

14. See the *Camp-Volant* for 7 March 1819.

15. *Quotidienne*, 7 April 1819. The critic for the *Camp-Volant* (15 April 1819), unable to resist a few joking references to Andrew's usual fellow actors—i.e., horses—and the size of his customary stage, conceded that "on the whole he displays above-average ability and as much sensitivity as may be expected in an English artist." It should also be noted that Ducrow never appeared in the pantomime *Le Tombeau magique*, presented the following November after he had left the Franconis, as Thétard and Lyonnet have erroneously reported in their histories.

16. See the *Journal de Lyon* for 3 September and the *Camp-Volant* for 12 September 1819; cf. the account of the accident in *Oxberry's* "Memoir," pp. 7–8.

17. See, e.g., the *Journal de Paris* for 4 October and the *Fanal des Théâtres* for 6 November 1819.

18. *Camp-Volant*, 3 October 1819. For other pointed references to Ducrow's nationality in this periodical, see the issues of 20 December 1818 and 15 April 1819.

19. *Oxberry's* "Memoir," p. 7.

20. B., J.-E. [Bouteiller, Jules Edouard], *Histoire complète et méthodique des théatres de Rouen* (Rouen, 1860–80), III, 75; cf. the *Journal de Paris* for 10 November 1819.

21. I must here admit to having at one time uncritically accepted and repeated this story myself in an article for *Theatre Research/Recherches Théâtrales*.

22. See, e.g., the Astley's bills for 26 December 1822 and 19 May, 30 June, 21 July, 18 August, 1 and 2 September 1823 in BM Playbills 170; 23 May and 11 November 1822 in BM Playbills 171; 25 September, 4 November, and 13 December 1822, V&A.

23. *Oxberry's* "Memoir," p. 7. Cf. Egan, pp. 267–68, whose description of Ducrow's company in "1818" is actually of the Franconis' or Ducrow's troop at a much later date.

24. *Miroir des Spectacles*, 1 August 1822; *Ami de la Charte*, 20 June 1823.

25. *Courrier des Spectacles*, 23 March 1821.

26. Reproduced in color in Marian Hannah Winter, *Le Théâtre du Merveilleux* (Paris, 1962), opp. p. 168. Another early but smaller colored print of "Mr. Ducrow as the Roman Gladiator" (plate 1) is in the Stone Collection of the Theatre Museum, V&A. No information as to the artist or the publisher is given on the engraving, but it may be this too is after a drawing by Andrew, published sometime before his departure for the Continent in 1818.

27. It seems obvious the act was also influenced by Charles Didelot's ballet *Flore et Zéphire*, which had been a favorite for some two decades prior to Ducrow's interpretation. The role of Zéphire—whose aerial flights were aided by invisible wires—eventually became one of the most famous in the repertoire of the dancer Antoine Paul, who performed it around the same time as Andrew. See Winter, *The Pre-Romantic Ballet*, p. 123 and passim; and compare the poses and costume of Paul in the illustrations on pp. 233 and 276 with those of Ducrow.

28. The sequence of poses is also described in a later Astley's bill for 6 July [1829], V&A.

29. *Mémorial Bordelais*, 30 April 1822.

30. Laurent Lalanne, born in 1785, was a year older than his famous sister. There was also a younger brother Baptiste, however, born around 1793, who eventually served as Madame Saqui's manager, and in time brought her to ruin. See Paul Ginisty, *Mémoires d'une danseuse de corde: Mme. Saqui (1786–1866)* (Paris, 1907), pp. 27, 44, 154, 164–70.

31. Bill for 31 July 1826, V&A. Although Andrew was performing his "Grand Flight of Mercury" by the time of his debut at the Cirque Olympique in 1818, the character itself was not original with him. Philip Astley had posed as Mercury while riding in the eighteenth century, as did any number of equestrians both before and after Andrew. For this reason, too, the claim made by some writers that Ducrow was the "inventor" of poses plastiques on horseback obviously must be considered an exaggeration. Another popular pose at the turn of the century was that of "Renommée" or "Fame," which Andrew also eventually added to his repertoire.

32. *Journal de Lyon*, 13 April 1820. For an anecdote concerning a production of this pantomime at the Cirque Olympique in 1851, see *Enter Foot and Horse*, p. 8.

33. Information culled from issues of the *Journal de Lyon* for 21 April and 2 and 16 May 1820.

34. *Journal de Lyon*, 21 April 1820; cf. the *Courrier des Spectacles*, 30 April 1820.

35. *Oxberry's* "Memoir," p. 9.

36. Archives Nationales F^{21} 1142. For this and all subsequent references to archival materials dealing with Ducrow's career in France, I am indebted to my colleague M. Tristan Rémy, whose own exhaustive study of these files led me to the pertinent information.

37. See the *Journal des Théatres*, 17 August 1820.

38. *Journal de Lyon*, 29 August 1820; and see the *Journal des Théatres*, 2 October 1820.

39. The letter was reprinted in the *Courrier des Spectacles* for 27 September 1820.

40. This regulation was an outgrowth of Napoleon's decree of 13 August 1811 under which governmental control was reestablished over the theatres, and the secondary houses of Paris, including the Cirque Olympique, were required to pay one-twentieth of their receipts to the Opéra. The exaction of the much higher proportion (one-fifth) from troupes touring the provinces was later amended in the case of the Franconis to the same "redevance" or tax they were subject to while at Paris—a dispensation that brought many protests from the directors of provincial theatres. It was, in fact, to placate one of these harried individuals that the Minister of the Interior ruled in 1813 that the Franconis could perform no more than fifteen days at Rouen, and it was this decision the equestrian managers were attempting to overturn in 1822. Ducrow, of course, was required to pay the usual twenty percent in the French towns he visited and therefore was not restricted to any set lengths of time. The history and explanation of these rulings is set forth in several documents in Archives Nationales F^{21} 1142.

41. *Oxberry's* "Memoir," p. 8.

42. Bills, with various cuts of Ducrow as Jacko [*sic*], are in BM Playbills 170 and Harvard I, 132. A capsule history of Mazurier's career, together with several illustrations of him in his various roles, is given in Winter, *Le Théatre du Merveilleux*, pp. 139–43. And for a curious, perhaps outrageous statement concerning his originality, see *Oxberry's* "Memoir" (p. 9), where it is said that "the ground work of all he [Mazurier] did he obtained from Parsloe, who was, at the period we speak of, with Ducrow." There was a Parsloe appearing as a Chinese buffoon at Astley's in 1825, and I assume this was the same Charles T. Parsloe who performed as a posturer at the Bristol Theatre Royal in 1827 (see Kathleen Barker, *The Theatre Royal, Bristol, 1766–1966* [London, 1974], p. 257) and who is depicted as "Master Parsloe" doing his "attitudes" in a print by W. West dating from 1812 (reproduced on p. 171 of David Mayer III, *Harlequin in His Element : The English Pantomime, 1806–1836* [Cambridge, Mass., 1969]). I find no reference to Parsloe by name during Ducrow's sojourn in France, though it seems likely he was the "jeune Chinois (Chinois quant au costume)" who is described in the *Mémorial Bordelais* for 14 April 1822 as assuming such difficult attitudes or postures that he gave the impression of being "deossified." From this description, too, it is apparent that the statement in *Oxberry's* "Memoir" refers specifically to Mazurier's interpretation of Polichinelle.

43. *Journal de Lyon*, 1 June 1820.

44. Bill for 13 September 1824, BM Playbills 171.

45. Reconstruction primarily based on the *Mémorial Bordelais* for 21 and 30 April 1822; the Edinburgh *Evening Courant* for 6 December 1827; "Ducrow's Horsemanship and the Carnival of Venice," *Theatrical Journal* for 30 August 1845 (the last source, a retrospective account written several years after Ducrow's death, is not always accurate). The Punch impersonation is also described in an Astley's bill for 25 May 1829, in which assurance is given that the illusion will be quite complete "if the Spectator will admit of the momentary supposition, that it is a Wooden Figure brought before him, with the joints hung upon wires and put in motion by pulling a string as the Toys of Children, differing only from the small play thing in point of size" (BM Astley's Scrapbooks III, 157).

46. See the *Schweizerfreund* for 15, 22, and 29 September 1820.

47. The *Gazzetta di Milano* of 29 November notes the arrival of Ducrow from Berne on this date.

48. See "Mr. Andrew Ducrow," Edinburgh *Opera-Glass*, 4 September 1840.

49. *Gazzetta di Milano*, 20 December 1820; cf. the *Journal de Lyon*, 9 January 1821. After one of the troop's performances, on the evening of 8 January, an attempt was made on the life of a well-known spectator. Colonel Browne, who during the previous fall had figured conspicuously in the unsuccessful divorce proceedings initiated by George IV against his wife Caroline of Brunswick, and who had earlier collected evidence of the Queen's indiscretions while she was living in Italy, was stabbed while he was walking home from the theatre—see *Oxberry's* "Memoir," p. 9; cf. the *Times* for 22 and 26 January 1821, with a letter from Browne in the later issue.

50. *Courrier des Spectacles*, 18 August 1821.

51. *Mémorial Bordelais*, 25 April 1822.

52. *Ami de la Charte*, 26 June 1823.

53. Ibid., 4 July 1823.

54. *Mémorial Bordelais*, 30 April 1822.

55. *Courrier des Théatres*, 22 April 1823; *Oxberry's* "Memoir," p. 9, n.

56. *Mémorial Bordelais*, 21 April 1822; cf. the issue for 30 April, where the critic reverts to the subject.

57. See, e.g., the Astley's bill for 11 April 1825, V&A.

58. *Mémorial Bordelais*, 30 April 1822.

59. See, e.g., the advertisement in the *Ami de la Charte* for 26 June 1823.

60. See the notices in the *Miroir des Spectacles* for 9 June 1823 and *Pandore* for 20 July 1823. The last also comments on the lack of "clarity" in Ducrow's production of *La Lampe merveilleuse*, a version of the Aladdin story.

61. But did not, apparently, take kindly to the role Ducrow had cast him for, which involved standing immobile amidst a barrage of fireworks—see the *Mémorial Bordelais* for 30 April 1822.

62. Advertisement and review in the *Mémorial Bordelais*, 25 April 1822; *Miroir des Spectacles*, 1 May 1822.

63. *Mémorial Bordelais*, 30 April 1822.

64. Ibid.

65. Quoted in the *Courrier des Spectacles*, 22 August 1821.

66. *Ami de la Charte*, 22 June 1823.

67. Agreement, signed by Ducrow as "Director of the Equestrian Troop lately of the Theatres at Milan," in Harvard I, 137. According to *Oxberry's* "Memoir" (p. 9), the offer was made by Charles Kemble, then manager of Covent Garden, upon meeting Ducrow in Paris. This may be true, but there can be no doubt the final terms were settled in London, for the agreement itself is dated there, and in his letter to the proprietors ten days later Ducrow tells of looking into the matters he discusses "on my arrival in France."

68. ALS, on paper with engraved letterhead "Direction du Cirque Olympique / De Mʳ Ducrow, / Premier Ecuyer de plusieurs Cours étrangères, sanctionné par / plusieurs Souverains," in Harvard I, 109. The title "Cirque Olympique" was as ubiquitous on the Continent as was that of "Olympic Circus" in Britain.

69. A copy of Robertson's reply is written on the above letter from Ducrow. On the subject of these negotiations, see *Enter Foot and Horse*, pp. 99–100.

70. [Bouteiller], III, 195–96; cf. *Pandore*, 11 October 1823. The Chinese acrobats were probably the "Turkish" ones who had been advertised the previous year, and who seem to have been no more stimulating then. "M. Ducrow," wrote the usually sympathetic reviewer for the *Mémorial Bordelais* on 21 April 1822, "would do well to suppress the act by his Turkish leapers. For too long they have bored spectators with their clumsiness."

4. *Triumph*

1. For the plot and reviews of *Cortez*, see *Enter Foot and Horse*, pp. 99–102; and for an extended discussion of the production of hippodramas in legitimate theatres and the opposition to them, see ch. 4, "Major Rivals," and pp. 222–27 in the same work.

2. *Museum; or, Record of Literature*, 8 November 1823.

3. See, e.g., the *London Magazine* for December 1823.

4. See *Enter Foot and Horse*, pp. 97–99.

5. Bill for 5 November 1823, V&A. In the bills for the Christmas pantomime of this year, the attendants of Flora include a Miss Griffiths, while a Collett appears among the male morris dancers.

6. Bill for 21 November 1823, V&A. For Cooke's connection with Ducrow on other occasions, see below, pp. 283, 373.

7. Bill for 26 December 1823, V&A.

8. See the *Times* for 27 December 1823 and the *Mirror of the Stage* for 5 January 1824. For an informative discussion of this and other pantomimes during the period, see Mayer, *Harlequin in His Element*.

9. *Times*, 28 December 1824.

10. Bills for this engagement are in vols. 3 and 4 of the Richard Smith Collection, "Bristol Theatre," in the Bristol Central Library, which also possesses two loose bills for the same engagement; and in BM Playbills 205.

11. See the *Mirror of the Stage* for 17 November 1823.

12. Bristol *Mercury*, 22 March 1824.

13. Ibid., 5 April 1824.

14. Loose bill in the Bristol Central Library.

15. Brayley, p. 64. At this time, too, the land on which the theatre stood was under lease from the Archbishop of Canterbury to John Chevalier Cobbold, who sublet the ground to the theatre's proprietors. Cobbold, to whom the ground lease had been first granted in 1819, continued as the Archbishop's lessee until well after the destruction of the third Astley's and death of Ducrow. At the time of the 1841 fire, in fact, he was described as the owner of the theatre itself, presumably owing to its having devolved to the ground landlord around 1838—see the valuations for 16 May 1833 and 23 October 1840 in the records of the archiepiscopal estates, Lambeth Palace Library; Brayley, pp. 64–65; *Examiner*, 13 June 1841. The annual license for the theatre's operation, issued during the Surrey Sessions the previous autumn, customarily included the names of the proprietors and their lessees. For Davis's quarrel with Hannah Astley and the Misses Gill over the license for the 1825 season, see the *Morning Chronicle* for 21 October 1824.

16. Dibdin, *Professional and Literary Memoirs*, pp. 138–39.

17. See *Enter Foot and Horse*, pp. 137–42.

18. *Columbine*, 11 July 1829.

19. Bon Gaultier [pseud. Theodore Martin], ed., *The Book of Ballads* (London, 1845), "The Midnight Visit." And for other references to Gomersal in this work, see "Don Fernando Gomersalez" and "The Courtship of Our Cid." Edward Alexander Gomersal (1788–1862), the son of a military officer, made his London debut at the Haymarket in 1811. By 1814 he had gravitated to Astley's, an association that was regretted by at least one critic, who compared his style to that of Kean—"impassioned, and natural: without any sepulchral solemnity, or statue like stiffness about him"—praised his voice and features for their variety of tone and serious expression, and suggested he would make a valuable second for Kean at Drury Lane (*The Stage*, 13 July 1816). Despite a hint by the same reviewer that the management of Drury Lane was scouting him, Gomersal spent the rest of his career at minor houses, most notably Astley's, where his finished and comparatively restrained style of acting was in marked contrast to that of his colleagues. For a description of his qualities during this later period—"an easy delivery—a good voice—and the power of making himself distinctly heard all over the house, without bawling"—see the *Weekly Dramatic Register* for 20 August 1825. Gomersal's wife was an actress who sometimes appeared at Astley's. His son William (d. 1902), who became a low comedian, lessee of several northern provincial theatres, and at one period toured America and worked for P. T. Barnum, left a volume of reminiscences entitled *No Chestnuts!*

20. Bill in BM Playbills 171. Other bills for this season are in BM Playbills 170 and at the V&A.

21. Unidentified clipping, hand-dated 7 September 1824, in V&A. For a reference to another of Ducrow's accidents this season, see the bill for 28 June in BM Playbills 170; and for mention of a near accident earlier in the season caused by breaking reins, see the unidentified clipping, hand-dated 8 May, V&A.

22. Dibdin, *Memoirs*, p. 131; BM Astley's Scrapbooks III, 132–33.

23. *Mirror of the Stage*, 15 December 1823; *Figaro in London*, 21 January 1837.

24. Bill for 28 October 1824, V&A; reviews in the *Times* for 29 October and the *Drama or Theatrical Pocket Magazine* for November. For a scathing article by John Lacy on the taste of the spectators who patronized such spectacles at the national houses and the "poets" who wrote them, see the *London Magazine* for December 1824.

25. "Theatrical Jockeying," *Morning Chronicle*, 26 October 1824. Cf. the later account by Elliston's biographer George Raymond, *Memoirs of Robert William Elliston, Comedian*, 2nd ed. (London, 1846), II, 373–74.

26. Folger Y.d.23 (133).

27. Folger Y.d.82 (242). In his diary for 4 July 1824, James Winston commented on this transaction and how, after signing the original agreement, "Ducrow applied for an engagement for himself and asked £50 a week. Seeing they were *done*, they were obliged to compromise the matter by giving him, Ducrow, £4.10 per week play house pay"—*Drury Lane Journal: Selections from James Winston's Diaries, 1819–1827*, ed. Alfred L. Nelson and Gilbert B. Cross (London, 1974), p. 91.

28. Letter, signed by Ducrow but in the hand of an amanuensis, Folger Y.d.23 (133).

29. *Drury Lane Journal*, p. 113.

30. An undated ALS from Ducrow at Holyhead to an unidentified manager in Ireland pertains, I believe, to this engagement. On account of a gale, he writes, the horses cannot be shipped, but he has nonetheless sent "Mr. Widdicomb one of my Company forward, and as he knows every Situation of the piece he may be of some service to you till I can get over"—Harvard Vauxhall Gardens Scrapbooks V, 83.

31. See the *Roscius* for 1 February 1825.

32. *Dramatic Argus*, 31 December 1824, 1 and 3 January 1825.

33. Bills for the Dublin engagement are in BM Playbills 211 and 212.

34. *Dramatic Argus*, 9 February 1825.

35. Davis did not disband his company immediately, for I find records of their performing at Bristol at the end of 1824 and at Glasgow and Newcastle in the following summer. The Makeens and the equestrian Fillingham were in this troop—see bills in BM Playbills 205 and 320.

36. *Times*, 2 February 1825; unidentified clipping in BM Astley's Scrapbooks III. The lease was later said to be at the annual rental of 1,400 pounds, an increase of 400 pounds over what Davis had been paying—Brayley, p. 65 and "Addenda," p. 3.

37. On West's sojourn in America, see, besides the standard histories of Odell and Ireland, Joe Cowell, *Thirty Years Passed Among the Players in England and America* (New York, 1845), p. 64; Isaac J. Greenwood, *The*

434 / NOTES TO PAGES 128–133

Circus: Its Origin and Growth Prior to 1835 (New York, 1898), pp. 94–95, 98; Robert William Glenroie Vail, "The Early Circus in America," *Proceedings of the American Antiquarian Society*, N.S., XLIII (1934), 179–81; and, most recently, Stuart Thayer, *Annals of the American Circus, 1793–1829* ([Ann Arbor], 1976), pp. 78–111.

38. *Opera Glass*, 16 October 1826.

39. See the obituary of North in the New York *Clipper* for 11 July 1885. On William West, see Frost (*Circus Life and Circus Celebrities*, p. 61), who mentions him as Ducrow's partner but nowhere refers to his father James; and Boase (*Modern English Biography*, III, col. 1281), who also writes of William only and gives his dates as 1812–90. The melo- and hippodramatist Edward Fitzball tells of William later stage-managing at Drury Lane, where he directed many of Fitzball's plays, then returning to the Amphitheatre, "of which he was once the leading star, and, in fact, continued so, in the undying 'Mazeppa'"—*Thirty-Five Years of a Dramatic Author's Life* (London, 1859), II, 139–40.

40. See *Enter Foot and Horse*, pp. 142–43.

41. Boase, I, col. 564.

42. See the *Figaro in London* for 21 April 1832 and the unidentified clipping, hand-dated 4 May 1839, V&A. For Cartlitch's later career in America, see *Enter Foot and Horse*, p. 187.

43. See, e.g., BM Playbills 165.

44. *Illustrated London News*, 20 May 1843.

45. *Era*, 12 July 1840.

46. *Sketches by Boz* (Oxford, 1957), pp. 107–108, "Astley's."

47. *Random Recollections of an Old Actor* (London, 1880), p. 121. Belton also claims Widdicombe married a "celebrated black equestrienne," the mother of Widdicombe's son Henry (1813–68), who became a well-known comic actor and worked at Astley's, the Haymarket Theatre, the Princess's, and elsewhere. The other references to Widdicombe's wife I possess make no mention of the lady's race; nor do I know of any celebrated black equestrienne in England around this time. The Widdicombes would also seem to have had a daughter in the profession, for in the spring of 1838 Ducrow announced a benefit for Miss Woolford and "Miss Widdicomb" during a visit of the company to the Equestrian Circus in Aberdeen (bill for 27 March [1838] in the King's College Library of the University of Aberdeen).

48. See the *Town* for 10 October 1840, which also describes Widdicombe's "dickey'd bosom, collared throat, a silken neckerchief arranged according to the nicest rules laid down by the authors of cravatina" and a bust and waist "of the most sublime pretensions to spider-like *nip-in-ity*, supported on the brawny legs of the far-famed Sturgeon of Garrat, and rejoicing in the jack-boots of Major Galbraith of Aberfoil." Widdicombe sometimes modified his military costume by wearing skintight breeches and trooper's boots, and in 1837 even combined these with a dress coat.

49. See, e.g., [David Prince Miller], *The Life of a Showman; and the Managerial Struggles of David Prince Miller* (London, n.d.), pp. 144–45.

50. [Renton Nicholson], *Rogue's Progress: The Autobiography of "Lord Chief Baron" Nicholson*, ed. John L. Bradley (Boston, 1965), p. 302. For other jokes on Widdicombe's antiquity, see "The Widdecomb [*sic*] Papers" in *Punch*, IV (1843), 74, 94.

51. The reviewer for the *London Magazine* (November 1825) seems to have taken a much lighter view of the scene: "Bonaparte was made a sort of Imperial Joseph Surface—a man of sentiment, with the addition of an outrageous humanity; and in his retreat he did nothing but console the sick and scatter cold fowls, blessings and brandy, among his suffering soldiers, to the unspeakable satisfaction of the spectators."

52. Clipping, hand-dated June 1825, in Disher Scrapbooks I.

53. *Weekly Dramatic Register*, 3 September 1825. Cf. the issue for 10 September, where the reviewer suggests Napoleon's expedition to Egypt would make a good subject for Astley's, although he does not wish to see this piece terminate, as usual, "with the final overthrow of Napoleon and the French arms. Why not do common justice, and *sometimes*, depict this astonishing man, as he *generally* was, a conqueror?"

54. Bill for 22 August 1825, V&A. An outline of the play's action is given in the *Times* for 23 August.

55. See above, p. 21. As Ducrow's bills sometimes stated, the entertainments were divided into "three distinct branches," by which he meant, however, (1) the two "splendid" dramas at the start and conclusion of every program, (2) "exhibitions of manly strength and activity in some of the branches appertaining to gymnastic and calesthenic [*sic*] exercises," and (3) demonstrations of riding and "horse-tuition"—see, e.g., the bill for 8 June 1829 and cf. those for 16 April 1827 and 23 April 1832, V&A.

56. Bill for 11 July 1825, BM Playbills 170.

57. See above, p. 32.

58. See the bill for 19 April 1824, BM Playbills 170. The "Mlle. Ducrow" in this announcement is probably Margaret.

59. Bill for M. Ducrow's Amphitheatre, 19 November [1825], in the John Johnson Collection of Printed Ephemera, Bodleian Library, Oxford University.

60. Bill for 30 January 1826, BM Playbills 244. The company had opened at the remodeled Olympic Circus on 26 December 1825—see Broadbent, *Annals of the Liverpool Stage*, p. 188.

61. See, e.g., the bill for 2 October 1829, V&A.

62. Bill for 23 July 1827, BM Playbills 170; *Morning Chronicle*, 28 March 1826. A bill for Ducrow's circus at Edinburgh in 1827 describes the ponies as partaking of their meal "with the strict observance of the most punctilious etiquette, previously playing at LEAP FROG, and jumping through and over several small circumferences, garlands, &c." (bill for 16 November 1827, British Museum Theatrical Cuttings 50).

63. Bill for 23 November 1825, Bath Municipal Library.

64. Bills for 25 and 26 November 1825, Bath Municipal Library.

65. Bill for 14 March 1826, BM Playbills 244.

66. Bill for 30 January 1826, BM Playbills 244.

67. See the review in the *Times* for 28 March 1826.

68. Bills for the premieres of all four of these pieces—on 27 March, 15 May, 10 July, and 28 August respectively—are in BM Playbills 170 and at the V&A.

69. Description of the first representation in the bill for 10 April 1826, V&A.

70. Billed for its first performance on 15 May, BM Playbills 170.

71. Bill for 11 September 1826, BM Playbills 171.

72. Bill for 19 June 1826, V&A. Cf., in the same collection, the unidentified review of Cline, hand-dated 1826, which also hints Ducrow is about to "give a specimen of his abilities in this way, at a benefit not far distant."

73. Unidentified clipping, hand-dated 1834, in Harvard II, 98. Cf. "Mr. Andrew Ducrow," *Actors by Daylight, and Pencilings in the Pit,* 14 July 1838. The anecdote bears out the earlier claim in *Oxberry's* "Memoir" (p. 14) that Ducrow "never asks any one to do any thing that he is unwilling to attempt himself. When Waterloo (we think) was rehearsing, one of his jumpers declining dropping from a rock piece, declaring it was too high for any one to attempt it, DUCROW ran up and jumped it (the difference between jumping and dropping is full six feet) and said, 'Now, Sir, will you try and drop it.' Example goes farther than precept, and the feat was performed." Cline later emigrated to the United States, where in August 1828 he was announced to dance on the elastic cord at the Bowery Theatre in New York on a bill that included the great Edwin Forrest—see Richard Moody, *Edwin Forrest, First Star of the American Stage* (New York, 1960), p. 86. Despite the "Herr" that always prefaced his name, and the Christian name "André" that appears in some accounts, according to the American manager Noah M. Ludlow, who employed him in 1830, Cline was actually an English Jew whose given name was John—see Ludlow, *Dramatic Life As I Found It* (St. Louis, 1880), p. 368. Like Ducrow's house author Amherst, who also eventually left England for America and died in a Philadelphia poorhouse in 1851, he seems to have fallen upon hard times in his later years. In his biography of the American manager Augustin Daly, Joseph Daly writes that "now and then I am reminded of my brother's care for old actors, and I find that at this period [c. 1876] he gave a place as doorkeeper to a venerable relic of bygone days—Herr Cline, the tight-rope dancer"—*The Life of Augustin Daly* (New York, 1917), p. 214.

74. Bill for 24 November 1826, Bath Municipal Library; cf. the bill for Ducrow's benefit on 27 November, on which occasion he was announced for his second appearance as Clown in the same pantomime.

75. See, e.g., Disher, *Greatest Show on Earth* (p. 112), who also confuses Louisa's brother with her father.

76. Bill for 27 December [1824], BM Playbills 322.

77. Advertisement in the Manchester *Gazette* of 17 March for Ducrow's benefit on the 19th.

78. BM Playbills 170.

79. See the bills for 9 July, V&A; 16 July, Harvard II, 6; cf. *Enter Foot and Horse,* pp. 36–37.

80. Unidentified review, hand-dated 26 August 1827, in Harvard II, 3.

81. *Oxberry's* "Memoir," p. 14.

82. Bill for 9 July 1827, V&A.

83. Bill for 14 May 1827, V&A.

84. See the bills for 14 May (premiere) and 9 July 1827, V&A.

85. See the bills for 4 June (premiere) and 23 July 1827, V&A.

86. Bill for 10 September 1827, BM Playbills 170.

87. Bills for Easter Monday [16 April] and 27 August 1827, V&A.

88. See, e.g., the bill for 23 July 1827, V&A; and cf. the review in the *Weekly Dramatic Register* (4 August 1827), which tells of the little fellow letting

the reins slip one evening and causing some confusion among the horses, "for which, as he was passing out after the performance, one of the Whippers-in (or whatever those gentlemen, who flog the horses round the circle, may please to call themselves) swore at the child with disgusting brutality."

89. He was identified as "Master Reuben" while the troop was performing at Newcastle in late 1829 (advance bill for the troop's first appearance on 26 November, BM Playbills 425) and as "Mr. Reuben Bridges Jr." in the Astley's bill for 4 July 1831 (V&A). Bridges senior, whose given name may also have been Reuben, was riding for Ducrow by 1829, and in 1831 was billed for Ducrow's act "The Chinese Enchanter" (see the bill for 29 September 1831, V&A). Frost (*Circus Life and Circus Celebrities*, pp. 110–11, 142, 299) mentions both an Anthony and John Bridges riding in acts similar to Ducrow's at Astley's and elsewhere during the late forties and fifties. One of them was married to an equestrienne named Amelia who performed the Cracovienne standing on horseback. The same Amelia was probably the niece of Ducrow's first wife mentioned above, pp. 78–79 and n.

90. Bill for 23 April 1827, BM Playbills 170.

91. *Weekly Dramatic Register*, 4 August 1827.

92. John Wilson et al., *Noctes Ambrosianae* (Edinburgh and London, 1868), II, 82 (January 1828). John Wilson, Professor of Moral Philosophy and one of Edinburgh's more notable characters at the time of Ducrow's visits there, originally published his dialogues, in which he figures as the character "Christopher North," in *Blackwood's Magazine*. When citing from this work, I shall therefore give the original dates of publication.

93. *Evening Courant*, 31 January 1828. Cf. the account of the last night of performing in the issue of 2 February 1828.

94. See, in particular, the 29 November 1827 issue of the *Edinburgh Dramatic Review, and Thespian Inquisitor*, whose critic was forced to conclude that "the inhabitants of this metropolis have not yet attained a very high pitch of civilization." The same periodical later changed course and, in an argument familiar to present-day circus managers, began harping on the "brutality or inhumanity" that presumably went into the training of the animals—a theme that was then taken up by the periodical's readers, not without some telling reflections on the sinfulness of going to places of amusement in the first place—see the issues of 7 and 10 December 1827.

95. A small handbill for the 1 January 1828 performance is in the Local History Department of the Southwark Public Library.

96. Such is the description of the act a few nights later when the company was performing at Glasgow—see the advertisement in the Glasgow *Herald* for 3 March 1828. The circus at Edinburgh, as previously mentioned, did not possess a stage.

97. On Lady Hamilton and the early history of tableaux, see Kirsten Gram Holmström, *Monodrama, Attitudes, Tableaux Vivants: Studies on Some Trends of Theatrical Fashion, 1770–1815* (Stockholm, 1967).

98. The earliest of these artists appears to have been the actor of nautical melodramas Frimbley, from the Glasgow and Edinburgh theatres, who exhibited "The Living Statue" at New York's Bowery Theatre on 1 and 5 October 1831—see Odell, III, 565. He was closely followed by the mime and man-monkey George Wieland, who on 12 October performed Ducrow's celebrated

statues at the Park Theatre on a benefit bill for Mrs. William Barrymore, the former Ann Adams of the circus family by that name. She and her husband had arrived at the Park some two months before to take up their duties as actress-dancer and stage manager. Mrs. Barrymore was herself an accomplished pantomimist and posed in some tableaux of her own during this season. Ireland describes her as "undoubtedly the best dancer of the English school known to our stage, and as a melo-dramatic pantomimist has been excelled by Celeste alone" (*Records*, II, 1–2, 23; cf. Odell, III, 544–45). The third of these interpreters was the actor John Fletcher. After trying out the act at London's Adelphi Theatre earlier in the year, he made his American debut in "The Living Statue" at Boston's Tremont Theatre on 28 November 1831 before moving on to repeat it at the Bowery in New York on 13 December—see T. Allston Brown, *History of the American Stage* (New York, 1870), p. 126; Ireland, II, 19; Odell, III, 569. The result of all this sudden activity, Odell informs us, was that tableaux vivants became a craze in America.

99. Bill for Ducrow's benefit on 25 August 1828, V&A.

100. Bill for 7 September 1829, V&A.

101. See the bill for 15 November 1828, BM Playbills 212.

102. [Herman Pückler-Muskau], *Tour in England, Ireland, and France, in the Years 1826, 1827, 1828, and 1829* [trans. Sarah Austin] (Philadelphia, 1833), pp. 489–90 (letter no. 40, 29 October 1828). For the account of the 1827 visit to Astley's, see p. 193 (letter no. 16, 19 July 1827).

103. Bill for 1 February 1828, BM Playbills 315.

104. Unidentified review in Harvard II, 21.

105. Ibid.; cf. the reviews in the *Times* and *Morning Chronicle* for 8 April 1828 and the bill for 7 April, V&A.

106. Bills for 15 November and 8 December 1824, BM Playbills 322.

107. *Town*, 17 October 1840. And see above, pp. 39–40.

108. *Town*, 21 November 1840.

109. Bills for 28 July and 12 May 1828, V&A.

110. See the advertisement in the Glasgow *Herald* for 12 December 1828.

111. An act which Ducrow also performed, especially in his younger years—see, e.g., the Astley's bill for 12 July 1824, BM Playbills 170; and the *Mémorial Bordelais* for 30 April 1822, which describes an instant in the act when "the two flags seem like two visible wings fitted to the shoulders of the rider. I say *visible* because it seems impossible to me that M. Ducrow is not concealing at least one small pair of them, imperceptible to profane eyes, in order to hover in space the way he does." The act is shown being performed in an engraving of the interior of Astley's published in *Londina Illustrata* and in many other prints of the period.

112. *Town*, 17 October 1840. The writer begins his article on trick equestriennes, it should perhaps be noted, with a cavalier remark about the "caducity or proneness to fall imputed to this class of Funambulists, by men of pleasure, who pretend to a far deeper insight into such matters than we either can or desire to boast of." He is careful to point out in his concluding paragraph, however, that his statements are not meant to apply to Madame Ducrow, who "has been mentioned merely to record our testimony that she is an exceedingly clever and highly respectable lady."

113. Bon Gaultier, "The Courtship of Our Cid." The action of this ballad again involves Gomersal, who is improbably cast as Woolford's partner in the ring. Either the writer had actually forgotten who Woolford's real partner was or (as is more likely) deliberately shifted his cast of characters in order to include once more his favorite figure of fun. Entering the circle and leaping his courser over the clown and master of the ring, "Gomersalez" is described as shedding layers of costume and impersonating four successive characters, until finally, as Mercury, he catches up with the horse of Woolford, who has been fleeing him all the while:

> One smart lash across his courser,
>   One tremendous bound and stride,
> And our noble Cid was standing
>   By his Woolfordinez' side!
> With a god's embrace he clasped her,
>   Raised her in his manly arms;
> And the stables' closing barriers
>   Hid his valour and her charms!

Gomersal was not a trick rider, and the equestrian described is—or should be—Ducrow.

114. Bill for 21 April 1828, V&A.

115. Bill for 14 July 1828, V&A.

116. Bill for 25 August 1828, V&A.

117. Unidentified review, hand-dated 4 September 1828, V&A; cf. the bill for 1 September, the date of the benefit, in the same collection.

118. See "The Late Mr. Ducrow," *Sunday Times*, 30 January 1842.

119. The Dublin *Morning Register* for 23 August 1828 contains a notice from Ducrow boasting of performances before the "entire" Royal Family on 13 May and 14 July, but the latter date is a printer's error for 19 June. The 13 May performance was by special command following a dinner party given by the Duke and Duchess of Clarence and is described in the advertisements and columns of the *Times* and *Morning Chronicle* of 13 and 14 May. The Duke again engaged the whole of the center box for the evening of 19 June when, following a grand dinner at the Admiralty, he and the Duchess, together with a party that included the Duke of Sussex and the children of Prince Esterhazy, visited the Amphitheatre to witness a performance of *The Battle of Navarino*—see the *Times* for 20 June. The Duchess of Clarence was herself a fairly regular patron of Astley's and sometimes attended with parties of her own. The bills for 6 July 1829, e.g., boast of one such visit the preceding 25 June.

120. See the advertisements in the *Times* for 18 and 20 June and the brief review in the issue of the 19th.

121. See the notice in the Dublin *Morning Register* for 23 August 1828, where Ducrow turns down an offer from "friends" to build him an amphitheatre in favor of Bunn's proposal.

122. See, e.g., the advertisement in the *Freeman's Journal* for 20 October and the puff in the *Evening Packet and Correspondent* for 7 October 1828.

123. William Frederick Wallett, *The Public Life of W. F. Wallett, the Queen's Jester: An Autobiography* (London, 1870), p. 10.

124. See the advertisements in the *Morning Register* for 13 November and the bill for 15 November 1828, BM Playbills 212.

125. Advertisement in the *Evening Packet and Correspondent*, 14 October 1828.

126. Advertisement for the opening night at Glasgow on 12 December 1828 in the Glasgow *Herald* of the same date; advertisements for the Edinburgh Theatre Royal in the Edinburgh *Evening Courant* for 20 and 22 December 1828.

127. See the advertisement and notice in the 15 and 19 December issues of the Glasgow *Herald*; cf. Walter Baynham, *The Glasgow Stage* (Glasgow, 1892), p. 119. At this time, too, the machinist Matthew Mackintosh, who had been working for Seymour, first joined Ducrow's company. He reports that Ducrow and Woolford left for Edinburgh without consulting Seymour and that the manager, threatening a breach of contract suit for 2,000 pounds, succeeded in having an embargo laid on the stud and properties. The escapade supposedly cost Ducrow 1,500 pounds—Mackintosh, *Stage Reminiscences*, p. 147.

128. See the advertisement in the Liverpool *Albion* for 15 December 1828.

129. Liverpool *Mercury*, 2 January 1829.

130. The speech, delivered on 10 April, is given in the *Albion* for 13 April.

131. Manuscript by J. G. Underhill in the Liverpool Free Library, cited in Broadbent, *Annals of the Liverpool Stage*, p. 244.

132. Advertisement in the *Albion*, 29 December 1828.

133. *Albion*, 16 February 1829.

134. *Mercury*, 2 January 1829; cf. the *Albion* for 19 and 26 January and 16 February 1829.

135. "Dramatic Feuilletons," *Sunday Times*, 22 June 1851, n.

136. Review in the *Dramatic Magazine*, 1 May 1829.

137. Bill in BM Playbills 170; cf. the review in the *Theatrical Examiner*, 22 April 1829.

138. Bill for 11 May 1829, V&A.

139. Bill for 8 June 1829, V&A; and see the review in the *Harlequin*, 13 June 1829.

140. Bill for 7 September 1829, V&A.

141. Bill for 6 July 1829, V&A.

142. See, e.g., the review of him as Tee-Tai-Chein, the Golden King of Ava, in his spectacle *The Burmese War*, in *Oxberry's Dramatic Biography and Histrionic Anecdotes*, 20 May 1826.

143. See the bill for 3 August 1829, V&A; and the review in the *Dramatic Magazine*, 1 September 1829. Price was one of the two New York partners who had bought out West in 1822.

144. Bills for Ducrow's engagement from 2 to 10 October 1829, V&A.

145. Bill for 14 September 1829, V&A.

146. Bill for 6 July 1829, V&A; cf. the bill for the premiere of the act on 8 June.

147. Bill for premiere on 15 June 1829, V&A.

148. Bill for 7 September 1829, V&A.

149. Archives Nationales F^{21} 1036. And see below, pp. 301–302.

150. ALS dated 17 September 1829, V&A.

151. Mlle. Lucie had indeed been riding at the Cirque Olympique prior

to her arrival in London, but whether she was a legitimate Franconi is another matter.

152. Bill for 2 October 1829, V&A.

5. *The Emperor of Horseflesh*

1. "The Crisis Examined" (16 December 1834), in *Selected Speeches of the Late Right Honourable the Earl of Beaconsfield*, ed. T. E. Kebbel (London, 1882), I, 23–24. The pertinent part of the speech is as follows:

> *The* Reform Ministry! I dare say, now, some of you have heard of Mr. Ducrow, that celebrated gentleman who rides upon six horses. What a prodigious achievement! It seems impossible; but you have confidence in Ducrow. You fly to witness it; unfortunately one of the horses is ill, and a donkey is substituted in its place. But Ducrow is still admirable; there he is, bounding along in a spangled jacket and cork slippers! The whole town is mad to see Ducrow riding at the same time on six horses. But now two more of the steeds are seized with the staggers, and lo! three jackasses in their stead! Still Ducrow persists, and still announces to the public that he will ride round his circus every night on his six steeds. At last all the horses are knocked up, and now there are half-a-dozen donkeys. What a change! Behold the hero in the amphitheatre, the spangled jacket thrown on one side, the cork slippers on the other. Puffing, panting, and perspiring, he pokes one sullen brute, thwacks another, cuffs a third, and curses a fourth, while one brays to the audience, and another rolls in the sawdust. Behold the late Prime Minister and the Reform Ministry—the spirited and snow-white steeds have gradually changed into an equal number of sullen and obstinate donkeys; while Mr. Merryman, who, like the Lord Chancellor, was once the very life of the ring, now lies his despairing length in the middle of the stage, with his jokes exhausted and his bottle empty.

2. Letter of 18 December 1835, in *The Letters of Charles Dickens*, ed. Madeline House and Graham Storey, I (Oxford, 1965), 109.

3. [William Clarke], *Every Night Book; or, Life After Dark* (London, 1827), p. 24.

4. *Oxberry's* "Memoir," p. 15.

5. "Mr. Andrew Ducrow," *Actors by Daylight*, 14 July 1838; "Mr. Andrew Ducrow," Edinburgh *Opera-Glass*, 4 September 1840.

6. "Dramatic Feuilletons," *Sunday Times*, 2 March 1851.

7. Ibid.

8. *Random Recollections of an Old Actor*, p. 122. A similar stratagem was later attributed to the American producer David Belasco, who used to come to rehearsals with a dollar watch which he would bring out and stamp upon

whenever the necessity arose to terrify his actors. The gesture, we are told, was "sobering"—see Brooks Atkinson, *Broadway* (New York, 1970), p. 47.

9. See, e.g., the *Town* for 10 October 1840.

10. *The Stage: Both Before and Behind the Curtain* (London, 1840), III, 66–67.

11. Entries for 30 June and 2 July, in "A Clown's Log: Extracts from the Diary of the Late Joseph Blackburn," ed. Charles H. Day, New York *Clipper*, 21 February 1880.

12. *Theatrical Journal*, 22 May 1841.

13. Ibid., 30 January 1841.

14. Bunn, I, 146–47.

15. "Dramatic Feuilletons," *Sunday Times*, 2 March 1851. A recent article on theatrical dressers in the New York *Times* mentions an unnamed American actor who insisted on female dressers ("he didn't want no man fussing over him"), so it would appear Ducrow was not unique in this preference—"In the Theater, the Best Dressers Don't Always Wear the Clothes," 2 January 1974.

16. On Broadfoot's reputation as a swearer, see Peter Paterson [pseud. James Glass Bertram], *Behind the Scenes: Being the Confessions of a Strolling Player* (Edinburgh, London, and Glasgow, 1859), p. 94; on Barrymore's, see the "Journal of Old Barnes, the Pantaloon, on a Trip to Paris, in 1830," pt. 2, *Bentley's Miscellany*, VII (1840), 628.

17. On the subject of Ducrow's language and mock refinement, see in particular Moncrieff's articles for 16 February and 22 June 1851.

18. Unidentified clipping, hand-dated 1834, in Harvard II, 98.

19. See, e.g., Disher, *Greatest Show on Earth*, p. 127; Saxon, *Enter Foot and Horse*, p. 53.

20. *Morning Chronicle*, 23 October 1838 (cf. the *Era* for 28 October, which also refers to Ducrow's use of the word "dialect"); Drury Lane bill for 22 October 1838 (premiere of *Charlemagne*), V&A. The anonymous author of *Charlemagne*, according to the *Sunday Times* for 21 October, was William Bayle Bernard, who had collaborated with Ducrow during the 1833–34 Drury Lane season on the spectacle *St. George and the Dragon*. As on the earlier occasion, too, both Ducrow and Bunn seem to have freely "improved" upon the playwright's work, for the same article reports them as having so cut, clipped, and altered the play "that we hear the concoctor (Mr. Bernard) does not know his child again."

21. Clarke, pp. 22–23; and see *Enter Foot and Horse*, pp. 53–54.

22. Unidentified review, hand-dated April 1835, in Disher Scrapbooks II. Cf. the obituary in the *Sunday Times* for 30 January 1842 where, in regard to Ducrow's achievements as a producer, it is claimed he "had no living rival."

23. *Odd Fellow*, 19 February 1842.

24. *The Stage*, I, 144–45, n.

25. "Ducrow at Rehearsal," *Behind the Curtain* (London, [1848]), pp. 100–102.

26. "Mr. Widdicombe at Rehearsal," Ibid., pp. 25–29.

27. Unidentified clipping, "Doings of Ducrow," in Harvard III, 4. The reference to Derby and Leicester would seem to point to the fall of 1840.

28. "Theatrical Sketch of Mr. A. Ducrow," p. 268.

29. "Dramatic Feuilletons," *Sunday Times*, 2 March 1851; cf. the article in the issue of 16 February 1851.

30. See the bill for 23 April 1832, V&A.

31. "The Late Mr. Ducrow," *Sunday Times*, 30 January 1842.

32. See, e.g., the bills for 22 August 1825 and 27 April and 15 June 1835, V&A.

33. *Recollections and Wanderings of Paul Bedford: Facts, Not Fancies* (London, 1864), p. 109. Cf. Egan (p. 266) who, referring to Andrew's younger days, writes that "as a rope-dancer, likewise, he was always classed as the first that had ever appeared in this country, of which he gave ample proof in his exhibitions during Madame Saqui's engagement at Covent-Garden Theatre; his performances in this line having been produced in the way of competition and rivalry."

34. Census returns for the Parish of St. Mary, Lambeth, Enumeration District no. 8, Amphitheatre Place—Public Record Office.

35. Will dated 10 November 1841, Public Record Office.

36. See, e.g., the preface to Charles Dibdin's *The High-Mettled Racer* (London: William Kidd, 1831), p. 6; and the plan of the theatre around this time reproduced in fig. 38.

37. Unidentified review, hand-dated 18 May 1834, Disher Scrapbooks II.

38. *Times*, 21 April 1829.

39. Unidentified article, hand-dated 1839, Disher Scrapbooks II.

40. The estimate of two million horses in England—with fewer than 1,000 blood or race horses among them—is reported in the Edinburgh *Advertiser* of 17 November 1837. The *Encyclopaedia Britannica* gives the horse and pony population for all of Great Britain in the 1960s as 200,000 and declining.

41. *Four Years in Great Britain: 1831-1835* (New York, 1835), II, 242–43. Not all love is boundless, however, and had Colton paid his visit to London ten years earlier he might have felt somewhat comforted by the reaction of several critics to the appearances of Ducrow's and Davis's horses on the boards of the national theatres. John Lacy was particularly outspoken at this time and has left an amusing if rather unflattering portrait of his countrymen who patronized and admired these performers: "Look at the grave, phlegmatic, taciturn, suicidal Englishman when the quadrupeds enter! Behold one of the most thinking people on earth,—the profound and sagacious islander,—the national brother of Newton and Bacon,—the consummation of sublunary wisdom, behold him in the middle of the pit when the snort and the tramp, the clang and the clatter, announce the ingress of a herd of equestrians! His right hand furnished with the symbol of solemnity—a snuff-box, and his nose bestridden by a pair of owl-eyed spectacles, behold him how he stretches his apoplectic neck towards the proscenium, and while drops of animal oil course one-another down his 'piteous nose,' groans or rather whinnies with delight as the fourfooted objects of his anxiety make their appearance!" (*London Magazine*, December 1824). Admittedly, the question was not one of horses as actors, but of the propriety of their nightly prancing across the boards of such shrines to Shakespeare as Drury Lane and Covent Garden. Lacy himself, in a moment of democratic candor, confessed he would "rather see Mr. Ducrow canter up to the clouds as a knight of a modern pantomime, than Mr. Young stalk across the stage as the hero of a modern tragedy."

42. Clarke, p. 24. For an earlier occasion when one of the actors nearly lost his "wig" in the midst of a performance of *Cortez*, see the *London Magazine* for December 1823.

43. Unidentified review, hand-dated 18 May 1834, Disher Scrapbooks II.

44. *Noctes Ambrosianae*, II, 82 (January 1828).

45. As both Phoenix and, a year later, Pegasus were billed as the "Enchanted Horse," it is likely these two were one and the same—see the bills for Liverpool, 30 January 1826 (BM Playbills 244), and Astley's, 14 May 1827 (V&A). Similarly, I should not be surprised if Ducrow's stags Salamander and Coco were in fact the same animal; the latter name duplicated that of the famous stag that performed at the Cirque Olympique in Paris.

46. Bill for 22 May 1837, V&A.

47. Bills for Easter Monday [16 April] 1827 and 26 December 1833, V&A.

48. See the bills for 4 June 1827 and 25 July 1836, V&A.

49. Review in the Edinburgh *Advertiser*, 31 October 1837.

50. *Spectator*, 18 September 1830.

51. Autograph signed by Ducrow and dated 26 February 1840, Disher Scrapbooks II.

52. Bill for 8 October [1838], BM Playbills 352. Cf. Moncrieff, who writes of Ducrow's delight in listing in the theatre's bills the names of the illustrious authors—Byron, Scott, Moore, etc.—on whose works several of the Amphitheatre's spectacles were based ("Dramatic Feuilletons," *Sunday Times*, 22 June 1851).

53. *Coureur des Spectacles*, 19 September 1843.

54. On the revolutionary nature of Ducrow's riding and how he differed from his predecessors, see, in addition to the sources cited in the text, the *Mirror of Literature* for 29 July 1826, which also contains a poem, "Ducrow, or The Matchless Equestrian"; *Oxberry's* "Memoir," pp. 13–14; Egan, "Theatrical Sketch of Mr. A. Ducrow," p. 268; "Memoir of Mr. Ducrow," *Owl*, 24 September 1831; Moncrieff, "Dramatic Feuilletons," *Sunday Times*, 2 March 1851.

55. "The Late Mr. Ducrow," *Sunday Times*, 30 January 1842.

56. "Memoir of Mr. Ducrow," *Owl*, 24 September 1831. Cf. *Oxberry's* "Memoir" (p. 13)—"there is no act that could be performed on the ground that he does not do on horseback"—and the sentiments of the critic for the *Mémorial Bordelais*, quoted above, p. 106.

57. "Ducrow's Horsemanship and the Carnival of Venice," *Theatrical Journal*, 30 August 1845.

58. *Oxberry's* "Memoir," p. 14.

59. Edinburgh *Evening Courant*, 15 December 1827. A number of critics went so far as to claim Andrew's mimic representations on horseback entitled him to the rank of dramatist. See, e.g., the *Mémorial Bordelais* for 30 April 1822 and the Edinburgh *Evening Courant* for 28 October 1837, whose reviewer this time, after acknowledging Ducrow to be the most accomplished equestrian ever to appear in Britain, writes that "his merit as an equestrian of the first order, which he undoubtedly is, is lost in our higher admiration of him as a dramatist."

60. *Noctes Ambrosianae*, III, 143–44 (February 1831). The dialogue continues with a description by Shepherd of Ducrow's attitudes as "The Gladia-

tor," looking "as if Mars himsel had descended in mortal guise, to be the champion o' his ain eternal city." For additional references to the "classical" nature of Andrew's performances, see the memoir in the *Owl*; the Aberdeen *Journal* for 20 October 1830; and Egan (p. 268), who writes of Ducrow's horsemanship as "not only original, but perfectly classical."

61. Bill for 13 September [1830], V&A.

62. Edinburgh *Evening Courant*, 19 November 1827; *London Magazine*, August 1824; *Mémorial Bordelais*, 14 and 21 April 1822.

63. Clarke, pp. 23–24; Edinburgh *Evening Courant*, 10 December 1827; bill for 3 October [1829], V&A.

64. Clarke, pp. 23–24.

65. See, e.g., the Edinburgh *Evening Courant* for 10 December 1827 and the *Mémorial Bordelais* for 30 April 1822.

66. *The Public Life of W. F. Wallett*, pp. 2–3.

67. Bill for 29 May 1826, V&A; Edinburgh *Evening Courant*, 19 November 1827.

68. A copy of the engraving with the verses is in Disher Scrapbooks II.

69. "Labour and the Poor," Letter 38, in the *Morning Chronicle*, 25 February 1850.

70. Bunn, I, 145, n.; I, 223, n.

71. "Theatrical Sketch of Mr. A. Ducrow," p. 268; Wallett, p. 61. Cf. the memoir of Ducrow in the 3 February 1872 issue of *All the Year Round* (p. 228): "The repertory of the riders of to-day is greatly indebted to Ducrow's skill and fancy. Whenever an especially attractive act of horsemanship is now presented, the spectator may safely conclude that he has witnessed a faithful following of an example set by Ducrow." In British Museum Theatrical Cuttings 50 there exists a curious printed interchange between the circus artists W. Powell and Richard Usher concerning a benefit night for the former at Gloucester. Powell, apparently, had falsely advertised he would be assisted by the well-known clown on this occasion and had also offended Usher by copying a celebrated act he performed with domestic cats. Defending the merits of his own act, Powell rhetorically asks, "Why does not Mr. Ducrow, who is the sole inventor of every New Scene, worth calling an *invention*, why does he not demand satisfaction of all those who copy, or *endeavour* to ride like himself." To which Usher sarcastically replies, "Because Mr. Ducrow well knows that such as Mr. Powell, who attempt to copy him or his scenes, are only held up to ridicule by all judges of the art who behold such puny efforts."

72. Bills for 11 January and 15 February 1836, in the King's College Library of the University of Aberdeen.

73. See M.-J. Vesque, "Le Cirque Olympique du faubourg du Temple, 1817–1826," *Cirque dans l'Univers*, no. 12 (1er trimestre 1953), p. 23; Tristan Rémy, "Les Héros du cirque et les ballons du siège de Paris," *Cirque dans l'Univers*, no. 100 (1er trimestre 1976), p. 19 and n. Despite an assertion in the latter article that Laribeau was himself the creator of the "Courier" or "Poste royale"—a common misapprehension among French historians—he did not perform the act until 24 January 1828, some eleven months after Ducrow had introduced it at Manchester. M. Rémy, upon receiving an inquiry from me, has generously confirmed this date.

74. *Oxberry's* "Memoir," p. 14.

75. Unidentified review, hand-dated 6 September 1832, BM Astley's Scrapbooks III, 179.

76. See, e.g., the bills for the Theatre, Sheffield, 7 December 1829 (BM Playbills 281), and the Bath Theatre Royal, 4 January 1830 (BM Playbills 180), both of which describe the "Venetian Statue" precisely as in Ducrow's bills, but without anywhere mentioning his name.

77. See, e.g., the bills for the Glasgow Theatre Royal, 7 January [1831] (BM Playbills 393), and the Queen's Theatre, Manchester, 9 November 1831 (BM Playbills 251).

78. *The Autobiography of Joseph Jefferson*, ed. Alan S. Downer (Cambridge, Mass., 1964), p. 9 and n.

79. A Prague bill advertising an act by the acrobats and perchists the Graffina Brothers, "first presented...in Ducrow's Circus, London," is in the Prague National Museum and is cited in a paper by Antony Hippisley Coxe written for the members of the Union des Historiens du Cirque—"A Study of Andrew Ducrow" (1957), p. 1. And thus the hyperbolical wording of an announcement for the first appearance of the American rider Levi North at New Orleans in 1841: "the Greatest Equestrian Rider in the World. . . . This gentleman was pronounced by Mr. Ducrow...to be the best Equestrian in Europe for daring Feats of Horsemanship" (bill for 14 December 1841, British Museum Theatrical Cuttings 50).

6. *Provinces and Provocations*

1. For especially descriptive accounts of Astley's and its popularity during Ducrow's period of management, see, besides the sources cited elsewhere, the *Morning Chronicle*, 12 June 1832; *Times*, 1 April 1834; *Town*, 10 October 1840; *Era*, 18 October 1840 and 18 April 1841; *Theatrical Journal*, 28 August 1841; F. G. Tomlins, *A Brief View of the English Drama, from the Earliest Period to the Present Time* (London, 1840), pp. 60–61; and the unidentified reviews in BM Astley's Scrapbooks III, 187 (hand-dated 20 May 1834) and Disher Scrapbooks II (hand-dated 25 August 1833).

2. Testifying before the Select Committee on Dramatic Literature in 1832, the actor and author Thomas J. Serle, asked which of the London theatres were principally supported by their own neighborhoods, replied that he thought the Pavilion and Coburg were examples, but that "Astley's, I think, draws from every part of the town, as having a peculiar performance of its own, to which most people go once a year" ("Report from the Select Committee on Dramatic Literature: With the Minutes of Evidence," in *Reports from Committees* for the 1831–32 session of Parliament, VII, 122).

3. *The Great Metropolis* (New York and London, 1837), I, 79.

4. "Astley's," in *Sketches by Boz*, pp. 104–105. (This sketch originally appeared in the *Evening Chronicle* of 9 May 1835.)

5. *The Old Curiosity Shop* (Oxford, 1951), p. 293. Cf. the letter to Daniel Maclise, written around 16 April 1840 when Dickens was at work on *The Old Curiosity Shop*, suggesting they spend the evening at Astley's (*Letters*, II, 59–60).

6. Grant, *The Great Metropolis*, I, 80.

7. See the *Theatrical Observer* for 24 June 1829.

8. See the bills for the engagement in BM Playbills 425.

9. Circular in BM Playbills 425.

10. *Tyne Mercury*, 22 December 1829. For other comments on performances at the Arena and Theatre during this period, see the issues of 1, 15, and 29 December.

11. *Dramatic Magazine*, 1 November 1830; bill for Ducrow's first performance on 11 October in BM Playbills 425.

12. See, e.g., Mayer, *Harlequin in His Element*, pp. 101–103; and for a detailed account of Chuny's career, death, and dissection, the *Mirror of Literature* for 11 March 1826.

13. Vail, "The Early Circus in America," p. 127.

14. The actor Joseph Cowell, in his *Thirty Years Passed Among the Players in England and America* (p. 64), tells of a similar "hydraulic experiment" at the New York Park Theatre in the 1820s. And surely it was with this and other considerations in mind that the Royal Minor Theatre at Manchester, in the summer of 1830, billed its production of *The Elephant of Siam* in the following words: "Third NIGHT of the ELEPHANT, Miss AUTOMATON, Who for Decency, Docility, Safety, & Sagacity, excels any *living* performer" (single bill for 25 and 26 June 1830, BM Playbills 251).

15. See the reviews in the *Corsair* and *Courrier des Théatres* for 5 July 1829; and for a description of the settings in the original production, see Winter, *Le Théatre du Merveilleux*, pp. 166–67.

16. *Dramatic Magazine*, 1 March 1830; Broadbent, *Annals of the Liverpool Stage*, p. 224, n.; bill for 13 September 1830, V&A.

17. See, e.g., the bills for the Bath Theatre Royal for 20 and 28 April and 1 May 1830 (BM Playbills 180) and the Dublin Theatre Royal for 30 May 1830 (BM Playbills 213). Notwithstanding her well-publicized obedience and gentleness, Mademoiselle—like all performing elephants—could be fatally unpredictable. At Newcastle, where she was brought by Yates, manager of the Adelphi, in August 1830, she killed one of her keepers who had somehow offended her and severely lacerated the leg of another—see the "Chronicle" of the *Annual Register* for 1830, p. 138.

18. See, e.g., the *Dramatic Gazette* for 30 October and 18 December 1830 and the Glasgow *Opera Glass* for 11 December 1830. For Djeck's appearances in New York, see Ireland, I, 657; Odell, III, 520–31.

19. Bill for 12 April 1830, V&A; reviews in the *Times* for 13 April and the *Dramatic Magazine* for 1 May 1830.

20. Bill for 10 May 1830, V&A.

21. Sheffield *Iris*, 22 November 1836.

22. See, e.g., the bills for 30 August and 13 September 1830, V&A.

23. Bills for 13 and 21 September 1830, V&A.

24. Bill for 19 July 1830, V&A.

25. See, e.g., the bill of 12 March [1838] for the Royal Olympic Arena, Aberdeen, in the collection of playbills in the King's College Library of the University of Aberdeen. In his *Reminiscences* (p. 145) Ducrow's machinist Matthew Mackintosh tells of an earlier meeting that supposedly took place between Ducrow and Scott at Edinburgh in 1827 (at which time, too, Mackintosh claims the French king Charles X—deposed in 1830—was living at Holyrood). He even embellishes his account with a description of Ducrow ludicrously wearing a court costume and waiting with silver candlesticks in his hands to light the novelist to his box! Like most everything by this writer, the tale is either a fabrication or hopelessly confused. Andrew himself never referred to any meeting with Scott prior to the 1830 one at the King's Theatre—although he did perform before the exiled French monarch at Edinburgh in 1830.

26. *Recollections and Wanderings of Paul Bedford*, p. 109.

27. See above, p. 26, and Hawkins, *Life of Kean*, I, 21.

28. See the Liverpool *Albion* for 2 February 1829.

29. Bedford, p. 37.

30. Both Fitzclarence and Wombwell are amusingly described in the series "Green Room Loungers" published in *Actors by Gaslight*, 14 July and 6 October 1838.

31. For a candid account of D'Orsay's early career, see the *Town* for 21 and 28 October and 11 and 25 November 1837.

32. Bedford, pp. 109–12.

33. *The Stage: Both Before and Behind the Curtain*, I, 145–47.

34. See Alan S. Downer, *The Eminent Tragedian: William Charles Macready* (Cambridge, Mass., 1966), pp. 147–48; and for Macready's own account of the notorious episode and its aftermath, *The Diaries of William Charles Macready: 1833–1851*, ed. William Toynbee (London, 1912), I, 301–303, 322–33.

35. Notwithstanding a comic duel between the two men in 1825—see Winston's *Drury Lane Journal*, pp. 116–17. For additional information on Westmacott, see, in addition to Macready's *Diaries*, Boase, *Modern English Biography*, III, col. 1284; the obituary in the *Bookseller* for 1 September 1868; "Green Room Loungers" in *Actors by Gaslight*, 22 September 1838; the *Letters* of Dickens (who sometimes served as an intermediary between Westmacott and Macready and his friends), I, 325, 344–45; and—for an especially devastating attack by a rival editor—the *Figaro in London*, 16 April 1836.

36. Book 4, chapter 10, "Supplementary Characters." Bulwer's attack on Westmacott (originally published in 1833), an exceptionally virulent piece of writing, hints at "another chastisement in reserve for him at the first convenient opportunity. It is a pity to beat one so often beaten—to break bones that have been so often broken; but why deny one's self a luxury at so trifling an expense—it will be some honour to beat him worse than he has been beaten yet"—*England and the English* (New York, 1857), II, 150. For a scathing critique by Westmacott of Bulwer's *Duchess de la Vallière* and Macready's acting in it, see the *Age* for 8 January 1837.

37. See the *Dramatic Magazine* for 1 November 1830.

38. See the Sadler's Wells bills for 1820 in BM Playbills 165. Two letters from Westmacott in the British Museum Perceval Collection (IV, 102–103),

dated 25 July and 12 August 1819, offer his services to Drury Lane and tell of his career in the provinces during the preceding four years. For his quarreling with Macready's father in 1819 at the Bristol Theatre Royal, see Barker, *The Theatre Royal, Bristol*, p. 99.

39. Wilson, *Noctes Ambrosianae*, III, 147 (February 1831).

40. *Morning Chronicle*, 13 October 1835. For the attribution of this review to Dickens, see the Oxford edition of his *Letters*, I, 76 and n.

41. See the bill for 19 July 1830, V&A.

42. British Museum Additional Manuscripts 42,925: Plays from the Lord Chamberlain's Office, vol. 61. The play was "allowed" or approved on 13 March 1834 for performance at Drury Lane.

43. The following reconstruction is based primarily on the MS (whose punctuation I have occasionally regularized) in the Lord Chamberlain's Collection, the Astley's bills for 13 September 1830 and 26 September 1831, and the bill of 21 March 1833 for Ducrow's Royal Arena, Birmingham.

44. *Noctes Ambrosianae*, III, 145.

45. Brighton *Guardian*, 7 November 1832.

46. See, e.g., the review in the *Spectator* for 18 September 1830.

47. See below, pp. 244–45.

48. Edinburgh *Caledonian Mercury*, 12 December 1839. Cf., on the same topic, the earlier remarks by the reviewer for the Edinburgh *Evening Courant*, 16 December 1830.

49. Bills for this engagement are in the collection of playbills in the King's College Library of the University of Aberdeen. The Aberdeen *Journal* carried appreciative reviews of Andrew's performances in its issues of 20 October and 17 November. See also Harry S. Lumsden's series of articles on the history of the circus at Aberdeen, "Circuses in the City from 1807 to 1897," pt. 2, in the *Northern Figaro* for 21 May 1898.

50. See the review in the Edinburgh *Evening Courant* for 4 December 1830 and the unidentified notice, hand-dated 2 January 1831, in Folger Y.d.23 (133). And cf. the account by Mackintosh referred to in note 25 above.

51. Bills for the engagement at the Theatre Royal are in BM Playbills 316. The Edinburgh *Evening Courant* for 16 December carried a long review of Ducrow's performance of *Raphael's Dream*.

52. See, e.g., the bill for 27 December 1830, BM Playbills 246; Broadbent, *Annals of the Liverpool Stage*, pp. 224–25.

53. For the history and detailed reconstructions of the various dramatic versions of Byron's poem, and the careers of notable actors who appeared in them, see *Enter Foot and Horse*, ch. 7, "The Wild Horse of Tartary." For further comments and reproductions of a setting and ground plan in one of these productions, see my article "John Howard Payne, Playwright with a System," *Theatre Notebook*, XXIV (Winter 1969–70), 79–84, with illustrations published in the Summer 1970 issue.

54. Unidentified clipping in BM Astley's Scrapbooks III, 18; *Owl*, 13 August 1831.

55. Charlie Keith, *Circus Life and Amusements (Equestrian, Dramatic, & Musical), in All Nations* (Derby, 1879), p. 47.

56. Bill for 15 August 1831, V&A.

57. Bill for 29 August 1831, V&A.

58. Bill for 12 September [1831], V&A.

59. Unidentified review, hand-dated 15 November 1831, in Drury Lane clippings, V&A. The reviewer for the *Times* (15 November) was of much the same opinion, but charitably suggested that if the piece were reduced to half its length, "it is likely to prove as attractive as any ballet of the kind we have seen, and Mr. Ducrow, who may be properly called the Roscius of the Ring, will ensure the applause to which his industry and ingenuity entitle him."

60. Advertisement in the Bristol *Liberal*, 29 October 1831.

61. The story is also told in the memoir "Mr. Andrew Ducrow" published in the Edinburgh *Opera-Glass*, 4 September 1840. Cf. Barker, *The Theatre Royal, Bristol*, p. 106.

62. The text of the play was eventually published in Pichot's *Mémoires d'un dompteur*, pp. 197–243. For an account of the Paris production, see M.-J. Vesque, "Le Cirque Olympique du boulevard du Temple (de mars 1827 à septembre 1836)," *Cirque dans l'Univers*, no. 15 (1953–54), p. 21. An unidentified review of the same production by an English correspondent is in Harvard II, 98.

63. Bills and reviews of these performances by Martin and Ducrow at Drury Lane are in the V&A.

64. R. J. Broadbent, "Annals of the Manchester Stage, 1735–1845," unpublished typescript in the Manchester Central Reference Library, pp. 496–98.

65. See, e.g., the advance bill for the opening on 26 December [1831] in BM Playbills 246. (Note that many of the Amphitheatre's bills in this volume for the months January–March 1832 continue to carry the printed year-date "1831" and have been bound with other bills from the actual 1830–31 winter season.)

66. Bills for the 1831–32 season in BM Playbills 246.

67. Liverpool *Journal*, 7 January 1832. Cf. the *Albion* for 9 January.

68. Liverpool *Albion*, 30 January 1832. In fact, it would appear even the title was old, for I find J. H. Amherst's *The Assassin Labourer, or The White Farm* billed for its premiere at Astley's on 14 May 1827. For the highly laudatory remarks of the same critic in earlier reviews of the Amphitheatre this season, see the *Albion* for 2 and 9 January.

69. *Albion*, 13 February 1832. The last were a problem common to all theatres of the early nineteenth century—the London Theatres Royal and Opera House included—for they could not be legally excluded if they paid their admission and did not solicit openly. A few managers, it was claimed, encouraged their attendance; others, like Macready when he was managing Drury Lane in 1842, attempted to restrict them to certain parts of the house (where, presumably, they would be isolated from potential customers—or at least from the better classes of playgoers) and saddled them with other inconveniences. Ducrow and West had themselves run into difficulties on the same score in 1826, when they were censured by a London magistrate for employing as a police officer a person who also kept a common brothel, whose girls were said to nightly infest the lobbies of Astley's—see the *Weekly Dramatic Register*, 16 September 1826. For another revealing complaint about prostitutes in the London theatres around this time, see the letter to the editor in the *Times* for 16 December 1825.

70. Letter dated 14 February, published in the Liverpool *Mercury* of 17 February 1832.

71. Letter dated 24 February, published in the Liverpool *Journal* of 25 February 1832.

72. Bill for 2 March [1832], BM Playbills 246. The same notices preface the advertisements taken in Liverpool newspapers at this time—see, e.g., the *Journal* for 3 March.

73. *Albion*, 27 February 1832. The "inferior" establishment, as the advertisements in the 30 January issue of the *Albion* reveal, was the Liver Theatre. The advertisements for the Amphitheatre in the *Albion* were discontinued after this issue, but continued in the other Liverpool papers, where Ducrow's notions of precedence were generally obeyed.

74. *Albion*, 5 March 1832.

75. The lease was due to expire on 30 May 1832, and Ducrow's decision not to renew it appears to have prompted the Amphitheatre's proprietor, Richard Armstead, to offer the building for sale—see the advertisement in the Liverpool *Journal* for 11 February 1832. During the 1832–33 season William Davidge, sometime manager of the Surrey Theatre in London, took the Amphitheatre. Among the artists who performed under his management was the equestrian William Batty, who eventually built and ran the fourth and final Astley's. In December 1834 Batty brought a company of his own to the Amphitheatre for a brief season and renamed the building after himself.

76. Advance bill for the opening on 23 April 1832, V&A.

77. Bill for 23 April 1832, V&A. Reviews of the production were carried in the *Times* and *Morning Chronicle* on 24 April.

78. For the history of this hippodrama, see *Enter Foot and Horse*, pp. 73–76.

79. *The High-Mettled Racer* (London: William Kidd, 1831), pp. 5–6. The preface is dated 28 November 1830. It was probably around this time, perhaps in the late twenties, that Cruikshank—not to be confused with his famous brother George—made several sketches of Ducrow's own scenes in the ring, most notably his "Courier of St. Petersburg," which served as basis for a series of miniature colored prints—see figures and the appendix "The Ducrow Iconography."

80. Bills for Ducrow's benefit, 24 September, and Mme. Ducrow's benefit, 5 October 1832, V&A.

81. Bill for 1 July 1833, V&A.

82. Bills for the 1832 season in V&A and BM Playbills 170 and 352.

83. Unidentified review, with printed date 26 September [1832], in V&A Astley's folders. The rest of the evening seems to have gone no better, for the same reviewer reports the "horses were disobedient, the assistants awkward, and the zebras intractable. The celebrated German rider [Lendemann] failed twice successively in attempting to leap over an extended piece of canvas, and was laid ingloriously sprawling in the sawdust. The zebras crushed down the palm trees and other scene-work, erected to enhance the effect of this exhibition; and one of the supposed hunters appeared seriously injured by a violent kick received from one of them."

84. Brighton *Herald*, 10 November 1832; cf. Henry C. Porter, *The History*

of the Theatres of Brighton, from 1774 to 1885 (Brighton, 1886), p. 61. For other reviews of the company during this engagement, see the *Herald* for 27 October and the *Guardian* for 24 October.

85. The performance was described in the Brighton *Guardian* for 21 November and Brighton *Gazette* for 22 November, with the former listing the complete program and reporting on Andrew's subsequent visit to the Pavilion. The *Court Journal* for 24 November carried a briefer description. Matthew Mackintosh's notoriously inaccurate account of the event is reviewed in the appendix "The Ducrow Apocrypha," to which I would add at this point that Ducrow did not—as Mackintosh claims—perform either "The British Sailor" or "The Courier of St. Petersburg," although Adams attempted the latter character and fell after the number of horses had been increased to six.

86. See the advertisement and review in the Birmingham *Journal* for 23 February 1833. The bills for this engagement are in BM Playbills 272.

87. Bill for 31 May 1833, BM Playbills 272.

88. *The Benefit System in the British Theatre* (London, 1967). For a detailed examination of Ducrow's charity benefits, from which much of the following is extracted, see my article "The Tyranny of Charity: Andrew Ducrow in the Provinces," *Nineteenth Century Theatre Research*, I (1973), 95–105.

89. Troubridge, p. 74. A practice that was not entirely restricted to the provinces, however, for around the end of the eighteenth century I find references to annual benefits at the Royal Circus for the London Humane Society (whose object was the resuscitating of persons apparently dead); and in 1826 Ducrow and West gave a much publicized benefit at Astley's under the patronage of the Duke of York for the distressed Spitalfields weavers—see the bills for 17 and 24 April 1826 (BM Playbills 170) and the unidentified clipping and letter to the editor, dated 19 April 1826, in Harvard II, 3. A letter from Sir Herbert Taylor, conveying the Duke of York's willingness to serve as patron on the occasion (he did not, however, actually attend) is in the Ducrow Album.

90. Liverpool *Journal*, 11 February 1832. The estimates ran as high as £700; the proceeds were £224.11s.6d.

91. Album, letter dated 16 June 1828.

92. See, e.g., Frost, *Circus Life and Circus Celebrities*, p. 241.

93. See the Aberdeen *Journal*, 17 November 1830.

94. Album: letter dated 14 December 1835 to Ducrow from the town clerk; bill of 16 December 1835 for Ducrow's Arena.

95. Dublin *Evening Packet and Correspondent*, 4 November 1828.

96. A letter in the Album from the Lord Provost of Edinburgh, dated 12 November 1827, acknowledges the receipt of thirty pounds for the charitable institutions of that city.

97. On Ryan's career, see Boase, III, col. 362; Keith, pp. 32–33. The "Shakespearean Jester" William Frederick Wallett had kind words for Ryan and his treatment of his employees—see *The Public Life of W. F. Wallett*, p. 61.

98. Hardly a unique instance in the case of Ryan, however, who was only one of the most persistent copiers of Ducrow's acts and programs—see, e.g., the bills for his Birmingham circus during the 1836–40 seasons, BM Playbills 272.

99. Birmingham *Journal*, 8 June 1833. The reference to Ryan's "canvas" is, of course, another slap at this rival's pretensions. The acrimony generated

by Andrew's settling with Ryan appears to have been highly contagious, for no sooner had he returned to Birmingham than he found it necessary to do battle with the Theatre Royal there as well. The last, reacting to an advertisement Ducrow had placed in the *Journal* of 25 May, circulated a "Caution to the Public" in which attention was called to an intended imposition at Ducrow's "booth"—namely, the production of the harlequinade *Puss in Boots* as given the previous winter at Covent Garden. Contrary to what Ducrow would have the public believe, the warning continued, the original performers, scenery, tricks, etc. were all destined for the Theatre Royal, which announced its own production for 30 May (copy of the notice in Disher Scrapbooks II). There was yet another party highly displeased by Ducrow's returning to Birmingham at this time. On 26 May William Charles Macready, scheduled to begin a run at the Theatre Royal on the following day, rode into town and made the following notation in his diary: "On approaching Birmingham I saw the terrible *affiches* of Mr. Ducrow's, which with other ill-boding circumstances prepared me for a bad week" (*Diaries*, I, 37).

100. Bill for 12 August 1833, V&A. The bill goes on to boast that at the 368th representation of *Mazeppa* on 5 August, 2800 persons were in the theatre.

101. Bill for 23 September [1833], V&A.

102. Bills for 8 April and 6 May 1833, V&A. See the reviews in the *Times* and *Morning Chronicle* of 9 April.

103. Bills for 22 April, 6 May, 17 June, 1 July, 5 and 26 August, and 23 September 1833, V&A.

104. For accounts of à Beckett's life, see the *Dictionary of National Biography* and M. H. Spielmann, *The History of "Punch"* (New York, 1895), pp. 272–80.

105. *Figaro in London*, 6 October 1832.

106. *Figaro in London*, 27 December 1834. À Beckett was succeeded by his friend the social historian and one of the founders of *Punch*, Henry Mayhew. Thereafter the notices of Ducrow and Astley's were consistently favorable. While priding himself that "our columns have been free from that reckless severity which used to be laid as a charge against this periodical," the new editor, however, had a few peculiarities of his own—among them an undisguised hatred of Jews, especially the "gang of Jews that have got into the Victoria" (23 January 1836). On an earlier occasion, reviewing Ducrow's production of *The Siege of Jerusalem* in the 16 May 1835 issue, Mayhew concluded his remarks with the jocular observation that "the only thing wanted to give a proper and a pleasant effect to the magnificent scenery and terrific combats...is the hanging of a few Jews." On the "merry prejudice" against Jews entertained by the original staff of *Punch*, see Spielmann, pp. 103–105, who also provides, on pp. 268–71, a biographical sketch of Mayhew.

107. *Figaro in London*, 21 April 1832.

108. Ibid., 12 May 1832.

109. See the issues of 16 June and 25 August 1832.

110. *Figaro in London*, 6 April 1833.

111. Ibid., 18 May 1833. And see the issue for 11 May.

112. Ibid., 17 August 1833.

113. Ibid., 27 April 1833. The business of the clown mixing with the

audience is as old as the circus itself, where even today one often sees them plopping down into the laps of embarrassed females and saluting them with resounding busses. It is uncertain whether the critic or his correspondent was complaining about John Ducrow, however, for traditionally there were two clowns to the ring each season, with the acrobat and leaper Williams seconding John in 1832 and 1833.

114. Unidentified review, hand-dated 19 May 1833, BM Astley's Scrapbooks III, 185.

115. See the bill for 27 May (V&A), which announces her reappearance after a "severe indisposition."

116. Macready, who did not want to attend the funeral but felt obligated to go, notes in his diary for 25 May that he "passed several pedestrian mourners on the road, and some carriages, Mr. Ducrow's" (I, 35–36).

117. Unidentified clipping, hand-dated 20 September 1833, Disher Scrapbooks I. According to a letter found in his rooms, his real name was not Yates and he apparently had several wives. Jealousy was ruled a contributing cause of his suicide.

7. Losses and Gains

1. See Charles Mackie, comp., *Norfolk Annals: A Chronological Record of Remarkable Events in the Nineteenth Century* (Norwich, 1901), I, 326–27.

2. Letter to J. Lunn, in the V&A Drury Lane boxes.

3. *The Stage*, I, 143–44; and see above, p. 181. A later account of Ducrow at the rehearsals of *St. George* describes him as hopping about on one leg up until the evening of the first performance, his left foot having been seriously burned in a recent accident ("Mr. Andrew Ducrow," *Actors by Daylight*, 14 July 1838).

4. Bill for 26 December 1833, V&A. For my earlier account of this production, see *Enter Foot and Horse*, pp. 103–106.

5. The following reconstruction is based primarily on the manuscript of the play, "allowed" and entered by the Lord Chamberlain on 20 December 1833—British Museum Additional Manuscripts 42,924: Plays from the Lord Chamberlain's Office, vol. 60. A good description of Bayard's struggle with the dragon, dating from the time of the play's revival at Astley's the following season, is contained in the unidentified clipping, hand-dated 20 May 1834, in BM Astley's Scrapbooks III, 187.

6. *Age*, 5 January and 9 March 1834.

7. *Examiner*, 29 December 1833. In his published diary Macready himself does not comment on the production, other than to mention some gossip he picked up at the Garrick Club: "Heard, among other observations on Messrs. Bunn and Ducrow from Mr. Meadows, that the language of the former [i.e.,

Ducrow?] to the women was so horridly revolting that had a relative of his been there he must have knocked him down"—*Diaries*, I, 90 (entry for 1 January 1834).

8. Bunn, I, 144; 223, n. The inscription on the vase, expressing Bunn's confidence in the "splendid talents" of Ducrow and the hopelessness of anyone ever succeeding him, was dated 26 December 1833 and reproduced in the *Age* for 5 January 1834. A number of engravings of the vase were also published, one of them at the bottom of a print depicting Ducrow on Bayard engaging the dragon in its den.

9. *Diaries*, I, 98.

10. See the *Age* for 5 January and the *Times* for 10 January 1834.

11. Bills for 17 February [1834] and succeeding evenings in British Museum Theatrical Cuttings 50 and V&A.

12. Bill for 17 March 1834, V&A.

13. See *Wemyss' Chronology of the American Stage, from 1752 to 1852* (New York, 1852), pp. 21–22; Brown, *History of the American Stage*, p. 10.

14. Bill for 31 March 1834, V&A. For some mixed reviews of the production, see the *Times* (1 April), *Examiner* (13 April), and *Figaro in London* (5 April). The last describes the theatre on Easter Monday as "of course crammed with Bacchanals, and a greasy collection of gin-swamped riff-raff."

15. Bill for the first night on Whitsun Monday [19 May 1834], V&A.

16. Bill for 4 August 1834, V&A.

17. Bill for 31 March 1834, V&A.

18. Bill for 21 April 1834 (premiere), V&A; reviewed in the *Theatrical Observer*, 22 April 1834.

19. Bill for 21 April 1834 (premiere), V&A.

20. Bill for 1 September 1834, V&A.

21. Census returns for the Parish of St. Mary, Lambeth, Enumeration District no. 8, Amphitheatre Place—Public Record Office.

22. "Dramatic Feuilletons," *Sunday Times*, 16 February 1851.

23. See the bill for 9 September 1834, V&A.

24. Descriptions of the funeral in the *Gentleman's Magazine* for July 1834 and the unidentified clipping, hand-dated 31 May 1834, in Folger Y.d.23 (133).

25. *Figaro in London*, 19 April 1834.

26. Ibid., 7 June 1834. And see, in the same issue, the attack on Bunn, who was supported by "all Ducrow's gang" at his benefit on 2 June.

27. Broadbent, "Annals of the Manchester Stage," pp. 521–22.

28. Bills for this engagement are in BM Playbills 237; and see the advertisements and reviews in the Liverpool *Journal* from 1 November 1834 to 3 January 1835.

29. See the explanation of these events, based on a letter from Ducrow, in the *Times* for 1 January 1835. An earlier letter from Sidney Foster, Andrew's treasurer at the time, published in the 23 December issue of the same paper was at pains to point out Ducrow was devoting all his time and attention to the Liverpool Theatre Royal. Cf. Westmacott's comments in the *Age* for 28 December; Bunn, I, 223–24; and the Drury Lane bills for 26 December 1834 (premiere) and 5 January 1835, which credit Ducrow with providing the stud and services of "some of the most eminent Performers & Artists of his Establish-

ment" and producing the "equestrian evolutions, grand tableaux, combats, and encounters of mounted knights."

30. Bunn, I, 224–25; *Enter Foot and Horse*, pp. 107–108.

31. See the *Town* for 21 November 1840.

32. *The London Theatre, 1811–1866: Selections from the Diary of Henry Crabb Robinson*, ed. Eluned Brown (London, 1966), p. 147 (entry for 6 February 1835).

33. Bills for these performances are in the V&A.

34. Bunn, I, 224, n.; "Mr. Andrew Ducrow," *Actors by Daylight*, 14 July 1838. The vase for this year, as an unidentified engraving in the Ducrow Album reveals, was surmounted by the figure of an armored knight standing with shield and spear.

35. Bunn, I, 225.

36. See the *Morning Chronicle* for 13 October and the *Times* for 14 October 1835. According to the bill for the evening in question, Adams was scheduled to perform "The Reaper," "The Milanese Voltigeur," and "The British Fox Hunter." During which of these the accident occurred is not recorded.

37. *London Amusement Guide*, 25 April 1836.

38. Bills for 20 April and 27 July 1835, V&A. Cf. the unidentified review in Harvard II, 98.

39. Bill for 8 June 1835, V&A.

40. *Figaro in London*, 15 August 1835. Cf. the bills for 10 August (premiere) and 29 August, V&A.

41. Bills for various dates in the V&A. For references to Woolford's career in America, see Greenwood, *The Circus: Its Origin and Growth Prior to 1835*, p. 112; and the bill for the American Theatre, Bowery, 17 March [1837], in British Museum Theatrical Cuttings 50.

42. See the bills for 31 August and 14 and 21 September 1835, V&A.

43. Bill for 29 June 1835 (premiere), V&A. A few months later, in a scene entitled "The Wizard of Peru, or The Senator and Barbary Courser," one of Ducrow's own steeds was performing all these feats—despite the fact, as the bills stated, that Franconi's Blanche had had the advantage of "three Years constant tuition." This prodigy of training appears to have been the work of the elder Ginnett, who interpreted the human character in the scene—see the bill for 28 September 1835 (first time), V&A.

44. Bill for 27 July 1835, V&A.

45. Bill for 4 May 1835, V&A.

46. See above, pp. 196–98; bill for Ducrow's benefit on 28 September 1835, V&A.

47. Advertisement in the *Morning Chronicle*, 12 October 1835; bill for the same date in the Guildhall Library. A description of the Colosseum and its panorama appears in the *London Magazine* for February 1829. For Dickens' comments on Ducrow's performance there, published in the *Morning Chronicle* of 13 October, see above, pp. 226–27.

48. Barker, *The Theatre Royal, Bristol*, pp. 119, 244. Cf. M. E. Board, *The Story of the Bristol Stage, 1490–1925* (London, n.d.), pp. 23–24; G. Rennie Powell, *The Bristol Stage: Its Story* (Bristol, 1919), p. 37. Most historians of the Bristol theatre, appalled by the type of entertainment Mrs. M'Cready

introduced to the boards of the Theatre Royal, look upon her period of management (1834–53) as a "dark" one and skip over it as rapidly as possible. Miss Barker's account of this remarkable woman's career is both sympathetic and corrective.

49. Letter to C. Westmacott at the *Age* office, in the collection of Mr. R. Toole Stott.

50. Bill for 23 November 1835, author's collection. Cf. the *London Amusement Guide* for 30 November 1835, which refers to Ducrow's new building at Hull, "embellished with taste."

51. Bill for the week of 28 December 1835, which announces the company will depart for Leeds following a final performance on 7 January (Disher Scrapbooks II); *London Amusement Guide*, 29 February 1836.

52. Bill for Saturday, 9 April 1836 (V&A), in which it is also claimed the Amphitheatre will open on this date. The bill was apparently printed while Andrew, who directed the spectacle, was having doubts about his ability to open on Easter Monday. The advertisements and review in the *Times* for 5 April indicate he made the traditional date after all.

53. Bills for 30 May, 13 and 20 June 1836 and 28 September 1835, V&A.

54. Bill for 11 April 1836, V&A.

55. Bill for 30 May 1836, V&A.

56. See the two different bills for 26 September 1836, V&A.

57. See, e.g., the bills for 25 April and 20 June 1836, V&A.

58. Bill in BM Playbills 246.

59. On Loyo's career, see, besides the standard history by Baron de Vaux, *Ecuyers et ecuyères* (Paris, 1893), H. Cazier-Charpentier, "Caroline Loyo," *Cirque dans l'Univers*, no. 86 (3ᵉ trimestre 1972), pp. 19–21; Henry Thétard, *La Merveilleuse Histoire du cirque* (Paris, 1947), I, 87; II, 193–94.

60. See the bills for 22 August and 5 September 1836, V&A.

61. For additional biographical data on Plège, see Tristan Rémy, "Notes pour servir à l'histoire de la famille Plège," *Cirque dans l'Univers*, no. 18 (1954–55), pp. 26–27.

62. Bunn, II, 84–86. Cf. Percy Hetherington Fitzgerald, *Chronicles of Bow-Street Police-Office, with an Account of the Magistrates, "Runners," and Police, etc.* (London, 1888), I, 245–47.

63. Bill in the V&A. Cf. the earlier, uncombative announcements for these performers in the bills for 30 May and 20 June.

64. Unidentified clipping, Disher Scrapbooks I. Cf. "Mr. Andrew Ducrow," *Actors by Daylight*, 14 July 1838.

65. *Owl*, 13 August 1831.

66. Hand-written extract from an unidentified source in the Winston materials at the Folger Shakespeare Library, Y.d.23 (133). A reference to Ducrow's "recent malady" in the same account would appear to date it sometime in late 1841.

67. Bunn, I, 146.

68. Copy in Harvard II, 86. Other copies of the menu are at the end of Harvard I; in the V&A (Westmacott's copy); in Disher Scrapbooks II; and in the Guildhall Library collection of Astley's bills.

69. Bunn, II, 86.

70. Undated bill in British Museum Theatrical Cuttings 50.

71. See "The Ducrow Apocrypha."

72. See the advertisement in the *Independent* for 12 November and the review in the *Iris* for 22 November 1836.

73. Review in the *Iris*, 29 November 1836.

74. See, e.g., the Newcastle *Journal* for 28 January 1837; cf. the reports in the issue of 21 January. Mackintosh (p. 161), in his account of this event, which he dates as occurring on 10 November 1835, attributes Margaret's death to a severe cold and inflammation of the lungs.

75. See, e.g., the notices in the Newcastle *Standard* for 21 January and the London *Age* for 22 January 1837. Copies of both were cut out and carefully pasted into the Ducrow Album, where they are followed by a mournful, perhaps original quatrain in Andrew's own hand:

> As Sorrow weeps, o'er virtues sacred breast,
> Our tears become us, our griefs are just,
> Such were the tears he shed, who grateful pays
> The last sad tribute of pure love and praise.

76. The North Country clown and showman Billy Purvis comments on Ducrow's visit to Newcastle in 1836–37 and the rivalry between them while Purvis was performing at his nearby theatre, the Victoria. Despite this competition, the two seem to have been on friendly terms, sending each other their "leavings" whenever one or the other house was too full; and Purvis reports another instance of Andrew's generosity: "Many evil things were circulated against him; but I must say that Mr. Ducrow always conducted himself with kindness towards me; in proof of which, when he left the town he ordered his set pieces of decorative paintings to be given to me; and this act I consider was kind in the extreme"—J. P. Robson, *The Life and Adventures of the Far-Famed Billy Purvis* (Newcastle-upon-Tyne, 1849 [for 1850]), pp. 184–85. See p. 160 for Purvis's recollection of the "late unrivalled equestrian" at an earlier date.

77. Broadfoot's letter to Westmacott, dated 17 January 1837 at the Royal Arena, Newcastle, is in Harvard II, 88.

78. *Reminiscences*, pp. 161–63. The hapless clergyman was E. Johnstone, according to the Bishop's Transcript of All Saints Cemetery, Kensal Green, 1837, entry no. 1117, which also gives the date of burial and Margaret's age. I am indebted to Mr. W. J. Smith, Head Archivist of the Greater London Record Office, for this information.

79. The manuscript, in the second volume of the Disher Scrapbooks at the University of Kansas, is dated 3 September 1839 and appears to be related to the far-flung materials of the noted collector of theatricalia James Winston, whose Drury Lane journals once belonged to Disher. For the use Disher made of the manuscript (which inaccurately reports the body was brought to London from Liverpool), see *Greatest Show on Earth*, pp. 141–42.

80. See the *Age*, 5 February 1837.

81. For additional correspondence on this matter, beginning as early as 20 February, with Frederick Gye of Vauxhall Gardens, see the two letters in Harvard II, 89 and the Harvard Vauxhall Gardens Scrapbooks V, 90.

82. Letter to Broadfoot at Ducrow's Arena, York, dated at Paris on 10

March 1837, in the R. Toole Stott Circus Collection at the University of California, Santa Barbara.

83. Letter to Duponchelle [*sic*] dated at London on 26 May 1837, loose letter with accompanying French translation in the Harvard Theatre Collection.

84. Petition, dated June 1837 *chez* M. D'harmonville, 170 rue Montmartre, and response in Archives Nationales F^{21} 1036.

85. See the unidentified reviews in the V&A and Harvard II, 98 and the bill for 27 March 1837, V&A. For a description of this production, see *Enter Foot and Horse*, pp. 61–63.

86. Bills for 3 July and 21 August 1837, V&A.

87. Bill for 1 May 1837, V&A. The original title was restored later in the season—see the bill for 31 July. And see, in the V&A, the bill for 20 August 1838, which carries a curious cut (fig. 67) depicting Ducrow reclining at the base of a tree in his Zephyr costume; Louisa Ducrow, as Cupid, seated atop the tree playing what looks like a recorder; Chaffé, as Puck or the Mischievous Sprite in a grotesque devil costume, both popping out of a basket and climbing a ladder set against the tree; and a third, unidentified infant (probably Miss Avery) as Rosebud rising from a flower and standing below Puck on the ladder. As is obvious from the illustration, the horses (which in 1838 numbered three) were not used throughout the act, and what one sees here are the decorations and machinery for "mechanical changes" and "metamorphoses" set up in the arena itself. This act, too, was copied by other riders and remained in circus programs for many years. Under the title "The Sprites of the Silver Shower," e.g., it was performed around 1857 by the American equestrian Burnell Runnells and his three children during the visit of Howes and Cushing's Great United States Circus to England. A handsome poster depicting several scenes from their act is in the British Museum.

88. Bills for 1 May and 25 September 1837, V&A.

89. Bill for 17 July 1837, V&A.

90. *Times*, 28 March 1837; cf. the bill for his debut on 27 March when he was advertised as "Herr Hicken." In later years there was a rider named Hicks who appeared as Mazeppa at Astley's and elsewhere; but the name of Ducrow's artist in 1837 seems to be correctly stated in the bills. As early as 1822 there was a master of the ring named Hicken at the Olympic Circus in Newcastle. His son, Master Hicken, was at this period billed for vaulting and performances on the flying (bounding) rope—see the bills in BM Playbills 322. I assume the latter was the Hicken Ducrow eventually engaged and who, during the 1836 season, was riding at Ryan's Royal Circus in Birmingham, where on 23 May he was billed to interpret "The Life and Death of Shaw, the Life-Guardsman" (BM Playbills 272), an act he repeated at Astley's the following 17 April (bill in V&A). Hicken seems to have enjoyed a long career in the ring. The clown Charlie Keith writes that around 1858, when he was appearing with Macarte's Circus in Bradford, Hicken was also there, "performing as an equestrian, and then about the oldest in England" (*Circus Life and Amusements*, pp. 26–27).

91. See the bills for 5 June and 21 August 1837, V&A.

92. Bills for 27 March and 4 October 1837, V&A.

93. See the bills for 7 August 1837 and 19 September 1836, V&A.

94. Bill for 3 April 1837, V&A.

95. Bills for 11 September and 3 July 1837, V&A.

96. Bill for 25 September 1837; for the run in the provinces, where the piece was sometimes announced as *The Council of Constantine*, see, e.g., the advertisement in the Sheffield *Independent* for 12 November 1836. Purvis also mentions Ducrow's production of the "Jewess" in connection with the 1836–37 season at Newcastle (Robson, p. 184). A blank verse rendition of the opera by J. R. Planché, also titled *The Jewess*, had been given at Drury Lane in the fall of 1835.

97. Unidentified review, hand-dated 10 June 1837, V&A; *Figaro in London*, 3 June 1837. Cf. the bill for 15 May, V&A.

98. Bills for 11 and 25 September 1837, V&A.

99. Bill for 25 September 1837, V&A.

100. B. F. Rayner, *The Dumb Man of Manchester* (London, n.d.), in Dicks' Standard Plays, no. 368.

101. Unidentified review, hand-dated 7 October 1837, V&A.

102. Unidentified review in the Ducrow Album.

103. Undated letter in the Ducrow Album. The words "in this manner" are inserted over a caret and apparently were a judicious afterthought of the anonymous young lady. Years later the painter and R.A. William Powell Frith retained a vivid—if somewhat inaccurate—impression of Ducrow's pantomime while reenacting the murder before the Chief Justice—see his *Further Reminiscences* (London, 1888), p. 109.

104. Advertisement in the Sheffield *Independent* for 9 June 1838 (with performances announced to begin on 11 June). Master and Miss Ginnett, "the youngest Female Equestrian in the Kingdom," were also with Ryan at this time.

105. Bill for 19 December 1838, in the collection of Theatre Royal playbills (1838–39) in the Glasgow Mitchell Library.

106. Bill for 1 December 1838, Glasgow Mitchell Library.

107. See the advertisements in the Edinburgh *Advertiser* for 7 and 14 November 1837; and the announcements in the Theatre Royal bills for 11 November and 14 December (for a return engagement of two nights), BM Playbills 317.

108. 10 November 1837. See the same reviewer's comments on Ducrow's "consummate art" as Figaro in the issue of 8 December.

109. See, e.g., the advertisement in the Edinburgh *Advertiser* for 19 December 1837; cf. the bill for Ducrow's Royal Olympic Arena at Aberdeen, 27 March 1838, in the volume of playbills in the King's College Library, University of Aberdeen.

110. See the advertisements in the Glasgow *Herald*.

111. Two clippings relating to this rumor—both hand-dated late January 1838—are in the Folger Shakespeare Library, Y.d.23 (133). Cf. Baynham, *The Glasgow Stage*, p. 126, who obviously had access to the same information and accepted it at face value.

112. See the advertisement and brief notice in the Aberdeen *Herald* for 3 March 1838. Several bills relating to this engagement are in the King's College Library at the University of Aberdeen.

8. Decline

1. Unidentified clipping, hand-dated 23 July 1837, Disher Scrapbooks II. The incident itself occurred on 12 July 1837.

2. Certificate of marriage in the General Register Office; Bunn, *The Stage*, III, 57.

3. Certificate of birth, General Register Office.

4. Certificate of marriage, General Register Office.

5. Letter in Harvard Vauxhall Gardens Scrapbooks V, 83.

6. *Thirty-Five Years of a Dramatic Author's Life*, II, 38–39.

7. Bill for 16 April 1838, V&A. Reviews in the *Times*, 17 April; *Actors by Daylight*, 21 April; *Figaro in London*, 2 June 1838.

8. See the *Figaro in London*, 28 April 1838; Brown, *History of the American Stage*, p. 65.

9. Undated advance bill, V&A.

10. As was not unusual for Ducrow's benefit nights, a number of variations of the same bill were distributed. Of the two preserved at the V&A, one is unillustrated and the other includes the cut (fig. 70) of him as the Idiot. A third variation in BM Playbills 352 contains the erudite effusion "Le Cheval Volant" discussed above, pp. 196–98.

11. *The Idiot of Heidelburg Castle*, "A Romantic Drama, in Three Acts, Arranged from the French Drama 'Le Pauvre Idiot,' with Alterations and Additions by Andrew Ducrow" (London, n.d.), Dicks' Standard Plays, no. 451. (The names of the play's characters and actors in the printed text differ slightly from those in the 8 October 1838 bills for the premiere.)

12. Bill for 4 June 1838, V&A, in which the author's name is given as Mr. Baxter.

13. See the bill for 4 June 1838, V&A.

14. See the bills for 2 and 9 July 1838, V&A, the latter with a cut of this feat.

15. See, e.g., the bill for 9 July in BM Playbills 170, in which the program is given in French, English, and German.

16. Parts of Blackburn's diary were edited by Charles H. Day and published in the New York *Clipper* for 14, 21, and 28 February 1880 under the title "A Clown's Log: Extracts from the Diary of the Late Joseph Blackburn." Efforts to locate the manuscript itself, which eventually became the property of Levi North, have to date proved unsuccessful.

17. For biographical information on Van Amburgh, see Boase, III, col. 1073; O. J. Ferguson, *A Brief Biographical Sketch of I. A. Van Amburgh, and an Illustrated and Descriptive History of the Animals Contained in His Menagerie* (New York: Booth, n.d.), which contains many pleasant absurdities concerning the "unnatural" history of the animals in Van Amburgh's collection; Vail, "Notes on the Early American Circus," pp. 148–52; and for an amusing, apocryphal account supposedly written by a fellow American, Ephraim Watts [pseud. of the poet and dramatist Richard Hengist Horne], *Life of Van Amburgh, the Brute Tamer* (Cheapside: Tyas, [1838]). A long extract from this last appears in the 2 February 1839 issue of *Actors by Daylight*.

18. Unidentified review, hand-dated 1 September 1838, V&A. See the review in the *Times* for 3 September and the bills for 27 August and succeeding weeks.

19. On Ducrow's rehearsal methods and reputed language on this occasion, see above, pp. 176–81.

20. The reviews of the production in the *Times* (23 October), *Actors by Daylight* (27 October), *Era* (28 October), and *Age* (28 October) were all favorable, while those in the *Sunday Times* (21 and 28 October) were especially destructive and seem to have led Bunn to lodge a complaint against this paper. The *Morning Chronicle* (23 October) and several other journals attempted to strike a balance but were generally disapproving.

21. *Actors by Daylight*, 17 November 1838.

22. See, e.g., the review in the *Times* for 27 December 1838.

23. The incident is reported in an unidentified clipping in Harvard II, 106. For Bunn's account of the royal visits, see *The Stage*, III, 117–23.

24. *Times*, 15 February 1839. Cf. Bunn, III, 175–79, who gives the date of the dinner as 13 March.

25. For two particularly horrified accounts of Victoria's visits to see Van Amburgh and the feeding of his animals, see the *Figaro in London* for 4 and 11 February 1839. *Actors by Daylight* (2 February 1839), which also commented on the Queen's display of "extraordinary wisdom and brilliant intellect" at the feeding and reported she was trying to decide if she should invite Van Amburgh's beasts to dine at the palace, gives a wildly funny description of her meeting with Bunn and the trainer and their supposed conversation: "'And that's Von Humbug, the man who has tamed them?' said the Queen, pointing to Bunn."

26. Bunn, III, 98. For Bunn's other remarks on the subject in this volume, and the number of performances reached by his various spectacles, see pp. 99–100, 104, 244–46.

27. *Diaries*, I, 473.

28. *Diaries*, I, 473–74 (entry for 25 October 1838).

29. See, e.g., *Actors by Daylight*, 6 October 1838.

30. Bill in BM Playbills 171; reviewed in the *Times* for 2 April 1839.

31. *Times*, 7 May 1839. Cf. the accounts in the *Age* for 28 April and the *Times* for 3 May.

32. Bills for 15 July (BM Playbills 170), 22 July, and 4 November 1839 (V&A).

33. See, e.g., the comments in the *Age* for 16 June, 18 August, and 17 November.

34. See, e.g., the bill for 23 September, BM Playbills 170. Van Amburgh himself by this time had gone on to Paris, where he and his lions were appearing at the Porte-St.-Martin Theatre in *La Fille de l'émir*. Théophile Gautier has left an amusing and highly descriptive review of the production—see his *Histoire de l'art dramatique en France depuis vingt-cinq ans* (Paris, 1858–59), I, 288–95 (18 August 1839). The celebrated feat with the lamb and Van Amburgh's thrusting his head into the lion's mouth were incorporated into the action of this play.

35. The Eglintoun Tournament, which was held on the west coast of

Scotland and lasted several days, received extensive coverage in the newspapers. For accounts of both it and the Astleian production, see the *Times* for 3 September.

36. Advance bill for 14 October 1839, BM Playbills 170; notices in the *Era* (of the private view for the press) for 13 October; *Times*, 15 October; unidentified article, hand-dated October 1839, Disher Scrapbooks II.

37. *Random Recollections of an Old Actor*, pp. 117–19. Upon being asked by Belton if he was ever afraid of his lion, Carter replied, "Never while performing; but in the depths of night and in silence I feel as if his fangs one day will drag me to a horrible death." The feeling was not prophetic.

38. See the *Age* for 5 July 1840 and the unidentified clipping in Harvard III, 4.

39. An extensive run of bills and reviews for the "Curriculum," which commenced on 2 July and ended on 30 August, is preserved in the fifth of the Vauxhall Gardens Scrapbooks at Harvard. See also the accounts in the *Era* for 7 July and the *Morning Advertiser* for 2 August 1839.

40. And like many another circus artist of the day—contrary to popular opinion—knew how to read and write, as is evidenced by a letter from him asking some unidentified person to take charge of two small monkeys while he was away on a winter tour—in British Museum Theatrical Cuttings 50. Hillier was sometimes billed as the "Milanese Youth" and "Mungo" Hillier, the latter designation presumably after the black character in Isaac Bickerstaffe's eighteenth-century comic opera *The Padlock*.

41. Belton, p. 121.

42. The same may be said of Jewish circus artists, of whom there was also a goodly number—some most eminent—in the nineteenth century. For reasons best known to themselves, many circus "fans" of the present day prefer to ignore or contest these facts, and one prominent American organization of such individuals has for many years systematically excluded Negroes from membership. The problem is compounded by the fact that descendants of some of these artists are still active in the circus.

43. See, e.g., the bill for 27 May 1839, V&A. And for a strange—perhaps apocryphal—tale about Andrew's carrying off an "ill-clad but innocent looking negro boy" whom he found selling "timber" on Waterloo Bridge the previous year, see the column "Our Miscellany" in *Actors by Daylight* for 28 July 1838. Since the writer goes on to state his belief that the child "is shortly to make his appearance in public as a *black tiger*," it may be he has sacrificed truth for a joke at Ducrow and Van Amburgh's expense. Yet the "Infant Pablo" did make his debut at Astley's the following season, and the chariots at Vauxhall were driven by "Africa's sons."

44. Bills for Ryan's Circus at Birmingham, 13 June and 4 July 1836, BM Playbills 272. For additional information on Fanque's career, see Boase, I, col. 1020; and the *Illustrated London News* for 20 March 1847, with an engraving of him performing haute école at Astley's.

45. See, e.g., the bill for 3 December 1849, Harvard III, 85.

46. See the *Age* for 6 October 1839.

47. See Mackie, *Norfolk Annals*, I, 390.

48. See the advertisement in the Edinburgh *Advertiser* for 17 December 1839; and above, p. 309.

49. Founded in 1838, the London Club abruptly broke up on 7 December 1839 following a heated argument in which Macready's toady the journalist John Forster was involved. For information on this club, see the *Dickensian*, XLI (1945), 40–41; Dickens, *Letters*, I, 392, n. and II, 231, n.; Macready's diary entries for 30 March and 8 December 1839; and, on the breakup, the *Age* for 22 December 1839. The industrial town of Sheffield, surprisingly, possessed its Shakespeare Club, which antedated the London one by nineteen years and was still flourishing in 1831—see, e.g., the "Historical Sketch of the Beginning and Progress of Theatrical Amusements in Sheffield" prefacing the first issue of the *Theatrical Examiner for Sheffield* (which was dedicated to the "Gentlemen of the Shakespeare Club"), 28 October 1824. The history of these societies, despite all the verbiage on Shakespeare that is annually ground out, remains to be written. Another of their functions—at least in provincial towns—was the support of local theatres.

50. Unidentified clipping in the Ducrow Album. The speeches reported in this article are not precise quotations, but appear to have been taken down by someone charged with making minutes of the proceedings.

51. Notice in the Liverpool *Chronicle* for 18 January 1840. For reviews of the season at the Amphitheatre, see the *Chronicle* for 28 December 1839, Liverpool *Mail* for 5 January 1840, and *Albion* for 20 January 1840.

52. Death certificate, General Register Office. Louisa's death and the cause of it were widely reported in the Liverpool and London papers. See, e.g., the Liverpool *Journal* and *Chronicle* for 4 April, the *Times* for 8 April, the *Theatrical Journal* for 18 April, and the *Gentleman's Magazine* for May 1840.

53. See the *Era* for 5 and 12 April 1840.

54. See, e.g., the *Age* for 13 September 1840.

55. Letter to Mrs. Leonard Wigan, dated 10 November 1840 at the Royal Amphitheatre, Lancaster, V&A.

56. Unidentified clipping, hand-dated 26 May 1840, Disher Scrapbooks II.

57. See the review in the *Times* for 12 September 1840.

58. See, e.g., the reviews in the *Times* for 21 April 1840 and the unidentified clipping in Harvard III, 4.

59. See the *Era* for 31 May 1840.

60. Bill for 15 June 1840 (second week), V&A. For another review of the production, see the *Theatrical Journal* for 27 June 1840.

61. See the *Era* for 28 June and 12 July 1840.

62. In Paris, Carter performed at the Cirque Olympique and Van Amburgh at the Porte-St.-Martin. For an interesting review of the former's performances, see Gautier, I, 334–38 (December 1839). Van Amburgh's new vehicle at the Surrey was *Mungo Park*—see the *Age* for 5 July 1840. There were any number of reviews comparing the merits of the two trainers and relative fierceness of their big cats.

63. See the *Theatrical Journal* for 25 July and 15 August 1840.

64. Manuscript in the Ducrow Album, signed "E. K."

65. See the accounts in the *Theatrical Journal* for 23 May and the *Era* for 24 May 1840.

66. See, e.g., the *Times* for 12 September 1840, the *Age* for 18 April 1841, and the *Actor's Note-Book* for 26 April 1841.

67. I have not succeeded in locating either the baptismal or birth certificate of this daughter. In the census returns of 7 June 1841, however, she is recorded as having been born in the county of Surrey and as then being eight months old.

68. See the review of the opening performance in the Edinburgh *Opera-Glass* for 25 December 1840.

69. The *Theatrical Journal* comments on the state of his health in its issues for 23 January, 27 March, 10 April, and 15 May 1841.

70. Edinburgh *Opera-Glass*, 26 February 1841.

71. Ibid., 12 and 19 February 1841. And see the Glasgow *Herald* for 12 February 1841.

72. See, e.g., the bills for 19 April, 26 April, and 7 June 1841, V&A.

73. *Age*, 18 April 1841.

74. See the bill for 7 June, V&A.

75. See the *Times* for 13 April and the *Era* for 18 April 1841.

76. Bill for 7 June 1841 (second week), V&A.

77. *Theatrical Journal*, 29 May 1841. And see the *Theatrical Chronicle* for 22 May 1841.

78. *Theatrical Journal*, 13 March 1841; unidentified clipping, hand-dated 14 March 1841, Disher Scrapbooks II.

79. The inquest was reported in the *Era* for 13 June 1841. The following description of the fire and its aftermath, unless otherwise noted, is based primarily on the following sources: the *Times* for 9, 10, and 11 June; the *Era* for 13 June; the *Examiner* for 13 June; the *Theatrical Chronicle* for 12 June; and the *Theatrical Journal* for 19 June 1841.

80. 1841 census return for Amphitheatre Place in the Parish of St. Mary, Lambeth, pt. 1, Enumeration District no. 8, p. 31. The 1841 census was actually supposed to list all persons, including visitors, sleeping over the previous night—that is, on 6 June—at the houses visited on the 7th. Another of its interesting features is that the ages recorded were supposed to be precise only in the case of persons 15 years old or younger. Above that figure ages were to be given as the "lowest of the term of 5 years within which the actual age falls." Thus Ducrow's and his wife's ages were recorded as 45 and 25, although Andrew was 47 at the time and Louisa around 27. There seems to have been considerable variation in the fidelity with which the enumerators followed their instructions, however, for Ducrow's apprentice Susan Beechdale (spelled "Bechtel" in the return) is listed as 16 years old and the ages of Ducrow's servants and cook (ranging from 17 to 30) appear to have been accurately recorded. Place of birth and profession were also included in the 1841 census. In the case of the latter, Andrew's was given as "gentleman" and Louisa's as "equestrian."

81. On Ducrow's "celebrated Cabinet of Art," see above, p. 208; and Edward Stirling, *Old Drury Lane: Fifty Years Recollections of Author, Actor, and Manager* (London, 1881), I, 177. Stirling tells of the collection containing some replicas of boars "from the famous Florentine bronze group" and of Ducrow remarking to a friend who was condoling with him over his loss, "Shouldn't have cared a straw for all the rest, if I could have saved the blessed pigs."

82. See the *Theatrical Journal* for 19 June 1841.

83. A copy of the printed subscription list is in the Local History Department of the Southwark Public Library.

84. See, e.g., Ducrow's letter of 19 June 1841 to S. W. Butler, who had offered his services for the Drury Lane benefit, in the Charles Swain Collection of the Manchester Public Libraries.

85. Drury Lane bill for 22 June 1841, BM Playbills 171. There was a last-minute change when Grisi replaced the singers Persiani and Rubini, who discovered they had to be elsewhere on the evening in question—see the *Era* for 27 June 1841, which also reports the evening's receipts. A letter dated 23 June from Ducrow to Mrs. C. Mathews (Mme. Vestris), thanking her and her husband for their services at the benefit, is in the V&A.

86. Bill for 26 June 1841, British Museum Perceval Collection XIII.

87. See the published subscription list and the *Theatrical Journal* for 19 June 1841.

88. Where the "dismounted cavalry" were not very successful—see the *Era* for 18 July and *Punch* for 7 August 1841.

89. See the *Theatrical Journal* for 17 and 24 July and *Punch* for 31 July 1841. Bills for the engagement are in British Museum Perceval Collection XIII.

90. Bill for 5 July 1841, Harvard Vauxhall Gardens Scrapbooks VI, 73. See Bunn's short-lived periodical *The Vauxhall Papers*, which was published three times per week during this period and gives the programs of entertainments. A pleasant drawing of the interior of the Rotunda and its ring, dating from around 1859 but possibly showing what the building looked like at the time of Ducrow's occupancy, has been discovered by Mr. George Speaight in the London Museum and is reproduced in *Theatre Notebook*, XXIX (1975), opp. p. 24. Mr. Antony D. Hippisley Coxe, in a privately published article for the Union des Historiens du Cirque—"The Lesser-Known Circuses of London" (1958; rpt. in *Theatre Notebook*, XIII [1959])—also comments on this circus and reproduces an illustration which he dates as 1847. The description by Southworth (*Vauxhall Gardens*, pp. 171–74), in which the writer would seem to believe Andrew himself was performing the "Chinese Enchanter," "Courier of St. Peterburg," etc. in the Rotunda is, of course, inaccurate. The same is true of his statement (p. 174) that the Gardens did not open in 1842, when the troop returned to the Rotunda.

91. See the advance bill dated 4 August and the bill for 9 August 1841 in the V&A. The *Times* for 10 August, in its review of the opening spectacle, describes the alterations and their carrying out, as does the *Theatrical Journal* for 14 August 1841.

92. The *Morning Herald* for 6 August 1841 gives a detailed description of events on the fateful day. And for subsequent reports on the state of Ducrow's health and progress, see the *Age* for 8, 22, 29 August, 12 September, and 31 October; and the *Theatrical Journal* for 14, 21, 28 August and 13 November.

93. *Punch*, in its 18 September notice of the production, even referred to Hicks as Cartlitch—evidently preferring to believe the latter was still with the company. And see the bill for 9 August 1841, V&A, and the reviews in the *Times* for 10 August and the *Theatrical Journal* for 28 August 1841.

94. Bills for the season at the Surrey are in the V&A and in British Museum Theatrical Cuttings 50.

95. Letter in the V&A.

96. See the *Times*, 21 October; *Theatrical Journal*, 30 October 1841.

97. See the *Theatrical Journal* for 13 November and 11 December 1841. And for notices of Batty's own activities and plans at this time, see the issues of 27 November, 4 and 18 December 1841 and the *Times* for 28 December 1841. An undated bill for Batty's "Olympic Circus" in Westminster Road is in the V&A.

98. Letter in the R. Toole Stott Circus Collection, University of California at Santa Barbara. This is the letter Broadfoot kept as a memento of Ducrow, pasting into it the sketch of a headdress Andrew had made for the 1838 production of *The Passage of the Deserts, or The French in Egypt and Siege of Acre* (fig. 37). It is doubly interesting on account of the postscript in the hand of Louisa, who also asks Broadfoot to give her love to the juvenile members of the troop.

99. Bill for Ducrow's establishment at the Amphitheatre, Humberstone Gate, author's collection.

100. *Theatrical Journal*, 1 January 1842; cf. the issue of 5 February 1842. The *Sunday Times*, in its obituary of Ducrow on 30 January, reported seeing him at the Olympic Theatre some three weeks before: "He appeared in good spirits, and, save a nervous contortion of the facial muscles, to which he had been long subject, in tolerable health."

101. Unidentified clipping, "Will of Mr. Andrew Ducrow," Disher Scrapbooks III.

102. See the *Era* for 30 January and the *Theatrical Journal* for 5 February 1842. Death certificate in the General Register Office.

9. Aftermath

1. Ducrow's will is in the Public Record Office: Prob. 10/6059 13086.

2. Descriptions of the funeral appeared in almost all the London journals and periodicals. The account given here is based mainly on the *Age* for 13 February, the *Morning Chronicle* for 7 February, the *Gentleman's Magazine* for April 1842, and extracts from various other journals in the Folger Shakespeare Library, Y.d.23 (133).

3. Unidentified clipping of a police report in Harvard III, 17.

4. *Diaries*, II, 157. In his entry for 3 February, Macready tells of declining Oscar Byrne's invitation to the funeral, "being compelled to attend the rehearsal of *Acis and Galatea*. Under any circumstances I should not have gone— to have met the company invited there."

5. See, e.g., the *Age* for 20 February 1842 and the *Gentleman's Magazine* for April 1842. The officially recorded value of the estate at the time the will was proved on 17 February was 45,000 pounds (Act Book, Public Record Office, Prob. 8/235).

6. Advertisements in the Liverpool *Albion* for these dates. A bill for Louisa's benefit, in BM Playbills 246, is headed "The Last Appeal to the Liverpool Public."

7. See, e.g., the *Theatrical Journal* for 16 September 1843 (commenting on the sale which had taken place much earlier).

8. Unidentified clippings and bill for 16 May 1842 in the V&A; *Theatrical Journal* for 30 April and 21 May 1842.

9. Bills for various dates in the V&A; British Museum Perceval Collection XIII; and British Museum Theatrical Cuttings 50.

10. Unidentified clipping in the V&A. Cf. the *Odd Fellow*, 6 August 1842.

11. Bills for 8 and 11 July 1842 in Harvard Vauxhall Gardens Scrapbooks VI, 122 and V, 79, with additional bills for July and August in VII; *Theatrical Journal*, 23 and 30 July 1842.

12. "Popular Places of Entertainment," *The Squib*, 30 July 1842.

13. Advertisement in the *Norfolk Chronicle and Norwich Gazette*, 10 September 1842.

14. Norwich *Mercury*, 24 September 1842.

15. *Norfolk Chronicle and Norwich Gazette*, 24 September 1842.

16. Bills for the Dublin engagement during February and March are in BM Playbills 214.

17. Astley's bill for 17 April 1843 in BM Playbills 170; unidentified clipping in Harvard III, 17.

18. See the *Theatrical Journal* for 1 April 1843.

19. Single bill for 20–22 April [1843] in British Museum Theatrical Cuttings 50; *Theatrical Journal*, 29 April 1843.

20. *Theatrical Journal*, 27 May 1843; single bill for 31 May and 2 June in BM Playbills 246.

21. Bills for 9 July and 10 August 1843, British Museum Theatrical Cuttings 50.

22. *Theatrical Journal*, 16 September 1843; unidentified clipping in Harvard III, 42. It would appear that the horses—or at least some of them—eventually made their way back to London, for a notice of a pantomime and the drama *Lelia* given at the Marylebone Theatre in 1844 contains the curious statement that "the introduction of Ducrow's horses is a great feature in the performances" (*Theatrical Journal*, 20 January 1844). How the horses came to be there, and who owned them, I do not know. Ducrow's famous mare Beda seems to have been spared the Hamburg disgrace. She was supposedly sold to the Negro equestrian Pablo Fanque while her master was still living, and Fanque later exhibited haute école with her.

23. *Theatrical Journal*, 30 September 1843. The *Coureur des Spectacles* for 19 September also terms Chaffé the "young son" of Ducrow.

24. *Histoire de l'art dramatique en France*, III, 276.

25. V. de Saint-Hilaire and A. Bourgeois, *Les Eléphants de la pagode*, no. 288 in Répertoire Dramatique des Auteurs Contemporains (Paris, 1845).

26. *Biographie des écuyers et écuyères du théâtre national du Cirque-Olympique*, "par un flaneur" (Paris, 1846), pp. 41–42.

27. Signor Saltarino [pseud. Herman W. Otto], *Artisten-Lexikon*, 2nd ed. (Düsseldorf, 1895), pp. 88, 91; Joseph Halperson, *Das Buch vom Zirkus* (Düsseldorf, 1926), p. 113.

28. Hillier did, however, apparently have a daughter in the profession, for in the Bibliothèque de l'Opéra there is a lithograph of "Grace Hillier, âgée de 6 ans 1/2, Ecuyère au Cirque National de Paris"—see Nicole Wild and Tristan Rémy, *Le Cirque: Iconographie*, Catalogues de la Bibliothèque de l'Opéra (Paris: Bibliothèque Nationale, 1969), p. 107.

29. Death certificate in the General Register Office.

30. See above, p. 31.

31. See, e.g., Disher, *Greatest Show on Earth*, p. 142.

32. *The Public Life of W. F. Wallett*, p. 81.

33. See, e.g., the *Theatrical Journal* for 26 April 1845 and 6 September 1849.

34. Death certificate in the General Register Office, Edinburgh; *Theatrical Journal*, 14 January 1852.

35. Birth certificate in the General Register Office.

36. R. J. Cruikshank, *Charles Dickens and Early Victorian England* (London, 1949), p. 242.

37. Marriage certificate in the General Register Office. Sarah Collett, who was billed as a singer and actress at Astley's during the 1837 season, was possibly the daughter of Ducrow's former teacher.

38. Death certificate in the General Register Office.

39. Letter written during the spring of 1940 by Iris Perrier (later Mrs. Rouls) to M. Willson Disher following the publication of his book *Greatest Show on Earth*. The original of Miss Perrier's letter is in the second volume of the Disher Scrapbooks at the University of Kansas.

40. Interview with Mrs. Joan Hoar of Cambridge on 15 November 1971.

41. Cruikshank, pp. 241, 243.

42. See "The Ducrow Apocrypha."

43. BM Playbills 251.

44. Peter Paterson [pseud. James Glass Bertram], *Glimpses of Real Life as Seen in the Theatrical World and in Bohemia: Being the Confessions of Peter Paterson, a Strolling Comedian* (Edinburgh, 1864), pp. 322–24. The same story is told by Paterson in his earlier *Behind the Scenes*, pp. 145–46. The misspelling of the family name is probably deliberate, since Paterson often made slight changes in the names of the persons he wrote about.

45. Louisa's will, dated 20 May 1897 and proved on 26 February 1900, is in the Principal Probate Registry at Somerset House.

46. See the *Illustrated Sporting and Dramatic News*, 27 March 1880; David Hoadley Munroe, *The Grand National, 1839–1930* (New York, 1930), pt. 2.

47. Much of the information concerning Peter Andrew John Ducrow and his family is contained in the letter of Miss Perrier to M. Willson Disher. Mrs. Nina Louise Trewin, another granddaughter of Peter Andrew John, has supplied me with additional facts.

48. Death certificate in the General Register Office; and see above, p. 340. Louisa is also mentioned in several accounts of her father's death and funeral.

49. Scattered references to Lucy occur in Craig's *Index to the Story of My Days* (New York, 1957) and Edward Craig's *Gordon Craig: The Story of His Life* (New York, 1968). A small text of *Hamlet*, once owned by Lucy and annotated by Craig, was formerly in the possession of Lucy's son, Mr. Peter

Ducrow. To her credit, Lucy Wilson seems to have been one of the few women who did not find Craig irresistible.

50. *Oxberry's* "Memoir," p. 15.

51. Frost, pp. 192–93.

52. Ibid., pp. 234, 246.

53. Saltarino, p. 91.

54. Information concerning William Ducrow's early career is based on a bill for Lent's circus for 12 September 1861 in the Bridgeport, Connecticut, Public Library; bills for Lent's circus at New York for 1865 (hand-dated) and 11 February and 2 March 1868 in the Moreau Scrapbook in the Harvard Theatre Collection; Frost, *Circus Life and Circus Celebrities*, p. 212; and scattered references to William's and George's New York City appearances in Odell, *Annals of the New York Stage*, VII–XI.

55. Programs and route books, 1887–1907, in the Circus World Museum at Baraboo, Wisconsin, and in the private collection of M. Jacques Garnier of Orléans, France. An illustrated program in the latter collection, for 30 November 1901 while the circus was playing at Paris, depicts the feat with the seventy horses.

56. Obituary notice in the New York *Clipper*, 9 October 1909.

57. Two obituary notices of Dan, one unidentified and the other from the Oakland *Tribune* for 31 August 1930, are in the Chindahl Collection at the Circus World Museum. The Pittsburgh *Press* carried a long front-page notice in its issue of 12 August 1930.

58. Note that all commas are actually points on the bronze-lettered tablet. Somerset's original composition, in which no mention is made of the "afflicted widow," runs as follows (punctuation and capitalization regularized): "Within this tomb, in the humble hope of a blessed hereafter through the merits of his Redeemer, repose the mortal remains of Andrew Ducrow, Equestrian, many years lessee of the Royal Amphitheatre. In him the arts and sciences deplore the loss of a generous patron, his family an affectionate husband and father, his friends a boon companion, the poor a constant and unwearied benefactor, and the world a strictly honorable man!" The letters of the inscriptions on the south side of the tomb have in many instances fallen victim to the encroaching ivy. The reader curious about these will find all of them transcribed by James M. Bulloch in the 16 March 1929 issue of *Notes and Queries*.

APPENDIX I: *The Ducrow Apocrypha*

1. Nor, I might add, is there any mention of Ducrow or the Champion in the Lord Chamberlain's accounts for the 1831 coronation, stored in the Public Record Office. Had the ceremony taken place, the Champion would have been entitled to the cup from which the King pledged him as his fee,

and Ducrow would no doubt have received some payment for his services as well. The *Court Journal*, in its descriptive accounts in the 3 and 10 September 1831 issues, makes no mention of the Ceremony of the Champion either.

2. See above, p. 161, for Ducrow's production at Vauxhall Gardens in 1828. That there was no reenactment of the Battle in 1829 is confirmed by advertisements in the London newspapers (see, e.g., the *Times* for 18 June) and a notice in the *Harlequin* for 4 July, in which the critic complains that the annual gala was less spirited than usual on account of the absence of the Battle itself.

3. See, e.g., the bills for the weeks of 15 June (during which Andrew was announced to dance a "Mariner's Ballet" with Louisa Woolford on the double rope), 22 June (by which date Andrew had been replaced on the rope by Master Bridges), and 6 July 1829, V&A.

4. *Tour in England, Ireland, and France, in the Years 1826, 1827, 1828, and 1829*, p. 566. Diavolo Antonio debuted at the Cirque Olympique on 16 December 1828—see Vesque, "Le Cirque Olympique du boulevard du Temple," p. 20.

5. Letter from Miss Jane Langton, 15 August 1972.

6. In the Guildhall collection of Miscellaneous Circus and Menagerie Playbills.

7. *The Public Life of W. F. Wallett*, pp. 28–29. The story was repeated a few years later in Frost's *Circus Life and Circus Celebrities*, pp. 63–64, and since then in any number of works on the circus.

8. Letter of 15 August 1972 from Mr. John Bebbington, City Librarian and Information Officer at the Sheffield City Libraries.

9. An extensive sampling of her letters may be found in Roger Manvell's *Sarah Siddons: Portrait of an Actress* (New York, 1971).

10. Letter in the Enthoven Collection, V&A. A later letter—still in a rough but legible script—addressed to Broadfoot on 22 November 1841 is reproduced among the illustrations at the end of vol. 1 of R. Toole Stott's *Circus and Allied Arts: A World Bibliography*.

APPENDIX II: *The Ducrow Iconography*

1. Sanger's will is printed in John Lukens' *The Sanger Story: Being George Sanger Coleman's Story of His Life with His Grandfather "Lord" George Sanger* (London, 1956), pp. 249–52.

2. See above, p. 79 and n.

3. See, e.g., the entry for Howe in Algernon Graves, *The Royal Academy of Arts: A Complete Dictionary of Contributors and Their Work from Its Foundation in 1769 to 1904* (London, 1905–06), IV, 173.

4. See above, p. 249.

5. According to a letter from the Antiquarian Horological Society to Mr. Coxe, other examples of the clock are extant. One of them—also of the brass-on-wood variety—came up for sale as I was penning these lines.

6. For illustrations of two figures depicting duets on horseback, see plate E-68, fig. 131 and plate E-100, fig. 194 in P. D. Gordon Pugh, *Staffordshire Portrait Figures and Allied Subjects of the Victorian Era* (New York and Washington, 1971); for a girl in a plaid skirt dancing the rope, plate E-146, fig. 305 in the same work; and for two male and female figures holding flags but without horses, perhaps also representing tightrope performers, plate E-24, figs. 50 and 51. A pair of equestrian figures, each showing a duet by standing male and female riders, also "said to be Andrew Ducrow and Louisa Woolford," is reproduced in fig. 235 in Anthony Oliver's *The Victorian Staffordshire Figure: A Guide for Collectors* (New York, 1972). The figures of the two children I have seen are in a private collection.

7. Cf. Pugh, plate E-68, fig. 131, who reproduces another example of the same figure.

Selected Bibliography

Note that information on archival materials; collections of ephemera, theatricalia, and circusiana; newspapers, theatrical and circus periodicals; and individual plays and poems is given in the text and notes.

BIOGRAPHICAL SKETCHES, OBITUARIES,
AND PREVIOUS STUDIES OF DUCROW

"Andrew Ducrow." *All the Year Round*, 3 February 1872.

Coxe, Antony Hippisley. "A Study of Andrew Ducrow." Privately published for members of the Union des Historiens du Cirque, 1957.

Egan, Pierce. "Theatrical Sketch of Mr. A. Ducrow, the Unparalleled Equestrian," in *Pierce Egan's Anecdotes of the Turf, the Chase, the Ring, and the Stage*, pp. 265–68. London: Knight & Lacey, 1827.

"The Late Mr. Ducrow." *Sunday Times*, 30 January 1842.

[Mackintosh, Matthew.] "Andrew Ducrow," ch. 11 in *Stage Reminiscences: Being Recollections, Chiefly Personal, of Celebrated Theatrical & Musical Performers During the Last Forty Years, by an Old Stager*. Glasgow: James Hedderwick & Son, 1866. First published in the Glasgow *Weekly Citizen*, Mackintosh's recollections are sometimes said to have been ghostwritten by the journalist John Stewart.

"Memoir of Mr. Ducrow." *Owl*, 24 September 1831.

"Mr. Andrew Ducrow." *Actors by Daylight, and Pencilings in the Pit*, 14 July 1838.

"Mr. Andrew Ducrow." Edinburgh *Opera-Glass*, 4 September 1840.

"Mr. Ducrow." *Actors by Gaslight; or, "Boz" in the Boxes*, 27 October 1838.

"Mr. Ducrow." Obituary in the *Gentleman's Magazine*, April 1842.

[Moncrieff, William T.] "Dramatic Feuilletons or, Leaves from the Common-Place-Book of an Old Stager." Four articles (part of a longer series) published in the *Sunday Times* for 16 February, 23 February, 2 March, and 22 June 1851.

[Rede, Leman Thomas.] "Memoir of Andrew Ducrow, Proprietor of the Amphitheatre." *Oxberry's Dramatic Biography and Green Room Spy*, N.S., II, no. 17 (4 August 1827).

Saxon, A. H. "Adventures in Nineteenth-Century Biography: Some Problems and Principles, with Examples from the Life of Andrew Ducrow." *Theatre Survey*, XVII (1976), 92–105. Paper read at the First Conference on the Nineteenth-Century British Theatre held at the University of Massachusetts, Amherst, in May 1974.

————. "Andrew Ducrow, England's Mime on a Moving Stage: The Years in France." *Theatre Research/Recherches Théâtrales*, XIII (1973), 15–21.

————. "La Carrière française d'Andrew Ducrow." *Cirque dans l'Univers*, no. 89 (2e trimestre 1973), pp. 3–11.

————. "L'Incendie de l'Amphithéâtre d'Astley et La Mort d'Andrew Ducrow." *Cirque dans l'Univers*, no. 100 (1er trimestre 1976), pp. 27–32.

————. "The Tyranny of Charity: Andrew Ducrow in the Provinces." *Nineteenth Century Theatre Research*, I (1973), 95–105.

Stott, R. Toole. "With Ducrow in the Provinces." Privately published for members of the Union des Historiens du Cirque, 1964.

Books, Articles,
and Frequently Cited Scrapbooks

Albach, Ben. "English Spectacles at Amsterdam During the Summer of 1814." Paper read at the Third International Theatre Conference ("Western Popular Theatre") held at the University of Manchester in April 1974. This and the other papers, presumably, will be published by Methuen.

Arnott, James Fullarton, and John William Robinson. *English Theatrical Literature, 1559–1900: A Bibliography*. London: Society for Theatre Research, 1970.

"Astley's, 1769–1880: A Collection of Views, Portraits, Autographs, Bills, Anecdotes, Advertisements, &c. Chronologically Arranged." Four superbly bound scrapbooks in the Harvard Theatre Collection, with the fourth volume a supplement. The bookplate of Clement Scott is in the second volume. Referred to in text as "Harvard."

"Astley's Amphitheatre: Collection of Over 1,000 Views, Portraits & Newspaper Clippings, Illustrating the Famous Astley's Theatre." Three scrapbooks, formerly the property of Charles B. Cochran and then M. Willson Disher, in the Kenneth Spencer Research Library at the University of Kansas. Referred to in text as "Disher Scrapbooks."

"Astley's Royal Amphitheatre, 1768–1833." Three quarto scrapbooks in the British Museum Theatrical Cuttings Collection. Only the third volume is paginated. Referred to in text as "BM Astley's Scrapbooks."

B., J.-E. [Bouteiller, Jules Edouard]. *Histoire complète et méthodique des théatres de Rouen*. 4 vols. Rouen: Giroux et Renaux (for vols. 1–3) and C. Métérie (for vol. 4), 1860–80.

Barker, Kathleen. *The Theatre Royal, Bristol, 1766–1966: Two Centuries of Stage History*. London: Society for Theatre Research, 1974.

[Barnes, James.] "Journal of Old Barnes, the Pantaloon, on a Trip to Paris, in 1830." *Bentley's Miscellany*, VII (1840), 457–68, 627–33; VIII (1840), 69–74, 195–201.

Baynham, Walter. *The Glasgow Stage*. Glasgow: Robert Forrester, 1892.

Bedford, Paul. *Recollections and Wanderings of Paul Bedford: Facts, Not Fancies*. London: Routledge, Warne & Routledge, 1864.

Belton, Fred. *Random Recollections of an Old Actor*. London: Tinsley Bros., 1880.

Biographie des écuyers et écuyères du théatre national du Cirque-Olympique, "par un flaneur." Paris: Chez l'Editeur du Répertoire Dramatique, 1846.

[Blackburn, Joseph.] "A Clown's Log: Extracts from the Diary of the Late Joseph Blackburn." Ed. Charles H. Day. New York *Clipper*, 14, 21, and 28 February 1880.

Board, M. E. *The Story of the Bristol Stage, 1490–1925*. London: Fountain Press, n.d.

Boase, Frederick. *Modern English Biography*. 6 vols. London: Truro, Netherton & Worth, 1892–1921.

Bon Gaultier [pseud. Sir Theodore Martin]. *The Book of Ballads*. London: William S. Orr, 1845.

Brayley, Edward Wedlake. *Historical and Descriptive Accounts of the Theatres of London*. London: J. Taylor, 1826.

Britton, John, and A. Pugin. *Illustrations of the Public Buildings of London*. 2 vols. London: J. Taylor, 1825–28.

Broadbent, R. J. *Annals of the Liverpool Stage from the Earliest Period to the Present Time*. Liverpool: Edward Howell, 1908.

————. "Annals of the Manchester Stage, 1735–1845." Unpublished typescript in the Manchester Central Reference Library.

Brown, T. Allston. *History of the American Stage...from 1733 to 1870*. New York: Dick and Fitzgerald, 1870.

Bulloch, J. M. "Andrew Ducrow." *Notes and Queries*, 16 March 1929. Transcribes the inscriptions on Ducrow's mausoleum.

[Bulwer-Lytton, Edward.] *England and the English*. 2 vols. New York: Harper & Bros., 1857.

Bunn, Alfred. *The Stage: Both Before and Behind the Curtain*. 3 vols. London: R. Bentley, 1840.

Campardon, Emile. *Les Spectacles de la foire...depuis 1595 jusqu'à 1791*. 2 vols. Paris: Berger-Levrault, 1877.

Catalogue of Additions to the Manuscripts: Plays Submitted to the Lord Chamberlain, 1824–1851. London: Trustees of the British Museum, 1964.

Cazier-Charpentier, H. "Caroline Loyo." *Cirque dans l'Univers*, no. 86 (3ᵉ trimestre 1972), pp. 19–21.

[Clarke, William.] *Every Night Book; or, Life After Dark*. London: T. Richardson, 1827.

Colton, Calvin. *Four Years in Great Britain: 1831–1835*. 2 vols. New York: Harper & Bros., 1835.

Cowell, Joe. *Thirty Years Passed Among the Players in England and America.* New York: Harper & Bros., 1845.

Coxe, Antony D. Hippisley. "The Lesser-Known Circuses of London." Privately published for members of the Union des Historiens du Cirque, 1958.

Cross, J. C. *Circusiana, or A Collection of the Most Favourite Ballets, Spectacles, Melo-Drames, &c. Performed at the Royal Circus, St. George's Fields.* 2 vols. London: Lackington & Allen, 1809. A second edition was published by Thomas Tegg in 1812.

Cruikshank, R. J. *Charles Dickens and Early Victorian England.* London: Pitman, 1949.

Curl, James Stevens. "Saving a Victorian Burial-Ground: Nunhead Cemetery, South London." *Country Life,* 17 July 1975, pp. 146–48.

———. *The Victorian Celebration of Death.* Detroit: Partridge Press, 1972.

Decastro, Jacob. *The Memoirs of J. Decastro, Comedian.* Ed. R. Humphreys. London: Sherwood & Jones, 1824. Contains, pp. 115–66, Decastro's *The History of the Royal Circus.*

Dibdin, Charles (the Elder). *The High-Mettled Racer.* London: William Kidd, 1831.

Dibdin, Charles Isaac Mungo (the Younger). *Professional and Literary Memoirs of Charles Dibdin the Younger.* Ed. George Speaight. London: Society for Theatre Research, 1956.

Dickens, Charles. *The Letters of Charles Dickens.* Ed. Madeline House, Graham Storey, and Kathleen Tillotson. 3 vols. (with others in progress). Oxford: Clarendon Press, 1965–

———. *Memoirs of Joseph Grimaldi.* Ed. Richard Findlater. New York: Stein & Day, [1968].

———. *The Old Curiosity Shop.* Oxford: Oxford University Press, 1951.

———. *Sketches by Boz.* Oxford: Oxford University Press, 1957.

Disher, M. Willson. *Clowns & Pantomimes.* London: Constable, 1925.

———. *Fairs, Circuses and Music Halls.* London: William Collins, 1942.

———. *Greatest Show on Earth.* London: G. Bell, 1937.

[Disraeli, Benjamin.] *Selected Speeches of the Late Right Honourable the Earl of Beaconsfield.* Ed. T. E. Kebbel. 2 vols. London: Longmans & Green, 1882.

Downer, Alan S. *The Eminent Tragedian: William Charles Macready.* Cambridge, Mass.: Harvard University Press, 1966.

Ducrow Album. A green leather scrapbook, with "A. Ducrow" stamped on its front cover, containing memorabilia assembled by Ducrow and his wives. Currently the property of Mr. Simon R. Bailey.

The Encyclopedia of the Horse. Ed. C. E. G. Hope and G. N. Jackson. New York: Viking, [1973].

Ferguson, O. J. *A Brief Biographical Sketch of I. A. Van Amburgh, and an Illustrated and Descriptive History of the Animals Contained in His Menagerie.* New York: Booth, n.d.

Findlater, Richard [pseud. Kenneth Bruce Findlater Bain]. *Grimaldi: King of Clowns.* London: MacGibbon & Kee, 1955.

Fitzball, Edward. *Thirty-Five Years of a Dramatic Author's Life.* 2 vols. London: T. C. Newby, 1859.

Fitzgerald, Percy Hetherington. *Chronicles of Bow-Street Police-Office, with an Account of the Magistrates, "Runners," and Police, etc.* 2 vols. London: Chapman & Hall, 1888.

Foote, Horace. *A Companion to the Theatres; and Manual of the British Drama.* 2nd ed. London: Marsh & Miller, 1829.

Frith, W. P. *Further Reminiscences.* London: Richard Bentley & Son, 1888.

Frost, Thomas. *Circus Life and Circus Celebrities.* London: Tinsley Bros., 1875.

———. *The Old Showmen and the Old London Fairs.* London: Chatto & Windus, 1881.

Gautier, Théophile. *Histoire de l'art dramatique en France depuis vingt-cinq ans.* 6 vols. Paris: Librairie Magnin, 1858–59.

Ginisty, Paul. *Mémoires d'une danseuse de corde: Mme. Saqui (1786–1866).* Paris: Charpentier & Fasquelle, 1907.

Gomersal, William. *No Chestnuts! Being Anecdotes of the Stage.* Worcester: Worcestershire Newspapers and General Printing Co., [1891].

Grant, James. *The Great Metropolis.* 2 vols. New York & London: Saunders & Otley, 1837.

Greenwood, Isaac J. *The Circus: Its Origin and Growth Prior to 1835.* Dunlap Society Publications, N.S., 5. New York, 1898.

Guest, Ivor. *The Romantic Ballet in England: Its Development, Fulfilment and Decline.* Middletown: Wesleyan University Press, 1972.

Halperson, Joseph. *Das Buch vom Zirkus*. Düsseldorf: E. Lintz, 1926.

Hawkins, F. W. *The Life of Edmund Kean*. 2 vols. London: Tinsley Bros., 1869.

Hazlitt, William. *Table Talk or Original Essays*. London & Toronto: J. M. Dent, 1908.

Highfill, Philip H., Jr., Kalman A. Burnim, and Edward A. Langhans, comps. *A Biographical Dictionary of Actors, Actresses, Musicians, Dancers, Managers & Other Stage Personnel in London, 1660–1800.* 4 vols. (with others in progress). Carbondale: Southern Illinois University Press, 1973–   . A useful, undocumented guide to many—but by no means all —performers associated with circuses and popular theatres in the late eighteenth and early nineteenth centuries.

Hill, Benson Earle. *Playing About; or, Theatrical Anecdotes and Adventures*. 2 vols. London: W. Sams, 1840.

Hodgkinson, J. L., and Rex Pogson. *The Early Manchester Theatre*. London: Society for Theatre Research, 1960.

Holmström, Kirsten Gram. *Monodrama, Attitudes, Tableaux Vivants: Studies on Some Trends of Theatrical Fashion, 1770–1815*. Stockholm: Almqvist & Wiksell, 1967.

"Hughes' Royal Circus." Three scrapbooks dealing with the history of the Royal Circus (later Surrey Theatre) from 1782 to 1831, in the Stead Collection of the Library of Performing Arts at Lincoln Center, New York. Formerly the possession of Henry B. H. Beaufoy.

Ireland, Joseph N. *Records of the New York Stage from 1750 to 1860*. 2 vols. New York: T. H. Morrell, 1866.

Jefferson, Joseph. *The Autobiography of Joseph Jefferson*. Ed. Alan S. Downer. Cambridge, Mass.: Harvard University Press, 1964.

Keith, Charlie. *Circus Life and Amusements (Equestrian, Dramatic, & Musical), in All Nations*. Derby: Bewley & Roe, 1879.

Keyser, Marja. *Komt dat Zien! De Amsterdamse Kermis in de negentiende eeuw*. Amsterdam & Rotterdam: B. M. Israel & Ad. Donker, [1976].

Loewenberg, Alfred. *The Theatre of the British Isles Excluding London: A Bibliography*. London: Society for Theatre Research, 1950.

Londina Illustrata. 2 vols. London: Robert Wilkinson, 1819–25.

Lukens, John. *The Sanger Story: Being George Sanger Coleman's*

Story of His Life with His Grandfather "Lord" George Sanger. London: Hodder & Stoughton, 1956.

Lumsden, Harry S. "Circuses in the City [Aberdeen] from 1807 to 1897." Series in 26 parts published in the *Northern Figaro* from 7 May to 5 November 1898.

Lyonnet, Henry. *Dictionnaire des comédiens français*. 2 vols. Paris: E. Jorel, [1908–12].

Lysons Collection. "Collectanea: or, A Collection of Advertisements and Paragraphs from the Newspapers, Relating to Various Subjects. Publick Exhibitions and Places of Amusement." Five scrapbooks, with the fifth a supplement, in the British Museum. Formerly the property of Daniel Lysons.

Mackie, Charles, comp. *Norfolk Annals: A Chronological Record of Remarkable Events in the Nineteenth Century, Compiled from the Files of the "Norfolk Chronicle."* 2 vols. Norwich: Norfolk Chronicle, 1901.

Macready, William Charles. *The Diaries of William Charles Macready: 1833–1851*. Ed. William Toynbee. 2 vols. London: Chapman & Hall, 1912.

Malcolm, James Peller. *Londinium Redivivum; or, an Ancient History and Modern Description of London*. 4 vols. London: John Nichols, 1802–1807.

Manning-Sanders, Ruth. *The English Circus*. London: Werner Laurie, 1952.

Mayer, David, III. *Harlequin in His Element: The English Pantomime, 1806–1836*. Cambridge, Mass.: Harvard University Press, 1969.

Meeks, Leslie Howard. *Sheridan Knowles and the Theatre of His Time*. Bloomington, Ind.: Principia Press, 1933.

The Microcosm of London. 3 vols. London: R. Ackermann, [1808–10]. Texts for vols. 1 and 2 by William Henry Pyne; for vol. 3 by William Combe.

[Miller, David Prince.] *The Life of a Showman; and the Managerial Struggles of David Prince Miller*. London: Edward Avery, n.d.

Molloy, J. Fitzgerald. *The Life and Adventures of Edmund Kean, Tragedian, 1787–1833*. 2 vols. London: Ward & Downey, 1888.

Moreau Scrapbook. A collection of playbills, etc., relating to the circus in New York City, formerly the property of Charles C. Moreau. Harvard Theatre Collection.

Munroe, David Hoadley. *The Grand National, 1839–1930.* New York: Huntington Press, 1930.

Murray, D. L. *Scenes & Silhouettes.* London: Jonathan Cape, 1926. Republished by Heinemann in 1930 under the title *Candles and Crinolines.*

Nash, George. "A Grand Chivalric Entertainment." *Victoria and Albert Museum Bulletin,* I, no. 4 (October 1965), pp. 36–40.

[Nicholson, Renton.] *Rogue's Progress: The Autobiography of "Lord Chief Baron" Nicholson.* Ed. John L. Bradley. Boston: Houghton Mifflin, 1965.

Odell, George C. D. *Annals of the New York Stage.* 15 vols. New York: Columbia University Press, 1927–49.

Oliver, Anthony. *The Victorian Staffordshire Figure: A Guide for Collectors.* New York: St. Martin's Press, 1972.

Paterson, Peter [pseud. James Glass Bertram]. *Behind the Scenes: Being the Confessions of a Strolling Player.* Edinburgh: D. Mathers; London: Henry Lea; Glasgow: Thomas Murray & Son, 1859.

———. *Glimpses of Real Life as Seen in the Theatrical World and in Bohemia: Being the Confessions of Peter Paterson, a Strolling Comedian.* Edinburgh: William P. Nimmo, 1864. An expanded version of the preceding work.

Perceval Collection. "Collections Relating to Sadler's Wells." Fourteen scrapbooks in the British Museum.

Pichot, Pierre-Amédée. *Les Mémoires d'un dompteur rédigés d'après les souvenirs personnels du célèbre Martin.* Paris: Bureau de la Revue Brittanique, 1877.

Planché, J. R. *The Recollections and Reflections of J. R. Planché (Somerset Herald): A Professional Autobiography.* 2 vols. London: Tinsley Bros., 1872.

Porter, Henry C. *The History of the Theatres of Brighton, from 1774 to 1885.* Brighton: King & Thorne, 1886.

Powell, G. Rennie. *The Bristol Stage: Its Story.* Bristol: Bristol Printing & Publishing Co., 1919.

Procter, Richard Wright. *Manchester in Holiday Dress.* London: Simpkin & Marshall; Manchester: Abel Heywood & Son, 1866.

———. *Our Turf, Our Stage, and Our Ring.* Manchester: Dinham; London: Simpkin & Marshall, 1862.

[Pückler-Muskau, Herman.] *Tour in England, Ireland, and France, in*

the Years 1826, 1827, 1828, and 1829. [Trans. Sarah Austin.]
Philadelphia: Carey & Lea, 1833.

Pugh, P. D. Gordon. *Staffordshire Portrait Figures and Allied Subjects
of the Victorian Era.* New York & Washington: Praeger,
1971.

Raymond, George. *Memoirs of Robert William Elliston, Comedian.*
2nd ed. 2 vols. London: John Ollivier, 1846.

Rémy, Tristan. "Les Héros du cirque et les ballons du siège de Paris."
Cirque dans l'Univers, no. 100 (1er trimestre 1976), pp. 19–24.

————. "Notes pour servir à l'histoire de la famille Plège." *Cirque
dans l'Univers,* no. 18 (4e trimestre 1954–1er trimestre 1955),
pp. 26–27.

Rendle, William, and Philip Norman. *The Inns of Old Southwark and
Their Associations.* London & New York: Longmans &
Green, 1888.

"Report from the Select Committee on Dramatic Literature: With
the Minutes of Evidence." *Reports from Committees* for the
1831–32 session of Parliament, VII.

Robinson, Henry Crabb. *The London Theatre, 1811–1866: Selections
from the Diary of Henry Crabb Robinson.* Ed. Eluned Brown.
London: Society for Theatre Research, 1966.

Robson, J. P. *The Life and Adventures of the Far-Famed Billy Purvis.*
Newcastle upon Tyne: John Clarke, 1849 [for 1850].

Saltarino, Signor [pseud. Herman W. Otto]. *Artisten-Lexikon.* 2nd
ed. Düsseldorf: Ed. Lintz, 1895.

Saxon, A. H. "Capon, the Royal Circus, and *The Destruction of the
Bastille.*" *Theatre Notebook,* XXVIII (1974), 133–35.

————. "The Circus as Theatre: Astley's and Its Actors in the Age
of Romanticism." *Educational Theatre Journal,* XXVII
(1975), 299–312.

————. *Enter Foot and Horse: A History of Hippodrama in England
and France.* New Haven: Yale University Press, 1968.

————. "John Howard Payne, Playwright with a System." *Theatre
Notebook,* XXIV (Winter 1969–70), 79–84 (with illustrations
published in the Summer 1970 issue).

Southworth, James Granville. *Vauxhall Gardens: A Chapter in the
Social History of England.* New York: Columbia University
Press, 1941.

Speaight, George. "The Circus at Vauxhall Gardens." *Theatre Notebook,* XXIX (1975), 3 (with illustration as plate 1 in same

issue). For further information on the topic, see the note by
M. Y. Williams, Borough Archivist of Lambeth, on pp.
145–46 of the same volume.

———. *The History of the English Toy Theatre.* London: Studio Vista,
1969.

———. "Master Saunders." Privately published communication to
the Union of Circus Historians (Union des Historiens du
Cirque), 1961.

Spielmann, M. H. *The History of "Punch."* New York: Cassell, 1895.

Stirling, Edward. *Old Drury Lane: Fifty Years Recollections of Author,
Actor, and Manager.* 2 vols. London: Chatto & Windus,
1881.

[Stone, Marcus.] "The Shakespeare Club: A Note by Marcus Stone,
R.A." *Dickensian,* XLI (1945), 40–41.

Stott, R. Toole. *Circus and Allied Arts: A World Bibliography.* 4 vols.
(with a fifth currently in progress). Derby: Harpur & Sons,
1958–   . The basic reference work for any study of the
circus.

Stratman, Carl J. *Britain's Theatrical Periodicals, 1720–1967: A
Bibliography.* New York: New York Public Library, 1972.
An expansion of the same compiler's *A Bibliography of
British Dramatic Periodicals, 1720–1960* (New York: New
York Public Library, 1962).

Strutt, Joseph. *The Sports and Pastimes of the People of England.* New
ed. London: Thomas Tegg & Son, 1834.

Thackeray, William Makepeace. *The Newcomes: Memoirs of a Most
Respectable Family.* 2 vols. London: Bradbury & Evans,
1854.

Thayer, Stuart. *Annals of the American Circus, 1793–1829.* [Ann
Arbor]: privately printed, 1976.

Thétard, Henry. *La Merveilleuse Histoire du cirque.* 2 vols. (with 500
sets accompanied by a third volume devoted to the Fratellini
clown family). Paris: Prisma, 1947.

Tomlins, F. G. *A Brief View of the English Drama, from the Earliest
Period to the Present Time.* London: C. Mitchell, 1840.

Troubridge, St. Vincent. *The Benefit System in the British Theatre.*
London: Society for Theatre Research, 1967.

Tuttle, George Palliser. "The History of the Royal Circus, Equestrian
and Philharmonic Academy, 1782–1816, St. George's Fields,
Surrey, England." Ph.D. dissertation, Tufts University,
1972.

Vail, Robert William Glenroie. "The Early Circus in America." *Proceedings of the American Antiquarian Society*, N.S., XLIII (1934), 116–85.

Valentine, Henry. *Behind the Curtain*. London: G. F. Frost, [1848].

Vaux, Baron Charles Maurice de. *Ecuyers et écuyères: Histoire des cirques d'Europe, 1680–1891*. Paris: J. Rothschild, 1893.

"Vauxhall Gardens: The History of Vauxhall Gardens from Its Commencement to Its Final Closing in July, 1859." Nine beautifully bound scrapbooks in the Harvard Theatre Collection. Referred to in text as "Harvard Vauxhall Gardens Scrapbooks."

Vesque, M.-J. "Le Cirque Olympique du boulevard du Temple (de mars 1827 à septembre 1836)." *Cirque dans l'Univers*, no. 15 (4e trimestre 1953–1er trimestre 1954), pp. 19–22.

———. "Le Cirque Olympique du faubourg du Temple, 1817–1826." *Cirque dans l'Univers*, no. 12 (1er trimestre 1953), pp. 22–23.

Wallett, William Frederick. *The Public Life of W. F. Wallett, the Queen's Jester: An Autobiography*. Ed. John Luntley. London & Derby: Bemrose & Son; London: Thomas Hailes Lacey; Edinburgh: John Menzies, 1870.

Watts, Ephraim [pseud. Richard Hengist Horne]. *Life of Van Amburgh, the Brute Tamer*. Cheapside: Tyas, [1838].

[Wemyss, Francis Courtney.] *Wemyss' Chronology of the American Stage, from 1752 to 1852*. New York: W. Taylor, 1852.

Wild, Nicole, and Tristan Rémy. *Le Cirque: Iconographie*. Catalogues de la Bibliothèque de l'Opéra. Paris: Bibliothèque Nationale, 1969.

Wilson, John, et al. *Noctes Ambrosianae*. 4 vols. Edinburgh & London: Blackwood & Sons, 1868.

Winston, James. *Drury Lane Journal: Selections from James Winston's Diaries, 1819–1827*. Ed. Alfred L. Nelson and Gilbert B. Cross. London: Society for Theatre Research, 1974.

Winter, Marian Hannah. *The Pre-Romantic Ballet*. London: Sir Isaac Pitman & Sons, 1974.

———. "La Prise de la Bastille, pantomime de cirque de 1789." *Vieux Papier*, fascicule no. 247 (janvier 1973), pp. 12–14.

———. *Le Théatre du Merveilleux*. Paris: Olivier Perrin, 1962.

Acknowledgments

During the several years this book was in preparation, my pursuit of Ducrow took me from the Riding School at Brighton to a basement of King's College in Aberdeen, from the shattered coast of North Devon to an isolated cottage in Essex, to Dublin and the sun-drenched valley of the Loire. I have ransacked both public and private circus collections abroad and in the United States, where my travels took me as far west as Wisconsin and Kansas. That I did not personally journey to and search through the libraries and collections of every locale in which Ducrow performed will perhaps be excused when the reader comprehends the number of towns he visited during a half-century of touring. My debt to the numerous institutions and individuals who aided me is considerable.

First, for money. There would have been little chance of my ever beginning, much less completing, so demanding a project without the support of the John Simon Guggenheim Memorial Foundation, which awarded me a Fellowship during the 1971–72 academic year and freed me to devote full time to research and travel. Messrs. Gordon N. Ray and James F. Mathias, president and vice-president respectively of the Foundation, continued to express a lively interest in the progress of my work and to aid me in various ways following the period of the initial award. I am proud to acknowledge my indebtedness to so prestigious and farsighted an institution, which has also provided a handsome subvention toward the expense of the illustrations in the finished work.

Second, to good friends and colleagues. Here, as in the past, I am especially grateful to Messrs. Antony D. Hippisley Coxe and R. Toole Stott, whose hospitality and fellowship, constant encouragement, hints as to where I might locate needed materials, and unfailing replies to my many inquiries considerably lightened my scholarly burden. Both also threw open their extensive private collections and served as readers of the manuscript in various stages of preparation. Dr. Marian Hannah Winter unstintingly gave me the benefit of her unrivaled knowledge of popular entertainments, dance history, and iconography and served as the third expert reader of the manuscript. To all three goes my warmest appreciation, but without any promise that I will never inflict such punishment on them again. In France I was again the recipient of much kindness and help, particularly from my fellow members in the Club du Cirque. M. L.-R. Dauven, vice-president of the Club and editor of its elegant journal *Le Cirque dans l'Univers*, has consistently shown himself to be one of my staunchest supporters—as is evidenced by his willingness to translate and publish the results of my research —and has moreover proven himself an excellent friend. My eminent colleague M. Tristan Rémy, who may properly be termed the *doyen* of circus historians, generously made available to me his own research notes, gave me the benefit of his wisdom on many occasions, and again accompanied me on my rambles about Paris. M. Jacques Garnier of Orléans was no less helpful in responding to my incessant demands and opened his vast collection to me. I shall never forget their splendid hospitality and camaraderie.

I am especially indebted to Miss Marja Keyser of Amsterdam, who volunteered to undertake the laborious task of searching out and sending me information on Ducrow's career in her country; and to Miss Elizabeth Leach in England, who responded to my many inquiries concerning Ducrow's activities in Manchester. Mr. George Speaight again permitted me to examine his fine collection of toy theatre prints and supplied me with several valuable leads and pieces of information, as did Professor William W. Appleton, who also played a key role in my obtaining several prints of Ducrow and my example of the Ducrow Clock. Mr. Peter Ducrow, great-grandson of Andrew, received me at his home in Thorpe-le-Soken and gave me free access to the album assembled by Ducrow and his wives and to other materials in his possession; Mrs. Joan Hoar, Mrs. Nina Trewin, and Mrs. Iris Perrier Rouls—also descendants of Andrew—were most helpful in supplying additional information and advice on the family and its genealogy. I salute the heroism of the gallant Christopher Calthrop, Esq., who unflinchingly agreed to lead a winter expedition to Nunhead Cemetery in search of the tomb of Ducrow's mother— after I myself had failed to find it during the summer months—and discovered only desecrated graves and the exposed remains of corpses. May he soon return to his friends.

Among other individuals who provided sundry bits of information and helped me in my work, I wish to thank Mr. Ben Albach, vice-president of the Amsterdam Toneelmuseum; Baron Sidney L. Bernstein and his able secretary Miss Josephine Moir; Mr. Townsend Brewster; Professor Oscar G. Brockett; Mr. David Cheshire; Mrs. Robin Craven; Mr. Robert Dick; M. José Dugardein of Belgium; Mr. Richard W. Flint, a walking mine of information on American circus collections; Dr. Alain Frère of Tourrette-Levens; Miss Mary Grahn; Mr. David Jamieson, editor of *King Pole*; Reverend Leslie D. Kelly, Vicar of St. John the Divine, Fairfield (Liverpool); Reverend Harold Lockyer of Hartland, Devon; Professor Edwin W. Marrs Jr.; Professor David Mayer III; Mr. Cyril B. Mills; Dr. Daniel F. Nalbach; Mr. Harry Nutkins; M. Robert Pesché of Tours, who seated me opposite a well-behaved poodle at a dinner party enlivened by automata; Mr. A. J. Pischl; Professor Arnold Rood; Miss Sybil Rosenfeld; Mr. Stuart Thayer, president of the Circus Historical Society; Mr. D. Thomas, Verger of Southwark Cathedral; and Mr. Cornelius Videler of Colorstats of Westport, who did much of the photographic work in its final stages. I am also pleased to acknowledge the aid given me at various times by my meticulous research assistants: Mr. Alvin Goldfarb in the United States; Mrs. Christine Markham in England; and Mr. Gerbert G. Beekenkamp in Holland.

Third, to the curators, librarians, and staffs of the many collections and libraries where my research was conducted. As will be readily grasped from the documentation, here I am indebted above all to three institutions, whose vast holdings are indispensable to any study of the English circus and theatre. At the Theatre Museum of the Victoria and Albert Museum, I was again made to feel at home by Mr. George Nash and Mr. Anthony Latham. The latter, in particular, was most attentive to my needs and helpful with his advice, instantly put at my disposal everything I needed, and promptly answered all my inquiries by post whenever I was not in London. Would that all curators were of his stamp! At the British Library in the British Museum, I availed myself of several departments with their valuable collections and am grateful to the many staff members who assisted me. Special thanks go to the men of the Newspaper Library at Colindale, who uncomplainingly trundled out the hundreds of heavy bound volumes of journals I consulted. At the third of these major institutions, the Harvard Theatre Collection, I received the usual cooperation from Miss Helen D. Willard and Dr. Jeanne T. Newlin and was excellently assisted by Miss Martha R. Mahard.

Mr. William J. Smith, Head Archivist of the Greater London Record Office, was most helpful in devising solutions to several recondite problems and courteously granted me access to the parish registers in his keeping; and Mr. K. A. Doughty, Librarian and Curator of the Borough of Southwark Public Libraries, was equally gracious in answering my inquiries and putting me on the track of much valuable information. At the Local History Department in Walworth Road, I was additionally assisted by Mr. Letton and especially Mrs. Dobson. Mrs. M. Y. Williams, Borough Archivist at the Minet Library, Lambeth; Mr. A. O. Meakin, Chief Librarian at the Central Library of Croyden; and Mr. E. G. W. Bill, Librarian of Lambeth Palace, also responded to several inquiries put to them. The Public Record Office, General Register Office at St. Catharine's House, Principal Probate Registry at Somerset House, and Guildhall Library were all on my London itinerary. Miss Constance-Anne Parker, Librarian of the Royal Academy of Art, kindly attempted to trace the bust of Ducrow for me. The Institute of Historical Research at the University of London admitted me as a reader so that I might work in its comfortable setting.

Outside London my research was accomplished primarily at the Bristol Central Library, whose Chief Reference Librarian, Mr. G. Langley, was most efficient and courteous; the Bath Reference Library; the John Johnson Collection of Printed Ephemera, presided over by Mr. M. L. Turner, at Oxford University; the Edinburgh Public Library, National Library of Scotland, and Edinburgh University Library; the Scottish Record Office; the Aberdeen Public

Library and King's College Library of the University of Aberdeen, where Miss Steven assisted me in tracing some circus materials; the Mitchell Library of Glasgow and the University of Glasgow Library; and the Trinity College Library and National Library of Ireland. As already noted, Miss Elizabeth Leach, Arts Librarian at the Manchester Central Library, was especially helpful in searching out information on Ducrow's career in that city, as was her assistant, Mrs. Jennifer M. Vyse. Miss J. W. Thompson, Local History Librarian at the Newcastle upon Tyne City Libraries, and Mr. R. Potts, Assistant County Archivist at the Newcastle upon Tyne County Record Office, replied to inquiries about the death of Ducrow's first wife in their city; Miss Jane Langton, Registrar of the Royal Archives at Windsor Castle, answered my questions about Princess, later Queen Victoria's relations with Ducrow; Mr. Yeoman, Chief Technician of the Anatomy Department of the University of Edinburgh Medical School, provided a stimulating explanation of the ancient practices at his institution. Others supplying me with odd pieces of information were Mr. John Bebbington, City Librarian and Information Officer of Sheffield; Mr. J. Smith of the Liverpool Record Office; and Dr. Felix Hall, County Archivist at Maidstone, Kent.

In France my research was conducted principally at the Bibliothèque de l'Arsenal, which is particularly rich in theatrical periodicals covering Ducrow's years in France; the Bibliothèque de l'Opéra, where I was again assisted by the charming Nicole Wild; the Archives Nationales and Archives de la Département de la Seine; and the Bibliothèque Nationale and its newspaper division at Versailles. M. A. Lökkös, Conservateur of the Bibliothèque Publique et Universitaire of Geneva, responded to my inquiries about Ducrow's visits to his city; and numerous other provincial librarians in France and Switzerland searched out and sent me copies of journals published in their towns.

In the United States I was able to gather much preliminary information in the Sterling and Beinecke Libraries of Yale University, the Widener and Houghton Libraries at Harvard University, the Library of Columbia University, and the Library of Performing Arts in New York City. The Rare Book Room of the Boston Public Library possesses many hard-to-find French and English theatrical periodicals of the early nineteenth century; the New England Deposit Library at Boston was useful for several French journals; and Mr. Donald Petty in the Reference Division of the Library of the City

College of New York promptly arranged for interlibrary loans or copies of those rare periodicals and journals I could not easily get to myself. Further afield, I was delighted to discover so much material relating to Ducrow in the Folger Shakespeare Library, although Mr. Alan Jutzi of the Manuscripts Department at the Henry E. Huntington Library and Art Gallery in San Marino, California, was less successful in turning up anything on him there. Mr. Robert S. Fraser, Curator of Rare Books in the Princeton University Library, responded to my inquiries and requests directed to his institution; as did Mr. Christian F. Brun, Head of the Department of Special Collections at the University of California, Santa Barbara, where the R. Toole Stott Circus Collection is now housed. Mr. John H. Hurdle, Curator of the Ringling Museum of the Circus at Sarasota, Florida, supplied me with information on the holdings in his collection; and Mr. William L. Joyce, Curator of Manuscripts at the American Antiquarian Society, made several suggestions relating to the circus in nineteenth-century America. In Baraboo, Wisconsin, I was particularly impressed by the formidable holdings of the Circus World Museum, whose librarian, Mr. Robert L. Parkinson, and former director, Mr. Charles Philip "Chappie" Fox, then assisted by Mr. Richard W. Flint, made my stay both profitable and memorable. To the south, Miss Alexandra Mason, Special Collections Librarian of the Kenneth Spencer Research Library at the University of Kansas, placed the three Astley's scrapbooks formerly belonging to M. Willson Disher at my disposal.

Parts of this book first appeared in articles published in the *Cirque dans l'Univers*, the *Educational Theatre Journal*, *Nineteenth Century Theatre Research*, *Theatre Research/Recherches Théâtrales*, and *Theatre Survey*. I welcome this opportunity to thank the editors of these journals for their interest and encouragement, and for providing a needed stimulus and focus for my thoughts during several difficult periods when I nearly despaired of ever seeing my lucubrations reach the light of day. It was perhaps only to be expected that an American press should be the first to appreciate the value and interest of a work dealing with the history of the English circus. That this press should in addition be a commercial one is, I believe, a tribute to its scholarly editor and president, Mr. James Thorpe III and Mrs. Frances T. Rutter respectively, whose enthusiastic reception of the manuscript, subsequent encouragement and advice, and concern over the quality of the publication itself were such as I could have expected from few, if any, university presses. Nor can I forget the sympathetic care lavished upon my work by Mr. William D. Rutter, whose own fine artistry is apparent in the design of this book.

Finally, I owe a debt of gratitude to my wife Gail and sons Jonathan and Eric—too often abandoned and made to suffer while I was driven and consumed by the shade of Ducrow. If they never come to understand my scholarly passion, I hope they will nonetheless forgive me for it.

Index of Persons

à Beckett, Gilbert Abbott, 265–68, 273–75, 282
Adams, Master (H.?), 234, 292, 314
Adams, Mrs. (Henry?), 355
Adams, Charles, 188, 234, 355
Adams, Master H., 302, 355
Adams, Henry, 161–62, 208, 234, 243, 245, 250, 263, 278, 283–85, 287, 290, 295, 299, 303, 452 n. 85
Adelaide (wife of William IV, later Queen Dowager), 284, 346. *And see* Clarence, Duchess of
Albert (Prince Consort), 339–40
Aldridge, Ira, 265
Alexander, John Henry, 340
Allard, Signor (equestrian), 355
Allen, Lord, 296
Amburgh, Isaac Van, 239, 321–24, 326–27, 339–40, 462 n. 34, 464 n. 62, fig. 71

Amherst, J. H., 134–35, 147, 164–65, 234, 264, 276, 398
Anderson, James, 346
Anderton, James, 354
Angoulême, Duchesse d', 28, 107, 379
Armstead, Richard, 451 n. 75
Astley, John, 23, 46, 49, 62, 71, 120, 248
Astley, Mrs. John (Hannah Waldo), 49, 120, 349
Astley, Philip, 17–18, 22–23, 46, 49, 51, 58–59, 62, 68–69, 108, 261, 396–97, 399, 414 nn. 1 and 8, 428 n. 31
Astley, Mrs. Philip, 17, 22
Atkins (architect), 289, 298
Avery (equestrian), 64, 314
Avery, Caroline, 188, 302, 314, 343, 459 n. 87

Index of Short Titles
(Plays, Scenes, Poems, Novels, &c.)

This book on Andrew Ducrow has been set in Plantin
by Asco Trade Typesetting Ltd of Hong Kong.
Christophe Plantin was French born but emigrated because of
religious persecution to Belgium where he began printing and
publishing books in 1555. He was the leading printer of the second
half of the sixteenth century. McNaughton & Gunn, Inc., of
Ann Arbor, Michigan, has lithoprinted the book on neutral pH factor,
long-lived paper. Short Run Bindery of Medford, New Jersey,
has bound this book.